1990

Criminology: Crime and Criminal Justice

Criminology: Crime and Criminal Justice

D. Stanley Eitzen
Colorado State University

Doug A. Timmer
University of Dubuque

JOHN WILEY & SONS
New York Chichester Brisbane Toronto Singapore

Cover design: Gina Davis
Text design: Loretta Saracino Marotto/Ann Marie Renzi
Production supervisor: Jan M. Lavin
Photo editor: Stella Kupferberg
Copy editor: Susan Winick

Library of Congress Cataloging in Publications Data:

Eitzen, D. Stanley.
  The sociology of crime and criminal justice.

  Bibliography: p.
  Includes indexes.
  1. Crime and criminals—United States. 2. Criminal
justice, Administration of—United States. I. Timmer,
Douglas A. II. Title.
HV6025.E47 1985   364'.973   84-13111
ISBN 0-471-09758-6

Printed in the United States of America

10 9 8 7 6 5 4 3 2

Preface:
From the Authors to the Student

The "first course" in criminology is among the most popular courses on many community college, four-year college, and university campuses. This popularity stems from a number of things. Among them are the inherent interest that many students have in crime-related topics, increased societal concern with crime rates or even perceived "crime waves," dissatisfaction with an often inefficient and ineffective criminal justice system, the recent growth in the number of schools and departments with specialized criminal justice programs leading to careers in law enforcement and corrections, and the close ties that criminology has with other areas of student study and career preparation, most notably law, political science, psychology, and social work.

We intend this book to be read and used in this introductory criminology course. We have provided a survey of the field of criminology, a description and explanation of crime and efforts to control it in American society, and a discussion of some of the most prominent and controversial crime-related issues in our society using a *sociological perspective*. We are convinced that both crime and its control are primarily *social problems* and are, therefore, best described, explained, and understood from a sociological point of view.

Our aim has been to provide a book that is both readable and interesting for students. To that end, we have incorporated a wide variety of sources: everything from newspapers and popular magazines to official government data to scholarly research and studies. This is reflected particularly in the use of special boxed materials or panels in each chapter. Our hope is that these panels will provide amplification and illustration of matters discussed in the body of the text, be especially interesting to students, and help to stimulate quality class discussions. We have tried to select panels, as well as statistics, graphs, tables, and other visual materials that are informative, insightful, thought provoking, and timely.

This book seeks to address not only the basic and traditional topics normally covered in an introductory criminology course, but also some of those topics that are emerging as especially important in the 1980s. Unlike other criminology texts, we have devoted entire chapters to each of six different kinds of crime—street, white-collar, victimless, organized, corporate, and political—expanding the discussion well beyond the limits of the more usual and narrower criminological concern with conventional property and violent crime. Also, since we contend that crime and attempts to control it can never be properly understood when approached separately, the last part of this text for introductory criminology is devoted to the criminal justice system. This section of the book focuses on the processing of those "selected" for criminal prosecution, the bias of the criminal justice system, and the consequences of crime and its control (or lack thereof) for American society.

Two other important ingredients, generally not found in other texts in the field, mold our discussion of the chapter topics. First, in addition to the description of contemporary crime-related phenomena, each phenomenon is examined historically to create an understanding of how both crime and criminal justice have emerged, leading to present conditions. Second, we use one or more of three sociological perspectives, as appropriate, to explain the various topics. These three perspectives are (1) traditional sociological explanations that focus on the immediate social environment of the criminal offender as the cause of crime, but still understand criminal acts as an expression of a pathological person who ultimately must be "readjusted" to society's requirements; (2) interactionist explanations, stressing the meanings that individuals, groups, institutions, and society attach to certain behaviors and the concrete encounters with social control agencies that define, manage, treat, control, and label "offenders"; and (3) radical explanations, emphasizing the ways in which the structure of society—especially inequities in wealth, power, and privilege, and the race and class bias of social institutions as presently organized—contributes to crime and our inability to control it.

Acknowledgments. Stan Eitzen would like to thank the following scholars for their contributions to his development as a sociologist and thus, indirectly, to his contributions to this project: Marston McCluggage, William Seiler, Charles Warriner, Gary Maranell, Ken Kammeyer, Bob Antonio, Norm Yetman, Maxine Baca Zinn, Nevell Razak, Jack Brouillette, T. R. Young, and Doug Timmer.

Doug Timmer would like to thank those who contributed in very direct, although highly diverse, ways to the completion of this book: Isabelle Johnston, Stan Eitzen, Mary Faino-Timmer, Bill Norman, and Ralph Scharnau. He also would like to express his gratitude to those whose contribution was more indirect, but certainly not less important: Ron Roberts, Steve Spitzer, Bill Chambliss, Dennis Mileti, Russ Nash and Harry Timmer.

D. Stanley Eitzen
Doug A. Timmer
May 1984

Contents

PART 1

CRIME, CRIMINAL JUSTICE, AND CRIMINOLOGY

1 Crime and Criminal Justice: A Sociological Perspective

CHAPTER OUTLINE

The Plan and Organization of the Book
The Sociological Perspective
A Sociological Perspective on Crime and Criminal Justice
Our Intention: Exploding Crime Myths

KEY TERMS

Private troubles
Public issue
Sociological imagination

If you have watched or listened to television or radio news today, or if you have read a local newspaper in the last 48 hours, you probably would agree that crime and successful and failed efforts to control it are major problems in American society. Media reports of both petty and heinous crimes, police corruption, dramatic courtroom trials and prison overcrowding and violence abound. And after the news, television crime dramas and crime-oriented motion pictures bombard us. Beyond this, hundreds of thousands of books and magazines—both fiction and nonfiction—provide commentary on some aspect of crime or the criminal justice system.

Almost inevitably then, there is a widespread interest in both criminal activity and efforts to prevent or reduce it in our society. But are these popular media portrayals and interpretations of crime-related phenomena always accurate? Do they actually reflect the realities of crime and criminal justice in the United States? Unfortunately, they do not and a primary reason for writing this textbook is to examine and expose the many stereotypes and preconceptions that sway and mislead most of us as we attempt to come to some sensible and rational understanding of crime and its control.

THE PLAN AND ORGANIZATION OF THE BOOK

We believe that to gain a more accurate view of crime and criminal justice at least four things need to be done:

1. *All* types of crime, not just conventional or traditional property and violent crimes (in other words, street crimes), should be recognized, described, analyzed, and explained. Therefore, after Part 1 of this text introduces criminological theory, criminal law, and crime rates, Part 2 consists of separate chapters on *all* types of criminal behavior in American society: victimless, white-collar, organized, corporate, and political crime, as well as conventional street crime.

2. In addition to the description and explanation of contemporary criminal activity and the present workings of the criminal justice system, the *history* of each kind of crime (from street to corporate) and each component of the criminal justice system (from police to prisons) needs to be explored. This is necessary so that the way in which current circumstances and current criminal justice practices surrounding crime have emerged can be fully understood. Therefore, each chapter in this text will endeavor to outline clearly the historical development of whatever topic is being considered. We are firmly convinced that you cannot understand where you are until you understand where you have been.

3. Since a complete understanding of crime necessitates an appreciation for the way in which a society fails, or is successful, in its attempts to control or prevent it, Part 3 of this introductory criminology text describes and explains the key components of the American criminal justice system. Separate chapters discuss the police, the criminal courts, punishment, and prisons. A sepa-

rate chapter on the recent "crisis" or "breakdown" in the justice system is also included. This part of the text focuses on the processing of criminals through the justice system, the biases of American criminal justice, and the consequences of crime and its control—or lack of control—for individuals and society.

4. Finally, to describe crime and the criminal justice system is to explain neither. Thus, we are careful to offer explanations for the phenomena we described: the origins of each kind of criminal activity discussed and the workings of each component of the criminal justice system that is dealt with. However, our explanations or *theories* will be limited to *sociological* explanations or *theories*.

But why do we choose sociological explanations or theories of crime and criminal justice over all others?

THE SOCIOLOGICAL PERSPECTIVE

Rather than starting with the individual, as biological or psychological perspectives might do, a sociological perspective focuses on the way in which individuals' behavior is influenced, conditioned, shaped, constrained, or determined by their social relationship to other human beings and to a variety of social institutions. From a sociological perspective, individual behavior is best explained in terms of its social setting and context.

A sociological view of human behavior emphasizes the organization or structure of the relations individuals have with other individuals and with social institutions. The patterns of social organization or social structures that most influence human behavior run the range from intimate and small groups to large institutional structures and relations; from intense and highly emotional relationships with one other person to family, friends, work groups, and neighborhood, to social classes and immense political and economic bureaucracies, to the entire society. Even though our more immediate, intimate, face-to-face, and small group encounters in everyday life are more visible to us and often seem more real, a sociological perspective will not let us forget how larger and more remote institutions shape and limit our behavior.

When the difficulties or problems that people experience in society are approached and analyzed using a sociological perspective, they are not seen simply as "private troubles." Rather, they become social problems or "public issues." For example, the unemployment of any one young black male in the United States is not just the private trouble of the man who is jobless. His unemployment is a public issue and is without question related to the fact that the unemployment rate for black males in this society is double that for white males and ranges as high as 40 to 80 percent in the ghetto areas of many large cities. One does not understand unemployment from a sociological perspective as a social problem until one can see it is not only a personal trouble but a public issue as well. It is not simply the individual traits and characteristics of the unemployed that are primarily responsi-

ble for joblessness; it is the structure of American economic and socia.
tions. It is this ability to see the connection between individuals having prob.
on the one hand, and the structure, organization, and workings of the institutions
and society that the individual is a part of on the other. The late American sociologist, C. Wright Mills (1959), called this ability the *sociological imagination*.

From a sociological perspective, then, individual problems reflect underlying
and deeper social problems. We will proceed in this text to describe, analyze, and
explain crime and criminal justice from a sociological perspective. For us, crime is
a profoundly social problem; the crime problem in our society is indeed a public
issue.

A SOCIOLOGICAL PERSPECTIVE ON CRIME AND CRIMINAL JUSTICE

If crime was somehow part of the constitution of certain people, was the property
of individual offenders, the result of the criminal biological or psychological
makeup of certain "criminal types," then it would be reasonable to suppose that
the incidence of crime would not vary appreciably from one place to the next,
from one time to the next. If something *inside* the criminal predisposes him or her
to act in a criminal way, then we could expect to find roughly the same level of
crime in all societies and throughout history. If crime just naturally occurs in that
part of the population, would we expect to find significant variation in the incidence of crime from culture to culture, from era to era?

Yet, the history of criminology, as well as its present, is littered with a host of
pre- and nonsociological theories and explanations of crime (we will examine
these in-depth at the beginning of the next chapter) that limit their (and our)
understanding of criminal behavior to the predisposing constitutional factors residing in the individual offender that are said to be the source of criminal activity.
This, in spite of the fact that tremendous variation in the amount and types of
crime between city and country, regions and cultures, has been known for sometime; in spite of the fact that the changes in crime and criminal justice brought on
by historical developments like industrialization, urbanization, and the emergence
of labor markets, for example, have been documented. We take this as evidence
that any accurate and reasonably complete understanding of crime and criminal
justice must go beyond the individual criminal offender, beyond the criminal type,
beyond pre- and nonsociological thinking, to an approach that focuses on the
social, economic, and political factors that give crime and criminal justice their
particular shape, and have done so in each particular society and in each particular historical period.

Crime and criminal justice must be examined and understood, from a sociological perspective, in the context of the society that surrounds them. We find ourselves in absolute agreement with these words from the preface of a recent criminal justice textbook written by Randall Shelden:

Crime and criminal justice do not exist in a social vacuum, divorced from other
aspects of our social system, particularly other pressing social problems. All

The poor lined up to receive some relief during the Great Depression. Crime and criminal justice must be examined and understood in the context of the society in which they are found.

one has to do is ride in a police squad car for a few nights, walk up and down city streets, sit in on court cases, or see the inside of a jail or prison to know that such social factors as race, class, age and sex play central roles in the criminal justice system and how crime and criminal justice are intertwined with such larger issues as racism, poverty, inequality and sexism. (Shelden, 1982, pp. xix–xx)

Another reason for adopting a sociological approach to crime and criminal justice, as opposed to one or another pre- or nonsociological perspective, is the way in which the latter has been used (and is currently being used) to recommend and implement a variety of failed criminal justice reforms. In Part 4 (Chapter 16) of this text we will make clear the connections between particular theories or explanations of crime and the criminal justice or crime control policies and practices that follow from each of them. Suffice it to say here, that the criminal justice policies and practices that have been derived from pre- and nonsociological approaches to criminal behavior—limiting the rights of the accused, more police, more prisons, more and longer prison sentences, more sophisticated technology for the "war on crime" and so on—have failed universally to control or prevent crime. In terms of generating a more rational and effective program to control crime in American society, these highly individualistic, predispositional perspectives on crime have led, and continue to lead, to a dead end. From our vantage point, only sociological explanations of crime have the potential to contribute to a more enlightened, progressive, rational, and effective criminal justice system and crime control strategy.

OUR INTENTION: EXPLODING CRIME MYTHS

From the beginning, we want to make our own perspective and intentions clear; we do not care to hide behind a thinly veiled and disguised claim to a disinterested and disengaged "scientific objectivity." Rather, ours is an often passionate commitment to those *sociological* explanations or theories of crime and criminal justice that go farthest in debunking a series of what we consider to be "half-truths" or misleading mythical descriptions and analyses of crime and the criminal justice system. Among the "crime myths" that these sociological perspectives will uncover and prove largely false are:

- That what is criminal at one time and in one place is always criminal, at all times, in all places.
- That the primary causes of crime are biological and psychological.
- That crime is predominately a lower-class phenomenon.
- That the most costly crime in American society is street crime.
- That the state and its criminal law are always neutral entities in society.
- That the criminal justice system is always organized to reduce and prevent crime.
- That the American criminal justice system is just.
- That the solution to the "crime problem" is more police and more prisons.

In short, our intention in this book is to instill a *sociological* understanding of what is most certainly a *social* problem.

2 Theories of Crime and Criminal Justice

CHAPTER OUTLINE

Pre- and Nonsociological Theories

   A critique of pre- and nonsociological theories

Sociological Theories of Crime and Criminal Justice: Traditional Perspectives

   A critique of traditional theories

Sociological Theories of Crime and Criminal Justice: The Interactionist Perspective

   A critique of labeling theory

Sociological Theories of Crime and Criminal Justice: Radical Criminology

   A critique of radical criminology

Understanding Crime and Crime Control

   Using theory
   Crime and criminal justice: dialectics and history

KEY TERMS

Anomie
Biosocial criminology
Blaming the victim
Criminal type
Criminogenesis
Differential association
Interactionist theory
Pre- and nonsociological theories
Primary deviance (crime)
Radical criminology
Secondary deviance (crime)
Surplus population

Your eye shall not pity; it shall be life for life, eye for eye, tooth for tooth, hand for hand, foot for foot.

Deuteronomy 19:21

So whatever you wish that men would do to you, do so to them; for this is the law and the prophets.

Matthew 7:12

Successful and fortunate crime is called virtue.

Lucius Seneca

In every case the laws are made by the ruling party in its own interest. . . . By making these laws they define as ''just'' for their subjects whatever is for their own interest, and they call anyone who breaks them a ''wrongdoer'' and punish him accordingly.

Thrasymachus, in Plato's *Republic*

An unjust law is no law at all.

St. Augustine

. . . we must not say that an action shocks the common conscience because it is criminal, but rather that it is criminal because it shocks the common conscience. We do not reprove it because it is a crime, but it is a crime because we reprove it.

Emile Durkheim

Law! What do I care about law! Hain't I got the power?

Cornelius Vanderbilt

From the beginning, a procession of the poor, the weak, the unfit, have gone through our jails and prisons to their deaths. They have been the victims.

Clarence Darrow

Don't get the idea that I'm one of those goddam radicals. Don't get the idea that I'm knocking the American system. . . . Capitalism . . . gives to each and every one of us a great opportunity, if we only seize it with both hands and make the most of it.

Al Capone

Law, in whatever name, protects privilege.

E. L. Doctorow

If a nigger kills a white man, that's murder. If a white man kills a nigger, that's justifiable homicide. If a nigger kills another nigger, that's one less nigger.

A Southern police department official

. . . We can never forget that everything Hitler did in Germany was "legal" and everything the Hungarian freedom fighters did in Hungary was "illegal."

Martin Luther King, Jr.

The inescapable conclusion is that society secretly wants crime, needs crime, and gains definite satisfactions from the present mishandling of it.

Karl Menninger

. . . unjust social arrangements are themselves a kind of extortion, even violence. . . .

John Rawls

Crime in the suites, not in the streets—take a look at who's really picking your pocket.

Painted on a Boston subway wall

I put to you this question: Is a society redeemed if it provides massive safeguards for accused persons including pre-trial freedom for most crimes, defense lawyers at public expense, trials, and appeals, retrials and more appeals—almost without end—and yet fails to provide elementary protection for its decent, law-abiding citizens?

U.S. Supreme Court Chief Justice Warren Burger

The crime problem has indeed become a matter of widespread concern, even among people of different philosophies. Today's hardliner on law and order is yesterday's liberal who was mugged last night.

Ronald Reagan

As these quotations indicate, crime and criminal justice have been problematic throughout history, from ancient Israel to contemporary America. But the quotations are instructive in another sense as well; they illustrate the tremendous diversity in the way crime and criminal justice have been explained and understood. This divergence in perspective continues today as social and political philosophers, sociologists, criminologists, politicians, policy makers, and everyday folk attempt to come to terms with the street, victimless, organized, white-collar, corporate, and political crime that grips our society.

This chapter will examine the diversity that characterizes the history of criminological thinking. We contend that much of what passes for criminology is either too descriptive (it offers much factual detail but no *explanation* for crime and criminal justice) or too limited in perspective (it offers only *one* explanation for crime-related phenomena, ignoring the diversity of perspectives in the field). Therefore, this book begins with an overview of the history of criminological theory, proceeding from pre- and nonsociological theories to contemporary sociological perspectives; from demonology to social structure.

A word of warning: throughout this chapter the word *theory* is going to be ever present. Criminological theory is what is to be described and analyzed in the next few pages. Do not panic. Theory, simply means the "ways of understanding and explaining crime and criminal justice." We have no interest in an overly scientific, technically sophisticated, highly abstract and intellectualistic discussion of theory that is divorced from the everyday and concrete reality of crime and attempts to control it. Theories of crime and criminal justice should be judged by their ability to enlighten our understanding of "crime in the streets and crime in the suites" and the practice of criminal justice in our society, and thus provide the most appropriate way of eliminating both of these things. We would encourage the reader, therefore, to accept this initial discussion of criminological theory and begin to understand how theory is always an important part of their own ongoing, everyday life. As one sociological theorist, Graham Kinloch, puts it:

> Theorizing is the process by which people account for their physical and social environments within the context of a specific setting, thereby defining their physical and social reality. The process applies to both science and everyday life; the perceived gulf between theory and reality is thus more apparent than real. (Kinloch, 1977, p. 48)

Theory, then, is merely our account of the world we have created and that now impinges upon and affects us all.

PRE- AND NONSOCIOLOGICAL THEORIES[1]

The earliest explanations of criminality relied on supernaturalism. These theories are "prescientific" and depend on religious faith and belief. Here, the criminal, like all other objects in nature, possesses a spiritual quality of one kind or another. Those committing criminal acts are inhabited by an evil spiritual force, a demon, and so on. The positive or morally good spirits are absent. Since one is either naturally afflicted by these corrupting influences on the one hand or by the proper religious and natural forces on the other, the practice of criminal justice or punishment becomes relatively clear-cut:

> Given such an explanation of crime, the only sensible solution was to try to exorcise the demons which were responsible for the behavior or, failing that, to do away with the criminal, either by exile or by execution. In a society where the gods were perceived as omnipotent and omnipresent, it was clearly a matter of the highest priority to appease them, no matter what the costs. (Huff, 1980, p. 156)

[1] This section draws extensively from the work of Ronald C. Huff, "Historical Explanations of Crime: From Demons to Politics" (1980).

In many ways the fate of the criminal in these "primitive" societies had more to do with conforming to the will of the gods than it had to do with either the rehabilitation of the individual offender or the protection of society. This was due primarily to the fact that the "failure of the group to punish the wrongdoer was believed to leave the tribe open to the wrath and vengeance of the gods" (Huff, 1980, p. 156).

This kind of thought concerning criminals and their control continued for the most part—in varying degrees of sophistication—until the emergence of criminology as a more or less organized and "scientific" approach to the study of crime-related phenomena. This classical period in criminology began in Europe about 1700.

Classical criminology was essentially based on utilitarian social philosophy and the notions of "rational man" and "free will." Crime, according to this perspective, is the rational choice of a criminal who is ultimately free to choose either criminal or noncriminal behavior. The demons are no longer in control of the individual. The individual of classical criminology is responsible for his or her actions. The idea of the reform or rehabilitation of the criminal offender is also incorporated into this body of thought. Classical criminologists held out the hope that the person choosing criminal behavior at one point in time might be transformed so as to choose noncriminal actions in the future. A systematic statement of what causes crime—what makes a "rational" and "free-willing" person choose criminal ways—however, is noticeably absent in this early criminological work.

The bulk of this early criminology focuses not on crime but on its control, that is, on criminal justice. Here, the work of Cesare Beccaria and Jeremy Bentham are particularly important. Both felt that the key to reforming an inhumane and brutal 18th-century European criminal justice system lay in the most basic of utilitarian principles: that all criminal justice practice should be geared toward "the greatest good for the greatest number." This view led these men to reject the idea of punishment of the criminal to either appease the gods or to gain society's revenge. Rather, they argued, the point of punishment is deterrence, to prevent crime and to rehabilitate the offender in the process. These are the things that lead to "the greatest good for the greatest number." Huff has concisely summarized the recommendation of Beccaria in particular for the overhaul of the criminal justice system of his day. Note how they are informed by utilitarian philosophy ("the greatest good for the greatest number") and the notion of punishment as deterrence, as well as how they foreshadow the modern "liberal" system of criminal justice in the United States. Beccaria:

> articulated the framework of what came to be known as the classical school of criminology, i.e.: (1) that the motivation underlying all social action must be the utilitarian value of that action. . .
> (2) that crime is an injury to society and can only be measured by assessing the extent of that injury. . .
> (3) that the prevention of crime is more important than its punishment. . .

(4) that secret accusations and torture should be eliminated while the trial process ought to be speedy and the accused treated fairly and humanely throughout the process. . .

(5) that the only valid purpose of punishment is deterrence, not social revenge. . .

(6) that incarceration should be utilized more widely, but, at the same time, conditions for those confined must be vastly upgraded and systems of classification developed to prevent haphazardly mixing all types of inmates. (Huff, 1980, p. 158)

A century later, around 1800, classical criminology began to undergo a significant revision. According to these "revisionists," it is not always the case that a rational person can choose between good and bad, right or wrong, noncriminal and criminal. Sometimes there are intervening factors, such as age, mental status, and physical condition, that impair the individual's responsibility for his or her behavior. Individuals may sometimes be only partially responsible for their criminal acts. (Notice, for example, how this is consistent with the way in which our present system of criminal justice absolves from criminal responsibility those found clinically insane.) Here, a partial determinism begins to replace the earlier notion of free will.

 In 1876, a book, *The Criminal Man,* published by an Italian psychiatrist, Cesare Lombroso, ushered in another phase in the history of criminological thought. This school of thought criticized classical criminology on the grounds that it had not been scientific enough and had not adequately dealt with the question of the causes of criminal behavior. It also had a quarrel with the revisionists; their idea of determinism had not been taken far enough. Criminality is often completely determined. But most important was the shift that this "positivist" (called this because of its reliance on the scientific method) criminology caused in the discipline's subject matter. No longer was crime the primary object of study. It was the criminal, *the criminal type,* that was to be analyzed. If this analysis were carried on properly, that is to say scientifically, knowledge of the criminal type would provide us with all of the information necessary for developing sound and effective crime control policies and methods.

This emphasis on the criminal, not on crime, has characterized a large part of criminology up to the present. Contemporary studies of the criminal type, however, have a long and varied history in the positivist or scientific criminology born in the late 19th century. Briefly, we will trace a bit of this history.

Lombroso made the initial contributions to the development of the criminal type. He said criminals are born criminals. They are inferior organisms, almost apelike. In Darwinian terms, they appear to be from "a lower phylogenetic level"; they have not evolved to the same level as the noncriminal portion of the species. Through observations inside Italian prisons and autopsies of other convicts, Lombroso concluded that those predisposed to criminal activity were characterized by receding foreheads, peculiarly shaped craniums, eye defects, big ears and lips, high cheekbones, long arms, and inverted sex organs. He also noted such anomalies as a lack of morality, excessive vanity, cruelty, and tattooing.

Later, a student of Lombroso, Enrico Ferri, attempted to formulate a universal typology of criminals. Constitutionally, Ferri claimed, criminals can be categorized in one of five ways: they are either insane, born, occasional, habitual, or passionate.

Charles Goring's 1913 study of 3000 English convicts also emphasized the physiology of criminals as the critical determinant of their criminal acts. He concluded that the convicts suffered from hereditary inferiority, low native intelligence, and were morally defective. In the United States, Harvard anthropologist Earnest Hooton, beginning in the late 1920s, studied 13,873 criminals and 3203 noncriminals over a 12-year period. Comparing criminals to noncriminals, Hooton's conclusions matched Goring's. Criminals were found to be "organically inferior." For Hooton, this meant they had low foreheads, pinched noses, compressed faces, and narrow jaws. More incredibly, Hooton also claimed that he could predict the type of crime certain persons would be prone to engage in based on their physical makeup. Murderers and robbers were tall and thin, forgers tall and heavy, and smaller men committed sexual assault and rape.

This search for the criminal body type has not abated in more recent times. William Sheldon (1940), for example, was a proponent of the idea that body types are closely related to temperaments that are, in turn, closely related to certain types of behavior, including crime. Even more recently, this kind of perspective on crime has focused on criminal families, criminal and noncriminal twins, the chromosome structure of criminals, and the chemistry of the criminal offender.

Family (see Panel 2.1) and twin studies have attempted to explain the propensity to criminal acts by concentrating on the criminal's genetic structure and the way in which it may be hereditarily passed from one generation to the next. The essential premise of twin studies is that if more identical twins (as compared with fraternal twins) are both criminal, then the effects of heredity would appear to be more significant in explaining criminality than would anything in the social environment (see, for example, Christiansen, 1968).

In the 1960s a chromosomal theory of crime enjoyed a short-lived popularity (used, for instance, by the mass media to help explain why Richard Speck murdered eight student nurses in Chicago). The view here was and is that prison populations tend to be made up disproportionately of males who carry an extra Y chromosome in their genetic code—the XYY syndrome.

The most extreme expressions of this tendency to reduce explanations of criminal behavior to physiology, genetics, and heredity are those that have concentrated on the neuroendocrine system. "The essential proposition of these theories has been that criminal behavior is often due to emotional disturbances produced by glandular imbalance" (Huff, 1980, p. 165). In sum, when the individual's body chemicals are out of balance, so is his or her behavior.

Not all of the criminological studies hoping to uncover the criminal type, however, have focused on physiology; some have focused on the innate psychology of the individual. Most of this work has been based on Sigmund Freud's theory of human behavior and personality. Here, criminal acts are understood as psychopathology. More specifically, the individual's unconscious leads to "personality deviation," which can, in turn, lead her or him to criminal acts. This

PANEL 2-1

A Contemporary Expression of Predispositional Theory?
The Criminal Family

PASADENA, Calif. (AP) It started out as a routine shoplifting arrest—two cousins, aged 8 and 9, picked up for stealing toy vehicles worth $3.97 from a department store.

But when police officer Tom Corey learned the culprits were members of a large family with a record of 150 arrests over three generations, he decided to try to "break the cycle of crime" by placing the youngsters in foster homes.

The Los Angeles Department of Public Social Services has filed precedent-setting petitions asking a court to take all 10 family members aged 18 or under from their parents.

The case, which goes to trial next month in the county's Juvenile Dependency Court, asks for a redefinition of what constitutes an unfit home.

In the past, children have been removed from parental custody for such reasons as the home's poor physical condition, parental abuse or lack of proper supervision. But never before has a court been asked to take the children primarily because the parents have criminal records.

Five of the nine counts filed against the family allege that the parents' criminal histories have involved the children "as an observer or participant."

"We were beginning to see the children follow the parents' pattern of behavior, so it specifically is a question of role modeling," said Bonnie Scales, social service caseworker. "We don't think it's in the child's best interest to be raised in a criminal environment."

Ron Marks, one of eight court-appointed attorneys assigned to represent various members of the extended family, believes a decision in favor of the county could set a dangerous precedent.

"It's possible the county will try to keep chipping away until finally, any parent with a criminal background can have his kids taken away," Marks said.

Corey, a 35-year-old former teacher, is sympathetic to the criticism. "However, at some point, there's got to be a way to break the cycle. It's up to the judge to decide that," he said.

Not all the family members are habitual criminals. One 23-year-old man operates a large janitorial business and employs three of his brothers. He doesn't agree with Corey.

"I didn't move away and I still got ahead," he says.

Source: Associated Press, "3-Generation Cycle of Crime Revealed in Routine Arrest," March 27, 1981.

approach to understanding criminal behavior has given rise to a plethora of mental and moral testing to determine who may have this tendency toward criminal psychopathology. "Using psychological tests such as the Rorschach, the Wechsler Adult Intelligence Scale, and the Minnesota Multiphasic Personality Inventory, the Thematic Apperception Test, psychologists have led in this attempt to construct causal theory" (Huff, 1980, pp. 165–166).

In case we may be inclined to dismiss these biological and psychological explanations of crime as outdated historic relics, we need only turn to their current resurgence within the disciplines of criminology and sociology. Albeit, in a more sophisticated and scientific way, *biosocial criminology* presently incorporates many of the tenets of the theories reviewed above. For example, Balkan, Berger, and Schmidt describe the work of C. Ray Jeffery, one of the foremost proponents of biosocial criminology in the United States today, in the following manner:

> The "biology" part of Jeffery's sociobiology emphasizes that each individual is genetically unique. Therefore, criminologists should look at brain codes and biochemical impulses indicating physical changes in the brain, which presumably produce such deviant behaviors as sociopathy (undefined) and alcoholism in those who have a "biochemical preparedness" for such behaviors. The biological condition of the individual is seen as crucial to that individual's learning pattern. Biosocial criminology renews old notions of a link between low intelligence and criminality. Jeffery suggests that the working-class poor are of low intelligence and criminal in part because of lower protein intake. (Balkan, Berger, and Schmidt, 1980, p. 17)

Unlike other conservative intellectuals who have recently been attempting to influence crime control policies in the United States—for example, James Q. Wilson (1975)—Jeffery advocates treatment, not punishment. The treatment, however, is medical, since crime originates in the biochemistry of the brain. Brain scans, blood tests, surgery, and psychotropic drugs need to be used to diagnose and treat the criminal population. This diagnosis and treatment must, of course, says Jeffery, be done by private business. If the state or federal government were to run such a program, a public outcry regarding an abhorrent loss of privacy would almost certainly ensue.

Again, it is important to remember that biosocial criminology offers nothing new regarding either the causes of crime or the practice of criminal justice. Balkan et al. conclude:

> Though much has been made of the "new" approach of biosocial criminology, in fact, nothing about this approach is new. It is, rather, a continuation of the tradition of looking for individual biological bases of criminal behavior. . . . . . . Jeffery's treatment model is nothing new; since the 1950s, a major form of treatment in prisons and mental institutions has been the use of drugs and psychosurgery. . . . (Balkan et al., 1980, p. 18)

A Critique of Pre- and Nonsociological Theories

 Pre- and nonsociological theories of crime and criminal justice from Lombroso to the currently fashionable biosocial criminology are wrought with many difficulties, some of them fatal. For instance, many studies done from these perspectives have been challenged on the grounds that they are nonscientific. Suspicious research procedures, methods, and findings abound. It simply has never been confirmed empirically that poor, minority, and working-class people—those who have historically had the most contact with the criminal justice system—are less intelligent, more emotionally disturbed, more morally defective, or more genetically defective than members of the middle, upper, and ruling classes. But pre- and nonsociological perspectives are flawed in ways that go beyond simple empirical inadequacies.

All of the pre- and nonsociological theories may be characterized as "predispositional" theories. That is to say, they all argue that somehow something "inside" the criminal person predisposes the person to criminal behavior. What is inside or predisposing may vary; it may be the genes, the unconscious, an evil spirit, or a free will, but the argument remains the same in its basic form: something *in* the individual is the origin of the criminal act. The role of social structure or society in criminogenesis is categorically ignored, or is at least uniformly absent.

Predispositional theories of crime severely limit the kinds of crime control policy or criminal justice practice that deal with crime appropriately and effectively. Since the source of crime resides within the criminal, the problem for criminal justice is what to do with this offender once apprehended. There are, for the most part, only three alternatives: physical elimination, extreme isolation and segregation, and treatment. Treatment, as conceptualized by predispositional theorists, does not entail a response particularly more humane or enlightened than elimination or isolation, since it primarily uses the ethically suspect medical technologies of psychotropic drugs and psychosurgery.

Predispositional theories have also focused almost exclusively on one kind of crime: what is today normally referred to as *street crime*—larceny, burglary, robbery, murder, rape, assault, auto theft, and so on. However, if we take account of all of the other kinds of crime that plague our society—victimless, organized, white collar, corporate, and political crime—it soon becomes apparent that most Americans must be genetically and morally defective; or at least many of those who supposedly exemplify the climb to success, the "best and the brightest" in American society, must have been so inflicted. Does the "biological-psychological criminal type" explain the behavior of politicians in the Watergate scandal or the criminal acts of corporate executives involved in price-fixing schemes? And what about the criminal and deviant acts of governments, multinational corporations, and labor unions? Can these organizations be genetically defective or psychopathological? Predispositional theory appears incapable of recognizing and explaining these "other" kinds of crime.

Finally, what of the political effects of this brand of criminological thinking? These theoretical perspectives do not admit to the role that social inequality, poverty, unemployment, the patriarchal organization of family life, socialization in mass-educational institutions, powerlessness, alienation, obstacles to full political participation and economic democracy, and other contradictions and crises in political, economic, and social life may play in both the generation of crime and the inability to control it. Thus, they have generally been put to conservative, or even reactionary, policy and political purposes. They have been used, as William Ryan (1976) puts it, to "blame the victim"—in this case, the street criminal—who has often suffered the injustices of both political and economic institutions and the criminal justice system and then been held solely responsible for his or her criminal behavior. Recently, it is not a historical accident that the resurgence of the predispositional tenets inherent in biosocial criminology, for example, have coincided with the election of a conservative national government (the Reagan administration) and its attempts to curtail the social supports and programs that have comprised the American welfare state since the Great Depression. As the individual offender is held more and more responsible for his or her crime, government-sponsored efforts to alleviate potentially criminogenic social and economic conditions are cut back.

Emphasizing the inadequacies of pre- and nonsociological theories, we reiterate that the focus of this book is sociological. We will concentrate on explanations for crime and its control that lie *outside* the individual. These sociological theories can be divided into three essential types: traditional, interactionist, and radical. Throughout this book, these three theoretical perspectives will mold our discussion of crime and criminal justice in America.

SOCIOLOGICAL THEORIES OF CRIME AND CRIMINAL JUSTICE: TRADITIONAL PERSPECTIVES

The first sociological perspectives on crime and criminal justice we will discuss are what we call traditional ones. These approaches probably continue to be the perspective of a majority of sociological criminologists at the present time. They are functional[2] perspectives in so far as their intellectual and theoretical roots are in the sociological theoretical orientation known as *structural-functionalism* (see Gouldner, 1970). Historically, this was the first specific theoretical orientation on crime and deviance and their control to emerge in American sociology. It represents a tremendous step forward in criminological thinking. Unlike pre- and nonsociological theory, these traditional sociological approaches do not locate the origins of criminal acts exclusively within the criminal person—in his or her physical, biological, or unconscious psychological makeup. Rather, the emphasis is on criminogenic *social* conditions. The *immediate social environment* is said to be primarily responsible for the criminality so rampant in our society: broken families, poor parenting, low-quality educational experiences, delinquent peer relations, poverty, lack of equal economic opportunity, inability to utilize those economic resources that are available, inadequate or unsuccessful socialization to the values implicit and explicit in American culture, and so on.

Turning to crime control, these traditional sociological perspectives are much more optimistic than predispositional theories. Generally, the contention is that correctional programs can be developed that will provide those who are arrested and convicted with the social skills necessary to overcome those aspects of their immediate social environment that led them to criminal acts in the first place.

[2] For an elaboration of the functional approach to crime, criminal law, and the consequences of crime for society see the essay by Chambliss, "Functional and Conflict Theories of Crime: The Heritage of Emile Durkheim and Karl Marx" (1976).

PANEL 2-2

A Comment on the Uses of Criminological Knowledge in American Society

A study nearing completion at the University of Michigan shows the ways in which the social sciences, no less than the physical sciences and mathematics, can be used by Government for potentially devious ends.

In 1978, the U.S. Law Enforcement Assistance Administration (LEAA) offered a $300,000 grant for a study of "collective disorders." In its request for proposals, the LEAA, an agency known for the billions it spent to outfit local police units with military hardware, said the information elicited from police agencies, dissidents, and reporters would be used by the Justice Department to "prevent and control" civil disturbances that might harm property or lives.

Of the six institutions that responded to the LEAA's request, the University of Michigan's Institute of Labor and Industrial Relations (ILIR) was selected. Although the LEAA itself was phased out by the Carter Administration, the Michigan research project continued under the auspices of the National Institute of Justice, which expects to receive the findings in June.

Activists in Detroit who were approached by the researchers included fast-food workers trying to organize, May Day demonstrators, Chrysler employes who had vandalized an assembly line when they learned they were to be laid off, and Iranian demonstrators. They were told, in letters sent out during the summer of 1980, that the University was interested in evaluating "the effectiveness of specific actions in the expression of issues and grievances."

Although many members of the 100 activist organizations contacted nationwide found the researchers sympathetic and sensitive to the civil liberties problems the study posed, none of the activists were told initially that the project was sponsored by the Justice Department. After being promised that their names would be kept confidential, many provided the requested information.

But if the names of those surveyed were protected, the age, occupation, marital status, and number of children of each was carefully noted. Although the interviewers had been cautioned not to ask, they were told to record each activist's sex and race. In addition, interviewees were encouraged to discuss the structure, recruitment methods, internal communications systems, and long-term objectives of their organizations.

The project's chief investigator, Lewis Ferman, says "great pains" have been taken to disguise the information, and promises to be "very, very careful that the data don't fall into the wrong hands."

But a member of the ILIR study's advisory panel has expressed reservations about use of the data. "I've been uneasy, very uneasy," said Charles Tilly, a

PANEL 2-2 (Continued)

sociology professor. "There's no question that there's a chance that what you will learn will be more valuable to law enforcement authorities than to those who want to open political processes."

University of Michigan graduate Jeff Alson agrees. "University of Michigan professors and the LEAA want to cloak the project in the objective appearance of a study," he said. "But my perception, knowing LEAA, is that it will be used to understand why protests take place and that knowledge will be used to suppress social and political dissent."

Alson's misgivings were underscored when he learned that a similar 1973 study resulted in guidelines to police intelligence units recommending that police collect the names of all activist organizations and their leaders. "Know their faces, addresses, cars, telephone numbers," the guidelines instructed. "Know the goals, strategy, and tactics of their organizations, the numbers of members, the level of their funding, and the sources of their funding."

Will the new study at Michigan bear similar fruit? Lois Mock, the study's coordinator at the National Institute of Justice, said the Justice Department does not expect the study to generate guidelines for the police, but she revealed some other disturbing possibilities.

The study might help cities formulate ordinances to regulate protest, she said, "so that people can't just go call a demonstration." She suggested that cities might require groups to state their purpose and estimate attendance at rallies before issuing permits. She added that although there would be legal problems, it would be ideal to put "limitations on the media" so the press would not help "escalate the situation into violence."

Ferman, however, sees different uses for his work. Instead of inhibiting social protest, he says, the study will help legal demonstrations remain peaceful.

People connected with the study obviously hold various opinions of how the information gleaned should be used. University of Michigan sociology professor William Gamson, who sits on the study's advisory panel, points out that there is no way of ensuring that any one view will prevail.

"There's no way we can really monitor the project," Gamson said. "It has a life of its own; it becomes a general social science research project." And while he, too, hopes some good will come out of the study, he says, "I'd feel more comfortable about [the study] if it were not sponsored by an agency whose mission is social control."

Source: Jeannie Wylie, "Social Science for Social Control," The Progressive, *June 1981, p. 27.*

Criminal justice, corrections, and punishment must be oriented to the reform and rehabilitation of the criminal. There is very little room in these perspectives for deterrence or retribution as appropriate responses for the criminal justice system. Notice, however, that even though the attention, in regard to crime causation, has shifted from biological and psychological to *social* factors in these traditional approaches, when the issue of crime control arises, the emphasis is still on the criminal, not on crime itself.

We characterize the theories discussed in this section as *functional* for three reasons. First, following the assumptions of other "order" or "consensus" understandings of society, these traditional perspectives tend to assume that all social institutions in general, and the criminal law and criminal justice system in particular, represent an agreed-upon and neutral organization and operation of American society that acts in the interest of all its members. Second, because traditional functional explanations share these assumptions with order and consensus perspectives on society, they also come to understand, for the most part, crime and deviance—even though social factors are said to cause them—as expressions of individual violations of the agreed-upon social order. Crime is still the property of an individual; it is ultimately an individual pathology. Third, since crime is "carried by" the individual criminal, these traditional sociological theories of crime and crime control, as we will see below, tend to advocate the readjustment of the individual to the requirements of what functional, order, or consensual theories of society hold most dear—the prevailing social order. The individual, not society, must be changed if crime is to be controlled.

We will proceed by briefly examining several examples of these traditional sociological theories. The discussion will delineate three distinct ways of understanding crime and criminal justice using this basic approach: social disorganization theories, social control theories, and socialization theories.

1. *Social Disorganization Theories.*   In the 1920s and 1930s several large American cities were hit simultaneously with the effects of a catastrophic economic depression, a devastating in-migration of both European immigrants and southern blacks (to urban centers in the midwest and northeast), and increasing rates of crime and deviance. Based on their experiences in Chicago, a group of sociologists residing there—later to be known in sociology as "the Chicago School"—developed their own particular explanation for increasing criminality: social disorganization (Park and Burgess, 1924). The Chicago School believed that the core areas of major cities—highly populated as they were with recently relocated and diverse European immigrants and black migrants, both often unemployed—were characterized by a high degree of cultural heterogeneity. Furthermore, the Chicago School believed that these diverse groups had not yet been able to incorporate the values and behaviors that made up the indigenous American culture. As a result, there was a breakdown in social organization that led to a pervasive confusion for these people in terms of cultural norms, that is, in terms of the "dos and don'ts," "rights and wrongs" of everyday behavior. Rapid social change led to social disorganization that led to *personal* disorganization—people became increasingly unsure of what was appropriate behavior in this new setting—which,

Social disorganization theory argues that the social disorganization found in the slums leads
to personal disorganization and a propensity toward criminal behavior.

in turn, led to deviant and criminal behavior. The role for criminal justice in the
Chicago School's estimation was straightforward enough: educate these culturally
diverse groups to the dominant American culture—to the "American Way." If
people were not adequately socialized to this culture, criminal and deviant behavior could not be controlled. "In this view, urban areas, being populated by such
maladjusted denizens as immigrants and the poor, criminals, dope addicts, the
mentally ill, and so on, had no coherent cultural standards and had to be incul-
cated with the dominant culture" (Balkan et al., 1980, p. 24). For this traditional
approach, crime and deviance are essentially the result of breakdowns in social
control that lead to social and personal disorganization, and the only way to
control these aberrant behaviors is to reconstitute control in each and every
individual by "filling them up" with the dominant culture.

Another variant of the social disorganization approach can be found in the work
of Thorsten Sellin (1938). Sellin concentrated on the culture conflict that the
Chicago School had discovered in the city; as a result of immigration and the rapid
pluralization of society, extremely diverse groups found themselves living side by
side. He found this to be the critical factor in generating a propensity to criminal
acts in the individual. The kind of breakdown that occurred in behavior norms that
led to criminal and deviant activities tended to exist in three different types of
situations, according to Sellin: when one or several groups' normative codes are
different but they find themselves in ongoing close contact, when the legal norms

of one group are extended to cover the behavior of another, or when one cultural group abruptly migrates to live with another.

2. *Social Control Theories.* Perhaps the best known theory of this type is Travis Hirschi's social bond theory (1969). Hirschi begins by admitting that his perspective has more to do with why people do *not* commit crime than it has to do with why they perpetrate criminal acts. According to Hirschi, we should assume that all individuals in society are potential lawbreakers and, therefore, what needs to be explained is why some people fail to commit deviant or criminal acts. The answer lies in the individual's social bonds: the ties that individuals have (or alternately, do not have) to parents, peers, and important social institutions like the school and workplace. When these ties or bonds are strong, individuals fear that deviant or criminal activity will jeopardize their relative position in society, and they refuse to run the risk of alienating and losing meaningful social relationships, careers, and security by engaging in illegal behavior. Conversely, when an individual's social bonds are weakened, they are more "free" to engage in criminal acts. Hirschi concludes then that it is the weakening of a person's social ties— usually beginning in their youth—that leads to criminality. Individual social bonds are the source of the social control of the individual that prevents crime.

Another classic expression of social control theory is Walter Reckless' containment theory (1967). This perspective is even more exaggerated in its turn toward the question of why people do not commit criminal acts and away from the question of why they do. It is also apparent that containment theory (as will be made evident below) is more oriented toward the individual offender and the role of nonsocial factors in crime causation than the other traditional sociological perspectives discussed in this section tend to be, including Hirschi's social control approach. In fact, we are somewhat tempted to label Reckless' theory a "psychological explanation of noncriminal behavior" rather than a "sociological explanation of criminal behavior."

Containment theory holds that society continually "pushes and pulls" individuals toward criminal acts. These pushes and pulls include everything from poverty, unemployment, and inequality to the presence of deviant and criminal subcultures, groups, and peers to more "personal" factors like hostility, rebelliousness, anxiety, restlessness, and mental conflict and problems. However, according to Reckless, both internal and external containments insulate and prevent many people from turning to crime. By external containments Reckless means the strong social bonds or ties that Hirschi believes provide the social control necessary to constrain the individual from criminal behavior. Internal containments, on the other hand, are those signs of "inner strength" that the many healthy individual personalities in society display: good self-concept, strong ego, goal oriented, and so on. Those with weak external and internal containment are, then, the most likely to engage in crime.

Before leaving this brief description of Reckless' containment theory, it should be pointed out that, in American society at least, Reckless believes that internal (i.e., individual, psychological) containments are the most effective crime controls. External containments are construed as necessarily weaker in a highly individuated society where most people spend a good share of their life away from the social bonds and ties that could control or contain them. Therefore, in the end, Reckless relies on the psychology of the individual offender for crime control.

3. *Socialization Theories: "Successful," "Unsuccessful," and "Different."* Perhaps the most classic expression of the idea that being completely and successfully socialized to a particular society's cultural values may turn out to be a source of deviant behavior is Robert Merton's (1968) theory of anomie. Merton assumes that American culture has been extremely successful at socializing all parts of the population to the desired goal of success, a success defined almost entirely in material terms. In other words, we nearly all agree that what we want is a good and secure career that will provide us with the material rewards (e.g., income) to allow the acquisition of all those material possessions that all Americans want (a split-level suburban home, two cars in the garage and two kids in the house, two weeks in the Caribbean). However, Merton also recognizes that American social structure—political, economic, and social institutions—does not provide all sectors of the populace with an equal opportunity to realize this "American Dream." Therefore, not everyone, for the most part not the poor and minorities, is able to attain the desired goal. And this situation is further confounded by the fact that not all poor folks and minorities have been socialized to the skills that would let them take advantage of all of the legitimate means that *are* available for the attainment of their desired goals.

The discrepancy between cultural values and goals (i.e., achieving material success) on the one hand and "limited legitimate opportunities" for attaining these ends made available by the social structure on the other, is what Merton calls *anomie*. Anomie, in turn, lessens the individual's commitment to legitimate means, since they are unequally distributed and often unavailable, and makes the person more open to the use of illegitimate means—criminal and/or deviant behavior—to attain the desired success.

Merton's theory of crime control revolves around his proposed solution to this anomic condition that differentially affects the population. There are at least two solutions: "(1) increase the opportunities to compete and resocialize people so they can make better use of the available legitimate means, and (2) reduce people's aspirations" (Balkan et al., 1980, p. 27). Although part of this first solution appears consistent with Merton's theory of crime causation, anomie (and, by implication, criminality) is the result of the contradiction between culture and social structure. Therefore, adjustments expanding legal and legitimate opportunities in the social structure will reduce crime and deviance. But it also points to the need to readjust the individual offender to the legitimate means (presumably however limited they may be) already available in the existing social structure. The latter involves the psychological adjustment of the individual offender and is less concerned with reforming the society that generates crime and criminals. Offenders must learn to make career choices that are more in line with the opportunities afforded them in existing social and economic institutions. (Much the same as the Carter and Reagan administrations went about managing "the lowering of the expectations" of the less advantaged in American society.) In other words, the poor and minorities should desire to be successful like everyone else, but not too successful; at least not take seriously a desire so strong that changes in the structure of society would be required to accommodate them. Here the criminal must ultimately "rehabilitate" psychologically and accept those limited legitimate means available to him or her.

An example of a traditional sociological theory of crime and criminal justice that is based on the idea of faulty, inadequate, incomplete, or unsuccessful socialization can be found in the work of Albert Cohen (1966). This approach analyzes the role of socialization to American cultural values and the way in which it contributes to criminality in almost the reverse fashion as Merton. Cohen's studies of delinquent gangs led him to conclude that the propensity to criminal behavior involves a faulty and inadequate socialization to the dominant cultural norms and values. According to Cohen, delinquent subcultures create and maintain value systems and behaviors that are intended to make a mockery of the dominant cultural values and codes for appropriate behavior. This is the real source of crime and delinquency; a sort of purposeful and hostile reaction against conformity to the wider culture. Cohen says of the gangs he has observed:

> They not only reject the dominant value system, but do so with a vengeance. They "stand it on its head"; they exalt its opposition; they engage in malicious, spiteful, "ornery" behavior of all sorts to demonstrate not only to others, but to themselves as well, their contempt for the game they have rejected. (Cohen, 1966, p. 66)

Needless to say, Cohen is not as optimistic as someone like Merton when it comes to rehabilitating or reforming this hard-nosed and disgusting commitment to antisocial behavior.

Yet another attempt to understand the source of criminal acts by examining the socialization process that surrounds it is E. H. Sutherland's theory of *differential association*. This attempt does not concentrate on either an "overly adequate" or a "too inadequate" socialization. From this perspective, criminal socialization is not "good or bad" in relation to some other kind of noncriminal socialization; it is merely a *different* socialization.

For Sutherland, *differential association* is the process by which deviant and criminal behavior and values are learned in criminal or deviant groups. Deviant or criminal subcultures are not socially disorganized, as the "Chicago School" would assert, but are simply socially organized in marked contrast to a society's dominant social and cultural organization. Each subculture, furthermore, has its own valued and socially approved behaviors, its own way of conferring status on its members. Deviant or criminal behavior is, therefore, *not* deviant or criminal at all in the context of the social group in which it is learned and valued behavior. In this context, it is normative. Individuals engaged in social interaction with others in social groups learn deviant and criminal values and techniques, rationalizations and justifications for their deviant or criminal actions, and to understand and value deviant and criminal behavior as a source of social status and prestige (Sutherland and Cressey, 1978). See Panel 2-3.

Sutherland contends that deviant or criminal behavior is socially learned in exactly the same way as all other "normative and law-abiding" behavior. It simply takes place in a *different* social context or subculture. In any social organization where "an excess of definitions favorable to violation of law over definitions unfavorable to violations of law" exists, the door is opened to criminal behavior (Sutherland and Cressey, 1970). In this social setting, people are quick to learn that crime is good, it is valued; it is a source of their own increasing status and prestige.[3] But in the end, Sutherland is liberal and optimistic; through a noncriminal differential socialization and association individual criminals can be rehabilitated and resocialized to noncriminal behavior patterns.

Another example of a theoretical perspective that relies on the idea of a "different" socialization is Sykes and Matza's *neutralization* or *drift theory* (see Sykes and Matza, 1957; Matza, 1964). Unlike Cohen (see above), Sykes and Matza do not believe that crime and delinquency (neutralization-drift theory is basically a theory of juvenile delinquency) are learned in a criminal or deviant subculture that for the most part rejects the larger, dominant culture around it. Unlike Sutherland, they do not believe that youth crime is the result of a "different" socialization consisting primarily of the acquisition of criminal techniques, values, and attitudes in a criminal or deviant subculture. Rather, these two theorists contend that most criminal, deviant, and/or delinquent subcultures and individuals adhere to quite conventional values and attitudes. What they learn in their "different" socialization in a subculture are rationalizations for those acts that allow them to temporarily "neutralize" conventional, accepted, and expected social norms and "drift" now and again into deviance and crime.

Sykes and Matza go on to identify certain basic "techniques of neutralization" that young people typically use to justify or rationalize their illegal behavior. These include denial of responsibility for criminal acts; denial that their illegal acts actually injure anyone; denial that their wrongful acts do indeed have victims; condemnation of the hypocrisy of school authorities, criminal justice system officials, and parents who condemn their criminal acts and the "higher" loyalty required by peer groups (as compared with society in general). Again, in this way, established social norms are neutralized and the individual is socialized in a manner that facilitates the drift toward crime and delinquency.

Walter Miller's theory of lower-class culture as a crime generating milieu (1958) contends, contrary to Sykes and Matza, that there is an identifiable and distinct culture, namely, lower-class culture, that socializes a greater proportion of those who live in its grips to crime than does the dominant, mainstream, American middle-class culture. Early Chicago school pioneers like Shaw and McKay (1972) attribute criminal behavior to youth groups and gangs in lower-class areas of large cities attempting to gain status and material rewards but still argue that most families in lower-class and slum areas actually subscribed to middle-class values and culture. Going a step beyond them, Miller believes that the whole of lower-

---

[3] In this regard, criminologist Gresham Sykes (1978) has suggested that crime is so pervasive in American society that even in the mainstream, dominant American culture and social organization, criminal activity is normative behavior. Americans in general, for example, are socially expected to cheat on their income taxes.

PANEL 2-3

Edwin Sutherland's Sociological Theory of Why Criminals Behave Like Criminals

The following statements refer to the process by which a particular person comes to engage in criminal behavior.

1. *Criminal behavior is learned.*   Negatively, this means that criminal behavior is not inherited, as such; also, the person who is not already trained in crime does not invent criminal behavior, just as a person does not make mechanical inventions unless he has had training in mechanics.

2. *Criminal behavior is learned in interaction with other persons in a process of communication.*   This communication is verbal in many respects but includes also "the communication of gestures."

3. *The principal part of the learning of criminal behavior occurs within intimate personal groups.*   Negatively, this means that the impersonal agencies of communication, such as movies and newspapers, play a relatively unimportant part in the genesis of criminal behavior.

4. *When criminal behavior is learned, the learning includes*   (a) techniques of committing the crime, which are sometimes very complicated, sometimes very simple; (b) the specific direction of motives, drives, rationalizations, and attitudes.

5. *The specific direction of motives and drives is learned from definitions of the legal codes as favorable or unfavorable.*   In some societies an individual is surrounded by persons who invariably define the legal codes as rules to be observed, while in others he is surrounded by persons whose definitions are favorable to the violation of the legal codes. In our American society these definitions are almost always mixed, with the consequence that we have culture conflict in relation to the legal codes.

6. *A person becomes delinquent because of an excess of definitions favorable to violation of law over definitions unfavorable to violation of law.*   This is the principle of differential association. It refers to both criminal and anticriminal associations and has to do with counteracting forces. When persons become criminal, they do so because of contacts with criminal patterns and also because of isolation from anticriminal patterns. Any person inevitably assimilates the surrounding culture unless other patterns are in conflict; a southerner does not pronounce *r* because other southerners do not pronounce *r*. Negatively, this proposition of differential association means that associations which are neutral so far as crime is concerned have little or no effect on the genesis of criminal behavior. Much of the experience of a person is neutral in

PANEL 2-3 (Continued)

this sense, e.g., learning to brush one's teeth. This behavior has no negative or positive effect on criminal behavior except as it may be related to associations which are concerned with the legal codes. This neutral behavior is important especially as an occupier of the time of a child so that he is not in contact with criminal behavior during the time he is so engaged in the neutral behavior.

7. *Differential associations may vary in frequency, duration, priority, and intensity.* This means that associations with criminal behavior and also associations with anticriminal behavior vary in those respects. "Frequency" and "duration" as modalities of associations are obvious and need no explanation. "Priority" is assumed to be important in the sense that lawful behavior developed in early childhood may persist throughout life, and also that delinquent behavior developed in early childhood may persist throughout life. This tendency, however, has not been adequately demonstrated, and priority seems to be important principally through its selective influence. "Intensity" is not precisely defined, but it has to do with such things as the prestige of the source of a criminal or anticriminal pattern and with emotional reactions related to the associations. In a precise description of the criminal behavior of a person, these modalities would be rated in quantitative form and a mathematical ratio be reached. A formula in this sense has not been developed, and the development of such a formula would be extremely difficult.

8. *The process of learning criminal behavior by association with criminal and anticriminal patterns involves all of the mechanisms that are involved in any other learning.* Negatively, this means that the learning of criminal behavior is not restricted to the process of imitation. A person who is seduced, for instance, learns criminal behavior by association, but this process would not ordinarily be described as imitation.

9. *While criminal behavior is an expression of general needs and values, it is not explained by those general needs and values, since noncriminal behavior is an expression of the same needs and values.* Thieves generally steal in order to secure money, but likewise honest laborers work in order to secure money. The attempts by many scholars to explain criminal behavior by general drives and values, such as the happiness principle, striving for social status, the money motive, or frustration, have been, and must continue to be, futile, since they explain lawful behavior as completely as they explain criminal behavior. They are similar to respiration, which is necessary for any behavior, but *which does not differentiate criminal from noncriminal behavior.*

Source: Edwin H. Sutherland and Donald R. Cressey, Criminology, *10th ed. Philadelphia: Lippincott, 1978, pp. 75–77.*

class culture—its attitudes, beliefs, values, schools, family, and neighborhood organization—gives rise to criminal activity.

For Miller, life in the slums is marked by the gradual development of a lower-class culture that then becomes highly stable and is passed on from one generation to the next. The people who live in this cultural setting are generally marginal to the established economic system and usually will not experience any success in the legal and legitimate social order. Consequently, says Miller, these people are socialized to a "different" culture: they learn to achieve personal satisfaction in those areas not closed off to them—in their own neighborhoods and culture. Lower-class individuals tend to adopt certain "focal concerns" that both fit the social and economic conditions of lower-class life and lead to criminal activity. These criminogenic focal concerns that lower-class individuals are socialized to in lower-class culture include an emphasis on getting into and staying out of trouble (both as sources of prestige in lower-class culture), male machismo or toughness, street savvy, excitement and adventure, casting your life to fate and luck, and a rebellious response to threats to individual autonomy and freedom that come from the authority bestowed upon police, parents, and schools.

In sum, Miller contends that crime is a normal reaction to the conditions, values, and norms of a unique lower-class culture.

A Critique of Traditional Theories

Traditional sociological theories, like predispositional theories of crime and crime control, have concentrated almost exclusively on conventional street crime. This leaves those perspectives open to the charge that since they tend to deal with only one particular kind of criminal activity, they are attempting to build a general theory of crime that ignores all of the other kinds of crime so rampant in American society. Closely related to this narrowness in perspective is what might be called "the myth of lower-class criminality" (see Tittle, 1983). Traditional theories have generally associated the immediate social conditions of poverty—poor schools, broken families, delinquent peer group relations, and so on—with criminality. In many instances, this argument has boiled down to little more than the notion that "poverty causes crime" (or at least that "the culture of poverty" causes crime). In a society where the corporate rich are normally the perpetrators of corporate and political crime (not to mention the many victimless, white-collar, and organized crimes committed by other relatively affluent people), this position makes very little sense.

The myth of lower-class criminality has also been exposed by recent "self-reported crime studies." From these kinds of studies it has become increasingly evident that "close to 100 percent of all persons have committed some kind of offense" and "[i]n a substantial portion of the offenses revealed by these studies, the crime was so serious that it could have resulted in imprisonment if the offender had been arrested" (Doleschal and Klapmuts, 1974, p. 15). In sum, much research indicates that no particular social class appears to be significantly more criminal—either in frequency or severity—than any other (see, for example, Hindelang, Hirschi, and Weis, 1979, 1981; Braithwaite, 1979; Tittle, Villemez, and Smith,

1978). Historically, it is true, however, that the structure and operation of the American criminal justice system have ensured that the vast majority of those arrested, convicted, and sentenced have been the poor, minorities, and members of the working class.

And, similar to predispositional approaches, the traditional sociological accounts of crime have emphasized the criminal, not the crime itself. "Blaming the victim" in pre- and nonsociological theories becomes "blaming the disorganized person" at worst, or "the immediate socially disorganized environment" at best, in traditional sociological theories. In this conception "the focus of attention remained the offender, . . . and correction still attempts to change him or his life situation to prevent repetition of his criminal behavior" (Doleschal and Klapmuts, 1974, p. 15).

Because of this focus on the criminal, traditional sociological theories have tended to become overly optimistic regarding the criminal justice system's ability to reform and rehabilitate the individual lawbreaker. As will be pointed out later in this book, there is literally no criminal justice practice or technique that has been successful in terms of consistently rehabilitating convicted American criminals. At least part of this unwarranted optimism comes from the inability of these traditional theories to take into account the historical and social-structural origins of crime and criminals. These theories do not appear to have developed a full appreciation of the extent to which crime may have its sources in wider and larger social, political, and economic institutions and forces in American society. Poverty, broken homes, and inadequate schools and health care may be only symptoms of larger obstacles to full economic, political, and social participation in society. They may, indeed, be caused by the same structural forces and institutional arrangements that produce crime: a racist and sexist class society, for example. At minimum, traditional sociological theories fail to make clear that rehabilitating the individual criminal and/or reforming her or his immediate social environment is exceedingly difficult without accompanying changes in the political, economic, and social institutions that lie at the very foundation of American society.

Finally, it has been reasonably contended that the theories of people like Sutherland, for example, are not theories of criminal behavior at all. That, in effect, they are very general theories of *all* human behavior that do very little, if anything, to advance our understanding of the particular sources of the behaviors that come to be called criminal.

SOCIOLOGICAL THEORIES OF CRIME AND CRIMINAL JUSTICE: THE INTERACTIONIST PERSPECTIVE

For the past 40 years the labeling or societal reaction view of both criminal and noncriminal deviance (and a majority of the research undertaken using this perspective has dealt with noncriminal deviance, e.g., mental illness, drug use, and homosexuality) has presented the strongest sociological challenge to the traditional theories that have just been reviewed.[4] In several ways, the labeling theorists have presented a more enlightened and progressive response to the problems of crime and criminal justice in our society than have most of the traditional approaches. Of course, labeling theory has also dismissed the central tenet of earlier predispositional theories that "something inside" the human individual causes or motivates deviant behavior. In fact, these societal reaction theorists have contended that motives are really nothing more than "after-the-fact" rationalizations or justifications for behavior, be it deviant or not (see Mills, 1940). Motives for behavior are not predisposing; they do not cause behavior of any kind.

The labeling perspective holds that crime and deviance are socially constructed (via people engaged in social interaction), not ontologically given or naturally occurring. That is to say, every human act is social, and no human act is inherently deviant or criminal. Crime is created and defined socially, in the process of social interaction. As Kai Erickson (1964, p. 11) has written, "Deviance is not a property inherent in certain forms of behavior; it is a property conferred upon these forms by the audience that directly or indirectly witnesses them." Furthermore, crime and deviance are relative to time and place. What is criminally deviant in one culture, may not be in the next; what is criminal at one point in history, may not be at another point, and vice versa. Howard Becker (1963) has summed up the labeling perspective on crime and deviance, a perspective that has for the most part analyzed the process of becoming deviant or criminal at the social-psychological level, "emphasizing the sequences of interaction through which deviant identities are built up and sustained" (Scull, 1977, p. 6):

> Social groups create deviance by making the rules whose infraction constitutes deviance, and by applying those rules to particular people and labeling them as outsiders. From this point of view, deviance is not a quality of the act the person commits, but rather a consequence of the application by others of rules and sanctions to an "offender." The deviant is one to whom that label has successfully been applied; deviant behavior is behavior that people so label. (Becker, 1963, p. 9)

Besides the notion that it may be a label, a social reaction, that ultimately creates crime and the criminal, labeling theory represents at least three other advantages over traditional approaches in its attempt to build a more empirically adequate sociological theory of crime and criminal justice:

1. *The Recognition That Crime Is a Political Phenomenon.* "The functional [traditional sociological] view of deviance, by ignoring the political aspects of the phenomena, limits our understanding" (Becker, 1963, p. 7). In other words, power is often the key variable in determining who labels the "criminal" and who

---

[4]This approach can be called *interactionist* in that it derives from a more general symbolic interactionist theoretical orientation in American sociology. Our discussion relies heavily on the excellent treatment of labeling theory in Andrew Scull, *Decarceration: Community Treatment and the Deviant: A Radical View* (1977).

gets labeled "criminal." Why is it, for example, that in our society the politically and economically powerful are the ones who can consistently label the "crimes" of the powerless?

2. *The Recognition That Social Relationships and Processes, Not Criminals, Must Be Rehabilitated.* Since, from this perspective, the source of crime is not the criminal or his or her immediate social environment, but rather an ongoing process of social interaction that labels and defines the criminal as criminal, it only makes sense that the surest approach to reducing criminality is not to attempt to change the criminal person, but to transform this social-definitional process. Scull (1977, p. 5) has said of labeling theorists in this regard, "Their more critical orientation produced a pronounced shift away from an obsessive concern with the attributes of individual deviants towards a more wide-ranging interest in social process."

3. *The Recognition That Crime and Crime Control Are Two Interrelated Parts of the Same Social Phenomenon.* The societal reaction and labeling theorists were the first to postulate what we will describe later in this chapter as "the dialectic of crime and crime control." Simply put, what this means is that labeling theory assumes that the agencies of social control—in this case, the criminal justice system—are probably even more important to an adequate explanation of the sources of crime in our society than are criminals and their criminal behavior. As Drew Humphries puts it, labeling theory:

> opened up a new line of inquiry for liberal criminologists: the contribution of the criminal justice system itself to the generation of crime. The argument is not complex: creation of deviant labels is the product of political conflict and the application of these labels sustains deviant behavior by informing an audience how to react to the labeled individual. (Humphries, 1979, p. 225)

Is the criminal justice system itself—obstensibly there to prevent and control crime—the ultimate creator and perpetrator of criminal activity?

Before returning to this question through a more detailed discussion of the labeling theorists' view of the American criminal justice system, the societal reaction conception of crime needs to be specified a bit more. In particular, the distinction between "primary" and "secondary" deviance must be drawn.

Primary deviance refers to any "original" behavior that may violate a rule or a law—drinking beer while teaching a course in criminology, smoking pot while taking a course in criminology, shoplifting at a local discount mart, stealing a car from a used-car lot, wife-beating, homicide, and so on. Although primary deviance occurs frequently and is common in our society, it has, from the societal reaction perspective, very little to do with the on-going problems of crime and deviance. What is critical is that "there occurs some sort of more or less organized societal reaction to some of this primary deviation, a reaction usually involving elements of stigmatization, punishment, and actual or symbolic segregation of the offender" (Scull, 1977, p. 5). In the case of an apprehended "criminal," the criminal justice system represents this "more or less organized response." At this point, the apprehended person may be labeled a "criminal." The criminal justice system will proceed by treating him or her like a criminal. The most likely

PANEL 2-4

Labeling Criminals

Another important sociological perspective, in which there has been a marked renewal of interest recently, emphasizes the role played by society's reactions to offending behavior in shaping social problem situations. Sociologist Howard S. Becker has stated this view succinctly:

> . . . social groups create deviance by making the rules whose infraction constitutes deviance, and by applying those rules to particular people and labeling them as outsiders. From this point of view, deviance is *not* a quality of the act the person commits, but rather a consequence of the application by others of rules and sanctions to an "offender." The deviant is one to whom that label has successfully been applied; deviant behavior is behavior that people so label. (1963:9)

This does not, of course, mean that the *acts* we commonly term homicide, theft, and drug use would never occur if they were not considered deviant or criminal. Rather, the point is that their nature, distribution, social meaning, and implications and ramifications are significantly influenced by patterns of social reaction. Society, in other words, determines what we make of these acts socially.

"Criminal" in this view is in some measure what sociologists call an "ascribed status." An individual's designation as an offender depends crucially on what *other people* do with respect to him and his behavior; it does not result simply and directly from his own acts. This means that research on crime problems must pay a good deal of attention to the substantive nature of these reactions (how and why we react to particular "offenses" as we do); the direct reactors and "labelers" (agencies of formal control, such as the police and the courts); and the typical processes of interaction between these control agents and the individuals they treat as criminals (with special reference to how this interaction may affect the development of criminal self-images and "careers" among the people so "labeled"). This point about interaction is important, because a great value of this orientation is the stress it places on *processes* involved in the development of criminal outlooks and behavior. Crime is not simply a matter of static conditions under which some individuals clearly "are" criminals (for all time and in all places) whereas others clearly "are not." On the contrary, both the individual's behavior and his self-conceptions are constantly undergoing change, and they are highly responsive to the reactions of others.

To a large extent, this view is little more than a recasting or amplification of a classic sociological dictum of W. I. Thomas to the effect that "when men define situations as real, they are real in their consequences"—a theme developed fur-

PANEL 2-4 (Continued)

Interactionists argue that since the agents of social control assume blacks to be more criminal than whites, their actions "fulfill that prophecy."

ther by Robert Merton as the "self-fulfilling prophecy." If we treat a person like a criminal, he is likely to become one. This point was nicely described by Frank Tannenbaum in an early work on crime and delinquency:

> No more self-defeating device could be discovered than the one society has developed in dealing with the criminal. It proclaims his career in such loud and dramatic forms that both he and the community accept the judgment as a fixed description. He becomes conscious of himself as a criminal, and the community expects him to live up to his reputation, and will not credit him if he does not live up to it. (1938:477)

We have already seen how the identification of young people as "troublemakers" by teachers and school officials may backfire—rather than acting as a preventive technique, such labeling may drive the child into new trouble and progressively greater alienation. Clearly, the police and the courts also have substantial power to activate and reinforce criminal careers and self-concepts. I have mentioned the ease with which we often "change" a person into a "criminal" (that is, our view of him changes) during the course of his trial on criminal charges. Indeed, the

PANEL 2-4 (Continued)

criminal trial is a prototype of what one sociologist has called the "status-degradation ceremony"—a ritualized process by which a condemned individual is stripped of his old identity and given a new (degraded) one. It is very difficult for an individual to sustain a favorable image of himself under the pressure of such public definitions. And if the defining process is clearly unfair . . . , then however unwilling the "offender" may be to define himself as such, and even if harsh sanctions are not invoked in his particular case, he is likely to develop a hostility toward the official "system" that may increase the likelihood of antisocial behavior on his part in the future.

Under the impact of negative social reactions, the individual may then be propelled from isolated acts of criminality into more complete involvement in criminal ways of life (heightened "commitment" to criminal roles), and he may come increasingly to view himself as an enemy of society (since society seems so determined to consider him one). Sociologist Edwin Lemert has suggested the distinction between "primary" and "secondary" deviation, the latter occurring when an individual comes to employ his deviance "as a means of defense, attack, or adjustment to the overt and covert problems created by the consequent societal reaction to him. . . ." (1951:75)

Concern with the impact of social reactions on individual self-conceptions and behavior (that is, focusing not on the pressures that initially drive the person into deviating behavior, but rather on the *consequences* for him of engaging in such behavior and being publicly identified as doing so) is but one aspect of this orientation to crime. Another involves examining the general impact, *on the society,* of

outcome is that society will so consistently label and treat the criminal as a criminal that through the "mechanism of the self-fulfilling prophecy" the person so defined will sooner or later change her or his identity and behavior to conform to the newly acquired label. This is secondary criminal deviance: the criminal deviance actually created and maintained by the criminal justice system. As Pretty Boy Floyd said, "I've got the name, so I'll play the game." Or, as Randall Patrick McMurphy found out in *One Flew Over the Cuckoo's Nest,* hospital patients came ultimately to regard themselves incapable of competence and assertive and independent behavior largely due to the incompetent, passive, and dependent definitions and labels given them by the hospital staff. (It is interesting to note that in the end, even the strong and forceful McMurphy was not able to overcome the institutionalized power and ability to define and construct reality and patient identities. That was the sole possession of the state hospital administration.)

For the labeling theorist, secondary deviance, and its intimate relationship to agencies of social control, is the crux of the "crime problem." As Edwin Lemert

PANEL 2-4 (Continued)

defining a particular form of behavior as criminal. I have already referred to a prime example of this sort of impact—seen in the consequences of treating as criminal various borderline "offenses." As we shall note in more detail, the "criminalizing" of certain types of behavior may exacerbate the social problems in question in ways that take us quite beyond the level of individual social psychology. Thus, we may find significant economic consequences flowing from "criminalization" (as when a society's reaction to some form of deviating behavior provides the groundwork for a thriving black market) and also significant effects on the behavior and outlooks of law enforcement officials, as well as the predictable proliferation of much "secondary" crime among the "offenders" themselves.

Finally, the emphasis on social reactions suggests still another broad area of research which should increase our understanding of crime problems. This has to do with the social meaning of the "creation" of crimes (by lawmaking), both generally and with respect to particular offenses. Thus we are led to ask what general functions are served by ensuring that there are *some* crimes and "criminals" in a society (do we, in other words, really need crime?). And we are also drawn to comparative and historical analysis of rule-making in particular behavior areas (for example, what led up to our present drug laws, why do they differ from those in other Western countries, etc.).

Source: Edwin M. Schur, Our Criminal Society: The Social and Legal Sources of Crime in America. *Englewood Cliffs, N.J.: Prentice-Hall, 1969, pp. 115–118.*

(1967, p. 17), the pioneering societal reaction theorist, has concluded, "In effect, the original causes of the deviation recede and give way to the central importance of the disapproving, degradational, and labeling reactions of society."

The labeled criminal is then essentially a victim of the criminal justice system. It is this system that catches the "criminal," publicly and legally brands him or her with a criminal label and then sits back and waits until the criminal incorporates his or her criminal identity as his or her own. The effects are devastating; as often as not the victim of criminal justice turns to a deviant or criminal career. The career, of course, is facilitated by both the wider community's reluctance to reintegrate the criminal into its ranks (who wants to live with or employ an ex-con?) and the way in which the process of public stigmatization and degradation inclines the criminal toward accepting criminal beliefs, values, and behaviors as morally justifiable. "In this fashion, the societal reaction allegedly produces a kind of role imprisonment which locks the deviant into a symbolic jail" (Scull, 1977, p. 6).

PANEL 2-5

Nine Key Assumptions of the Labeling Theory of Crime and Criminal Justice

1) No act is intrinsically criminal; 2) criminal definitions are enforced in the interest of the powerful; 3) a person does not become a criminal by violation of the law but only by the designation of criminality by authorities; 4) due to the fact that everyone conforms and deviates, people should not be dichotomized into criminal and noncriminal categories; 5) the act of "getting caught" begins the labelling process; 6) "getting caught" and the decision-making in the criminal justice system are a function of offender as opposed to offense characteristics; 7) age, socioeconomic class, and race are the major offender characteristics that establish patterns of differential criminal justice decision-making; 8) the criminal justice system is established on a freewill perspective that allows for the condemnation and rejection of the identified offender; and, 9) labelling is a process that produces, eventually, identification with a deviant image and subculture, and a resulting "rejection of the rejectors."

Source: Charles Wellford's summary of Clarence Schrag's assumptions of labeling theory, in Charles Wellford, "Labeling Theory and Criminology: An Assessment," Social Problems 23 (3), 1975, p. 333.

If the criminal is, in the main, the victim of criminal justice, what of this criminal justice system itself? Criminal justice is characterized by efforts that are contrary to its stated intention. The irony or paradox of this institution is this: the social control agency designed to prevent and control crime actually often creates and maintains criminality through the "stabilization and crystallization of primary deviance." "Stabilized and crystallized" primary deviance is secondary deviance, which is, in turn, the "manufacture" of those who "carry" crime in our society, those who have incorporated their criminal identity and embarked on a criminal career. Lemert has evaluated this tendency in social control agencies:

> . . . not only do reform and rehabilitative institutions in our society fail to demonstrate scientifically that their work actually accomplishes what is claimed for it, but their staffs would be hard put to prove that their efforts do not have effects opposite from what was intended. Many of the social welfare policies of post-Elizabethan England and nineteenth century United States created as many pauperized individuals as they eliminated. . . . Some observers are inclined to the belief that treatment in our mental hospitals precipitates psychoses in many patients and fixes and exaggerates the emotional disturbances of others. Certainly it is not hard to show that our penology and administrative policies toward criminals are important factors in recidivism. (Lemert, 1951, p. 68)

When it comes to the issue of solutions to this failing criminal justice system, the societal reaction theorists' response has taken at least two separate directions. First, there has been an essentially liberal response: efforts need to be made to humanize the bureaucratic, arbitrary, capricious, and often brutal social control response that meets the victims of criminal justice. A more respectful and sympathetic response to the "criminal underdog" must become an institutionalized part of our criminal justice system. Second, and more important, many labeling theorists have taken a libertarian position on this issue. For them, since the criminal justice system is ultimately the source of much of our "crime problem," the best criminal justice system is the one that intervenes in the lives of rule- and lawbreakers the least. Labeling theorists have especially pushed this approach in regard to victimless crime (see Schur, 1965, and Chapter 7). This kind of "noninterventionist" system is portrayed as best for both society (crime is reduced) and the individual victims of criminal justice (criminal identities are not as likely to be used to build alienated criminal careers). Many of these theorists have noted, for example:

> that the illegality of drug use may often force addicts into other illegal activities in order to support their habits, or that incarceration of deviants in prisons would only further socialize them into deviant and criminal subcultures . . . Schur . . . has gone so far as to recommend a program of "radical nonintervention" . . . . (Balkan et al., 1980, p. 32)

In many respects, the bottom line here is that if you ignore crime, that is, primary criminal deviance, it will tend to go away.

A Critique of Labeling Theory

Although labeling theory tells us much about the origins and development of secondary deviance, it provides little in the way of an explanation for the sources of primary deviance, that is, for the original rule- or lawbreaking.[5] Although societal reaction and labeling are undoubtedly involved in the stigmatization of deviants and often contribute to "secondary crime," labeling theorists have tended to downplay the conditions in society that lead to criminal behavior in the first place. This weakness in labeling theory is primarily a result of the theory's ahistorical and astructural perspective on both crime and criminal justice. Contrary to the contentions of many societal reaction theorists, crime is not simply the violation of a rule and the acquisition of a label. What is criminal in any society is always ultimately tied to the historical development of its social institutions.

Labeling theory's social-psychological orientation has led its research efforts to concentrate on the face-to-face, immediate encounters between those social control agents who label and those "underdogs" who get labeled. No attention is given to the role historical development and social structure may play in the ever-changing shapes and forms crime and its control take. This approach has led to a

[5] Gary Marx (1981) has argued, however, that social control must be seen as a cause of primary as well as secondary deviance.

neglect, and sometimes even a flat rejection, for example, of the relevance of things like the division of American society into social classes or the nature of its political and economic system to an adequate explanation of the sources of crime (Scull, 1977). Put another way, labeling theory has often failed to take full account of the larger social and historical contexts in which face-to-face labeling encounters take place. Although these theorists have very adequately and elaborately detailed, in rich and concrete terms, the impact of the criminal justice system on the labeled and processed victim, they have not adequately analyzed the structure of criminal justice organizations themselves, their interrelations with other key societal institutions, especially the economy and the polity, and the role they play in determining who and what comes to be socially constructed as criminal.

This ahistorical and astructural approach has led to a characterization of the social control that emanates from the criminal justice system as arbitrary. Scull comments:

> In turn, this narrowness of vision inevitably leads to work which depicts social control as arbitrary. For want of a larger perspective, the actions of the agencies come to be seen either as free-floating and apparently perverse, or as determined simply by the immediate interests of the first line controllers. . . . (Scull, 1977, p. 10)

The question of exactly *who* it is that labels and *who* it is that gets labeled has not been central for labeling theory:

> Of course there are definers and defined but what do the definers represent? What interests are they defending? How do their actions reinforce the existing nature of capitalist society? No answers to such questions are provided: the definers are a group of freefloating "baddies." (Taylor and Taylor, 1968, p. 30)

It is more likely that instead of being arbitrary the control inherent in the criminal justice system is both patterned and purposive. Ample empirical evidence exists to support such a view. Without question it is the powerless in American society who wear the overwhelming majority of deviant and criminal labels. William Chambliss has summarized those studies that have researched the class bias of the American criminal justice system:

> The lower class person is (1) more likely to be scrutinized and therefore be observed in any violation of the law, (2) more likely to be arrested if discovered under suspicious circumstances, (3) more likely to spend the time between arrest and trial in jail, (4) more likely to come to trial, (5) more likely to be found guilty, (6) if found guilty, more likely to receive harsh punishment than his middle- or upper-class counterpart. (Chambliss, 1969, p. 86)

At least part of this difficulty in labeling theory, the characterization of social control as random and arbitrary, is due to the absence of another critical variable in explaining crime and criminal justice—power. It is true that labeling theorists have often acknowledged or paid lip service to the politics of labeling power. That is to say, they have long recognized the importance of power in determining who defines and who gets defined "crazy" or "criminal." As a practical matter, however, labeling theorists have seldom taken account of social power beyond the relatively modest power and authority of criminal justice professionals and administrators. The realities of class power in a corporate-dominated society, for example, have been left untouched. In short, it is not enough to merely recognize the role power plays in creating and maintaining crime, criminals, and efforts at their control. For labeling theory:

> The acknowledgment of the role of power remains formal rather than substantive, with little effect on theory or analysis. And the ritual acknowledgment that those who label (or who construct and impose new labels) are more powerful than those who are labeled represents a dismal substitute for the analyses of power structures and their impact. (Scull, 1977, p. 11)

Labeling theory can also be criticized for its rather exclusive concentration—perhaps an inadvertent one (one where the theoretical approach necessarily and logically leads)—on street and "victimless" crime. The crimes of the powerful—organized, corporate, and political—are notoriously missing in labeling theory studies. Instead, labeling theory has focused our attention on the "nuts, sluts, and perverts" that walk our downtown streets (Liazos, 1972). It leaves us with a bad taste in our mouths; with the impression that crime and deviance are the sole property of minorities, slum dwellers, and street gangs. By overlooking the criminal qualities of American social institutions and the powerful individuals who direct them, labeling theory contributes to a serious injustice. As Alexander Liazos has explained:

> We should banish the concept of "deviance" and speak of oppression, conflict, persecution, and suffering. By focusing on the dramatic forms, as we do now, we perpetuate most people's beliefs and impressions that such "deviance" is the basic cause of many of our troubles, that these people (criminals, drug addicts, political dissenters, and others) are the real "troublemakers"; and, necessarily, we neglect conditions of inequality, powerlessness, institutional violence, and so on, which lie at the bases of our tortured society. (Liazos, 1972, p. 119)

Two final criticisms of labeling theory are pertinent. First, many of this perspective's pronouncements on crime and criminal justice are grounded in research on noncriminal deviance. It may indeed be the case that crime and noncriminal deviance entail such different social processes that this kind of convenient sliding from one to the other is unwarranted. Crime and noncriminal deviance (alcoholism, gambling, mental illness, etc.) may be two separate things. Second, as was the case with some traditional sociological theory, labeling theory is open to the charge that it is a theory of behavior in general; that it is not a specific theory of crime and criminal justice at all.

SOCIOLOGICAL THEORIES OF CRIME AND CRIMINAL JUSTICE: RADICAL CRIMINOLOGY

Just prior to World War I, a Dutch sociologist and economist, Willem Bonger (1916), began to put together a theory of crime that emphasized the role of the organization of economic production and distribution in its causation. This historically represents the first extensive application of Marxist theory in criminology. Bonger concluded that capitalism, more than any other economic system, is characterized by a rampant inequality stemming from a control of the industrial and economic means of production by an extremely small number of people (the capitalist ruling class). The masses (the working class and below) are deprived of any control of these economic processes. They merely sell, in an extremely dependent fashion, their labor to the owning and controlling class for a wage. It is this structural subjugation of the masses in capitalist society that is at the source of criminality.

> The economic subjugation of the masses, he (Bonger) argues, stifles men's 'social instincts' and leads to unlimited egoism, insensitivity, and a spirit of domination on the part of the powerful, while the poor are subjected to all sorts of pathogenic conditions: bad housing, constant association with 'undesirables,' uncertain physical security, terrible poverty, frequent sickness, and unemployment.'' (Huff, 1980, p. 166)

Further, Bonger attempted to discern causal connections between certain types of crime, for example, prostitution and theft, and the economic inequality fostered by a capitalist class society. And since, for Bonger, crime is causally related to the economic structure of society, this structure—not the criminal or her or his immediate environment—must be radically transformed in order to reduce crime.

After Bonger, however, there was a long drought. This perspective in criminology has only recently (for the most part, within the past 15 years) been more fully developed, refined, and solidified into a prominent theoretical perspective in criminology in the United States and Europe. Taylor, Walton, and Young (1973) and Chambliss and Seidman (1982) provide more in-depth and much more detailed introductions to these developments than will be provided in this text. But more than anything else, this perspective is characterized by its emphasis on the historical and social-structural (particularly political and economic structures, i.e., the political economy) origins of crime and the way attempts to control it are socially organized.

Most Marxist, radical, or critical[6] analysis done in criminology would suggest that the historical development of capitalism was, and is, intimately linked to the historical development of our particular criminal law. The criminal law, in turn, is primarily responsible for the origin and development of crime itself. Capitalism, criminal law and crime are, therefore, inseparable social and historical pro-

---

[6]Not all of the criminological research done from this point of view is explicitly Marxist; hence the words "radical" and "critical."

cesses—the dialectic of crime and crime control is to be taken seriously—and are all relatively recent and modern phenomena.

Drew Humphries (1979) has argued, in this regard, that for crime to emerge three conditions must be met. First, a state (some kind of institutionalized and organized government) must develop. Second, a dominant economic class must emerge that then comes to at least indirectly control the state in general and its criminal law in particular. Third, a marginal economic class with no secure relation to the means of economic production and distribution and without the means to sustain and reproduce itself (its own social life) needs to have developed. In short, crime emerges when a ruling class is able to utilize a state and its criminal law to control a working class and maintain its exclusive ownership and control of economic, political, social, and cultural life.

Illustrative of the above is the Wood Theft Law in 1840 Germany. The state sold public forests to corporate interests and wealthy individuals who wanted to sell lumber for profit. This interfered with the tradition of peasants and small farmers having the free use of the trees in the public forests to build and heat their homes. The solution to the problem was passage of the Wood Theft Law, which made criminals of people who took wood from these formerly public lands.

From this perspective it is also highly unlikely that abolitionists (white or black) and humanitarian values "freed" hundreds of thousands of black slaves. Rather, the American state made slavery illegal, made it a crime, when capital- and technology-intense agricultural production replaced earlier forms of less automated labor-intense agriculture. The dominant (and at that time, Northern) economic class had realized that labor-intense slavery was not the most efficient and profitable agricultural practice. What was needed were money, machines, and marginal wage-laborers, not slaves. To aid in this process, the state criminalized slavery; and slaves, slave owners, and plantations gradually began to disappear (both examples are from Humphries, 1979).

From a radical perspective, what then can be said of the role of the state and its criminal law and criminal justice system? First, criminal law and criminal justice are primarily tools for enforcing social and public order (in more explicitly Marxist versions this may be conceptualized as "imposing the conditions for the maintenance of a dependent 'wage-laboring' class"). For example, it is thought that the municipal, public police force was originally—and still is—a response to the public disorder that threatens a capitalist industrial society, not a response to criminality per se. Radical criminology points to the myth of crime control (via local law enforcement) as a protective community response to increased felonious activity. This view is evidenced by the fact that probably about 80 percent of U.S. municipal policing activity has to do with minor and misdemeanor offenses (see Timmer, 1981).

But while the state's criminal law and criminal justice apparatus are quick to punish those who attempt to exist outside of the legal and institutionalized organization and operation of social institutions that break down social and public order, it tends to ignore the crimes of the rich and powerful. Corporate crime goes largely unpoliced. As the radical criminologist might ask, "When was the last time a corporation went to prison or was put on probation?"

PANEL 2-6

An Historical and Structural Analysis of Crime in the United States

In 1973 . . . in America . . .

. . . Drug usage was said to be epidemic, seeping out from decaying ghettos to the suburbs. Murder and assault were reported rising at an unparalleled rate. Corporate fraud and chicanery had made headlines and sent Wall Street reeling. And Watergate, the apparent crime of the century, was in full flower. The harder we struggled to place these phenomena in a cultural and political context, the more we found ourselves driven to examine the roots of American crime.

The record of crime in America is of course voluminous . . .

. . . we have tried to draw the lines of authority between the individual and the state, to discover how it is that particular actions are determined to be crimes, who defines them as such, how those definitions change and for what reasons, and how as a consequence America has evolved a criminal subculture unmatched anywhere in the world. It is our thesis that the rulers and leading intellectuals of the nation have through the years often diffused our most disturbing social and personal issues and redefined them as the combat between crime and social stability. Episodes of rebellion and dissent, complemented by the pervasiveness of poverty and violence, have until recently escaped public-school texts. Recent "discoveries" of these themes have themselves demonstrated the peculiar opaqueness that has so obscured the American past—an opaqueness that in large part has resulted from the way in which individual and social challenges to the dominant culture have been deflected through the mechanism of the criminal court. To challenge the established order, established customs, or established ideologies was to attack society—just as in the original Puritan settlements to act without the approval of the church "elect" was to act as an agent of the devil, and therefore as a criminal. Public preoccupation with "the crime problem," we believe, has been a recurring method by which America's social elites have defined the boundaries of acceptable moral and political behavior.

PANEL 2-6 (Continued)

Europeans, who acknowledge a centuries-old class system, have described their social conflicts in overtly ideological terms as the combat among competing groups within society. Believing themselves free of these class conflicts, however, Americans were always convinced that challenges to the singular authority of the state resulted from flaws within the individual. A political system that declared class antagonism to be criminal on the face of it thus sought to eliminate conflict by eliminating its individual instigators, labeling them criminal. At the same time, through the invention of the penitentiary as the critical punitive device, the elites sought to reform lower-class miscreants by making them dependent and reshaping their moral deficiencies. That the courts and reformatories seldom achieved their immediate goal of reforming petty criminals has been secondary to their effect on the discourse created around crime and their symbolic importance as institutions of public order.

Control over the definition of crime and the administration of the criminal justice system has been, we argue, the dominant means by which the nation has addressed a broad range of public dilemmas. Not merely obvious crimes like murder, burglary, assault, and fraud are left to the courts, but the ever changing power relations among individuals—sex, job opportunities, family structure—are finally codified through criminal case law. Thus in 1978 a Michigan woman who burned her husband alive after he had repeatedly beaten her and denied her an independent career was acquitted of murder—largely because the movement for political and personal liberation among American women had grown powerful enough that homicide could be considered a legitimate self-defense against the crime of wife beating. Until recently, however, wife beating was considered a matter of male privilege within the family, far beyond the purview of the criminal courts. And in colonial times a woman who struck her husband could be tried for treason.

Contemporary issues of crime and social conflict are matters of ongoing debate that reflect profound cleavages within American society and that continue to be played out as issues of crime and punishment. . . .

Source: Frank Browning and John Gerassi's The American Way of Crime. *New York: Putnam, 1980, pp. 9–13.*

Criminology from this vantage point is also interested in crime and criminal justice as an ideology. The perceived seriousness of street crime and the media's announcement of "crime waves," for example, are said to organize broad support for the state's criminal justice practices. One need only consider how crime is depicted on television, where we (all of *us* decent citizens) are on the "right" (no political pun intended) side and street criminals (all of *those* immoral and irresponsible "nasties") are on the "wrong" side.[7] "We" must do something to suppress "them." In short, the ideology of crime and criminal justice is used to legitimate criminal justice practices employed by the state; practices, again, that one class uses to control another.

In many ways, crime and criminal justice are, from the point of view of radical criminology, so interrelated that they can be defined simultaneously. Crime and criminal justice ultimately represent the legal instruments of the state, legitimating its use of force and coercion (Humphries, 1979). For this reason, the state's attempts at law enforcement and criminal justice become in the main, "technologies" of social control. Crime control becomes a technique, a technique for enforcing the state's authority. Controlling crime begins to have little to do with the informal and more humane processes of social control inherent in community life (as is thought to have existed in many precapitalist and prestate societies).

Radical criminology has conceived of this technical system of criminal justice as (1) institutionalized oppression of the poor and working class and (2) a system organized and structured to fail. Criminal justice "structured to fail" refers to the process whereby the criminal justice system absorbs an ever-expanding surplus population (that part of the population that expands as economic processes in advanced capitalist societies make more and more people economically and socially redundant, that is, not needed, surplus to economic production and distribution) even while failing to control crime and thereby maintaining a large and visible "criminal class" that supposedly threatens all of society. This serves to divert attention away from social and economic problems created at the top of society by ruling groups benefiting from the established order of things and focuses it on the "dangerous classes" at the bottom of society. The failure is also found in the many types of crime in American society that go unpoliced because they actually contribute to the social and public order so desired by the state and ruling class: organized, corporate, and political crimes. But the system fails because failure serves the status quo and those who gain advantage from it. In this sense at least, failure is success (see Reiman, 1979).

If the criminal justice system maintains the status quo in American society by failing to police some kinds of crime but not others, what do we know specifically about which crimes are policed and which are not? A radical criminological perspective would suggest the following typology (see Table 2-1) of policed and unpoliced crime when the logical possibilities of social control and crime control are considered.

---

[7] Sociologist Emile Durkheim, a radical criminologist by no stretch of the imagination, had in the early part of this century already pointed to the way in which crime helped to create "moral boundaries" (the morally respectable distinguished from the immoral criminal) in society and functioned to instill a stronger social solidarity in the noncriminal community.

TABLE 2-1

Radical Criminology and a Typology of Policed and Unpoliced Crime: Organized Crime Control as Social Control

		SOCIAL CONTROL	
		Activity contributes to control	**Activity does not contribute to control**
	Activity is legal	All legal and normative behavior	Street "crime": legal political dissent, demonstrations, etc.
		NOT POLICED	POLICED
CRIME CONTROL	**Activity is illegal**	White-collar, organized and corporate crime, political crime by the state	Street crime, "victimless" crime, and political crime against the state
		NOT POLICED	POLICED

Given this kind of perspective on what is policed and what is not policed in American society, coupled with the reality of limited police resources, a radical perspective in criminology would probably contend that it is, indeed, more likely that pot-smoking workers in a General Motors plant would be policed than would a ghetto homicide, where one poor, unemployed black has killed another poor, unemployed black. Seriousness of the offense aside, pot smokers on an assembly line bear a closer relationship to the means of economic production and hence are more potentially disruptive to the social order than are people who have already been forced to become completely marginal to political and economic life.[8]

More than traditional or interactionist theories, radical criminology has looked beyond street crime to other important forms of criminal activity in our society: white-collar, organized, corporate, and political crime. In this regard, Young (1978) has suggested that while radical criminology should continue to locate the sources of all crime in the organization of the economic modes of production and the state's political intervention into this economic organization (i.e., locating the sources of crime in the political economy), it should also realize that a general theory of crime is inconceivable. Rather, the concrete and historical reality of each type of crime in American society may require its own theory.

For example, street crime is best conceptualized as emanating in a surplus population that has been marginal to, or completely excluded from, any meaningful participation in social and economic life (Humphries, 1979). Those in the surplus population (basically the large city black or brown ghetto, the "marginal"

---

[8] In fact, a few criminologists of this persuasion have speculated that an "unofficial" policy of "decarcerating" (as opposed to incarcerating) herds of criminals and other deviants into the core areas of large U.S. cities to prey upon each other (as opposed to preying on the middle and upper classes) has emerged within the past decade. See Scull (1977) and Chapter 15 for a more detailed analysis of this "deviant ghettoization."

working class, and those already processed by the criminal justice system, i.e., in prison, etc.) have been separated from both economic production and distribution. They have no labor power, no productive power (they cannot secure a wage in exchange for their work); neither have they the ability to consume goods and services (they lack the money that others' labor commands). Under these conditions, street crime may represent "the forcible reunification" of economic production and consumption (working and welfare representing more "peaceful," less forceful, reunifications of these things) (Young, 1978).

White-collar crime, however, may require a different explanation. Economic production, consumption, and mass-media advertising in capitalist societies encourage the "morality of private accumulation" in the private citizen. Rampant consumerism is the rule. Often crime, cheating the Internal Revenue Service, for example, may be the only way to make a car and house payment, send the kids to college, and otherwise survive economically. This is especially the case at present, as various economic factors mean that many in the "middle-income population" are faced with the prospect of adjusting their standard of living downward.

The sources of corporate crime are to be found primarily in the contradictions of capitalist economic development itself and in the role of the state in advanced capitalist societies. Logically and historically, capitalist enterprise has tended toward conglomeratization and monopolization. Over time, remaining financially secure and economically competitive become more and more difficult for more and more firms (some estimate that less than 200 financial and industrial corporations are now in control of the American economy). Also contributing to the hostile fiscal, legal, and economic environment of the American corporation is the state. Socially beneficial regulations, such as controls on air and water pollution, cost the private corporation. What all of this leads to is a "profit squeeze." U.S. corporations that had roughly a 15 percent profit margin before World War II, now profit at a rate around 5 percent. Corporate crime, through the sale of dangerous, unhealthy, and otherwise shoddy products, price-fixing, violation of worker's health and safety rights, environmental pollution, illegal trust-building, and illegal political campaign contributions, is used to help restore part of this declining profit margin.

For radical criminology, an adequate analysis of organized crime in the United States needs to abandon the limited leads that traditional and interactionist studies have provided concerning this phenomenon. First of all, the myth of an ethnically based (Sicilian or Italian) Mafia should be laid to rest. Organized crime is a state, corporate private sector, large labor union (e.g., the Teamsters) coalition. Furthermore, organized crime is best characterized as an unregulated, untaxed, high profit, capital- and technology-intense growth industry. It is so large—it probably does more than $150 billion worth of illegal business a year—that William Chambliss (1978) has contended that the advanced capitalist economy of the United States is actually crime dependent. It is not that we have an essentially legal and smooth-functioning economy with a little crime here and there; rather, our economy could not function as it does without both its criminal and legal foundations. We have one economy, with its legal aspects dependent on its illegal dimensions and vice versa. Furthermore, as profitable and secure investment opportunities in the legal economy shrink (as they have been for some time in the U.S. economy), the illegal sector is likely to expand even faster.

A radical analysis of organized crime also points to the "myth of victimless crime." Organized crime sells its commodities—sex, drugs, and money—to its victims. Addicts and prostitutes, for example, are directly victimized by the institutions of organized crime.

Radical criminology has also begun to analyze explicitly political crime. Although "crimes against the state" (illegal dissent, riot, revolt, etc.) have not garnered much attention, "crimes by the state" have. Human rights violations, war, unemployment, poverty, racism, and sexism have all been characterized as criminal activities that the American state is obliged to engage in as it protects the economic interests of the corporate sector both at home and in the Third World. Along these same lines, radical and Marxist criminologists have also been quick to focus attention upon the crimes committed by the criminal justice system itself, crimes like police brutality and class-biased, racist and sexist criminal court sentencing and correctional policy.

A Critique of Radical Criminology

Although radical criminology represents the first and fullest appreciation of the historical and structural nature of crime and criminal justice, making this perspective the most truly sociological view in criminology, it is not a perspective without flaws. We will discuss four of these flaws here. The first two, if not resolved properly, could prove to be intellectually and politically fatal for radical criminology. The last two, although probably not deadly, could lead to serious intellectual and political mistakes.

1. *Links to the Marxist "Prophetic Tradition."* Some explicitly Marxist work in criminology has become infused with the "revolutionary eschatology" of its informing perspective. The contention here is that capitalist societies will inevitably be transformed, first to socialism and then to a classless communist society. Richard Quinney, a Marxist criminologist, has described the inevitable dissolution of criminal justice (and by implication crime as well) that will accompany the inevitable transformation of society:

This takes us far beyond criminal justice. To transcend the capitalist economy and the capitalist state is also to transcend criminal justice. In the transition to socialism there is a dialectic between criminal justice and a popular justice movement beyond the control of the state. Developing consciousness among the working class involves a consciousness about social control. Working-class institutions will create forms of dealing with the problems that accompany class struggle, including protection from the repression of the capitalist state. These forms will be in the hands of the working-class, not in the jurisdiction of the state. The forms of control and human transformation will become apparent only in the movement toward socialism and in the movement from one state of socialism to another. The only thing we can be certain of now is that the forms of "justice"—or whatever the conceptualization that will be created—will be appropriate to the emerging society. The movement is clearly beyond criminal justice. (Quinney, 1977, pp. 158–159)

Any criminology that adheres to a prophetic vision of the future over and above concrete social and historical realities, does so at its peril. History is not predetermined in this fashion. Earlier Eitzen (1978, pp. 201–202) criticized this prophetic-Marxist view of the future of crime and criminal justice as "too utopian . . . like Marx's final stage of history . . . a statement of faith rather than one based on proof." This kind of Marxist criminology, in spite of its methodological emphasis on historical study, abandons historical reality when it becomes politically convenient to do so.

2. ***The Present Lack of an Adequate Empirical Base for Testing the Validity of the Key Proposition in Radical Criminology.*** This key proposition is, essentially, that capitalist-class society, replete as it is with class conflict and struggle, is the source of crime and the state's repressive attempts to control it. The corollary to this is, of course, that some form of a relatively classless, democratic-socialist society will effectively reduce crime and thus eliminate the need for repressive controls. And there is, indeed, evidence that those societies and governments that provide the most protection for their members from vast income and power inequalities tend to have lower property and violent crime rates (see Braithwaite, 1979, for example).

But socialist revolutions around the world (in the U.S.S.R., the East European block, Cuba, the People's Republic of China, etc.) generally have not yet attained fully classless, democratic, and socialist institutions. There are plenty of capitalist (advanced and "developing") societies currently available to study and test empirically radical criminology's perspective on the ultimate sources of crime and criminal justice practices. But no truly democratic-socialist society is available for testing its theory of crime reduction and elimination. The question, "would crime and other forms of deviance disappear under such a socialist system?" (Eitzen, 1978, p. 202), must necessarily remain empirically unanswerable at this point. Unfortunately, this often reduces the critical stance of the radical criminologist to philosophy and ideology.

This has been a source of tremendous irritation to traditional criminologists who have tended to react to it with strong, and in our estimation, often inappropriate, ideological tools of their own. Witness Charles McCaghy's comments:

In addition to its dubious assertions about the sources of crime, radical criminology rests uneasily on the assumption that crime will be drastically curtailed only upon the dissolution of capitalism. Radical criminologists believe that since class divisions create crime, only the transition to socialism and eventually to classless communism will diminish crime. However, the belief that the economic and social difficulties within the capitalist system are insoluble is purely ideological speculation, as is the notion that noncapitalist societies can be relatively crime-free in the absence of repressive governmental measures. The existing examples of the socialist transition—the U.S.S.R., Cuba, and the People's Republic of China—are ruled by strict regimes which provide no clue of the extent of crime in their societies. Thus the validity of radical criminology as an explanation of criminal behavior is uncertain at best. . . . (McCaghy, 1980, pp. 64–65)

3. *Controlling Street Crime.* Street and violent crime, even though they may be committed by an exploited and oppressed surplus population and marginal working class, do victimize and terrorize poor and working-class people who are its usual victims. Radical criminology has not paid enough attention to immediately controlling this sort of crime. (Since the transformation and full democratization of society takes time, what can be done about crime in the meantime?) It may be that this lack of attention to the protection of the poor and working class is contributing to (or at least, not deterring) the poor and the workers'—many of whom face the fear and reality of mugging, assault, burglary, and robbery on a daily basis—tendency to embrace conservative "law and order" solutions (like more policing, harsher sentencing, erosion of the legal rights of the accused, etc.) to the "crime problem." It is exactly these kinds of solutions, of course, that were offered by the Reagan Administration in the United States and that radical criminologists found so abhorrent.

Put in this context, Gresham Sykes' assessment of radical criminology has some merit:

In the administration of the criminal law in our society today, there is ample evidence that our ideals of equality before the law are being compromised by the facts of income and race in an industrial, highly bureaucratized social order. If a "critical criminology" can help us solve that issue, while still confronting the need to control crime, it will contribute a great deal. (Sykes, 1974, p. 213)

4. *Hanging on to Labeling Theory's Insights.* With its emphasis on social structure, radical criminology may fail to retain and complement itself with the social-psychological insights of labeling theory. More specifically, labeling theory's analysis of the impact of criminal justice control agencies on the everyday lives, reality, and identity of those labeled and processed as criminal and deviant, as well as their impact on the formation of criminal careers, should be carefully integrated into a radical perspective.

UNDERSTANDING CRIME AND CRIME CONTROL

Using Theory

As elaborated upon earlier, this book will dismiss pre- and nonsociological theories as incapable of explaining crime and criminal justice in American society. We will state again, quite categorically, that these kinds of theories are logically inadequate, empirically suspect, and unable to generate any humane and workable social policy for controlling crime.

On the other hand, we will employ throughout the text each of the three sociological approaches to crime and criminal justice that we have discussed in this chapter. Whenever and wherever one, all, or some combination of these theories appears to hold some illustrative or explanatory power for the problem under consideration, they will be applied. These applications will occur, when appropriate, in our treatment of all types of crime—street, white collar, victimless, organized, corporate, and political—and all components of the criminal justice system, that is, the criminal law, police, courts, and corrections.

Crime and Criminal Justice: Dialectics and History

Besides the consistent use of theory to understand crime and criminal justice, this text will also systematically examine the historical development of all types of crime and all parts of the criminal justice system within a context of the "dialectic of crime and crime control."

Crime and crime control are not separable social phenomena. They are characterized by their interrelatedness. Richard Quinney has explained this "dialectic" and given us the rationale for its use in our analysis of crime and criminal justice:

> The basic problem in any study of the meaning of crime is that of integrating the two sides of the crime phenomenon: placing into a single framework (1) the defining of behavior as criminal (i.e., crime control) and (2) the behavior of those who are defined as criminal (i.e., criminality). Thus far, the analysis of crime has focused on one side or the other, failing to integrate the two interrelated processes into one scheme. (Quinney, 1977, p. 33)

But this dialectical approach also has an historical side. Social phenomena, such as crime and criminal justice practices, are not often understood and defined by what they have been in the past and are now becoming. An adequate and enlightened analysis of crime and criminal justice in the United States must be one that takes full account of the historical development of these aspects of social life. Again, we will take Quinney's admonition seriously:

> The dialectical method allows us to comprehend the world as a complex of processes, in which all things go through a continuous process of coming into being and passing away. All things are studied in the context of their historical development. (Quinney, 1977, p. 32)

Let us begin then, our exploration of the world of crime and its control.

CHAPTER REVIEW

1. Pre- and nonsociological theories of crime contend that something *inside* individual criminals predisposes them to criminal acts. These theories are all predispositional theories whether or not they point to body type, genes and

heredity, body chemistry, or innate psychology as the primary cause of crime. The prominence of pre- and nonsociological perspectives in criminology has led to the continuing search for the *criminal type*.

2. Pre- and nonsociological theories of crime tend to limit available crime control strategies to physical elimination, extreme isolation and segregation, and/or medical treatment.

3. Pre- and nonsociological theories of crime are inadequate to the extent that they are empirically suspect due to suspicious research procedures and methods, empirically unconfirmed, ignore criminogenic social structural forces, focus only on street crime (leaving all "other" kinds of crime unexplained), and put to conservative (even reactionary) political purposes.

4. Traditional sociological theories of crime look *outside* the individual for the causes of crime. These theories basically locate the source of criminal acts in the immediate social environment. More specifically, traditional sociological perspectives can be characterized as social control theories (where crime is the result of weakened ties, bonds, controls, and constraints on the individual), social disorganization theories (where rapid social change and culture-conflict lead to the personal disorganization that causes crime), or socialization theories (where either a "too adequate," or "inadequate," or "different" socialization to the dominant culture in society is held to be the primary source of crime).

5. Traditional sociological perspectives on crime control tend to be liberal and optimistic: through the reform and rehabilitation of the individual offender's immediate social environment, crime, according to these perspectives, can be significantly reduced and controlled.

6. Weaknesses of traditional sociological perspectives include the tendency to concentrate only on street crime; the tendency to accept "the myth of lower-class criminality"; the focus on adjusting (reforming or rehabilitating) the individual offender to the social order even after identifying social factors as the primary cause of crime; failure to consider the "wider and larger" political, economic, and social sources of crime in American society that stem from the structure of racist, sexist, and class-biased institutions.

7. From the interactionist perspective, crime is not a characteristic or property of the individual criminal or of a particular criminal act. Rather, what makes a person criminal is the way society, or some group or agency in society, reacts to him or her. Individuals and acts become criminal only when they are so labeled and treated. Primary deviance—the "original" violation of a rule or law—is not the most significant source of the "crime problem." Secondary deviance—the deviance that is socially constructed when powerful interests in society stigmatize the acts of the powerless with deviant or criminal labels that, through the mechanism of the self-fulfilling prophecy, often lead to deviant and criminal identities and careers—is the primary source of crime. The irony here, of course, is that the agency charged with the prevention and control of crime, the criminal justice system, is actually seen as an "organized societal reaction" that helps to manufacture crime.

8. Interactionists argue that a criminal justice system that either intervenes the least, that pursues a "policy of nonintervention" in the lives of apprehended

offenders (the libertarian view) or that intervenes in a much more humane, sensitive, and sympathetic way vis-à-vis offenders (a liberal approach), will control crime much more effectively than the present system.

9. Like traditional sociological perspectives, the interactionist perspective has concentrated almost solely on street and "victimless" crime, and also similar to traditional approaches, has failed to take full account of the "wider and larger" historical and structural origins of crime. In addition, interactionists have failed to explain adequately the causes of "primary deviance" and the way in which power is used to criminalize the acts of the poor and minorities systematically and purposefully.

10. Radical criminology is perhaps the most fully sociological perspective on the sources of crime in society. This approach goes beyond characteristics of the individual criminal, his or her immediate social environment, or his or her face-to-face encounters with agents and agencies of social control, and locates the origins of crime in the "wider and larger" historical development and structure of society's institutions. More specifically, this perspective holds that the mode or organization of economic production and the state's intervention in that economy, particularly in a fully developed capitalist society, creates the class inequality and conflict that ultimately leads to crime. Radical criminology also contends that a general theory of crime is unattainable and that its basic orientation or framework can and should generate separate theories for different kinds of crime (street, victimless, white collar, organized, corporate, and political crime).

11. Since radical criminology holds the structure of economic, political, and social institutions responsible for the contradictions, conflict, and inequality that generates crime, the prescription for more effective criminal justice and crime control is to transform the very structure of the basic institutions of capitalist society to democratize the economy and society. For radical criminology, the reform, or rehabilitation of the individual offender and/or his or her immediate environment will ultimately fail to control crime.

12. Weaknesses of radical criminology include instances of close association with the Marxist "prophetic tradition," the lack of an empirical base that could satisfactorily test the proposition that classless, democratic-socialist societies would be relatively crime-free, a failure to address the immediate question of controlling street crime, and a tendency to become so thoroughly structural in its analysis that the sound social-psychological insights of labeling theory into crime causation are often ignored.

3 Criminal Law

CHAPTER
OUTLINE

Principles That Guide the Criminal Law
Law and Sociological Theory: Functional and Radical Views

The Functional Approach
Law from the Radical Perspective

Summary and Evaluation: Functional and Radical Views of the Law

Definition of Crime
The Bias of the Law
The Nature of Law and Punishment by Type of Society
Assessment of the Functional and Radical Views of the Law

KEY TERMS

Common law (English)
Ex post facto laws
General deterrence
Mala in se crimes
Mala prohibita crimes
Mens rea
M'Naghten rule
Police power
Rehabilitation
Retribution
Specific (special) deterrence
Stare decisis

There are two contrasting views of the law. One is that the law is neutral, a force for the common good. The following quotes support this view:

Where law ends, tyranny begins.

William Pitt the Elder (1708–1778)

The law is reason free from passion.

Aristotle (384–322 B.C.)

Law is experience developed by reason and applied continually to further experience.

Roscoe Pound

The law that will work is merely the summing up in legislative form of the moral judgment that the community has already reached.

Woodrow Wilson

The law is not an end in itself, nor does it provide ends. It is preeminently a means to serve what we think is right.

Justice William J. Brennan, Jr.

Order is the first requisite of liberty.

Georg Wilhelm Hegel (1770–1831)

The contrasting view, that the law is the tool of the powerful, is the theme of these statements:

Where the weak or oppressed assert the rights that have been so long denied them, those in power inevitably resist on the basis of the necessity of tranquility.

Chief Justice Earl Warren

Law is merely the expression of the will of the strongest for the time being.

Brooks Adams

The French law in its majestic equality prohibits both rich and poor alike from sleeping under the bridges of the Seine.

Anatole France

Laws are spider webs through which the big flies pass and the little ones get caught.

Honoré de Balzac (1799–1850)

Law and order are always and everywhere the law and order which protect the established hierarchy.

Herbert Marcuse

Crime, formally, is conduct that the law has labeled illegal. The study of crime and crime control must begin, then, with an understanding of the law. Since law is a social product, we must comprehend the historical and contemporary forces that shape it. Most fundamentally, we must address the question illustrated by the contrasting statements above—*do the laws reflect some interests more than others?* This is the central question addressed in this chapter and the answer provides the foundation for understanding the role of the state in the patterns and vagaries of crime and its control in American society. We begin, however, with an overview of the principles of American criminal law, their origins, and the problems with each.

THE PRINCIPLES THAT GUIDE THE CRIMINAL LAW

The immediate sources of the law in the United States are the U.S. and state constitutions, federal and state legislation, judicial decisions in the federal and state courts, administrative regulations by federal, state, and local agencies, and local ordinances. Despite this diversity and obvious inconsistencies and conflicts among the laws from different sources, there is a general unity to the American legal system. This unity stems from our legal heritage—from ancient Greece, ancient Rome, and Judeo-Christian tradition, and especially from England. The early American colonists brought the English legal system with them, and although there has been modification, the present system "still growing and slowly changing, bears the stamp of this complex legal history" (Sykes, 1978, p. 44). Central to the English and American legal systems is what is known as the *common law*. The common law developed in England as judges ruled that certain actions were crimes even though there were no existing laws making them so. In the eleventh century these unwritten, customary laws were codified by the king's courts into a set of legal rules—the common law.

The English common law is the basis for much of the U.S. legal system. Unlike England, however, the common law has been standardized and put in statutory form by state legislatures. Of course, these legislatures have also gone beyond the common law to define crimes not considered under the common law.

While there are legal differences within the United States, the English common law, the federal criminal code, and the U.S. Constitution provide for a unity. This occurrence in the legal system is reflected in the major principles that guide the federal and state laws.

Fundamental is the principle that there is no crime without law, no punishment without law (in Latin, *nullem crimen sine lege, nulla ponna sine lege*). This provides fairness since individuals are forewarned about what acts are criminal and if violated how they will be punished. Thus, *ex post facto* laws (i.e., laws passed after the act is committed making it illegal) are prohibited. This provides an important guarantee to citizens against arbitrary government actions.

The problem with this principle is that if powerful interests are able to keep certain acts from being crimes—such as pollution, misleading advertising, and disregard for worker safety—they are exempt from sanctions. So, too, are harmful acts by the government.

A second principle guiding the American legal system is that the state has the power to prohibit conduct deemed harmful to society. This is the fundamental power of the state to regulate in order to protect public health, safety, welfare, and morals. This power to create criminal laws to prevent harm in the public interest is called the state's *police power*.

Two types of laws are made under the state's police power. There are laws that make crimes of acts that are commonly considered evil in and of themselves such as rape, murder, robbery, kidnapping, arson, and assault. These acts, considered violations of traditional morality, are prohibited by *mala in se* laws. In contrast, there are also laws (*mala prohibita*) that prohibit acts that are criminal only because the law so states. Such crimes as speeding, driving on the left side of the road, the violation of a zoning ordinance, and disorderly conduct are *mala prohibita* offenses.

There is considerable debate over whether the legal codes in a heterogeneous society should demand conformity to the morality of the majority. There was no debate over this in Puritan New England. The Bible was the guide for lawmakers as they equated sin with crime (Erickson, 1966). The Puritan legacy continues in modern America as assumed *mala in se* laws prohibit the use of recreational drugs, gambling, prostitution, and other "victimless" crimes. Religious fundamentalists won significant political victories in 1980 and at the center of their political agenda was the passage of more laws reflecting their version of morality.

Another principle is that the criminal law stipulates that violators must be punished. Punishment has five potential uses. The first is general deterrence. This is the public punishment of criminals to deter potential criminals by example. In the past punishment was often public to accomplish this goal. There were public floggings and the placing of criminals in the stocks in the town square (a favorite in Puritan New England) to restrain others from committing crimes.

The second use of punishment is specific deterrence, which is to punish the criminal so that he or she will not repeat the offense. Hard labor, torture, limited diet, and solitary confinement are assumed to accomplish this goal. The Prisons Act of 1865 in England provided for these punishments as well as such meaningless but painful tasks as the shot drill to make prison life something no one would chance again. The "shot drill required the prisoner . . . to lift heavy cannonballs, keeping the elbows away from the body and the knees straight, moving the ball a few paces and then placing them on the ground, only to repeat the performance endlessly" (Chambliss and Seidman, 1971, p. 198).

Punishment is also used to isolate the perpetrator from society to protect against his or her antisocial acts. Fourth is the goal of rehabilitation—to change criminals into conforming members of society. Fifth is retribution or vengeance ("an eye for an eye"). Sykes (1978, pp. 59–60) has argued that whereas vengeance continues to shape much of the public's thinking about criminals, the official rationale for punishment is deterrence. Most criminologists, however, agree that this societal tactic of using the fear of punishment to deter subsequent criminal behavior only has a minor deterrent effect of crime (Balkan et al., 1980, p. 123). Chapter 13 will explore this question in detail.

Another principle guiding our legal system is that criminal responsibility, and the need for punishment, is not just a function of committing an illegal act. There must be deliberate intent for the criminal act to be criminal. The principle expressed in Latin is *actus non facit reus nisi mens sit rea* ("an act does not make one guilty unless his mind is guilty"). The accidental killing of another, for example, is not murder. An involuntary crime that occurs while the defendant was sleepwalking or having a seizure is not punishable under the *mens rea* principle.

Insanity is another legal defense since mental disorder negates criminal responsibility because the individual is not conscious of wrongdoing or able to control himself/herself. This is a controversial defense because the legal rules relating to the use of insanity are as uncertain as the psychiatric profession's understanding of mental disorder. The fundamental test for criminal responsibility involving insanity is the M'Naghten Rule. In 1843, an Englishman Daniel M'Naghten was tried for the murder of the secretary of the prime minister of England. M'Naghten was found "not guilty, by reason of insanity" as the court agreed that he suffered from paranoid delusions. Because of the unpopularity of the decision the British Parliament asked the court to define under what conditions individuals are not responsible for their acts. In essence the ruling, known as the *M'Naghten Rule,* was that a person is insane if he or she is unable to distinguish between right and wrong as a result of some mental disability (Senna and Siegal, 1978, p. 82). The M'Naghten Rule was adopted in the United States and continues to guide decisions today in about one-half of the states but not without considerable controversy. Many questions are unanswered since many individuals are mentally disturbed but can distinguish between right and wrong. Most fundamentally, what is mental illness? And, who should decide on the mental illness of a defendant, a judge, jury, or psychiatric experts? The latter would seem the most appropriate, but there is basic disagreement among them as evidenced by considerable research (see Eitzen, 1983), and the typically contradictory testimony by psychiatrists and psychologists for both sides in a trial involving the criminal insanity of a defendant.

The twists of logic used in the insanity defense are shown in the 1901 Supreme Court ruling in *Hotema v. United States*. The defendant in this case killed an alleged witch in obedience to what he believed to be a biblical demand. "The court approved a charge which directed that if the defendant's belief in witches was simply the conclusion of a sane mind, he was to be convicted, but if the result of a disordered mind, acquitted. Insanity as a ground of defense exculpates only when the defect is a mental disease and not merely one of training" (Chambliss and Seidman, 1971, p. 206).

Criminal responsibility is also tempered significantly by immaturity. Mentally retarded persons and children are generally exempt from responsibility for their otherwise criminal acts because they are unable to understand the full meaning of their actions. Although the principle is firm, the application of the age exemption, for example, varies by jurisdiction, especially over the exact age of accountability.

Individuals are also relieved of responsibility for their acts if they have acted in self-defense. Those making the claim of self-defense in the courts must prove they were in danger and that the amount of force used in the counterattack was reasonable.

Finally, another condition affecting responsibility is intoxication whether by alcohol or other drug. Generally, the courts and juries tend to reduce punishment for defendants who commit criminal acts while intoxicated.

There is another and quite different problem with the *mens rea* principle that we must recognize; it promotes bias. This guiding principle of our legal system demands that the court prove that the defendant *intended* to commit the offense. Hopkins has argued successfully that this is relatively easy to prove in street crimes but much more so when the offenses are corporate and white-collar crimes. Thus, there is "a bias against conventional, largely working-class criminals and in favor of white collar offenders, a bias which is inherent in the very law itself" (Hopkins, 1981, p. 386).

Another principle, adopted from the English common law, that guides the American legal system is that court decisions shall be based on precedent (*stare decisis*). Once a decision has been made by a court, that decision is considered binding in subsequent applicable cases, unless there is an unusual mitigating circumstance. The advantage of this principle is that it promotes stability and predictability in legal decisions rather than capriciousness. Thus, if general deterrence is to occur (a dubious assumption), potential criminals must know beforehand of the severity of the punishment. The disadvantage is that in reinforcing tradition, the courts find it difficult to adapt to changing conditions, right a wrong decision, or deal adequately with long-standing discrimination.

A final principle guiding our laws is that there are constraints on the arbitrary powers of government. There are procedural laws that direct the government to treat the accused fairly. Defendants in criminal cases are guaranteed due process, the assumption of innocence, the right to cross-examine witnesses, legal defense, and a trial by jury. Unfortunately, as we will see in Chapter 11, the accused especially if poor does not always get these rights in practice.

These procedural laws, which protect individuals when accused of crimes from the arbitrary actions of the government, are also the result of our English legal legacy. When William became King of England in 1066, he and subsequent monarchs were faced wth unifying the country under one ruler, the king. A number of compromises were made between the king and his subjects over 100 years or so, to bring about this unity, and to appease the barons and the Catholic Church, which lost power. Among these compromises were a number of procedural guarantees limiting the king's power such as rules of evidence, the right of appeal, and the right to be judged by a jury of peers (Hartjen, 1978, pp. 27–28).

In contemporary America the Supreme Court has made a number of decisions reaffirming the rights of persons accused of crimes. A few of these celebrated cases are:

- *Gideon v. Wainwright* (1963) where the court ruled that a lawyer must be provided for indigent (poor) defendants in felony cases going to trial.

> **INTERROGATION WARNINGS TO PERSONS IN POLICE CUSTODY:**
>
> THE FOLLOWING WARNINGS MUST BE GIVEN TO THE SUBJECT BEFORE THE INTERROGATION BEGINS:
>
> 1. "You have the right to remain silent and refuse to answer questions." Do you understand? Subject replied _____.
>
> 2. "Anything you do say may be used against you in a court of law." Do you understand? Subject replied _____.
>
> 3. "You have the right to consult an attorney before speaking to the police and to have an attorney present during any questioning now or in the future." Do you understand? Subject replied _____.
>
> 4. "If you cannot afford an attorney, one will be provided for you without cost." Do you understand? Subject replied _____.
>
> 5. "If you do not have an attorney available, you have the right to remain silent until you have had an opportunity to consult with one." Do you understand? Subject replied _____.
>
> 6. "Now that I have advised you of your rights, are you willing to answer questions without an attorney present?" Subject replied _____.

The police at the time of arrest must inform suspects of their constitutional rights—the so-called Miranda Rights.

- *Escobedo v. Illinois* (1964) ruled that counsel must be provided prior to the police interrogation of a suspect.
- *Miranda v. Arizona* (1966) insisted that the police at the time of arrest must inform suspects of their constitutional rights.

These and other decisions have come under increased attack by political conservatives because they are viewed as too lenient. The war against violent crime, in their view, will not be won as long as the liberal courts side with the accused. Thus, conservatives favor repeal of the exclusionary rule (which limits what can be used as evidence by protecting individual rights), more pretrial detention without bail, and mandatory minimum sentences. To the degree that the political composition of the court reflects this view, the procedural rules guaranteeing the rights of the accused are in jeopardy. Even assuming that the court's earlier decisions stand, it must be recognized that the constitutional guarantees of fairness, however admirable in the abstract, do not, in practice, protect effectively the members of the relatively powerless segments of society from the awesome power of the government.

The questions raised for each of these guiding principles are meant to indicate that for all its strengths, the American legal system is sometimes inconsistent, occasionally ambiguous, and often biased. The law is continually debated by political and economic elites, members of the legal community and concerned citizens alike on such legal issues as the goal of punishment and what forms are most effective, the appropriateness of laws governing morals, the degree to which the accused should be protected, and the conditions under which individuals are not accountable for their acts. Central to understanding these and other legal debates are two basic views: functional theory and radical theory. The presentation and implications of these two theoretical perspectives on criminal law are the subjects of the remainder of this chapter.

LAW AND SOCIOLOGICAL THEORY: FUNCTIONAL AND RADICAL VIEWS

Society creates crime by passing laws that make certain acts illegal and their perpetrators criminals. Political authorities in a society specify and describe those acts that are crimes and the punishment that the guilty will receive in the name of the state. Criminal law, then, is inherently political (Hartjen, 1978, p. 24). There are two contrasting ways to view this political nature of law (and crime). One is that when rulebreakers are singled out and punished, the norms of society are being reaffirmed and legitimated. From this angle the laws represent the views of the majority and serve their interests by providing order, stability, and the protection of the moral stance of the community. Juxtaposed to this functional view of the law is the radical position that the powerful control the powerless by imposing their definition of morality on them. What is a crime and who is a criminal is a consequence of who is doing the defining (Skolnick, 1969). The important point of this view of the radical theorists is that the powerful use their power in the criminal-defining process for their advantage. Each of these perspectives is important and has important implications for the understanding of crime and crime control in American society. We begin by describing the functional approach to law, which has been the dominant view in traditional sociology.

The Functional Approach

Proponents of this model view law as the formalization of the values of society (Sumner, 1906). The laws are the agreed-upon rules necessary for social order. They are the instrument for the protection of society's members. The law, because it reflects the common consensus, is neutral. Chambliss has summarized the basic assumptions of functional theorists regarding the law:

The law represents the value consensus of the society.
The law represents those values and perspectives that are fundamental to social order.
The law represents those values and perspectives that it is in the public interest to protect.
The state as represented in the legal system is value-neutral.
In pluralistic societies, the law represents the interests of the society at large by mediating between competing interest groups (Chambliss, 1976, p. 4).

To understand this paradigm more clearly we will examine briefly the arguments of three of its most important advocates—Emile Durkheim, Roscoe Pound, and Talcott Parsons.

Emile Durkheim (1855–1917) was a French sociologist whose scholarly work was devoted to understanding the integrative bonds in society. He believed that the central feature of crime is that it is universally disapproved of by the members of society because it offends the collective conscience of the community (Durkheim, 1949, p. 73). When a crime is committed, then, the central values of the society are attacked. The violators must be punished because this punishment reinforces the values of society and the solidarity of the collective conscience by preserving the moral boundaries of society (Durkheim, 1949, p. 102).

Durkheim disinguished between two extreme types of society that differ in size, homogeneity, and complexity. Small, homogeneous societies such as preliterate tribes are characterized by mechanical solidarity. People in these societies are bound together by tradition, the similarities of their everyday activities, and by a common morality. There is a compelling consensus on group values reinforced by tradition, religious beliefs, and by all of the members of the community. Thus, there is a clear and consistent message on what behaviors are appropriate and which are not. The people in these societies are governed by custom, not by codified laws. Minor deviations from the norms in these close-knit groups are generally sanctioned by informal controls such as gossip, ridicule, and other forms of humiliation. When acts offend the collective consciousness, however, the punishment is repressive since the social solidarity of the group must be protected and preserved. The community is saying that these forms of deviance will not be tolerated. The concern, then, is with community solidarity, not the rehabilitation of offenders.

Although Durkheim (1949) longed nostalgically for an era when societies were simple and highly integrated, he realized that the modern world was much different. Societies now are large, heterogeneous, industrialized and urbanized. The complexity in these societies results from a high degree of differentiation. This division of labor is the source of integration in these societies by connecting specialized workers in an interdependent network. Thus, Durkheim characterized these societies as integrated through organic solidarity. Durkheim believed that integration is tenuous in these societies because pluralism leads to greater individual freedom than found in simpler societies. Many individuals in these settings experience anomie, which means ''normlessness.'' In effect, these persons, because of rapid social change, geographical or social mobility, become unsure of what the rules are, and this leads to their personal disorganization. Therefore, it is essential to control individuals to hold their potentially deviant behavior in check. This is accomplished by the enforcement of formal laws (Ritzer, Kammeyer, and Yetman, 1982, p. 81). The emphasis is different, however, in these large, impersonal societies than in small, homogeneous ones. Instead of repressive law now, Durkheim asserted, there is restitutive law. Punishment tends toward restitution and compensation for harms done to the victim. Punishment is given by the legal system in such societies in terms of what is beneficial for the offender's rehabilitation.

The ideas of Roscoe Pound (1870–1964), a highly influential American legal scholar, are in the tradition established by Durkheim. He argued that the law was a social product, reflecting the consciousness of society (Pound, 1942). He viewed the law as a necessary means of social control to constrain individuals, to uphold civilized society, and to deter them from "conduct at variance with the postulates of social order" (Pound, 1942, p. 18). The law for Pound was also an integrative mechanism since it resolved conflicting interests and maintained order in society.

> Looked at functionally, the law is an attempt to satisfy, to reconcile, to harmonize, to adjust these overlapping and often conflicting claims and demands, either through securing them directly and immediately, or through securing certain individual interests, so as to give effect to the greatest total of interests or to the interests that weigh most in our civilization, with the least sacrifice of the scheme of interests as a whole. (Pound, 1943, p. 39)

In a pluralistic society there are different and sometimes opposing interests. The law provides the neutral framework within which these conflicting claims are reconciled fairly and in an orderly manner. The law is the instrument that controls diverse interests according to the requirement of social order (Quinney, 1970, p. 34). The only bias of the law is toward social order; those interests are served by the law that are in the best interests of society. Since the law functions for socially worthwhile purposes, only right laws could develop in a civilized society (Quinney, 1979, p. 20).

Talcott Parsons (1902–1979), probably the most influential American sociologist of the past 40 years, gave contemporary emphasis to Durkheim's view of the law. He, too, was principally concerned with societal order. Also, like Durkheim and Pound, his model of society is based on the assumption of societal-wide consensus. His logic was that:

1. Every society is a relatively persisting configuration of elements.
2. Every society is a well-integrated configuration of elements.
3. Every element in a society contributes to its functioning.
4. Every society rests upon the consensus of its members (Dahrendorf, 1958).

Parsons (1977) believed that societies evolve with differentiation being the basic evolutionary principle. Preliterate societies have an undifferentiated elite controlling simultaneously in religious, political, and economic matters. In modern societies, in contrast, there are specialized elites in each institutional arena. As societies become more differentiated, crime becomes more salient because the integrative mechanisms of modern societies are more problematic than in undifferentiated societies where cohesion is virtually automatic. Stability in modern societies is ensured by the "institutionalization of a set of norms defining the limits of legitimate action" (Parsons, 1951, p. 118).

According to Parsons, the emergence of legal systems helps to integrate societies that would otherwise be bogged down in ethnic particularism. Law is one of the handful of evolutionary universals on the way to modernity. With the institutionalization of criminal law, deviance is *criminalized*—imperfectly, to be sure, and to a varying extent in different societies. The price societies pay for the universalism of the criminal law is the inevitable discrepancies between parochial moralities of subgroups, especially ethnic groups, and the universalistic codes embodied in the law. To put it another way, it is necessarily more difficult to control crime in a complex society than it is to control deviance in a less differentiated society. (Toby, 1979, p. 387)

Law from the Radical Perspective

The founding principle for radicals is that the law is biased to protect the dominant class in society. In short, the law is not the reflection of moral boundaries, as the functionalists assert, but is a weapon in class conflict. The intellectual giant of this view is Karl Marx (1818–1883). Although Marx did not develop a systematic theory of crime, his conflict model provides the essential insights for understanding crime and the law.

The Basic Premises of Marx

For Marx the starting point for the understanding of society is the organization of economic production. Every society has a specific mode of production based on the combination of tools, raw materials, technical knowledge, human labor, and

Radical criminologists argue that the law is a weapon of the ruling class used to perpetuate its advantage.

those who own all of these elements. In economic systems such as slavery, feudalism, and capitalism, there are those who own the forces of production and at the other extreme, those who work for these owners. The owners are advantaged materially from the status quo and obviously work to maintain it. The powerless are disadvantaged both materially and in other exploitative ways. Thus, classes result from the ownership (or nonownership) of the means of production.

The mode of production—the way the economy is organized—is the foundation for the way other institutions work. As Marx put it:

> The sum total of these relations of production constitutes the economic structure of society—the real foundation, on which rises legal and political superstructures and to which correspond definite forms of social consciousness. The mode of production in material life determines the general character of the social, political, and spiritual processes of life. (Marx, 1904, p. 11)

In other words, the economy provides the infrastructure of a society that shapes the political system, educational system, religion, and other forms of social thought.[1]

An essential element of the superstructure is the state. The state, according to Marx, is not value-neutral; it is a weapon in the hands of those who control it (the owners of the means of production).

> The State consists of the institutions of coercion: the police, the army, prison officials. These are the principal weapons in the hands of the ruling class. Law, which rests finally upon the State's self-perpetuating monopoly of violence or instruments of coercion, therefore represents the will of the ruling classes; in more modern terms, we would say that it embodies the values of the ruling class. This is a view which conceives of society in terms of sharp conflict between different classes, each with its own set of values, and the State as a weapon in the hands of the class in control of it. (Chambliss and Seidman, 1971, p. 53)

In essence, the state, and in particular for our needs, the law, exist as tools of the ruling class to maintain its advantage over the lower class. Speaking of the ruling class Marx and Engels (1966, p. 47) said: "Your jurisprudence is but the will of your class made into a law for all, a will whose essential character and direction are determined by the economic conditions of your class."

Contemporary criminologists in the Marxian tradition view the law as a creation of the powerful in society, rather than as a reflection of community custom. The law for them reflects, rather, underlying class division. In the words of William Chambliss (1978, p. 193), "What makes the behavior of some criminal is the

---

[1] We are cautioned by interpreters of Marx that the base—the infrastructure metaphor—is not meant by Marx to be fully deterministic. Politics, law, philosophy, and the like are *based* on the economic foundation; they are *shaped* by economics but as they evolve and interact they are not reducible to the economy (Greenberg, 1981, p. 15). These other institutions and social processes do have a certain amount of autonomy, "but they cannot be studied in isolation from the political economy of the time" (Balkan, Berger, and Schmidt, 1980, p. 41).

coercive power of the state to enforce the will of the ruling class. . . ." Or as Richard Quinney has put it:

> Law is made by men, representing special interests, who have the power to translate their interests into public policy. Unlike the pluralistic conception of politics, law does not represent a compromise of the diverse interests in society, but supports some interests at the expense of others (1970:35). . . . As an act of politics, law and legal decisions do not represent the interests of all persons in society. Whenever a law is created or interpreted, the values of some are necessarily assured and the values of others are either ignored or negated. (Quinney, 1970, p. 37)

The basis for this assertion is that interest groups are grossly unequal in power. If they were similar in power, as the functionalists contend, the law would more likely represent compromise and the common interests. But this has not been the case. Nor is it the situation now.

Evidence for the Law Protecting the Ruling Class

From the beginning the law has had a class bias. The earliest known legal code, the Code of Hammurabi, was formulated as early as 2270 B.C. in Babylonia. Included was a section that justified vengeance ("an eye for an eye, a tooth for a tooth"). Most significant, though, this principle was asymmetrical—a noble could punish a commoner for an offense, but a commoner was not permitted to do so when harmed by a noble (Hartjen, 1978, p. 28).

Criminal law in England and the United States has not been as blatant in its bias as this. Many of the laws have benefitted the interests of commoners by promoting order. But, nonetheless, the law has tended to favor certain interests. Our task in this section is to provide some examples of how special interests have shaped the laws for their benefit.

The Laws of Vagrancy   Vagrancy laws appeared in England in 1349. These original statutes made it a crime to give money to any able-bodied adult who was unemployed. The rationale, which was included in the law, was that idle people are prone toward vice and theft and thus should be encouraged to work. But the intent of the law, according to Chambliss (1964, 1976), was quite different. The plague known as the Black Death, which struck England in 1348, killed at least half of the population creating a tremendous labor shortage and a press for higher wages for workers. The vagrancy laws were intended to offset these consequences by forcing all idle people to work and at low wages. It was even unlawful to refuse an offer of work or to leave the community. As Foote described it:

> By the Statutes of Labourers in 1349–1351, every able-bodied person without other means of support was required to work for wages fixed at the level preceding the Black Death; it was unlawful to accept more, or to refuse an offer of work, or to flee from one county to another to avoid offers of work or to seek

higher wages, or to give alms to able-bodied beggars who refused to work. (Foote, 1956, p. 615)

Thus, feudal landowners were able to continue to control and exploit the serfs (peasants).

The vagrancy laws were altered significantly in the 1500s. England by this time was shifting from a feudal and agricultural society to one of commerce and trade. Merchants were increasing the traffic of valuable goods and these shipments required protection. There was, from the merchants' perspective, a clear need for laws and law enforcement to control persons who might jeopardize such trade. The new vagrancy laws now assumed that idle people were potential "rogues" and "vagabonds." The 1547 law read:

Whoever man or woman, being not lame, impotent, or so aged or diseased that he or she cannot work, not having whereon to live, shall be lurking in any house, or loitering or idle wandering by the highway side, or in streets, cities, towns, or villages, not applying themselves to some honest labour, and so continuing for three days; or running away from their work; every such person shall be taken for a vagabond. And . . . upon conviction of two witnesses . . . the same loiterer [shall] be marked with a hot iron in the breast with the letter V, and adjudged him to the person bringing him, to be his slave for two years. (quoted in Chambliss, 1976, p. 74)

People suspected of criminal activity were now often punished as vagrants. And the punishment was increasingly severe. The laws called for, depending on the situation, public whippings, cutting off of an ear, and even death (Chambliss, 1976, p. 73).

Clearly, these vagrancy laws in England reflected the wishes of the powerful. Under feudalism there was the need for cheap labor. Later with the growth of a mercantile class, the vagrancy laws were used to protect commercial trade from potential troublemakers. The vagrancy laws, with this latter bias, were adopted in the American colonies with only minor changes.

In America as in England, the central purpose of the vagrancy laws has been to control criminals and other undesirables. Vagrancy statutes provide a handy excuse for apprehending a suspect when evidence of wrongdoing is lacking or hard to come by . . . the use of vagrancy laws in contemporary society to keep bums and other undesirables off the streets, or at least out of respectable neighborhoods, suggests the influence of middle-class desires and power to shape criminal law. (Hartjen, 1978, p. 33)

In fact the vagrancy laws have even been used in recent times in agricultural states to provide cheap labor during harvest (Spradley, 1970).

The Law of Theft   Prior to the 15th century there was no legal conception of theft as we know it. A landmark English case, the Carrier Case in 1473, resulted in a legal definition of theft that reflected the interest of the powerful of that time and continues to the present (Hall, 1952).

The defendant in the Carrier Case, a foreign merchant, had been hired to carry bales of wool and cloth to Southampton. However, he took the goods to another place, opened the bales and took the contents. He was apprehended and charged with a felony. Under the laws of that time the act was not a crime because anything that was lawfully in someone's possession belonged to that person. Theft at that time only involved trespass and the illegal removal of someone else's property. The only protection for a merchant was to hire someone to transport goods who was trustworthy. In feudal times this worked because the landowners were the masters of the economic resources of society, and others dared not betray them. Although the informal modes of feudal order were once adequate, the advent of capitalism required the protection of private property. The new economy was based on commodity exchange and change required legal changes for such protection. The court so ruled in the Carrier Case. The ruling was that while the bales were in the custody of the carrier, he did not legally possess the contents. By taking the contents that were not his, he was guilty of theft. This decision was required by the new economic conditions of capitalism and was demanded by the growing power of the merchant class and by King Edward IV who was very active in domestic and foreign trade. These powerful interests dictated a rule for their protection. As Hall has summarized it:

> On the one hand, the criminal law at the time is clear. On the other hand, the whole complex aggregate of political and economic conditions described above thrusts itself upon the court. The more powerful forces prevailed—that happened which in due course must have happened under the circumstances. The most powerful forces of the time were interrelated very intimately and at many points: the New Monarchy and the *nouveau riche*—the mercantile class; the business interests of both and the consequent need for a secure carrying trade; the wool and textile industry, the most valuable, by far, in all the realm; wool and cloth, the most important exports; these exports and the foreign trade; this trade and Southampton, chief trading city with the Latin countries for centuries; the numerous and very influential Italian merchants who bought English wool and cloth inland and shipped them from Southampton. The great forces of an emerging modern world, represented in the above phenomena, necessitated the elimination of a formula which had outgrown its usefulness. A new set of major institutions required a new rule. The law, lagging behind the needs of the times, was brought into more harmonious relationship with the other institutions by the decision rendered in the Carrier's Case. (Hall, 1952, p. 54)

The Carrier Case decision, shaped as it was by changing social conditions and emerging social interests, provided the foundation for further enlargement on the law of theft. As banking and the use of paper currency expanded, for example, the theft laws were expanded to include embezzlement by employees. These and other laws provided further protection of the mercantile interests. As Quinney (1970, p. 73) has put it: "The legal protection of property has always been to the interest of the propertied segments of society."

Laws to Curb the Excesses of Corporations A number of major laws have been passed in the last 100 years or so in the United States that were aimed at restricting private enterprise. The Sherman Act of 1890 prohibited monopolies. The Federal Food and Drug Act of 1906 was an effort to stop the adulteration and misbranding of food and drugs. The many regulatory laws instituted under the New Deal of President Franklin Roosevelt curbed other abuses of big business. These and related government efforts would seem to negate the argument that the law represents the interests of the most powerful segments in society. They, too, however, are found to be congruent with the interests of the powerful.

With respect to the antitrust (anti-monopoly) legislation, the aim was not to change the economic system but to preserve a competitive system demanded by the principles of free enterprise. President Theodore Roosevelt, self-styled trust-buster, said in this regard:

> We can do nothing of good in the way of regulating and supervising these corporations until we fix clearly in our minds that we are not attacking the corporations, but endeavoring to do away with any evil in them. We are not hostile to them, we are merely determined that they shall be so handled as to subserve the public good. (quoted in Morison, Eliot, and Commager, 1950, p. 391)

Similarly, when the legislation and actions of President Franklin Roosevelt's New Deal instituted considerable governmental planning and regulation of the economy, these actions were not antibusiness. On the contrary, these actions strengthened the business interest. As historians Morison, Eliot, and Commager have argued:

> Indeed it is certain that the New Deal did more to strengthen and to save the capitalist economy than it did to weaken or destroy it. That economy had broken down in many nations abroad, and its collapse contributed to the rise of totalitarian governments which completely subordinated business to the state. The system was on the verge of collapse in the United States during the Hoover administration, and it is at least conceivable that had that collapse been permitted to occur, it might have been followed by the establishment of an economy very different from that to which Americans were accustomed. Historically Franklin Roosevelt's administration . . . saved the system by ridding it of its grosser abuses and forcing it to accommodate itself to larger public interests. History may eventually record Franklin D. Roosevelt as the greatest American conservative since Hamilton. (Morison, Eliot, and Commager, 1950, p. 630)

As an example, pure food and drug legislation set standards for purity, quality, and uniformity in the products as well as the control of false labeling and misleading advertising. All of these demands raised the cost of production but it was in the interest of the largest producers to do so because this would drive out the smaller competitors. The same thing happened in the meat-packing industry as new federal controls simultaneously destroyed smaller companies and improved the quality of the products so the larger American firms could compete in the European markets (Kolko, 1963, p. 106). The largest meat-packing firms actually lobbied for these federal regulations (Chambliss, 1976, p. 78).

A similar situation occurred in the railroad industry. The railroads in the late 1800s were in chaos because of labor strife, intense competition, and national economic crises. Profits were low and bankruptcies common. Under these circumstances the major railroads sought federal intervention to regulate prices (guaranteeing profits) and to set routes.

> Price and policy regulation by the federal government reduced competition and thus eliminated the possibility that a small company might take business away from a larger one. Although widely touted as antimonopoly legislation, the establishment of the Interstate Commerce Commission and enactment of the statutes controlling railroad activities were essentially moves to encourage monopolies within the railroad industry. (Chambliss, 1976, p. 77; see also Kolko, 1965)

As a final example of a law appearing detrimental to powerful business interests, let's consider briefly the laws outlawing child labor. Many manufacturing industries employed children during the 19th century. This was considered inhumane by many and laws were passed eventually prohibiting the practice. But the largest manufacturers favored such a law because to do so gave them a competitive edge over marginal companies (Platt, 1972, p. 39). The credibility of this argument is increased when we observe that there are exceptions to child labor laws. Some industries today allow child labor to be exploited—particularly agriculture,

> where large corporations as well as small farmers rely upon children of all ages to pick potatoes, strawberries, and other agricultural products during the harvest season. The fact that it would be humane to abolish these practices has apparently fallen on deaf ears where the use of child labor remains profitable for large and small producer alike. (Chambliss, 1976, p. 79)

In sum, the attack on corporations, which has occurred over the past 100 years or so "has not been against business but has been inspired and led by the business interest itself" (Quinney, 1970, p. 77).

Drug Laws   The current laws concerning the purchase and use of drugs make some psychoactive drugs legal such as caffeine, nicotine, and alcohol, others require a doctor's prescription (e.g., amphetamines and barbiturates), and still others are illegal (psychedelics, marijuana, heroin, and cocaine). The legal status of a drug, ironically, is not related to its health dangers to individuals or its costs to society.[2] Alcohol and nicotine, for example, can be legally obtained and used indiscriminately, while marijuana and heroin, which are less dangerous, are illegal. Why are some drugs legal whereas others are not? Why is some drug use

[2]This section is taken primarily from Eitzen (1983, Chap. 14).

considered "abuse" but other use is simply use? Why are some drugs illegal now that once were legal? The explanation for these questions and anomalies has to do with the role of powerful interest groups—corporations, agricultural lobbies, religious groups, and government bureaucracies. In short, the answer has to do with the politics of drugs.

The early 1900s were characterized as a period of reform. A number of individuals and groups agitated to legislate morals (e.g., the 18th Amendment to the Constitution prohibiting the sale and use of alcohol was passed in 1919 after pressure from these reform forces). These groups rallied against psychoactive drugs because they believed them to be sinful. They fought against "demon rum" and "demon seed" as well as other moral evils such as gambling and prostitution. They believed that they were doing God's will and that if successful, they would provide a better way of life for everyone. Therefore, they lobbied vigorously to achieve their goals (appropriate legislation and enforcement of the laws to rid the country of these demons).

> All of these evils violated the ethical and philosophical foundations of the religious and moral culture which dominated political power at that time. Narcotics use, like alcohol use, led to a lack of rationality and self-control which were the cornerstones of proper "WASP" behavior. (Reasons, 1974, p. 388; see also Becker, 1963, pp. 147–163)

As a result of these reform efforts, Congress passed the Harrison Narcotics Act of 1914. This was basically a tax law requiring people who dispensed opium products to pay a fee and keep records. The law was relatively mild. It did not prohibit the use of opium in patent medicines or even control its use. It did, however, establish a Narcotics Division in the Treasury Department (which eventually became the Bureau of Narcotics). This department assumed the task (which was not part of the formal law) of eliminating drug addiction. Treasury agents harassed users, doctors, and pharmacists. The bureau launched a propaganda campaign to convince the public of the link between drug use and crime. Finally, the bureau took a number of carefully selected cases to court to broaden its power. In all these endeavors, the bureau was successful. The net result was that "what had been a medical problem, if a problem at all, had become a legal one; patients became criminals practically overnight" (McCaghy, 1976, p. 292).

This point cannot be overemphasized; prior to the Harrison Act drug addicts were thought (by the public and government officials) to be sick and in need of individual help. They were believed to be enslaved and in need of being salvaged through the humanitarian efforts of others. But with various government actions (laws, court decisions, and propaganda) and the efforts of reformers, this image of addicts changed from a "medical" to a "criminal" problem.

> The addict's image was being transformed rapidly from the "sick" and "repentent" deviant, to the "enemy" deviant. . . . Subsequently the addict would be viewed as the "enemy" deviant, indulging in drugs for his own pleasure in defiance of the values of those in power. Furthermore, he was increasingly

perceived in criminal terms as a threat to the personal safety and moral well-being of "good citizens." While the early imagery was primarily one of a moral degenerate, increasing emphasis was being placed upon the user's affiliations with the criminal class. The user of the drugs became associated with the "dangerous classes" and was viewed as manifesting disrespect for the dominant mores and values of society. (Reasons, 1974, p. 397)

The source of our arbitrary drug laws is the power structure in society (Himmelstein, 1978). There is evidence that elites in complex societies ban the use of psychoactive drugs because they link them with subversion. This is because dissident groups often use drug-induced experiences to affirm social solidarity in opposition to the powerful.[3] Himmelstein has summarized how this has worked throughout history:

We find again and again that elites try to suppress drug use because they link it to subversion and that drugs actually are important elements in many oppositional movements. Egyptian pharaohs (c. 2500 B.C.) fought a continual battle against beer and wine use in the temples of Memphis, which were centers of political unrest. The time-honored image of the coffee house as a center of subversion goes back at least to the sixteenth century Moslem world, where the death penalty was levied for visiting them. Peyote (in the Native American Church), marijuana (in the Jamaican Ras Tafari movement and of course in the 1960s in the U.S.), and alcohol (in the Afro-Brazilian movement) all have served as the foci for culturally and politically subversive movements. (Himmelstein, 1978, p. 45)

The powerful in society also direct their repression at the drugs used primarily by minority groups, the poor, and the criminals (Bonnie and Whitebread, 1974, pp. 13–31). The Chinese workers, not opium, were the targets of early antiopium laws. Similarly, the reform movements aimed at prohibition of alcohol were the attempts by the old middle class (rural, Protestant, native born) against the urban workers, largely Catholic, and immigrants who threatened their privileged status.

In this context, the movement against alcohol turned from reform to prohibition and from concern to moral indignation. Alcohol became a symbol of everything in the new society that threatened the old middle class, and Prohibition became a symbolic way for that class to reassert its cultural and political dominance. (Himmelstein, 1978, p. 46)

This connection between drug laws and social class is also apparent in the laws against the opiates. The change from "illness" to "crime" occurred as the drug use shifted from middle to lower class in the early 1900s (Duster, 1970, pp. 9–10).

---

[3] This is not to say that drugs are always used to unify resistance groups. While this is true in some cases, as Himmelstein has shown, some resistance groups reject drug use entirely for two basic reasons. First, they reject drugs *approved* by society because they symbolize the majority's power. Second, radicals claim that drugs dull the revolutionary urge, destroy commitment, and undermine discipline.

As a final example of this relationship between social class use and drug policy, let's look at the current drive to liberalize marijuana laws. When marijuana was used primarily by the lower classes (Mexican-Americans were prominent users as were deviant groups), the laws against its use were highly punitive. But the use shifted in the 1960s primarily to middle-class, white, affluent, college youth. Although their parents probably disagreed with their marijuana use, they did not want their children treated as criminals and stigmatized as drug users. The ludicrousness of punishment for marijuana use and legality for alcohol became readily apparent to the educated. Hence, there was a push to liberalize the laws by white, affluent, and powerful people in most communities and states.

Powerful economic interests promote drug laws favorable to them. For example, a significant part of American agriculture and industry is engaged (with government support) in the production and marketing of nicotine and alcohol products. Even though it is well known that tobacco is harmful to users, the government will not ban its use because of the probable outcry from farmers, the states where tobacco is a major crop, the tobacco manufacturers, wholesalers, retailers, transporters, and advertisers. Marijuana, on the other hand, is merchandized and sold illegally, so there is no legitimate economic interest pushing for its legality. As Etzioni has said, "There are no pot equivalents of tobacco states, wine growers, cigarette manufacturers, and their allies in the U.S. Department of Agriculture or friends on the Hill" (Etzioni, 1973, p. 4).

Similarly, the pharmaceutical industry works diligently to persuade Congress to keep amphetamines and other pills from being restricted too much. Americans spent in 1979 some $16.5 billion on prescription drugs and packaged medication. Naturally it is in their best corporate interest to continue this lawful and very profitable enterprise. In 1970, Congress, pushed by President Nixon, passed The Comprehensive Drug Abuse Prevention and Control Act. There were attempts by some forces to include amphetamines in the dangerous drug category in that bill, but they were not successful. The law did declare marijuana possession a serious crime but did not do the same for amphetamines, although the evidence was irrefutable that they are more dangerous to the user than marijuana. This inconsistency led one observer to conclude: "The end result is a national policy which declares an all-out war on drugs which are *not* a source of corporate income. Meanwhile, under the protection of the law, billions of amphetamines are overproduced without medical justification" (Graham, 1972, pp. 14–15).

Because some drugs are illegal, some illicit economic interests flourish. The underworld suppliers of drugs oppose changes in the law because legalization of drugs would seriously reduce their profits. They, therefore, promote restrictive legislation. This means, often, an "unholy" alliance between underworld economic interests and religious/moral interests who seek the same end—prohibition of the drug—but for opposite reasons. So a member of Congress could safely satisfy religious zealots and organized crime by his or her "morally correct" vote for stricter drug laws.

The law enforcement profession is another interest group that may use its influence to affect drug policy. If drugs and drug users are considered menacing, then budgets to trap them will be increased. If drug users are criminals, then more arrests will be made, proving the necessity of enforcement and, not incidentally, the need for higher pay and more officers to combat this evil. Perhaps the best example of this syndrome is provided by the Narcotics Bureau created by the Harrison Act of 1914. As mentioned earlier, this bureau was instrumental in changing opiate use from a "medical" problem to a "criminal" problem. The bureau used a number of tactics to "prove" that its existence was necessary: it won court cases favorable to its antidrug stance; it vigorously used the media to propagate the "dope fiend" mythology; and it used statistics to incite the public or prove the effectiveness of the bureau. The bureau, for example, was instrumental in getting the Marijuana Tax Act of 1937 passed. The arguments for enacting the law were based on moral grounds but some observers have suggested that it represented a case of a bureau wanting to increase its size and importance and that marijuana, which was an unregulated drug at the time, was a convenient tool to accomplish that goal. The head of the bureau, Harry J. Anslinger (who served in that post from 1930 to 1962), led an assault on marijuana in which he depicted the drug as an assassin of youth leading to heroin addiction. Stories of "marijuana atrocities" by "dope fiends" were supplied to the media. The bureau even sponsored a movie, "Reefer Madness," which pictured marijuana users as people who would do anything to obtain the "killer weed." Anslinger's campaign was successful with the passage of the Marijuana Tax Act. There is evidence, however, that Anslinger's crusade was motivated not by the drug but by Congress' budget cut in each of the preceding four years. It is safe to say that the bureau's attack on marijuana was not exclusively based on morality (Sloman, 1978; Anderson, 1981).

To summarize, the current laws concerning drugs are illogical. The severity of the drug laws is not related to the danger those drugs pose to individuals and society. The laws reflect, rather, a political mix—the consequences of interest groups with varying amounts of power having their way, with the less powerful suffering the consequences.

SUMMARY AND EVALUATION: FUNCTIONAL AND RADICAL VIEWS OF THE LAW

The functional and radical perspectives are theoretical opposites. Although they agree that modern society is composed of different groups and interests, functionalists perceive these diverse groups as in harmony and cooperation while radicals depict them as in competition and conflict. The former assume the interest groups to be more or less equal in power and willing to compromise while the latter, in contrast, argue that the groups are divided into dominant and subordinate positions (Eitzen, 1982, Chaps. 3 and 17). Stemming from these fundamental assumptions about the structure of society, functional and radical theorists have very different views on the law.

Definition of Crime

From the functional perspective a crime is any violation of laws enacted and enforced by the state. The state defines the law; *ipso facto* the state is above the law and therefore it cannot be criminal. Proponents of both theoretical perspectives agree that the law exists to maintain societal order and stability. But the radicals ask of the functionalists: in maintaining order, does the order that is preserved serve all of the people equally? Are some categories negatively affected whereas others are advantaged? Is the state itself guilty of doing harm? In this regard, some radical theorists as well as others argue that crime should be redefined to include violations of human rights (Schwendinger and Schwendinger, 1970). The following statement by the American Friends Service Committee (1971, pp. 10–11) argues the radical position:

> Actions that clearly ought to be labeled "criminal," because they bring the greatest harm to the greatest number, are in fact accomplished officially by agencies of the government. The overwhelming number of murders in this century has been committed by governments in wartime. Hundreds of unlawful killings by police go unprosecuted each year. The largest forceful acquisitions of property in the United States have been the theft of lands guaranteed by treaty to Indian tribes, thefts sponsored by the government. The largest number of dislocations, tantamount to kidnapping—the evacuation and internment of Japanese-Americans during World War II—was carried out by the government with the approval of the courts. Civil-rights demonstrators, struggling to exercise their constitutional rights, have been repeatedly beaten and harassed by police and sheriffs. And in the Vietnam war, America has violated its Constitution and international law.

Thus, the strict adherence to a legal definition of crime, as used by the functionalists, excludes from scrutiny many of the harms done by the state. Also, to the degree that the powerful are successful in keeping certain of their activities out of the criminal code, they, too, escape the criminal label and punishment. The corporate sector has, in this regard, been able to keep the laws weak or nonexistent concerning their promotion of racism and sexism, the marketing of unsafe products, the extortion of excessive profits, and their reluctance to eliminate hazardous working conditions (Greenberg, 1981, p. 6).

Finally, from the radical position, what is a crime and who is a criminal are the result of the powerful's ability to determine the law. This bias in the law against the powerless elements of society, means that political dissent, which the powerful will define as criminal, may be, from the radical's perspective, appropriate to change an unjust system.

The Bias of the Law

Functionalists posit that the law is socially neutral, reflecting a common consensus of the members of society and providing them equal protection. This is the heart of their view—the laws are the formalization of the shared understandings of what are appropriate behaviors. The law is created by the representatives of the people to serve the general good. The order determined by these neutral laws and fair law enforcement serves everyone.

Morever, the functionalists assert that American society is a well-ordered system with many interests vying for control. The law, from this perspective, is a form of social compromise and social control that regulates and integrates these competing interests. As Parsons (1962, p. 72) has put it, the "law has a special importance in a pluralistic liberal type society. It has its strongest place in a society where there are many different kinds of interests that must be balanced against each other and that must in some way respect each other." Such a view has a fatal flaw; a plurality of interests does not mean that all groups will compromise and share equally in the law-making process. Nor does it mean that the enforcement of the law is neutral, treating all interests alike. The radical perspective takes the opposite and more realistic position. In the words of Quinney:

> Law is a *result* of the operation of interests, rather than an instrument that functions outside of the particular interests. Though law may control interests, it is in the first place created by interests. (Quinney, 1970, p. 35)

> Although law is supposed to protect all citizens, it starts as a tool of the dominant class and ends by maintaining the dominance of that class. Law serves the powerful over the weak; it promotes the war of the powerful against the powerless. Moreover, law is used by the state (and its elitist government) to promote and protect itself. (Quinney, 1974, p. 24)

Or as Chambliss and Seidman have asserted:

> Far from being primarily a value-neutral framework within which conflict can be peacefully resolved, the power of the State is itself the principal prize in the perpetual conflict that is society. The legal order—rules which the various law-making institutions in the bureaucracy that is the State may hand down for the governance of officials and citizens, the tribunals, official and unofficial, formal and informal, which determine whether the rules have been breached, and the bureaucratic agencies which enforce the law—is in fact a self-serving system to maintain power and privilege. In a society sharply divided into haves and have-nots, poor and rich, blacks and whites, powerful and weak, shot with a myriad of special interest groups, not only is the myth false because of imperfections in the normative system: It is *inevitable* that it be so. (Chambliss and Seidman, 1971, p. 4; see also Quinney and Wildeman, 1977, p. 12)

The Nature of Law and Punishment by Type of Society

Durkheim, a functionalist, argued that in simple societies the punishment of rule breakers is repressive because their acts offend the collective conscience. In complex and modern societies punishment, he argued, tends to be restitutive rather than repressive. This form of punishment is not punitive but rather stresses compensation of victims and efforts to rehabilitate offenders so that they will once again be acceptable to society.

Chambliss and Seidman (1971, p. 32), two radical theorists, have argued the opposite—"the lower the level of complexity of a society, the more emphasis will be placed in the dispute-settling process upon reconciliation [and mediation and compromise]; the more complex the society, the more emphasis will be placed on rule-enforcement.'' Their argument goes further than Durkheim by adding an important variable—the extent of economic stratification present in society. ''The more economically stratified a society becomes, the more it becomes necessary for the dominant groups in the society to enforce through coercion the norms of conduct which guarantee their supremacy'' (Chambliss and Seidman, 1971, p. 33). The evidence from 51 societies ranging from nonindustrial to highly industrialized sides with the radical perspective—the more industrial the society, the more repressive the laws (Chambliss, 1976a, p. 17; see also Chambliss, 1976b, p. 97; Kadish, 1967).

Assessment of the Functional and Radical Views of the Law

The evidence strongly supports the radical perspective of the law. Clearly, as we have seen, powerful interest groups have great influence in the law formation process. When the interests of the powerful clash with the interests of the powerless, we should not be surprised that the interests of the former are served. This means that the law supports the existing social arrangements that benefit the advantaged and leaves the powerless vulnerable to a biased criminal justice system and exploitation by the powerful.

The radicals are also correct in pointing to the lack of consensus over the criminality of certain acts. There is a wide variation in beliefs in the United States concerning whether some acts are inherently criminal, for example, failure to register for the draft, personal use of recreational drugs, sexual acts between consenting nonmarried adults, owning a handgun, abortion, and industrial pollution.

Although the radical perspective on the law most fits reality, several caveats are appropriate. For example, there is considerable empirical evidence that there *is* a general consensus in the United States concerning crimes such as murder, rape, robbery, burglary, and arson (see Hagan, Silva, and Simpson, 1977; Rossi et al., 1974). In effect, many criminal laws are *not* the result of the activity of some self-serving interest group but are created for the benefit of the larger community (Hartjen, 1978, p. 49).

The acceptance of the radical perspective does not automatically mean that there is a monolithic ruling class which possesses absolute power and passes laws reflecting only its own interests. There is a clear consensus among radical criminologists that the laws reflect the interests of the powerful segments in society. There is disagreement among them, however, over the ways that the powerful maintain their advantage. One position in the debate is held by the instrumentalists who hold the law is an instrument of the ruling class. This position rests on two assumptions. First and foremost, there is a ruling class in capitalist society, and second, the ruling class actively manipulates the government and public opinion for its own advantage. The other side in this debate and the more plausible one, is made by the structuralists, who argue that the law (and other parts of the system) work to the advantage of the ruling class because of structural factors, irrespective of the active involvement of a unified power elite. The ruling class is not a unified group. Moreover, the common people have some influence on public policy. As Greenberg has queried:

> Why does the ruling class choose to rule through *law* rather than naked and arbitrary terror? Having made the choice, might it not have some consequences for the manner in which the class rules? If law embodies the will of the ruling class, why do members of that class sometimes violate the law? Here the existence of corporate and governmental crime becomes mysterious. (Greenberg, 1981, p. 191)

There are structural constraints that keep the advantaged segments of society from overwhelming the disadvantaged. "If law is to be legitimated to the masses, it cannot appear to be nothing more than an instrument of their oppression; it must appear to be fair. And to appear fair, it must sometimes *be* fair" (Greenberg, 1981, p. 192).

There are other structural constraints that bias the political and economic system in favor of the already advantaged without the advantaged being organized and conspiratorial.[4] For example the choices of decision makers are often limited by what have been called systemic imperatives (i.e., the institutions of society are patterned to produce prearranged results regardless of the personalities of the decision makers). In other words, there is a structural bias that pressures the government to do certain things and to avoid others. Inevitably, this structural bias favors the status quo, allowing those with power to continue to have this power. For example, no change is always easier than change. The current political and economic systems have worked and generally are not subject to question, let alone change. Thus the propertied and the wealthy benefit, whereas the propertyless and the poor continue to be disadvantaged. Parenti has shown how this is related to the legal system:

> The law does not exist as an abstraction. It gathers shape and substance from the context of power, within a real-life social structure. Like other institutions, the legal system is class-bound. The question is not whether the law should or should not be neutral, for as a product of its society, it *cannot* be neutral in purpose or effect. (Parenti, 1978, p. 188)

In addition to the inertia of institutions, there are other systemic imperatives that benefit the already advantaged. One such imperative is for the government to provide an adequate defense against our enemies (real or imagined), which stifles any external threat to the status quo. Domestically, government policy also is shaped by the systemic imperative for stability. The government promotes domestic tranquility and the existing distribution of power by squelching political dissidents.

In sum, this chapter provides the foundation for our analysis of crime and crime

---

[4]This section is taken from Eitzen (1983, Chap. 2).

control in American society. Foremost, it suggests the theoretical synthesis that most closely fits with reality and informs the analyses in this book. This theoretical approach is vital to the understanding of the politics of crime rates, the overemphasis on street crimes, and the class bias that pervades the criminal justice system.

CHAPTER REVIEW

1. The formal definition of crime is conduct that is illegal. Since crime is determined by the law, the critical question is whether the law is biased or not. In short, does the law reflect some interests in society more than others?

2. The unity in the American legal system derives from the legal traditions of the ancient Greeks, Romans, and Hebrews and especially from English common law. There are six guiding principles to the American legal system emanating from these traditions.

3. The first principle is that there is no crime without law, thus prohibiting *ex post facto* laws.

4. The second principle is that the state has the power (police power) to prohibit acts deemed harmful to society and its citizens.

5. The third principle is that criminal violations must be punished. Punishment has several uses: to deter potential criminals (general deterrence), to deter further criminal acts by the criminal (specific deterrence), to protect society, to change criminals (rehabilitation), and retribution (vengeance).

6. The fourth principle guiding the American legal system is that individuals committing criminal acts are only considered criminals and punished if they are responsible. There must be deliberate intent (*mens rea*). Insanity, immaturity, and self-defense are all justifications for relieving responsibility for otherwise criminal acts.

7. The fifth principle is that court decisions are guided strongly by precedent (*stare decisis*). This reinforcement of tradition promotes stability but also makes necessary changes difficult to attain.

8. The last principle is that there are procedural constraints limiting the arbitrary powers of government over individuals.

9. Since society creates crime by passing laws, criminal laws are inherently political. The functionalist and radical perspectives provide two contrasting ways to view this political nature of the law (and crime).

10. The functionalists argue that the law is not biased because it represents the consensus of society. Durkheim, furthermore, argued that the law integrates because as rulebreakers are punished the rules and values of society are reaffirmed.

11. The radicals argue, in contrast to the functionalists, that the law is used by the powerful to impose their definition of morality on the powerless. For them what is a crime and who is a criminal are consequences of who is doing the defining. Thus, for Marx and his later-day followers, the law is biased and is used as a weapon of those who dominate to maintain their domination.

4 The Social Organization of Official Crime Rates

CHAPTER OUTLINE

Official Crime Statistics

The history of crime statistics
The FBI's crime index

Other Measures of Crime

Victimization surveys
Self-reported criminality

Crimes Omitted from Traditional Sources of Criminal Statistics

Tax evasion
Fraud
Corporate crime
Political crime

Three Theoretical Views of Crime Rates

The traditional sociological perspective: Official crime rates as a reflection of criminality in society
The interactionist perspective: The social construction of crime rates
The radical perspective: The politics of crime rates
Conclusion

KEY TERMS

Crime index (FBI)
Defounding
Politics of crime rates
Self-fulfilling prophecy
Self-report surveys
Social construction of crime rates
Unfounding
Uniform crime reports (UCR)
Victimization surveys

Think of a crime, any crime. Picture the first "crime" that comes into your mind. What do you see? The odds are you are not imagining a mining company executive sitting at his desk, calculating the costs of proper safety precautions and deciding not to invest in them. The odds are that what you do see with your mind's eye is one person physically attacking another or robbing something from another on the threat of physical attack. Look more closely. What does the attacker look like? It's a safe bet he (and it is a *he,* of course) is not wearing a suit and tie. In fact, my hunch is that you—like me, like almost anyone in America—picture a young, tough, lower-class male when the thought of crime first pops into your head. You (we) picture someone like the Typical Criminal described [above]. And the crime itself is one in which our Typical Criminal sets out to attack or rob some specific person. (Reiman, 1979, p. 57)

Why do we have these images of specific crimes and criminals? One reason is that we are reminded by politicians of the dangers of particular kinds of crimes. Attorney General William French Smith under President Reagan has said, for example, that "violent crime is out of control" in the United States (cited in Ostrow, 1981, p. 3). Similarly, the attorney general of California speaking before a civic club said:

Today [1981] in California you are four times more likely to be a victim of murder, four times more likely to be a victim of robbery and three times as likely to be a victim of rape than you were in 1960. (reported in Kerby, 1981)

Apparently the message is getting across to Californians as evidenced by the growth of the self-defense industry. In that state in 1980 some 108,000 tear gas permits were issued. *In the first six weeks of 1981 the number of permits issued jumped to more than 400,000.* In January 1980 Californians bought 24,000 handguns and in January of 1981 handgun sales increased to 35,000 in that state (Kerby, 1981).

The heightened fear of crime is not limited to Californians. The Figgie Report (1982), a random survey of adults in 1980, found that: (1) 40 percent of those surveyed considered themselves "highly fearful" that they will become victims of murder, rape, robbery, or assault; (2) 24 percent said the threat of crime prevents them from going out at night to places in their neighborhoods they used to visit; and (3) 52 percent owned a gun to protect themselves.

The data on crimes and criminals that are used by politicians and reported in the media are supplied by the government. These data and their meanings are the subject of this chapter. The understanding of these rates and what they mean and do not mean are extremely important as background to the analysis of crime and its control. The chapter is divided into four parts: the history and description of the official crime rates, the sources of crime rates, crimes not emphasized by the government but nevertheless revealing about the extent of crime in society, and the interpretation of official crime rates from three theoretical perspectives.

OFFICIAL CRIME STATISTICS: THE FBI CRIME INDEX

Accurate record keeping regarding the incidence and types of crimes is an important activity for governments. The information is necessary for governments to accomplish their mandate of maintaining a minimum level of crime control. However, there are problems with data gathering and interpretation when it comes to crime statistics. These difficulties will become apparent as we trace the history of crime statistics in the United States.

The History of Crime Statistics

No crime statistics were collected in the United States from colonial days to the mid-19th century (Maltz, 1977). New York, Massachusetts, and Maine were the first states to collect crime statistics (see Ferdinand, 1967), but for the most part, record keeping by state and locality during the early years of American history was haphazard or nonexistent. Federal record keeping was authorized in 1870 when Congress created the Department of Justice. The states and local police establishments, however, tended to ignore this task either because of indifference or fear of federal control over them (Maltz, 1977, p. 33). This tendency began to be reversed in 1927 when the International Association of Chiefs of Police created a committee on Uniform Crime Records. The committee soon found that no two states defined all crimes alike. It also raised several important issues concerning the collection of crime data that continue to be problems today.

Which data most accurately reflect crime? One source would be data provided by the police based on the complaints received. This, it was argued, would be an accurate index of the actual extent of crime. Another data source was police arrests, but this is dependent on the discretion of the police and therefore not always reliable (Black, 1970). A more common method of measuring crime is to limit the data to court records. The argument for the use of these data is that they deal with *known* offenders and victims and therefore are more reliable than police records. The main argument against the use of court records is that they would *understate* the amount of crime because so many criminals are never processed by the courts.

The second issue involves who would collect the data on crime. By the late 1920s there was general agreement that "crimes known to the police" was the most accurate measure. The question was which agency should compile, analyze, and disseminate the crime statistics—the Federal Bureau of Investigation (FBI), the Census Bureau, or some other federal agency? The decision was made in 1930 that the record system would be housed in the Department of Justice, with the collection, analysis, and reporting done by the FBI (Maltz, 1977, p. 36).

Although the FBI was given the mandate to collect the data, its source of the data was local police agencies. From the beginning in 1930, though, these agencies supplied the data to the FBI on a voluntary basis. Since 1969, 47 states have standardized their reporting and participate in the program. In the 3 states without statewide collection efforts, data are submitted directly to the FBI by local agen-

Each of approximately 15,000 local jurisdictions supplies data to the FBI on the extent of crime in their district.

cies. This data collection network now represents about 15,000 units and 98 percent of the nation's population (Zolbe, 1980, p. 7).

The third issue involving official crime statistics was what crimes to include. What has evolved is a list of 29 types of crimes, which the FBI divides into two parts (see Table 4-1).

Part I crimes are the most serious and Part II crimes are considered less so by the FBI. Interestingly, the FBI uses crimes "known to the police" for Part I offenses but uses the number of persons arrested to assess the magnitude of Part II offenses.

Part I crimes, except for arson (see Table 4-1), are used by the FBI to comprise what it calls the Crime Index. The Crime Index is used by the FBI to show the amount of crime in a given year compared with previous years. These statistics provide the public with its image of the level of criminal activity and whether it is growing or declining. Let's look at this index and its meanings in greater detail.

Crime in the United States: The FBI's Crime Index

In September of each year, the FBI releases to the public its annual report of serious crimes. The part that is typically reproduced in the media is the "crime clock," where we are able to see how often each of the crimes making up the FBI's Crime Index is committed. Figure 4-1 presents the "crime clock" for 1982. Presented in this form the data on crime are indeed alarming.

TABLE 4-1

The Classification of Criminal Offenses by the FBI

The Part I offenses:

1. *Criminal Homicide.* (a) Murder and nonnegligent manslaughter: the willful (nonnegligent) killing of one human being by another. Deaths caused by negligence, attempts to kill, assaults to kill, suicides, accidental deaths, and justifiable homicides are excluded. Justifiable homicides are limited to: (1) the killing of a felon by a law enforcement officer in the line of duty; and (2) the killing of a felon by a private citizen. (b) Manslaughter by negligence: the killing of another person through gross negligence. Excludes traffic fatalities. While manslaughter by negligence is a Part I crime, it is not included in the Crime Index.

2. *Forcible Rape.* The carnal knowledge of a female forcibly and against her will. Included are rapes by force and attempts or assaults to rape. Statutory offenses (no force used, victim under age of consent) are excluded.

3. *Robbery.* The taking or attempting to take anything of value from the care, custody, or control of a person or persons by force or threat of force or violence and/or by putting the victim in fear.

4. *Aggravated Assault.* An unlawful attack by one person upon another for the purpose of inflicting severe or aggravated bodily injury. This type of assault usually is accompanied by the use of a weapon or by means likely to produce death or great bodily harm. Simple assaults are excluded.

5. *Burglary-Breaking or Entering.* The unlawful entry of a structure to commit a felony or a theft. Attempted forcible entry is included.

6. *Larceny-Theft (Except Motor Vehicle Theft).* The unlawful taking, carrying, leading, or riding away of property from the possession or constructive possession of another. Examples are thefts of bicycles or automobile accessories, shoplifting, pocket picking, or the stealing of any property or article that is not taken by force and violence or by fraud. Attempted larcenies are included. Embezzlement, ''con'' games, forgery, worthless checks, and so on are excluded.

7. *Motor Vehicle Theft.* The theft or attempted theft of a motor vehicle. A motor vehicle is self-propelled and runs on the surface and not on rails. Specifically excluded from this category are motorboats, construction equipment, airplanes, and farming equipment.

8. *Arson.* Any willful or malicious burning or attempt to burn, with or without intent to defraud, a dwelling house, public building, motor vehicle or aircraft, personal property of another, and so on.

The Part II offenses:

9. *Other Assaults (Simple).* Assaults or attempted assaults where no weapon was used or which did not result in serious or aggravated injury to the victim.

10. *Forgery and Counterfeiting.* Making, altering, uttering, or possessing, with intent to defraud, anything false which is made to appear true. Attempts are included.

11. *Fraud.* Fraudulent conversion and obtaining money or property by false pretenses. Included are larceny by bailee and bad checks except forgeries and counterfeiting.

12. *Embezzlement.* Misappropriation or misapplication of money or property entrusted to one's care, custody, or control.

13. *Stolen Property—Buying, Receiving, Possessing.* Buying, receiving, and possessing stolen property, including attempts.

TABLE 4-1 (Continued)

14. *Vandalism.*   Willful or malicious destruction, injury, disfigurement, or defacement of any public or private property, real or personal, without consent of the owner or person having custody or control.

15. *Weapons—Carrying, Possessing, and so on.*   All violations of regulations or statutes controlling the carrying, using, possessing, furnishing, and manufacturing of deadly weapons or silencers. Included are attempts.

16. *Prostitution and Commercialized Vice.*   Sex offenses of a commercialized nature, such as prostitution, keeping a bawdy house, procuring, or transporting women for immoral purposes. Attempts are included.

17. *Sex Offenses (Except Forcible Rape, Prostitution, and Commercialized Vice).*   Statutory rape and offenses against chastity, common decency, morals, and the like. Attempts are included.

18. *Drug Abuse Violations.*   State and local offenses relating to narcotic drugs, such as unlawful possession, sale, use, growing, and manufacturing of narcotic drugs.

19. *Gambling.*   Promoting, permitting, or engaging in illegal gambling.

20. *Offenses Against the Family and Children.*   Nonsupport, neglect, desertion, or abuse of family and children.

21. *Driving under the Influence.*   Driving or operating any vehicle or common carrier while drunk or under the influence of liquor or narcotics.

22. *Liquor Laws.*   State or local liquor law violations, except "drunkenness" (offense 23) and "driving under the influence" (offense 21). Federal violations are excluded.

23. *Drunkenness.*   Drunkenness or intoxication. Excluded is "driving under the influence" (offense 21).

24. *Disorderly Conduct.*   Breach of the peace.

25. *Vagrancy.*   Vagabondage, begging, loitering, and so on.

26. *All Other Offenses.*   All violations of state or local news, except offenses 1–25 and traffic offenses.

27. *Suspicion.*   No specific offense; suspect released without formal charges being placed.

28. *Curfew and Loitering Laws.*   Offenses relating to violation of local curfew or loitering ordinances where such laws exist.

29. *Runaways.*   Limited to juveniles taken into protective custody under provisions of local statutes.

SOURCE: Federal Bureau of Investigation, *Uniform Crime Reports for the United States,* Washington, D.C.: U.S. Government Printing Office, 1982, Appendix II, pp. 340–341.

Figures 4-2 and 4-3 depict graphically the trend lines for the various crimes included in the Crime Index from 1960 to 1982. The data in these figures reveal two trends. The first is that the growth rate in crimes known to the FBI has been explosive. The crimes counted as violent by the FBI (assault, robbery, rape, and murder—see Figure 4-2) show an increase of 340 percent over the 22-year period, whereas the property crimes included in the other figure rose more than 290 percent in the intervening two decades.

Data like these are sufficiently grave and alarming to make the public understandably concerned and fearful of the rising tide of crime in American society. Politicians generally capitalize on these fears by pledging to reduce the crime problem. In 1965, for example, President Johnson established a new advisory group, the President's Commission on Law Enforcement and Administration of

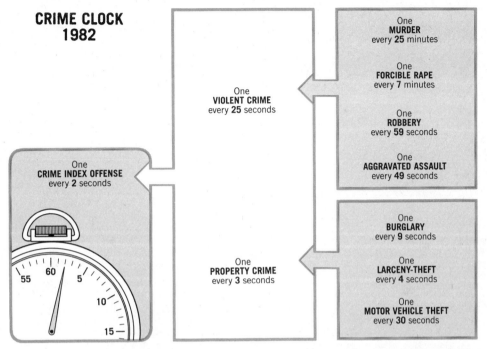

Figure 4-1 The crime clock should be viewed with care. Being the most aggregate representation of UCR data, it is designed to convey the annual reported crime experience by showing the relative frequency of occurrence of the Index Offenses. This mode of display should not be taken to imply a regularity in the commission of the Part I Offenses; rather, it represents the annual ratio of crime to fixed time intervals.

SOURCE: Federal Bureau of Investigation, *Uniform Crime Reports: Crime in the United States 1982*, Washington, D.C.: U.S. Government Printing Office, 1983, p. 5.

Justice, and pledged the resources of the federal government to "banish crime from the United States of America." During the next 10 years the expenditures by all levels of government on the criminal justice system (the police, courts, and jails) rose over 200 percent. In that same decade, however, the FBI's crime index rose 160 percent for property crimes and 190 percent for violent crimes (Skogan and Klecka, 1977, p. 1).

Subsequent presidents (Nixon, Ford, Carter, and Reagan) have made commitments similar to Johnson's to battle the crime wave facing the nation. Recently, President Reagan's special task force on crime called for new legislation to battle the growing danger from crime by allowing evidence in trials previously excluded by the Constitution, by denying bail to persons presenting a danger to the community and providing $6.5 billion in federal grants to help the states build prisons.

The second trend found in Figures 4-2 and 4-3 is the recent decline in each type of crime. In 1981 the long-term upward trend leveled off and in 1982, although there were 12.9 million Crime Index offenses, these represented a 3 percent decline from the previous year's total of 13.3 million crimes. This was the first significant annual decrease since 1977 and the trend appeared to continue in the

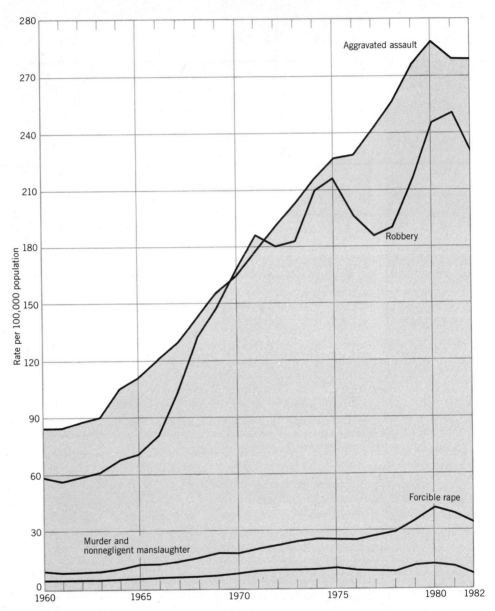

Figure 4-2   Violent crimes reported to the Federal Bureau of Investigation by type: 1960 to 1982.

SOURCE: Bureau of the Census, *Social Indicators III*, Washington, D.C.: U.S. Government Printing Office, 1980, pp. 216, 241; and Federal Bureau of Investigation, *Uniform Crime Reports: Crime in the United States 1982*, Washington, D.C.: U.S. Government Printing Office, 1983, p. 43.

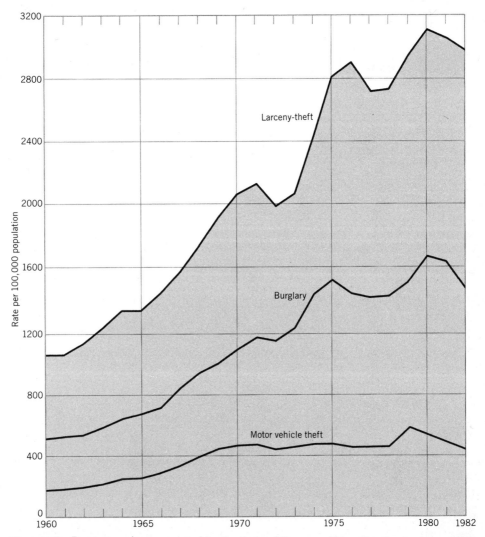

Figure 4-3   Property crimes reported to the Federal Bureau of Investigation by type: 1960 to 1982.

SOURCE: Bureau of the Census, *Social Indicators III*, Washington, D.C.: U.S. Government Printing Office, 1980, pp. 217, 242; and Federal Bureau of Investigation, *Uniform Crime Reports: Crime in the United States 1982*, Washington, D.C.: U.S. Government Printing Office, 1983, p. 43.

first six months of 1983 as reported crimes were down another 5 percent (compared with the first six months of 1982). Although these recent declines may be a short-lived aberration similar to what occurred in 1977,[1] there are some intriguing speculations for this abrupt and encouraging shift. FBI Director William H. Webs-

---

[1] The long-term trend for Crime Index crimes is up. Even with the 3 percent dip from 1981 to 1982, the 1982 rate per 100,000 inhabitants was still 9 percent greater than in 1978 and 34 percent greater than in 1973 (Federal Bureau of Investigation, 1983, p. 40).

ter attributed the drop to greater vigilance by citizens in neighborhood watch programs (cited in *USA Today,* 1983, p. 8A). A second possibility is that the recent trend toward mandatory sentencing, crackdowns on repeat offenders, and other "get-tough" measures by the police and the courts are having the desired effects by locking up more criminals and possibly deterring others. The prison population, for example, increased 12 pecent in 1981 and another 12 percent in 1982, thus making it impossible for these additional offenders to victimize the public, at least in the short run. A third possible explanation for the decline in crime is that the baby-boom generation is moving out of the crime-prone years into adulthood. Figure 4-4 compares the age structure of the American population

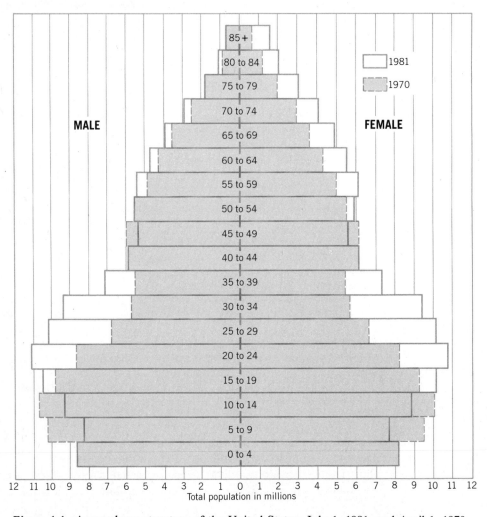

Figure 4-4 Age and sex structure of the United States: July 1, 1981, and April 1, 1970.

SOURCE: Bureau of the Census, "Population Profile of the United States 1981," *Current Population Reports,* Series P-20, No. 374, September 1982.

for 1970 and 1981. In 1970 the largest age category was 10 to 14. In 1981 it had shifted to ages 20 to 24. About half of all reported violent crimes are committed by males between the ages of 15 and 24. In 1980 there were 42.4 million Americans in this category and by 1990 there will be only 35.5 million, ensuring, if this hypothesis is correct, a continued decrease in the crime rate throughout this decade and beyond (Alter, 1983).

But before we go too far trying to explain the various crime trends, we must address a major problem: the official statistics supplied by the FBI are not necessarily reliable indicators of criminal behavior in the United States. Let's examine some of the major difficulties with these official statistics on crime.

As noted earlier, the data gathered for the FBI come from about 15,000 local agencies, which will vary in their rigor, care in keeping records, and the importance they attach to various criminal behaviors. Local officials, furthermore, may record fewer crimes than actually reported to hide problems with their organization or they may inflate the data to win public support for a larger budget to fight against the rising tide of crime in the community (Sykes, 1978, p. 75).

Because they are based on police statistics, the FBI data are subject to the vast discretionary powers of police officers. Police constantly interpret and make judgments. There are situations that can be processed as criminal or not, depending on the mood of the police officers at the scene (Black, 1970). In this regard, official FBI data are better used as measures of police output than as the measure of crimes (Maxfield, Lewis, and Szoc, 1980).

Crimes known to the police exclude many criminal activities, thus masking the actual extent of crime. There are those crimes that occur between consenting individuals that rarely come to the attention of the police. As willing participants they are not "victims" and obviously will not themselves inform the police. Some examples of criminal activities where this occurs are illegal transactions between a bettor and bookie, john and hooker, and junkie and pusher (McCaghy, 1980, pp. 34–35). Another major source of crimes missed by the police are those that go unreported by the victims. Unreported crimes occur for a variety of reasons, such as the belief that the police will do nothing about them, fear of reprisal, concern that the resulting court appearances and the like will be too time consuming, or the victims may report it to authorities other than the police (Myers, 1980). Victimization surveys, as we will see shortly, indicate that the FBI statistics only reflect about between one-fourth and one-third of the actual crimes (violent and property).

A fundamental problem with the FBI statistics on crime is that they direct attention solely to "street crimes." The FBI's official crime index focuses the attention of the media, public officials, and the public toward violent and property crimes of a certain type, which tend to be committed by certain categories of persons (lower class, poor, minorities). Attention is thus officially directed *toward* one type of crime and *away* from others—from corporate crimes, white-collar crimes, organized crime, political crimes, and other crimes of society's well-to-do.

In sum, the FBI statistics on crime are the single source of the public's image of crime. Although, as we have seen, the *Uniform Crime Reports* are an inaccurate barometer of crime, "they are taken by the public as valid and reliable indicators of lawlessness. Therefore, increases in crime noted in the media may incite the public, even though there may be little basis for such fears" (Reasons and Perdue, 1981, p. 317). The public, then, has images of the amount of crime present in society and the type of criminals to fear. But these images are faulty because they stem from the official emphasis on selected offenses. Because the statistics are so selective and are distorted further by the media and politicians, crime waves, that is, the heightened social awareness of crime, are creations of forces other than actual criminal behavior (Fishman, 1978).

OTHER MEASURES OF CRIME

Given the problems with the FBI Crime Index, how can we determine the extent of crime? There are two other indicators of crime—victimization surveys and self-report studies—both of which suggest a much higher rate of crime than the FBI official data. They indicate the existence of a vast reservoir of unrecorded crime.

Victimization Surveys

In 1972, the Census Bureau began victimization studies to determine as accurately as possible the estimate of crime in the United States. Their surveys involve a number of procedures (Skogan and Klecka, 1977, pp. 7–13). The largest component of the program is the National Crime Panel, which involves the interviewing and reinterviewing of a national sample of 60,000 households every six months for up to $3\frac{1}{2}$ years. Data from these individuals are used to determine estimates of the national frequency of the same crimes as found in the FBI's Crime Index (except for murder).

The second procedure is the interviewing of the owners, managers, and clerks of a sample of 42,000 business establishments. This tactic produces an estimate of commercial robbery and burglary rates.

Finally, the Census Bureau conducts victimization surveys in 26 major U.S. cities. Housing units in the central city in each of these cities are randomly selected and each member in the household 12 years or older is questioned about his or her experiences as a victim of crime. Also by random sampling, one-half of the respondents are asked their perception of crimes, the extent of their fear, and other attitudes regarding criminal activities.

The data from these yearly surveys are quite revealing. Foremost, they indicate that most crimes are never reported to the police and, therefore, not included in the FBI's Crime Index. Table 4-2 provides the data for 1979, which is typical for the years studied. Most startling, these data show that over 6 out of 10 crimes go unreported to the police.

A second finding from the victimization studies is the remarkable stability in the various crime rates from year to year (see Table 4-3). This lack of fluctuation is inconsistent with the message of the yearly FBI Uniform Crime Reports that crime is rising rapidly. "To the contrary, these data suggest that members of

TABLE 4-2

Estimated Distribution of Reported and Unreported Crimes in the United States, 1979

Crime	Reported to the Police		Not Reported to the Police	
	Number	**Percent**	**Number**	**Percent**
Rape	96,874	51	91,624	49
Robbery	619,230	57	471,464	43
Assault	2,053,192	44	2,610,189	56
Burglary	3,178,510	48	3,404,268	52
Larceny	2,673,247	25	7,888,167	75
Auto theft	949,878	69	420,061	31
Totals	9,570,931	39	14,885,773	61

SOURCE: Timothy J. Flanagan, David J. van Alstyne, and Michael R. Gottfredson (eds.), *Sourcebook of Criminal Justice Statistics—1981* (U.S. Department of Justice, 1982), p. 232.

society are not falling to criminal acts more frequently now than they were a few years ago'' (Census Bureau, Social Indicators III, 1980, p. 206). This finding has been interpreted by Eugene Doleschal, the director of the Information Center of the National Council on Crime and Delinquency, as suggesting that the FBI's rising crime rates reflect a "crime reporting wave rather than a rise in criminal activity" (Census Bureau, 1979, p. 1). The crime epidemic suggested by the FBI statistics is perhaps an artifact of greater diligence and effective reporting by the police. "The phenomenon of drastic increase in crime rates is explained by the fact that law enforcement agencies have been dipping ever deeper into the vast reservoir of unreported crime" (Doleschal, 1979, p. 3).

Criminal victimization surveys should be viewed with some caution, however. There is the potential for both over- and underreporting with the greater likelihood

TABLE 4-3

Number and Percent of "Households Touched by Crime," by Type of Crime, 1975 to 1980

	1975	1976	1977	1978	1979	1980
Households total (in thousands)	73,123	74,528	75,904	77,578	78,964	80,622
Percent of households touched by						
all crimes	32.0	31.5	31.3	31.3	31.3	30.0
Rape	0.2	0.2	0.2	0.2	0.2	0.2
Robbery	1.4	1.2	1.2	1.1	1.2	1.2
Assault	4.5	4.4	4.7	4.6	4.8	4.4
Burglary	7.7	7.4	7.2	7.2	7.1	7.0
Larceny	10.2	10.3	10.2	9.9	10.8	10.4
Auto theft	1.8	1.6	1.5	1.7	1.6	1.6

SOURCE: Timothy J. Flanagan, David J. van Alstyne, and Michael R. Gottfredson (eds.), *Sourcebook of Criminal Justice Statistics—1981* (U.S. Department of Justice, 1982), p. 276.

of the former. Distortion in the information about crimes may occur as respondents misunderstand or forget what transpired, are ignorant of legal definitions, and as they fabricate the facts (Levine, 1976). Underreporting is especially likely for certain crimes where the victim may be ashamed or wishes to protect the perpetrator, such as in the case of rape, spouse abuse, or child abuse.

Victimization surveys have the same bias as the FBI data. They ask for and receive information about "street"-type crimes while ignoring those types perpetrated by more powerful individuals and organizations.

Self-reported Criminality

Another method to determine the extent of criminal activities in society is to ask representative samples of the public to tell about their own criminal activities. A number of investigations, principally by sociologists, have found that juvenile and adult criminality is widespread. In a classic study by Short and Nye (1958), the investigators compared the self-reported criminal behavior by students in three midwestern high schools with the reported crimes of delinquents in a midwestern juvenile detention center. They found that the high school students engaged in numerous criminal activities similar to those found among the institutionalized delinquents. Another study of 700 middle-class adults asked the respondents if they had ever committed (after age 15) any one or more of 49 crimes that were punishable in New York State by at least one year in prison. The results were that 91 percent admitted committing at least one such offense. The average number of offenses by men in the sample was 18 and by women, 11. Moreover, about two-thirds of the men admitted at least one serious crime—a felony—as did about one-third of the women (Wallerstein and Wyle, 1947).

Many studies of self-reported criminality substantiate the findings of these classic studies. The consistency of the results leads to two conclusions. First, the official crime statistics of the FBI, and even those from the victimization studies, actually understate the amount of crime. And second, not only are criminal acts frequent but they are found throughout the social class structure. This runs counter to the consistent finding from official sources that the distribution of criminality is in the direction of minorities and the poor. What the official data reflect then is the bias of the criminal justice system in apprehending and processing as criminals disproportionate numbers from the underclasses.

Although very helpful in establishing that crime is not overrepresented among the poor, there are problems with self-report surveys that lessen the impact of their findings. Essentially there are three problems. The first is that the results may not be valid because the respondents may have had inaccurate recall or may have deliberately provided false information, either reducing or enhancing the number and types of criminal acts.

A most important criticism of these studies involves sampling. Most of the studies involve youth or of adults, asking them to recall their activities as youths. This focus on the young is primarily because schools provide settings where many subjects can be surveyed simultaneously and inexpensively. Also, since attendance is mandatory, it is assumed that such a survey will provide a reliable estimate of all youths in a given community. This propensity to use school youth as subjects may lead to misleading or inaccurate conclusions. The data may be unreliable because of the tendency of some to inflate their criminality, whereas others may be fearful of revealing their illegal activities. Many of the crimes of youth are only crimes for youth (underage drinking, truancy, running away), which unduly inflates the crime rate. Another problem with using school populations is that the sample may not represent youth because it omits those not in attendance on a given day (delinquents, when compared to nondelinquents, are least likely to attend school regularly or to have dropped out altogether). As a result, there are problems with generalizations about the criminal behaviors of youths and especially about the criminal behaviors of adults.

A final problem is that not only have self-report studies tended to neglect the criminal behavior of adults, those few that have, have focused on traditional crimes. But what about white-collar crimes and the decisions by corporate executives that do harm to consumers and the public? As Randall Shelden has asked:

> Is stealing a car more serious than the manufacture of thousands of unsafe cars which result in serious injuries or even deaths? A related problem is that no study has yet focused on the deviant activities (undetected) of corporate executives or other high-status persons. Rather, these self-report studies have focused almost exclusively on rather conventional criminal and delinquent behavior. (Shelden, 1982, p. 35)

CRIMES OMITTED FROM TRADITIONAL SOURCES OF CRIMINAL STATISTICS

A fundamental problem with the official crime statistics is that they direct attention toward certain crimes and away from others. In doing so, they inform us as to what crimes are the most important. But are these officially recognized crimes (the FBI index crimes) the most important? Are they the most violent? Are they the most expensive in terms of property loss? Let's look at four areas of considerable criminal activity that are all but overlooked by official crime counters and crime stoppers: tax evasion, business fraud, corporate crimes, and political crimes. Since entire sections and chapters are devoted to these crimes later in the book, they will only be introduced at this point.

Tax Evasion

There is an irregular economy in the United States where millions of individuals and companies evade billions of dollars in taxes. Involved are thousands of small businesses—bars, restaurants, retail stores, repair shops, and other legal enterprises as well as illegal activities such as gambling, drug sales, prostitution, and the sale of stolen property—that deal with cash customers. Because there are no official records, businesses can skim off a portion of the cash receipts, thus reporting a lower-than-actual amount of income. Employees can be paid in cash thereby helping the employer to evade Social Security payments, the cost of unemployment insurance, worker's compensation, and medical insurance. The employee, in turn, need not report this income because there is no record. Employees who receive cash from customers for services (e.g., waiters, cab drivers, music teachers) often do not report all or a part of their income to the government, thereby avoiding taxes they should legally pay. The amount involved in this underground economy is not trivial. One estimate in 1981 was $275 billion annually or 10 percent of the Gross National Product (Gersten, 1981). The number of people involved in this vast underground has been estimated at 20 million (*U.S. News & World Report,* 1979). The amount of money these persons failed to pay in taxes involved, at minimum, $50 billion (Schultz, 1980). It is important to note that most of the activities involved here occur in legitimate business activities. The Internal Revenue Service has estimated that only 25 percent of the underground economy involves illegal activities (reported in Tuky, 1981).

In addition to the failure to report income, there are other forms of tax cheating. In 1979 the IRS estimated that some $18 billion was overdeclared in deductions on income tax returns. The IRS conducted a nationwide study of 5000 households and found that 27 to 32 percent of those interviewed admitted to being "less than absolutely honest" in completing their 1979 tax returns. Moreover, the study found that about half considered understating income or overstating expenses or charitable deductions as acceptable behaviors (reported in Rankin, 1980).

The amounts of money lost in government revenues by these various means of tax evasion clearly surpasses the amount of property stolen and reflected in the FBI official statistics. Yet, because income tax evasion is not included in the Crime Index, the public is unaware of the magnitude of this type of criminality. Also, once again their ire is directed away from the criminal activities of the middle and upper classes and toward those of the less affluent.

Fraud

Another area of criminal activity that often goes undetected, unreported, and/or unpunished is fraud. Some criminologists have argued that fraud—the use of deceit, lies, or misrepresentation in the marketplace—is "the most prevalent crime in America" (Sutherland and Cressey, 1974, p. 42). Some examples of recent fradulent schemes are (see Simon and Eitzen, 1982, pp. 89–91):

- A 1979 government study found that motorists were overcharged an average of $150 per car per year for repairs.
- Medicaid abuses (overcharges to the government and underservice to patients) by doctors, hospitals, nursing homes, and druggists was estimated in 1979 to total $8 billion annually.
- Stock in the Equity Funding Corporation rose from $6 a share to $80 a share from 1967 to 1972. This phenomenal growth was the result of faked reports about assets, sales, and earnings including the issuing of 64,000 phony life insurance policies. The company actually had *never* earned any money since

1967 and when this became known, shareholders lost between $2 and 3 billion (Dirks and Gross, 1974; Blumdell in Moffett, 1976, pp. 42–89).

The important point concerning the crime of fraud is that the economic costs to the victims and the public (higher prices for goods, increased taxes for government activities) are huge when compared with the relatively small economic costs of street crimes.

Corporate Crimes

The crimes of corporate America are much more costly and violent to Americans than are street crimes, yet they are not included in the official statistics on crime. Let's look briefly at the economic magnitude of some of these illegal activities first.

Price fixing by companies supposedly in competition costs consumers billions. In 1980, for example, the Federal Trade Commission, after an eight-year study, released data showing that consumers were overcharged by 15 percent for ready-to-eat cereals over a 15-year period. These overcharges in the cereal industry, it was alleged, were the direct result of the monopoly held by Kellogg, General Mills, and General Foods. Their parallel pricing and control of the market resulted

Ralph Nader's famous book indicted America's largest automobile manufacturers for their willful production and sale of dangerous products.

PANEL 4-1

Crimes That Do Not Count

Jeffrey Reiman has argued that the most dangerous antisocial behaviors are not counted as crimes by the government and the public. The costs of crime in 1974 were roughly 20,000 deaths and 500,000 instances of serious bodily harm short of death, and the total value of property stolen in 1974 was somewhere between 3 and 3½ billion dollars. Compare these totals with the following "noncriminal" acts:

- The Vietnam War resulted in 50,000 American dead and several hundred thousand wounded, hundreds of thousands of Vietnamese killed—all at a cost to the taxpayers of roughly $164 billion.

- Job-related deaths from industrial disease account for 390,000 illnesses and 100,000 deaths annually. For every murder recorded in 1974 by the FBI Crime Clock, six workers died "just from trying to make a living"!

- A congressional committee in 1976 estimated that more than 2 million medical operations performed in 1974 were not only unnecessary but also killed about 12,000 patients and cost nearly $4 billion. In 1974, the FBI reported that a "knife or other cutting instrument" was the weapon used in 17.6 percent of the 20,600 murders that year. That works out to 3626 murders due to "cutting or stabbing." Obviously, the FBI does not include the scalpel as a "knife or other cutting instrument."

- More than 350,000 people die yearly of cancer and between 60 and 90 percent of those cases result from preventable, environmental sources such as exposure to chemicals, food additives, air pollution, and cigarette smoking. For example, Deer Lodge County in Montana, where Anaconda's copper smelting works is located, ranks ninth out of 3021 U.S. counties in lung cancer rates. Salem county in Delaware, home of DuPont's Chambers Works, which has been manufacturing chemicals since 1919, has the highest bladder cancer death rate in the nation.

in consumers paying $100 million more annually than they would if there were true competition (Associated Press, October 3, 1980). One review of cases of proven price fixing between 1963 and 1972 revealed that the practice occurred among companies producing and marketing the following: steel wheels, pipe, bed springs, metal shelving, steel casings, refuse collection, swimsuits, structural steel, baking flour, fertilizer, acoustical ceiling materials, beer, gasoline, asphalt, book matches, linen, school construction, plumbing fixtures, dairy products, auto

PANEL 4-1 (Continued)

● The average American consumes one pound of chemical food additives annually. We are, in effect, guinea pigs testing the effects for nearly 3000 food additives. Many of these chemicals, alone or in combination, are strongly suspected of producing cancer, gallbladder ailments, hyperkinesis in children, and allergies. They may also adversely affect the rate of DNA, RNA, and protein synthesis.

Our affluent society allows poverty to exist, which means that we have caused suffering and premature death. The poor suffer more from poor health and die earlier than do those who are relatively well off. The babies born to the poor are more likely to die in infancy and to have permanent brain damage because of the inadequate diets of their mothers. In short, poverty kills. And a society that could remedy its poverty but does not is an accomplice in murder.

In sum, Reiman says: "The criminal justice system does not protect us against the gravest threats to life, limb, or possessions. Its definitions of crime are not simply a reflection of the objective dangers that threaten us. The workplace, the medical profession, the air we breathe, and the poverty we refuse to rectify lead to far more human suffering, far more death and disability, and take far more dollars from our pockets than the murders, aggravated assaults, and thefts reported annually by the FBI. And what is more, this human suffering is preventable. A government really intent on protecting our well-being could enforce work safety regulations, police the medical profession, require that clear air standards be met, and funnel sufficient money to the poor to alleviate the major disabilities of poverty. But it does not. Instead we hear a lot of cant about law and order and a lot of rant about crime in the streets. It is as if our leaders were not only refusing to protect us from the major threats to our well-being but trying to cover up this refusal by diverting our attention to crime—as if this were the real threat."

Source: Jeffrey H. Reiman, The Rich Get Richer and the Poor Get Prison, *New York: John Wiley & Sons, 1979, pp. 62–87.*

repair, athletic equipment, ready-mix concrete, shoes, and wholesale meat (Hay and Kelley, 1974). What the extra cost is to consumers of these illegal practices in these industries (and the list is a partial one) is unknown but surely runs into the several billions of dollars.

Corporate crimes also do violence to human life (see Simon and Eitzen, 1982, pp. 97–130). Corporate violence occurs from the production and sale of unsafe products (e.g., the Corvair and the Pinto), to the sale of adulterated foods (the meat-packing industry, among others, has a history of this), and the refusal to eliminate or improve dangerous working conditions (e.g., in the mines, the production of asbestos and vinyl chloride, and in the textile industry). Corporations also place people in jeopardy by the indiscriminate waste of resources and the pollution of the environment. Panel 4-1 illustrates a number of corporate crimes and their economic and human costs.

Political Crimes

There are a number of crimes committed by government officials that do harm to people. They involve the illegal use of power for political purposes by those in positions of legitimate authority. Sykes has listed the following misuses of power as political crimes:

> The dismissal of persons from their jobs for revealing governmental corruption; discriminatory prosecution on the basis of political opinions; the manufacturing of evidence, including the use of perjured testimony; unlawful sentencing; the premeditated and unlawful repression of legal dissent; entrapment; illegal wiretapping; illegal search and seizure; unlawful arrests; illegal treatment of prisoners; illegal denial of the right to vote; illegal awards of state and federal contracts; bribery to influence the political process; unlawful use of force by the police; and military war crimes. (Sykes, 1978, p. 221)

When the public relies on government data for crime rates there is the problem that the government does not report its own wrongdoings. The FBI, whose index informs us of the extent of crimes annually, is, in fact, itself guilty of numerous crimes listed above by Sykes (Simon and Eitzen, 1982, pp. 204–211; Sykes, 1980, pp. 55–58).

Political crimes point to two problems: who monitors the monitors? and the facts of political deviance are generally hidden from us because we are dependent on the government for data, that if revealed, would damn them.

The crucial question raised by examining crimes outside the FBI index is: Why do some crimes "count" while others do not? There are several possible answers. Among them:

1. Acts of violence are universally abhorred in American society.
2. In a capitalist society the laws and law enforcement exist to protect private property.
3. Focusing on street crimes reinforces the commonly held belief that the poor and minorities are threats to stability and must be controlled.
4. Street crimes are easier to identify and control than other types.
5. Crimes are defined by the poweful, therefore, the actions of the powerless are monitored whereas those of the powerful are not.
6. Law enforcement agencies are more secure if they control the powerless rather than challenge the powerful.

Which of these possibilities or which combination provides the answer? As you become more acquainted with the three theoretical perspectives used throughout this book, you will see that the answer depends on one's point of view.

THREE THEORETICAL VIEWS OF CRIME RATES

There are several ways to interpret official crime rates, which coincide with the three sociological theories that we are using to understand crime and crime control in society.

The Traditional Sociological Perspective: Official Crime Rates as a Reflection of Criminality in Society

Scholars holding this view tend to accept the official crime rates as a reflection of the amount of criminal behavior in society. They accept the criticism that these rates may not be completely accurate but they believe them to be at least highly correlated with what actually occurs. Beyond this, the traditional sociologists tend to view official crime rates in one of two ways (Quinney and Wildeman, 1977, pp. 96–97). The approach of conservatives is based on the assumption that crime statistics indicate the amount and kinds of people who willfully violate the rules of society. The official rates indicate, further, that criminal behaviors tend to be concentrated among the lower social classes who have a weaker commitment to society. It follows that the solution to crime involves efforts to socialize the lower segments of society so that they have a greater acceptance of the laws and customs of society. Furthermore, because the lower classes have more need for the external control of their behavior, the efforts of the police should be concentrated in their neighborhoods.

The more liberal wing of this perspective also accepts crime rates as correlated with actual behavior. They vary from conservatives in their assumption that the causes of crime are a complex set of social and psychological forces beyond the control and/or even the recognition of the individual (Quinney and Wildeman, 1977, p. 97). The task of the researcher is to use the statistical measures to find the determinants of criminal behavior.

The Interactionist Perspective: The Social Construction of Crime Rates

The interactionists reject the equating of criminal acts with official crime rates. They point to the self-report criminality studies, which show that almost everyone is guilty of criminal behavior. If the official statistics were accurate they would be very much higher and would be randomly distributed in the population. But neither is true. Self-report studies and victimization surveys both indicate an actual crime rate several times greater than the official FBI data and indicate that crime is by no means a "lower class" phenomenon.

What the official crime statistics indicate, then, is "the reaction of society to certain kinds of offenses [rather] than as measures of the amount of criminality in society" (Quinney and Wildeman, 1977, p. 109). Certain types of offenses are emphasized and certain kinds of people differentially receive the label "criminal." What is a "crime" and who is a "criminal" are therefore the products of a selection process by authorities throughout society. Conceived in this way, crime is socially created. Perceived in this way, the rates of crime reported by official agencies are accurate; they measure perfectly "the amount of social labeling taking place in society. They measure the productivity of official agencies" (Hartjen, 1978, p. 200).

A number of factors are involved in the social production of crime rates. There is a self-fulfilling prophecy, for example, when certain crimes are identified as the most troublesome for society, as in the case of the FBI Crime Index, and the efforts of the police are directed at detecting them. As Hartjen (1978, p. 201) puts it: "As the number of police increases, the probability that more crimes will be detected increases." Since more officials are looking for crime, more of it is likely to be found. This explains, at least in part, the higher crime rates in urban areas than in rural areas and the greater proportion of violent and property crimes in poorer neighborhoods when compared with more affluent ones.

Crime rates are also produced when the official agencies change their procedures. In the 20 years from 1960 to 1980, the rate of violent crimes per 100,000 population increased 340 percent and the rate of property crimes per 100,000 increased 290 percent. Does this rapid growth reflect changes in criminal behavior or are other factors involved? Obviously, the rate of crime may have increased faster than the population in those two decades. But the increase may also be the result of more police personnel, more accurate record keeping, political pressures to crack down on crime, and the like. Moreover, crime rates are readily manipulated. At the municipal level, for example, police bureaucracies can easily manipulate crime rates and it is in their interest to do so (Timmer, 1981, pp. 16–18). Local police bureaucracies are dependent on municipal, state, and federal bureaucracies for their funding. The extent of this funding depends on local crime rates. Rates, in this context, are extremely political creatures. Rates must prove the police effective; the bureaucracy must at least be perpetuated at present levels. But rates must not convey the impression of an overly effective police department; the crime problem is still not under control, and increased funding and bureaucratic expansion are necessary. In short, rates (including those presented above) are manipulated for political and bureaucratic purposes.

Municipal police departments routinely rely on two related procedures for constructing "satisfactory" statistical rates: unfounding and defounding. Unfounding refers to the process of "statistically declaring" that particular unsolved crimes were never crimes committed in the first place. Defounding involves "statistically lessening" unsolved felonies to misdemeanors. Both procedures, of course, effectively raise clearance rates.

Most often, organized crime control efforts lower the official crime rates. The levels of crime, though, are usually unaffected.

The Nixon administration's early 1970s "law and order" rhetoric led to the establishment of a "national crime control laboratory" in Washington, D.C. Given the necessary financial resources and police personnel, the city was to become a model in efficient and effective crime control. Crime statistics (rates) were used to measure the success of this program. Crime rates did fall, particularly burglary and larceny. Crime rates did not fall because of increased police activity and resources, however, but fell because of defounding. Seidman and Couzens (1974, p. 476) conclude that:

> at least part of the decline in crime statistics for the District of Columbia is attributable to increased downgrading of larcenies and, to a lesser extent, of burglaries. This appears to be a pure case of the reactivity of a social indicator: the fact that the statistic is used as a measure of performance affects the statistic itself. The political importance of crime apparently caused pressures, subtle or otherwise, to be felt by those who record crime, pressures which have led to the downgrading of crimes.

A decrease in New York City's crime rate provides another illustration of this process. In a recent year, the city's crime rate decreased and the clearance rate increased, both at very significant levels. This occurred when both of these rates in all other large American cities were proceeding in the opposite direction. When a reform police administration finally brought unfounding and defounding under control, the effects on crime in New York City were astounding: within one month's time both robbery and assault increased by 200 percent, larceny by 300 percent and burglary by 500 percent (Lundman, 1980, pp. 65–66).

The interactionists also argue that crime is created because the kinds of crime emphasized and the kinds of people considered to be "criminal" are not as dangerous as other acts and persons escaping the perjorative labels. Avoiding these labels are the more affluent individuals and the corporations engaging in costly and violent acts. The powerful in society—powerful by their economic resources and their ability to influence the labeling process—misdirect our collective attention away from the criminal acts of their social class and toward those of the powerless. Reiman has said it well:

> By calling crime created, I want to emphasize the human responsibility for the shaping of crime, not in the trivial sense that humans write the criminal law, *but rather to call attention to the fact that decisions as to what to label and treat as crime are not compelled by objective dangers and thus that to understand the reality of crime, we must look to the motives and interests of those who shape those decisions.* (Reiman, 1979, p. 55)

In sum, interactionists look at crime rates very differently than traditional sociologists. Crime rates do not reflect crime but society's construction of crime rates and, by implication, crime. Their emphasis is on the labeling process. Why is it that certain crimes are defined and labeled as more serious than others? Why are certain persons—the poor, the marginal—disproportionately called "criminal"? As Hartjen puts it:

> A labeling approach . . . leads one to explain the likelihood that some persons' behavior will be labeled a crime while others' goes unquestioned. It is not why people act as they do but why some individuals are selected to be defined as having acted in particular ways while others are not that is of major issue. (Hartjen, 1978, pp. 200–201; see also Kitsuse and Cicourel, 1963; Black, 1976)

The Radical Perspective: The Politics of Crime Rates

Official crime statistics reveal to the public that street crimes against persons and property are on the rise. The radical perspective argues that such a view is naive. A prominent sociologist of this persuasion, Richard Quinney, has argued that we must understand the political context of crime rates:

> Crime rates . . . have to be understood for their political construction and the political uses they serve. It is for political purposes that criminal statistics are gathered and for political needs that criminal statistics are recorded and interpreted. For that reason, American crime rates are subject to great manipulation, from their inception to their use. It is impossible to know from any statistic the "true" rate of crime. Whether crime is increasing or decreasing in the United States is a question that can never be answered objectively without considering the politics of the times. (Quinney, 1979, p. 65)

There are several political uses of crime rates. As we noted in the previous section, the police need high crime rates to justify their existence. They need appropriations from various political units for higher salaries, better equipment, and more personnel. They cannot let crime get out of hand, however, or the public will call for a purge of the old policies and personnel. Thus, "the police have a [political] interest in maintaining both a high and a low rate of crime" (Quinney, 1979, p. 65).

The crimes stressed by the FBI Crime Index are aimed at certain categories of people and divert attention away from the criminal activities of others. The focus is on the criminal acts of the underclass. Blacks, for example, are disproportionately arrested (between three and four times the rates for whites) and imprisoned (about 1 in every 20 black men between the ages of 25 and 35 is either in jail or prison on any day, compared with 1 of every 163 white men in the same age group) (Quinney, 1979, p. 344). As Quinney has stated:

> To overrepresent the amount of crime by blacks is to make a political statement: that blacks are inferior (at least socially) and that they must be further controlled. *Racism is thereby maintained by the legal system in the recording and reporting of crime rates.* (Quinney, 1979, p. 66) (Emphasis added.)

The singling out of other members of the underclass means that the legal system, through its institutionalized selectivity regarding crime rates, reinforces and maintains the system of inequality.

By focusing on street crimes, the message is that these are the most serious of crimes. As we have noted, however, by far the most serious crimes in both property loss and violence to human life are corporate and political crimes, not street crimes. To reemphasize that point: in 1977 the Joint Economic Committee of Congress estimated that the total cost in 1976 of crimes against property (robbery, larceny, burglary, and auto theft), the crimes we are most worried about, totalled $4 billion. Yet, we tend to ignore those property crimes of the affluent—fradulent bankruptcy, bribery, kickbacks, embezzlement, consumer fraud, and computer crime—which in 1976 totalled $44 billion, 11 times the amount for street crimes (cited in Doleschal, 1979, p. 5). The adherents of the radical perspective interpret the official emphasis on street crimes as a deliberate means to protect the interests of the wealthy and powerful. It is important to the advantaged to have society's social problems viewed by the populace as centered among the underclass. As long as this happens, the system that advantages some and disadvantages others goes unchallenged, and the efforts at crime control are directed at the "enemy" criminal class in our society. In the view of radical criminologists, then, crime is not a behavior found unusually among the lower classes, although street crime is. Street crime is a lower-class phenomenon because of restricted opportunities in society. From this view, both the street criminals and their victims are victims. The problem, then, is the structure of society that perpetuates inequality. The greatest danger to the social order is not crime by the underclass, but the crimes by the powerful (Dod, Platt, Schwendinger, Shank, and Takagi, 1976, p. 1).

The emphasis on street crimes and solutions aimed at changing criminals, and stricter penalties to punish them, also deflect attention away from the social conditions that promote criminality. Although we know that there are social and political factors that artificially inflate the rates of street crimes by members of the underclass, the fact remains that they are most likely to engage in these types of crimes. The next chapter is devoted to this question, so we will only anticipate the argument from the radical perspective. Although President Reagan, in his war on crime, attacks the moral deterioration of America's families and schools, he ignores the structural reasons that account for the prevalence of street crimes by the underclass: slums, overcrowding, economic exploitation, unemployment, subordination, and institutional discrimination, all of which offer members of certain segments of society no reason for hope and no stake in the system. Advocates of the radical perspective argue that capitalism and the organization of the economy is the probem rather than the solution. As Jerome Skolnick has put it:

For people who are fearful of crime (and which of us isn't?), the hard line rhetoric sounds appealing. It might even cut crime by a few percentage points, or it might not, depending upon how well the economy does in the next few years. The steadfast refusal of the Administration, however, to even consider the causes of crime may be politically safe, but it is hard to see how it will make our streets and homes significantly safer. (Skolnick, 1981, p. 3)

Conclusion

What are we to make of the official data on crime? Each of the three theoretical perspectives provides insight as to how they should be interpreted. First, the official data on crimes do inform us, although not very accurately, about a limited, but nonetheless important, range of crimes. Second, the official data report accurately on the official reaction to certain types of crimes. The interactionists also point to the negative impact of labeling that occurs in the processing of certain kinds of people for certain kinds of offenses. Most important, they point out that the crime statistics do not reflect the reality of crime but that they actually have a hand in *creating* the reality we see (Reiman, 1979, p. 51). Finally, the official data reveal a class bias; they direct our collective attention toward crimes of the underclass and away from those of affluent individuals and powerful corporations.

Official data on crimes, for all their limitations, do tell us something about crime, particularly its political nature and how it is defined and controlled. Knowledge of this should make us less susceptible to the shrill editorials in the media and the political rhetoric backed by official statistics on how crime is rising at such an alarming rate. A more realistic understanding of what crime rates tell us and what they do not tell us also provides an important foundation for the understanding of crime and its control in society—the goal of this book.

CHAPTER REVIEW

1. The government provides the official data on crime to the media and the public. Since 1930, the data on crime have been collected from the states and local law enforcement agencies by the FBI. The crimes are divided into 29 categories, 7 of which are considered the most important (murder, rape, robbery, aggravated assault, burglary, larceny-theft, and motor vehicle theft). These 7 crimes constitute the FBI's Crime Index.

2. The FBI's Crime Index has some major flaws: (a) it is comprised of data collected from more than 15,000 local agencies, which vary in their rigor and diligence in record keeping, and it deliberately inflates or deflates crime rates for political reasons; (b) it is based exclusively on crimes known to the police, thereby excluding crimes between consenting adults, and crimes unreported by victims; and (c) it directs attention solely to "street crimes" and "street criminals."

3. The Census Bureau provides another estimate of crime with its victimization surveys. Individuals from 60,000 households, 42,000 businesses, and 26 major cities are randomly selected for interviews concerning their experiences as victims. The results reveal that (a) about one out of three households is touched by crime annually; (b) about 6 out of 10 crimes go unreported to the police; and (c) the crime rate is relatively stable over time (in contrast to the widely fluctuating, but mostly upward rates reported by the FBI).

4. Victimization studies have two flaws. The first is that individuals may provide distorted information that is taken as fact. Second, there is an emphasis

in the questions asked by the surveys on street crimes and an avoidance of crimes by the affluent and powerful.

5. Social scientists have provided a third indicator of crime: self-report studies. This technique asks respondents to reveal (anonymously) their past criminal activities. These studies reveal consistently that criminality is much more widespread than the FBI and Census studies indicate. Moreover, they show that crime is found throughout the social class structure not just in the underclass, as the FBI data show.

6. Self-report studies have three methodological flaws that lessen their impact: (a) respondents may not provide accurate information; (b) the studies tend to be of youth or of adults asked to remember their activities as youths (to do so inflates the crime figures because youths tend to commit more crimes and many of their criminal activities are not criminal if done by adults, such as truancy and underage drinking); and (c) those few studies that have focused on adult crimes have focused on street crimes, neglecting white-collar crimes.

7. A fundamental problem with the FBI statistics on crime, the victimization studies, and the self-report studies is that they direct attention toward certain crimes (street crimes) and away from others. Neglected are such important crimes as tax evasion, fraud, price fixing, corporate disregard for human safety, and the illegal use of political authority.

8. The traditional sociological perspective on official crime rates has been one of acceptance. There is a basic understanding that these rates may not be completely accurate but that they are at least highly correlated with what actually occurs.

9. Interactionists reject the official crime rates as indicators of actual crimes given the findings from self-report studies. They argue that the official crime statistics indicate how society reacts to certain kinds of offenses and disproportionately labels the poor and minorities as criminals. This is one way that crime rates are socially constructed. This occurs in two other ways as well. There is a self-fulfilling prophecy as certain crimes are identified by the FBI as the most troublesome. This directs the attention of the police to these crimes and they then find them to the exclusion of those crimes in which the police are relatively inactive. Also, official agencies may deliberately increase or decrease crime statistics for political reasons. Two ways to lessen rates and thus appear more efficient are unfounding (declaring that unsolved crimes never occurred) and defounding (lowering felonies to misdemeanors).

10. The radical approach to official crime rates focuses on their political nature. Similar to the interactionists, radicals point to the manipulation of crime rates for political and bureaucratic purposes. Most significant, the radicals argue that official crime rates are used to divert attention away from the criminal activities of certain categories of people (the affluent and the powerful) and organizations (corporations and polities) and toward the powerless. It is not only a diversionary tactic but also one that helps to maintain the current balance of power. The underclass is seen as the enemy and efforts are directed at keeping them in line rather than viewing the structure of society as the culprit.

PART 2 TYPES OF CRIME

This section describes a wide range of criminal activities in American society. Separate chapters on street, white-collar, victimless, organized, corporate, and political crime focus on the nature and extent of each of these types of criminal activity, as well as on their perpetrators and their victims. As we use the three theoretical perspectives on crime and criminal justice developed in Chapter 2 to explain each of these different types of crime, it will become apparent that some sociological theories offer better explanations than others for particular kinds of crime. In general, traditional sociological, interactionist, and radical criminological perspectives all have some usefulness in explaining the "disorderly" crimes of *individuals*—street, white-collar, and victimless crime. However, radical criminology has the most potential when it comes to understanding the origins of the "orderly" crimes of *organizations*—organized, corporate, and political crimes.

5 Street Crime

CHAPTER OUTLINE

The Historical Development of Street Crime
Contemporary Street Crime

Rates
Social conditions and street crime

Types of Street Crime

Crimes of accommodation
Crimes of resistance

Theory and Street Crime

The traditional approach
The interactionist approach
The radical approach

Punishing Street Crime

The productivity of crime

KEY TERMS

Crimes of accommodation
Crimes of resistance
Dual labor markets
Predatory crime
Personal crime
Street crime

"Watch teams"—groups of neighborhood residents patrolling their own streets, homes, and businesses—are springing up all over the country. Millions of Americans are investing in home alarm systems, burglar bars, watchdogs, paralyzing sprays and, of course, handguns. Increasingly, we have become a people fearful of our own communities and convinced that "crime has overwhelmed all traditional defenses" (*U.S. News and World Report,* July 13, 1981, p. 53).

And, not all of this fear is unfounded. In 1980, the FBI found that "thirty percent of all households in the United States experienced some type of crime and 6 percent suffered a violent crime" (reported in *U.S. News and World Report,* July 13, 1981, p. 53). The bureau has reported roughly the same kinds of figures for each year since 1980.

But before turning to a fuller description and analysis of the contemporary and aggravating problem of crime in the streets, however, it is necessary to examine the historical development of this type of crime. For it is not accidental that certain behaviors and acts have come to be defined as criminal (and, thus, proper targets of official control) in our society and others have not. The history of street crime is instructive on this matter: how and when did the categories of conventional or traditional street crime emerge?

THE HISTORICAL DEVELOPMENT OF STREET CRIME

The development of street crime in the United States coincides historically with a period of rapid and intense social change. The sources of this devastating change were many. "As westward expansion, urbanization, immigration, industrialization, and the conflict over slavery remade the face of American society, uprooting established patterns of life and challenging old values, Americans launched what historian Robert Wiebe called a 'search for order' " (cited in Walker, 1980, p. 56). The consequence of this change, however, was rather consistent: social disorder.

Westward expansion in this country was essentially a lawless process. As the West was settled—usually involving the expropriation of Indian lands—the new "landowners" discovered that they often needed to take the law into their own hands in order to protect their recently acquired property. Increasingly, vigilante groups imposed their own brand of "law and order." No government authority existed. "In the absence of law, violence arose" (Walker, 1980, p. 57), a violence that needed to be regulated and curbed if America was to expand its borders and its economy.

By the time the U.S. Constitution was being written, fear of losing the power, privilege, and property generated by the new political and economic order was widespread among those who had been fortunate enough to have profited from it. Those who had gained wealth and property during America's early independence came to influence the new government. Those who had not gained these things were perceived generally as "threatening rabble." The Federalists were not without a solution: a constitutionally mandated national legal system that could not only aid in the integration of the new economy—something the new commercial classes desperately wanted in order to quell "nonprofitable" and destructive economic chaos and competition in the growing American free-market system—but would also begin to enforce order among the "dangerous classes" who threatened the smooth functioning of the new order.

The 19th century brought even more disorder in the United States. The urban east coast began to experience unprecedented chaos and rioting. Capitalist industrialization and the accompanying institutionalization of the factory organization of work, urbanization, and the immigration from Europe of a largely unskilled labor force began to take their toll. Walker has depicted the pervasiveness of the disorder:

> Philadelphia and Baltimore competed for the dubious title of "mob city," as both had a dozen major disturbances between 1834 and 1860. New York experienced three major riots in 1834 alone. Nor was the problem confined to the East; Cincinnati, St. Louis, and Chicago had their own riots. (Walker, 1980, p. 57)

The "dangerous classes" were composed of "America's transient mass of poor, expendable, unskilled workers" who "were perceived as the source of America's expanding pool of criminality" (Browning and Gerassi, 1980, p. 128). The under- and unemployed, created by a growing industrialization became an ever threatening source of disorder. Those in control of the government and economy began to see a way out of this dilemma: control this source of disorder by defining its actions as criminal. In effect, "the new Republic found no other way of dealing with its great injustice, poverty" (Browning and Gerassi, 1980, p. 133).

Immigration was an important catalyst in this process. As western, and then southern and eastern, Europeans arrived in the United States, ethnic conflict, suspicion, and hatred increased. Divergent religions, languages, cultural practices, and class backgrounds all helped to "fuel the fire" in an already conflict-ridden society.

But economic problems continued to generate the most severe and violent disorder, the kind of violence and disorder that would be criminally defined and controlled by a still emerging criminal justice system. Walker has described those particular "criminal" actions:

> Investors destroyed banks that had failed and lost their savings, and working-men retaliated with violence against the injustices of the new industrialism. By the second half of the century, industrial violence began to take on the aspect of class warfare. The worst episode was the railroad riots of 1877, when angry workers attacked and destroyed railroad properties in dozens of cities across the country. In Pittsburgh, law and order completely collapsed, and the mob destroyed an estimated $5 million worth of property. (Walker, 1980, p. 58)

And when workers attempted to organize against the new industrial capitalists and managers, they were often met with "official" violence. Panel 5-1 describes one of these instances: the Haymarket Square affair in Chicago where labor leaders organized a rally supporting an eight-hour work day but became the victims of police violence.

The institution of slavery that marred American society in the 18th and 19th centuries was also a source of violence, lawlessness, riots, and other forms of public disorder. By 1830, the antislavery movement had already begun to arouse racial passions and the vigilante actions that often followed in both the North and the South. Both "free" blacks and white abolitionists were attacked and terrorized by white supremacists in Boston, Cincinnati, Philadelphia, and other cities. Vigilantes everywhere attempted to suppress any and all opposition to slavery. This violence also spread to the western frontier where, for example, "Bleeding Kansas" erupted into a virtual civil war between pro- and antislavery forces. Not all of the mob violence, however, came from proslavery movements. In 1850, antislavery leaders began to defy and resist openly any enforcement of the Fugitive Slave Act, often utilizing both public demonstration and mob action. Later on, the Civil War unleashed the disorder and violence that went with the division of many communities in border and southern states into warring pro-Confederacy and pro-Union factions. And after the Civil War, during Reconstruction, groups like the Ku Klux Klan emerged, employing violence to property and persons as a way of attempting to reestablish white supremacy.

Although American criminal law has been most concerned historically with those behaviors deemed "disorderly" by ruling economic and political groups, this does not imply that the law has remained static. Changing social, political, and economic conditions have dictated (and continue to dictate) specific changes in the criminal law and in the definition of those criminal behaviors that "need to be controlled." For example, the criminal court in Colonial America was primarily concerned with issues of religious conformity and sexual morality. By the time the U.S. Constitution was complete, however, sexual and religious indictments had virtually disappeared and been replaced primarily with the prosecution of property crimes. Browning and Gerassi have documented this shift:

> In Massachusetts, the "Bible Colony," sinful offenses against God and offensive public behavior had always burdened the criminal docket . . . A study of Middlesex County cases showed that 210 of the 370 prosecutions between 1760 and 1774 were for fornication, 3 were for cohabitation and adultery, and 27 were for violation of the Sabbath. By 1789, when a new code was put into effect, 5 people were convicted of fornication; in 1791, 1 and after that, none. Clearly the courts of Middlesex County—like most of the nation's prosecutors, cared little about who went to bed with whom. Religious indictments also declined, so much so, that by 1816 a court publication noted that "thousands of violations occurred every year, with scarcely a single instance of punishment." . . . [S]till the courts were not left without work, for a new trend was developing—prosecution for crimes against property. Throughout the colonial decades, a gradual increase in theft and burglary had been recorded in the larger port cities. But after the Revolutionary War, the increase was phenomenal. In Middlesex County, for example, the records show that theft and burglary prosecutions

PANEL 5-1

The Haymarket Square Affair

On the morning of May 1, a bright balmy Saturday, the *Chicago Mail* asked for blood. "There are two dangerous ruffians at large in this city; two skulking cowards who are trying to create trouble," the paper editorialized. "Mark them. . . . Make an example of them." One was Albert Parsons, thirty-eight, whose solid middle-class Yankee family had moved to Montgomery, Alabama. He had fought with the Confederacy, had been radicalized by the depression of 1873, and had become a socialist during the police riot of 1877 when he had been warned by the police chief to leave town or be hanged "to a Camppost." The other "ruffian" was August Spies, thirty-one, a German-born socialist, newspaper editor, and labor leader. Throughout the day Pinkertons and militia men, armed with rifles,

When the Haymarket "conspirators" were hanged, November 11, 1887, their last words were reported by Police Captain Schaack. August Spies said, "You may strangle this voice but my silence will be more terrible than speech." Adolph Fischer said, "Hoch die Anarchie!" George Engel said, "Hurrah for anarchy!" Albert Richard Parsons said, "O men of America, let the voice of the people be heard . . . ." Just then the trap was sprung.

PANEL 5-1 (Continued)

were stationed on rooftops, and 1,350 National Guardsmen in full battle gear and equipped with Gatling guns were waiting in the armory ready to attack. But the rally for an eight-hour-day, led by Parsons and Spies, was peaceful, and the *Mail* did not reap its blood. Two days later, after Spies finished addressing six thousand strikers near the McCormick Harvester Works, where fourteen hundred workers had been locked out for joining a union, a scuffle developed when scabs headed into the plant. Almost immediately two hundred Chicago policemen surged out of side streets and began beating and shooting the strikers, killing four and wounding scores. Spies responded by calling for a mass protest rally for the next day, to meet at Haymarket Square. The big press in America has rarely been on the side of the workingmen, and even more rarely on the side of justice, but this time it indulged in overkill, describing the labor leaders as mad anarchists and the crowd as "liquor-crazed. . . ."

May 4, 1886, was an ugly day in Chicago. No sooner had Parsons, Spies, and other labor leaders spoken to the three thousand workers assembled at Haymarket Square than it started to rain. As most people began to leave, Captain John ("Clubber") Bonfield showed up with 180 policemen and ordered them to hurry up. At that moment a bomb exploded in the front ranks of the police. The cops then went mad, clubbing and shooting. Some of the strikers fired back, but the crowd dispersed fast. It was all over in a flash. Yet that began the real Haymarket affair, for, though some strikers were dead and hundreds wounded, what mattered was that one policeman had been killed on the spot and seven more died from wounds later. The *New York Times* cried murder and demanded vengeance. All further rallies and demonstrations were forbidden—except, of course, in support of the police. Hundreds of radicals and labor leaders were arrested as state's attorney Julius S. Grinnell told his law enforcers: "Make raids first and look up the law afterwards." Finally, on June 21, Parsons, Spies and six other radicals were charged with conspiracy and being accessories to murder—punishable by death. . . .

The Haymarket trial represents one of the most disgusting episodes in the American system of justice. Even Illinois governor John Peter Altgeld, risking his political career, said so publicly in 1893, accusing Judge Joseph E. Gary of flagrant prejudice. Indeed, of the twelve jurors not one was a worker, four said they hated radicals, and every single one admitted having formed an opinion about the guilt of the defendants before the trial—yet the judge, the defense having exhausted its preemptory challenges, disqualified none. "Much of the evidence given in the trial was pure fabrication," Governor Altgeld said later, adding that testimony was gained from "terrorized, ignorant men" whom police had threatened "with torture if they refused to swear to anything desired." Seven of the eight were con-

PANEL 5-1 (Continued)

demned to hang, the eighth getting fifteen years. Lucy Parsons and the two Parsons children were arrested and jailed for trying to see Parsons before his execution. Appeals for clemency or pardons were denied. The Supreme Court refused to hear the case. Spies, Parsons, and two others were hanged on November 11, 1887. A fifth had committed suicide in jail. The two others had their sentences commuted to life imprisonment. The *New York Times* was jubilant. Six years later, Governor Altgeld refused an "act of mercy." Either the men were innocent or they were guilty, he said. For five months he studied the record. On June 26, 1893, describing the trial as a complete sham and condemning Judge Gary as a bigot, he freed the last three defendants. America's press condemned him. In Chicago, New York, Philadelphia, Detroit, he was called unfit for the governor's chair. Everywhere big business donated funds to defeat him in 1896. He lost the election, and the workers lost their eight-hour day.

Source: Frank Browning and John Gerassi, The American Way of Crime, *New York: Putnam, 1980, pp. 228–230.*

rose about four times from 1775 through 1784. Prosecutions remained at that level until 1790, decreasing slightly during the economic boom years of the 1790s; but during the depression of 1807 they doubled again. . . . (Browning and Gerassi, 1980, p. 123)

And who was the object of these emerging prosecutions for property crimes? For the most part, they were the urban, unemployed surplus population and poor laborers; 75 percent during the 1780s and 71 percent in 1807 in Middlesex County (Browning and Gerassi, 1980, p. 123).

Popular discontent with the new economic order and the institutions of private property was commonplace in America after 1790 and was further aggravated with each ensuing period of economic depression (in 1807, 1819, 1837, and so on). The most important new function of the criminal law became the protection of individual and corporate property. By 1810, the prosecution of assaults on private property became the primary activity of the nation's criminal courts. As Massachusetts Governor John Hancock put it in 1793, the object of criminal law was the "good order" of the government and "the security" of private property (Browning and Gerassi, 1980, p. 125).

The institution of criminal law in the United States, then, bears a close relation to the historical (and contemporary) concern with property crime. In contrast to the earlier colonial period, the violation of someone's property (a neighbor, a landlord, an employer, for example) also became a violation of the law, of the state's power and authority. The criminal—that person engaged in acts threatening the established public order and the maintenance of private property—was no longer simply a person violating the community's code of decent and moral behavior. "He was now characterized as an enemy of the state bent on the willful destruction of its authority" (Browning and Gerassi, 1980, p. 126).

Another more recent example of the way in which changing political or economic factors influence the determination of what is criminal and what is not in our society has to do with the historical processes by which drug use has been criminalized. As Helmer (1975) has argued, business cycles, labor markets, and unemployment are not unrelated to the sale and consumption of *illegal* narcotic drugs. More specifically, by documenting the history of drug use in the United States, Helmer has concluded that it has been, and is now, an undeniably working-class phenomenon. Not insignificantly, he further insists that this working-class characterization of illegal drug use "has been a specific cause, not a general consequence, of narcotics prohibition when it has been enacted" (Helmer, 1975, p. 7).

Historically, as labor-market conditions—the supply of and demand for workers—in the United States have responded to the needs of industry (specifically the owners and managers of capital), not only have the conditions of workers' lives changed, but so has the membership of this working class. Wherever and whenever labor supply has vastly exceeded demand in the American economy and drug use has followed, it has been declared illegal through the institutions of criminal law. In this way, legal control of group who has become surplus to the American economy and society is facilitated. After they had finished building the railroads in the West, the American economy could no longer accommodate the Chinese. Opium was declared illegal and the exclusionary campaign against the Chinese was begun. Later on in the 19th century when the menial labor of Mexicans was no longer needed in the Southwest, their use of marijuana was made criminal. And more recently, when the labor surplus residing in the economically depressed (and potentially politically explosive) black, brown, and Latino ghettos in many large cities began to threaten public order, yet other narcotics were criminalized.[1]

The crimes that plague our streets these days—assault, burglary, larceny, arson, homicide, manslaughter, robbery, auto theft, shoplifting, rape, vandalism, drug use—have their roots in an historical propensity toward social and public disorder. These crimes, however, may not always have been crimes and may not always be crimes in the future. Social, political, and economic forces, along with those in society powerful enough to affect these forces, will continue to play a major role in the determination of what is criminal and what is not.

---

[1] For a more detailed discussion of the use and sale of illegal drugs in the United States, see Timmer (1982) as well as Chapter 8.

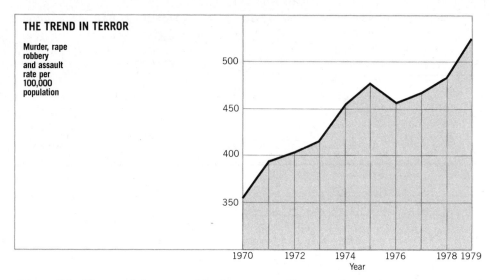

THE TREND IN TERROR

Murder, rape robbery and assault rate per 100,000 population

Figure 5-1 The trend in terror. Murder, rape, robbery, and assault, rate per 100,000 population.

SOURCE: *FBI Uniform Crime Reports*, from Ed Magnuson, "The Curse of Violent Crime," *Time*, March 23, 1981, p. 19.

CONTEMPORARY STREET CRIME

Rates[2]

As pointed out in Chapter 4, the FBI's official crime rate divides street crime into two categories: violent crime and property crime. It is important to note that as long as the Bureau has gathered these data, property crimes have been much more numerous than violent crimes.

Although the rate of increase in the FBI Uniform Crime Reports for violent crimes ("crimes against persons": robbery, aggravated assault, rape and murder) fluctuated throughout the 1970s (see Figure 5-1), the overall trend in street crime, when property crimes (theft-larceny, auto theft and burglary) are included, was one of significant increase. In 1970, the FBI reported an overall street crime rate of 363.5 per 100,000 population. By 1979, it listed an overall rate of 535.5. Table 5-1 reflects the way in which the FBI documented this increase in crime over the decade of the 1970s. Notice how the victimization surveys (again, see Chapter 4) administered semiannually by the Bureau of the Census and the Bureau of Justice Statistics (BJS) do not reflect a rapidly growing criminality over this decade. These crime data, both generated by the U.S. Department of Justice, document a sizable increase in reported crime but not in criminal victimization. The fact that

[2]When considering the crime statistics to be presented here—be they from the FBI Uniform Crime Report, the National Crime Survey, or victimization surveys—the reader should keep in mind all of the potential inaccuracies and political and bureaucratic biases that plague them, as discussed in the previous chapter.

TABLE 5-1

Violent Crime Indexes (Percentage Change Over Previous Year)

Year	FBI	BJS	Year	FBI	BJS
1971	10.5	—	1976	−3.9	1.9
1972	2.3	—	1977	2.3	1.9
1973	4.9	—	1978	5.2	2.1
1974	11.3	2.4	1979	11.0	1.9
1975	5.3	1.9	1980[a]	10.0	—

SOURCE: Department of Justice, in Editorial Research Reports, "Violent Crime's Return to Prominence," Vol. I, No. 10, March 13, 1981, Washington, D.C.: *Congressional Quarterly,* p. 195.
[a] Based on first six months.

the FBI Crime Index reported a 50.1 percent increase in crimes reported to the police between 1970 and 1979—from 8,098,000 crimes to 12,152,700—whereas victim reports of crime remained fairly constant throughout the period, has led some observers to the ironic conclusion that the 1970s represented a "crime wave without victims" (see Browning, 1982, for example).

Figure 5-2 concentrates on the eight large urban areas that contributed most to the FBI's increasing crime rate during the 1970s.

By 1980, FBI statistics showed even more pronounced increases in street crime. These are the data still being used by the mass media and others to create the impression of a crime scare or wave in the United States. Crime wave or not, a researcher at the Bureau of Justice Statistics (again, whose own victimization surveys do not confirm the reality of the latest crime wave) put it as well as it can be put: "Our figures do not show a new crime wave—but they show there's a hell of a lot of crime" (quoted in Magnuson et al., 1981, p. 17). A hell of a lot of crime, indeed.

In 1979, after several years of relatively modest increases, the FBI's crime rate began to show sizeable advances. In 1980, it appears as though the rates escalated by leaps and bounds. New York, Los Angeles, Miami, and Dallas all recorded record levels of murder, robbery, and burglary. Detroit, which had experienced a declining street crime rate since 1976, reversed itself and showed increases in every category of crime measured by the Uniform Crime Report. For the nation as a whole, the FBI estimated a 10 percent jump in serious crime during the first six months of 1980 (Press, 1981, p. 46).

Figures for the first six months of 1980 also indicated that New York City probably experienced its most criminal year in history. Street crime in New York ran 60 percent above the national average. In 1980 the city topped the nation in robbery rate and posted a record number of murders: 1814 (Magnuson et al., 1981). If that murder rate were to go unchanged, predicted an M.I.T. study, "one out of every 61 babies born in the city last year can expect to die at the hands—or gun—of a killer" (Magnuson et al., 1981, p. 18).

Los Angeles experienced much the same thing at the same time: murder up 27 percent, armed robbery 20 percent, burglaries 16 percent, and rape 10 percent.

THE TRAGIC VICTIMS OF CRIME

Attempted Murder

Two shotgun blasts destroyed the eyes of Jim A. Tucker and drove the Vietnam veteran into despair and seclusion.

His assailant is unknown. So is the reason he shot Tucker. Even today, four years later, a BB occasionally works its way from Tucker's skull. And at night Tucker, alone with his shadows, wonders if maybe, just maybe, a pellet might one day work its way downward into his brain.

"It took me a year to figure out I wasn't going to be able to see again . . . I never realized what a problem blind people have."

These days Tucker sits in his rented home in Firestone, Colo. In the daytime his back is to the sun for warmth. "It feels pretty good."

His roommate reads for him. Unable to read music, Tucker attempts to master a borrowed piano—by ear.

"I don't go out at all, I don't have any desire to. I don't have any ultimate goals . . .

"I keep living with this idea that tomorrow may not come. I think the experience (being shot) could happen again. I guess you could say I'm paranoid. After four years I still haven't gotten it out of my head."

Purse Snatching

Nancy's purse was recently snatched by two street thugs. She's terrified.

"I'm getting so paranoid," says the middle-aged state employee from Denver.

Her purse contained her keys, identification, credit cards, some $30—the usual flotsam and jetsam a woman accumulates in a handbag.

Losing her keys and all her identification awakened Nancy to the world of street crime. It made her feel genuinely vulnerable.

"Someone tried to get in (break into) our house last night . . ."

"Now I feel quite vulnerable. It's come home to me . . . I thought I knew how to handle myself in all sorts of situations. And now I don't think people can (handle themselves) when that sort of thing happens . . .

"I've learned a lesson. Women have to know they can't carry purses anymore. The same thing has happened to three other women in my office building."

"I had a can of Mace in my purse, but it didn't do me any good. I was walking down the sidewalk and I didn't hear a thing. They (two juveniles) came running and ripped my purse off my arm as smooth as silk. I wasn't pushed down or anything . . .

"It's not the dark you have to be afraid of anymore. It's all the time."

Burglary

Harold and his wife live in a large home in one of Denver's posher neighborhoods. Recently while his wife was gone, Harold decided to shop for lunchmeats. When he returned an hour later his home had been burgled and he and his wife were missing $22,000 in jewelry and silver flatware.

A neighbor had seen a suspicious individual lolling about the curb and later noticed that Harold's living room drapes were pulled closed, which was not the family's custom. She called police, who apparently arrived while the burglar was still inside the house. The cops poked about Harold's yard, rattled his doors then left.

"I asked the detective what their report was," Harold says. "He told me: 'They just goofed!' "

Harold says the incident has caused him to investigate installation of a burglar alarm. He has't done it yet, but he chats about the merits of various security systems.

Harold installed security doors several weeks before the burglary. But the burglar simply broke and entered through a window.

He is a member of a neighborhood association which several years ago distributed an electric pencil-like device to mark valuable metal items. But Harold only marked his television and stereo gear, not the family jewelry or silver, the burglar's primary target.

"The whole thing doesn't bother me as much now as it did at first . . . It used to bother me when I went to bed. I couldn't sleep.

"It hasn't altered our lifestyle too much, I guess . . . It's . . . just one of those things."

Assault

Patricia Ruelas, of Denver, wasn't a crime victim. But her pain is no less real. Her brother is serving an eight-year sentence for assault. And it has almost destroyed the Ruelas family.

"It was devastating to us when they arrested him . . . The hardest thing was that they had him in jail, let him out for a month or so, then arrested him a second time . . .

"They (the police) came to my mom's house, searched it at 4 a.m. and impounded her car the second time. She about had a nervous breakdown. It was a month before he (the brother) would see any of us. And when we finally saw him, he just cried and cried, like a baby . . . It was like rocking a baby in my arms. It was so sad . . ."

The experience on the family has "been totally devastating," Patricia says. "My father in Texas has turned so cold-hearted toward my brother . . . It has just about destroyed our lives . . ."

Manslaughter

Ayleen Salazar's brother was beaten to death with a tire iron allegedly wielded by a family friend.

"We had known him (the friend) for about 18 years," she says.

Authorities filed a first degree murder charge, "but what we can't understand is why the charge was dropped to manslaughter."

Ayleen said she had asked that the Denver district attorney refile the murder charge, "but (DA Dale) Tooley was real rude . . . he told me I should get myself a lawyer and take a lesson in law."

"My brother was drunk and he had a small police record. The guy who killed him was a white guy and never had a police record. (One of the assistant district attorneys) handling it told me my brother would be on trial, not the white guy . . .

"If you're a drunk Chicano and have a police record you can be beaten to death by a white person who has no police record."

Her brother's death has shattered Ayleen's family.

"My dad is beginning to have nightmares. He just can't figure out why nobody seems to give a damn. He feels like this guy (the killer) should pay. I've had to talk to him, to tell him he should be strong . . .

"I'm a nervous wreck. I could have related to the fact that he died. But the way everybody has acted has been (worse) on me mentally than the fact he died . . ."

Source: The Rocky Mountain News, *Denver, Colo., February 25, 1981.*

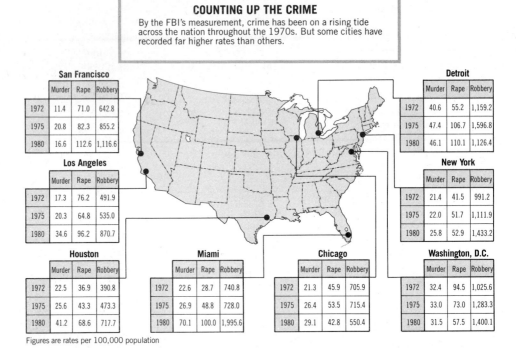

COUNTING UP THE CRIME

By the FBI's measurement, crime has been on a rising tide across the nation throughout the 1970s. But some cities have recorded far higher rates than others.

San Francisco

	Murder	Rape	Robbery
1972	11.4	71.0	642.8
1975	20.8	82.3	855.2
1980	16.6	112.6	1,116.6

Detroit

	Murder	Rape	Robbery
1972	40.6	55.2	1,159.2
1975	47.4	106.7	1,596.8
1980	46.1	110.1	1,126.4

Los Angeles

	Murder	Rape	Robbery
1972	17.3	76.2	491.9
1975	20.3	64.8	535.0
1980	34.6	96.2	870.7

New York

	Murder	Rape	Robbery
1972	21.4	41.5	991.2
1975	22.0	51.7	1,111.9
1980	25.8	52.9	1,433.2

Houston

	Murder	Rape	Robbery
1972	22.5	36.9	390.8
1975	25.6	43.3	473.3
1980	41.2	68.6	717.7

Miami

	Murder	Rape	Robbery
1972	22.6	28.7	740.8
1975	26.9	48.8	728.0
1980	70.1	100.0	1,995.6

Chicago

	Murder	Rape	Robbery
1972	21.3	45.9	705.9
1975	26.4	53.5	715.4
1980	29.1	42.8	550.4

Washington, D.C.

	Murder	Rape	Robbery
1972	32.4	94.5	1,025.6
1975	33.0	73.0	1,283.3
1980	31.5	57.5	1,400.1

Figures are rates per 100,000 population

Figure 5-2   Counting up the crime. By the FBI's measurement, crime has been on a rising tide across the nation throughout the 1970s. But some cities have recorded far higher rates than others.

SOURCE: Aric Press et al., "The Plague of Violent Crime," *Newsweek*, March 23, 1981, p. 52.

Miami, in the middle of the world cocaine trade and its warring factions, the arrival of thousands of Cuban exiles, and political turmoil and social unrest in its black ghetto, had to call in 100 state troopers to aid local police. It did not seem to help however; in 1980, homicides rose 60 percent and robberies 80 percent (all figures reported in Magnuson et al., 1981, p. 18). Las Vegas experienced a 21.3 percent increase in reported street crime in 1980, whereas crime in Phoenix was up 17.8 percent and in Tucson 16.7 percent in the same year (Ostrow, 1981, p. 1). Figure 5-3 locates what appears to be the "capitals of American violent street crime."

But not all of the dramatic rise in official street crime rates had its source in large metropolitan centers. Violent crime in America's suburbs climbed 7.4 percent in 1979 (U.S. Department of Justice, 1980). In 1980, violent crimes in rural areas increased by 13 percent (Magnuson et al., 1981, p. 18). Although rural America did not see a significant increase in muggings, shootings or murders, reported house break-ins and thefts of autos and other farm equipment skyrocketed. (The extent to which this may reflect urban perpetrators traveling to rural areas has not yet been established.) In addition, many of the energy boomtowns in the Rocky Mountains and far West are continuing to experience staggering increases in reported street crime.

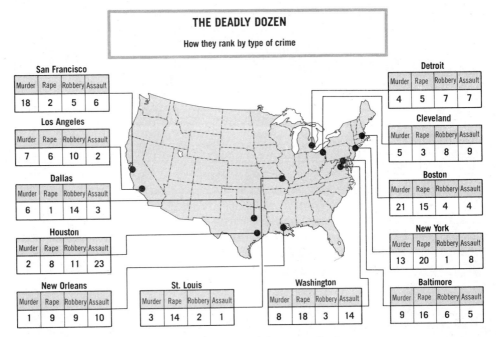

THE DEADLY DOZEN

How they rank by type of crime

San Francisco

Murder	Rape	Robbery	Assault
18	2	5	6

Los Angeles

Murder	Rape	Robbery	Assault
7	6	10	2

Dallas

Murder	Rape	Robbery	Assault
6	1	14	3

Houston

Murder	Rape	Robbery	Assault
2	8	11	23

New Orleans

Murder	Rape	Robbery	Assault
1	9	9	10

St. Louis

Murder	Rape	Robbery	Assault
3	14	2	1

Washington

Murder	Rape	Robbery	Assault
8	18	3	14

Detroit

Murder	Rape	Robbery	Assault
4	5	7	7

Cleveland

Murder	Rape	Robbery	Assault
5	3	8	9

Boston

Murder	Rape	Robbery	Assault
21	15	4	4

New York

Murder	Rape	Robbery	Assault
13	20	1	8

Baltimore

Murder	Rape	Robbery	Assault
9	16	6	5

Figure 5-3 The deadly dozen. How they rank by type of crime.

SOURCE: A survey of the 25 largest cities for the first six months of 1980, done by the Citizens Crime Commission of New York.
SOURCE: Ed Magnuson et al., "The Curse of Violent Crime," *Time*, March 23, 1981.

Overall, an analysis of 1980 FBI Uniform Crime Index data (based on reports from roughly 12,000 law enforcement agencies) indicate that reported street crime increased by 10 percent in the United States, as compared with 1979 data.[3] Violent crime—assault, murder, rape, and robbery—increased by 13 percent: assault, 8 percent; murder, 7 percent; rape, 9 percent; and robbery, 20 percent. Property crime—burglary, larceny-theft, and motor vehicle theft—increased by 9 percent: burglary, 14 percent; larceny-theft, 8 percent; and motor vehicle theft, 2 percent. This overall 10 percent increase in reported street crime in 1980 represented the most significant annual rise since 1975 (all figures in Ostrow, 1981, p. 1).

Moving closer to the present, in 1981, the number of FBI Crime Index offenses reported to the police was approximately the same number as were reported in 1980. Violent crime, the Uniform Crime Report said, increased 1 percent in 1981 (as compared with 1980) while property crime remained at roughly the same level as the year before (U.S. Department of Justice, 1982).

The first six months of 1982 showed an actual decrease in street crime as measured by the FBI Index: a 3 percent decline in violent crime and 6 percent dip in the more numerous property crimes. But, as the Justice Department itself has

[3] The FBI added an eighth crime to its Index in 1979—arson. Data on arson, however, are still sketchy and incomplete when compared with data on the other seven index crimes. For that reason, we will not include arson in any of our discussion and analysis of the Uniform Crime Report.

warned, any leveling off or small declines in the 1982 (or beyond) Uniform Crime Index must be understood in light of the fact that they represent a stabilization or decrease from the two highest official crime rates in our history—in 1980 and 1981 (Associated Press, October 20, 1982).

We close this general discussion of official street crime rates by citing the findings of the Justice Department's 1982 National Crime Survey. This survey is in a sense the most comprehensive official crime data available since it includes crimes that have been reported to the police as well as those that have not.[4] The National Crime Survey, again, gathered its data by interviewing some 50,000 American households in 1982 in regard to their criminal victimization during that year. Probably the most significant information that has emerged from the National Crime Surveys in recent years is that while the FBI's Uniform Crime Report (counting only police reported crime) between 1975 and 1982 showed wide fluctuations ranging from one annual increase of up to 10 percent to a small decline in 1982, the National Surveys during this same period showed no significant difference from year to year in the percentage of American households that were victimized by crime (Associated Press, June 13, 1983).

The Most Violent Crime

Since the Reagan administration pledged that its law enforcement, judicial, and correctional policies would focus primarily on the control of violent crime, we should take note of the data available on the most violent of crimes: murder. As we have already noted, America's reported murder rate has most definitely been on the upswing.

Table 5-2 gives 1980 murder rates for the 20 largest cities in the United States. But even when the murder-prone large cities are mixed in with small cities and towns and rural areas, the nation's overall homicide rate remains high. In 1974, the homicide rate in the United States reached what was then an all time high—9.8 per 100,000 population. The rate was 9.7 per 100,000 population in 1979 and even higher in 1980 (Magnuson et al., 1981, p. 18). In every year since 1973 there have been about 20,000 murders in the United States (U.S. Department of Justice, 1982).

In an average week, about 400 Americans are murdered. Most are slain as the result of a family quarrel or neighborhood argument. Many die in gang or drug wars. Recently, as many as a third of all murders appear to be the work of strangers (to the victim). However, the most devastating statistics having to do with murder in the United States are related to handguns. Handguns have never been banned in America and only a handful of states have any meaningful and restrictive registration procedures for handgun owners. The result: more than half

---

[4]Of course the National Crime Survey can only count crimes for which a victim can be interviewed. Therefore, NCS crime statistics do not include the approximately 20,000 murders reported to the police in 1982.

TABLE 5-2

Murder Rates

How the 20 Largest Cities Compare			
	Population Rank	Homicides During 1980	Homicides Per 100,000 Persons
1. Cleveland	18	280	**48.9**
2. Detroit	6	548	**46.0**
3. Houston	5	644	**41.4**
4. Dallas	7	322	**35.7**
5. Los Angeles	3	1,042	**35.3**
6. Washington, D.C.	15	202	**31.7**
7. Chicago	2	863	**29.1**
8. Baltimore	9	216	**27.5**
9. Philadelphia	4	437	**26.0**
10. Memphis	14	166	**25.7**
11. New York	1	1,790	**25.5**
12. San Francisco	13	110	**16.3**
13. Boston	19	91	**16.2**
14. Columbus, Ohio	20	91	**16.2**
15. Indianapolis	12	107	**15.4**
16. Phoenix	11	105	**13.4**
17. Milwaukee	16	80	**12.6**
18. San Diego	8	108	**12.4**
19. San Jose	17	62	**9.9**
20. San Antonio	10	69	**8.8**

SOURCE: *USN&WR* table—Basic data: Police reports, U.S. Dept. of Commerce, in *U.S. News and World Report,* "Violence in Big Cities: Behind the Surge," February 23, 1981, p. 63.

the people murdered in Chicago since 1970 have been the victims of handguns; more than half of all murders that result from domestic and neighborhood arguments involve handguns (Press, 1981; Isaacson, 1981).

The murder rate in the United States in 1979 was 9.7 per 100,000, which was probably the highest homicide rate anywhere in the world. In 1979, Japan had 1.6 murders per 100,000 population; Britain, 1.3; West Germany, 1.3—all countries, incidentally, that have legislated and enforced very restrictive handgun regulations.[5]

[5] In spite of the Reagan administration's purported desire to control violent crime, it remained uniformly and absolutely opposed to any and all gun control legislation in the United States. The attempted assassination of Reagan himself, done with a handgun, makes this position even harder to understand. It is also true that an August 1981 Gallup Poll revealed that 91 percent of the American people favor tougher handgun controls. Even U.S. Attorney General William Smith's Reagan-mandated Task Force Report on Violent Crime concluded that "crime committed by individuals using handguns is perhaps the most serious problem of violence facing our nation today." This report also recommended outlawing the importation of handgun parts to the United States, tightening federal law

The number and severity of street crimes are increased by the relatively easy access to hand guns.

A Cross-cultural Comparison

As measured by the official rates of violent crime in each society, Ross and Benson (1979) have completed a study that indicates that the United States is a much more violent society than other urbanized, industrialized nations. Table 5-3 shows that the U.S. homicide rate in 1976, for example, was 5 times higher than that in Japan and 8 times higher than in England. The robbery rate in the United States was 17 times that of Japan and 8 times that of England; for rape, the U.S. rate was nearly 10 times greater than in Japan, 12 times that of England. (As pointed out in Chapter 4, and again at the beginning of this chapter, however, we cannot simply accept these official data at face value.)

to allow for easier tracing of firearms, making it more difficult for convicted felons to purchase handguns, and strengthening the 1968 federal gun-control law (a law that the National Rifle Association, an antigun control lobby that probably represents the most powerful and effective single-issue political lobby in the United States, wants to gut). All of this because "in 1978, . . . firearms were used in 307,000 murders, robberies, and aggravated assaults reported to the police; 77.8 percent of the guns used to murder were handguns. . . ." Yet, when President Reagan (September, 1981) spoke to the International Chiefs of Police in New Orleans, he verbally supported only one task force recommendation: mandatory prison terms for felons using guns, the only task force recommendation supported by the National Rifle Association, We will take up the wider issue of the relationship between guns and street crime in the section "Social Conditions and Street Crime" below.

TABLE 5-3

Crime Rate for Selected Crimes in the United States, Japan, and England and Wales: Offenses Known to the Police, 1976 (per 100,000 population)

	United States	Japan	England/ Wales
Homicide	8.80	1.74	1.16[a]
Robbery	196.00	11.20[b]	24.84[c]
Rape	26.4[d]	2.68	2.24

SOURCE: Ruth A. Ross, and George C. S. Benson, "Criminal Justice from East to West," *Crime and Delinquency* 25, January 1979, p. 77.
[a] Includes manslaughter and infanticide.
[b] Includes robbery involving homicide and rape.
[c] Includes aggravated burglary.
[d] Includes attempted rape.

How are these disparities to be explained? It could be that there are significant differences in the compilation of crime statistics, with crime in Japan and England being underreported. However, both of those countries have highly centralized police systems (whereas data on officially reported crime in the United States are taken from over 12,000 law enforcement agencies each year) that probably result in more accurate crime statistics than our own.

Density of population (measured as the number of persons per square mile) is often considered a factor causing street crime; the hypothesis contending that overcrowding heightens social tensions, which in turn lead to criminal acts. The Ross and Benson data, however, reveal almost the opposite. The least densely populated nation—United States—has the highest crime rate. And, as Table 5-4

TABLE 5-4

Crime Rate for Selected Crimes in New York, Tokyo, and London: Offenses Known to the Police, 1976 (per 100,000 population)

	New York	Tokyo	London
Homicide	17.50	1.96	1.96[a]
Robbery	915.00	23.00[b]	76.30[c]
Rape	37.20[d]	3.29	2.45

SOURCE: Ruth A. Ross and George C. S. Benson, "Criminal Justice from East to West," *Crime and Delinquency* 25, January 1979, p. 78.
[a] Includes manslaughter and infanticide.
[b] Includes robbery involving homicide and rape.
[c] Includes aggravated burglary.
[d] Includes attempted rape.

illustrates, even though population density is essentially the same in New York City, Tokyo, and London (the largest city in each of the three nations under study), New York's murder rate is approximately nine times higher than it is in either of the other two cities.

Why is it that the United States appears to be the most violent urban-industrial society? This is an important question to ask and an even more important one to answer, both theoretically and politically. It is certainly a question we will put to each theoretical perspective—traditional, interactionist, and radical—when we consider theories of the causes of street crime later in this chapter.

Social Conditions and Street Crime: Perpetrators and Victims

What are the social conditions or factors that appear to be most closely related to the occurrence of street crime? What social conditions tend to be experienced by those who commit street crime and those who are victimized by it? The President's Commission on Law Enforcement and Administration of Justice has answered these questions like this:

> Study after study in city after city in all regions of the country have traced the variations in the rates for these crimes. The results, with monotonous regularity, show that the offenses, the victims, and the offenders are found most frequently in the poorest, and most deteriorated and socially disorganized areas of cities. (President's Committee on Law Enforcement and Administration of Justice, 1967, p. 35)

Indeed, the Justice Department's 1982 National Crime Survey showed that the households most vulnerable to crime during that year were in the central cities. In 1982, the Survey noted, at least one third of all urban households were victimized by street crime, due for the most part to higher burglary and violent crime rates than were found in the suburbs and rural areas. Violent crime—rapes, robberies, assaults by strangers—and burglaries victimized 13 percent of city households, 10 percent of households in the suburbs, and 8 percent of rural households (Associated Press, June 13, 1983).

Within the context of the ecology of the "inner city" then, we will examine street crime's association with social class, race, sex, age, addiction, gangs, and guns.

Class.   Three aspects of class inequality appear to be significantly related to street crime: unemployment, poverty, and income inequality. M. Harvey Brenner's (1976) studies have revealed, for example, that between 1920 and 1940 and again between 1947 and 1973, in California, Massachusetts, and New York (as well as outside the United States—in Canada, England, Wales, and Scotland) there has been a significant and direct relationship between unemployment and nearly every measure of criminal activity. As unemployment has risen, so has the number of crimes known to the police; the number of arrests, trials, and convictions; and the number of imprisonments.

A U.S. Bureau of Prisons' (1975) report has confirmed Brenner's work. The bureau examined the relationship between the number of persons incarcerated in federal prisons and the Department of Labor's unemployment index for the period 1952 to 1974. Each year's official prison population was matched against the unemployment rate of 15 months earlier (to allow the time necessary for the unemployment to have an effect on incarceration rates). The findings clearly indicated that as the unemployment rate grew higher, so did the number of persons in prison. Since then, important and well-respected studies by Jankovic (1977), Greenberg (1977), and Yeager (1979) have found a strong positive relationship between unemployment and prison commitments. But since unemployment rates tend to underestimate the actual number of people out of work, labor-force participation rates may be better measures of joblessness. Using these later rates, Phillips, Votey, and Maxwell (1972) found an even stronger relationship between unemployment and crime.

More recently, other studies have made clear the links between unemployment and crime. Under a National Institute of Justice Research Agreements Program, the Vera Institute in New York City has extensively and intensively interviewed a random sample of inmates leaving that city's Rikers Prison. They found their sample to be typical of other prison and jail populations in the United States: male, young, native to the area, single, largely from minority groups (primarily black and brown), either unemployed before their arrest or working at a low-level, low-paying job. The group studied by the Vera Institute is also representative of the U.S. prison population in another respect: they had been heavily involved with the criminal justice system in the past. Among the Rikers inmates, one half of those who had been arrested before their most recent offense had been arrested eight times before. One half of the sample studied had been incarcerated at least once before and a third had been imprisoned more than four times (reported in *Society*, 1980). Why do these men turn to crime in the first place? Why do so many return to it again and again, even after being caught and punished? Perhaps this response by a recently released inmate at Rikers explains much of it:

> If the job pays good, I'll go to the job. If the street is good, I'll go to the street. (quoted in *Society*, 1980, p. 2)

Allen Calvin (1981) has even more recently pointed out the erroneous conclusions that many criminologists have drawn in regard to unemployment and crime. After analyzing the relationship of black youths to unemployment and crime, Calvin has charged that several propositions presently found in the criminological literature simply are not true. Among them:

(1) Unemployment rates for black youths went down markedly in the 1960s. (2) Crime will drop significantly in the 1980s because there will be fewer youths in the age range that is critical with respect to criminal activity. (3) The simultaneous improvement in the economic condition of blacks in the 1960s because of "Great Society" programs and rapid rise in the crime rate indicates that there is no immediate relationship between economic factors and crime, at least among

blacks. (4) With respect to street crime, there is something inherent in the black culture that differentiates it from other cultures in the United States. (Calvin, 1981, p. 234)

Calvin is able to show that the data belie each of the four points above, and his study documents an extremely strong association between the unemployment of black youth and street crime. The Department of Labor reported that in December 1982 black teenage unemployment was over 53 percent in the United States and is higher than at any previous time in its recorded history (since 1954).

It is important to note here that Calvin's work empirically challenges two "noneconomic" perspectives on the causes of crime: a demographic theory and a subcultural one. A fair number of American criminologists have been attracted to the idea that since most street crime—both property and violent crime—is committed by young persons, a great majority between 18 and 24 years old, the current U.S. "crime wave" is due to the fact that a relatively high proportion of our present population belongs to this age group. Because we know that this age group will be smaller in the coming decades, the argument goes, we know we will have fewer criminals and thus, less crime. But Calvin's research leads us to question this analysis. When crime rates are high and criminals young, it does not necessarily follow that age causes crime. Age may be only coincidental to the unemployment, poverty, and racism experienced by many 18- to 24-year-olds in our central cities. These oppressive social and economic factors may have more impact on this group than on any other, and furthermore, will continue to have their devastating effects whether or not this particular age group is becoming a greater or lesser proportion of the overall population. It would be nice if crime were a function of naturally occurring population patterns that would "self-correct" and thus slowly but surely eliminate criminal activity. However, it seems safe to say that this is not the case.

In addition, Calvin's research casts doubt on theories that contend that a subculture's differing values—vis-a-vis the dominant culture—are the primary causal impetus for crime. He found nothing about black youth subcultural values that differ substantially from other subcultures—both criminal and noncriminal—in regard to criminal behavior. Instead, he found that when the members of any subculture, in this case black youth in the ghetto, have their lives threatened with the uncertainty and insecurity of unemployment, poverty, and racism, crime is a readily available response. In effect, subcultural theories of crime only serve to confuse and obscure the institutionalized social and economic factors in criminogenesis.

Unemployment is, of course, intimately related to poverty, and poverty, in turn, appears to influence directly the incidence of crime; as poverty increases, crime increases. This is true at both the aggregate and individual levels, as is made clear in a study by Berk, Lenihan, and Rossi (1980).

This study focused on 2000 ex-offenders randomly selected in Texas and Georgia. Each of the ex-offenders in the chosen sample was given unemployment benefits (through the Transitional Aid to Released Prisoners program supported by the U.S. Labor Department) immediately upon their release from prison. Berk et al., over a one-year follow-up period, then concentrated on understanding the relationships between unemployment payments (transfer payments), unemployment, arrests for property and nonproperty crimes, and time spent in jails or prison. The researchers found:

> several important implications for the relationship between poverty and crime among ex-offenders. First, it appears that . . . unemployment does increase arrests for both property and nonproperty crimes. Moreover, the effect is direct and nontrivial; ex-prisoners who are unemployed have more difficulties with the criminal justice system. Second, modest transfer payments appear to reduce arrests for property and non-property crimes. Poverty is apparently causally related to crime at the individual level. . . .
>
> For ex-offenders at least, unemployment and poverty do cause crime on the micro level. Modest amounts of financial aid can reduce recidivism among ex-felons . . . unemployment can increase recidivism. (Berk et al., 1980, p. 784)[6]

Much research indicates, however, that another aspect of class inequality in American society—income inequality—may have even more to do with the incidence of street crime than unemployment and poverty do. Braithwaite (1979), after an extensive review and analysis of available data, has concluded that the widening of the income gap between rich and poor is the economic factor that most often and most profoundly leads to increases in street crime. More specifically, he has found that U.S. cities with the widest income gaps between low- and average-income earning parts of their populations consistently have the highest street crime rates. Further, Braithwaite has reported that this relationship between high levels of income inequality and high levels of criminality holds up regardless of city size, geographic region, or the proportion of the city population that is made up of minority groups.[7] A recent study by Carroll and Jackson (1983) has confirmed Braithwaite's findings. Using 1970 *U.S. Census and Uniform Crime Report* data on 93 nonsouthern cities of over 50,000 population in 1960, these researchers have found the level of income inequality to be an important predictor of the level of violent crime.

Another study by Blau and Blau (1982) has pointed to the importance of economic inequality—particularly socioeconomic inequality between races—in explaining violent street crime and has at the same time raised serious questions about the validity of certain explanations of violent crime that have gained fairly widespread acceptance in contemporary criminological literature. Among these latter explanations are the ideas that criminal violence is a regional cultural tradition or a subcultural value and life-style. For example, criminal violence has been

---

[6] For a more in-depth look at the findings of those researchers see Rossi, Berk, and Lenihan (1980).
[7] On the international level, Braithwaite has found that nations with the highest levels of income inequality tend to have the highest homicide rates. Also, his research has revealed that nations with the lowest levels of expenditure on social welfare programs (programs that tend to reduce income inequality) have the highest homicide rates.

attributed to geographic location in the South where a "southern tradition of violence" is supposedly at work. In addition, violent street crime has also been said to be the result of the proportion of urban populations that is black because a "subculture of violence"—where, according to Wolfgang and Ferracuti (1967) blacks are socialized to violent values, life-styles, expectations, and problem-solving behaviors—purportedly festers there. Using data on the 125 largest metropolitan areas in the United States, Blau and Blau have found that socioeconomic inequality between races, and other economic inequality in general, increases rates of criminal violence, but they have been unable to find any significant support for the "southern tradition of violence" or the "subculture of violence" explanations. They have concluded that if there is some "culture of violence" that contributes to the incidence of violent crime, it too has its roots in pronounced economic inequalities.

Class inequality has important effects on street crime through yet other mechanisms. In a fascinating study, Humphries and Wallace (1980) found that the financial investment patterns of dominant and ruling groups and classes in society—those who own, control, and manage American industrial and business affairs—at least from 1950 to 1971, are related to street crime rates. Where profits are accumulated and some portion of them reinvested, jobs are gained (the size of the urban manufacturing labor force increases) and the crime rate is low. Conversely, Humphries and Wallace have shown, when profits are not forthcoming, deindustrialization (disinvestment) occurs, jobs are lost, and street crime rates are high. In this way, extreme inequality concentrates property, power, and control of investment decisions in the hands of a relatively small class whose actions then impact other less powerful and privileged classes (like the poor and the working class who are, as we shall see later, the primary victims of street crime) and the community in general (including its crime rate).

Finally, another aspect of class inequality in American society that undoubtedly is related to the incidence of street crime is the existence and operation of a "dual" labor market (see Bonacich, 1976). What this refers to is the segmentalization of the American labor force into one class that is primarily white and works at skilled or professional, career-oriented, secure, well-paying occupations and another that is primarily black, brown, poor white, and female and labors at unskilled, temporary, part-time, menial, dirty, alienating, and poor-paying jobs—unless, of course, there are *no* jobs available, as often there are not. This latter segment of the "dual" labor-market (we will discuss this market at a greater length in Chapter 16) is, of course, where the bulk of under- and unemployment, poverty, racism, and income inequality in American society is found and hence, where the bulk of street crime is found (again, as we shall see below, both its perpetrators and its victims).

As the bulk of street crime perpetrators are poor, unemployed, or working at low-level, low-paying menial jobs, so are its victims. Street crime tends to be an intraclass phenomenon: poor and working-class folks tend to victimize other poor and working-class folks. The Presidential Commission on Civil Disorders (1968) found that predominantly white working-class neighborhoods had crime rates more than five times greater than more affluent white neighborhoods. Elliott Cur-

TABLE 5-5

Victimization Rates for Persons Age 12 and over, by Type of Crime and Annual Family Income of Victims (Rate per 1000 Population Age 12 and over)

Type of Crime	Less Than $3,000 (7,598,000)	$3000–$7499 (24,760,000)	$7500–$9999 (12,115,000)	$10,000–$14,999 (28,582,000)	$15,000–$24,999 (48,028,000)	$25,000 or more (38,406,000)
Crimes of violence	64.3	40.1	35.1	32.9	30.6	29.3
Rape	2.9	1.5	1.3	1.2	0.4	0.6
Robbery	14.3	10.6	7.2	6.3	4.9	4.8
Robbery with injury	5.7	3.9	2.1	2.1	1.5	1.5
From serious assault	3.1	1.8	1.1	1.2	0.7	0.8
From minor assault	2.7	2.1	.9	0.9	0.8	0.7
Robbery without injury	8.6	6.7	5.1	4.3	3.5	3.3
Assault	47.0	28.0	26.7	25.3	25.2	23.9
Aggravated assault	18.1	10.5	10.3	9.2	9.1	7.9
With injury	6.6	4.2	4.4	3.4	3.1	2.3
Attempted assault with weapon	11.6	6.3	5.8	5.8	6.1	5.6
Simple assault	28.9	17.5	16.4	16.1	16.1	15.9
With injury	9.0	5.9	5.0	5.0	4.4	3.9
Attempted assault without weapon	19.9	11.6	11.4	11.1	11.8	12.0
Crimes of theft	87.4	65.5	78.4	78.5	83.7	103.5
Personal larceny with contact	6.7	4.8	2.8	3.3	2.5	1.9
Purse snatching	3.0	2.3	0.6[a]	1.0	0.8	0.5
Pocket picking	3.7	2.4	2.2	2.3	1.7	1.4
Personal larceny without contact	80.7	60.7	75.6	75.3	81.2	101.7

SOURCE: U.S. Department of Justice Bureau of Justice Statistics. *Criminal Victimization in the United States, 1980.* Washington, D.C.: U.S. Government Printing Office, 1982.

Note: Detail may not add to total shown because of rounding. Numbers in parentheses refer to population in the group; excludes data on persons whose income level was not ascertained.

[a] Estimate, based on about 10 or fewer sample cases, is statistically unreliable.

rie has summarized a series of victimization studies done by LEAA (the Law Enforcement Assistance Administration) during the 1970s by noting that:

> A woman whose annual family income is below $3,000 is roughly seven times as likely to be raped as a woman whose family income is between $15,000 and $25,000. A man with an annual income above $25,000 is only half as likely to be robbed as a man making less than $3,000, and less than one-third [as likely to be] injured in a robbery. . . . (Currie, 1977, p. 5)

Table 5-5 summaries victimization rates for various categories of crime and annual income utilizing the most recent available government data. Note how, with the exception of "personal larcenies without contact" that go in an opposite direction, the generalization "that the poorer you are the greater the likelihood you will be victimized by street crime" seems to hold up.

Race.   Those criminalized in our society are not only overwhelmingly poor, unemployed, underemployed and/or members of the working class, they are also overwhelmingly from minority groups. Balkan et al. have pointed out that:

> the 1976 FBI Uniform Crime Reports show that approximately 35 percent of all arrests are of nonwhite persons despite the fact that the 1970 U.S. Census shows nonwhites comprising only 12.5 percent of the total population. Overrepresentation of minorities in prisons is even greater . . . the disparity between white and black increases as one moves from arrests to court convictions to prison sentences. . . . (Balkan et al., 1980, p. 64)

Charles Reasons (1974) found that, in 1970, nonwhites made up 49 percent of the U.S. prison population (all state and federal correctional facilities). He then calculated the ratio of particular racial groups in prison to their presence in the overall U.S. population. He found the ratio to be only 0.6 for whites but 1.8 for Hispanics, 3.2 for blacks, and 3.4 for Native Americans.

Every state in the United States has a lower incarceration rate for whites than for blacks. The median incarceration rate for minority groups in each state is at least double the rate for whites. Nevada has the highest incarceration rate for whites, 191.7 per 100,000 population, but the rate is lower than that for blacks in 49 states (Ricchiardi and Moore, 1980).

One state, for example, Iowa, which ranks 32nd among the 50 states in incarcerating whites, 1st in imprisoning native Americans, 4th in imprisoning blacks, and 16th in jailing Hispanics, has racial disparities that are more extreme than in many other states but yet are typical of patterns throughout the country. In 1980, more than 1 percent of Iowa's blacks and Indians were in the state's prisons: 1157.1 blacks per 100,000 black Iowans and 1036 per 100,000 Native American Iowans were imprisoned. The comparable rate for Hispanics was 185.7 but only 60.8 for whites (the national median for whites is 70.8). Iowa has a 3 percent black population and a 25 percent black prison population (of a total prison population of roughly 2800). Twenty-eight out of one hundred inmates serving life sentences in the state are black. Evidence also exists that there is a much higher rate of incarceration without parole for Iowa's minorities as compared with white inmates (Ricchiardi and Moore, 1980).

Although racial minorities have more contact with the criminal justice system than whites do, this does not mean that race causes crime. Race, like age, is more coincidental to crime. Many crimes on the street are committed by blacks, for example, because the social conditions of unemployment, poverty, and racism fall more heavily on their shoulders. On the whole, these social forces negatively impact black communities more than they do white communities.

Not only do the perpetrators of street crime come disproportionately from minority groups, so do its victims. Again, Elliott Currie has summarized a series of LEAA victimization studies:

> Black women are more than twice as likely to be raped as white women. Black men are two and a half times as likely to be robbed as white men. . . .

A black family making below $7,500 a year is about half again as likely to have its home burglarized as a white family making over $15,000. (Currie, 1977, p. 5)

The U.S. Department of Justice's Bureau of Justice Statistics has also confirmed that Hispanics more often than non-Hispanics are the victims of most types of street crime:

Based on National Crime Survey data from 1973 through 1978, the Bureau's advance report on the Hispanic victim noted that households headed by Hispanics have higher average rates for residential burglaries, household larcenies, and motor vehicle thefts. Individuals of Hispanic origin also are more likely than non-Hispanics to be victims of robbery. (in *Society,* 1981)

Table 5-6 summarizes victimization rates for blacks and whites in 1980. Notice that with the exception of "simple assault" and "personal larceny without contact," blacks are significantly more victimized by all types of street crime. In

TABLE 5-6

Victimization Rates for Persons age 12 and over, by Type of Crime and Race of Victims (Rate per 1000 Population Age 12 and over)

Type of Crime	White (157,081,000)	Black (19,691,000)
Crimes of violence	32.2	40.2
Rape	0.9	1.1
Robbery	5.7	13.9
Robbery with injury	2.0	4.3
From serious assault	1.0	2.5
From minor assault	1.1	1.8
Robbery without injury	3.7	9.6
Assault	25.5	25.2
Aggravated assault	8.7	12.3
With injury	2.8	5.0
Attempted assault with weapon	5.9	7.3
Simple assault	16.9	12.9
With injury	4.7	3.8
Attempted assault without weapon	12.2	9.1
Crimes of theft	83.2	79.1
Personal larceny with contact	2.6	6.2
Purse snatching	0.9	2.8
Pocket picking	1.7	3.5
Personal larceny without contact	80.6	72.9

SOURCE: U.S. Department of Justice Bureau of Justice Statistics. *Criminal Victimization in the United States, 1980.* Washington, D.C.: U.S. Government Printing Office, 1982.

Note: Detail may not add to total shown because of rounding. Numbers in parentheses refer to population in the group.

1982, according to the National Crime Survey, black households were more likely than white households to be victims of robbery or aggravated assault, and 10 percent of all black households as compared with 6 percent of all white households were victims of at least one burglary or attempted burglary (Associated Press, June 13, 1983).

The data suggest that street crime is far from being an interclass race war, as has sometimes been alleged. Minorities, to a large extent, are victimizing minorities.

Sex. Until very recently, female street crime rates as measured by the FBI's Uniform Crime Reports consistently showed a low level of female arrests. At present, much debate is going on in criminological circles as to whether or not female crime is on the upswing. Balkan et al. (1980) have contended that for violent crime there is no evidence that female criminality has been increasing whereas for property crime there is some evidence of an increase:

> Recent analyses of the Uniform Crime Reports arrest data show that the proportion of female arrests for violent crimes has not changed significantly over the last twenty years; in fact, it actually decreased from 11.6 percent in 1954 to 10.2 percent in 1974. . . . However, over the same period, property crimes by women increased from 8.2 percent to 21.2 percent. . . . (Balkan et al., 1980, pp. 217–218)

On the other hand, Steffensmeier and Cobb (1981) have analyzed sex differences in urban arrest patterns from 1934 to 1979, as they have appeared in the FBI's Uniform Crime Reports, with different results. They have concluded that although women have made large gains on men in terms of arrests for some petty property crimes (larceny in particular) and small gains in arrests vis-a-vis men for a number of other offenses, when changes in both the reporting and statistical analysis of crime trends and alternative sources of crime data are taken into account, the increase in female arrests over the past four and one half decades are more apparent than real. In sum, Steffensmeier and Cobb have argued that there is little solid evidence that female crime is increasing in relation to still much more prevalent male crime (see also Steffensmeier, 1980).

Another debate concerns the relationship between increased female property crime and the advent of the Women's Movement for social, political, and economic equality in our society. There are those criminologists holding to the view that the increased sex-role equality of women in the past few years has not only increased their participation in the legitimate and legal economy but has also opened up new opportunities, traditionally reserved for criminal males, in the illegitimate and illegal work force. The argument is that the Women's Movement itself has contributed to an increase in female criminality. Female crime is, in a sense, from the perspective, the by-product of a wider "masculinization" of female sex roles.

Others believe that the impact of the Women's Movement on female crime, although real, is less direct. It may be, for example, that law enforcement agencies have paid more attention to women in general, and the criminal activities of women in particular, since the advent of the Women's Movement (Balkan et al.,

1980). Or it may be, since the present increase in female crime appears limited to property crime only, that the increased labor force participation of women has moved many women closer to oppportunities to commit certain criminal offenses.

Steffensmeier, Rosenthal, and Shehan (1980) have attempted to test the theory that increased sex-role equality for women is primarily responsible for any increases in female criminality. More specifically, these researchers wanted to test the proposition that the narrowing of differences in male and female crime rates during World War II was due mainly to war-time equalization of sex roles and the expanding occupational roles of women. Their research suggests that sex-role equality did not explain the narrowing of the differences in male and female crime rates during the war. Rather, it can be shown first that much of the narrowing in differential rates was due to the fact that the most criminal part of the male population—the young males—was at war and unable to commit domestic crime. Second, if the types of crime that women were increasingly arrested for at this time are considered, sex-related crimes like prostitution and adultery "that reflect the paternalism and double standard of sexual morality in society, the narrowing of the sex differential disappears" (Steffensmeier et al., 1980, p. 403). Female arrests for this type of crime, rather than reflecting an increased sex-role equality, can be attributed to a very stable political, economic, and social inequality. Finally, these researchers have shown that the increased labor-force participation of women during World War II did not increase their arrests for property crimes.

Whatever the extent of a recent increase in female criminality and whatever its relation to the Women's Movement and sex-role equality, a sensible response to any increase in female property crime has been offered by Balkan et al.:

> We see the rise in women's property crimes as related to the current economic crisis, which is reflected by the high incidence of unemployment, especially among women and minorities, who are the "last hired, first fired." The fact that increasing numbers of women are divorced single parents, heads of households, and in dead-end, low-paying jobs, intensifies their economic hardship. (Balkan et al., 1980, p. 218)

Chapman (1980) has suggested that most of whatever recent increases in female crime that have occurred are due to increases in petty property crime, not to increases in white-collar and occupational crime. This indicates, she says, that women commit more economic or property crimes when jobs are *unavailable,* not when they are more available, as the sex-role equality explanation maintains. This view is supported by a study of a program referred to above: the Transitional Aid to Released Prisoners project. Generally, the "TARP" experiment found that offenders who were released from prison without any economic means tended to be rearrested at a higher rate than those who were given some means of economic support (see the section on class above). Specifically, Jurik (1980) found that those *female* offenders released from prison with either unemployment compensation or support from an employed male tended to be rearrested less often.

If the Women's Movement has called into question the relationship between social, political, and economic conditions on the one hand, and women as perpetrators of street crime on the other, it has, with even more authority and success, directed attention to the way in which women are routinely victimized in this society. Rape, wife beating and battering, forced sterilization, and sole responsibility for birth control have historically constituted (and continue to do so at present) the most brutal and inhumane crimes against women; although only one of them—rape—has ever been officially designated and counted as crime by any official crime statistic like the FBI Uniform Crime Index.

Rape is legally defined as the sexual penetration of a woman's body without her consent and always includes either the use or threat of force. It is not a crime of sexual passion, but rather an act of physical violence and aggression. Although it is not difficult in our society to find men who believe that the only women who get raped are women who want to be raped, who enjoy being assaulted, degraded, and humiliated, studies have shown that the number of rape cases that are in *any* way precipitated by the victims—by women themselves—are very small, even less than 5 percent (see, for example, Griffin, 1976).

During the 1970s, the number of rapes increased more than any other violent crime (Balkan et al., 1980). Despite the fact that the FBI's Uniform Crime Reports have recently shown overwhelming increases in reported rapes, it is still the case that many of them go officially unreported. This has been confirmed by victimization surveys throughout the 1970s and 1980s that have indicated a significantly greater number of rapes than have been reported to the police. Rape victims are still afraid of being labeled "promiscuous" (as deserving what they've received) and stigmatized by friends, relatives, and husbands. If the victim does report a rape, she has often been subjected to insensitive, distrusting, and even hostile police, medical personnel, and defense attorneys. A victim of rape describes her experience in Panel 5-3.

There is also ample evidence that reporting rape often may do little or no good. Rape still appears to have the lowest conviction rate of any violent crime. DeCrow (1975) reports, for example, that as late as 1968, in New York City, there were 1840 reported rapes and *one* conviction.

Rape occurs in all social classes. However, it does disproportionately victimize poor, working-class and minority women. As with other violent street crimes, both rape victims and rapists tend to come from the most economically deprived segment of American society. After reviewing a series of U.S. Justice Department victimization studies—a 1971 to 1972 survey of 8 large cities, a 1973 survey of 13 large cities, a 1974 to 1975 study of 8 large cities, and another study of 26 large cities in the same time period, and two nationwide surveys in 1977 and 1978—Schwendinger and Schwendinger (1983) have concluded that the lower the family income, the greater the likelihood that women will be raped. The great majority of women who have experienced rape or attempted rape have come from families with annual incomes of less than $10,000 (Schwendinger and Schwendinger, 1983).

Rape victims and rapists may have any of a variety of "prerape" relationships: strangers, acquaintances, friends, intimate, even married. It has been estimated that about one half of all rapes are committed by men known by the victim. LeGrand (1973) found, for instance, that in only 37.6 percent of the rapes she studied was there no prior relationship between rapist and victim. Also, there is evidence that most rapes are planned (see Schwendinger and Schwendinger 1983, p. 46), that almost all involve the use of force, that many are extremely brutal, that rapist-victim intimacy usually means more violence is involved, and that a majority of victims are passive during the rape. Balkan et al. have summed up research on rape:

> In addition, few rapes are spontaneous; in over 80 percent of the cases reported by Amir (1971), the rapes were entirely or partially planned. Physical force was used in 85 percent of all reported cases, and brutal beatings occurred in one fifth. When there was a close relationship between the rapist and his victim, greater violence was used. Over one-half of all victims were submissive during the rape, which is not surprising considering the potential for harm involved. (Balkan et al., 1980, p. 235)

What of husbands who rape their wives? Legally, husbands may still, in many states, victimize their wives. Rape laws in the United States have historically been related to the notion of women as property (in this case, sexual property) and have served to protect the males who "own" them, rather than the women themselves:

> Even within a marriage, where women exchange their sexuality for economic security, wives often unwillingly submit to sexual intercourse . . . but . . . it is within the confines of the law for a husband to forcibly penetrate or "rape" his wife. The reason for the legality of such infractions is related to the belief that a woman is part of a man's property. Historically, as well as in present times, rape laws have attempted "to regulate male ownership of women's sexual capacity"—to protect the rights of men as possessors of "their women's" bodies, and not the rights of women to control their own bodies. . . . (Balkan et al., 1980, p. 235)

Instead of focusing on the individual characteristics, traits, and behaviors of rape victims and rapists, as has normally been the case when criminologists, other social scientists, and those in the mass media have sought explanations for this heinous crime, Schwendinger and Schwendinger (1983) have taken a more sociological, more social-structural approach. Their analysis is instructive in terms of the social conditions that we have identified as contributing to the incidence of street crime earlier in this chapter. These criminologists cite evidence that confirms that the same social conditions that increase the incidence of all other street crimes—both violent and property crime—also increase the incidence of rape. According to the Schwendingers, the greater the degree of class inequality in society in general (class inequality expressed in and through those things described above: un- and underemployment, poverty, income inequality, racism, a "dual" labor market and so on), and the economic and political inequality between sexes in particular, the greater the general level of violence in society and the greater the incidence of violence between men and women; therefore, the greater the incidence of rape.

'On a warm night last August, I was raped . . .'

JANE DOE

On a warm night last August, I was raped in my sixth-floor apartment by a young man I had never seen before. He climbed through the window of my "safe" apartment, which has a dead-bolt lock on the door, stood before me as I lay in bed, and said, "Don't scream or I'll kill you." Seven months later, long after I had identified him to the police, a grand jury threw the case out.

It is no accident that my case took this long, and no accident that my assailant was not indicted. He had enough money to hire three lawyers and as a white middle-class student he was able to persuade the district attorney's office to delay his case for months instead of bringing it to the grand jury within weeks, as usually happens in rape cases. He was also able to arrange for other nice middle-class people to testify for him. Since I was not permitted to read the grand jury transcripts I will never really know why he was not indicted, but I gather that his fraternity brothers told the jury he was with them in the fraternity house for at least part of the time during which I was raped.

I am 30 years old, white, middle-class and single. I live on a nice street on New York's Upper West Side, in a building that has a doorman. I am, in short, what the detectives call a "real person"—not the stereotypical welfare mother, lonely divorcee, teen-age girl or bored suburban housewife who society thinks, unfairly, are "asking for it."

In this past year I have learned some interesting lessons about rape and criminal justice in New York City. My case started auspiciously. When the police arrived, I calmly gave them a precise physical description of my assailant, down to the colors of his T-shirt, and description of the jewelry he stole from my apartment. Less than one hour after the rape, while I was being examined at the hospital, the police picked up a man fitting my description—two blocks from my apartment. When I saw him sitting in the back of the police cruiser, a huge grin on his face, I identified him immediately. He turned out to be a student at the university where I teach. The police laboratory later discoved that he had semen in his underwear at the time of his arrest.

My identification, I was assured by the detectives, would be enough to get an indictment. Such was not to be the case. Though, to their credit, the police treated me with great sensitivity, they failed at something equally important: They did not gather evidence at the only time they could. They didn't, for example, obtain a warrant to search the suspect's apartment for my stolen jewelry and would not have taken the sheet from by bed for forensic analysis had I not reminded them to do so.

Perhaps police headquarters or city hall should take part of the blame for this well-meaning but inept performance; the police department's special rape unit had been disbanded, for budgetary reasons, in August. That month, I learned later, is the time of the year when rape is most frequent.

My frustrations were compounded when my case reached the Manhattan district attorney's office. For three months nothing happened except that I was made to feel more like the accused than the victim. The prosecutor assigned to the case seemed more intent upon undermining my account of the incident than learning more about it; he never even asked me to tell my story in person. Only after another month of waiting and some pressure from an influential private attorney was another, more sympathetic, assistant district attorney assigned to my case.

I was soon to discover, however, that the new prosecutor was solicitous only as long as she thought she had a ''strong'' case. Identifying your rapist and circumstantial evidence do not constitute a ''strong'' case. One should leave a scar on your rapist's body or offer him a drink—taking care not to smudge the fingerprints on the glass. Also, when the accused is white and middle class he is more likely to be believed than the usual rape suspect or victim. Had my assailant's name been ''Hector Lopez,'' the assistant district attorney later suggested to me, things might have turned out differently.

Evidence in rape cases is limited by the objective reality of rape; there are no witnesses and assailants rarely leave fingerprints. So, why is an impossible burden of proof placed on the victim? No one wants to convict innocent men, but why should a positive identification of the assailant and verified evidence of rape not be sufficient to bring an accused rapist to trial?

Throughout it all, I came to realize that being an inquisitive, insistent victim was more of a disadvantage than a benefit. Whenever I called to be apprised of the progress of my case, the authorities treated me as little more than an unwanted intruder.

Seven months after I was raped, the charges against the suspect were dropped. I still do not know why. But I suspect that the long delay and the palpable lack of enthusiasm from the prosecutor's office did not help. The Manhattan DA's office is not interested in getting an indictment unless it is 99-percent sure of a conviction.

The experience has left me feeling twice victimized; first by a sole assailant, second by the criminal-justice system. Having taught my students that the struggle for justice should be waged within the system, I wonder how much I should revise this year's lecture notes. Meanwhile, my assailant walks free—free not only to register for my classes but free to rape again.

Jane Doe—a pseudonym was requested—teaches in New York City. This article was distributed by the New York Times News Service

Source: Jane Doe, "On a Warm Night Last August, I Was Raped. . . ," Des Moines Register, September 6, 1982, p. 7a.

In sum, the Schwendingers maintain that their data indicate that the more class and sex inequality in society, the more rape. This proposition seems particularly sound because not only do those women who experience the most class inequality experience rape most often, but the perpetrators of rape, like the perpetrators of other violent and property street crimes, tend to be those males most victimized by class inequality. Rape is, of course, an "intersex" phenomenon, but it is *not* primarily an interclass or interracial crime.

Recent increases in reported rape rates, however, have not been nearly as severe as the epidemic indicated by increases in reported wife batterings and beatings. Increased police domestic disturbance calls, hospital emergencies, and family homicides are all indications that violence is being inflicted on women in their own homes. Again, Balkan et al. have summarized what is known about the incidence of violence against women in the family:

> There is evidence that wife beating affects as many as three times the number of women as rape. . . . The FBI indicates that ten times more rapes are committed than are reported, and the number of wife beatings are even more frequent and less often reported. . . . The Boston police, for example, receive more than 45 wife-beating calls a day or 18,000 a year . . . , and in 1974 they responded to 11,081 domestic disturbance calls, almost all of which included physical violence. . . . In addition, Boston City Hospital reports that close to 70 percent of the assault victims who come in for emergency treatment are women who have been attacked in their homes, in most cases by husbands or lovers. . . . (Balkan et al., 1980, p. 244)

In fact, Del Martin has written that:

> because of the increase in the crime of rape (62 percent in the five-year period ending in 1973), American women are often advised to "stay at home where they won't get hurt." But people who would impose such a curfew on a woman's freedom of movement might change their tune if they had access to local police reports on domestic violence, which suggest that women may be even less safe in their homes than they are in the streets. (Martin, 1976, p. 10)

Yet another dimension of criminal violence against women is related to the fact that responsibility for birth control has fallen on their shoulders. They, not their husbands or male friends, have been the ones who have suffered the physical and psychological damage of unproven and unsafe birth control practices and technologies. The negative medical side effects of "the pill," for example, have contributed to high blood pressure, heart disease, birth defects, and emotional disturbances in many cases. When women resist "voluntary" birth control, it has sometimes been followed with "involuntary" birth control—forced sterilization. The social control of "problem" persons or groups that forced sterilization can bring has not failed to impress medical and political authorities in the United States. The forced sterilization of poor "welfare mothers," primarily Hispanic and black, has not been an infrequent occurrence.

Finally, with respect to victimization by sex, we find that men continue to be victimized by violent street crime much more often than women. In 1980, men were robbed and assaulted twice as often as women. They were also much more likely to be victims of "personal larceny without contact." Women were, however, the principle victims of all of the specific "crimes against women" discussed above. But rape, the only one of these crimes measured by the National Crime Survey, was the least frequently occurring violent crime in 1980.

Age. As adherents of the demographic theory of crime discussed above are quick to point out, a disproportionate amount of street crime in the United States is perpetrated by relatively young persons. An Associated Press (August 17, 1981) report on an Office of Juvenile Justice and Delinquency Prevention (a part of the U.S. Department of Justice) study stated that 23 percent of the violent crime in the United States between 1973 and 1977 was committed by juveniles (18 years of age and under). In spite of the fact that these young people made up only 14.6 percent of the total population, they were credited with committing 17.8 percent of all reported aggravated assaults, 24.2 percent of all robberies, and 30.4 percent of all personal larcenies (primarily purse snatchings and pocket pickings). The study also found that juveniles and youths (persons 18 to 20 years old) taken together committed the vast majority of all reported larcenies, and that the highest overall crime rates were found among young offenders between the ages of 18 and 20.[8]

But again, if the perpetrators of street crime are young, so are their victims. A study in Chicago by the Chicago School Board and the National Institute of Education found that during a two-month period in the spring of 1980, nearly 25 percent of the city's public junior and senior high school students were victims of theft (United Press International, October 24, 1981).

Government victimization statistics show that, relative to their number, young people are the most frequent victims of criminal attack. In 1980, persons between the ages of 12 and 24 had the highest victimization rates for crimes of violence (robbery, assault, rape, and murder) and theft (burglary, larceny, and auto theft) while the elderly (age 65 and over) had the lowest victimization rates for those crimes (U.S. Department of Justice/Bureau of Justice Statistics, 1982). 1978 victimization studies had shown that persons under the age of 25 were 2.7 times more likely to be victimized by violent crime than were persons age 25 to 64 and 8 times more likely to be victimized by crime of this sort than persons 65 years old or older, while for crimes of theft the ratios were roughly 1.7 to 1 and 6.5 to 1 (U.S. Department of Justice/Bureau of Justice Statistics, 1980). The public image of the elderly in our large cities being the primary victims of indiscriminate street muggings, robberies, and violence is not justified, at least not by official statistics.[9]

---

[8] This study was done using National Crime Survey data (see Chapter 4).

[9] Recently some sociologists and criminologists have noted that although the elderly are among the segments of the American population least likely to be victimized by street crime, the FBI Uniform Crime Reports indicate they are becoming more criminal: a 257 percent increase in arrests for the elderly (compared with a 177 percent increase in the general population) between 1964 and 1979 with more increases more recently (see Kotulak, 1982). This so-called geriatric crime wave is more apparent than real. The UCRs still show that the elderly account for only 2.5 percent of all felony arrests. Increases in elderly street crime seem quite probable at present though, as more and more aged persons not only experience the economic deprivation of forced retirement but also cuts in social programs such as Social Security and Medicare.

These government data also indicate that both male and female young persons are more susceptible to criminal victimization than their adult counterparts. However, "Young males were particularly susceptible to robbery and assault, having higher rates than any other age/sex grouping" (U.S. Department of Justice/ Bureau of Justice Statistics, 1980, p. 2).

1980 government victimization statistics also show that young persons were more often the brunt of household crimes:

> With respect to the residential crimes, households headed by young persons (age 12–19) clearly had the highest rates for burglary and household larceny. Those headed by persons age 12–34 had the highest rates for motor vehicle theft. Households headed by senior citizens had the lowest rates for each of those offenses. In fact, the rates for burglary and household larceny decreased significantly as age of household head increased. Motor vehicle theft rates based on the number of vehicles owned also decreased significantly for each older age group. (U.S. Department of Justice/Bureau of Justice Statistics, 1982, p. 5)

Much as women are victimized by some especially vicious and violent street crimes (rape, beating, and battering) so are young persons. Child abuse, for example, is a serious problem in our society. The results of a national study of child abuse done in the mid-1970s suggested that more than 1 million children in the United States are the victims of neglect or physical violence each year, including at least 2000 deaths. But again, child abuse is not an officially designated crime and does not turn up in the official crime statistics that serve to establish local, regional, and national crime rates.

The recent disappearance and eventual murder of some 28 black children and teenagers in Atlanta points to yet another way in which young people are victimized by violent street crime. Victims of this kind of violence across the country are far more likely to be poor and black than affluent and white (see Panel 5-4), and the incidence of this type of crime is far more widespread than it is commonly thought to be. For instance, although the situation in Atlanta was a well-publicized story in the mass media, it is not widely recognized that 20 other cities in the United States have a youth murder rate that surpasses that of Atlanta (Browning, 1981).

Browning has summed up the frightening officially gathered statistics on this phenomenon:

> A recent report from the Washington-based Children's Defense Fund outlines the grim profile. One of every seventeen nonwhite men and one of every thirty-two nonwhite women between ages sixteen and nineteen are the victims of a serious crime each year. For every white male teenager murdered in America, five young nonwhites are killed. Almost fifty of every 100,000 nonwhite children under the age of four are murdered, according to a 1975 report of the U.S. Department of Health, Education and Welfare. Since then, police officials say, the figures have only grown worse. (Browning, 1981, p. 34)

PANEL 5-4

The Rising Death Rate of Black Americans

The rising death rate of American blacks—one recent Chicago study found a 300 per cent increase in black homicides between 1964 and 1973—has spawned new fears among blacks throughout the nation. And within the last year alone a spate of apparently racial killings in a half dozen cities has brought the level of fear and paranoia to new heights.

In Buffalo, five black men were viciously murdered, apparently at random, in one three-week period last fall. Two had their chests carved open and their hearts ripped out. More recently nearby Rochester police brought a sealed indictment against a white man who was overheard in Georgia boasting of blacks he had killed in that northern city.

In Cincinnati, two black teen-agers were shot down by an unknown assailant with a .44 caliber carbine.

In Indianapolis last January, two men were murdered by sniper fire as they stood before large plate glass store windows.

In Salt Lake City, two young joggers were shot and killed while they were out running. Their killer, convicted this spring, is a self-confessed white supremacist who was also questioned in connection with the shooting last year of Vernon Jordan, president of the National Urban League.

In several suburban communities surrounding Oakland, California, black families have been subjected to gunfire, fire bombings, and open assaults on their children in the public schools.

The cumulative effect of these renewed anti-black attacks, of the rising death rate among black teen-agers, of resurgent Ku Klux Klan activity, and of the morbid litany pouring out of Atlanta, has been profound. It is the sort of all-pervasive fear suggested by Kennel Jackson, a black historian at Stanford University: "When you pick up the newspaper and read about this black being killed here and another black being killed there, it does something to your psyche, something bad. It leads to the perception that it's suddenly hunting season on blacks again."

Source: Frank Browning, "Life on the Margin: Atlanta Is Not the Only City Where Black Children Are Dying," The Progressive, September 1981, p. 37.

Addiction.[10] The purported linkage between addiction to narcotic drugs and street crime has caused some disagreement among American criminologists.

[10]Heroin addiction itself is, of course, a crime. The way in which this particular street crime is intimately linked to two other types of crime, "victimless" crime (the addict may only be harming him/herself; not contributing to any social or criminal harm or injury) and organized crime (those persons and organizations involved in the manufacture and sale of the narcotics the addict buys and uses), is analyzed in Chapter 7 on victimless crime and Chapter 8 on organized crime.

Some have argued that there is a very close relationship and that, indeed, addiction causes crime. U.S. Attorney General William French Smith, spearheading the Reagan Administration's "attack" on violent crime, announced that a primary government strategy would be to reduce and eliminate illicit and illegal drug traffic (United Press International, October 24, 1981).

Two recent studies commissioned by NIDA (the National Institute on Drug Abuse) have supported the idea of a causal link between addiction and crime. James Inciardi, Director of the University of Delaware's Division of Criminal Justice, has found that 239 heroin users in the Miami area reported committing 80,644 street crimes in the 12-month period preceding his interview with them. The likelihood of arrest for this group, however, was very low. Only 0.2 percent of the 80,644 self-reported crimes—1 out of every 427 crimes—resulted in an arrest (reported in Alcohol, Drug Abuse, and Mental Health Administration News, 1981).

A Temple University research team found that 237 addicts committed more than 500,000 crimes during an 11-year period in which they were not imprisoned and were using heroin. These researchers stated the relation between addiction and street crime in no uncertain terms: "It is opiate use itself which is the principal cause of high crime rates among addicts." The study also found that when addiction stopped, crime rates dropped markedly. An overall 84 percent decrease in criminality occurred for all types of crime and all types of offenders when "addicts" who were not incarcerated were not using heroin (reported in Ostrow, March 21, 1981, p. 1).

The federal government has for sometime accepted the notion that heroin addiction and street crime are causally related. In the 1970s, for example, the then still functioning LEAA formulated, funded, and oversaw the operation of the TASC Project (Treatment Alternatives to Street Crime Project). This program was founded on the conviction that at least 50 percent of street crime in the United States was due to heroin addiction. By attempting to divert convicted felons (some of whom had been convicted and had served time in prison on as many as four or five previous occasions) away from state and federal prisons and into "secure" drug abuse treatment centers, the LEAA hoped that the "drug-crime lockstep" of going into prison addicted, leaving prison addicted, returning to crime to support an ever-present habit, of returning to prison again, could be halted and reversed.

The official government position on the relationship between addiction and crime was based upon what appeared to be sound research. A survey conducted by the Harlem Small Business Chamber of Commerce in 1970 found that 51.2 percent of those Harlem residents interviewed had been criminally assaulted during that year. Sixty-nine percent of these people identified a heroin addict as the offender. This same study revealed that theft and burglary to support heroin addiction amounted to $1.8 billion in 1970 in Harlem alone, and that 90 percent of all Harlem businesses had been robbed in the recent past (findings reported by Congressman Charles Rangel in Sohn, 1976, p. 39). A Ford Foundation Report found that a group of ex-addicts in New York City rarely used legally obtained funds to purchase heroin. Approximately 5 percent of the money used to buy heroin came from legal sources. The remainder was raised by selling heroin, prostitution, theft, burglary, and robbery (Holahan and Henningsen, 1972). The fence factor—the thief's inability to sell the goods he or she has stolen at more than one eighth to one fifth of their original cost or present market value—of course, escalates the amount of street crime required of the addict. Supposedly, the addict with a $300 a day heroin addiction would need to steal at least $1500 a day if he or she was to finance his or her addiction with theft (see Timmer, 1982).

However, data on the relationship between heroin addiction and heroin-related thefts are questionable. Indeed, many ghetto, barrio, and working-class heroin users are also petty entrepreneurs (using two ''caps'' of heroin and selling the other eight) and may not always engage in theft to support a habit. Federal Bureau of Investigation and police data on this question, for example, may be particularly inflated owing to what Helmer has identified as the ''utilitarian'' legitimation of U.S. criminal law and public policy regarding drug use. ''The typical utilitarian approach to the narcotics problem is the same one today it has always been: narcotics cause crime'' (Helmer, 1975, p. 12). This argument holds that although narcotics may not cause social harm in and of themselves, they do cause crime (an obvious social harm) and thus, must be controlled. What is not considered here is that the undeniable association between drug use and street crime may be due to their being caused simultaneously by other factors such as racism, poverty, unemployment, obstacles to full democratic participation in government and the economy. In short, figures related to the costs associated with drug use and street crime should probably be approached with Helmer's caution, ''They are highly speculative, and are noted here only to indicate how much narcotics officials thought they were chasing with what they were spending'' (Helmer, 1975, p. 4).

Gangs.   It is undeniably true that much of the reported street crime perpetrated by young persons is done in the social context of street gangs. Juveniles, for example are much ''more likely than adults to commit crimes in gangs or groups of three or more'' (Associated Press, August 17, 1981). The Reagan Administration's Task Force on Violent Crime estimated both the size of these gangs and the proportion of street crime committed by young persons that is gang related:

> It is estimated that these disruptive youth groups involve perhaps up to 20 percent of eligible boys in cities over 10,000 population and that about 71 percent of all serious crimes by youths are the product of law violating groups . . . there are about 2,200 gangs with 96,000 members located in approximately 300 United States cities and towns. (reported in Elsasser, 1981)

The Task force also cited statistics indicating that approximately 3400 gang-related homicides were recorded in 60 U.S. cities between 1967 and 1980 (reported in Elsasser, 1981).

A U.S. Justice Department Office of Juvenile Justice and Delinquency Prevention report (referred to above), however, suggests that the stereotypical view of the ''wild-eyed, violence-prone, gang member without a conscience'' as the primary culprit in our efforts to reduce or eliminate street crime may be inaccurate. This report found that juvenile crime ''is less serious in terms of weapons use, theft, financial losses, and injuries than is adult crime'' (in Associated Press, August 17, 1981). It is also the case that during the five-year period 1973 through 1977, the FBI Uniform Crime Index indicated that crime rates for juveniles remained relatively stable and that, for that period at least, U.S. citizens were twice as likely to be victimized by adults as juveniles. The Office of Juvenile Justice and Delinquency Prevention reported yet other statistics that challenged ''the myth of savage and irrational street youth'':

> Guns rarely were used by juveniles, and the rate in which they were used did not increase during the 1973–1977 period . . . the vast majority of rapes were committed by adults. . . . Elderly people were more than twice as likely to be victimized by adults as by juveniles, and the offenses were less serious when juveniles commited the crimes. (in Associated Press, August 17, 1981)

Noting that youthful offenders are much more likely to perpetrate property crimes—as against violent crime—Elliott Currie challenges the conventional view of ''violence-prone urban youth'' in Panel 5-5.

But where do these gangs come from? Quinney (1979, p. 227) has written that ''Violent gang activity may become a collective response of adolescents in slums to the problems of living in such areas of the city.'' Balkan et al. (1980) tend to agree with this assessment, pointing out that criminal street gang activity is most often found in those places where poverty, unemployment, drugs, and police encounters are commonplace. In these places, gangs become not only the source of members' only meaningful social relationships, but also a source of protection where ''life on the streets'' has made survival an issue.

Other commentators have argued that particular institutions in our society—the schools, for example—play a role in inciting a criminal and/or violent response on the part of some youth gangs. Along these lines, Liazos (1978) has contended that increasing vandalism of school property may be an indication that youths view schools as ''alien territory.'' Further, in an ironic twist, it may be the case that school attendance, rather than truancy, is a contributing factor in the production of delinquent activities:

> contrary to the common belief that idleness and an unstructured environment cause delinquency, some statistics indicate that delinquency actually decreases when schools are not in session. For example, a study conducted by the Los Angeles Probation Department on seasonal trends of the juvenile detention population found that, from 1972 to 1978, there was a higher rate of delinquency during the academic year than during summer vacation. In 1978, the number of youths detained in juvenile hall steadily increased from 900 in September to a peak of 1,190 in May, with the exception of the two-week Christmas holiday, which showed a reduction in detainees from the previous month. Beginning in June, the number of detainees steadily decreased until the fall semester began. . . . (Balkan et al., 1980, p. 71)

Again, as with the class, race, sex, and age characteristics of those who commit crime and those who are its victims, the youthful perpetrators of gang-oriented street crime are also most likely to suffer its consequences. A study of the Chicago Public Schools (referred to above), for example, found that many students are carrying weapons to school as a self-protective device primarily because of their fear of street gangs throughout the school system.

Guns.   Handguns are very much implicated in the high levels of criminal violence in the United States:

- The United States today has probably the most heavily armed citizenry in history.
- At least one half of all American households own at least one gun.
- The total number of weapons belonging to private individuals is well over 100 million (all reported in Wright, Rossi, and Daly, 1983).

And . . .

- FBI statistics have indicated that of the 23,044 homicides committed in 1980, 50 percent, or 11,522, were handgun shootings.
- In 1980, 1426 children were killed with handguns.
- Sixty-six percent of law enforcement officers killed in 1980 were slain with handguns.
- One in nine Americans has been threatened or attacked with a handgun.
- About 2.5 million new handguns are added to the arsenal of private arms in the United States each year.
- In some areas, as many as one half of the weapons used in handgun crimes are stolen.
- Information gathered by the FBI and from foreign consulates has shown that nations with strong handgun registration and control laws have fewer per capita handgun-related deaths. In 1979, for example, 10,728 persons were murdered by handguns in the United States, but only 52 people were killed by handguns in Canada, 48 in Japan, 42 in West Germany, 21 in Sweden, and 8 in England (all of this reported in The Committee for the Study of Handgun Misuse, 1983).

Although it is no doubt true that when handguns are available, the likelihood of homicidal injury and/or death increases, this does not necessarily mean that guns cause crime. In fact, Wright et al. (1983), in an important and very recent study exploring the relationships between guns, crime, and violence, have concluded that there is little evidence to show that owning a gun is a primary cause of criminal violence. They have also argued that there is little or no evidence to either *support* or *refute* the idea that private gun ownership serves to reduce crime by deterring offenders who fear gun-wielding citizens. There is evidence, however, which suggests that households with guns present are about seven to eight

PANEL 5-5

Is the Image of Violence-Prone Urban Youth a Bum Rap?

Since the looting in the wake of New York City's power blackout last summer, the image of a violence-prone urban youth has brought fear and concern to American cities. Legislators, newspaper editors and criminal justice professionals have used the same image of a rising wave of juvenile violence as the rationale for a "get-tough" policy toward youthful offenders.

That policy has led to stiffer sentences for juvenile criminals, accelerated youth prison construction and a new emphasis on control instead of rehabilitation in the juvenile justice system.

But is the image a fair and accurate one? Recent evidence from the Justice Department offers a different, less dramatic picture. Contrary to the standard myths, the most recent FBI Uniform Crime Reports show that:

- Juvenile crime is less serious and widespread than adult crime, which still accounts for most crimes of violence. Juvenile offenses are most often aimed at property, not people.

- Juvenile crimes of violence, while serious, are not increasing. In fact, of the four major crimes of violence—murder, rape, robbery and aggravated assault—the statistics show a marked decrease in juvenile offenses.

- Juvenile offenses are not directed disproportionately against the elderly and the helpless, as often portrayed. Actually, juveniles themselves are most often the victims of juvenile crime.

It remains true that teen-agers do commit more crime than their proportion of the total population would indicate. In 1976, according to the FBI's statistics, youths under 18 accounted for about 25 percent of all arrests across the country, while they constituted about 31 percent of the total population. While these figures seem to suggest that young people commit fewer crimes than their proportion of the population, they ignore the fact that youth crime is concentrated in the higher age brackets, from 15-18.

Still, the statistical portrait of youth crime provides a different picture than the myth: In 1976, people under 18 accounted for only 9.2 percent of all murder arrests—while people over 45, supposedly the least crime-prone segment of the population, accounted for 13.5 percent. Youths under 18 committed 1,302 murders in 1976, while the much smaller 25-to-29-year-old group committed more than twice that number.

For most other crimes of violence, the picture is similar. The only officially designated violent crime in which teen-age youths are overrepresented is robbery—33.5 percent of arrests in 1976 were of youths under 18. Significantly, robbery is a property-related crime. It is in crimes against property that juveniles are clearly overrepresented, accounting for slightly more than half of all arrests for burglaries and motor vehicle thefts, and about three-fifths of arrests for vandalism.

PANEL 5-5 (Continued)

In terms of violent crime, juvenile offenses are actually declining, both in the nation as a whole and in the cities. Between 1975-76, the number of juvenile arrests nationwide dropped 17.3 percent for murder and 19.32 percent for robbery. Youth arrests for rape and aggravated assault also dropped by 3.4 percent and 4.4 percent respectively. For murder, juvenile arrests have been declining since the early 1970s; between 1972-76, juvenile murder arrests dropped by more than 27 percent.

Not only are the stereotypes about juvenile criminals misleading, but so are those regarding the victims of juvenile crime. Data from recent surveys by the Law Enforcement Assistance Administration show clearly that life is far more threatening for juveniles than for adults—and, in general, least threatening for the elderly.

In 1975, men aged 16-19 nationwide were victimized by robbery at a rate three times that of men aged 35-49. They suffered an assault rate three-and-a-half times that for 35-to-49-year-olds and an astonishing 18 times the assault rate for men over 65.

A 16-to-19-year-old woman is twice as likely to be raped as a 25-to-34-year-old. A boy aged 12-15 in San Francisco is more than three times as likely to be assaulted or robbed as a man aged 50-64, and, if the youth is white, six times as likely as a white man over 65.

In a recent study of crime patterns in a Philadelphia ghetto, University of Pennsylvania criminologist Leonard Savitz found that 46 percent of black teenagers interviewed had been robbed, assaulted or extorted in the course of a single year, and 60 percent had over two years. The study found that juvenile criminals were as liable to be crime victims as law-abiding youths; between a third and two-fifths of both delinquents and nondelinquents had been robbed in one year.

The study also turned up evidence that, for inner-city youth, belonging to a fighting gang may reduce the danger of criminal victimization. Fighting gang members were found to suffer fewer robberies, assaults and extortions, to be less fearful of their neighborhoods, and to be no more seriously involved in criminal acts than their peers.

Another common belief regarding urban crime in general—that it will decrease as a result of a predicted decline in the youth population—is also, unfortunately, apt to be wrong. For one thing, adults account for most of our urban violence. And Harvard criminologist Walter Miller has calculated that the part of the youth population most "at risk" in terms of violent crime—urban minority youth—is on the increase in major American cities. Similar calculations by Franklin Zimring of the University of Chicago Law School suggest that the minority youth population in big cities will increase from 12-20 percent of the total urban population from 1970 to 1990.

Source: Elliott Currie, "Is the Image of Violence-Prone Urban Youth A Bum Rap?" Pacific News Service, in The Des Moines Register, *March 7, 1978.*

times as likely to experience a handgun death as are households that do not own guns. In this sense, at least, handgun ownership appears to make households less, not more, safe.

Indeed, it may be that "crime causes guns" comes closer to the truth than "guns cause crime." Wright et al. (1983) have found a lack of pervasive evidence to support the claim that private individuals are arming themselves out of a fear of violent crime. Another recent analysis by McDowall and Lifton (1983), however, provides some of this evidence. These sociologists have found that in Detroit, between 1951 and 1977, there was a direct relationship between perceptions of declining collective security and the citizen demand for legal handguns. They found that high violent crime rates, civil disorders, and negative changes in police strength led to increases in gun ownership. It is worth noting that high violent crime rates (as seen above) and civil disorders (as will be seen below) are both related to a complex of class inequalities. This suggests that the following "causal chain" might explain, particularly in the absence of any meaningful national gun control policy, high levels of gun ownership: high levels of class inequality lead to high levels of crime, violence, and disorder, which in turn increases perceptions of collective insecurity and then, gun ownership.

Conclusion: Perpetrators and Victims

The preceding discussion of those who commit crime and those who are its primary victims leads to the conclusion that those who are the perpetrators of street crime are normally its victims as well. With the obvious exception of those violent crimes that specifically victimize women, a young minority male who is either un- or underemployed is not only most likely the person to be apprehended and punished for the commission of a street crime, but he is also most likely to be victimized by these kinds of acts. The leading cause of death for young black males in our society does, for instance, continue to be murder (see Harris, 1981).

TYPES OF STREET CRIME

Sociologist Richard Quinney (1977) has suggested that the meaning of street crime may vary with the type of crime it actually happens to be. He divides street crime into two basic varieties: crimes of accommodation and crimes of resistance. Both kinds of street crime are the result of the way in which dominant political and economic groups in our society deprive the poor, minorities, and workers of economic security and democratic political participation. When these deprived sectors of society engage in accommodationist street crime, however, their criminal activity does not take on an explicit political character. That is to say, although their criminal acts are a reaction to social, political, and economic exploitation and inequities, they are not directly aimed at correcting or alleviating this exploitation and inequality. In fact, most of this kind of crime is intraclass crime: it consists of the exploited poor and working class criminally attacking or taking advantage of other exploited poor and workers, not the criminal victimization of members of ruling groups in society. Quinney further breaks down crimes of accommodation into predatory crimes and personal crimes:

> Much criminal behavior is of a parasitical nature, including burglary, robbery, drug dealing, and hustling of various sorts. . . . These are the predatory crimes . . . pursued out of the need to survive. . . . Most police activity is directed against these crimes.
>
> In addition to the predatory crimes there are the personal crimes that are usually directed against members of the same class. These are the conventional criminal acts of murder, assault, and rape. . . . (Quinney, 1977, p. 54)

Oftentimes, however, what appear to be ordinary, or even senseless, criminal acts, have on closer inspection a rather clear-cut political dimension. They are criminal acts "on the street" that are either directly or indirectly intended to transform the social, political, and economic conditions and circumstances that keep the poor, minorities, and workers poor and exploited. Those acts are crimes of resistance. The uprisings, rioting, and violence in the ghetto areas of many large American cities during the 1960s were not entirely apolitical criminal events. Blacks living in impoverished inner cities were not simply engaging in deviant and criminal activity. As Horowitz and Liebowitz (1968) have pointed out, blacks were a politically marginal group whose revolt should be understood in terms of the way in which deviance, crime and the only available means of political expression—riotous and violent revolt—constituted their response to the desperation brought on by the conditions of ghetto life.

Beginning in 1981, the Reagan administration went about dismantling the American welfare state and began to reduce or eliminate the minimal social supports provided to politically marginal groups in American society since the New Deal. Because of this, a sociological understanding of present circumstances would lead one to the conclusion that the crimes of resistance so prevalent in the black ghettos of Chicago, Los Angeles, Miami, Cleveland, Detroit, Memphis, Louisville, and other urban areas during the 1960s could very well reappear. Cuts in Social Security expenditures, supplemental security income, ADC (Aid to Dependent Children), food stamps, Medicaid, CETA programs (Comprehensive Employment and Training Act), federal government loans to small business (particularly minority small businesses), among others, will no doubt increase the chances of a riotous and rebellious response on the part of disenfranchised blacks in the same cities that witnessed it over a decade ago. And this criminal activity would again involve, at least in part, a political dimension.

As mentioned earlier in this chapter, unemployment and street crime are intimately related. In fact, in an appearance before a U.S. House of Representatives' subcommittee on crime, economist and sociologist Harvey M. Brenner testified that his studies showed that every 1 percent increase in the overall unemployment rate results in a 6 percent increase in the number of robberies and a 4 percent increase in homicides (reported in Harris, 1981). Unemployment in the United States is at present having the most severe impact on blacks living in the deteriorating core of our largest cities. Anthropologist Marvin Harris has uncovered the full extent of this unemployment by combining "official" and "hidden" joblessness:

> Officially, the unemployment rate for blacks stands at about 14 percent. But that figure includes only people who are actively looking for work. It does not include blacks who have part-time jobs but who want full-time jobs, nor does it include those who have stopped looking for work because they cannot find anything acceptable. Adding the hidden unemployed to the officially unemployed raises the black unemployment rate to 25 percent (compared with 12 percent for whites, calculated on the same basis). But that is still only the tip of the iceberg. Ronald H. Brown of the National Urban League calculates that more than half of all black teenagers are unemployed; and in the ghettos like Harlem, the rate among young blacks may be as high as 86 percent. (Harris, 1981, pp. 124–125)

These kinds of economic conditions (and the resultant social conditions) in the ghetto seem to ensure high rates of individual criminal activity. The potential economic benefits of street crime easily outweigh the relatively low risks entailed. The street criminal probably will not be caught by the police and punished by the criminal justice system. The odds are in his or her favor.[11] The economic and social condition of ghetto residents makes crime more of an opportunity than either legitimate and legal employment or welfare. As John Conyers, a member of the U.S. House of Representatives and the Congressional Black Caucus, has written: "When survival is at stake, it should not be surprising that criminal activity begins to resemble an opportunity rather than a cost, work rather than deviance, and a possibly profitable undertaking that is superior to a coerced existence directed by welfare bureaucrats" (quoted in Harris, 1981, p. 126). Crime becomes the most attractive career.

As the conditions of ghetto life in the United States ensure high rates of individual crime in the streets, they also lead to periodic outbursts of collective rioting and revolt. Indeed, the revolt in the ghettos of American cities is not nearly as amazing as—given the realities of everyday ghetto life—the fact that it has not happened more often. As Charles Silberman has put it, "had the blacks not had the guts to withstand the daily diet of institutionalized abuse, the United States would have gone up in smoke long ago" (quoted in Model, 1981, p. 31).

But the smoke has rolled over our cities before and has begun to again in the 1980s. Rioting in the Liberty City section (we will not comment on the irony of this name other than to note that it was bestowed on ghetto residents by a white real estate developer) of Miami in 1980, for example, left 18 people dead and resulted in more than $100 million in property damage. Another Miami ghetto, Overtown, erupted similarly in December 1982 and again in March of 1984. This "criminal" rioting was not without a political undercurrent; a political statement was being made. This time ghetto blacks "knew their enemy." It was, again

---

[11] For a discussion of the relatively small proportion of all criminal acts that culminate in an arrest, see Chapter 11.

according to Charles Silberman, "more like Sampson shaking the temple and bringing it crashing down. The fact that Blacks violated the age-old Southern taboo against killing whites left no doubt that this time they were seeking vengeance . . ." (quoted in Model, 1981, p. 32).

Arthur McDuffie, a black insurance salesman living in Miami, was beaten to death by four white police officers in December of 1979. The police officers were later acquitted of the crime by an all-white jury. Soon the disturbance broke out in Liberty City, and white businesses became the principal target.[12] Violence came to Overtown after a police officer shot and killed a young black playing a video game in a neighborhood arcade. It was later determined that the youth was unarmed, although the police officer initially claimed he only fired his gun as the youth was drawing his. Again, an all-white jury acquitted the charged Hispanic police officer and the Overtown black ghetto erupted yet another time.

Crime and unemployment in Miami ghettos—it is estimated that at least one half of all unskilled young black males are unemployed—both remain high. Blacks continue to view the police as an occupying army capable of the kind of unchecked brutality that led to the last round of rioting. The police tend to view any excursion into Miami ghettos as extremely dangerous and as "a potential ambush."

Both white and black community leaders are fearful that an already explosive situation will be made worse with more federal government cutbacks in both social services and aid to small black businesses. The head of a tenant council in a "large and troubled" Liberty City housing project explained this fear: "The President talks about cutting down to the bone. . . . Hell, there ain't no bone for us to cut" (in Ramirez, 1981, p. 1).

Among the impacts of proposed cuts in Liberty City were the loss of over 1000 CETA jobs and decreases in public housing and rent subsidies when over 20,000 people were on waiting lists (some for as long as eight years) for those services (Ramirez, 1981). Overtown faced the possibility of having a $6.9 million commercial development project going unfinished. A *Wall Street Journal* staff reporter reports a conversation with a black community leader in Liberty City:

> "Reagan has fired the shot, but we have yet to feel the wound," says . . . Mr. Pitts. He notes that after the 1968 riot, little was done to change basic conditions in the ghetto. But after last year's devastation, he says. "We won't have 12 years to appease black folks." (Ramirez, 1981, p. 16)

It is interesting to note that while largely unorganized political activity like rioting and revolt may lead to increases in criminality, *organized* political participation actually tends to lead to decreasing involvement in deviant and criminal behavior. Social movements for political and economic justice may indeed be the most effective "therapy" or "treatment" for deviant or criminal behavior, as well as a "spontaneous and efficient" crime control practice.

Whereas the low rate of success experienced by most mental health, drug and

---

[12] Street gangs still taunt the police with "Are you going to McDuffie me?"

alcohol abuse, and correctional treatment programs in the United States has long been noted,[13] the potentially positive impact of political activism on "reform" or "rehabilitation" has only more recently been recognized. For instance, the rise of the free and independent (free and independent of Communist Party and government control) trade union movement in Poland, called Solidarity, has meant that more and more Polish workers have become involved in political activities designed to gain control over their working lives and the future direction of Polish society. Soon after a summer of labor crises in Poland's cities (in 1980), Polish farmers began their own movement to form a trade union called "Rural Solidarity." As soon as this happened, there was a noticeable drop in the consumption of vodka in the Polish hinterlands. As a parish priest in the Zbrosza-Duza region put it:

> Before the strikes, the peasants were inclined to keep to themselves and spent a lot of their time in hard drinking. . . . If I upbraided them for it, they replied that there was no point in doing anything else. Now, they are ashamed to get drunk because they are aware that the countryside has come awake and that there may be a chance to do something about their poverty. (quoted in Kaplan, 1981)

A similar relation between political activism and crime has been noted in the United States. Solomon et al. found that those communities and individuals who were involved in the civil rights movement's political protests against the intolerable injustices of white racism during the early 1960s experienced lower rates of criminal activity. These researchers have summed up their findings in this way:

> Data are presented which suggest a substantial reduction in crimes of violence by Negroes in three cities during periods of organized protests and "direct action" for civil rights in those cities. The findings are based on official crime reports, medical records, newspaper accounts, and interviews with residents of the three communities (two cities in the Deep South and one in a border state). It is hypothesized that Negroes release long damed-up resentment of segregation by asserting themselves (directly or vicariously) in direct action for civil rights. Such emotional expression, when it occurs in a framework of community organization may reduce the need for aggressive outbursts of a violent sort, thus reducing the incidence of such crimes. (Solomon et al., 1980, p. 35)

Street gang warfare also tends to decrease when movements for social, political, and economic justice can channel frustration and hostility toward ruling political groups who are most responsible for injustice. During the 1960s and early 1970s, for example, Chicano and black community organizations in Los Angeles, that were politically agitating the city's white power structure, provided many minority youths with an identity and "cause" that went beyond their frequent intra- and intergang street violence. However, as these movements gradually

---

[13] For a detailed discussion of the failure of the American correctional system to rehabilitate criminal offenders, see the relevant sections of Chapters 13, 14, and 15.

weakened and all but disappeared in the middle and late 70s, ethnic and racially motivated gang violence began to escalate again (Balkan et al., 1980).

Indeed, the high rates of individualistic, accommodationist, predatory street crime that characterize the United States—as compared with, say, Western Europe or Japan—may be at least partially explained in terms of the historical lack of a firmly established, progressive, opposition party or movement. Criminologist Milton Mankoff has suggested that:

> It can be argued that the growth of a mass radical political movement in the United States could provide a constructive alternative to misdirected, individualistic, and unjustified attacks on persons who are often equally oppressed by the social order. A lower incidence of violent crime in Western European capitalist societies might possibly reflect the fact that the working classes there generally have a much higher degee of class consciousness, a greater involvement in trade unions (most likely with Socialist or Communist leadership), and a greater allegiance to Socialist or Communist political parties than their American counterparts. The United States is virtually the only advanced capitalist society in the world which does not have a powerful Labor, Socialist or Communist party representing the working class. (Mankoff, 1976, p. 192)

THEORY AND STREET CRIME

A Gallup Poll in April 1981 reported that

- ''A 54 percent majority of Americans say there is more crime in their community than there was a year ago. . . .''
- ''Fear of crime has grown to the point that 45 percent of the public now say they are afraid to walk alone at night near where they live and as many as one in six admits being fearful even while at home. . . .''
- ''An increase in victimization also has occurred, with almost one-fourth of Americans the victims of a serious crime. . . .''
- ''Virtually all survey participants (92 percent) report having taken some step to protect themselves from criminals—from the simple expedient of making sure the doors are locked (84 percent) to buying a gun for protection (16 percent).''

But enough of our extended description of the realities and perceived realities of street crime and its victims in the United States. Describing crime is not enough; in fact, describing crime is useless unless we begin to explain it, that is, understand it from one or another theoretical perspective. In this regard, George Gallup asked the 54 percent of Americans in his random sample who had earlier stated that there was more crime in their neighborhood or community than there had been the year before: ''In your opinion, why is there more crime in this area than there was a year ago?''

Gallup's respondents tended to assign primary responsibility for increases in the crime rate to the American economy. Forty-three percent (higher than any other response category) blamed economic conditions. Specifically, 21 percent pointed to unemployment (in this estimate of public opinion, unemployment was the most often mentioned, single, specific cause of crime), 16 percent pointed to the higher cost of living, and 6 percent to poverty (Gallup, 1981).

Next to the economy, the public then held the criminal justice system most responsible for increases in criminality (26 percent). Here, lenient criminal courts and judges (15 percent) and inadequate police protection (11 percent) were cited by the respondents. Other ''causes for crime'' identified by significant numbers of respondents included excessive drug and alcohol use (18 percent), lack of parental guidance and discipline (12 percent), and overcrowding in cities (11 percent).

If this is a fair representation of the public conception of what causes street crime, how does it compare or contrast with the explanations of sociologists and criminologists? When they genuinely contribute to our increased understanding, as was pointed out in Chapter 2, each of the three dominant sociological perspectives on crime and criminal justice will be used to explain each of the crime and criminal justice-related phenomena dealt with in this book. In the case of street crime, the traditional, the interactionist, and the radical theoretical approaches all enhance our knowledge of the particular social, economic, and political sources or origins of this particular kind of crime. For this reason, we will present below examples of the explanations and analyses of street crime offered by persons working in each of these theoretical domains.

The Traditional Approach to Street Crime

As can be recalled from our earlier discussion of this theoretical perspective, it has tended to focus on the immediate social environment that is said to foster a primarily lower-class criminality. Although ''self-report studies'' (see Chapter 4) indicate that no class in American society is probably more or less criminal than any other class, it is also true, as we have seen in this chapter, that it is primarily lower-class street criminals who are singled out by the mechanisms of criminal justice for arrest, conviction, and sentencing. In Panel 5-6, Richard Cloward and Lloyd Ohlin (1980) adhere to this traditional emphasis on the immediate social environment of the lower class in their analysis of the social sources of delinquent subcultures. Their approach combines Merton's theory of anomie and its emphasis on ''differential access to legitimate and legal means in the attainment of culturally desired goods'' with Sutherland's theory of differential association and its notion of ''differential access to illegitimate and criminal means.''[14] Cloward and Ohlin go on to illustrate the way in which differential opportunities—both legitimate and illegitimate—have structured the immediate social environment of youth in the core and ghetto areas of the largest American cities. This structuring has forced the emergence of three distinct delinquent subcultures in a manner described in Panel 5-6.

[14] For a review of the theoretical work of Merton and Sutherland, see Chapter 2.

PANEL 5-6

A Traditional Sociological Account of Delinquent Subcultures

. . . there appear to be three major types of delinquent subculture typically encountered among adolescent males in lower-class areas of large urban centers. One is based principally upon criminal values; its members are organized primarily for the pursuit of material gain by such illegal means as extortion, fraud, and theft. In the second, violence is the keynote; its members pursue status ("rep") through the manipulation of force or threat of force. These are the "warrior" groups that attract so much attention in the press. Finally, there are subcultures which emphasize the consumption of drugs. The participants in these drug subcultures have become alienated from conventional roles, such as those required in the family or the occupational world. They have withdrawn into a restricted world in which the ultimate value consists in the "kick." We call these three subcultural forms "criminal," "conflict," and "retreatist," respectively. . . .

The extent to which the delinquent subculture organizes and controls a participant's allegiance varies from one member to another. Some members of the gang are almost totally immersed in all the perspectives of the subculture and bring them into play in all their contacts; others segregate this aspect of their lives and maintain other roles in the family, school, and church. The chances are relatively slight, however, that an adolescent can successfully segregate delinquent and conforming roles for a long period of time. Pressures emanate from the subculture leading its members to adopt unfavorable attitudes toward parents, school teachers, policemen, and other adults in the conventional world. When he is apprehended for delinquent acts, the possibility of the delinquent's maintaining distinctly separate role involvements breaks down, and he is confronted with the necessity of choosing between law-abiding and delinquent styles of life. Since family, welfare, religious, educational, law-enforcement, and correctional institutions are arrayed against the appeal of his delinquent associates, the decision is a difficult one, frequently requiring either complete acceptance or complete rejection of one or the other system of obligations. . . .

The Criminal Pattern . . .   In the central value orientation of youths participating in this tradition, delinquent and criminal behavior is accepted as a means of achieving success-goals. The dominant criteria of in-group evaluation stress achievement, the use of skill and knowledge to get results. In this culture, prestige is allocated to those who achieve material gain and power through avenues defined as illegitimate by the larger society. From the very young to the very old, the successful "haul"—which quickly transforms the penniless into a man of means—is an ever-present vision of the possible and desirable. Although one may also achieve material success through the routine practice of theft or fraud the "big score" remains the symbolic image of quick success.

The means by which a member of a criminal subculture achieves success are clearly defined for the aspirant. At a young age, he learns to admire and respect older criminals and to adopt the "right guy" as his role-model. Delinquent episodes help him to acquire mastery of the techniques and orientation of the criminal world and to learn how to cooperate successfully with others in criminal enterprises. He exhibits hostility and distrust toward representatives of the larger society. He regards members of the conventional world as "suckers," his natural victims, to be exploited when possible. He sees successful people in the conventional world as having a "racket"—*e.g.,* big businessmen have huge expense accounts, politicians get graft, etc. This attitude successfully neutralizes the controlling effect of conventional norms. Toward the in-group the "right guy" maintains relationships of loyalty, honesty, and trustworthiness. He must prove himself reliable and dependable in his contacts with his criminal associates although he has no such obligations toward the out-group of noncriminals.

One of the best ways of assuring success in the criminal world is to cultivate appropriate "connections." As a youngster, this means running with a clique composed of other "right guys" and promoting an apprenticeship or some other favored relationship with older and successful offenders. Close and dependable ties with income-producing outlets for stolen goods, such as the wagon peddler, the junkman, and the fence, are especially useful. Furthermore, these intermediaries encourage and protect the young delinquent in a criminal way of life by giving him a jaundiced perspective on the private morality of many functionaries in conventional society. As he matures, the young delinquent becomes acquainted with a new world made up of predatory bondsmen, shady lawyers, crooked policemen, grafting politicians, dishonest businessmen, and corrupt jailers. Through "connections" with occupants of these half-legitimate, half-illegitimate roles and with "big shots" in the underworld, the aspiring criminal validates and assures his freedom of movement in a world made safe for crime.

The Conflict Pattern . . .   The role-model in the conflict pattern of lower-class culture is the "bopper" who swaggers with his gang, fights with weapons to win a wary respect from other gangs, and compels a fearful deference from the conventional adult world by his unpredictable and destructive assaults on persons and property. To other gang members, however, the key qualities of the bopper are those of the successful warrior. His performance must reveal a willingness to defend his personal integrity and the honor of the gang. He must do this with great courage and displays of fearlessness in the face of personal danger.

The immediate aim in the world of fighting gangs is to acquire a reputation for toughness and destructive violence. A "rep" assures not only respectful behavior from peers and threatened adults but also admiration for the physical strength and masculinity which it symbolizes. It represents a way of securing access to the scarce resources for adolescent pleasure and opportunity in underprivileged areas.

Above all things, the bopper is valued for his "heart." He does not "chicken out," even when confronted by superior force. He never defaults in the face of a personal insult or a challenge to the integrity of his gang. The code of the bopper is that of the warrior who places great stress on courage, the defense of his group, and the maintenance of honor.

Relationships between bopping gang members and the adult world are severely attenuated. The term that the bopper uses most frequently to characterize his relationships with adults is "weak." He is unable to find appropriate role-models that can designate for him a structure of opportunities leading to adult success. He views himself as isolated and the adult world as indifferent. The commitments of adults are to their own interests and not to his. Their explanations of why he should behave differently are "weak," as are their efforts to help him.

Confronted by the apparent indifference and insincerity of the adult world, the ideal bopper seeks to win by coercion the attention and opportunities he lacks and cannot otherwise attract. In recent years the street-gang worker who deals with the fighting gang on its own "turf" has come to symbolize not only a recognition by conventional adult society of the gang's toughness but also a concession of opportunities formerly denied. Through the alchemy of competition between gangs, this gesture of attention by the adult world to the "worst" gangs is transformed into a mark of prestige. Thus does the manipulation of violence convert indifference into accommodation and attention into status.

The Retreatist Pattern   Retreatism may include a variety of expressive, sensual, or consummatory experiences, alone or in a group. In this analysis, we are interested only in those experiences that involve the use of drugs and that are supported by a subculture. We have adopted these limitations in order to maintain our focus on subculture formations which are clearly recognized as delinquent, as drug use by adolescents is. The retreatist preoccupation with expressive experiences creates many varieties of "hipster" cult among lower-class adolescents which foster patterns of deviant but not necessarily delinquent conduct.

Subcultural drug-users in lower-class areas perceive themselves as culturally and socially detached from the life-style and everyday preoccupations of members of the conventional world. The following characterization of the "cat" culture, observed by Finestone in a lower-class Negro area in Chicago, describes drug use in the more general context of "hipsterism". . . . Thus it should not be assumed that this description in every respect fits drug cultures found elsewhere. We have drawn heavily on Finestone's observations, however, because they provide the best descriptions available of the social world in which lower-class adolescent drug cultures typically arise.

The dominant feature of the retreatist subculture of the "cat" lies in the continuous pursuit of the "kick." Every cat has a kick—alcohol, marijuana, addicting drugs, unusual sexual experiences, hot jazz, cool jazz, or any combination of these. Whatever its content, the kick is a search for ecstatic experiences. The retreatist strives for an intense awareness of living and a sense of pleasure that is "out of this world." In extreme form, he seeks an almost spiritual and mystical knowledge that is experienced when one comes to know "it" at the height of one's kick. The past and the future recede in the time perspective of the cat, since complete awareness in present experience is the essence of the kick.

The successful cat has a lucrative "hustle" which contrasts sharply with the routine and discipline required in the ordinary occupational tasks of conventional society. The many varieties of the hustle are characterized by a rejection of violence or force and a preference for manipulating, persuading, outwitting, or "conning" others to obtain resources for experiencing the kick. The cat begs, borrows, steals, or engages in some petty con-game. He caters to the illegitimate cravings of others by peddling drugs or working as a pimp. A highly exploitative attitude toward women permits the cat to view pimping as a prestigeful source of income. Through the labor of "chicks" engaged in prostitution or shoplifting, he can live in idleness and concentrate his entire attention on organizing, scheduling, and experiencing the esthetic pleasure of the kick. The hustle of the cat is secondary to his interest in the kick. In this respect the cat differs from his fellow delinquents in the criminal subculture, for whom income-producing activity is a primary concern.

The ideal cat's appearance, demeanor, and taste can best be characterized as "cool." The cat seeks to exhibit a highly developed and sophisticated taste for clothes. In his demeanor, he struggles to reveal a self-assured and unruffled manner, thereby emphasizing his aloofness and "superiority" to the "squares." He develops a colorful, discriminating vocabulary and ritualized gestures which express his sense of difference from the conventional world and his solidarity with the retreatist subculture.

The word "cool" also best describes the sense of apartness and detachment which the retreatist experiences in his relationships with the conventional world. His reference group is the "society of cats," an "elite" group in which he becomes isolated from conventional society. Within this group, a new order of goals and criteria of achievement is created. The cat does not seek to impose this system of values on the world of the squares. Instead, he strives for status and deference within the society of cats by cultivating the kick and the hustle. Thus the retreatist subculture provides avenues to success-goals, to the social admiration and the sense of well-being or oneness with the world which the members feel are otherwise beyond their reach. . . .

Source: Richard A. Cloward and Lloyd E. Ohlin, "Differential Opportunity and Delinquent Subcultures," in Delos H. Kelly, ed., Criminal Behavior: Readings in Criminology, *New York: St. Martin's Press, 1980, pp. 210–215.*

The Interactionist Approach to Street Crime

The example of an interactionist analysis of crime presented here also begins with the organization of street gangs. What William Chambliss has focused on, however, is the way in which the fate of these gangs and their individual members determines the probability of adult criminal activity later on. The interactionist concern with the development of deviant or criminal identities—and ultimately deviant or criminal careers—and the importance of a societal reaction to the formation of these identities and careers is emphasized in Chambliss' classic study of "the Saints and the Roughnecks." Two gangs violating "rules and regulations" with roughly the same degree of severity, with roughly the same frequency, experience vastly different societal reactions. The disparate labels attached to the behaviors and activities of these groups by their families, neighborhoods, communities, schools, and criminal justice system legitimates and "makes legal" one group and criminalizes the other. In this way, Chambliss has found the self-fulfilling prophecy that accompanies a societal reaction and the application of criminal labels to be the social source of crime and criminals. Secondary deviance is born: "I've got the name, so I'll play the game." Babbie (1980) summarizes Chambliss' research in Panel 5-7.

The Radical Approach to Street Crime

Although radical criminology would not deny that certain features of the immediate social environment—poverty, broken families, delinquent peer relations, declining sense of community—and the social definitional process that stigmatizes the "underdog" with a criminal label are important factors that are often associated with the incidence of street crime, it is more likely to view these factors as "symptoms," not "causes." Poverty and unemployment; inadequate schools; deteriorating family, peer, neighborhood, and community relationships; the ability of the "powerful" to utilize control agencies like the criminal justice system to process and define the activities of the "powerless" as criminal; as well as crime itself, are all symptoms related to a more fundamental cause of crime: the historical and social-structural development of capitalist society. All of these symptoms are the result of an increasingly corporate-dominated class society. There is an historically evolving political economy of street crime. For these reasons, the radical explanation of street crime appears to be more comprehensive than the traditional or interactionist explanations.

In Panel 5-8, Tony Platt identifies the ultimate origin of street crime as the accumulation of capital for purposes of profit that marginalizes an historically varying proportion of the labor force and makes them surplus to the production of, as well as the consumption of, goods and services. Platt traces the historical development of capitalist societies from the original displacement of the feudal system to industrial capitalism and on to the present organization of economy and society in the United States—monopoly capitalism. He illustrates the way in which the "surplus population" is created under each of these stages of capitalist development and also points out how those in these "surplus populations" are "forced" into those activities that have emerged under the rubric "street crime."

PANEL 5-7

An Interactionist Account of the Origins of Adult Criminality

The Saints and the Roughnecks

Sociologist William Chambliss presents a graphic instance of the selective labeling of deviants in his study of two teenage gangs, the ''Saints'' and the ''Roughnecks,'' which he observed over a two-year period.

The Saints were a group of eight upper-middle-class boys. By school officials, teachers, townspeople, and police, they were viewed as fine, upstanding youngsters, bound to do well in later life. But behind the backs of parental authorities they were a delinquent gang. Truancy was a daily occurrence for members of the group. One boy would ask to be excused from class. He would then go to the class of a fellow gang member and tell the teacher that his friend was needed at an activities meeting. The teacher would usually oblige, having defined the boys as good students and as honest and responsible. As a group, the boys were never caught in their subterfuge. When individual members were stopped, they would admit their error, apologize, and be forgiven.

Once the boys managed to escape school, they drove to a pool hall or a cafe outside town, where they'd horse around or harass the proprietor. On weekends, the boys would drive to a nearby city, get drunk, play ''chicken,'' vandalize buildings, or uncover potholes and watch while motorists drove into them. The boys were never caught at any of their more serious activities; when they were stopped by the police, they were very polite and contrite, and were released.

In school, the students cheated heavily but were never caught. Since the teachers had decided these were good students, even when the boys didn't do well, they could expect to be given high grades anyway.

The six Roughnecks were perceived quite differently by the community. They came from lower-class families, they didn't act as politely as the Saints did, and they didn't dress as well. Unlike the Saints, too, they were constantly in trouble with the police, who saw them as delinquents and picked them up frequently. Townspeople perceived them as drinkers, fighters, and petty thieves. They assumed that the Roughnecks were on their way to a lifetime of crime. Although the

---

Also, note in Panel 5-8 how Platt argues that the present conditions of monopoly capitalism are destined to result in ever higher street crime rates.

PUNISHING STREET CRIME

Historically, street crime in the United States has been the most policed crime. Rather than vigorously pursuing and prosecuting other kinds of crime (white-collar, organized, corporate, and political crimes), law enforcement, criminal

PANEL 5-7 (Continued)

members of the group got passing marks in school, the teachers felt the boys would never "make something of themselves." Some told Chambliss that they were passing members of the gang only because they thought it would be worse for everyone if they didn't.

In terms of their actual delinquency, Chambliss judged the Saints and Roughnecks as about equal, although the Saints were able to indulge themselves more frequently because they had the cars and the money to do so. Community members viewed the two groups in radically different ways, Chambliss suggested, because the Roughnecks were more visible, expressed their attitudes toward those in authority more openly, and committed acts that people of higher classes thought particularly offensive. All these selective perceptions, Chambliss noted, are related to the different social-class origins of the boys.

As a labeling theorist might suspect, most members of the different gangs grew to confirm the community's expectations of them. Almost all the Saints graduated from college and went on to become managers or professionals. Of the Roughnecks, the two who had been star football players got scholarships to attend college and went on to become high-school teachers. Two of the other boys were later charged with and convicted of murder, and a third became a small-time gambler.

In Chambliss's view, the labeling of deviants becomes a self-perpetuating process—unless the magic circle is broken, as, for instance, by the scholarships offered the two Roughnecks. The Roughnecks accepted the community's definition of themselves as delinquents and became increasingly alienated from the values of the community; the Saints, on the other hand, accepted the community's definition of themselves as basically good, ambitious boys who only wanted to occasionally enjoy a harmless prank, and they eventually became solid citizens.

In what other ways do you think economic and social standing affects the labeling of deviants?

Source: Earl R. Babbie, "The Saints and the Roughnecks," in Sociology, *Belmont, Calif.: Wadsworth, 1980, p. 159.*

court, and corrections resources have been directed primarily toward the violent and property crimes of street criminals.

An increasingly conservative and repressive approach to the policing of street crime has recently been recommended from the highest levels of American government. At U.S. Attorney General William French Smith's request, his Task Force on Violent Crime, appointed in 1981, purposely avoided considering any sociological explanations for the "wave of serious, violent crime we are now experiencing." (Elsasser, 1981). Thus, the Task Force recommended a series of

Radical Criminology, Social Class and Street Crime

The current high level of crime and victimization within the marginalized sectors of the working class can be partly understood in the context of the capitalist labor market. The "relative surplus population" is not an aberration or incidental by-product. Rather it is continuously reproduced as a necessary element of the capitalist mode of production and is, to quote Marx, the "*lever* of capitalist accumulation. . . . It forms a disposable industrial reserve army that belongs to capital quite as absolutely as if the latter had bred it at its own cost. Independently of the limits of the actual increase of population, it creates, for the changing needs of the self-expansion of capital, a mass of human material always ready for exploitation."

For this population, the economic conditions of life are unusually desperate and degrading. The high level of property crime and petty hustles cannot be separated from the problems of survival. Commenting on the process of primitive accumulation in 15th and 16th century England, Marx observed that the rising bourgeoisie destroyed the pre-existing modes of production through the forcible expropriation of people's land and livelihood, thus creating a "free" proletariat which "could not possibly be absorbed by the nascent manufactures as fast as it was thrown upon the world." Thousands of peasants were "turned *en masse* into beggars, robbers, vagabonds . . . and 'voluntary' criminals. . . ." For these victims of capitalism, crime was both a means of survival and an effort to resist the discipline and deadening routine of the workhouse and factory.

But crime was not only a manifestation of early capitalism, with its unconcealed plunder, terrorism and unstable labor market. Crime was endemic to both the rural and urban poor in 18th century England. And at the peak of industrial capitalism in the mid-19th century, Engels vividly described the prevalence of theft, prostitution and other types of widespread victimization in working class communities. "The British nation," he concluded, "has become the most criminal in the world."

With at least 41 million persons annually victimized by serious "street" crimes in the United States, it is clear that monopoly capitalism has aggravated rather than reduced the incidence of crime. Recent studies, prepared for the United Nations report on *Economic Crises and Crime,* support the argument that the rate of criminal victimization is not only correlated with crises and "downturns" in the capitalist economy, but also with the "long-term effects of economic growth," thus giving support to Marx's "absolute law of capitalist accumulation—in proportion as capital accumulates, the lot of the laborer, be his payment high or low, must grow worse." The economic underpinnings of "street" crime are underscored by the findings of the Victimization Surveys that over 90% of serious offenses are property-related (theft, burglary, robbery, etc.). Not surprisingly, most "street" crime is disproportionately concentrated in the superexploited sectors of the working class where unemployment rates of 50% are not uncommon.

But "street" crime is not only related to economic conditions; nor is it solely restricted to working class neighborhoods. A series of national studies, conducted by Martin Gold and his colleagues, found little difference in rates of juvenile delinquency between blacks and whites or working class and petty bourgeois families. Their latest study reports that "white girls are no more nor less frequently or seriously delinquent than black girls; and white boys, no more nor less *frequently* delinquent than black boys; but white boys are *less seriously* delinquent than black boys. . . ." Moreover, when delinquency is correlated with socioeconomic status, it is found that "higher status" boys (i.e., the sons of the petty bourgeoisie for the most part) are more likely than working class boys to commit thefts, steal cars and commit assaults.

"Street" crime, like white chauvinism and male supremacy, is most brutal in (although by no means limited to) the superexploited sectors of the working class. Monopoly capitalism emiserates increasingly larger portions of the working class and proletarianizes the lower strata of the petty bourgeoisie, degrades workers' skills and competency in the quest for higher productivity, and organizes family and community life on the basis of its most effective exploitability. It consequently makes antagonism rather than reciprocity the norm of social relationships.

Under monopoly capitalism, family and peer relationships become even more brutal and attenuated. The family as an economic unit is totally separated, except as a consumer, from the productive processes of society. Adolescents are denied access to the labor market and forced to depend on their parents, who bear the costs of their subsistence and education. As a result, millions of youth, including many of the children of the petty bourgeoisie, "become subject to an extraordinary variety of social problems that accompany the statuses of dependent able-bodied persons in our society."

"It is only in its era of monopoly," writes Harry Braverman in *Labor and Monopoly Capital*, "that the capitalist mode of production takes over the totality of individual, family, and social needs and, in subordinating them to the market, also reshapes them to serve the needs of capital." While more and more of the population "is packed ever more closely together in the urban environment, the atomization of social life proceeds apace. . . . The social structure, built upon the market, is such that relations between individuals and social groups do not take place directly, as cooperative human encounters, but through the market as relations of purchase and sale."

As more family members are required to work and the pressures of urban life intensify, the family is required to "strip for action in order to survive and 'succeed' in the market society." Thus, urban life, governed by capital and the profit motive, "is both chaotic and profoundly hostile to all feelings of community." The "universal market," to use Braverman's appropriate term, not only destroys the material foundations of cooperative social relations, but also permeates even the most private domain of personal life, setting husband against wife, neighbor against neighbor. "In short," as Engels observed over a century ago, "everyone sees in his neighbor an enemy to be got out of the way, or, at best, a tool to be used for his own advantage. . . ."

Source: Tony Platt, " 'Street' Crime: A View from the Left," Crime and Social Justice 9 (Spring/ Summer), 1978, pp. 30–31.

measures to be taken that would seriously erode the constitutional rights now guaranteed to those accused of criminal acts. Proposals relaxing existing legal protection against unreasonable search and seizure and denying liberty without due process of law would make it easier for state and federal courts to obtain and uphold criminal convictions. Among the recommendations of this Task Force were:

- Changes in federal law which presently allows criminals to appeal their state convictions in federal courts.
- Elimination of the "exclusionary rule" which forbids the use of illegally obtained evidence in criminal convictions.
- Elimination of the U.S. Parole Commission by revising sentencing laws so that offenders with "comparable" backgrounds receive "comparable" punishments for the commission of "comparable" crimes.
- Establishment of a verdict "guilty but mentally ill" requiring convicted criminals released from treatment for mental illness to serve the remainder of their criminal sentence in prison, thereby giving courts an alternative to the "innocent by reason of insanity" verdict.
- Allowing judicial discretion in denying bail for those awaiting trial, sentencing or appeal who have been deemed "a danger to the community" by the passage of a "nationwide preventive detention law."
- Expanding federal forces to prosecute the "serious criminal activities" of youth street gangs in large cities (all reported in Elsasser, 1981).

The underlying premise of these proposals is that we must sacrifice certain civil and personal liberties, that is, democratic rights, in order to police a rising tide of crime. But even if we were to consent to this erosion of constitutional rights, we would have no guarantee that these kinds of proposals would control and reduce crime. Consider, for example, the only recommendation made by the Task Force on Violent Crime that would increase federal funding for the criminal justice system—$2 billion to be given to states over a four-year period for prison construction.

The nation's overcrowded prisons were cited by the Task Force as the premier problem facing the American system of criminal justice. Indeed, the population explosion in state prisons has led some federal judges to order convicts released and other judges to refuse to sentence convicted criminals to prison on the grounds that it violates the constitutional protection against cruel and unusual punishment.

But the construction of more prisons does not, in and of itself, address the problem of controlling street crime. We are faced with a situation in which more crimes are committed than are reported to the police, more crimes are reported than suspects are arrested, more suspects are arrested than are tried and convicted, and more offenders are tried and convicted than actually go to prison. In effect, what this means is that only a very small percentage of those engaging in street crime end up in prison. How is it sensible, then, to propose to control street crime by building "more and better" prisons? And, even if every offender presently on the street could be identified, arrested, and sent to prison for life, this would not alleviate the social, economic, political, and legal factors that lead to street crime in the first place. New offenders would appear and replace the older and incarcerated ones.

New York Times columunist Tom Wicker concluded that, none of the Task Force recommendations addressed the real issue:

> Even former Attorney General Griffin Bell, the co-chairman (of the Task Force), acknowledged that these (the Task Forces' recommendations) would affect few cases and were largely symbolic—calculated, that is, at whatever constitutional cost, to placate an American public always eager for a "quick fix" for intractable problems. (Wicker, 1981).

The kind of approach to street crime and its control that informs the Attorney General's Task Force Report on Violent Crime is also apparent in the control and domination of the U.S. Congress by conservatives and neoliberals and their calls for longer prison sentences and restoration of the death penalty. Simply put, "The country is becoming more conservative and punitive," says John Matthews, a sociologist for the Houston Police Department (quoted in Leo et al., 1981, p. 30).[15]

The Productivity of Crime: Why Isn't Street Crime Policed More Effectively?[16]

The difference between a stagnant economy—or even full-fledged recession or depression in the American economy—and prosperity may be the relative health of the nation's "criminal economy." This is to say, an efficient and effective policing of street crime might have a negative impact on the smooth and orderly functioning of the American economy.

Stealing, for example, may have as its most critical economic function the ability to "loosen" and recirculate capital that has become frozen in already purchased goods. Usually, the stolen goods fenced are sold to persons with marginal incomes, thus bringing them back into the economy. At the same time, the cars, bicycles, televisions, and other stolen items must be replaced. This may add a crucial margin to the income of local merchants and businesses.

As discussed in Chapter 2, Young (1978) has pointed out how in advanced capitalist societies people have only limited opportunity to "reunite" production and distribution, separated as they are by considerations of profit. Of course, the preferred mode of "unification" is to sell one's labor power, that is, to work. But in times of simultaneous inflation and recession and under conditions of high unemployment, this is particularly difficult, especially for young ghetto and other economically marginal working-class people. Of the other means available to "reunite" production and distribution, welfare is too meager, charity too unde-

[15] A more in-depth description and critique of recent conservative and repressive changes in official state and federal crime control policies appears in the conclusion to this text, Chapter 16.
[16] This section is taken from Timmer (1982).

pendable, and kinship networks too fragile. Street crime prevails as the most available, workable, and secure alternative.

The theft generated in this context leads to the replacement of stolen goods through tax write-offs, insurance, and personal and corporate spending. All of these modes of replacement, in turn, stimulate consumption—and thus, production—in the "legal economy." Replacement purchasing alone, it is estimated, creates in the neighborhood of $30 to $40 billion of added consumption in the U.S. economy each year. Other indications of the economic productivity of street crime include the mugging insurance that is offered by America's largest insurance companies and the locks, chains, dogs, alarm systems, tear gas canisters, and handguns that are produced and purchased. And, of course, street crime is primarily responsible for the economic productivity of the criminal justice system itself. Without street crime, where does the labor of countless correctional employees, probation and parole officers, clerks, judges, and police go?

In all these ways, production, consumption, and employment are created and the American economy expands and benefits. Perhaps at least part of the failure of the American criminal justice system to control and reduce the incidence of street crime is explained by the "positive" effect this failure has on the organization and functioning of the American economy.

CHAPTER REVIEW

1. Contemporary street crimes in our society—like assault, burglary, larceny, arson, homicide, manslaughter, robbery, auto theft, shoplifting, rape, vandalism, and drug use—have not always been defined as criminal and were criminalized only when and to the extent that they were perceived as threatening to the established social order. Social, political, and economic forces, together with those powerful enough to affect these forces, have played a major role in determining what is criminal and what is not criminal in American society.

2. Official street crime rates vary by how they are measured. The FBI Uniform Crime Report (based on police reported crime) indicates a fluctuating, but generally increasing, violent crime rate throughout the 1970s, with a steadily rising property crime rate during this same period; street crime rates in general (both violent and property crime) reaching their peaks in 1980, leveling off in 1981, and decreasing a bit in 1982 and 1983. National Crime Surveys (victimization surveys), on the other hand, indicate little or no change in street crime rates between 1975 and 1982. All official and unofficial measures of street crime consistently document much more property crime in the United States than violent crime.

3. There are approximately 20,000 murders in the United States each year. The American homicide rate appears to be the highest in the world. In fact, overall U.S. violent crime rates appear to be among the highest in the urban-industrial world.

4. In the main, research shows that as unemployment, poverty, and income inequality increase, so does street crime. Class inequality also appears to

contribute to street crime in other ways; for example, the investment patterns of the dominant economic class (those who own, control and manage major industries and financial institutions) in the United States and the existence of a "dual" labor market have both been shown to be positively related to high street crime rates.

5. Race, sex, and age, although highly associated with the incidence of street crime, do not necessarily cause it. Rather, young minority males are disproportionately victimized by the various forms of class inequality—unemployment, underemployment, poverty, racism, and so on—that do seem more causally related to crime.

6. Rape is a violent act of physical aggression, not a sexual act. Poor, working-class, and minority women are victims of rape more often than other women. Rape is related more to the level of inequality in society than to the individual characteristics and traits of rapists and/or rape victims.

7. Addiction, gangs, and guns—like race, sex, and age—are often associated with the incidence of street crime but do not necessarily cause it.

8. With the obvious exception of those violent crimes that specifically victimize women, the arrested and convicted perpetrators and the victims of street crime tend to be very similar: young, minority males.

9. There are at least two basic types of street crime: crimes of accommodation and crimes of resistance. Crimes of accommodation are individualistic property crimes that are committed basically to insure the survival of the perpetrator (called *predatory crimes*) and individual violent crimes (called *personal crimes*). Crimes of resistance are those street crimes, such as riot and revolt, that have a much more explicitly political character.

10. All three of the dominant sociological perspectives in criminology appear relevant to explaining street crime: traditional theories emphasize the role of the "immediate social environment" (poverty, unemployment, broken homes, inadequate schools, peer relationships, deteriorating neighborhoods and communities, etc.) in causing street crime. Interactionist theory focuses on the way in which the "powerful" react to the behavior and activities of the "powerless" with labels and actions that stigmatize them as "criminals" as the source of street crime. Radical criminological theory points to the way in which the historical and structural development of capitalist society marginalizes a segment of the population, making them surplus to both the production and consumption of goods and services and "forcing" them into street crime.

11. Historically, street crime in the United States has been policed more than any other type of crime. During the present era, a host of conservative and repressive measures have either been proposed, or have already been made a part of, official crime control policy. These changes and proposed changes not only threaten civil and individual rights and liberties that are constitutionally guaranteed, but also appear to be ineffective crime control strategies.

12. At least part of the reason for the failure to effectively reduce and control street crime in American society may have to do with the economic productivity of this criminal activity.

6 White-Collar Crime

CHAPTER OUTLINE

Nonoccupational Crimes

Income tax evasion
Other efforts to defraud the government
Insurance frauds
Credit card fraud
Computer theft

Crimes by Employees against Employers

Time theft
Employee pilferage
Kickbacks
Embezzlement

Occupation-Related Frauds

Fraud in maintenance and repair businesses
Fraud in automobile and appliance repair
Fraud in health care
Fraud in land sales
Fraud in the sale of used automobiles
Miscellaneous frauds

The Costs of White-Collar Crime

The comparative economic and physical costs of white-collar and street crimes
The financial costs to the public
The social costs

The Punishment of White-Collar Crime Offenders
Explanations for White-Collar Crime

Criminogenic social conditions
The interactionist perspective
The radical perspective

KEY TERMS

Caveat emptor
Embezzlement
Fee splitting
Fraud
Kickback
White-collar crime

When politicians, journalists, and citizens talk about crime they typically refer to street crimes such as robbery, murder, assault, and other traditional violent crimes. Official statistics on crime, as we have shown, also focus exclusively on these types of illegal acts perpetrated primarily by members of the lower socioeconomic groups in society. These traditional crimes have also drawn most of the attention of criminologists who attempt to develop theories to explain criminal behavior. But to look only at street crimes ignores crimes of much greater economic and social cost. Moreover, such neglect disregards crimes that occur with much greater frequency. The irony is that though these crimes are extremely important, they are relatively unnoticed and if the perpetrators are apprehended, they usually go unpunished. This neglected area of crime—white-collar crimes by individuals—is the topic examined in this chapter.

The crimes of concern in this chapter often are called *white collar* because they are most typically committed by "respectable" members of the community. The famous criminologist, Edwin Sutherland, coined the term "white collar crime" in his presidential address to the American Sociological Association in 1939 (Sutherland, 1940). Although largely ignored, this address was very important in the history of American criminology because it challenged analysts of crime to examine the criminal activities in the corporate, commercial, professional, and political spheres. Sutherland pointed out that the majority of crimes are not committed by members of the lower class, hence, explanations of crime that use poverty or the sociopathic conditions of poverty are wrong. This important legacy of Sutherland was tempered by his lack of conceptual rigor in defining white-collar crime. As a result, the concept of white-collar crime today continues to be a sponge word that combines all sorts of occupational and nonoccupational crimes, crimes by individuals for self-gain as well as crimes by corporations that collude to fix prices or pollute the environment.

Since we will devote separate chapters to corporate crime and political crime, this chapter will focus on only one aspect of what Sutherland and others have included under the rubric of white-collar crime. Our attention is directed to nonviolent crimes by individuals. The crimes we will consider have been delineated by Herbert Edelhertz and Gresham Sykes as illegal acts committed by relatively high-status persons using nonphysical means, concealment or guile to obtain money or property, business or personal advantage (Edelhertz, 1970, p. 12; Sykes, 1978, p. 86).

There are two types of victims of these crimes. The first victim is employers: employees commit crimes in the course of their jobs that violate their employers. These include pilferage, embezzlement, padded expense accounts, and the selling of secrets to competitors. The second victim is the general public, customers or clients who are defrauded. Or it may be the government that is victimized by income tax evaders.

This chapter is organized to examine three categories of white-collar crimes by individuals: (1) nonoccupational crimes, (2) crimes committed by employees in violation of their duty and loyalty to employers, and (3) fraudulent behaviors in occupations. After these categories are discussed, we will assess their societal and personal costs, the punishment of violators when apprehended, and the possible explanations for these widespread illegal behaviors.

NONOCCUPATIONAL CRIMES

The central theme of the crimes in this category is the attempt to "put something over" on the government, the public, corporations, or others through misrepresentation, breach of trust, and the lack of fair dealing (Schur, 1969, p. 163). Examples of crimes included here are fraudulent claims for insurance, bankruptcy fraud, purchases on credit with no intention to pay, income tax evasion, and the like. We will examine some of these to illustrate the methods and scope of these personal crimes outside of one's occupation.

Income Tax Evasion

Tax evasion involves some form of fraud. Money may be "laundered" into what appears to be a legitimate business expense. For instance, the owner of a small firm paid $30,000 to a lawyer for allegedly providing public relations services. No such services were performed and the lawyer returned the money minus a percentage for his services as a front for tax purposes (Bequai, 1978, p. 121). Other methods used to defraud the government involve the use of two sets of books (one set of actual records and another set of misleading records for the Internal Revenue Service), shifting funds from one bank to another, the use of fake invoices, and concealing assets by placing them in the names of friends or relatives. A favorite ploy is to place funds in a foreign bank where the Internal Revenue Service cannot subpoena records. This use of tax havens costs the U. S. Treasury an estimated annual loss of 25 billion dollars in tax revenues (Kelly, 1983). Other schemes involve the use of W-2 forms with fabricated amounts of earnings and tax deductions, declaring dependents who are nonexistent, and the like.

As mentioned in Chapter 4, a nationwide survey by the IRS revealed that approximately 3 out of 10 persons admitted to cheating on their taxes. The Government Operations subcommittee of the House of Representatives estimated in 1982 that the government loses about $80 billion annually because of such widespread tax cheating (Jackson, 1982). Some examples (Kelly, 1983) include:

- Unreported income from individual business: $26 billion.
- Unreported income from farmers: $1.4 billion.
- Unreported capital gains: $9.1 billion (approximately one half of all capital gains income goes undeclared).
- Unreported dividends and interest: $7.7 billion.
- Unreported income and padded expenses from partnerships and small business: $7.2 billion.

The Internal Revenue Service has found that about 30 percent of Americans admit to cheating on their taxes.

Another $100 billion or so in lost taxes occurs because of the underground economy. This is where workers and entrepreneurs dealing in cash (e.g., waiters, artists, musicians, physicians) simply do not report all or part of their earnings and the government cannot prosecute because there are no records. Peter Gutman of Baruch College estimated that in 1982 as many as 30 million people were involved in unreported income totalling $450 to $470 billion (reported in *U. S. News & World Report,* 1982, p. 48; see also Greenwald, 1982).

Other Efforts to Defraud the Government

The government is involved in numerous social programs, many of which are available to the middle classes. These programs are sometimes abused by individuals for unlawful gains.

Item   Many government subsidized student loans have never been repaid. For example, an audit by the Health and Human Services Department in 1982 revealed that 63,000 doctors and nurses owed $30.6 million in overdue loans, a 20 percent delinquency rate (United Press International, 1982).

Item   Vietnam veterans accepted $329.6 million in educational benefits without going to school (King, 1975).

Item   The government estimated that in 1981 unemployment-benefit cheaters were overpaid by $219.9 million. The common ways used to bilk the system included collecting benefits and working at the same time, claiming falsely to be looking for suitable work, overstating wages or length of employment to qualify for larger benefits, and setting up fake companies and collecting benefits for fictitious "laid off" employees (Sheler, 1982).

Insurance Frauds

The magnitude of falsifying insurance claims is revealed in the estimate by the U.S. Chamber of Commerce (1977, p. 344) that 10 percent of all claims are fraudulent, costing $1.5 billion (in 1974). This results in insurance premiums being 15 percent higher than would be the case if fraud did not exist.

Many people routinely falsify insurance claims so they can be reimbursed for damages they are not entitled to. They may claim that the damage to their car was from a single accident when only part occurred at the time of the claim. A claim may be made for hail damage to a car for dents that occurred from other means. Nonexistent items may be listed as stolen. The cause of death may be altered to receive benefits fraudulently. Most arson, the deliberate and illegal burning of property, is done to defraud insurance companies.

Credit Card Fraud

Another method to make illicit gains is to purchase goods, services, or receive loans through fraudulent credit card use. This is done mostly (60 percent) by using cards that were either lost or stolen. Twenty percent occur when legitimate applicants are issued cards but never receive them, and the other 20 percent through fraudulent application. As an example of one elaborate credit card scheme, consider the case of John Spillane who obtained more than 1000 credit cards and $660,000 in loans by establishing at least 300 phony identities.

In July 1970, Spillane set up several fraudulent businesses by incorporating, securing post office boxes, and ordering telephones. Somehow, he managed to get five New Jersey banks to give these "businesses" loans, and because he was prompt with interest payments, the loans were increased. To pay the interest, Spillane needed more income, so he began creating the fraudulent personal identities to get credit cards—mostly BankAmericard [Visa] and Master Charge—he could get cash advances of between $500 and $1,500 from banks. To set up the phony identities, Spillane needed two things: jobs for his aliases and good credit ratings for them. The jobs were easy. He set up several more phony businesses that consisted of just a telephone. Lieutenants would receive calls from credit card companies, pretend to be personnel department workers, and give verifications of employment for the aliases. (reported in Vetter and Silverman, 1978, pp. 239–240)

Losses from credit card fraud have increased from $177 million in 1973 to about $265 million in 1982. Thieves using fake credit cards stole more from banks in 1982 ($128 million) than banks lost to holdups ($46.8 million) (*USA Today,* May 19, 1983). Significantly, one fifth of all credit card fraud is by merchants using phony billing, requests for reimbursement from nonexistent businesses, and knowingly accepting stolen cards for a kickback (Pitts, 1983).

Computer Theft

The computerization of business and government has increased manyfold the potential for crime. These crimes are different from other crimes in the FBI's Index of Crime, and they are difficult to detect. They are invisible, since the transactions are electronic rather than face-to-face. They are nonviolent. The perpetrators are intelligent, educated, creative, and considered responsible members of the community. And these crimes are unusually safe since detection is infrequent, and prosecution, if detected, tends to be lenient. Most important, the financial rewards are greater. Considered in this section are those computer-assisted crimes involving the theft of property by nonemployees (computer theft by employees is a special case of embezzlement, which is considered later in this chapter).

The forms that computer theft take are varied. They may involve fraudulently gaining time on a computer, time that will benefit the perpetrator. Or it may involve gaining access to secret files, the contents of which can be sold to competitors, used for blackmail, or be altered (a favorite is to change the grades kept in a school's computer).

Banks use a magnetic-ink-character-recognition system on checks and deposit slips enabling them to be read by computer and automatically sorted and processed. Understanding this system, a depositor in a Washington, D.C. bank took blank deposit slips and had his account number printed in magnetic ink on them. Periodically he placed these forms on the pile of bank deposit slips in the bank. Other customers would innocently take these slips and record their own deposits in the usual way. The tellers accepted these slips and they were machine sorted. In this way the computer funneled over $250,000 of the deposits of other customers into the criminal's account. Before anybody took notice, the man withdrew $100,000 and vanished (Whiteside, August 22, 1977, pp. 49–50).

In a more ingenious scheme, Jerry Schneider stole telephone equipment from the Pacific Telephone and Telegraph Company. It started in high school when he began collecting documents thrown away by the company. He eventually accumulated a complete library of the company's operating guides. With this information he was able to instruct the company's computer by telephone to deliver telephone equipment to a company drop-off point. Over a seven-month period, Schneider was able to steal over $1 million in equipment, which he stored in a warehouse and sold to private suppliers and users of telephone equipment. After he was caught, having been turned in by a disgruntled employee, he was sentenced to 60 days in prison, and ordered to pay Pacific Telephone $8500 over a five-year period at $141.50 a month (Parker, 1976, pp. 59–70). This light sentence is typical (actually Schneider only served 40 days in jail because of good behavior) for perpetrators of these kinds of crime. We will consider why later in the chapter.

CRIMES BY EMPLOYEES AGAINST EMPLOYERS

The crimes in this category are fundamentally abuses of trust in the employee-employer relationship. They involve some form of theft by employees such as embezzlement, theft of petty cash and supplies, padded expense accounts, accepting bribes and kickbacks, and the selling of corporate secrets. These crimes by insiders involve many billions of dollars resulting in higher costs to consumers and great inflationary pressures on the economy.

Time Theft

A common employee practice is the deliberate waste and abuse of on-the-job time. Robert Half has conducted a survey of 312 corporations since 1970 to assess the amount of employee time wasted and his findings as of 1980 were that (1) the average time theft per employee was 4 hours and 5 minutes per week, (2) office workers wasted 30 percent more time than manufacturing workers, (3) executives wasted as much time as other employees, and (4) this practice cost the American economy at least $120 billion annually (in Willis, 1982).

Time theft occurs for a variety of reasons. The norms of the workplace may encourage it. Employees may feel that wasting time may be partial payment for their being underpaid. Or it may be an expression of the alienation workers feel for the monotony and meaninglessness of their work.

Employee Pilferage

Inventory shrinkage occurs illegally from shoplifting by outsiders and theft by insiders. Although the former accounts for huge losses, for every dollar of merchandise lost to shoplifters, company employees steal $15 worth (Porter, 1982) for a total of $10 billion annually (Gest, 1983). A common assumption is that most of this employee theft is done by those with relatively low status in the organization. However, a recent national survey of internal company theft found that while executive-level employees were involved in about 15 percent of the thefts, they were responsible for 85 percent of the total dollar loss (cited in Porter, 1982).

The reasons for employee pilferage vary according to the individual circumstances of the perpetrators. Donald Hornung investigated blue-collar theft at an electronics plant and found that 91 percent admitted having pilfered at least once. He also found that most of the theft involved property of uncertain ownership such as nails, screws, and scrap metal. The employees felt justified in taking these items, although company property, because they were considered inconsequential and the company would likely never miss them (Hornung, 1970).

A recent survey for the National Institute of Justice reported that one third of employees admitted stealing (cited in Gest, 1983). There are several other reasons why employee pilferage occurs with such frequency. Foremost, the employee work group generally accepts certain pilfering activities as legitimate and others as illegitimate. "Acceptable" pilferage involves what the work group feels individuals are entitled to take in quality and quantity (Altheide, Adler, Adler, and Altheide, 1978). Co-workers, thus, tend to set the standards of what is appropriate, for example, selling products to friends for "discounts," labeling merchandise "damaged" and buying it at a much lower cost, and taking home "surplus" items. Conversely, co-workers also set the limits beyond which the pilferage is viewed as theft. Thus, the work group simultaneously promotes and limits employee theft.

Another reason for widespread employee pilferage is that employees may "steal" to compensate for what they feel are unfair wages. Such a practice may even be condoned by employers, who are able to keep wages low and write off their losses for tax purposes or collect from insurance.

In a variation of the above, employees may steal for revenge and dignity. "They see their wages-in-kind as not only something they are entitled to, but also as a way of 'getting back' at a boss or supervisor who made an unkind remark or probably more common, insisted that a worker show up for overtime" (Altheide et al., 1978, p. 102).

Kickbacks

Persons in authority may use their positions of power and trust to make illegal gains. As part of their job, they may, for example, purchase equipment or give a contract for services to those who give them money or other favors. The guilty parties who take money "under the table" are typically purchasing agents or other officials in a company, organization, or government. Government officials are included here because in a very real sense they, like officials in a corporation, are taking advantage of their employer—in this case voters—for their personal economic advantage. Some examples from the political arena are:

Item A Mississippi State Senator and a former State Senator were found guilty of receiving $300,000 in kickbacks for awarding a $600,000 Mississippi Department of Public Welfare contract (Webster, 1979).

Item A U.S. Chamber of Commerce (1977, p. 326) study reported that in a certain city every contract signed over several years was inflated by 10 percent to allow for kickbacks to municipal officials.

Item In a most famous case resulting in his resignation as the Vice President of the United States, Spiro Agnew pleaded "no contest" to accepting kickbacks for the awarding of contracts for the building of streets, sewers, and bridges in Baltimore County when he was the county executive.

Item Between 1977 and 1979 the Dallas school system lost $10 to $15 million in a series of illegal activities. "A number of administrators and employees in the Support Services Division, under the guise of carrying out a school desegregation order, awarded contracts without competitive bidding, wrote job specifications so that only one contractor could qualify, arranged for overcharging and charging for work never done, received kickbacks, and used more expensive equipment than necessary'' (Linden and Beck, 1981, p. 574).

Kickbacks also occur with regularity in the business world. Employees in positions of power because they are in charge of hiring or purchasing are subject to the temptations of taking money ''under the table'' for making the right decisions. For a price, they direct the company's business toward a single supplier (e.g., an airline, food outlet, or product). One researcher estimated that in large urban centers like New York, $1 out of every $7 that changes hands may be tainted with commercial bribery (Bequai, 1978, p. 42).

Embezzlement

This type of theft involves a violation of employer trust for personal gain. The techniques may vary, from bookkeeping manipulations to the pocketing of cash out of the cash register. The amounts may be major or petty. We will concentrate here on major amounts stolen by trusted employees.

To accomplish embezzlement the perpetrator must have a comprehensive understanding of a company's financial operations and access to the records so that accounts can be manipulated. Those with jobs such as bank teller, electronic data processor, loan officer, treasurer, accountant, and company president have the potential for embezzling large sums from their companies. By definition, then, embezzlers of large amounts are respectable and important employees. If they were not, they would not be in the position to commit such a crime.

The amount embezzled in the United States is large but the exact figure is unknown. These crimes are severely underreported primarily because the victims (businesses) are afraid that public disclosure will harm their reputation. Also they may fear an increase in insurance rates. As a result, for example, only about 15 percent of computer-assisted thefts are ever reported to the police (*U.S. News & World Report,* 1980, p. 40). Nevertheless, there are some estimates of the magnitude of this form of crime. A 1977 study conducted by the American Management Association for the federal Law Enforcement Assistance Administration found a total of $4 billion lost to embezzlement (cited in Pope, 1978).

Recent computer technology has made it possible to manipulate a company's books with thousands of entries daily, making embezzlement more difficult to trace and more lucrative. Some examples of computer-assisted embezzlement are:

Item In 1978 Stanley Mark Rifkin, a computer consultant to Security Pacific National Bank, was able to transfer $10.2 million from that bank into an account at the Irving Trust Company of New York.

Item The chief teller of New York City's Union Dime Savings Bank manipulated the computer to cover thefts of $1.5 million over three years. When caught, the perpetrator pleaded guilty, expressed remorse, and was sentenced to 20 months. He served only 15 months because of good behavior (Whiteside, August 22, 1977, pp. 43–49).

Item   The greatest bank robbery in history occurred when Wells Fargo was taken for $21.3 million by computer over a two-year period.

Item   Exxon lost $20 million worth of fuel over seven years because a computer expert manipulated the records of oil transfers and oil gauges.

Item   In 1982 a claims agent in the Social Security Administration manipulated the system's computers to issue $104,000 in unauthorized checks.

The important question is why do trusted employees embezzle? As McCaghy has asked,

> Who are these embezzlers? Because they have been entrusted with funds in the first place, they are often the nicest of people. . . . Embezzlers are often quiet, unassuming, faithful employees plugging away at their jobs year after year without vacations (to take a vacation is to permit someone else a chance to see the books). Good embezzlers must be good employees who have earned the trust to be in a position where no one worries about them. So what goes wrong? (McCaghy, 1980, p. 254)

Donald Cressey (1953, pp. 164–165), a sociologist who studied embezzlers, concluded from his study that three conditions are present in cases of embezzlement: First, the individual is faced with a financial problem that cannot be resolved by the help of others. For example, the individual may face an unusual medical expense or gambling debts (the chief teller of Irving Trust Company, noted above, had an annual salary of $11,000, yet was placing bets on horse races and other sporting events of as much as $30,000 *a day*), is trapped in an overcommitment to high interest rates, or is attempting to maintain a standard of living beyond his/her salary. Second, there is the identification of opportunity. These individuals recognize that they can secretly resolve the problem by taking advantage of their trusted position in the company. Third, the individual rationalizes and justifies his or her illegal actions as noncriminal. Some possible rationalizations are: "It is all right to steal a loaf of bread when you are starving." "All people steal when they are in a tight spot." "I'm only going to use the money temporarily, so I am borrowing, not stealing." These vocabularies of motive serve to make the criminal behavior seem appropriate in the circumstances (Cressey, 1965).

Another possible reason is the employees' belief that they are underrewarded and therefore only taking what rightfully belongs to them. The excitement of pitting one's computer and/or bookkeeping skills against the company and its auditors may compel some people to embezzle. Regarding computer embezzlement, McCaghy has said:

> The computer is an unexplored frontier; it presents a challenge to discover just how much it can do, and the extent to which it can be manipulated by those

exploiting it. For some programmers the security measures designed to protect the computer's data are a red flag—a dare that the computer's secrets cannot be penetrated. Trying to break those defenses becomes a game in which ethics are of secondary concern. (McCaghy, 1980, pp. 259–260)

OCCUPATION-RELATED FRAUDS

This section focuses on a special type of economic crime: those illegal activities by which individuals obtain money or property under false pretenses. These are crimes by a seemingly legitimate entrepreneur against a client or customer. The frauds are organized by industry. It is important to note that the fraudulent behaviors included here are not exhaustive. Fraud is prevalent throughout American society. Sutherland and Cressey, two renowned criminologists, have informed us of the magnitude of this form of crime:

> Most recorded crimes are crimes against public order or public morality, such as disorderly conduct and drunkenness. . . . It is probable that if all cases of fraud could be recorded, fraud would rank close to drunkenness and disorderly conduct in frequency. (Sutherland and Cressey, 1978, pp. 19)

Fraud in the Maintenance and Repair Businesses

Many of the things we own such as automobiles, electrical appliances, and even our homes are sophisticated and beyond our expertise so that when they need repair we are dependent on the expertise of others. Some unscrupulous operators take advantage of this dependence by overcharging their customers, convincing them to purchase unnecessary materials, or by selling items that are faulty.

Home repairs are fraught with fraudulent schemes. Frauds occur in chimney repair, furnace repair, painting, basement waterproofing, termite control, roofing, and the like. People are charged for work undone, shoddy workmanship and materials, and promises that go unfulfilled.

A common home improvement scheme involves the "model home pitch." A salesperson for a home siding firm, for example, alleges to represent a major aluminum company. He/she tells a prospect that a few homes in selected areas are being chosen to demonstrate a new form of home siding. The "fortunate" homeowner is to receive the siding at a much reduced cost. In return for this bargain, the homeowner agrees to allow the company to photograph the house before and after the siding is installed. These photographs are to be used in local newspaper and television advertisements. The homeowner will also benefit by receiving a commission for each potential customer who responds to these ads. This scheme is typically fraudulent because: (1) the salesperson does not represent a major manufacturer; (2) the siding material is inferior to the siding already on the house; (3) the "bargain" price is higher than one would pay if comparable siding were sold and installed by a reputable firm; (4) there are no local ads and no commissions; and (5) there are no model homes; everyone in the neighborhood receives the same pitch (Cartwright and Patterson, 1974, pp. 18–20).

As an example of another scam, witness the activities of the Holland Furnace Company of Michigan. This company employed 5000 people in 44 states. The primary tactic to sell their wares was to scare potential customers about the safety of their present furnace. Typically, the Holland employees would gain entrance into a home by claiming to be government agents or gas and utility company inspectors. Then they would tell the homeowner, falsely, that the present furnace would asphyxiate the people living in the house or the house would burn up or blow up (Hills, 1971, p. 159).

Fraud in Automobile and Appliance Repair

In 1941, *Reader's Digest* disconnected a coil from an automobile engine and took the car to 347 garages in 48 states. The results of this investigation were that 63 percent of the garages either overcharged, did unnecessary work, or charged for unneeded parts. In a similar investigation, *Reader's Digest* found that nearly two thirds of 304 radio repair shops overcharged for a radio with a loosened tube and that nearly one half of the jewelry stores they took a watch with a loose screw to deliberately cheated them (Riis and Patric, 1942, pp. 53–184). Lest one think that these practices no longer occur with such frequency, the National Highway Traffic Administration revealed that in 1978 nearly 40 percent of all auto repairs were the result of fraud or waste (reported in *U.S. News & World Report,* 1978, p. 72). In 1979, a government survey found that car owners were overcharged an average of $150 per car annually for repairs. The result is that 53 cents of every dollar spent on car repairs is wasted because of overcharges, work not performed, unnecessary work, wrong repairs, and incompetent work performed (Associated Press, 1979).

One practice, common to the auto and other repair industries, that is responsible for much of the padded costs is the use of flat rate labor costs. This means that labor for repairs is charged according to the standard amount of time a given job is supposed to take, not the time actually taken. The result is that customers typically pay for shop and mechanic time that is never used.

Fraud in Health Care

Medically related fraud occurs in a number of ways, a few of which are cited here. One form is unnecessary surgery. The House Subcommittee on Oversight and Investigation reported that unnecessary surgery in 1976 cost $3.5 billion and led to an estimated 12,000 deaths (cited in Claiborne, 1978, p. 12). Another report estimated that the number of unnecessary operations at 3 million annually, resulting in 16,000 deaths (Winter, 1978). *The New York Times* noted that in one year 260,000 of the 787,000 hysterectomy operations were unnecessary, as were 500,000 of the 724,000 tonsillectomies (cited by Cousins, 1976). Not all of these unnecessary operations were performed because of doctors' greed since ignorance or ineptitude are also to blame. "But no one supposes that the fact of financial dishonesty is totally absent from the picture" (Allen, 1979, p. 122).

Another fraudulent practice by doctors is fee splitting. This is a kickback arrangement whereby doctors pay those who refer patients to them (commonly other doctors but also lawyers and insurance brokers). Of course, to make these payments, the doctor will pad the patient's bill so that all in the chain are adequately compensated. The practice is illegal in many states because of the danger to patients when a referral is made on the basis of the size of the fee rather than the competence of the doctor or surgeon. Doctors also receive kickbacks from laboratories, x-ray clinics, and pharmacies for directing business their way.

Widespread fraud by medical practictioners has occurred in federally funded health programs for the poor and the elderly, especially those paid through Medicaid and Medicare. One practice is to have two sets of prices—one for private patients and a higher bill for Medicaid recipients—since the government will pay. An audit of over 20,000 bills submitted by medical laboratories showed a median overcharge of 116 percent on the tests paid by Medicaid (cited in Allen, 1979, p. 123). An investigation by the Department of Health, Education, and Welfare revealed the following audacious examples of Medicaid abuse (all are cited in Allen, 1979, p. 127):

Item   A druggist who dispensed more than 100 pills a day to the same patient for 204 consecutive days.

Item   A doctor who billed the same patient for six tonsillectomies.

Item   A gynecologist who charged a patient for a complete hysterectomy and later for an abortion.

Item   A physician who submitted 26,000 bills for a year's work on Medicaid patients (to accomplish this feat would require that the doctor complete the work on a patient every 10 minutes, 16 hours a day, all year).

Fraud has been even more prevalent in the nursing home business, which is largely funded by Medicare-Medicaid funds. The Senate Subcommittee on Long-Term Care investigated alleged nursing home abuses and found that profiteering occurred in several ways: operators confiscated the $25 monthly allowance provided every nursing home patient on Medicaid; they used hidden charges and cut expenses by reducing staff, restricting the use of heating in winter and air conditioning in the summer, spending as little as 50 cents per patient per day for food, and doing infrequent laundering. Another common method of illegal profiteering was to get Medicare or Medicaid to pay for medical treatment that never happened (Mendelson, 1974; Percy, 1974).

A widespread form of health swindle is the selling of alleged disease cures to persons suffering from ailments that legitimate medicine cannot cure. Victims of arthritis, for example, experience great pain, and medical science has not been very helpful in finding relief, let alone a cure, for the intense suffering. Desperate for relief and hope, the victims are susceptible to the appeals of health quacks who promise "cures" through the use of copper bracelets, zinc shoe disks, sitting in

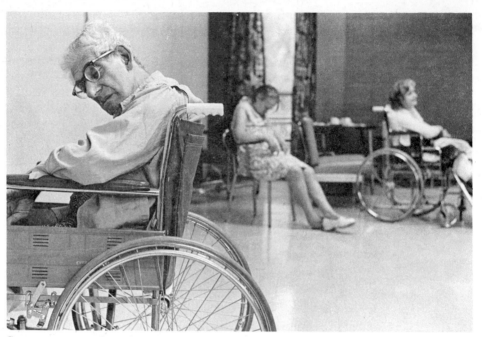

Some operators of nursing homes have abused their patients for profit by not providing adequate services and by accepting Medicare or Medicaid payments for medical treatment never administered.

uranium mines, exotic foods, and other schemes. The situation is similar for victims of other crippling and fatal diseases such as multiple sclerosis and cancer.

The common concern for looking youthful and attractive is another weakness on which medical quacks prey. Millions of dollars are spent annually on "cures" for baldness, acne, skin wrinkling, small breasts, and obesity. This last cure, weight reduction, is an especially lucrative area for swindlers. There are exaggerated advertising claims for the use of slimming devices such as weighted belts, wraps, running suits, machines that shock the body to harden muscles, and for dietary aids such as pills and certain foods that are guaranteed to "burn away fat." Not only are these claims usually false and costly, but they are sometimes dangerous.

Fraud in Land Sales

Land hustlers have tended to be concentrated in areas with special allure such as in the deserts, mountains, near lakes, or by the sea. People living in large cities with high rates of violent crime, pollution, and traffic congestion or living in places where the climate is too harsh are especially attracted to advertisements claiming wide open spaces, friendly neighbors, continuous sun, and nearby fishing, hunting, boating, and golf. Unscrupulous land promoters have taken advantage of the unwary through deceptive sales techniques, delay or default on development promises, multiple sale of the same property, and misrepresenting the value and amenities of the land. For some examples of sales deception in land sales, consider the following:

Item   A newspaper ad for Lake Mead Rancheros claimed "The Rancheros are livable now. . . . You can own a king-sized estate with roads and electricity, water and phones available. . . . Build now and move in." In actuality, though, power and phone lines were six miles away and the nearest water was from a coin-operated pump 12 miles away (cited in Snow, 1978, p. 138).

Item   Stonewood Ranch, a 4000-acre barren tract near the petrified forest in Arizona, was completely sold out in 40-acre parcels yet there was no access to the property (Snow, 1978, p. 138).

Item   A woman was told her Florida lot included water and sewer lines and was close to a freeway only to discover that the land was so remote that she could only view it from a helicopter (Cartwright and Patterson, 1974, p. 37).

Several tactics are used to get investors to take the plunge for land they have not seen, or if they have seen it, to accept the promoter's plans to transform the land into a recreational paradise. One popular scheme is to invite potential buyers to a free dinner and entertainment at a local restaurant. Guests are paired with a company representative for a constant sales pitch during the evening. The entertainment is a movie or slides about the land development. After the movie, a map with the lots for sale is shown, giving the guests a "chance to get in on the ground floor." Employees of the company, posing as guests ("shills"), then rush forward to "buy," pretending to take advantage of this fantastic bargain. This "band-wagon" atmosphere leads real prospective buyers to fear that they had better act quickly or miss out.

Other tactics include "free" vacations and other prizes. As an example, the promoter for Port Mille Lacs in northern Minnesota held a free drawing. Each of those who participated was notified that he or she had won a consolation prize of a $50 certificate to be applied to the purchase of $695 lot, which was described in glowing terms. When the customer arrived in Port Mille Lacs the prize lot was found to be far from the lake and in a swamp. The sales representative then would switch the customer to a lake-front lot selling for seven times as much money (cited in Cartwright and Patterson, 1974, pp. 40–41). This "bait and switch" scheme is common in the sale not only of land but also cars, furniture, sewing machines, and the like.

Fraud in the Sale of Used Automobiles

This industry is especially rich in fraudulent behavior. A common practice to increase sales is to do cosmetic changes on cars rather than to improve their mechanical condition. This tactic is based on the knowledge that customers are especially impressed by observables such as the paint job and seat covers. To give a car a paint job is not a deviant act in itself but it may be used to hide known defects from prospective buyers. Extensive body work and a paint job, for example, may be done to disguise the signs that a car has been in a wreck.

In an indirect admission by the auto industry of its tendency to misrepresent a car's condition at the time of sale, the National Automobile Dealers Association gave campaign contributions to members of Congress of $825,000 over three years to defeat a rule recommended by Federal Trade Commission that would have required used car dealers to disclose to customers in writing all known major defects and the warranty rights the dealer offered. The lobbying efforts were successful; Congress vetoed the FTC ruling in May 1982 (Mayer, 1982).

Another subterfuge employed by dealers to misrepresent the cars they sell is to tamper with the mileage reading on the used-car odometers. By reducing a car's mileage by say 40,000 miles, an unscrupulous dealer may be able to sell the car for hundreds maybe even thousands of dollars more than if the true mileage were used.

Miscellaneous Frauds

The list of fradulent schemes for dishonest profit is practically endless. To name a few that we have not discussed, there are fraudulent ministers and charitable fundraisers; swindlers in door-to-door sales of everything from pots and pans to encyclopedias; trade schools that promise adequate training and guaranteed jobs but do not deliver; phony employment agencies; stocks and commodities sold fraudulently; dishonest practices in the funeral industry where the grief and guilt of the bereaved are used to increase the cost of burying the dead; people who misrepresent themselves as handicapped to increase their sales; and fraudulent art schools and dance studios. Clearly, fraud is endemic to business in American society, and we have not even considered the deceptive advertising, price fixing, and price gouging at the corporate levels (see Chapter 9).

Telephone-sales scams (known as *boiler room* operations) are designed to lure the greedy and the gullible into investing in such "lucrative" areas as oil lease lotteries, the purchase of cheap stocks, and mining ventures. One outfit out of Fort Lauderdale, the International Gold Bullion Exchange, bilked customers for more than $140 million in three years. Another, the U.S. Oil and Gas Corporation of Coral Gables, Florida, swindled some 66,000 people of about $60 million (Harris, 1983).

Another and related area of fraudulent activity involves the use of the mails to advertise false charities, offer bogus jobs, and bargain products. The Council of Better Business Bureaus reports that in 1982 there were more than 76,000 complaints registered against mail-order firms for shoddy merchandise, misrepresented items, and the like. The Postal Service found one scheme in which 50,000 people invested $650,000 in a bogus "work at home project" of stuffing envelopes for a profit (Diggs, 1982).

The remaining sections of this chapter examine the societal and personal costs of fraud and the other forms of white-collar crimes, the penalties for getting caught, and the reasons for these behaviors.

THE COSTS OF WHITE-COLLAR CRIME

One conclusion is evident from the descriptions of white-collar crimes—these criminal behaviors are widespread in American society. Because they are so prevalent, the costs to society are immense.

There is no way to know precisely the financial costs of these crimes. They are much more likely to be underreported and undetected than traditional street crimes. Often the data are concealed by victims. Those who succeed in cheating on their income tax are, by definition, unknown to the authorities. Also, the excessive amounts that consumers pay as a result of fraud are just crude estimates. Despite these limitations, let's examine some important dimensions of the social and economic costs of these crimes.

The Comparative Economic and Physical Costs of White-Collar and Street Crimes

The costs of white-collar crimes far exceed those of traditional street crimes. The following estimates show the magnitude of the difference:

Item   White-collar crime, narrowly defined as crimes against business, cost an estimated $50 billion in 1981—nearly 10 times more than the monetary loss from all street crimes (Ruhl, 1981, p. B1).

Item   A study in Florida showed that the average amount involved in a street crime in that state was $35, while the average loss from a white-collar crime was $621,000 (Ruhl, 1981, p. B1).

Item   The FBI reported that 3459 bank robberies, burglaries, and larcenies netted $22,100,000 during the first half of 1980. During that same six months, the agency completed investigations of 5174 fraud and embezzlement cases involving $103,300,000 in loot (cited in *Changing Times,* 1980).

Item   The director of public health in California estimated that medical quackery kills more persons than all crimes of violence taken together (cited in Geis, 1974, p. 125).

The Financial Costs to the Public

The widespread cheating and fraudulent behavior in American society puts a great financial burden on the public. As noted earlier, insurance costs are considered to be 15 percent higher because of these crimes. Dishonesty by executives and employees increases the retail cost of merchandise by about 15 percent (McCaghy, 1980, p. 245). Most significantly, the estimated $180 billion (1982) in lost tax revenues from various forms of tax cheating and evasion places a great tax burden on the noncheaters. When businesses and banks go bankrupt because of fraud or embezzlement, employees, customers, investors, and the public suffer economic setbacks as well.

The Social Costs

The view of some is that even greater than the financial and physical costs of nonviolent crime is the destructive impact of these crimes on public confidence in commercial activity. The President's Commission on Law Enforcement and Administration noted this possibility:

> Most people pay little heed to crimes of this sort when they worry about "crime in America," because these crimes do not, as a rule, offer an immediate, recognizable threat to personal safety. However, it is possible to argue that, in one sense, those crimes are the most threatening of all . . . because of their corrosive effect on the moral standards by which American business is conducted. (President's Commission on Law Enforcement and Administration, 1967, pp. 4–5)

Put even more forcefully this time by the executive vice-president of a firm specializing in the security of corporations in a speech to the Executives Club of Chicago:

> While seemingly innocent since there is no physical violence, white collar crime is a hundred times more destructive to our society, since it destroys the vitality of our economy. It ruins our corporations financially, creates further unemployment, and contributes to inflation. But above all, white collar crime warps the moral fiber of society where honesty and decency have been traditionally valued. . . . (Britton, 1981, p. 488)

These crimes demonstrate an extreme disrespect for the rights and property of others and they are committed, for the most part, by persons respected in the community. Thus, these people (and their criminal acts) set an example of lawlessness for the general population. When such crimes are committed by the well-to-do and go relatively unpunished, as we will see in the next section, they serve as rationalizations for the lower classes to justify their own behavior. Bitterness at class and racial discrimination in the criminal justice system also makes traditional offenders resistant to rehabilitation. Unpunished violations by white-collar offenders create disrespect for the law and engender a desire for revenge against those who protect their own but punish society's outcasts (Conklin, 1977, p. 8).

THE PUNISHMENT OF WHITE-COLLAR CRIME OFFENDERS

The previous section established that white-collar crimes are much more widespread and expensive than street crimes. Yet, when the punishment of street criminals is compared with that of white-collar crime offenders, the former receive disproportionately more harsh sentences. For example, although banks lose six times as much through embezzlement than through robbery, only 17 percent of those convicted of embezzlement go to jail while 91 percent of those convicted of bank robbery go to jail (Ruhl, 1981, p. B15). Another study found that 22 percent of convicted embezzlers go to jail for an average of less than two years while 71 percent of convicted auto thieves went to prison (for three years) and 64 percent of those convicted of transporting stolen property went to jail for an average of four years (Fleetwood and Lubow, 1975).

Later in the book there will be a discussion of the punishments common to traditional criminals. For the moment, though, let's raise some hypotetical questions comparing the punishment of a street criminal with that of a perpetrator of a white-collar crime.

- What would be the punishment if someone robbed a bank of $21 million? Ben Lewis, the insider at Wells Fargo who helped two others embezzle that amount, was sentenced to five years in prison.

- What would be the punishment if someone robbed the government of $148,000? Former Secretary of Agriculture Earl Butz fraudulently understated his 1978 income tax by that amount and was fined $10,000 and given 30 days in jail.

- What would be the punishment for someone who took $250 million from a bank by force? C. Arnhold Smith, the chairman of U.S. National Bank, entered a plea of "no contest" to charges of conspiracy, misapplication of bank funds, filing false statements, and making false entries in his bank's books—estimated to be about $250 million. His penalty for these crimes was a $30,000 fine to be paid at the rate of $100 a month for 25 years—with no interest. He was also placed on probation for five years (Forbes, 1975).

Clearly, in each of these cases the perpetrator of the violent crime would have received much more severe penalties (see Table 6-1). The wide gap in punishment

TABLE 6-1

Average Length of Sentence for Those Imprisoned in Federal Prisons, 1980

Offense	Average Sentence (Months)
Street Crimes	
Assault	39.9
Auto theft	47.2
Extortion	69.5
Robbery	143.4
White-Collar Crimes	
Income tax fraud	17.8
Lending institution fraud	27.3
Bribery	29.8
Embezzlement	32.4

SOURCE: Timothy J. Flanagan, David J. van Alstyne, and Michael R. Gottfredson (eds.), *Sourcebook of Criminal Justice Statistics—1981*, Washington, D. C.: U. S. Government Printing Office, 1982, pp. 410–413.

is tolerated by most in society. There is little public outcry over nonviolent crimes, especially those committed by the well-to-do. Some possible reasons for this are:

1. The crimes are not threatening to life.
2. These crimes are usually committed at the expense of a large organization that is wealthy, powerful, and impersonal. Public attitudes toward stealing vary according to the nature of the organization. One study found, for example, that respondents would steal with the least reluctance from a large business firm, with more reluctance from a government agency, and with the most from small businesses (cited in Schur, 1969, p. 175).
3. The perpetrator is often perceived as bright and creative causing many to actually admire the act (Vetter and Silverman, 1978, p. 242).
4. The perpetrators are educated and respectable members of the community. The criminals typically have character traits that make them appear to their associates and superiors as reliable and trustworthy. After all, that is how they got the positions of trust which gave them the opportunity for such crimes.
5. There may be a reluctance to prosecute these criminals because of the social relationships between those who violated the trust and the officers of the company (Haskell and Yablonsky, 1974, p. 77).

The relative nonpunishment of white-collar criminals in American society raises a serious question: Is there a difference between street criminals and nonstreet criminals? Are purse snatchers and land defrauders different? Are bank robbers with guns in their hands and stocking masks different from bank embezzlers sitting at their computer consoles dressed in three-piece suits? The public and the criminal justice system clearly have a double standard—one with a class bias. As William McCullough has argued: "Something is out of kilter. Somewhere our criminal justice priorities have gotten scrambled. When a sizable segment of our supposedly better citizens can loot and steal with relative impunity, justice has been horribly abused" (McCullough, 1981).

Some feel that nonviolent criminals should be punished but by a fine rather than a jail term. This is the position of University of Chicago law professor Richard Posner who argued that fines that vary progressively with the affluence of the perpetrator would act as a deterrent and be less costly to society than prison (Posner, 1980; see also Buckley, 1981).

Allen Dershowitz, Harvard law professor, has argued the opposite position:

Under existing alternatives, it's essential that white collar criminals go to jail . . . imprisoning economic offenders is a symbolic punishment but it's precisely the absurdity of it that serves as the form of punishment. (quoted in Fleetwood and Lubow, 1975, p. 35)

Similarly, Fleetwood and Lubow have argued that "if the deterrent theory of punishment has any validity at all, it should apply best to white-collar criminals, who are usually motivated by greed rather than need or passion'' (Fleetwood and Lubow, 1975, p. 35). This view is supported by research. Albrecht found, for example, that convicted white-collar criminals who went to jail tended not to revert to crime when they returned but those who were not jailed had their dishonesty reinforced and tended to go back to their criminal activities (Albrecht, 1979).

A third position is that there should be differential punishment but that the well-to-do should be punished *more* than violators of traditional crimes. There are two different arguments for this position. One is that the well-to-do have had the benefits of education, wealth, and opportunity, while street criminals usually have not. The second argument is that crimes by the affluent cause more social disruption than traditional crimes (Geis and Meier, 1977, p. 18).

The relative lack of law and law enforcement regarding white-collar crimes leads us to consider why this is the case. We have shown that white-collar crimes have greater social and economic costs than street crimes, yet they go relatively unnoticed and when noticed by the authorities, relatively unpunished. Very likely this anomaly is because white-collar crimes, while illegal, are not viewed as threatening to the fabric of society. Indeed, white-collar crimes are not policed with the same vigor as street crimes because they are, generally, part of the normal ways the economy works in American society (Timmer, 1981).

EXPLANATIONS FOR WHITE-COLLAR CRIMES

The types of crimes included in the category "white collar" are varied, as we have seen. Some, such as income tax evasion, are done by people from all social strata. Some occur outside of one's occupation while others are directly tied to making a living. The variation means that one theory will not apply universally. Each of the three theoretical perspectives used in this book alone and in combination with others adds to our understanding of this complex phenomenon.

Criminogenic Social Conditions

The traditional sociological explanation for crime—poverty and social disorganization—are invalid explanations for the crimes considered in this chapter. They do not explain, for example, fraud, embezzlement, and computer theft, which are crimes committed by the affluent. White-collar criminals tend to have been brought up in affluent neighborhoods, in intact families, have college degrees, and have plenty of economic opportunities. Thus, the social conditions considered criminogenic by many criminologists, such as broken homes, low-quality education, poverty, lack of opportunity, and social disorganization just do not apply.

Sutherland's theory of differential association has some explanatory power when fraudulent practices are considered. Sutherland explained his theory:

The hypothesis of differential association is that criminal behavior is learned in association with those who define such behavior favorably and in isolation from those who define it unfavorably, and that a person in an appropriate situation engages in such criminal behavior if, and only if, the weight of the favorable definitions exceed the weight of the unfavorable definition. (Sutherland, 1949, p. 234)

In the business of used car sales or the selling of land, taking unfair advantage of customers may be normative. As Newman has described it,

Incumbents in these occupations, being relatively isolated from possible other association when this criminal activity is not common, learn attitudes, values, motives, rationalizations, and techniques favorable to this type of crime. . . . [The individual] through associations with colleagues who define their offenses as "normal" if not justified, learns to accept and participate in the antilegal practices of his occupation. The emphasis is on a fundamental learning process and does not rely on personality deficiencies as the root of such crime. (Newman, 1977, p. 58)

Differential association, however, is not a helpful theory for understanding a crime like embezzlement. Embezzlers, by definition, have violated a trust agreement with their employers. They tend to commit their crimes in isolation. Embezzlers do not learn their technologies and adopt their deviant values from other embezzlers.

Merton's theory of anomie, if stretched,[1] is a relevant theory that applies in a general way to many white-collar crimes. Given the values of the society, the goal of success is more important than the means of succeeding. So in the quest for economic success many will cheat on their taxes, steal from work, lie to potential employers about their academic credentials, or misrepresent the facts about a sale to a customer. These fraudulent behaviors are encouraged by two facts: the stakes are high and the chances of being punished are low.

The Interactionist Perspective

This perspective is less informative about white-collar crimes than the other two theoretical perspectives. Two insights from this perspective are relevant, though. The first stems from the interactionist proposition that crime is socially constructed. Crime is created by the laws. The powerful in society make the laws that curb certain behaviors by particular categories of people and omit others. Thus, the laws and the activities of the protectors of those laws—the police and the courts—are aimed particularly at traditional crimes. This is not to say that the powerful have decriminalized the illegal acts by the affluent. But the weaknesses in the statutes regarding business crimes and the relative lack of punishment given

[1]Technically, Merton's theory only applies to those who do not have access to the socially approved means to achieve success. Middle- and upper-class people, since they have the socially approved means, have no reason, according to Merton, to deviate. Some white-collar people, however, may, like those in the lower classes, feel that they are trapped with little hope of upward mobility through legitimate means.

to the few who are caught when compared with the rigor applied to traditional crimes is a clear indicator of how power is exercised in society. As criminologists Clinard and Quinney have noted:

> In the laws directed at the behavior of businessmen and other occupational members there has been a strong tendency to enact lenient statutes and to enforce them in a similar fashion, showing favoritism to offenders of high social status. Many of these laws provide no criminal sanctions, and where sanctions are included, they have been used hesitantly. Thus, the laws outlawing occupational offenses differ from conventional laws of crime not only in their origin, but in philosophy, in the determination of responsibility or intent, in enforcement and prosecution procedures, and in the sanctions used to punish the violators. (Clinard and Quinney, 1973, p. 198)

The second insight of the interactionist perspective pertinent to this discussion is related to the first. The affluent, because of their status in the community and their resources and power, are able to escape the stigmatization of being labeled criminal. The affluent can hire the best lawyers to fight for them plus judges tend to be lenient with these people who are their social equals.

The Radical Perspective

The radical perspective directs the analyst's attention to the economic and political structure of society as the source of white-collar crime. The culprit in this view is the culture of capitalism. Steve Allen, the comedian, composer, and author has written a book about the extent of corruption in America. Although by no means a radical, Allen has argued that the source of the prevalence of scandal and fraud in American society is capitalism:

> [Capitalism] is a generally free-market structure in which it is perfectly possible for honest people to make a living, to make a profit—possible, for some, to accumulate great wealth. But it is a structure under which considerable advantages also can accrue to the ruthless, unscrupulous, and dishonest person. . . . I prefer our system to the Communist alternative. . . . But [is capitalism] holy? Sanctified in any sense? Nonsense. The loose structure of economic practices generally connoted by the terms free enterprise or capitalism is useful, practical, productive. That is one side of the ledger. But to refuse to examine the other side is stupid. Capitalism has also been responsible for the worst sort of selfishness, cruelty, suffering, poverty, hunger, sickness, thievery and chicanery of which man is capable. (Allen, 1979, pp. 37, 39)

What is there about capitalism that promotes certain types of crime? Sociologist Edwin Schur has argued that the underlying values of American life promote and shape criminality. His position is that there is a duality in society—cultural values that pull in opposite directions (Schur, 1969, pp. 185–188). In the business world there are the principles of honesty, public accountability, and concern for the public interest. But these are countered by the values that support such business activities as secrecy and deception to maximize profit without regard for customers, clients, or the public.

The principle of *caveat emptor*—let the buyer beware—is a traditional feature of capitalism that is an open invitation for fraud in the marketplace. The assumption of *caveat emptor* is that:

> The buyer must accept full responsibility for a sales transaction; the seller accepts none. He must rely upon and trust nothing but his own personal inspection of his purchase, ignoring any representations of the seller which he does not confirm for himself. Any buyer who does other than this must suffer all consequences of purchases which turn out badly. (Preston, 1975, pp. 32–33)

A primary tenet of capitalism is that the maximization of profits supersedes all other considerations. This means that there is a strong tendency for employers to pay their employees as little as possible in wages and benefits. The result is that employees tend to feel abused and underpaid, have feelings of personal alienation, disloyalty to the company, and resentment toward management. In this climate, employees may steal to punish the company and/or to bring their wages up to what they consider fair.

The culture of capitalism also promotes materialism (the accumulation of capital), which is manifested in a competitive consumerism (''keeping up with the Joneses''). For many, this results in a pattern of buying on credit and overspending on items of conspicuous consumption. This tendency for many to overcommit their limited resources may motivate them not to report cash income or to overreport charitable contributions to the Internal Revenue Service. There may be another reason for employee pilferage or even embezzlement.

Similarly, the economic conditions generated by capitalism in American society are conducive to widespread white-collar crimes. The recent past has been characterized by an ever-increasing pace of economic contradictions—simultaneous inflation and recession; the decline of some industries (autos and steel) and the increase in others (high technology); the growth of some regions (sun belt) and the decline of others (industrial northeast and midwest); higher taxes and reduced services; and the reduction in real wages and purchasing power for the majority while the few increase their advantages. This uncertain and declining economic climate means that the American Dream of upward mobility is ever more elusive. When the legal avenues to achieve this dream are blocked, then many choose illegal means—white-collar criminality—to be successful.

Finally, the conditions of mass society combine with the culture of capitalism to promote white-collar crimes. Most Americans live in metropolitan areas and work in huge bureaucracies. Social relations in these settings tend to be impersonal, segmentalized (i.e., we deal with others in a limited way, knowing them only in a particular role, such as client or merchant, rather than the person as the sum of all his or her roles), and instrumental (goal oriented). When the individualism, competitiveness, and materialism of capitalism are added to the conditions of mass society, we can readily see how such a climate fosters "me-first/goals regardless of the means" attitude in individuals. The result is a climate in which fraud flourishes.

CHAPTER REVIEW

1. White-collar crimes—those illegal acts committed by relatively high status persons using nonphysical means, concealment, or guile to obtain personal advantage—are more costly socially and economically than street crimes. The victims are employers and the general public as customers or clients or the government.

2. Individuals may engage in white-collar criminal activities outside of their occupations by illegally evading taxes, falsifying insurance claims, using credit cards illicitly, and by fraudulently using computers.

3. Crimes by employees against employers include time theft, employee pilferage, kickbacks, and embezzlement.

4. Fraudulent behavior occurs commonly in a number of occupations such as in the repair of homes, appliances, and automobiles; health care, land sales, used car sales; and in telephone, postal, and door-to-door sales.

5. The social costs of white-collar crimes include: (a) the reduction of public confidence in commercial activities, (b) the setting of an example of lawlessness within the "respected" segments of the community, and (c) the disrespect for the criminal justice system as the perpetrators go relatively unpunished.

6. The relative lack of punishment for white-collar criminals is possibly due to: (a) the crimes are not life-threatening; (b) the crimes are often committed at the expense of large, impersonal organizations; (c) the perpetrators are often perceived as bright and creative, and they are educated and respected members of the community; and (d) the perpetrators are friends with the officers of the company violated.

7. No one theory explains white-collar crime. The traditional sociological explanations for crime—poverty and social disorganization—are invalid. Sutherland's theory of differential association and Merton's theory of anomie have limited application.

8. The interactionists provide two helpful insights. First, since crime is created by the law and the powerful make the laws, the law and the enforcers of the law are directed away from business crimes and toward crimes by the powerless. Second, the affluent use their status and financial resources to escape the stigmatization of being labeled a criminal.

9. The radical perspective directs attention to the economic and political structure of society as the source of white-collar crime. Capitalism, with its emphases on the maximization of profit, materialism, and competitiveness cultivates the climate where white-collar crime flourishes. So, too, are the economic conditions fostered by capitalism and the conditions of mass society.

7 Victimless Crime

**CHAPTER
OUTLINE**

Crime Without Victims: A Short and Sordid History
The Extent and Status of Victimless Crimes

Sex crimes: adultery, homosexuality, prostitution, and pornography
Abortion
Gambling
Drug use and addiction
Vagrancy, disorderly conduct, and public drunkenness

The Ideology of Victimless Crime

The traditional sociological view
The interactionist perspective
A radical approach

The Medicalization of Crime and Deviance
Punishing Victimless Crime: Five Costs of Criminalizing

Enforcement costs
Secondary crime costs
Police corruption
Constitutional costs
The fiscal crisis of the state

KEY TERMS

Complainantless crime
Consensual transaction
Criminalization
Decriminalization
Fiscal crisis of the state
Legalization
Medicalization of crime and deviance
Overcriminalization
Victimless crime

The Manhattan District Attorney's office in New York City has declined to use a controversial type of evidence in prosecuting prostitutes that was offered to it by a special mayor's task force appointed to assist in midtown "clean-up" efforts. To use the rejected evidence, private investigators hired by the task force to elicit the necessary sexual acts or overtures would have provided the incriminating testimony. A recent obstacle to the long-time use of plainclothes "decoys" has been that the prostitutes now will rarely even talk about sex until a "customer" has undressed; yet, under a New York City police regulation, officers cannot disrobe while on duty. In rejecting the proffered testimony of private decoys, an assistant district attorney described the practice of using private investigators to perform sexual acts in order to get evidence as "offensive" to high law enforcement standards and said he would be unwilling to present such a case to a grand jury, whom it would "repel and disgust." For his part, the task force director termed such rejection "ridiculous," a missed opportunity to enforce the law.[1]

Is the prostitute a criminal? Is prostitution a crime? Is anyone victimized by the prostitute's activity? Is there a complaining victim, a complainant? Should the criminal law be used to enforce a private morality that may not be shared by the prostitute? Are laws prohibiting prostitution enforceable? Can the police arrest and the criminal courts prosecute prostitutes without corrupting themselves in the process and increasing public disrespect for the law and the criminal justice system? Do Americans really believe that prostitution is a crime? Should prostitution be decriminalized? Legalized?

These are the kinds of questions and issues that will be addressed in our discussion of "victimless crimes."

CRIME WITHOUT VICTIMS: A SHORT AND SORDID HISTORY

The use of criminal law to attempt the prohibition of morally deviant acts among and between willing and consenting adults has long been a subject of intense legal debate. Indeed, the early defenders of this use of criminal law tended to see the very issue of societal survival at stake. As Kadish has written "Stephens in the last century . . . and Lord Devlin in this century have urged the legitimacy of criminal intervention on the ground that 'society cannot ignore the morality of the individual any more than it can his loyalty; it flourishes on both and without either it dies' " (Kadish, 1971, p. 58). But from John Stuart Mill in the 19th century up to the present, the contrary view of this "illegitimate" use of criminal law has been stated vigorously. In 1957, a study of homosexuality and prostitution commissioned by the British government—the Wolfenden Report—stated this position

---

[1]From Edwin M. Schur, *Interpreting Deviance: A Sociological Introduction,* New York: Harper & Row, 1979, p. 343. (Schur's adaptation is based on a news article in *The New York Times,* December 2, 1976, p. 47.)

succinctly, "Unless a deliberate attempt is to be made by society, acting through the agency of the law, to equate the sphere of crime with that of sin, there must remain a realm of private morality and immorality which is, in brief and crude terms, not the law's business" (Great Britain Committee on Homosexual Offenses and Prostitution, quoted in Kadish, 1957, p. 58).

It was not until the 1960s, however, that the legal idea of the illegitimate intrusion of the criminal law into the individual's private life and actions emerged as a sociological concept—"crimes without victims" (see Schur, 1965; Duster, 1970; Kittrie, 1971; Geis, 1972; Schur and Bedau, 1974). This notion of "victimless crime" has tended to be defined in three distinct ways, all of which have provoked public and political controversy.

The first of these approaches has taken the meaning of "victimless" quite literally; understanding it as "lack of harm to others" or "the absence of victimization." The problem with this approach is that little consensus has emerged in the United States concerning which crimes are, and which crimes are not, victimless in this sense. Although some have argued that prostitution, drug addiction, and abortion are "crimes" that do not have victims, others have argued "that the prostitute is a victim (of social conditions, of her pimp, or of exploitation by men), that the illegal drug user is a victim of the drug, that the fetus is a victim of abortion" (Schur, 1979, p. 450).

A second approach to the issue of whether or not we have made criminal certain acts that are victimless and therefore should not be criminalized evolves around the notion of the improper legislation of private morality. It has often been heard in American society that "we should not, or cannot, legislate morality." The problem here is twofold. On the one hand, it is hard to contend that we should not legislate morality, since all criminal law imposes some morality. To outlaw homicide and rape, for example, is to proscribe these behaviors both legally and morally. To outlaw these behaviors is to evaluate them morally; as wrong. On the other hand, if we make a distinction between public and private morality and hold to the view that it is only private morality that should not be legislated we are confronted with another obstacle: "How are we to determine what morality is private in order to know that its legislation was improper?" (Schur, 1979, p. 451).

Sociologist Edwin Schur, an ardent advocate of decriminalizing victimless crimes, has argued that there is a third and more fruitful way in which to describe and understand crimes that are victimless. This involves the ideas of "complainantless crime" and "consensual transaction":

Some "offenses" consist of willing exchanges of strongly desired (though legally proscribed) goods or services. The crucial point about these situations is that, regardless of whatever victimization judgments outside observers might make, the participants do not see themselves as being directly victimized by the illicit transaction. As a consequence, nobody directly involved in the situation is likely to initiate enforcement of the law by complaining to the police. In the ordinary course of events, the drug-user does not wish to complain about the pusher's illegal drug-selling; the illicit gambler does not feel victimized by the bookie who facilitated his or her betting. In other words, these are characteristically "complainantless crimes." (Schur, 1979, p. 451)

From this perspective, the "victim" may be a victim in some "objective" sense, from someone else's point of view, but does not experience him/herself as a victim in a "subjective" sense, from his/her own point of view. No complaint is made by a person who perceives that they have been victimized by an "illicit" transaction or exchange. In fact, since the so-called victim is a willing participant in the exchange, the transaction is a consensual transaction. In the United States, at the present time, a diverse array of criminal offenses are characterized by this lack of a complainant and by consensual transaction. Among them are adultery, homosexuality, prostitution, pornography, abortion, gambling, drug use and addiction and to a lesser extent, vagrancy, disorderly conduct, and public drunkenness.

But as we have already noted, these crimes have only recently emerged as "victimless crimes," crimes that some contend should not be crimes at all. In Chapter 5 we pointed out how what is criminalized in a particular society changes over time.[2] This is as true of victimless crime as it is of street crime. A critical question then becomes, "Which victimless crimes are presently criminalized (or have been in the past) and which are not (and have not been in the past) and why?" As Bedau has asked:

Why, for example, do we allow persons to gamble with their money, so long as they spend it on some risky ventures (the stock market), but prohibit them if they wish to spend it on others (off track betting, the numbers pool)? Why do we license the sale of some personal services (escort services, massage parlors) and not others ("massage parlors," prostitution)? Why do we allow some demonstrably harmful substances to be sold without prescription and merely tax them (tobacco, alcohol) whereas some others (marijuana, cocaine) are unavailable over the counter at all? (in Schur and Bedau, 1974, pp. 100–101)

Bedau has answered his own questions by saying that the explanation of these apparent contradictions in what is criminalized and what is not has more to do with history than it does with morality; more to do with ideology than logic. In other words, we have not consistently and logically applied a particular morality to determine what victimless crime should or should not be criminalized in American society. Rather, the ongoing historical change and transformation of political and economic institutions, and the ideologies that support and justify them, best explain the changing vicissitudes of criminalization and decriminalization in our society. Skolnick and Dombrink (1978) have referred to this as the "political economy of the societal reaction to deviance." By this they mean that the way a society responds to a particular activity—whether or not this societal reaction criminalizes this activity—is primarily dependent upon the historical development of that society's political and economic institutions and the requirements of their "smooth functioning" at any given time. Along these same lines, Taylor, Walton, and Young (1974, p. 274) have pointed out that we need to begin to understand "the political and economic imperatives that underpin on the one hand the 'lay

[2] See the section "The Historical Development of Street Crime" in chapter 5.

ideologies' and on the other the 'crusades' and initiatives that emerge periodically either to control the amount or level of deviance or else (as in the cases of prohibition, certain homosexual activity, and most recently, certain 'crimes without victims') to remove certain behaviors from the category of 'illegal' behaviors.''

As was pointed out in Chapter 5, drug laws in the United States reflect particular class interests. So too, have laws prohibiting certain victimless crime. Vagrancy laws, for example, first emerged in 14th-century England to help supply labor for landowners. Later on, vagrancy laws were used to control ''undesirable and disruptive elements'' in the industrializing communities of England, the United States, and Canada (see Chambliss, 1964). Only very recently have vagrancy statutes been attacked as unconstitutional and as an unnecessary criminalization of a victimless activity, and been expunged in several states (Reasons and Perdue, 1981).

Another example of the criminalization of what is perhaps an inherently victimless behavior concerns the place of alcoholic drink and drunkenness in U.S. history. Reasons and Perdue have argued that prohibition was definitely ''more than just a cultural victory for the puritans'' in that the criminalization of alcohol was linked intimately to the political and economic interests of a corporate class in charge of industrializing the United States:

> While drunkenness has been increasingly eliminated as a crime, historically it was established to uphold middle-class, rural Protestant puritanical beliefs about drinking. In fact, such interests led to the ''noble experiment'' of prohibition. . . . Not to be ignored is the historical fact that the temperance movement emerged during the post-Civil War period and continued on until the institutionalization of prohibition in 1919. This was a time when the immigrant workers (men, women, and children) were savagely exploited in the urban factory system. The image of the drink-dependent workers seeking escape from toil was hardly comforting to the industrial elite. Thus, it is plausible to argue that prohibition was more than a cultural victory for the ''puritans.'' Rather, it was consistent with corporate industrial interests. (Reasons and Perdue, 1981, p. 338)

The current trend in the United States, however, may be tipped in favor of decriminalizing or legalizing many of the criminal and deviant activities that appear to be victimless. Skolnick and Dombrink have reminded us, for example, that:

> Americans wagered more than $17 billion in 1974—on lotteries, horse racing, bingo, legalized numbers, and casino games—in the more than 40 states that permit one form or another of legal gambling . . . the liquor industry produced a billion gallons of alcoholic beverages in 1976, on which $4.5 billion in taxes was collected by the government. . . . One third of the adult citizens of the United States were able to light up a joint, fearing, in most cases, the maximum penalty of a $100 citation for that activity. . . . Consenting adults in California were able

PANEL 7-1

The Criminalization of Video Games: An Emerging Victimless Crime?

MESQUITE, TEXAS "Insert coin. The evil Gorfian robot empire has attacked. Your assignment is to repel the invasion and launch a counterattack."

So go the instructions for the video game Gorf as they flash repeatedly on the screen at the one-room Aladdin's Castle amusement center in the Town East shopping mall in this Dallas suburb.

Nearby, on a rainy afternoon, adults with bored expressions are meandering slowly through the stores, fumbling for their credit cards to buy shoes and wigs, cheese and books, water beds and designer jeans.

Inside Aladdin's Castle, the pace is quicker. Teen-agers from a nearby high school stare intently at the screens of Gorf, Asteroid Deluxe and Space Fury. To the accompaniment of high-pitched electronic blips and whirs, for 25 cents a try, they repel enemy invaders.

It is a scene that could be found anywhere in the United States—and there are some parents and local officials who believe it adds up to a new version of Trouble in River City. They complain that the video games may serve as a breeding ground for truancy and unhealthy influences that could contribute to the ruination of America's youth.

This week, the U.S. Supreme Court will take up a test case involving Aladdin's Castle that may help decide the future of the growing, and highly lucrative, video-game industry.

The justices will hear arguments on the constitutionality of a Mesquite town ordinance that bars any person under the age of 17 from playing a coin-operated video

or pinball game unless a parent or guardian is present.

Mesquite's law is not unique. A number of other cities and towns across the nation have placed similar restrictions on video-game rooms and pinball parlors. But the 5th U.S. Circuit Court of Appeals in New Orleans ruled a year ago that the Mesquite ordinance violated the constitutional rights of persons under 17 to associate with one another.

High-priced Legal Talent

Mesquite officials appealed that decision to the Supreme Court. Now the video-game industry is employing high-priced legal talent and pulling out all stops to prevent a Supreme Court ruling that might put a crimp in its remarkable growth.

One worried video-game giant, Atari Inc., retained Robert H. Bork, a former U.S. solicitor general and one of the nation's leading constitutional scholars, to file a friend-of-the-court brief that warned of the "obvious financial harm" Atari might suffer if Mesquite's ordinance is upheld.

Years ago, many American cities and towns had similar debates over pool halls. Detractors contended they were a waste of time and provided an unwholesome environment for young persons who gathered in them. It also was said that unsavory adults might use the pool halls to introduce teenagers to alcohol, tobacco and other vices.

"That the keeping of a billiard hall was a harmful tendency is a fact requiring no proof," the Supreme Court declared in

PANEL 7-1 (Continued)

1912 in a case upholding a ban on pool halls by the city of South Pasadena, Calif.

Almost seven decades later, some officials and citizens in Mesquite are contending that the video-game rooms are similarly harmful.

"Breeding Ground"

"It's not that the machines themselves have any inherent evil," said the Rev. Ronnie Yarber, pastor of the Gross Road Baptist Church. "But they're a breeding ground for other things that our cities do not need—drug traffic and the abuse of alcohol among teen-agers or even pre-teens."

"It's the lure of these things," City Councilman Bill Blackwood complained. "I've seen kids as early as 6:30 in the morning, pumping all their lunch money into these machines."

Mesquite's law, passed in 1973, applies to all "coin-operated amusement machines."

Elland Archer, the Mesquite city attorney who drafted the law eight years ago and is defending it before the Supreme Court, said the ordinance was enacted because police officials believed that "these places were badly in need of regulation."

"We have documented cases of truancy," Archer said. "The police department said there had been numerous incidents of drug transfers, and that some pushers used these places to ply their trade. We had many, many parents come in and tell the City Council that children were spending lunch money on these games."

Despite the claims about drug use and/or sales in video-game rooms, there is little evidence available about such activity.

Although Mesquite police and city officials—and some citizens—are upset about the video-game rooms, the city is hardly in an uproar. At no time, either before or after the 1973 ordinance was passed, has an organized group been formed to try to limit the spread of video games.

R-rated Movies

In contrast, noted Mark Manroe, editor of the Mesquite Daily News, a coalition of religious and civic leaders was quickly formed last year to fight the introduction of R-rated movies on cable television in Mesquite. Mesquite voters nevertheless decided to permit the movies. "Compared to the cable-TV fight, the video games just aren't a big deal," Manroe said.

The video game store at the Town East shopping center is one of 250 Aladdin's Castle centers across the United States—almost all of them located in large, enclosed regional shopping malls.

Aladdin's is owned by Bally Manufacturing Corp., which reported revenues of $38.3 million from Aladdin in 1980. Glenn Seidenfeld, a Bally vice president, expects a "substantial increase" this year. Seidenfeld estimated the single, one-room outlet in Mesquite earns well over $100,000 a year.

Aladdin's Castle itself is merely a tiny part of what has become a huge industry.

The Amusement and Music Operators Association told the Supreme Court recently that there are now as many as a million coin-operated amusement games and jukeboxes in 300,000 stores and other public facilities in the United States.

Estimates of the amount of money Americans spend on video games each

PANEL 7-1 (Continued)

year range from $3 billion to $9 billion. Industry officials believe that anywhere from 50 percent to 75 percent of their customers are 18 or younger.

Aladdin's Castle filed suit against Mesquite in 1977, seeking the right to operate at the shopping center without interference.

"Criminal Elements"

The company challenged two different parts of the Mesquite ordinance: the requirement that persons under 17 be accompanied by an adult, and a separate provision requiring Mesquite police to investigate possible "connections with criminal elements" before a license for any amusement center is granted.

Two lower federal courts have held that the law on "criminal elements" is so vaguely worded as to be unconstitutional. And although U.S. District Judge William M. Taylor originally upheld Mesquite's age restriction, the federal appeals court in New Orleans concluded last year that this was unconstitutional, too.

Source: Jim Mann, "Trouble with a 'V' for Video Games," Los Angeles Times, *reprinted in the* Des Moines Register and Tribune, *November 14, 1981, pp. 6a and 6b.*

to commit sexual acts that previously were prohibited by criminal law. . . . Over 800,000 legal abortions were reported performed in 1975. . . . (Skolnick and Dombrink, 1978, p. 193)

But historically, changing ideological, social, political and economic conditions not only meant that "old" victimless crimes disappeared, that is, were decriminalized or legalized, but that other "new" crimes without victims may have emerged. Panel 7-1 illustrates how this criminalizing process might begin.

THE EXTENT AND STATUS OF VICTIMLESS CRIMES

In Chapter 4, we pointed out the many obstacles involved in compiling accurate crime statistics. Measuring crime is an even more difficult proposition when it comes to constructing victimless crime rates. By definition, these crimes often involve no victim and thus, no complainant. In fact, the victims are normally "willing victims," they are, in some sense desirous of participating in their "criminal" activity. It is unreasonable, therefore, to expect these willing victims to incriminate themselves and report the full, or even partial, extent of their criminal activity to any public law enforcement agency.

There are, however, "unofficial" data available which indicate that the following victimless crimes are quite pervasive in American society.

Sex Crimes: Adultery, Homosexuality, Prostitution, and Pornography

Many states still have statutes "on the books" that prohibit extramarital and "abnormal" sexual intercourse (or other sexual acts) between consenting men and women. Kinsey's classic studies of American sexual behavior (see Kinsey, Pomeroy, and Martin, 1949) have made various estimates of the degree to which Americans actually participate in these legally proscribed activities; at one point suggesting that as much as 95 percent of the American adult population is potentially criminal in regard to these kinds of statutes.

Consensual adult homosexuality has also remained criminal to varying degrees in many states and localities. The limited data available suggest that homosexual activity may be much more widespread than is commonly thought to be the case:

> Kinsey . . . found that about 10% of all males in the United States had "extensive" homosexual experience, although only 4% had an extensive commitment to homosexuality as an adult. Kinsey's studies may have somewhat underestimated the incidence of male homosexuality. It is difficult to say. Female homosexual activity is even harder to estimate than male. At any rate, Kinsey . . . found that 5% of married women had had homosexual experiences to the point of orgasm with another woman. (from Roberts, 1978, p. 202)

There is also evidence that homosexual marriage is currently on the increase. Although "the law is very hazy about the legality of such arrangements" (Roberts, 1978, p. 209), it can be expected to continue to be criminalized in various ways in the foreseeable future.

Indications are that both prostitution and pornography capture the attention and dollars of many Americans every year. In regard to prostitution, Kadish has written:

> Prostitution has endured in all civilizations; indeed few institutions have proven as hardy. The inevitable conditions of social life unfailingly produce the supply to meet the ever-present demand . . . . (Kadish, 1971, p. 60)

He goes on to add that "it has been estimated that over two-thirds of white males alone will have experience with prostitutes during their lives . . ." (Kadish, 1971, p. 60). At a very minimum, it appears as though prostitution and pornography taken together represent a $2 billion annual income for organized crime in the United States (Eitzen, 1980). Other estimates claim that pornography alone is as much as a $5 billion-a-year industry (Graham, 1981).

Abortion

At the time of this writing, efforts are still under way in the U.S. Congress to criminalize those abortions that were made legal by a 1973 U.S. Supreme Court decision. Many of these recent efforts have centered around amending the U.S.

A highly charged contemporary issue is whether women have the right to terminate a pregnancy or not. For some this is a right while for others it is a crime.

Constitution with an anti-abortion amendment of one sort or another or with the "Human Life Amendment." Even the historic 1973 decision of the high court, however, did not represent anything close to a full and complete decriminalization or legalization of abortion. The ruling only stated that a woman could, during the first "trimester" of her pregnancy, abort the fetus and that no state could infringe on this right. States have remained relatively free to regulate abortion procedures in the second trimester of pregnancy and to prohibit, with the criminal law, abortion during the third trimester (provided the woman's life is not endangered by the full-term pregnancy).

This partial decriminalization of abortion has not, however, been uniformly applied to all women. In June 1980, the U.S. Supreme Court introduced a class bias into the decriminalization of abortion that discriminates against poor women. Reasons and Perdue explain this legal ruling:

On the last day of June 1980, the United States Supreme Court declared that federal Medicaid funds for the poor need not be used to pay for abortions if such be the will of Congress. At present, highly restrictive criteria must be met. Federal Medicaid abortion law stipulates that federal money can be used for abortions only if (1) the mother's life would be endangered if the fetus were carried to term, (2) the pregnancy resulted from rape or incest promptly reported to a law enforcement agency, or (3) two physicians certify that the continuation of the pregnancy would produce severe and long-lasting physical health damage to the mother. . . . (Reasons and Perdue, 1981, p. 646)

Thus, poor women who do not meet these eligibility criteria, but still choose to have an abortion, often must turn to more affordable illegal and unsafe operations. There are, of course, no reliable figures available on the number of illegal abortions performed each year; estimates have, in fact, ranged all the way from 100,000 to well over 1 million. It is safe to continue to assume, nonetheless, that the demand for abortions—both legal and illegal—by both married and unmarried women "is urgent and widespread" (Kadish, 1971, p. 61).

Gambling

Americans probably engage in illicit gambling more often than they participate in any other illegal activity. Panel 7-2 documents the pervasiveness of this phenomenon in general and the ubiquity of illegal sports gambling in particular in American society.[3]

Drug Use and Addiction

In many ways, American society is a "drugged society"—drugged with both legal and illegal substances. The illegal substances purchased and consumed are many and varied: marijuana, cocaine, amphetamines, barbiturates, hallucinogens, heroin, and other narcotics. The number of persons and dollars involved in the use of just one of these drugs—heroin—gives one a sense of the extent of illegal drug use and in this case, the extent of addiction to illegal drugs, in the United States. According to Block and Chambliss:

> The average heroin addict in the United States in the early 1970s was spending $30,000 a year on heroin. . . . Although this is a very high figure, it is noteworthy that it is an average based upon the fact that not all heroin addicts are "street people." Many addicts are wealthy professional and business people who no doubt pay considerably higher prices for their "shit" than do the people in the ghettos and the slums.
>   Accepting, for the sake of argument, this average expenditure per addict enables us to also estimate the gross volume of business from heroin. If, as most experts agree, there are at least one million addicts in the United States, then this means that the annual gross sale of heroin in the United States today exceeds $30 billion. . . . (Block and Chambliss, 1981, p. 33)

[3]The pervasiveness of illegal gambling in the United States often takes curious twists. In July of 1981, for example, the Internal Revenue Service reported that "bookies" in Tennessee had paid federal income tax on over $1 million worth of bets in the previous year. Even though Tennessee state law prohibits all gambling, the IRS record shows that the state ranks fifth in the nation in terms of the amount of income generated by professional gamblers (Associated Press, July 1, 1981).

GAMBLING ON SPORTS COMES OUT OF THE CLOSET

It invoked memories of 1951, when college basketball provided the focal point for New York's gambling underworld. Then, star players from the City College of New York were found to have accepted bribes for shaving points in a 1950 tournament.

Thirty years later, James Sweeney, playmaker and captain of the 1978–79 Boston College basketball team, an academic all-American and nominee for a Rhodes Scholarship, sat before a federal jury in New York and admitted that he should have informed his coach of an alleged point-shaving scheme, but he was afraid that "the bettors would get to me first."

Sweeney, who testified Nov. 3, is a government witness in the Boston College case, not one of the five men indicted for conspiring to manipulate the scores of Boston College games so that a syndicate of bettors could profit. However, Richard Kuhn, a former teammate of Sweeney's, is one of the five. If convicted, Kuhn could face a 20-year prison term.

Those who defend Kuhn's position contend that American society has increasingly accepted the inevitability of gambling. Indeed, gambling on sports has come out of the closet. Betting lines and gambling columns appear almost daily in most major American newspapers. Studies indicate that as many as eight out of every 10 adult Americans gamble. One-fourth of those bet regularly on organized athletic contests. While most gamblers wager only occasionally for recreation and stake small amounts of money, for some, gambling is a compulsion.

Fyodor Dostoyevsky, the Russian novelist who was a compulsive gambler, wrote in 1866: "The main point is the game itself. . . . On my oath, it is not greed for money, despite the fact that I need money badly."

Studies support his view. They indicate that, contrary to popular belief, gambling activity increases with income level. Nonetheless, evidence of corruption in sports suggest that money, more often than the game itself, motivates gamblers.

Perhaps the most celebrated incident of all was the 1919 "Black Sox" scandal, in which eight members of the Chicago White Sox baseball team were accused of conspiring to throw World Series games. They were later acquitted of the charges, but banned from baseball nonetheless.

Baseball still is not immune from gambling involvement, though ever since the 1919 scandal, punishments for even the slightest association with gambling have been severe. Pitcher Dennis McLain, then of the Detroit Tigers, was suspended for half of the 1970 season for his involvement with a Michigan bookmaking operation.

Clete Boyer, while a player with the Atlanta Braves, was fined $1,000 in 1968 by Baseball Commissioner Bowie Kuhn for having bet on football games three years earlier. And Willie Mays was forced to dissociate himself from the New York Mets organization by Kuhn in 1979 for promoting a legal casino operation.

Kuhn's action against Mays indicates the hypocrisy of athletic officialdom, which often denies that games are the objects of big-time betting. Simply, millions of Americans love to bet, especially on their favorite teams. For most, its allure is the game itself. For others, the greed for money steals the game out of the sport.

Source: Joseph Kessler, "Gambling on Sports Comes out of the Closet," Editorial Research Reports, reprinted in the Des Moines Register and Tribune, *November 14, 1981, p. 5a.*

Those arrested for vagrancy are typically the unemployed, poor, and minorities.

Vagrancy, Disorderly Conduct, and Public Drunkenness[4]

The "offense" of vagrancy usually includes one or some combination of the following: "living in idleness without employment and having no visible means of support; roaming, wandering, or loitering; begging; being a common prostitute, drunkard, or gambler; and sleeping outdoors or in a residential building without permission" (Kadish, 1971, p. 66). Since their historical origin in feudal Europe, vagrancy laws have been put to a variety of uses (see Chambliss, 1964). "Today, they are widely and regularly used by police as a basis for arresting, searching, questioning, or detaining persons (who otherwise could not legally be subjected to such interventions) because of suspicion that they have committed or may commit a crime or for other police purposes, including clearing the streets of undesirables, harassing persons believed to be engaged in crime, and investigating uncleared offenses" (Kadish, 1971, pp. 66–67).

Both vagrancy laws and laws against "disorderly conduct" have been, and currently are, one of the most important and frequently used tools for those charged with policing American cities. Because the penalties for these offenses

---

[4]These crimes may, under certain conditions, be more likely than other victimless crimes to have a victim other than the perpetrator (the vagrant, the drunk, etc.) him/herself.

are generally minor (they are usually simple misdemeanors) and because those arrested are normally unemployed, poor, minorities, or marginal members of the working class, the use and abuse of these statutes by the police has not generally been subject to either judicial review or public criticism.

In most U.S. urban areas, arrests for disorderly conduct exceed the number of arrests for every other crime except public drunkenness. More than any other group of persons, "drunks" and "winos" who populate city streets and alleys are processed each day by the American criminal justice system. As many as 35 to 40 percent of all arrests made by the police are for public drunkenness. Taken together, vagrancy, disorderly conduct, and public drunkenness probably constitute as much as 60 to 80 percent of all arrests and certainly occupy a large proportion of police attention, time, and resources.

THE IDEOLOGY OF VICTIMLESS CRIMES

As alluded to earlier, there has never been any generalized agreement regarding whether or not certain crimes are best understood as "victimless crimes." This controversy has extended itself to include not just philosophers, sociologists, and criminologists but politicians, policy makers, and the public as well. In this section we will examine the range of opinion concerning "crimes without victims" as it is expressed in each of the three dominant sociological perspectives on crime: traditional, interactionist, and radical. In sum, it is apparent that the very idea of victimless crime is problematic.

The Traditional Sociological View

This perspective is not usually prepared to concede to the victimless nature of most crimes that have been so identified earlier in this chapter. Here the prostitute, the addict, the gambler are all seen as legitimate criminals who have as their primary victim "society."

From this point of view, all cultures consider some behaviors to be inherently deviant. In modern societies, these cultural values are codified in the criminal law which, in turn, is used to ban, or at least significantly inhibit, these "threatening activities and behaviors." All crime is perceived as a threat to the social order and the values that support it; crime is not simply a threat to individuals as potential or actual victims.

Because of this, the vice squad is probably going about the right work. In fact, the existence of the vice squad is not the issue at all; the primary issue or difficulty is making it more efficient. "Control of vice is an especially delicate political problem because . . . vital social values that the community insists its members accept in outward practice and at least give lip service to are at stake—the case of children, including the unborn as well as the underaged dependent against what cultural norms deem threats to their well-being (abortion, drugs, and pornography); and the integrity of the family unit, as opposed to individual sexual opportunity, gambling, prostitution . . ." (Rhodes, 1977, pp. 192–193).

Since criminal law prohibiting vice reflects the established social and cultural values in American society, any behavior that challenges the law in this regard also challenges these societal values and in this way begins to "victimize" society. For this reason, any attempt to tamper with these laws and decriminalize or legalize any of the so-called victimless crimes will, from this perspective, be met with considerable, if not insurmountable, resistance. And, it may not matter how reasonable or rational the case for decriminalization or legalization is.

Arguments that police are wasting valuable time and resources closing down sex shops, arresting prostitutes, and pinching numbers runners fall on deaf ears. Protests that vice corrupts police and courts and leads to violation of civil liberties and hostility from cultural minority groups are to little avail. . . .
. . . Frequently, it makes little difference that the forbidden behaviors are regularly indulged in, or that one social class proscribes for another less powerful class. Even when prestigious commissions accumulate evidence that no one suffers from a victimless crime to a degree that can be ameliorated by invoking a criminal sanction, recommendations based on decriminalization for reasons of social harmlessness are met, a priori, with a studied rejection. Such was the attitude of the White House toward the recommendations from both the *Report of the Commission on Obscenity and Pornography,* . . . commissioned by President Nixon, and the *Report of the National Commission on Marihuana and Drug Abuse* . . . [Indeed, former Attorney General John Mitchell rejected any recommendation to "legalize marijuana" even prior to the final report of the National Commission on Marihuana, whose members were appointed by President Nixon.] (Rhodes, 1977, p. 192)

There is a problem with using vice laws to ensure that society is not victimized, however. A vigorous enforcement effort designed to "clean the streets" of this sort of "criminal" activity may not benefit or protect the entire society but rather may only serve the interests of a relatively small political elite. Panel 7-3 illustrates how this "class bias" may have recently had its impact—legitimating the city administration—in New York City.

The Interactionist-Liberal/Libertarian Perspective

Representatives of this perspective, more than any of the others, have made the case for the reality of victimless crime. From this vantage point, abortion, addiction, adultery, drunkenness, gambling, homosexuality, pornography, prostitution, and vagrancy do not victimize anyone or anything. There is no victim and, therefore, there is no crime. In fact, our society suffers from overcriminalization. We should begin to decriminalize most, if not all, of those victimless activities that are now against the law. Or, as Kadish (1971, p. 60) has put it, "Only the judgment that the use of the criminal law for verbal vindication of our morals is more important than its use to protect life and property can support the preservation of these laws as they are." Furthermore, any act that is forbidden by criminal law but does not victimize anyone or produce any identifiable individual or social

PANEL 7-3

The Ideology of Enforcing Vice Laws: Who Benefits?

Assessing a change he insisted did not begin until he started speaking out on the matter, Mayor Koch last week congratulated New York judges for their tougher attitude on crime. "This is not an open city," he said, promising that the stern measures, including arrests for such "quality-of-life" offenses as prostitution, gambling and low-level drug trafficking, would continue.

Arrests there certainly have been. Data gathered by the state Office of Court Administration show that of the 67,365 cases filed in Criminal Court last year, 21,357 involved the kinds of crimes to which Mr. Koch referred.

But while these misdemeanors are punishable by up to a year in jail and a $1,000 fine, it is hard to find a judge on Centre Street who doesn't exhibit a strong aversion to such sentences. "We do not treat these offenses with the same degree of gravity as we do others because they are not so offensive as to demand our time," said one, who, like many on the bench, was reluctant to be quoted by name for fear it might compromise him when one of these cases comes before him.

Other statistics drive home the point:

- Of the 2,311 gambling convictions last year, 1,892 resulted in non-jail sentences (including probation, conditional and unconditional discharge or fine), 259 in sentences of "time served" (the time a suspect is detained between arrest and arraignment, generally about 23 hours) and only 160 in longer jail terms.
- Of the 6,519 convictions for low-grade narcotics offenses, including possessing a hypodermic needle and possessing or selling marijuana, 4,550 resulted in non-jail sentences, 974 in time served and 995 in longer jail terms.
- Of the 9,136 prostitution convictions, 4,559 resulted in non-jail sentences, 4,016 in time served and 561 in longer jail terms.

Why, given sentences like these and the city's limited prosecutorial resources, are persons arrested for such crimes in the first place?

harm is an act that, according to Jeffrey Reiman, is prohibited by an "unconstitutional" statute. He has said that:

it seems reasonable that the Supreme Court should strike down as unconstitutional any criminal law that prohibits an act that does not cause demonstrable harm, with the burden of proof lying with the state to demonstrate the palpable harm the law seeks to prevent.

Whether as a legislative or a judicial criterion, however, this principle would undoubtedly rid our law of the excrescences of our puritan moralism. It would bring our law more in line with a realistic view of what is harmful, and it

PANEL 7-3 (Continued)

One widely discussed reason is that nearly every component of the criminal justice system seems to benefit from the frequent roundup of gamblers, prostitutes and drug dealers: police officers, who can earn overtime between arrest and arraignment; district attorneys, whose conviction rates and caseloads, important in determining budgets, are inflated; judges, who can swiftly clear these cases from their calendars, and, of course, private defense attorneys who specialize in such cases.

"It enables the Police Department, the Mayor and the District Attorney to say that they are doing everything in their power to improve the quality of life in New York city, and that it is only because of judges like Erdmann that their effort goes for naught," said Judge Martin Erdmann.

Even if they gave lengthier jail terms, some judges say, defense lawyers would simply demand trials, bringing the entire system to a halt. After all, last year there were 12,464 arrests for prostitution alone. Furthermore, some defend sentences of "time served" as inherently more honest than conditional discharges. In theory,

one so sentenced must follow certain rules or prosecutors can restore the case to the calendar for trial. In practice, this seldom occurs.

Levying fines is also viewed by some on the bench as putting them in the position of becoming, as one put it, "the ultimate pimp." The assumption is that if they do indeed pay the fine, and often they do not, prostitutes simply earn the money by "turning more tricks."

While some say the answer is to decriminalize these offenses, others contend it lies in a more coordinated criminal justice system. Much could be gained, they say, if the courts, the prosecutors and the police all would adopt similar priorities. Others, though, lean toward the tougher approach Mr. Koch has repeatedly advocated. "I'm beginning to question the wisdom of the courts exercising triage in these situations," said Judge Jeffrey M. Atlas. After a year and a half on the bench, Judge Atlas said he has become exasperated with defendants who repeatedly appear before him on the same charges, and he has developed, he said, a "conform or be punished" attitude toward them.

Source: E. R. Shipp, "Quality-of-Life Offenses: City Makes a Big Issue of Little Crimes," New York Times, August 30, 1981, p. 6e.

would eliminate the forced induction into criminality of the individuals—mainly those of the lower class—who get arrested for "victimless crimes." (Reiman, 1979, pp. 197–198)

It should be pointed out that decriminalization does not mean that the acts decriminalized are not social problems. It does, however, insist that any efforts aimed at ameliorating perceived social problems like abortion, addiction, gambling, prostitution, and the like, not employ the criminal law and its sanctions. This is seen as a potently counter-productive step, since as Schur has said, "The basic idea behind decriminalization is, quite simply, reducing the amplification or

[handwritten margin note: If we decriminalize we reduce secondary deviance]

secondary expansion of various deviance problems'' (Schur, 1979, pp. 460–461). In other words, the criminalization of this deviance typically exacerbates the deviance and the end product is more, not less, deviant activity. The organized societal reaction to deviant behavior that the criminal law and criminal justice system represents and embodies can create the phenomenon of secondary deviance, or more specifically in this case, ''secondary crime.''[5]

In this regard, Reiman (1979) has pointed out how the purposeful design of an inefficient and failing criminal justice system (failing in terms of its official stated purpose and ideology of protecting society, distributing justice, and reducing and preventing crime) would necessarily include a number of ''irrational laws'' that would prohibit victimless acts and then not aid in the actual prevention of these same acts. According to Reiman, these laws only serve to make ''criminals'' out of many people who do not regard their activity as such. But more importantly, it increases ''their need to engage in secondary crime.'' Since addiction is illegal, organized crime can inflate and set the ''market price'' of narcotics and the addict is compelled to steal to support his or her habit. Criminalizing addiction produces theft (a more serious offense?). Since prostitution is illegal and the prostitute cannot rely on police protection, she must use the services of a pimp—thus, a new form of criminality is thus created. In sum, ''secondary crime'' refers here to the fact that the criminalization of victimless crime generates yet more crime.

[handwritten margin note: Secondary crime]

In recent years, many states have moved significantly in the direction of decriminalization. Schur (1979) has summarized some of the changes: By the late 1970s at least 10 states, California and New York among them, had decriminalized the possession of small amounts of marijuana for personal use. These states began substituting fines for the previously used probation and jail sentences. In Ann Arbor, Michigan, possession of under 1 ounce of marijuana became a ''crime'' similar to a parking or traffic violation and was handled with a citation or ticket.

[handwritten margin note: decriminalization in certain states]

Legal abortions are now available in many states, again including New York. (Of course, as mentioned earlier, this decriminalization has been ''class-biased'' in that the use of federal funds for abortions for poor women has been banned unless very restrictive eligibility criteria are met.) Beginning in Illinois in 1962, some states have removed the criminal sanction for homosexual acts between consenting adults.[6] Gambling has been increasingly legalized in the past decade as state and local governments experiencing budgetary problems and ''fiscal crisis'' have entered into competition with illegal gambling enterprises for what they

---

[5] See Chapter 2. This concept, ''secondary crime,'' will be further elaborated upon later in this chapter.

[6] It is not clear whether the decriminalization of homosexuality has continued to occur since the 1960s and early 1970s or has been reversed by a growing ''anti-gay backlash'' in the United States. Schur (1979) has argued that the overall trend in the direction of decriminalization is probably continuing, ''the ongoing struggle over gay rights continues to generate specific political controversies in various localities which tend to exhibit highly fluctuating outcomes. For example, whereas the 1977 vote overturning a gay rights ordinance in Miami was widely viewed as a major setback for gay liberation, the November 1978 repudiation by the California electorate of an initiative that would have permitted the firing of homosexual public school teachers in that state represented a considerable victory. Despite some occasional indications nationally of an anti-gay backlash, the overall trend still seems to be in the direction of decriminalization and further expansion of the rights of homosexuals . . .'' (Schur, 1979, p. 458).

perceive to be an extremely lucrative business.[7] State- and city-sponsored casinos and state- and city-run lotteries and off-track betting operations have become numerous. Nevada has experimented with legalized prostitution. Some cities have established "adult zones" where "porn shops," "triple XXX theaters," and "massage parlors and escort services" can operate free of local law enforcement interference.

The victimless "crime" that has most resisted this trend toward decriminalization is addiction. Possession, use, manufacture, and sale of heroin in the United States remains as illegal and criminal, if not more so, than it was when it was criminalized by the Harrison Act in 1914. But

> everyday in which we keep the acquisition of heroin a crime, we are using the law to protect the high profits of heroin black marketeers, and we are creating a situation in which large numbers of individuals are virtually physically compelled to commit theft. Since there is little evidence that heroin is dangerous beyond the fact of addiction itself, there can be little doubt that our present "cure" for narcotics use is more criminal (and criminogenic) than the narcotics themselves. (Reiman, 1979, p. 193)

Indeed, the resistance to the decriminalization of heroin is probably related to "the high profits of heroin black marketeers." As the chapter on organized crime will point out, illicit and illegal industries in the United States (like the heroin industry) are so vast and so intimately linked to the licit and legal economy that the decriminalization of their criminalized goods and services would have a profound impact on the stability of the U.S. economy—and by implication, the entire society. Nonetheless, proponents of decriminalization argue that when addicts cannot obtain heroin legally, they obtain it illegally and "since those who sell it illegally have a captive market, they will charge high prices to make their own risks worthwhile" (Reiman, 1979, p. 193). Without a legal alternative source of heroin, addicts must often turn to more street crime to pay the inflated prices set by the monopolistic and illegal heroin industry.

Several proposals have been made concerning the most appropriate decriminalization of heroin in the United States. Most revolve around the treatment of addiction as a medical problem and the controlled legalization of the production and sale of heroin. Some have suggested following the British system of providing regulated dosages of heroin to officially registered addicts. Some have argued that the drug be sold by prescription in pharmacies (Morris and Hawkins, 1970). Still others have suggested that heroin be sold at a low and state-regulated price—labeled in regard to contents, recommended dosage, and addictive potential—without prescription, to anyone of "legal age" (Baridon, 1976).

In sum, the interactionist perspective leads to the liberal/libertarian position that certain crimes are without question victimless and should, therefore, be

---

[7] The way in which legal gambling operations have begun competing with illegal gambling operations to generate revenue that can be used to help resolve "the fiscal crisis of the state" will be dealt with in more detail in Chapter 8.

decriminalized or made legal. As Edwin Schur has eloquently made his case for decriminalization below, we are reminded that the issue of decriminalization is not purely a moral one; nor does it involve a decision to "allow" or "not allow" particular activities or behaviors. Abortion, addiction, adultery, drunkenness, gambling, homosexuality, pornography, prostitution, and vagrancy will continue to thrive whether they are made legal or illegal. The real issue is the development of a rational social policy that effectively reduces real individual and social harm:

> One might believe, for example, that "drug addiction is immoral" or at least highly undesirable and, nonetheless, also conclude that on balance and in actual operation restrictive narcotics laws make a bad situation worse rather than better. If the basic concern is to develop policies that work to minimize the overall social harm associated with a given problem, then using the criminal law merely to express moral disapproval when the actual result of such use will be an exacerbation of the disapproved conditions readily becomes counter-productive. Furthermore, and this is another point that is sometimes obscured in the heat of debate, the realistic choice facing policymakers and, indirectly, the electorate that mandates their actions is usually not one of either "allow-ing" or "not allowing" the offending behavior. Opponents of decriminalization sometimes insist that "we cannot allow" such and such a deviating activity, glossing over the fact that such activity will in fact persist if not thrive under criminalization as well as decriminalization. To cite a major example, despite the strong feelings and moral dilemmas relating to abortion, large numbers of women will take actions to terminate their pregnancies whether this behavior is legal or not. The real policy choice is not between "legalizing" the practice and "refusing to permit it." It is between enabling women to have safe and compe-tent pregnancy terminations or driving them to dangerous attempts at self-induced abortion or the almost equally serious risks involved at the hands of many illegal practitioners. (Schur, 1979, p. 460)

The Radical Approach

This approach focuses on victimless crime as an economic and political phenome-non. In a significant way, victimless crime is a myth; there is indeed a crime and a victim. But the crime is not that of the addict or the prostitute. They are not the criminals; they are the crimes' victims, the ones suffering the political and eco-nomic exploitation and criminal acts of both the state, through selective and class-biased law enforcement and organized crime, through the provision of illegal goods and services. Also, from this perspective, so-called victimless crime in-volves "the exploitation of the weakness of vulnerable people." For example, "in the case of gambling, [it] often results in economic loss and personal dislocations of substantial proportions" and "the major physical and emotional hardships imposed by narcotics addiction raise even more serious evils" (Kadish, 1971, p. 63).

Victimless crimes victimize the lower classes in another way as well. Their behavior is, in effect, criminalized by the creation and application of vice laws that police their ''private lives.'' This represents a profound extension of the mechanisms of social control in capitalist-industrial societies that did not exist in earlier preindustrial societies (see Parks, 1976). For radical criminology, the creation and selective enforcement of vice laws are thus singled out as a vehicle through which societal elites are able to control the activities of the underclasses (Mankoff, 1976).

A ''radical'' perspective on victimless crime differs from a ''liberal'' view not only in regard to its political understanding. Philosophically as well, the approaches are quite distinct. A radical perspective is prone to define harm as any and all suffering, independent of whether or not the person has freely chosen to undertake the activity he or she is involved in (a prime consideration in the interactionists' liberal analysis of victimless crime). So too, a radical view might extend this conception of harm to the entire community: any and all acts that limit individuals' virtue or ability to serve their society may be seen as harmful (Reiman, 1979). But most importantly, ''an illiberal conception of harm might allow an individual or group to hold an action harmful because, for example, it would thwart desires that people would feel if they were truly rational or truly human'' (Reiman, 1979, p. 56). Victimless crime is harmful in this regard since those exploiting the vulnerable, such as the addict, the prostitute, the gambler, are thwarting the human potential of these members of the lower, dispossessed classes, even though their victims may be ''willing victims.''

As outlined in Chapter 2, the radical theory of street crime can be applied to the problem of victimless crime. As with street crime, the so-called criminal here (who is really a victim)—the addict, the prostitute, and so on—has been made surplus to the modes of production and distribution in an advanced capitalist society. Reiman applies this radical theory to victimless crime: ''Prostitution is the incarnation of the degradation of the modern citizen as producer, while addiction captures his degradation as unfree producer and ultimately as consumer'' (Reiman, 1979, p. 66). Left without alternatives, ''redundant'' and ''excluded'' members of a society may turn to addiction and prostitution.

The criminalization of victimless crimes actually sets the stage for the illegal sale of sex, drugs, and money by organized criminal operations to certain members of the surplus population. In this way, it can be seen that victimless and organized crime are significantly interrelated. The sale of these commodities is particularly exploitive in that illegality, scarcity, the provision of special skills and complex organization, and a growing surplus population of potential consumers combine to insure high prices and profit margins:

Illegality provides strong economic incentives for illicit trafficking in the proscribed goods and services, for taking the risks involved in being part of such a black market. It is this illegality and the attendant risk for the illicit operators that, given persisting strong demand, pushes up prices and profits . . . in the case of drugs, most distinterested observers are convinced that such a profitable illicit enterprise could not easily prevail in competition with legal provision at cost of the currently illegal goods or services . . . where the goods wanted are or become reasonably scarce (e.g., heroin) or where the services desired involve special skills (abortion) or complex organization (large-scale gambling), the stage is set for a thriving illicit market. (Schur, 1979, p. 454)

From this perspective, then, victimless crime is rooted in organized crime. Only the elimination or reduction of organized criminal industries and activities will significantly control or prevent victimless crime.

Nevertheless, the present economic, physical, and emotional victimization of the poor and minorities by organized crime, and the selective law enforcement that accompanies it, reinforces the political and economic inequalities typical of a class society like the United States. "In short, what often happens under victimless crime laws is that those deviators whom many observers would see as already having been most victimized socially are selected out for further victimization through the law" (Schur, 1979, p. 455).

In terms of direct economic exploitation, for example, it is apparent that when heroin is illegal, the ability to pay becomes a primary determinant of the addict's activities. The "affluent addict" need not resort to the capital-producing street crime of the "ghetto addict" and thus may keep his or her victimless crime hidden. Another example that illustrates the class bias perpetuated by victimless crime is abortion. Middle- and upper-class women can afford to pay for safe and competent abortions, whereas poor, black and brown women run the risks of injury and death that often are associated with illegal abortions performed by "unskilled and unscrupulous practitioners" (Schur, 1979).

This very direct exploitation of the underclasses is further institutionalized by a class-biased law enforcement effort. Indeed, the police have generally come to regard addiction, prostitution, and numbers-running as lower-class phenomena, ignoring their frequent occurrence in "respectable" society:

police focus on the most publicly visible and seemingly most offensive manifestations of the proscribed behavior. Faced with an untenable and overwhelming enforcement task in areas where both the statutory provisions and the immediate situations afford wide discretion in deciding which particular instances will be selected-out for treatment as "offenses," the police necessarily establish working priorities. Here . . . we see operating indirectly the role of differential power resources in shaping individual deviant careers, for the better-off deviators have a much stronger chance of shielding themselves from police interference. In the case of drug-law enforcement, for example, the main thrust of policing activity has been felt by the poverty-stricken "street addicts," who frequently are driven to "pushing" as well as other money-producing crime to finance their habit. Both the more fortunately situated drug-users (physician-addicts, college students, etc.) and the remote (and usually not-addicted) drug distributors have usually maintained relative immunity from interference. Similarly, enforcement activity is routinely directed against street-walkers rather than the relatively more affluent "call girls," against "numbers" operators rather than upper-class gamblers. . . . (Schur, 1979, p. 455)

THE MEDICALIZATION OF CRIME AND DEVIANCE

Sociologists Peter Conrad and Joseph Schneider (1980) have pointed out that decriminalization does not necessarily include the decreasing use of class-biased social control mechanisms in American society. Rather, decriminalization may more often entail a shift in the locus of this control, from criminal justice to medicine, for example. The contention here is that if an act is decriminalized but retains its deviant character and definition in society, then it is extremely likely that the responsibility for its control will shift from criminal justice institutions to medical institutions. To the extent that other major political, economic, or social changes do not occur, decriminalization, it is argued, will only lead to an increasing understanding and treatment of crime and deviance as medical problems (Conrad, 1980).

In fact, it is the medicalization of certain crimes, such as public drunkenness, that actually allows for their decriminalization. This is the case since medicalization permits the decriminalization of behaviors that can still be defined as deviant, that is, as sick, and thus do not become "socially vindicated" or "approved," while simultaneously providing an alternative form of social control, that is, medicine and medical institutions. While medicalization speeds decriminalization, the bureaucratization of American health care facilitates yet more medicalization. Although it is true that "bureaucratic organizations reduce medical professional power, the institutional structure of the hospital is better suited to function as an agent of social control than the singular office practice" (Conrad, 1980, p. 200).

The decriminalization of alcohol use and public drunkenness illustrates this process of medicalization. During the industrialization of Europe and the United States (the 18th and 19th centuries), alcoholic drink, then generally believed (at least by the emerging bourgeois class) to be a primary cause for crime, disorder, and public riots, was, for the first time, criminalized. Ironically, the crime of public drunkenness was unknown until the emerging market economy encouraged the commercial sale of alcohol. When this occurred, drinking was torn from communal and family-oriented (usually mealtime) use. Drinking was no longer primarily for the purpose of creating and sustaining community stability and solidarity but now became an expression of the private individual attempting to escape the alienation of industrial labor and life.

The medicalization of drunkenness first appeared with the rise to prominence of "the disease model of alcoholism." But this did not transpire until alcohol use in general was, in fact, decriminalized—until the repeal of prohibition in the United States (Schneider, 1978). The progressive decriminalization of public drunkenness has followed on the heels of the decriminalization of alcohol use, reaching its pinnacle in the 1960s and 1970s. In 1950, only 4.7 percent of the entire in- and out-patient mental health institution population in the United States was reported to be suffering "alcohol or drug psychoses" of one kind or another. By 1975, "alcoholism" represented the largest diagnostic category in U.S. state mental hospitals: nearly one half of all state hospital patients (Redlich and Kellert, 1978, p. 26). It is apparent that "the decriminalization of 'public drunkenness' (e.g., police now bring drunks to the mental hospital instead of the drunk tank) is in part reflected by this enormous increase of alcoholics in the mental health system'' (Conrad, 1980, p. 198).

But does the decriminalization and medicalization of a victimless crime like public drunkenness represent anything other than a politically and economically convenient shift in the control of the criminal or deviant, a shift that nevertheless continues to blame the victim? Reasons and Perdue (1981, p. 338) have suggested that it does not:

> The current movement toward decriminalization and involuntary civil lock-up represents . . . the new ideology of the medical model rather than the criminal. The emphasis is still one of blaming the victim rather than examining the structural nature of alienation . . . and the relationship between a ''privatized'' society and alcohol abuse.

In short, decriminalization may not have always delivered on its promise. Instead of the elimination of ''unnecessary'' controls, one kind of control may simply be replacing another.

PUNISHING "VICTIMLESS CRIME": FIVE COSTS OF CRIMINALIZING

A New York appellate court judge, in arguing for the legalization of gambling, has written:

> The existence of gambling crimes are a gross hypocrisy. They congest the courts, they encourage corruption, they are a primary source of income for organized crime, they lead to disrespect for the law, and they deny the state an important source of legitimate revenue. . . . (Wachtler, quoted in Geis, 1978, p. 274)

No matter what one's theoretical or ideological perspective is on the reality of victimless crime and the desirability of decriminalizing it, the social problems resulting from the punishment of these ''offenses'' with the criminal law are undeniable. Schur (1979, pp. 452–453) has identified these problems as ''the costs of criminalizing'':

> *the laws on balance do more harm than good* . . . they have produced unintended consequences that *have overall, increased the amount of social harm* associated with the problems they aim to control. Such largely ''secondary'' consequences can be conveniently discussed as *''costs of criminalizing . . . .''*

Let us examine these costs in some detail.

Enforcement Costs

In regard to victimless crime statutes, "It seems fair to say that in few areas of the criminal law have we paid so much for so little" (Kadish, 1971, p. 63). This conclusion is warranted given the difficulties encountered in the enforcement of vice law. Not only are victimless crimes usually "consensual" crimes, they most often occur "in private" as well.

Since these acts are normally consensual and private, there is no complainant involved. If the police are to come up with evidence in these cases they will have to go about finding it themselves. This has often involved the use of highly questionable or, in fact, illegal investigative practices. Detective work in and around victimless crime normally includes the use of decoys, informants, "bugging devices," wiretapping, and "no-knock raids." Narcotics police have relied almost exclusively on paid informers—sometimes addict informers. Police decoys, posing as "Johns," have been used to entrap prostitutes. Attempts at enforcing antihomosexuality laws have utilized hidden surveillance. Raids have been used to surprise those involved in illegal abortions, both practitioners and recipients of the service. Wiretapping has been prominent in the enforcement of anti-gambling statutes (Schur, 1979). It is evident that "the use of such low-visibility tactics increases the likelihood of corruption and arbitrariness in the enforcement of the law" (Reiman, 1979, p. 196). When the police engage in such suspicious and perhaps illegal activities themselves while enforcing the law, the end result can only be a waning respect for the law and those who attempt to enforce it among those who are policed in such a manner. Particularly when those policed in this fashion are the poor and oppressed minorities, feelings of resentment toward the law and the hypocrisy of law enforcement may result. "There is, after all, what can reasonably be taken for hypocrisy in formally adhering to the constitutional, statutory, and judicial restrictions upon the power of the police to arrest, search, and otherwise intervene in the affairs of citizens on the streets, while actually authorizing disregard of those limitations, principally against the poor and disadvantaged, through the subterfuge of disorderly conduct and vagrancy laws" (Kadish, 1971, p. 67). This situation may actually create the conditions for more, not less, street crime:

> The practical costs of this departure from principle are significant. One of its consequences is to communicate to the people who tend to be the object of these laws the idea that law enforcement is not a regularized, authoritative procedure, but largely a matter of arbitrary behavior by the authorities. The application of these laws often tends to discriminate against the poor and subcultural groups in the population. It is unjust to structure law enforcement in such a way that poverty itself becomes a crime. And it is costly for society when the law arouses the feelings associated with these laws in the ghetto—a sense of persecution and helplessness before official power and hostility to police and other authority that may tend to generate the very conditions of criminality society is seeking to extirpate. (President's Commission on Law Enforcement and Administration of Justice, 1967, pp. 103–104)

PANEL 7-4

The Financial Costs of Enforcing Vice Laws: Prohibiting "Victimless Crimes"

Perhaps more than their moral concerns, opponents of decriminalization concentrate on the fiscal unfairness of their having to support the sinful in their self-indulgent ways. Their argument suggests that allowing legalized gambling, for instance, will ensnare marginal earners and welfare clients, and that these persons will lose what little money they have on reckless wagering, thus forcing hard-working taxpayers to render up even greater portions of their wages to support them and their impoverished families. Similarly, legalizing marijuana, it is said, will induce large numbers of potential contributors to social well-being to opt for drug-induced nirvanas, and thereafter these dropouts too will have to be supported by escalated food stamp subsidies and welfare doles.

Perhaps so—perhaps not. But we do have some information regarding the present cost of processing victimless crimes within the criminal justice system, one of the foremost considerations that would have to be entered into the ledger before striking a fiscal balance.

The Public Safety Systems research group in Santa Barbara, California (Poole, 1973), calculated the costs involved in the prevention, detection/apprehension, adjudication, and correction of four categories of offenders in Ventura County, California. Detection and apprehension costs, for instance, involved expenses for the police dispatchers, patrol officers, detectives, and laboratory services. Corrections included costs associated with probation investigations, adult and juvenile hall, honor farm, juvenile camps, and ward placement program.

Offense categories include crimes against persons (7 percent of the County's reported crimes) and crimes against property (60 percent), non-victim crimes (24 percent), and miscellaneous crimes (9 percent). Non-victim crimes were primarily drug offenses, gambling, consensual sex offenses, public drunkenness, and delinquent-tendencies adjudications. Miscellaneous crimes included offenses such as drunk driving and illegal possession of weapons.

Enforcement costs that result from the attempt to enforce victimless crime laws that are, at least to some extent, "unenforceable," are economic as well, that is, they involve the loss of real dollars and cents. Limited crime control resources—money, personnel, time, and energy—are diverted away from those crimes that may be much more potentially harmful to a community's people and property, and toward those activities that may be relatively harmless and victimless. Victimless

PANEL 7-4 (Continued)

The two major cost findings of the study were these:

(1) Non-victim crimes accounted for the greatest expenditure of funds among the different offense categories. Some 33 percent of the total of $19 million spent annually in the County on its criminal justice system went for such offenses. Crimes against persons accounted for 15 percent, and miscellaneous crimes for 24 percent of the expenditures.

(2) Non-victim crimes were particularly expensive to deal with in the areas of detection/apprehension and corrections. The cost of victimless crimes to the criminal justice system broke down as follows: prevention (8 percent); detection/apprehension (36 percent); adjudication (20 percent); and corrections (36 percent). The corresponding figures for all offense categories taken together were: prevention (12 percent); detection/apprehension (34 percent); adjudication (24 percent); and corrections (30 percent).

It should be noted that Ventura County's per capita crime rate is not too different from that of other metropolitan areas. For homicide, robbery, aggravated assault, grand theft, and auto theft, the reported crime rates are somewhat below the national average, while they are slightly higher than that average for burglaries and forcible rape. Since Ventura County (1970 census figures) contains 376,430 persons, the cost per person per year of criminal justice concerns with victimless crimes comes to $16.63. If this figure is extrapolated to the national scene, the cost for the United States amounts to $3.4 billion. Obviously, rural conditions might deflate this figure, while megalopolitan considerations might raise it, and other things—such as salary levels—might alter it somewhat. More obviously, the costs will not disappear totally with decriminalization. Nonetheless, it seems worth putting on record an approximation of the financial costs within the criminal justice system of the enforcement of laws against crimes without victims in the United States today.

Source: Gilbert Geis, "The Criminal Justice System Without Victimless Crimes," in Peter Wickman and Phillip Whitten (eds.), Readings in Criminology, *Lexington, Mass.: D.C. Heath, 1978, pp. 273–274.*

crime statutes are not only difficult but costly to enforce. Again, in the absence of citizen complainants and with the "crime" being committed "behind closed doors," the police must rely on their own resources and ingenuity (not always legal ingenuity) to gather the evidence needed for a successful prosecution (Schur, 1979). Panel 7-4 documents the tremendous economic cost that one local law enforcement jurisdiction incurred in the pursuit of victimless crime. We may legitimately ask whether this kind of expenditure is justified in the light of over-worked police, overburdened courts, overcrowded prisons, and an underfinanced criminal justice system.

Secondary Crime Costs

Punishing victimless crime is also costly to society in that it often creates more crime and criminals than it inhibits. Ultimately, of course, it is always the case that criminal statutes define and make criminals. But particularly in the area of victimless crime law it is apparent that the relevant statutes make "criminals" of those who would not be so labeled on any other grounds. This deviance or crime "amplification" is often directly harmful to the individual "victimless criminal" and in the long-run, perhaps, to society as well. "The policy of labeling as criminals otherwise respectable and law-abiding people has been especially condemned in such areas as marihuana use (where it has been felt to promote antisocial outlooks), abortion (where it has produced postabortal guilt, not so typically found in less repressive legal situations), and homosexuality (where it is widely held responsible for impairing the self-esteem of a great many Americans)" (Schur, 1979, p. 456).

The amplification of crime and deviance that the application of criminal sanctions to victimless crime ensures is typified by, as mentioned earlier, the addict's need to engage in more crime—property theft—to finance his or her habit. Another more subtle manifestation of this is the victimless criminal who, if finally sent to prison, associates with other inmates and learns to be a "better criminal." Vice laws produce secondary crime in yet another way. Again, as noted above, the pimp arrives to "protect" the prostitute since her criminal status precludes any legal police protection. This "occupational growth and opportunity" originates in the enforcement of victimless crime laws. "Such ancillary roles include virtually all people involved in the provision of the banned goods or services as well as others who benefit from their illegality—from the professional heroin-trafficker to the pimp, from the landlords of premises used for prostitution to manufacturers and sellers of pornography, from those who operate illegal gambling establishments to people who devote themselves to robbing or blackmailing homosexuals" (Schur, 1979, p. 456). All of these crimes and criminals are dependent on the criminalization, in the first place, of some victimless offense. And finally, when the police and other law enforcement agencies are forced to violate the law to enforce it (as so often is the case in vice law enforcement), yet more secondary crime is generated.

Police Corruption

The consensual nature of most victimless crime, the typical lack of a complainant, and the fact that vice is often accomplished in private mean that enforcement of victimless crime law is exceedingly difficult. This difficulty, in turn, has precipitated widespread police corruption. Indeed, corruption appears to be inherent in the sociology of the victimless crime enforcement situation. Schur (1979) has identified the characteristic features of these situations that contribute to police corruption:

1. Police discretion in identifying specific victimless offenses and offenders.
2. Police recognition of highly ambivalent public attitudes toward victimless crimes.
3. Police awareness of the tremendous amount of money and profits that accrue in the distribution of illegal goods and services.
4. The eagerness of the organizers of organized crime to bribe the police not to enforce vice law.
5. The police realization that many arrests for victimless offenses do not result in prosecution or conviction.
6. The atmosphere of hypocrisy that generally surrounds the entire victimless crime enforcement effort.

Large-scale graft has been evidenced in the payoffs to the police made by illegal gamblers, narcotics distributors, those running "houses of ill-repute," and illegal abortion "clinics." The source of this graft, again, is significantly linked to the effort to enforce the unenforceable. A former New York City Police Commissioner, Patrick Murphy, has said in this regard:

> The policeman would be more effective in his crime prevention duties and he would be held in higher public esteem if he were not required to enforce so many regulations which attempt to control morals—the so-called victimless crimes. . . . By charging our police with the responsibility to enforce the unenforceable we subject them to disrespect and corrupting influences. And we provide the organized crime syndicate with illicit industries on which they thrive. . . . (quoted in Geis, 1978, p. 275)

The illegal sale of drugs and illegal gambling have probably been the two areas most significantly involved in widespread police graft and corruption. In regard to the sale of illegal drugs, for example, former U.S. Supreme Court Chief Justice Earl Warren has said, "The narcotics traffic of today . . . could never be as pervasive and open as it is unless there was connivance between authorities and criminals" (quoted in Geis, 1978, p. 274).

Concerning gambling, the Knapp Commission Report (1972) on police corruption in New York City found that police acceptance of bribes from illegal gambling interests—in exchange for *no* enforcement or relaxed enforcement—was well organized and persistent over time in spite of occasional scandals exposed by the media, police department reforms and reorganization, frequent and massive transfers in and out of gambling enforcement units in the police department, and the periodic closing down of some illicit gambling operations. The report also noted that many "bribed" police officers did not consider their activity particularly illegal since so much of the public enjoys placing bets of one kind or another and actually relies on this illicit service for its enjoyment:

In 1971 in New York, fifty of the 450 plainclothesmen in the Police Department's 17 divisions who were charged with enforcing the gambling laws had been transferred out of their units on suspicion of misconduct. Police officials were considering having officers with ten years or more in the Department, rather than younger men, assigned to gambling, on the presumption that veterans would stand to lose more by accepting bribes; to cut the opportunity for temptation they were also planning to reduce tours of duty in gambling enforcement from four to two years. . . . (in Geis, 1978, p. 275)

Since many police are willing to accept the bribe, illegal professional gambling organizations are willing to pay for it. Payoffs are normally understood to represent a "necessary business expense," much like the legal business organization's purchase of insurance or tax payments (Schur, 1979).

Constitutional Costs

Over the past two decades, a series of judicial restraints have been put on law enforcement practices.[8] Nearly all of these restrictions have come in response to the methods used by the police to enforce laws against victimless crimes. Many "unfortunate" experiences with illegal search and seizure, wire-tapping, bugging, entrapment (usually with "decoys"), and other forms of electronic surveillance and interception have made this court activity necessary.

Norval Morris, a noted legal scholar in the United States, has suggested that the judicial restraints on law enforcement that have resulted from "illegal" attempts to enforce victimless crime statutes may, in the end, actual foreshadow the erosion of our constitutional rights of privacy and due process rather than secure them. Morris has reiterated the difficulties involved in policing victimless crime, noted how the attempts to police vice are responsible for most of the constitutional consideration of civil liberties in the United States, and commented on how the Constitution's ability to protect individual rights and privacy may be the ultimate victim of the attempt to police victimless crime. "Effective" law enforcement may take primacy over civil liberties:

Police work is almost by definition more difficult in cases of victimless crime; the best evidence is lacking, no injured citizen complains to the police and serves as a witness. The police must therefore "develop" cases with unreliable informers, undercover work, tapping and bugging, entrapment and decoy methods, swift seizure of evidence, and forceful interrogation. Drug cases account for most of our constitutional difficulties with search and seizure. Organized crime and gambling account for most instances of wiretapping and other invasions of privacy. Attempting to balance, in these tilted scales, constitutional concerns for privacy and due process with a concern for police effectiveness has lessened for the rest of us the protection of our constitutional

[8]More recently, of course, conservative national and state governments have been engaged in dismantling some of these restraints.

rights. In the long run, this enervation of the power of the Constitution may not be the least of the harms flowing from the overreach of the criminal law. (Morris, quoted in Geis, 1978, p. 274)

The Fiscal Crisis of the State

Burgeoning budget deficits have recently meant a "fiscal crisis" for many governmental units in the United States. City and state governments, as well as the federal government, have increasingly "gone broke" as revenues have not kept pace with expenditures (see O'Connor, 1973). One way of alleviating at least part of this crisis would be to decriminalize and legalize many activities, goods, and services that presently are outlawed by victimless crime statutes and allow the state (government) to engage in the lawful provision of these consumer goods and services. The enormous profits generated in the sale of these commodities would thus be transferred from organized criminal interests to legally constituted and operating governments. As noted earlier, some cities and states have, for example, begun to compete with illicit organized gambling operations for their share of the market. This phenomenon will be explored further in the next chapter.

CHAPTER REVIEW

1. "Victimless crime" has been defined in essentially three different ways: (1) as the absence of victimization, (2) as the improper legislation of private morality, and (3) as complainantless crime involving consensual transactions.

2. Examples of victimless crime in contemporary American society include adultery, homosexuality, prostitution, pornography, abortion, gambling, drug use and addiction, and to a lesser extent, vagrancy, disorderly conduct, and public drunkenness.

3. As with street crime, changes in those behaviors criminalized as victimless crime, from one time to another, from one place to another, indicate that victimless crimes (at any given time and place) are the result of historically changing social and economic institutions and ideologies. Similarities between acts that are criminalized and those that are not illustrate further that particular acts do not become criminalized as victimless crimes out of the consistent application of society's moral standards.

4. Each of the three dominant sociological perspectives on crime and its control take varying perspectives on the issue of whether or not there is such a thing as victimless crime. The traditional sociological view is that although some crimes may not have individual victims, all crime represents a threat to society's laws and values and thus to the established social order. From this perspective, even the so-called victimless crimes have a victim—they victimize society. The interactionist perspective, more than other sociological perspectives, has held that a significant number of crimes in American society are victimless and that since it cannot be readily demonstrated that they result in any individual or social harm, many of these acts should be decriminalized

or legalized. Not to do so only leads to more crime—"secondary crime." For radical criminology, victimless crime is, to a significant extent, a myth. But the perpetrators of this kind of crime, not society, are the real victims. They are victimized by both organized crime's provision of illegal goods and services and by the states' selective and class-biased law enforcement practices. The real victims of victimless crime are those in the underclass whose political and economic exclusion from "legal society" leads them to these acts.

5. In some cases, the decriminalization of victimless crimes does not lead to the elimination of "unnecessary" social controls. Instead, one kind of social control may simply replace another. Recently, decriminalization in the United States has often meant that the control of some criminal or deviant behavior has shifted from the criminal justice system to medical institutions. This process has been referred to as the *medicalization of crime and deviance*.

6. Criminalizing victimless offenses costs both individuals and society dearly. These costs include loss of respect for the law, loss of valuable police resources (personnel, time, and money), more crime (secondary crime), police corruption, the potential loss of constitutionally guaranteed rights and liberties, and the loss of a lucrative source of state revenue.

8 Organized Crime

CHAPTER OUTLINE

The History of Organized Crime
Organized Crime in the United States: Its Nature and Extent
Using Theory: The Political Economy of Organized Crime

The myth of the Mafia
Links to legitimate business and the legal economy
The productivity of crime
Corruption: police, politics, and foreign policy

A Case Study in Organized Crime: The U.S. Heroin Industry
Punishing Organized Crime: Economic and Political Obstacles

Corruption
Linkages to the legal economy
"Orderly" crime
The fiscal crisis of the state

KEY TERMS

Crime tariff
Disorganized crime
Mafia
Organized crime
Underground economy

LEGITIMATE BUSINESS INFILTRATES THE RACKETS[1]

By Nicholas Von Hoffman

They had the Godfather on TV again recently, the classic gangster genre movie. Very enjoyable but with about the same relationship to organized crime as "High Noon," "Destry Rides Again," or one of those sanguinary Sam Peckinpah epics has to the daily life of the old West as it was lived by wheat farmers and cattle drivers.

NBC repeatedly inserted announcements that we viewers were not to take this highly romanticized, prettied up depiction of gangsterism as an ethnic slur. In truth, the Black Hand or the Mafia isn't an Italian institution but a Sicilian one. Al Capone assuredly was the king of the gangsters, but just as assuredly wasn't a member of the Mafia. Scarface Al was an equal opportunity slugger who had Poles, Irish, Jews and even ordinary killer WASPs on his payroll.

The mystical mumbling of Italian words and the incantations of bloody Sicilian vendettas is fun and one shouldn't knock it as entertainment as long as it's not accepted as anything close to what organized crime in America is about. By organized crime is meant people who form themselves into profit making concerns to provide goods and services by illegal means.

Most such organizations seldom if ever are 100 percent criminal. A substantial amount of what they do offends no law, something we all admit implicitly when we discuss the "problem" of gangster penetration into legitimate business. Such irony when you think of the millions of dollars we spend on ineffectual social work programs to get crooks to go straight.

Some organizations, however, may derive a larger percentage of their cash flow from activities that offend the law than others. Thus people who hijack merchandise might be said to spend more of their time earning their living by crime than the retail stores who buy the stolen goods. The amounts involved go into the billions and it's all around you. You can be reasonably sure that those ads with incredible discounts for appliances mean the store in question is peddling hot stuff.

It is as Business Week magazine said the other day, "When a consumer finds Pepperidge Farm stuffing at Milwaukee's Seven Mile Fair flea market selling for $4.15 a case versus the $5.33 a case the company is charging wholesalers, as one customer did a few years ago, it should be obvious the goods are stolen."

Gangsters also supply venture capital, naturally at high interest rates, but often a loan at high rates is better than no loan at low rates. In the trucking industry, or segments thereof, economists have long noted that the Teamsters Union operates as a price rigging mechanism that controls or even eliminates competition so that less efficient companies don't go out of business. This is a job that the Interstate Commerce Commission used to handle, but now, with deregulation, the Teamsters may be the only wall left protecting the industry from the dangers of a free market.

Business Week points out another important motive for illegal activities by legal corporations or legal activities by illegal corporations however you care to define it: "At every major shipping terminal in the country—rail, truck, air—theft on a scale too big to be random continues at appallingly high levels. That is what some unions offer in exchange for their members' docility." A free, honest, and earnestly representative trade union is a pain

[1]Source: King Features Syndicate in the Rocky Mountain News, November 25, 1980, pp. 33 and 36.

in the ass to the boss, whether he's a capitalist in Pittsburgh or a commie in Gdansk.

These examples give the impression that it is the seamier side of corporate America that, like the Corleone family, sometimes makes it on the up-and-up and sometimes takes it from under the table. Not so. A recent study by Fortune Magazine of 1,043 "major corporations" reveals that in the past decade 117 or 11 percent "have been involved in at least one major delinquency," by which is meant things like kickbacks, bribery, illegal campaign contributions, fraud, tax evasion and conspiracy to rig prices. Here are a few of the names on what the magazine calls its "Roster of Wrongdoing": Textron, U.S. Steel, Owens-Illinois, ITT, Greyhound, Gulf & Western, General Dynamics, Tenneco and PepsiCo.

Ashland Oil is apparently unable to go straight. Here's its record of repeat offenses: ". . . pleaded guilty to making a $100,000 illegal political contribution. It was also convicted, after a nolo plea, of fixing the price of resins. This year its construction subsidiary pleaded guilty in three cases of rigging bids for highway construction work . . ."

How are we going to stop legitimate business from infiltrating the rackets? Or is it that it's not organized crime but disorganized crime we fear?

Why is it that Americans have tended to fear "disorganized street crime" more than "organized crime" when the costs of the latter may far surpass the former? What is organized crime anyway? Is it the legal corporation frequently engaging in illegal acts? Is it illegal enterprise sometimes profiting from legal activities? "Is it legitimate business infiltrating the rackets" or the rackets moving in on legitimate enterprise? Is organized crime a national crime syndicate; a "mafia"? Should we police and control organized crime as vigorously as we have disorganized crime?

These and other related issues will be pursued in this chapter. As will be evident in the discussion that follows, the organized sale and distribution of such illegal goods and services in American society as sex, drugs, money, and violence are both vast and profitable. Organized crime encompasses a wide range of criminal operations: gambling, narcotics, prostitution, loan-sharking, extortion, securities and financial fraud, labor racketeering, the corruption of city, state, and national governments and their criminal justice system; as well as more recent and "innovative" involvements like urban sweatshops and marketing goods in the Third World that have been declared illegal in the United States.

There is a profound link between this chapter and the previous one. A good share of the activity of organized crime involves "selling to victims"—the victim of addiction, for example—or "the sale of the victim"—the victim of prostitution. In short, organized crime is, to a significant degree, often dependent upon victimless crime. As victimless crimes remain, or are increasingly criminalized, organized crime flourishes. Indeed, wherever and whenever goods, services, or activities are declared illegal, the potential for a "black market" exists. And these new markets have the potential to become highly lucrative ones. An organized criminal interest is able to secure, with relative ease, a monopoly control (it is in many instances the sole provider of the goods, services, or activities) and thus can inflate the prices it charges and further victimize its victims. Prices and profits for organized crime are increased still further by the operation of "the crime tariff" (see Packer, 1968): the surcharge warranted by the legal risks undertaken in providing illegal goods, services, and activities. It has been estimated, for example, that a street purchase of $150 worth of illegal heroin in an American city would cost about 20 cents if made directly from one of the world's opium-producing regions.

But the criminalization of victimless crimes is not the only reason for the prosperity enjoyed by those in our society who are "organizing crime." Organized crime's position and role in the ongoing functioning of the American economy—both legal and illegal—must also be examined. But before we turn to this problem, it is necessary to understand the historical development of organized crime in the United States, for organized crime has not always been so organized.

THE HISTORY OF ORGANIZED CRIME

In many ways the interlude between feudal society and capitalist society in Europe provided the beginnings of what is now referred to as organized crime in America. As the earlier social forms began to decay and disappear, the feudal landlords could no longer assert a total control of the peasantry and since the capitalist economy and national governments were not yet firmly in place, a political void was created. Without an effective or governing ruling class in society, law and order became problematic: where was it to come from and who was to provide it? In Sicily, in the early 19th century, it was a group that came to be called the "Mafia" that intervened. This group began renting land and estates from the absentee feudal lords and then leasing them for a profit to the landless peasants. Through this activity, the emerging Mafia was able to solidify more economic and political power than other societal groups and became, for a short period, the only reliable source of law and order. In time, the peasants were paying "the individual boss and his army of followers" not only for their rented land but also for protection. The Mafia, then, represented an alternative and unofficial system of law, order, power, and economic opportunity in the absence of strong and official mechanisms for the provision of these things (see Hobsbawn, 1959).

This Sicilian Mafia was characterized by networks of groups or "families" that controlled limited geographical areas. When these groups were connected to each other at all, the connections were extremely loose. It was this rather unorganized "organized crime" that came to be in control of the "vice districts" of American cities beginning in the late 19th century. As one immigrant and minority group after another found their new society wanting in terms of a just system of law, order, power, and opportunity, the Mafia became an attractive alternative.[2] Ini-

---

[2] As will be pointed out later in our discussion of the "myth of the Mafia," the word *Mafia* may be legitimately used to describe the ethnically controlled unorganized "organized crime" of this historical era but it does not accurately describe organized crime in the United States after the era of Prohibition. The reasons for this will become clear as we develop the history of organized crime.

tially the Irish were in charge, then the Jews. As these ethnic groups were assimilated to the official machinery of law, order, power, and opportunity, Italian-Americans emerged as the primary organizers of on-going criminal activities. But until Prohibition, American organized crime was still characterized by rival ethnic groups fighting for the control of local marketplaces—the vice districts (Balkan et al., 1980).

Beginning in 1920, the conditions that would allow organized crime to become more organized and expansive appeared. The Volstead Act of 1920 implemented the 18th amendment to the U.S. Constitution. For all intents and purposes, wine, beer, and liquor were outlawed. Organized criminal interests made certain that Americans did not have to do without these commodities. An incredibly vast market became available to organized crime. But there is perhaps a more important reason for the growth and development of organized crime[3] in this era. Between the two world wars, the American economy underwent a profound transformation, whereby local and labor-intense small-scale production and distribution gave way to highly centralized mass production and chain-store retailing:

> the American economy no longer revolved around the corner groceries and neighborhood shops where most household items had been crafted and sold. Just as the steel, oil, and rubber magnates had already forged an industrial system based on "efficient" production for the nation as a whole, so, too, the war had mobilized the nation's economy to streamline the production of consumer goods. Never before had industry realized it could produce so much for so many. . . . What had been a nation of regional economies was now consolidated into a unified economic system, which would soon wipe out most of the personalized, community factories and businesses that had characterized the America of Whitman and Twain. Everywhere corporate mergers were becoming the order of the day. The consolidations of the twenties brought about such giant food, soap and automobile combines as Maxwell House, Colgate-Palmolive, and Chrysler. Greatest of the new conglomerates were the chain stores, an entirely new invention for retail marketing. Their success was phenomenal, a growth from some 29,000 units in 1918 to 160,000 units in 1929. . . . (Browning and Gerassi, 1980, p. 362)

Before long, organized crime leaders like Al Capone, John Torrio, and Lucky Luciano began to understand the tremendous profit that could be gleaned from the application of mass-production techniques to criminal enterprise. Until then, individual neighborhoods and vice districts had been in the hands of individual gangs and their leaders. The competition—often warring competition—inherent in this small-scale organization prevented the cooperation necessary for organization on a larger scale. "Bookies, prostitutes, and the thieves tended to work within a

---

[3] One of the reasons we continue to think of organized crime in the United States as a Mafia controlled primarily by Italians or Sicilians (in spite of the evidence that suggests the mythical nature of this belief) is that Italians were involved disproportionately in organized crime at precisely that historical moment when it experienced its first thrust toward real growth, development, and organization.

single neighborhood'' (Browning and Gerassi, 1980, p. 363). But it became increasingly apparent that Prohibition and the lucrative business it would generate meant that efficient management and centralized control would benefit organized crime. The old vice district, replete with the uncertainties of local competition and organized primarily as ''a feudal system of territorial control,'' was eliminated, often with the gangland violence that was so much a part of the ''roaring 20s''[4] (Browning and Gerassi, 1980, p. 365). The Prohibition era signaled a profound change in the organization of organized crime: criminal operations were increasingly citywide, national, and even international in scope. In short, organized crime was becoming more and better organized:

> The significant phenomenon of the twenties was that vice, the provision of illegal goods and services, become big business. The emergence of *organized* crime involved the adoption of big-business techniques: consolidation, national organization, and the elimination of competition. (Walker, 1980, p. 180)

The unprecedented accumulation of criminal wealth soon followed. Federal agents estimated, for example, that the annual bootlegging revenues in 1927 from the Capone organization in Chicago alone may have surpassed $60 million. Beyond this, Capone's enterprise had begun to diversify and was believed to include $25 million in annual gambling revenues, $10 million from the control of labor unions and the extortion of businesses, and a $10 million annual take from other ''miscellaneous vice services'' (reported in Walker, 1980, p. 182).

The attack on alcohol and drinking that resulted in Prohibition had also been an attack on the saloon or tavern in particular, and working-class culture and politics in general. For urban working-class communities, the saloon was not merely a place to relax and drink, it was also a political institution, where the ruling political machines met, patronized, and organized their working-class constituencies. The working class was angry about this moralistic attack—''thou shall not drink''—on their culture and institutions, and since many of the urban political machines were politically dependent on these communities and neighborhoods for their continued control of city government, they and their police departments were not overly prone to enforce Prohibition. If this was not enough to ensure a lack of enforcement, organized crime's corruption of the police and the machine through bribes and payoffs was (Walker, 1980).

The organized crime that the corruption of the municipal police and municipal government allowed had something for just about everyone. Consumers, entrepreneurs, police and municipal officials all benefitted:

> The ''consumers'' could have their liquor, gambling, and sex. Providing these services offered access to small-business careers for working-class entrepre-

---

[4] Organized crime also began to prosper from its efforts to aid in the removal of competition in the legal sector of the American economy. Racketeering served in bringing small-labor intensive family industries into the mass-production economy, which according to Walter Lippmann, was nothing more than ''a perverse effort to overcome the insecurity of highly competitive capitalism'' (cited in Browning and Gerassi, 1980, p. 366). See the discussion of labor racketeering later in this chapter.

PANEL 8-1

Prohibition: Organized Crime in Chicago

With the demand for alcohol unabated and the risk of punishment rather low, prohibition opened up an enormously profitable field of endeavor. It was the special genius of Johnny Torrio, the most prominent figure in Chicago's vice business, to recognize that profits could be increased through oligopoly. Torrio drove smaller competitors out of business (through bombing or murder) and established agreements for the orderly division of territories with other large operators. It was the classic style of American big business. Torrio assumed his leadership in Chicago in 1920 upon the death of James Colosimo in the same year that prohibition went into effect.

The Torrio arrangement rested upon a corrupt relationship with the Chicago police and the rest of city government. The mayoral administration of William ("Big Bill") Thompson between 1919 and 1923 happily complied. The system broke down with the election of Mayor William Dever in 1923. Promising to clean up the city, Dever ordered his police chief to crack down on the bootlegging industry. This set off the famous "beer wars." With Torrio's power challenged by the authorities, smaller operators decided to carve out a larger portion of the business for themselves. The result was violent competition for control of the Chicago bootlegging industry. Chicago criminals murdered an estimated 215 of their colleagues between 1923 and 1926, while the police killed another 160 suspected gangsters.

Al Capone assumed control of the Torrio organization in 1925, after Torrio suffered both a short jail term and a nearly fatal gunshot wound. Far more ruthless than his predecessor, Capone established complete dominance of the Chicago crime syndicates by 1929. The Capone organization murdered one major competitor, Hymie Weiss, leader of the North Side organization, and then brought the gangland wars to a brutal climax with the famous St. Valentine's Day "massacre." The reelection of the corrupt "Big Bill" Thompson as mayor in 1927 helped to restore order to the crime business.

Source: Samuel Walker, Popular Justice: A History of American Criminal Justice, *New York: Oxford University Press, 1981, pp. 181–182.*

neurs. The police and other municipal officials obtained handsome pay-offs for ignoring illegal activity. And the trade-off between vice and non-enforcement provided a solid foundation for the political machines. Protest as they might, the middle-class moralists could not break this potent combination of mutual self-interest. (Walker, 1980, p. 107)

In such a setting enforcement was bound to fail and organized crime was destined to profit.

But if organized crime's "economic takeoff" and initial prosperity was so dependent on prohibition, why didn't it collapse (or at least suffer) when prohibition was repealed by the Roosevelt Administration and the 21st amendment in 1933?

Organized crime not only weathered the repeal of prohibition but survived the simultaneous imprisonment of many of its leaders (including Al Capone for income-tax evasion in 1931) and the Great Depression.[5] Through it all, organized crime flourished. Much like the modern, legal, bureaucratic corporation, organized crime adapted to changes in both leadership and economic conditions (Walker, 1980).

Prohibition had done several things for organized crime, not the least among them being the development of a large cadre of skilled managers and the accumulation of large sums of capital. The loss of the market for illegal booze found organized crime ready, willing, and able to make new investments and diversify its operations. For example, even before repeal, organized crime was responding to the anticipated loss of business: exclusive distribution contracts with legal distilleries who would soon be selling legal whiskey were negotiated (Browning and Gerassi, 1980). This represents the beginning of the formal and widespread intrusion of organized crime into legitimate business, an intrusion that would increasingly come to characterize the activity of organized crime, intensifying during and immediately after World War II and continuing at present. The links to legitimate business were profitable from the start:

> The two most notorious gangsters to get an early lock on legal liquor were Torrio and Frank Costello. . . . In December 1933, the month repeal was ratified, Torrio paid $62,000 for the newly organized import firm of Prendergast and Davies Co. Ltd. According to the Internal Revenue Service that firm was "the biggest corporation of its kind in New York City . . . until well into the middle of 1935." Apparently Torrio did as well with his "legitimate" business as he did with bootleggers, for by the time the IRS decided to launch an investigation, it claimed the company was grossing several million dollars each month. (Browning and Gerassi, 1980, p. 368)

Along with these initial inroads into legitimate business, organized crime's diversification also included new illegal enterprise. Bars and restaurants in New York City began to use organized crime's control of certain labor unions in the city to arrange "sweetheart" contracts with their employees. Also in New York, organized crime interests had control not only of the garment industry's workers and their unions, but management as well. Management used "the Jewish Mob" to ensure docile unions, and labor used it to make management more responsive to its demands. On the famed "waterfront," organized crime used its control of

---

[5] Neither has the most recent recession—beginning in 1980—brought hard times to organized crime. In fact, as will be argued later in this chapter, organized crime in the United States has often represented, as it does at present, a "growth industry" in an otherwise stagnating legal economy.

the International Longshoremen's Association (ILA) to control the labor market—that is, who worked and who didn't—on the docks. Chicago movie houses came to pay for organized crime's influence in the actors' and theatrical employees' unions. Extortion money was paid by the nation's largest film distributors to avoid employee strikes, among other things. Organized crime interests also became influential in the trucking business and its largest union, the Teamsters. Indeed, the 1930s brought the full-fledged development of two profitable organized crime operations that would continue to prosper over the next few decades: extortion and labor racketeering.

As alluded to earlier, whenever and wherever *criminalization* occurs, a potential market for the illegal provision of criminalized goods or service by organized crime is born. Indeed, new markets for organized crime are often dependent on new criminalizations. With the *decriminalization* of liquor, organized crime turned to other criminalized markets. One of these markets identified as having enormous potential was the sale of illegal narcotics, most significantly, heroin. Heroin was in the process of becoming completely criminalized in the United States, beginning with the passage of the Harrison Act in 1914. The illegal heroin industry expanded, developed, and profited as never before in the 1930s. Also beginning in the 1930s and 1940s, organized crime became involved in illegal gambling, particularly horse racing—via off-track bookmaking—and the sale and operation of slot machines.

Everywhere organized crime went, loansharking followed. Bridled with more cash than it knew what to do with, the underworld used its money to make more money. "A Russell Sage Foundation report issued in the mid-thirties estimated that loansharks grossed $10 million a year" (in Browning and Gerassi, 1980, p. 373).

Prostitution, too, constituted a lucrative trade in many large cities, particularly New York. Again, prostitution, like all of the other "new" post-prohibition product lines that organized crime offered, was organized just as the modern business corporation was. Lucky Luciano's instructions to one of his "lieutenants" regarding the operation of New York City brothels indicated clearly how "disorganized crime" was becoming "organized crime":

> "All right, Davie. Let it go for a couple of months. Let's see what happens. But you haven't got the racket up well enough to make it worth while. Here's what we'll do. We'll put all the madams on salary. No more fifty percent stuff. We'll syndicate every house in New York. We'll run them like chain stores." (quoted in Browning and Gerassi, 1980, pp. 374–375)

But even this more organized "organized crime" of the 1920s, 30s, and early 40s is not the organized crime of the 1950s, 60s, 70s, and 80s. Organized crime received yet another boost to its already secure and established profitability: World War II and the postwar prosperity that followed. For the most part, "crime networks benefitted from the same economic and political climate that benefitted other businesses from 1945 on" (Chambliss, 1978, p. 153). In short, the postwar boom represents yet another major development in the history of organized crime. The profits, capital, wealth, and assets of organized crime in both Prohibition days and the late 1930s and early 1940s pale when compared with the next 40 years:

> In the mid-forties, organized crime was alive and prospering . . . but the real turning point came with the return of prosperity. . . . First during the wartime economic boom and then even more so during the affluent post-war years . . . Americans had more money to spend and, with the shortening of the work week, they had more time to spend it. . . . (Walker, 1980, p. 206)

By 1950, neither individuals nor networks of individuals, leaders, or "gangs" could control organized criminal interests in America. The gangster, the Mob, the Mafia, the Cosa Nostra were all being replaced with a crime increasingly organized and corporate in structure. As will be seen below, this structural change would facilitate and make more complete organized crime's linkage to the licit and legal economy.

ORGANIZED CRIME IN THE UNITED STATES: ITS NATURE AND EXTENT

At the most general level, we define organized crime as "business enterprises organized for the purpose of making economic gain through illegal activities" (Ianni and Ianni, 1976, p. xvi). This illegal enterprise is dependent upon at least three interrelated phenomena for its continuing existence: (1) consumer demand for goods, services, and activities that are illegal, (2) an organization capable of producing and supplying these goods, services, and activities on an ongoing basis, and (3) the corruption of political and law enforcement officials who provide protection—for their own profit or gain—for these illegal organizations and operations (Clinard and Quinney, 1973). The specific activities of organized crime in the United States can be broken down into at least three, partially distinct, categories: the illegal control of the illegal sale and distribution of particular goods, services, and activities (primarily gambling, narcotics, loansharking, and prostitution and pornography); the illegal control and sponsorship of legal activities and legitimate businesses (everything from loaning money to owning and operating resort casinos and hotels, to investment in and control over real estate development and firms and federal reserve banks), and the illegal operation of numerous "rackets" (primarily labor union racketeering and extortion from legitimate businesses) (Quinney, 1970).

In this section we not only delineate what sorts of activities characterize the workings of organized crime in the United States, but we also attempt to document its size. That is to say, how vast, how expansive, how profitable are these criminal operations?

Figure 8-1 compares estimates of organized crime revenues for the year 1979 with the revenues of several of the largest legal industries in the country for that

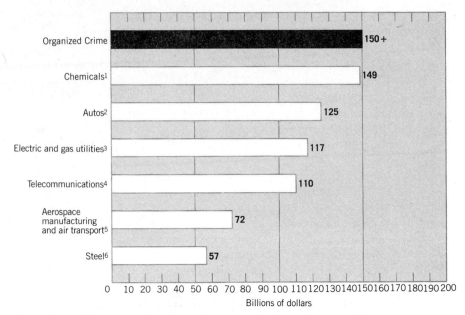

Figure 8-1 Crime pays. The figure gives a rough idea of how organized crime revenues—from drugs, illegal gambling, loansharking, cigarette bootlegging, and the like, as well as income from legitimate businesses—compare with those of some of America's largest industries. Only the oil industry's revenues—''365 billion in 1979, with $57 billion shipped overseas to pay for imports—are bigger. Organized crime's profits, some $50 billion a year—are in a class by themselves. [1]Figures From E. I. Du Pont de Nemours; [2]General Motors, Ford, Chrysler, AMC; [3]Edison Electric Institute and American Gas Association; [4]Edelson Technology Associates; [5]Aerospace Industry Association and Air Transport Association; [6]American Iron and Steel Institute.
SOURCE: James Cook, ''The Invisible Enterprise,'' *Forbes*, September 29, 1980, p. 61.

same year.[6] The information presented here suggests that when organized crime's revenue—from both illegal and legitimate business ventures—is compared with all other legal industrial and financial corporations in the United States, only the oil industry's revenues surpass it. And, when profits (instead of revenues) are compared, no legitimate industry appears to come close to the estimated annual $50 billion generated by organized crime. It has also been estimated that the gross income derived from organized crime is probably at least twice that derived from any other illegal activity (President's Commission on Law Enforcement and Administration of Justice, 1967). In addition, the IRS maintains that the tax revenue lost to the federal government from the illegal sale of drugs, gambling, and pros-

---

[6]These figures represent estimates drawn, for the most part, from government and popular (newspapers, magazines, etc.) sources. These remain, however, due to a general lack of independent social science research, literally the only data available regarding the size of organized criminal operations in the United States. Nevertheless, these data should be considered ''suspect'': those who collect and report them may suffer not only from less than reliable investigative and statistical techniques but may also have a ''vested interest'' in over- or underreporting. For a discussion of these problems see Galliher and Cain (1974).

titution was between $6.1 and $9.8 billion in 1981 (Associated Press, March 23, 1982).

Of $150 billion in annual organized crime revenues, it is estimated that $100 billion of it comes through the "illegal sale of illegal goods, services and activities": $63 billion from the sale and distribution of narcotic drugs (as will be seen below, over $30 billion annually from the sale of heroin alone), $22 billion from gambling, $8 billion from prostitution and pornography, and the remainder from activities like cigarette bootlegging (in those parts of the world where cigarettes are either scarce or to escape high taxes), loansharking (often at interest rates in excess of 200 percent a year), and, as mentioned earlier, more "subtle" and "innovative" enterprises, including the operation of the resurgent sweatshops in the garment and other industries in New York City and Los Angeles (see Panel 8-2) and the illegal dumping of toxic wastes (see Panel 8-3) (Simon and Eitzen, 1982, p. 182; Cook, 1980).

Other income then comes from organized criminal activity that involves the "illegal control and sponsorship of legal activities and legitimate business" and the "organized criminal operations that profit via labor racketeering and the extortion of legitimate business." In regard to the first of these, organized criminal interests are able to take capital accumulated in illegal and illegitimate enterprises and reinvest it in legal and legitimate enterprise. It is extremely difficult to determine whether a dollar (or billions of dollars) is "legal" or "illegal" once it has been invested in a legal and legitimate fashion. Consider for a moment capital generated through the illegal sale of sexual services that can then be transferred to a legal investment portfolio on Wall Street; money illegally gathered that becomes a source of legal capital for the largest industrial and financial corporations in the world. Typical and specific examples of this legal use of illegal capital include the reported partnerships of a number of large corporations—Pan American Airways and Howard Hughes Corporation among them—with organized criminal interests in gambling casinos, resort hotels, and restaurants in both Las Vegas and the Caribbean (Reid, 1969; Kohn, 1976). And, recent senate hearings (1980) have confirmed that profits originating in the illegal sale and distribution of cocaine have now been able to gain a significant interest and control of the Miami, Florida real estate market and that the attempt by organized criminal interests to purchase Federal Reserve member banks in South Florida has actually been made. At present, it is safe to say that no one understands the full extent of the "legal" uses of illegal capital in the United States, but nevertheless, it seems reasonable to argue that:

> Organized crime has grown into a huge business in the United States and is an integral part of the political economy. Enormous amounts of illegitimate money are passed annually into socially acceptable endeavors. An elaborate corporate and financial structure is now tied to organized crime. (Quinney, 1975, p. 145)

Other evidence documenting the intrusion of organized crime into the legal economy includes such diverse enterprises as the operation of "chop-shops" that dismantle and "sell for parts" (see Panel 8-4) most of the $3 billion in autos stolen each year (Cook and Carmichael, 1980); the recirculation of stolen goods in the

PANEL 8-2

Organized Crime: Running the Sweatshops

NEW YORK (AP) Garment industry sweatshops, nearly eliminated after a notorious factory fire in 1913, have grown from fewer than 200 to 3,000 in the last decade in New York City, with organized crime the "linchpin" in the proliferation, a state senator said Thursday.

"We thought we got rid of the sweatshops after the Triangle Shirtwaist fire, when 146 garment workers perished," state Sen. Franz S. Leichter said at a Chinatown street corner news conference as he released a report his staff prepared on sweatshops.

"But, in fact, there are probably more now than there were then," he said. He said about 50,000 people, mostly illegal aliens, are employed in these shops, often working under hazardous conditions for less than minimum wage.

Seventh Avenue designers often send out their fabrics to be sewn in reputable garment factories, either here, in other states or overseas on a contract basis.

Using sweatshop-type factories—generally characterized by poor working conditions and low wages—for this work is not illegal as long as the workers earn the minimum wage. However, they are deplored because they usually violate American labor, health and safety laws.

There are rising numbers of illegal aliens from Asia, Latin America, the Dominican Republic and Haiti who are a perfect "pool of exploitable labor," Leichter said.

The sweatshops no longer are limited to Chinatown. They have spread to northern Manhattan, the South Bronx and Queens, he said.

The senator charged that trucking firms with organized crime ties dominate the sweatshop business.

"They set up the shops, provide the leases and even some of the Seventh Avenue business and then rake in the profits of carrying the garments back to Seventh Avenue," the heart of New York's garment industry, he claimed.

legal and legitimate market through their resale in flea markets, supermarkets, department and discount stores (Cook and Carmichael, 1980); the nearly complete control of the U.S. mozzarella cheese business and Wisconsin's giant Grande Cheese; securities and exchange fraud (most often and typically involving either the artificial inflation of stock value or the sale of unauthorized and illegal stocks); and the use of labor union pension funds to underwrite illegal activities. In regard to this last mentioned activity, the Teamsters Union and its Central States Pension Fund have been used effectively by organized criminal interests to produce capital needed for other business ventures. For example, one organized crime "agent," Allen Glick:

seemed to represent the new breed in Las Vegas. In 1972 a San Diego real estate promotor bankrolled his acquisition of one ailing Vegas casino, and Glick was on his way. In 1974, when Glick was 31, his Argent Corp., with only $66,000 in

Panel 8-2 (Continued)

Leichter said in Chinatown alone the truckers, by "carving out territories" and "charging exorbitant freight charges" to haul garments from the sweatshops to the manufacturers, collected more than $9 million a year in overcharges. His allegations were based on information from law enforcement agencies, he said.

"Nobody changes truckers here," said one sweatshop owner who did not wish to be identified. "We just pay what they charge." To do otherwise, he said, could result in harm to the shop or the goods.

Leichter said the workers generally earn about $100 a week, which is below the minimum wage. Most workers are too afraid to complain for fear of being deported, he said.

A spokesman for the International Ladies' Garment Workers Union, who did not wish to be identified, said, "I do not know of any situation where union shops are not paying the minimum wage." Many of the shops that Leichter says have sprung up are not unionized.

A visit Thursday to a shop where sportswear is made found 20 Asian women seated side-by-side at a long table in a small room on the second floor of an old building. One section of the ceiling was beginning to sag and bales of fabric were stored everywhere.

Each woman was hunched over an old-fashioned sewing machine, each with a large box of material at her side. All declined to answer questions.

Steam from an industrial clothes presser made the air in the small room seem tropical.

Leichter said many of the Seventh Avenue garment firms are "widespread and regular" users of sweatshops, and he accused all levels of government of not enforcing existing laws.

In response, city officials say budgetary cutbacks have caused a reduction in its inspector force.

Source: The Associated Press, "Mob Linked to Growth of Garment Sweatshops," The Rocky Mountain News, February 27, 1981.

assets, nonetheless borrowed $63 million from the Teamsters to buy out the Stardust and Fremont casinos. (Cook, 1980, p. 96)

Indeed, in recent times organized crime has found a new appeal in organized labor:

the billions piled up in the union pension funds. At least a few have unquestionably come under the influence of the mob, including the Teamsters Central States Pension Fund, once billed as "the biggest, baddest, most abused and misused pension fund in America." (Cook, 1980b, p. 70)

In the mid-1970s, approximately one half of the Central States Pension Fund real estate loan portfolio was committed to about a half-dozen investors. Among them, the heir apparent to organized crime "executive" Meyer Lansky (as noted

PANEL 8-3

Organized Crime: Dumping Toxic Waste

The Mob has moved into a lucrative racket spawned by public concern over the environment: Underworld-connected firms are engaged in the illegal dumping of poisonous and explosive industrial wastes for unethical businessmen who want to get around the new controls that go into effect this month.

These new federal regulations require an accounting of toxic wastes that may have been stored for years on the premises of chemical and other industrial plants. To avoid the ruinous expense of proper disposal, these firms are rushing to get rid of the wastes any way they can. That's where the Mob comes in, according to law-enforcement authorities.

A typical example illustrates the savings that can be made by breaking the law: A tank-truck load of chemical waste that costs $40,000 to send to a legitimate disposal site can be disposed of for half that amount by the Mob, which can drive an 8,000-gallon tank truck to a wooded area like the New Jersey Pine Barrens and dump it in eight minutes flat.

State and federal investigators have found dumping operations linked to organized crime in New Jersey, New York, Connecticut, Rhode Island and Massachusetts:

—A Bridgeport, Conn., trucking company, owned by associates of the late crime boss Carmine Galante, dumped 6,000 barrels of poisonous, explosive waste on a Connecticut farm. The same company was also involved in illegal dumping near a Rhode Island pig farm, where the waste blew up and burned out of control for three days.

—An alleged waste dumping tycoon on the East Coast is John Albert, owner of the Samson Tank Cleaning Co. of Bayonne, N.J. The company was recently indicted for illegal dumping in New Jersey and Massachusetts. According to a police affidavit obtained by my associate Tony Capaccio, Albert has "an extensive criminal history and is a known associate of New Jersey and New York crime members."

— . . . trucks hauled poison-saturated industrial filters to a dump site operated by the Chelsea Terminal Co. The waste was then deposited in bins owned by Jersey Sanitation Inc., which, in turn, is owned by organized crime figure Frank Stamato Sr. and George Katz, a New Jersey businessman indicted in the ABSCAM scandal. Among the substances illegally dumped at the site—as identified by New York organized crime investigator John Fine—were lye, radioactive waste, PCB-laden oil, explosive petroleum ethers and a highly flammable suspected carcinogen, epichlorohydrin. The toxic materials seeped into a creek flowing into the Arthur Kill waterway.

Source: Jack Anderson, "The Mob's New Racket," United Features Syndicate, The Rocky Mountain News, *November 17, 1980, p. 51.*

PANEL 8-4

The Stolen Car Industry

BALTIMORE, MD. (AP) Car thefts now cost Americans about $4 billion a year, and make up a lucrative—and growing—illegal industry, insurance and law enforcement officials said Wednesday.

One of every 43 registered vehicles in the United States will be stolen or broken into for parts or accessories in 1982, the National Automobile Theft Bureau meeting here was told. And experts said that organized crime increasingly is getting into the stolen car business.

"The increase in car thefts is attributed to professionalism among thieves," said Tim Kett of the auto theft bureau. "Organized crime is highly involved, especially in major metropolitan cities."

He said 1.1 million car thefts were recorded nationwide in 1980, up 1.6 percent from 1979.

"There's a change in the crime profile," Kett said. "Twenty years ago law enforcement agencies were recovering 90 percent of the stolen vehicles. Last year, only 55.5 percent of the vehicles were recovered, many of them stripped."

Officials said the car theft business has turned from one in which cars are stolen for joyrides and abandoned, to a "steal-to-order" business in which a professional thief locates and steals the type of car requested by a customer. Many other cars are stolen and broken into parts for distribution in "hot shops" across the country.

Police and insurance officials say the keys are left in the ignitions of the majority of cars that are stolen.

The National Automobile Theft Bureau, which is affiliated with more than 500 insurance companies, is based in Palos Hills, Ill. It aids law enforcement agencies and is a clearinghouse for stolen car information.

Source: The Associated Press, "Business Boom in Car Thefts Costs $4 Billion a Year," Des Moines Register and Tribune, March 25, 1982.

below, prominent in the international narcotics trade), a St. Louis lawyer, a San Diego real estate developer with criminal interests in Las Vegas, and a former "director" of organized crime operations in Cleveland (Cook, 1980).

Legitimate loan companies have been particularly susceptible to the intrusions of organized crime. This susceptibility is, of course, not unrelated to the fact that one of the two most important services provided legitimate business by organized crime is the loaning of money, albeit "high-risk" money at high interest rates (Cook and Carmichael, 1980).

The other critical service organized crime has been and is able to provide business, in exchange for handsome profits, is revealed by examining the last of the three categories used to describe organized crime's activities earlier in this section: labor racketeering and the extortion of legitimate business.

This establishment in New York City is reportedly operated by Carmine Galante, an alleged leader of organized crime in that city.

"Labor peace" has, since World War I, been a commodity successfully and profitably sold to American business and governments by organized crime. Labor unions controlled by organized criminal interests have long been preferred (over "uncontrolled" unions) by many representatives of the business and political elite.[7] These elite sectors have been more than willing to pay those criminal interests to infiltrate unions and their leadership to guard against union unrest, strikes, and militant agitation for more and better wages, benefits, protection from the health and safety hazards of the workplace, job security, and democratic participation in the ongoing operations of American industry:

> In Detroit in the 1940s the automobile companies used gangsters to suppress the efforts to unionize the auto industry. Gangsters like D'Anna and Adonnis were given a monopoly over the haulaway business at the Ford Motor Company in return for gaining control of the auto worker unions in the city. And even after the AFL succeeded in unionizing the auto industry, Ford still hired mobsters for use as strike breakers. In 1945 and 1946 there were more strikes in the U.S. (41,750) than in the previous ten years combined, so the need for strike breakers was clear. Use of gangsters for this purpose was curtailed in the 1950s as unions supported governmental policies related to the Cold War, and militant unionism, often associated with communism, declined. (Simon and Eitzen, 1982, p. 60)

[7]A more complete discussion of the ways in which organized crime has assisted ruling groups in American society with the suppression and control of powerless parts of the population follows in the next section.

But labor racketeering did not disappear with the onset of the Cold War. In the 1960s, for example, former Attorney General Robert Kennedy reported on his time spent tracking down this kind of activity in the Teamsters Union, which was then under the tutelage of the notorious Jimmy Hoffa:

> We found that a close relationship existed between Jimmy Hoffa and employ-ers. We found that he was more than willing to do favors for them. Big favors, such as settling strikes against the wishes of his men. And we found that em-ployers were anxious to do favors for him. Big favors, such as setting him up in business so that he could reap big profits. He helped them. They helped him. And they always insisted that the exchange of favors was coincidental. . . . (quoted in Roberts, 1978, p. 147)

After Prohibition, another "racket" gradually became part of the repertoire of American organized crime. "Protection rackets" developed around the distribu-tion of a wide variety of goods and services in many large cities. Organized crime came to extort legitimate American business by "asking" them to pay for the protection and continued well-being of their enterprise. Failure to pay for this protection could end in the destruction of property, physical injury, or even death.

By 1968, the National Emergency Committee on Crime and Delinquency had identified the following industries and businesses as victims of the protection and extortion rackets:

auto agencies	garment manufacturing
bakeries	groceries
banking	horses
bars	hotels
coal	produce
construction	race tracks
entertainment	real estate
food importers	restaurants
funeral homes	trucking
garbage disposal	vending machines

It is important to note that American consumers pay for all of this "protection" and extortion. Goods and services grow more expensive and costs are "passed on" when the intrusion of organized crime in the marketplace extracts its price.

USING THEORY: THE POLITICAL ECONOMY OF ORGANIZED CRIME

Our description of the historical development and the contemporary nature of organized crime in the United States indicate that this type of crime is essentially an economic and political phenomenon. The primary purpose is the pursuit of economic gain and advantage. Beyond this, it is intimately intertwined with the legal economic system. And its ongoing operation and well-being has been dependent upon the protections afforded it by political bodies: city, state, and federal governments and their criminal justice agencies and institutions.

Descriptions of the activities of American organized crime do not lead us to those factors identified as the sources of crime by traditional sociological perspectives. Sociological factors in the "immediate social environment"—poverty, broken families, inferior quality schools, under- and unemployment; "differential association" in delinquent, deviant, or criminal subcultures, or inadequate socialization to the "American Dream"—are not associated frequently with the operations of organized crime. In fact, our description of organized crime reveals crime "at the top" of society, not "at the bottom." Rather than occurring in a context of poverty, deprivation, and deviant subcultures, organized crime carries out its activities in the context of the financially lucrative sale of illegal goods and services, the profitable investment in legitimate business enterprise (utilizing illegally generated capital), and labor racketeering and the extortion of business, many times involving some of the largest and most successful unions and industrial and financial corporations in the nation.

We should also remember that these traditional approaches have tended to understand crime as a response of the *individual* to his or her "immediate social environment."[8] In other words, they represent more of a theory of disorganized crime, than a theory of organized crime. Our discussion to this point has revealed an organized crime growing more and more organized, until it has reached the corporate organization that characterizes it at present. What is needed is a theoretical perspective that understands and analyzes criminal activity as the response of criminal *organizations* to "the wider organizational, political, and economic environment." For all of these reasons, organized crime cannot be explained from the perspective of traditional sociological theories of crime.

The interactionist perspective also has tended to concentrate on the labeled and stigmatized *individual,* as well as his or her commitment to a deviant identity and ultimately his or her commitment to a deviant or criminal career. The interactionist is not at all convinced that the primary source or origin of deviance or crime is found in the original breaking of rules or laws, that is, in primary crime or deviance. Rather, the crux of the "crime problem," the more significant source of crime, involves the process of secondary crime or deviance. Secondary crime refers to the application of a criminal label by the criminal justice system that stigmatizes the individual offender. The stigmatized offender, then, lives up to the expectations of his or her criminal label and through the mechanism of the self-fulfilling prophecy takes on an increasingly criminal identity. Labeling, stigmatization, and criminal identity ensure exclusion from the non-criminal or "respectable" community and because of the lack of any available non-criminal alternatives, the individual offender is well on his way to a criminal career. Ironically then, the criminal justice system itself produces and sustains crime and criminals. But crime is the property of the individual and his or her encounter with

---

[8]This individualistic orientation is evident even when representatives of these perspectives leave their more usual focus on the traditional street crimes associated with the "lower class" and focus instead upon white-collar or corporate crime. See, for example, Sutherland's (1949) application of his theory of differential association to these crimes.

a system of social control, that is, the criminal justice system. It represents, in effect, an individual-oriented social-psychological explanation of crime that is hard-pressed to account for the origins of the crimes of organizations.

The interactionist approach argues that the origin of crime is dependent upon the stigmatization that sets in motion the process of secondary deviance or crime. As we have already seen, organized criminal activity in the United States has by and large escaped any and all stigmatization. Indeed, organized crime has a relative degree of status and prestige, often tied to the highest levels of political and economic power and status in the United States. For the most part, the organized crimes of organized crime simply have not been criminalized by our system of criminal justice—not policed, prosecuted, or sentenced. They are criminal nevertheless. For this reason, and the one outlined above, organized crime is not best explained from the perspective of interactionist theory.

The theoretical framework provided by radical criminology can best explain (1) crimes that are inherently economic in nature, (2) crimes that are *organized,* and (3) crimes that are an integrated part of American political and economic institutions and therefore escape significant criminalization.[9] The focus of this perspective, after all, is the political economy. Let us now turn to an elaboration of this theoretical perspective on organized crime. We will refer to it as "the political economy of organized crime."

The Myth of the Mafia

One of the first tasks of this perspective is to unmask what it considers to be "the myth of the Mafia" (or "Cosa Nostra," "Mob," etc.). Purportedly, organized crime is the product of the conspiratorial activities of about 24 families in the largest American cities. Further, the operations of these families are thought to be international in scope, unusually violent, and literally unstoppable. Membership in this criminal endeavor is believed to be limited in terms of ethnicity with most "family" members presumed to be Italian or Sicilian, as it was at the time of Prohibition. In the main, this "image of organized crime, as presented in the mass media, is of a secret international organization of Italian and Sicilian gangsters, who, via corruption and violence, are quite successful in exerting their will in almost any task they undertake" (Simon and Eitzen, 1982, p. 59).

In 1950, a special U.S. Senate Committee under the leadership of Senator Estes Kefauver, investigated organized crime in the United States and interviewed a number of Italian "gangsters," concluding that a small and sinister organization called the Mafia was at the center of organized crime's illegal activities (see Smith, 1975). In 1957, the meeting of a group of "Italian racketeers" in upstate New York was exploited by the media to help persuade the American public that the Mafia was, indeed, not a myth. In 1963, a "small-town hoodlum" by the name of Joe Valachi testified that a secret, conspiratorial organization called the "Cosa Nostra" did, in fact, exist. In 1972, many Americans were reading and watching

---

[9]These will also be our criteria for adopting an appropriate theoretical framework for understanding and explaining corporate crime. See Chapter 9.

The Godfather, which was soon followed by a flood of books and movies devoted to describing the ritual ceremonies and criminal behaviors of the "Mafioso," "Mafia," "Cosa Nostra," "Mob," and so on (all reported in Roberts, 1978). Incidents such as these, according to radical criminology, have contributed to "the myth of the Mafia," a myth that takes us far from the real issues of organized crime.

The focus on organized crime as a "Mafia" prevents our understanding the political economy of organized criminality in American society. It might be extremely interesting and fascinating to study the sensational rituals and exotic behaviors of particular "gangsters" or "families," but it prevents a full appreciation of the extent to which organized crime represents a corporate bureaucracy that depends for its survival upon intimate relations with legal and legitimate political and business organizations:

> The major tasks of the illicit entrepreneur are to obtain neutralization of government machinery so that illicit patron-client arrangements can continue, and to generate sufficient internal control of the illicit marketplace. The former task entails primarily corrupt relationships, whereas the latter task entails primarily violent intimidation . . . illicit enterprise is a game that anyone can play. It does not require a total commitment . . . executives in the electrical industry (until some of them were caught price-fixing in 1962) can operate in both legitimate and illicit areas simultaneously. Nor does it require Italian ethnicity. . . . We can focus on a group of entrepreneurs who have a common ethnic heritage, but the combination of entrepreneurial skill, a sense of patron-client relationships, and a kinship milieu is not similarly limited. . . . The future course of illicit enterprise will depend upon the imperatives of marketplace economics. . . . The use of the Mafia label may influence the future of the entrepreneur, but it will not determine the future of illicit enterprise. . . . (Smith, 1975, pp. 322–323)

Other radical criminologists have argued that the idea of a Mafia is credible only because it serves a scapegoating function: we have someone or something to blame for at least part of "the crime problem" (Galliher and McCartney, 1977). The "Mafia myth" does appear to have an ideological function in American society. That is to say, the myth creates an image of organized crime that does not correspond to its reality. Specifically, making the Mafia responsible for organized crime hides the institutionalized relations between legitimate business people, political figures, and the "agents" of organized criminality. Put another way, this image "is a form of mystification; a mask which conceals the relationship between organized crime and the workings of the capitalist system" (Simon, 1981, p. 355). Or still another way: "Our interest and concern with the 'organized underworld' has directed our attention away from the 'organized upperworld' " (Reasons, 1974, p. 230).

But to argue that the control of organized criminal activity does not belong to an Italian or Sicilian Mafia is not to argue that the control of organized crime in the United States is faceless or invisible. There may not be a Godfather, but there is a national crime network at work in our society.[10] William Chambliss' field study of organized crime in Seattle, for example, led him to conclude that

> Despite the mythical character of the idea of a Mafia, there is nonetheless a national crime network . . . that is to say, it is a loose affiliation of businessmen, politicians, union leaders, and law enforcement officials who cooperate to coordinate the production and distribution of illegal goods and services, for which there is a substantial consumer demand. (Chambliss, 1978, p. 151)

Panel 8-5 is part of Chambliss' report of this "loose affiliation" he found in Seattle. Figure 8-2 (on page 264) displays the Seattle crime network. Note how this network includes not only representatives of the Mafia—the racketeers—but also includes powerful financial, business, political, and law enforcement officials in Seattle, throughout the surrounding area, and across the state of Washington. (Chambliss later found this "local" network to be part of a national, and even international, network as well.)

Links to Legitimate Business and the Legal Economy

The identification of organized crime with this "national crime network" requires that an empirically adequate theory of organized crime must be able to explain its many and varied interrelations with the legal and legitimate economy. Indeed, it may be the case that organized illegal enterprise is required by the ongoing functioning and survival of legitimate and legal enterprise operating in the American economy. Organized crime may not represent an aberration, a pathology, or a blight on an otherwise healthy, moral, and legal economic system. Rather, organized crime "must be thought of as a natural growth, or as a developmental adjunct to our general system of private profit economy" (Vold, 1958, p. 240). And these "interrelations" may result in both illegally generated capital being invested in legal ventures and legal capital finding its way into illegal business operations. One reason that many American economists have recently appeared to be puzzled over the refusal of the American economy to respond to monetarist control and policy, that is, to "tight money," may be the impetus given the inflationary economy—even in periods of deep recession and high unemployment—by the investment in a large and growing criminal economy (Timmer, 1982).

The Productivity of Crime

Organized crime's integration into the American economy leads, logically, back to a theme that is struck again and again in our analysis of crime in the United States: one of the primary reasons for crime's pervasiveness and our inability to control it

---

[10] For a classic work in criminology which argues that the structure and operation of organized crime is determined essentially by a "Mafia," see Donald R. Cressey's *Theft of a Nation* (1969).

PANEL 8-5

The Seattle Crime Network

There were over a thousand people in Seattle who profited directly from the rackets, bootleg whiskey, organized theft and robbery, drug traffic, abortion rings, gambling, prostitution, land transactions, arson, phony stock sales, and usury. Everyone who successfully engages in these criminal activities must share the profits with *someone* or some group of people. The more regulated the criminal activities and the more successful the participants, the more systematized the profit sharing. The entire system is simply a collection of independent operators who cooperate and compete according to their ability, their power, and their interests.

Disparate as it is, widely distributed among people in different walks of life, and changing all the time, there is nonetheless a hierarchy. Some people are more important than others. In times of crisis some people have the power to make critical decisions while others do not. Not surprisingly, those who profit the most from the rackets and who also have the power to take action are the most likely to meet and discuss problems and prospects. In Seattle the group of power-holders who controlled and set policy for the illegal business enterprises varied. Over the years the more active participants included a King County prosecutor, a Seattle city council president, an assistant chief of police, city police captains, the King County sheriff, the King County jail chief, undersheriffs, the president of the Amusement Association of Washington (who had the only master's license for pinball machines in the county), a Seattle police major, and an official of the Teamsters Union. In addition there were persons from the business and professional community who were members of the network and who in a quiet, less conspicuous way were as influential over illegal business activities as were the more visible operatives listed above. They included a leading attorney who defended network members and joined them in investments in illegal enterprises, a realtor who arranged real-estate transactions and shared investments, an officer of one of the state's leading banks, a board member of a finance company that loaned money exclusively to businesses or individuals who were either members of or under the control of the network, and various labor union officials—mostly in the Teamsters Union, but high-level officials of other labor unions were also involved from time to time.

One of the problems with determining the real power sources in an enterprise as inherently secretive and variable as a crime cartel is of course the line between active participant (or policymaker) and compliant benefactor. For example, a prosperous retail store-owner in the city often invested in and profited from illegal enterprises ranging from real-estate frauds to drug traffic. He also financed and

Panel 8-5 (Continued)

arranged for the transportation of stolen jewelry out of the United States to Europe, where it could be recut and sold on the European market. He never set policy, never became involved in the day-to-day decisions, never allowed himself even to be consulted about the handling of a particular problem within the ongoing enterprises. Yet he knew of most of the problems and could well have been influential had he cared to make his wishes known. He preferred to remain silent. His decision, he told me, was based on the "good old American tradition of self-preservation." He felt that the less he was involved in "administration," the more likely he was to remain unconnected publicly with the "seamy side of business." He acknowledged, however, that when a newspaper reported the death of a member of the network due to "accidental drowning," he knew it was no accident.

A further problem is to decide the point at which one has enough information to feel confident that the rumors and allegations being put forward as "facts" by informants match sufficiently with other data to be acceptable. The people mentioned so far were all well established in the minds of all my informants in a position to know. These people also exhibited life-styles which clearly showed incomes in excess of anything they could have had from their legal incomes. (The county prosecutor claimed publicly that his standard of living exceeded that which his salary could support because of monies his wife had inherited.)

But it was also alleged by some informants, who should have known, that the real power in the illegal business enterprises lay with high-ranking officials in state politics, a close associate in Seattle, and a former Seattle city council member. I was unable to establish the validity of these claims. In the end the consistency of informant reports convinced me that the governor was indeed a beneficiary of heavy political campaign contributions from network principals. He, like many others, benefitted from the profits and left the management to others.

At one time (1963-65) it was fairly easy to identify seven people who constituted the backbone of the network. This group shifted, however, and some of the seven became less involved while some new people emerged as principals. Both composition and leadership are variable; success is determined by connections and profits. When drug trading becomes more precarious, the people involved may lose considerable influence; when cardrooms come under fire, those people whose profits or payoffs are principally in cardrooms lose their influence.

Whatever the composition, this coalition of shifting membership (but fairly constant leadership) persisted and had more to say about how the rackets were run than anyone else. It also met more or less regularly, but here too the pattern was not akin to a monthly board of directors' meeting but was more a series of meetings between key players from different walks of life. Politicians who were

Panel 8-5 (Continued)

deeply involved in the network met regularly at their "businessmen's club" with members of the city council, the county board of supervisors, and several key businessmen who were profiting from the rackets. Law-enforcement officers met monthly with a pinball operator who was the head of the Amusement Association, an association of pinball operators which was the official lobby for the pinball machine owners. The head of the Amusement Association in turn met with other businessmen, at least one of whom was reputed to be the bagman for state politicians.

Some sense of the organized–disorganized nature of the rackets can be gleaned from a series of incidents in the mid 1960s which involved an attempt by Bill Bennett (P) to take over part of the pinball operation in the city. Bill's brother Frank was one of the prominent racketeers in town, a man generally believed to be involved in prostitution and the collection of payoffs for state officials (including the governor) as well as the police. Bill decided that he wanted a piece of the action in the pinball business. He tried at first to demand a territory but he met with resistance. Pinballs were at the time concentrated pretty much in the hands of several people. The only master license in the county was held by the Amusement Association. As president, Ben Cichy represented not only his own interests as the major pinball operator in the state, but also the interests of other pinball operators. Ben Cichy was well protected in his position. As president of the association that looked out for the pinball interests, he met regularly with and allegedly paid substantial sums of money to politicians, to Frank Bennett (P), and to members of the police department. In addition, the Amusement Association collected from all pinball operators a monthly fee that was used to ply state and local politicians with liquor, parties, and women for favors, not the least of which were large campaign contributions to politicians who worked in the interests of pinball owners. Thus Bill Bennett was taking on some formidable opponents when he tried to muscle into the pinball business. On the other hand, Bill and his brother Frank were well connected in political and business circles. Among others, Frank

is its economic productivity. Crime, and particularly its organized variety, spurns and stabilizes the American economy by providing alternative forms of growth and profit. In short, crime is good business both inside and outside of the legal American economy.

Besides generating capital that can be invested in both legal and illegal business ventures, organized crime's economic productivity serves a "control function" in society. Radical criminologists maintain that corporate capitalist societies characterized by the near monopoly control of industrial capital and production inevi-

Panel 8-5 (Continued)

was closely allied with politicians who were the political and personal enemies of the county prosecutor and might well have been favorably disposed toward an attempt to undermine part of his political base.

When Bill's efforts to gain part of the pinball operation were turned down by Cichy and the other owners, he filed what is referred to as an "underworld antitrust suit." He and some of his men began throwing Molotov cocktails through the windows of places containing Cichy's machines. Some restaurant owners were roughed up. This caused some attention in the press, so people were getting nervous. To calm things down, the pinball operators offered to let Bill in if he would agree to pay them twenty thousand dollars for the loss of their territory plus a fee of two dollars a month for each machine over and above the fifty cents per machine that went to the Amusement Association for lobbying.

The agreement reached by the other pinball operators was, however, not satisfactory to the chief of police, who saw Bill as a "hoodlum." This was one of the few occasions when the chief put his foot down. An informant in the police department said that "in all likelihood" the chief vetoed the agreement as a result of support and instructions from the county prosecutor. Because of the trouble Bill had caused, the chief insisted that he leave the state, which he did.

Several features of this event are important. First, it underlines the competition between different persons acting primarily as individuals out to increase the size of their business and their profits. It also illustrates, however, that when the entire enterprise is threatened, it is possible for a coalition of the more powerful members of the rackets to force less powerful members to acquiesce. The incident also indicates an important element in the way any network protects itself. The two-fifty a month which Bill would have to pay for each machine was divided between protection (two dollars a month) and lobbying (fifty cents a month). The one activity is presumably criminal (by statute), the other legal.

Source: William J. Chambliss, On the Take: From Petty Crooks to Presidents, *Bloomington: Indiana University Press, 1978, pp. 61–66.*

tably lead to more and more of the population growing surplus to the processes of production and consumption.[11] Organized crime serves to absorb some of this "surplus population" by putting them to work—criminal work. A surplus population "out-of-control" can thus be brought "under control," and as the present worldwide and domestic economic downturn continues and the surplus popula-

[11] See the section "Radical Criminology" in Chapter 2 and "Theory and Street Crime" in Chapter 5.

Financiers

Jewelers	Attorneys
Realtors	Businessmen
Contractors	Industrialists
Bankers	

Organizers

Businessmen	**Politicians**	**Law-enforcement Officers**
Restaurant owners	City Councilmen	Chief of Police
Cardroom owners	Mayors	Assistant Chief of Police
Pinball machine license holders	Governors	Sheriff
Bingo parlor owners	State legislators	Undersheriff
Cabaret and hotel owners	Board of Supervisors members	County Prosecutor
Club owners	Licensing Bureau Chief	Assistant Prosecutor
Receivers of stolen property		Patrol Division Commanders
Pawnshop owners		Vice Squad Commanders
		Narcotics Officers
		Patrolmen
		Police Lieutenants, Captains, and Sergeants

Racketeers

Gamblers	Pimps	Prostitutes	Drug distributors	Usurers	Bookmakers

Figure 8-2 Seattle's crime network.

SOURCE: William J. Chambliss, *On the Take: From Petty Crooks to Presidents*, Bloomington, Indiana: Indiana University Press, 1978, p. 74.

tion becomes larger, we can only expect an expansion in organized criminal activity.[12]

Radical criminologist Stephen Spitzer (1975) has argued that organized crime has succeeded in creating a "parallel opportunity structure"—employment opportunities in illegal activities for persons who would otherwise be unemployed—that is able to hold in check the political discontent and/or dissent that might originate among members of the surplus population. He contends that the goods and services provided the surplus population by organized crime serve to prevent them, the surplus population, from readily identifying the sources of their political and economic exploitation in society. Organized crime's monopoly over the production and sale of illegal goods and services actually contributes to the public order in society that proves beneficial to elite and ruling groups or classes.[13]

---

[12] Even in the communist-planned state or city, organized crime flourishes: the Communist mayor of Naples, Italy, for example, explained recently that he would not dare move to enforce the law prohibiting the illegal cigarette trade in his city. Even with all of those employed in this illegal trade, the city's official unemployment rate exceeds 30 percent.

[13] And therefore, tends not to be policed. For an elaboration of this point of view, see the section below "Punishing Organized Crime: Economic and Political Obstacles."

More specifically, Michael Tabor (1971) believes that organized crime has been particularly effective in controlling American ghettos. Tabor's contention focuses on the organized distribution of heroin in ghetto areas. Heroin addiction affects primarily that portion of the surplus population that one could expect to present a serious threat to the prevailing social order: young, black, and unemployed. The illegal sale, distribution, and use of narcotic drugs can help to keep potential political actors in "a state of perpetual escapism from inhumane conditions in the ghetto" (Simon and Eitzen, 1982, p. 61).

The social control that is a consequence of organized crime's operations and tends to benefit ruling interests in society is, by and large "unconscious," not the end product of some grand conspiracy. However,

> There is some evidence that the theses of both Spitzer and Tabor are correct. We know that heroin addiction is highly concentrated in the ghetto areas of America, and that certain illegitimate gambling activities, such as numbers running, not only give poor people a source of hope that they will become wealthy, but also provide a source of employment. . . . (Simon and Eitzen, 1982, p. 61)

Corruption: Police, Politics, and Foreign Policy

Organized crime's perpetual survival and prosperity are dependent ultimately upon the relationships it can foster with law enforcement agencies and local and national governments to ensure the protection of its operations. An empirically adequate theory of organized crime must, therefore, be able to take full account of the glaring lack of enforcement and control vis-a-vis organized criminality in American society. A "political economy of organized crime" approach focuses in this regard on the processes of police and political corruption.[14]

Corruption may, at some levels at least, be so pervasive because organized crime is more powerful than government and its enforcement agencies. For example, Walter Reckless (1973) believes that organized crime "has more power and exerts more control over local government than local government exerts over it." But whatever the level of government, or the relative degree of organized crime's organized influence and power, it is safe to say that police and political corruption has increased steadily since Prohibition. Organized crime has increasingly replaced violence with corruption. Organized crime is less violent in the 1980s than it was in the 1930s and this is due primarily to its ability to replace guns and brass knuckles with payoffs and bribes.

To ensure its survival and continued profitability, organized crime corrupts police departments and governments with bribery, payoffs, kickbacks, campaign contributions, and the delivery of voters, and all public officials need do is "look the other way." Police officers and administrators, prosecuting attorneys, judges,

---

[14]In fact, it has been reported that most organized criminal operations include a position known as "corrupter" (see Cressey, 1969).

media personnel, city-council members, and legislators can all be corrupted in this way.

Historically, political corruption has served not only the economic interests of organized crime but the political interests of those corrupted as well. The criminal corruption of the political machines that has characterized so much of political life in urban America—particularly in the largest cities like Chicago and New York—has, for example, served to benefit both organized crime and political authority. The costs have included not only the suppression of populist and socialist opposition but also perversion of the essence of the democratic process:

> The first major services were those that they (organized criminals) rendered to political machines. . . . Their efforts in electioning may not have been uniformly successful, but the overall affect of the machine politics that they supported was to produce a city government that treated favorably the powerful business groups which also supported it and gave no openings for political participation to emergent socialist or populist groups. Indeed it was the racketeers themselves who mediated the demands of the proletariat to city hall. The rewards for these political services came in quite direct fashion since it was the politicians they served who protected their freedom to develop other markets. (McIntosh, 1973, pp. 63–64)

What emerged was the corruption of government officials that benefitted powerful criminal, political, and business interests. And, we can expect this to continue since "a few significant and continuing services to big business will be enough to create a context in which corrupt politicians and police can safely permit racketeering at all levels" (McIntosh, 1973, pp. 65–66). Since the effects of this criminal-police government-business coalition are essentially nondemocratic, radical criminologists have described this situation as one "in which criminal syndicates support the ruling class in a capitalist society via the suppression of genuine democracy among the relatively powerless in society"[15] (Simon, 1981, p. 359).

American foreign policy has also been corrupted by organized criminal interests. In exchange for protection of certain of organized crime's operations—both domestic and international—organized criminals have been willing to engage in the following kinds of activities: providing counter-intelligence for the U.S. Navy during World War II by monitoring German submarines, arranging for foreign agents and immigrants from the New York docks to assist the Allies invasion of Sicily in 1943, hiring out terrorist services to the CIA that were designed to "encourage" socialist dockworkers in Marseilles to abandon their refusal to move U.S. armaments bound to aid the French army in their war on Vietnam, assaulting communist picket lines across Europe, and becoming involved in the CIA's plan to assassinate Fidel Castro in Cuba[16] (Simon and Eitzen, 1982).

---

[15] This is, of course, quite contrary to the more conventional notion that organized crime is, for the most part, a Mafia that secretly threatens and is a foe of democratic institutions in American society.
[16] Of course organized crime had some real interest in removing Castro because he closed the casinos down during the revolution in Cuba. Batista, Castro's predecessor, had been a much closer friend of organized crime, inviting them and their casinos to Havana in the 1930s.

A CASE STUDY IN ORGANIZED CRIME: THE U.S. HEROIN INDUSTRY[17]

The heroin industry is a mainstay of the political economy of much of the capitalist world and it shall not be eliminated any more readily than will the automobile, banking or construction industries.

William J. Chambliss

Not only are millions of Americans addicted to drugs, many banks are addicted to drug money.

Senator William Proxmire

[The banks] all handle a big flow of narcotics money and they're not interested in whether it's narcotics money. They're just interested that it's money that they can use to make more money.

House Committee Staff Member

There is in the United States a growing *underground economy* that is becoming an ever-increasing and significant part of the Gross National Product. Money, capital, funds for investment, are increasingly accumulated in this sector of the economy, albeit illicitly and illegally. The media (NBC Nightly News: A Special Segment, in April 1980 for example) have reported on the Internal Revenue Service's estimation of the size of this "alternative" economy. The IRS estimates an underground economy of $275 to $300 billion in untaxed goods and services per year in the United States. Furthermore, the IRS believes that at least one third of the underground economy is generated by organized crime's illegal sale of illegal goods and services (loansharking, gambling, drugs, prostitution) and street crime. If these figures are accurate, these two types of crime are at least one fifth as productive in the United States economy as the entire federal budget. And it should be pointed out that the IRS is using an extremely conservative indicator of the size and productivity of the criminal portion of the underground economy since it must rely on "reported crime rates" (that always reflect high levels of "unreported crime") as a basis for calculating untaxed goods and services.

Economists have used other "unofficial" indicators to arrive at estimates of the size of this "alternative" economy. In 1977, Gutmann derived a $200 billion figure for the underground economy. Later, Feige argued that a more accurate figure was probably closer to $700 billion, approximately 30 percent of the 1980 U.S. gross national product (see Brom, 1980).

Although the links between legal and illegal business enterprise are becoming increasingly visible (as is pointed out below), identification of those engaged in these activities has not always been entirely clear. However, the coordinating and controlling interest in the underground economy appears to reside in a national crime network.

---

[17] The case study material presented here is a slightly revised version of material that appeared in Doug A. Timmer, "The Productivity of Crime in the United States: Drugs and Capital Accumulation," *Journal of Drug Issues*, Summer, 1982.

Since World War II, the economic growth in crime networks has been unmatched by the growth rate of any sector of the legal economy. While the nation's legal economy was booming with the extension of credit and expropriation of Third World resources, markets for illegal goods and services were expanding even faster. Profits in the illegal sector of the economy were (and remain) extremely high and federal, state, or local regulatory restrictions were (and continue to be) virtually nonexistent.

As profit rates fall in the legal sector of the American economy (from about 15 percent in 1940 to about 5 percent in 1980)[18], due not only to the internal contradictions of the U.S. economy (inflation, recession, stagflation) but also to increasing Third World resistance to the expropriation of its resources and capital (via producer cartels, socialist liberation movements, etc.), investment in the illegal sector becomes more attractive. Windfall profits in the underground economy are unconstrained by taxation, high labor costs, retirement and pension plans, profit sharing, large advertising budgets, consumer safety laws and worker health and safety regulations and directives from OSHA (Occupational Safety and Health Administration). In sum, in times of profit squeeze, the illegal economy flourishes and assists business in establishing former rates of profit.

Crime and other forms of the underground economy, then, present a more advantageous mechanism for the private accumulation of investment capital and profit under certain historical, social, and economic conditions. Recently, these conditions have encouraged increasing levels of investment in illegal enterprise in the United States. There are at least four reasons for this. First, the illegal accumulation of private profit and funds for investment are characterized by technologically intense production and high rates of growth (i.e., illegal industries tend to be "growth industries"). Second, these kinds of illegal business activities result in untaxed and unusually (as compared with licit and legal investment) high profit margins. Third, there are significant links between illegally generated capital and profit on the one hand, and legally obtained capital and profits on the other. And finally, a "stagflating" U.S. economy (where inflation and recession occur simultaneously) deepens conflict between classes and is responsible for changes in labor-market conditions that have grown increasingly favorable to the sale of illicit and illegal commodities. Indeed, without these exaggerated shifts in local, regional, national, and international labor supply and demand, the three processes described above would probably not be able to assure the high levels of profitability that now characterize illegal enterprise in American society. (We will explain all of this in more detail below.)

The entire process can be illustrated by examining the political economy of drug trafficking in the United States, the most profitable heroin market in the world.[19]

Capital, Technology, and Growth

There can be no denial that significant amounts of capital—in fact, even great fortunes—have been amassed via the sale of opium. China was opened to the

[18] These estimates are from URPE (the Union of Radical Political Economists).
[19] For a concise summary of the historical development of the U.S. heroin trade, see Chambliss (1977).

West through a series of wars fought essentially for the control of poppy fields, and many British and American fortunes were based almost exclusively on the opium trade (e.g., the Peabodys, the Cabots, the Delanos). World leaders like Chiang Kai-shek got their start in the underworld dealing in opium (Yurick, 1970).

In the United States today, heroin sales are booming. For instance, on one street in Harlem alone:

> Conservative estimates indicate that for at least four hours a day, 365 days a year, $400 worth of heroin is sold per minute on 115th Street. This is $24,000 an hour, $96,000 a day, $672,000 a week. Here 13-, 14-, and 15-year-old black kids sell heroin almost as fast as McDonald's sells hamburgers. (Nelson, 1980, p. 12)

The New York City police have reported that from November 1976 to November 1979, 50,598 bags of heroin, 7779 bottles of methadone (heroin's government-sponsored legal "alternative"), and 61,820 hypodermic needles and syringes were seized in Harlem's 28th precinct.

If, as Chambliss (1977) estimates and most experts agree, there are roughly 1 million heroin addicts in the United States who must each spend approximately $30,000 a year to support their habits, then the gross annual sale of heroin in the U.S. exceeds $30 billion.[20] This does not represent an insignificant part of the national economy. In 1970, for example, General Motors, Exxon, IBM, ITT and the six other largest multinational corporations in the world had gross sales of less than $30 billion (Chambliss, 1977, p. 68). Today, only the international petroleum industry may surpass the heroin industry in volume of business. If these figures are correct, in 1970, only 20 countries in the world generated a Gross National Product in excess of U.S. heroin sales (Chambliss, 1977, p. 68).

By 1970, about 90 percent of the U.S. heroin supply came from the opium fields of the "fertile triangle," the geographic intersection of Burma, Laos, and Thailand in Southeast Asia. This area was still controlled by elements of the Kuomintang who dealt the opium through Taiwan and American middlemen. Transportation of the raw opium to heroin processing plants in the large cities of Southeast Asia and on to the United States for consumption was generally provided by two CIA (U.S. Central Intelligence Agency) "contract" airlines: Air America and Air Continental (Yurick, 1970; McCoy, 1972).

American technology transformed the Southeast Asia opium trade and thus increased the economic productivity of heroin in the United States. According to the Committee of Concerned Asian Scholars:

> The old opium trade moved slowly by caravan down from the hills and then by riverboat, winding its way down the Mekong Valley through Laos, Cambodia and Vietnam. The trade was dangerous and the opium might pass through many

---

[20] Other illicit and illegal drugs also generate large quantities of capital and profit. For example, drug trafficking is now the largest industry in South Florida. The DEA (Drug Enforcement Administration) now estimates the total gross value of the cocaine trade in the Miami area to be in excess of $7 billion annually. Tourism, the largest licit and legal industry in South Florida, had a gross value of $5.2 billion in 1979 (U.S. Senate Committee on Banking, Housing, and Urban Affairs, 1980).

middlemen before reaching its destination, thus increasing risk and reducing profit. . . . (CCAS, 1972, pp. 62–63)

But later, American supplied airplanes could transport opium and heroin between major collection, processing, relay, and marketing points. Electronic communication helped coordinate travel, integrate supplier networks, orchestrate dealerships, and transfer funds. The old labor-intensive routes were bypassed. A technologically intense heroin industry consolidated trade, reduced risk, and increased profit (CCAS, 1972).

Also, heroin (like many of the other commodities of organized crime) is an ideally profitable commodity. Economic growth is built into the sale and distribution of heroin. Its market necessarily expands: the addict must steal or "push" to finance an addiction. To the extent that the heroin industry is able to "coerce" addicts into being advertisers, sales persons, and distributors of their product so as to finance their own addiction, it is truly a "growth industry."

Profit Margin

Heroin may be the most profitable enterprise in the United States. It is probably also the nation's second largest consumer import (oil being the largest). The business is so lucrative that its control may be impossible within the structure of a capitalist economy, no matter what the legal penalties. Where millions of dollars can be made in a technologically-intense growth industry in periods as short as six months, many in this illegal enterprise are willing to risk even mandatory death penalties for their employees. One source reports that

A $2,000 investment in Rangoon, Beirut or elsewhere is worth about $30,000 as soon as it reaches the United States. And it's worth nearly $500,000 when broken down and sold on the streets. (Bunker, 1976, p. 596)

Another estimates that:

Ten kilos of opium (22 lbs.) bring hill-tribe growers in Laos only a few hundred dollars, but they can be refined into heroin worth some $16,000 when imported into this country. Watered down and divided up, it's worth about $300,000 on the streets of our cities. (CCAS, 1972, p. 12)

Whenever U.S. Customs makes a seizure of 50 or 100 pounds of heroin, the mass media proclaim its value to be millions of dollars. It is important to remember that this is the drug's street value, its market value as a commodity for consumption. It does not represent its cost, the initial capital investment. In effect, something worth 20 cents in the international market converts to a U.S. market value of $50 to $75. Clearly, this kind of crime is a good investment and it pays well.

Organized crime is vitally involved in the drug traffic in the United States. Only a small percentage is stopped by government efforts, such as this cocaine bust at Miami International Airport.

The Economic Productivity of Illicit Drugs: Linkages to the Legal Economy

Via the heroin trade, money/capital is formed and then takes a variety of paths—some legal, some illegal—the world over. These paths multiply the economic effects of heroin and further establish it as part of the capitalist economy. Besides the obvious links to street crime, other illegal spinoffs of the heroin industry generating still more capital and private profit include crime in the criminal justice system itself.

Police incomes are supplemented by the heroin industry. Bribes are taken in exchange for protection, and confiscated heroin is resold on the illicit open market. This flow of capital does not stop with the police; it proceeds upward throughout the criminal justice system and beyond to corrections officials, district attorneys, judges, and the political coffers of federal, state, and local officials. This results in discretionary income for police and other criminal justice officials that may be converted to "luxury" items and other conspicuous consumption, as well as to more productive investment: second homes, small income properties, second cars, occasional vacations, small investment portfolios, college expenses for children. A whole new line of consumption is supported.[21]

[21] Other "minor" market activities spring up in and around the heroin industry. An excellent example of this is the sale of clean (drug-free) urine to heroin addicts who must maintain abstinence or face further criminal proceedings initiated by probation and parole officers, jailors, prison officials, or the criminal courts.

But the economic productivity of this illegal sector of the economy is not separate from, or contradictory to, the legal economy. Legality and illegality exist as one system. Historically, capitalism has commanded the international economy by working the entire range of legal and illegal economic activity.

In regard to the heroin industry, the linkages between legal and illegal enterprise are strong. Legal capital and profit accumulation dependent upon *illegal* activity, that goes beyond the replacement purchasing (replacing stolen goods) and the development of the home-security products industry already discussed in Chapter 5, includes:

1. *Development of police personnel and technology.* Increased alarm over the spread of heroin use and abuse and its relationship to growing street crime rates has led to police requests for more funds for improvements and expansion in crime control personnel and technology. For example, this has led to the development of a new police role or position: the undercover agent or ''narc.'' In short, lines of production for expanding police technologies (e.g., new and better equipment for undercover surveillance of suspected drug users) are supported and jobs are created.

2. *Medical and drug company growth.* While medical and pharmaceutical industries rush to develop the ''cure'' for heroin addiction, one should remember that heroin was invented to cure the problem of morphine addiction medically. The state supports this productive activity. Federal government subsidy to the drug industry produced methadone, now taking its turn as the legal medical treatment for a ''newer'' illegal narcotic addiction—heroin. Also with the increased market competition of illicit drugs like heroin, large drug companies devote more and more resources to the production and distribution of legal alternatives (i.e., legal narcotics and barbiturates).

3. *Drug prevention and therapy industries.* All over the United States, clinics, half-way houses and counseling programs run by federal, state, and local governments, private hospitals, and churches have sprung up. Scientific theories of the causes of addiction abound. Theories of its cure proliferate. Research is financed; experimental programs funded. The point of scientific activity in this ''therapy market'' is to invent, sell, and fund a treatment program. As Yurick (1970) has put it:

> Again, each psycho-social theory of the cause and cure of the habit doesn't have to be valid: what is valid is the ability to sell the theory, to get funding for the theory, to convince some legislator (and possibly addicts) that the program works, to demonstrate some successes, and to generate in the wake of failures still further programs. Social scientists compete fiercely on the open market for funding, and competition is the spur to the growth of a body of scientific capital: the point is to get that program on the market first and sell it. This has also given rise to a new job category: the professional junkie who goes from program to program getting funds to keep alive, demonstrating the success of each program. (Yurick, 1970, p. 35)

With these programs comes jobs for multitudes of program administrators, clerical workers, social workers, drug counselors, psychiatrists, clinical psychologists, sociologists of drugs and drinking, and reformed addict lecturers. Also, since the heroin addict is criminally defined in the United States, and since he or she is at least somewhat dependent on some kind of street crime to support an addicted life-style, occupational expansion in the criminal justice system occurs. More court and corrections (probation, parole, and prison) employees are needed. Job prospects for criminologists improve.

Even a conservative on domestic social policy and programs such as former President Richard Nixon asked the U.S. Congress to allocate $155 million to heroin rehabilitation projects. A sizeable share of this money went to the LEAA (Law Enforcement Assistance Administration) to create the TASC (Treatment Alternatives to Street Crime) Project. This program was intended as a nationwide effort specifically designed to address the problem of the relationship of heroin addiction and street crime; the aim was to divert addicted offenders into heroin treatment facilities and away from prison where their addiction was typically maintained.

An additional component of the economic productivity of therapy is the infrastructure of treatment programs. Heroin rehabilitation requires a physical plant. Millions of dollars are spent purchasing land and building new centers or remodeling old ones. Architects and contractors are hired. Plans are paid for even though they may never materialize.

Labor-Market Conditions: Drugs and the Accumulation of Private Profit and Investment Capital

Helmer (1975) has argued that business cycles, labor markets, and unemployment are not unrelated to the sale and consumption of narcotic drugs. More specifically, he concluded that the history of drug use in the United States has been, and is, an undeniably "working-class phenomenon." As we have pointed out, he further insists that this working-class characterization of illicit drug use "has been a specific cause, not a general consequence, of narcotics prohibition when it has been enacted" (Helmer, 1975, p. 7).

Historically, as labor-market conditions (the supply of, and the demand for, labor) have responded to the dictates of the investment practices of big business, not only have the conditions of working-class life changed, but so has the membership of this class. Consumption of illegal drugs in the United States has followed the labor surplus, and organized crime's sale of these drugs has served to control and "anesthesize" an historically varying surplus population. Illegal drug use and addiction was associated first with exclusionary campaigns against the Chinese and Mexicans when their labor was no longer needed (to build the nation's rail system, for example), then with economically depressed (and potentially politically explosive) black, brown, and Latino ghettos, and even more recently, with the labor surplus represented by the American army's return from the war in Vietnam. (The latter is historically unique in its introduction of a relatively large number of *white* working-class young men into the addict population.)

At present, a U.S. economy plagued with inflation, unemployment, and generalized economic slowdown helps create the labor-market conditions for expanded illegal capital and profit accumulation through the sale of illicit drugs. As the labor surplus grows in the ghettos of all colors, and increasingly creeps into white working-class neighborhoods and communities made marginal to economic production and consumption, the illicit and illegal market for drugs expands. Indeed, without these shifts in labor-market supply and demand, it is highly unlikely that the illegal accumulation of capital and profit characterized by technologically intense production, high growth rates, untaxed and unregulated profit margins, and significant linkages with legal business would be nearly as successful and efficient as presently is the case.

The Structured Failure of Law Enforcement and Crime-dependent Capitalism

When a Citizen's Commission to Investigate the FBI obtained the files of a Bureau office in Media, Pennsylvania, they found only 1 percent of the active caseload to be concerned with the organized crime network in the United States. On the other hand, more than one half of the cases dealt with draft resistance, the antiwar movement, AWOL GIs, black community organizations, and other progressive political and labor groups (CCAS, 1972).

Clearly, all-out law enforcement efforts vis-a-vis the trafficking and marketing of heroin in the United States do not occur. More serious effort in this direction would not only make the drug's transportation and distribution by a national crime network more difficult but might also slow the spread of heroin addiction. In both 1968 and 1969, less than 200 pounds of illegal heroin entering the United States were seized by federal law enforcement officials. By 1970, the Nixon administration had decided to crack down on the international heroin traffic (an explanation for this stepped-up law enforcement effort is presented below); over 600 pounds were seized. In 1971, 1600 pounds of heroin were confiscated. In 1972, the efforts of the U.S. Customs Office and the Bureau of Dangerous Drugs resulted in the seizure of 2700 pounds of illegal heroin. But the figures fell to 900 pounds in 1973 and less than 600 pounds in 1974 (Chambliss 1977, p. 72). The point is that, even during peak periods of federal law enforcement activity, insignificant amounts of heroin entering the United States have been seized. It has been estimated by the Federal Bureau of Narcotics that at least 25,000 pounds of heroin enter the United States each year (CCAS, 1972). Others estimate that 1 pound of heroin that makes it into the United States would make up for the seizure of 20 pounds, and that U.S. law enforcement efforts have never seized more than 5 percent of the imported heroin in any given year (Bunker, 1976).

Roughly 5 tons of pure heroin are required annually to supply about 1 million American addicts. "How," Bunker has asked, "can we stop 5 tons spread among the 100 million tons of imports, among the 100 million persons arriving on 300,000 airplanes and 150,000 ships?" (Bunker, 1976, p. 596). The odds against the enforcement of drug laws are staggering.

But the costs of nonenforcement, too, are high. Again, there is the street crime related to heroin traffic and addiction. The estimated total cost of heroin addiction in the United States is between $7.5 and $10 billion annually. This cost includes financial loss from crimes, lost tax revenue, law enforcement expenditure, and added expense for criminal courts and correctional facilities. But, it must be remembered, that these are public costs, incurred as private interests accumulate capital and profit through the sale of heroin. The public loses; private, organized criminal interests win.

Chambliss (1978) has pointed out how what may appear as strict law enforcement vis-a-vis domestic and international heroin trafficking, may actually be a political shift in the control of the national crime network: from the Democratic to Republican Party, for example. He has described the Nixon administration's war on organized crime in general, and on Meyer Lansky, a prominent figure in the national crime network, in particular:

> The final attack on Lansky was probably the most successful and the most serious. The Republicans attempted to close off his sources of heroin. They did this by pressuring the Turkish government to enforce the law prohibiting the growing of opium. . . . At that time . . . Turkey accounted for probably 90 percent of the opium processed into heroin and shipped to the United States. By 1972 . . . Lansky had lost control over a major source of his financial empire. The Republican administration also pressured the Latin American governments whose countries were layover points in the heroin route to America, and Lansky's principal Latin American coordinator of heroin traffic, Auguste Ricord, was forced out of Argentina, where he had been managing the traffic for years. . . . Meanwhile, the heroin traffic from Southeast Asia, especially from the Golden Triangle of northern Thailand, Burma, and Laos, expanded production and a new source of heroin for the incredibly lucrative American market opened up. It is unknown whether this new heroin source was linked to Republican politicians, but the fact that the CIA and the South Vietnamese governments under generals Ky and Thieu actively aided the development of this heroin source suggests that such a link is not beyond the realm of possibility. . . . (Chambliss, 1978, pp. 165–166)

There are essentially two reasons why law enforcement, as it relates to the heroin industry, is structured to fail. The first is international politics; the second has to do with the political economy of U.S. law enforcement and crime control.

In the international arena, the U.S. government has normally not encouraged or pressured foreign governments to reduce heroin traffic. In places like Indochina and Turkey, for example, the U.S. government has been politically and militarily dependent on the government officials, military generals, and businessmen who profit from the opium trade. The U.S. government has not wanted to offend regimes in these countries because they represent a counter-revolutionary force instrumental in the control of popular peasant, nationalist, and socialist movements and organizations. These movements and and organizations, of course, have been a constant threat to American-based transnational corporations and U.S. military bases located in these countries. Thus, the "CIA, instead of tracking down and breaking up the international heroin network, spends most of its time and . . . tax dollars propping up these right-wing governments'' (CCAS, 1972, p. 9).

Finally, data on the heroin trade and its relationship to the legal economy in the United States confirm Chambliss' (1978) contention that the very foundation of advanced capitalist-democratic societies like the United States is both criminal and legal. Societies such as these are not characterized by basically smooth functioning economies that are only mildly and occasionally irritated by a pathological criminality. Rather, the political economy of the United States (and societies structured similarly) utilizes the processes of both the legal and illegal private accumulation of both legal and illegal capital and profit. And the crime necessary for the accumulation of this illicit and illegal capital and profit is not only tolerated and condoned, it is generated and required by the structure and operation of American society. There are not two economies in advanced capitalist-democratic societies; there is one, with two highly interrelated spheres—one legal, one illegal. Furthermore, the relationship of law enforcement and crime control to the illegal sphere of the economy, because of this sphere's interrelation with the legal economic sphere, often structurally ensures the failure to police or control the U.S. heroin trade. More likely law enforcement responses in this area are nonenforcement and/or covert facilitation (Marx, G., n.d.).

In sum, the advanced capitalist economy of the United States is not only crime ridden, but crime dependent. We have attempted to describe and analyze the processes involved in the illegal accumulation of capital and profit and their impact on the ''legal'' economy by examining the sale and distribution of heroin in the United States.

PUNISHING ORGANIZED CRIME: ECONOMIC AND POLITICAL OBSTACLES

There are at least four obstacles to any significant and effective crime control or law enforcement applied to organized crime in American society. Three of them— organized crime's corruption of governments and the police, the extent of the integration of organized criminal interests into the licit and legal economy, and organized criminality's contribution to ongoing processes of order and control— have been discussed earlier in this chapter. The other—organized crime's potential to assist the state (particularly local and state governments) in resolving its present fiscal crisis—is mentioned for the first time in this section. Let us consider each of the four obstacles in turn:

Corruption

We have attempted to document the corrupting influence of organized crime on local, state, and national governments and law enforcement agencies throughout this chapter. We only want to reiterate and reemphasize the point here: organized crime's existence and profitability are dependent on the corruption of government and law enforcement. After an extensive documentation of the incredible expanse of organized crime's activity and enterprise, the writers of a special series of articles on organized crime for a leading business publication in the United States contended that to launch an "all-out attack" on the operations of organized crime could well mean an "all-out attack" on many of our most legitimate, legal, and "sacred" institutions as well. The corruption runs deep: "You cannot move against such an invisible enterprise without destroying the most valuable parts of the visible society that protects it" (Cook and Carmichael, 1980, p. 158).

In one last example of the kind of political obstacle that the corruption of governments and law enforcement creates for the effective control of organized crime, historian Samuel Walker describes former FBI Director J. Edgar Hoover's manipulation of the agency that could perhaps have stood the best chance of combating crime networks that were national in scope:

> The FBI was logically the agency best equipped to attack organized crime. Yet, it did virtually nothing. For reasons that are not entirely clear, Hoover chose to ignore organized crime and continue his emphasis on bankrobbers and Communists. Perhaps organized crime was too formidable a foe. This touched off a long and bitter struggle within the Justice Department. One faction urged a vigorous attack on organized crime, while Hoover marshaled his support in Congress against it. . . . Critics of the FBI argued that the bureau had almost completely ignored organized crime. . . . (Walker, 1980, p. 207)

Linkages to the Legal Economy

Much of this chapter on organized crime has been concerned with illustrating the linkages between legal and illegal economic enterprises in the United States. Again, these interrelations are so pervasive that some sociologists and criminologists have concluded that the very structure, organization, and operation of the American economy is a criminal-legal one; that the American economy is not only crime ridden, but crime dependent. Others have begun to argue that although a few economic enterprises may be purely legal or illegal, the more typical American business represents some mix or combination of legal and illegal activities (see, e.g., Smith, 1980).

Not surprisingly then, long-time students of organized crime like Ralph Salerno say, "Businessmen deal with organized crime on whatever terms they have to. . . . But there is no demand from the business establishment to say, 'Hey, goddammit, do something about organized crime' " (quoted in Cook and Carmichael, 1980, p. 145). In other words, even independent of the corruption of government and law enforcement, there are serious economic obstacles blocking the effective control of organized crime: the business community's welfare and profitability are often linked to and dependent upon organized criminal activity and, therefore, this very powerful and influential part of the community is often uninterested in any kind of genuine law enforcement effort.

"Orderly" Crime

We have discussed in this chapter some of the ways in which organized criminal operations can serve to aid the social control of so-called problem populations. The increasing numbers of persons who find themselves excluded from both economic production and consumption in advanced capitalist societies make up, according to the perspective of radical criminology, a surplus population. This part of society—lest it organize and protest its plight (thus threatening those in charge of political and economic institutions run in their interest)—must be controlled. Organized crime may assist in this control effort to the extent that some of this surplus population can be absorbed into the illegal marketplace via illegal employment and thus have its potential for dissent diluted and diverted. And, as we have seen, in some cases the consumers of organized crime's products (e.g., narcotic drugs) may become so "anesthetized" in their consumption that any and all political organizations and activities that would challenge their exploitation in society are thwarted.

Through its ability to assist in the securing of social order and control, any crime that can contribute this much to the political and economic status quo, radical criminology warns, will tend to go unpoliced. Here we refer the reader back to Table 2-1 in Chapter 2. This "typology of policed and unpoliced crime," it should be remembered, suggests that social control is as important a variable in predicting whether or not a particular kind of activity is policed in the United States as is whether or not the activity is illegal. The typology also suggests that crimes that are disorderly (as well as some legal behaviors), that disrupt and disturb the social order, are policed: street crime and victimless crime. On the other hand, crimes that are "orderly"—crimes that are corporate and organized—are not policed. This has led radical criminologists to the conclusion that as long as law enforcement is characterized primarily by its interest in social control—as opposed to crime control—efforts to police and control organized criminal interests will remain largely ineffective and symbolic (see Block and Chambliss, 1981).

The Fiscal Crisis of the State

At the end of the previous chapter we argued that by criminalizing and punishing the so-called victimless crimes (e.g., gambling, prostitution, addiction), the state (particularly local and state governments) deprives itself of a source of revenue that could aid in the resolution of budget deficits and fiscal crises. These revenues, we suggested, are gathered instead by organized crime. Because of this, some observers have predicted that we can expect governments at all levels in the United States to legalize some of this crime in the near future (e.g., Skolnick and Dombrink, 1978). There is evidence that this is happening already in selected cities and states. This could mean that as the state begins to compete with organized crime for a part of its revenues, its enforcement and control effort vis-a-vis its primary competitor would pick up. However, it may be even more likely that governments will become more corrupted by, and integrated with, organized

PANEL 8-6

An Editorial on Organized Crime's Corruption of U.S. Foreign Policy: Who's "Soft on Crime"?

William Kennedy, the U.S. attorney in San Diego, was fired this week because he took his job seriously. That's not the way the Justice Department described it, of course. Attorney General William French Smith said the action was taken because Kennedy had made "improper comments" about a pending case. Those comments, he said, "were highly prejudicial to the interests of the United States."

If Smith really believes that, he has peculiar ideas about what those interests are. Kennedy got in hot water because he confirmed disclosures in the San Diego Union that Justice Department officials blocked prosecution of a former Mexican official who had been implicated in a multi-million-dollar stolen-car ring. Kennedy confirmed that the prosecution was halted after the Central Intelligence Agency reported that the official was a key U.S. intelligence source.

If Kennedy had kept his mouth shut, or if he had leaked the information anonymously (which is how it frequently is done in Washington), he would still be U.S. attorney. Kennedy was fired because he played it straight.

The CIA has a right to protect the iden-tities of its informants. But those informants are not entitled to a license to steal from the American people. In this case, the need for secrecy seems silly. The official in question was formerly the chief of the national police in Mexico. Surely, it is not surprising for the head of a friendly intelligence service to exchange information with U.S. intelligence services.

Kennedy was caught up in the Reagan administration's obsessive drive to suppress information that the public has a right to know. The administration has sought to weaken the Freedom of Information Act and has supported legislation making it a crime to disclose the names of intelligence agents.

Kennedy said he was aware of the need to keep secrets, "but I'm concerned about the victims—car owners or the insurance companies that have paid off claims."

It says a lot that Smith was more interested in protecting the possible perpetrators of crimes than in protecting the victims of crimes, and that to achieve that end he was willing to fire a diligent and candid public servant. It makes one wonder who in Washington is "soft on crime."

Source: "Who's 'soft on crime'?" The Des Moines Register and Tribune, *Opinion page, April 10, 1982.*

crime as it enters into these new ventures. To assume otherwise might underestimate significantly the relative power and influence of organized criminal interests in the United States:

To its proponents, both within and without the gaming industry, legalized casino gambling seems a painless way to raise government revenues, take pressure off the tax payer and avert cutbacks in vital government services. But even if these dubious propositions should hold, it's a virtual certainty that these worthy goals cannot be realized without funneling additional hundreds of millions of dollars into the coffers of organized crime. (Cook, 1980b, p. 104)

Yet another obstacle to the control of organized crime in American society may be in the offing.

In conclusion, we quote William Chambliss to summarize the political and economic obstacles to controlling and punishing organized crime, and also to pull together the perspective employed throughout this chapter—*the political economy of organized crime:*

> Money is the oil of our present-day machinery, and elected public officials are the pistons that keep the machine operating. Those who come up with the oil, whatever its source, are in a position to make the machinery run the way they want to. Crime is an excellent producer of capitalism's oil. Those who want to affect the direction of the machine's output find that the money produced by crime is as effective in helping them get where they want to go as is the money produced in any other way. Those who produce the money from crime thus become the people most likely to control the machine. Crime is not a by-product of an otherwise effectively working political economy: it is a main product of that political economy. Crime is in fact a cornerstone on which the political and economic relations of democratic-capitalist societies are constructed.
>
> In every city of the United States, and in many other countries as well, criminal organizers sell sex and drugs, provide an opportunity to gamble, to watch pornographic films, or to obtain a loan, an abortion, or a special favor. Their profits are a mainstay of the electoral process of America and their business is an important (if unrecorded) part of the gross national product. The business of organized crime in the United States may gross as much as one hundred billion dollars annually—or as little as forty billion—either way the profits are immense, and the proportion of the gross national product represented by money flowing from crime cannot be gainsaid. Few nations in the world have economies that compare with the economic output of criminal activities in the United States. (Chambliss, 1978, pp. 1–2)

CHAPTER REVIEW

1. The history of the development of organized crime in the United States can be described roughly in terms of three distinct stages: (1) the pre-Prohibition era when there was intense competition for the "right" to provide illegal goods and services in the vice districts of most large cities, and organized crime was primarily made up of small-scale operations; (2) the Prohibition era when the provision of illegal booze led to the consolidation (largely through the process

of gangland violence) of organized crime's many small-scale enterprises into a more profit-efficient, large-scale, corporate organization; and (3) the post-Prohibition era (up to and including the present) when organized crime, using the management and organizational techniques of modern corporate bureaucracies and the enormous wealth and assets gained during Prohibition, not only branched out and began providing new illegal goods and services but also became significantly integrated with legal business activities.

2. Organized crime can be defined as "business enterprises organized for the purpose of making economic gain through illegal activities."

3. Organized crime is dependent on at least three interrelated phenomena for its continued existence: (1) consumer demand for goods, services and activities that are illegal; (2) an organization capable of producing and supplying these goods, services, and activities on an ongoing basis; and (3) the corruption of political and law enforcement officials who will provide protection for these illegal organizations and operations.

4. The activities of organized crime in the United States fall into three categories: (1) the illegal control of the illegal sale and distribution of particular goods, services, and activities (e.g., illegal gambling, illegal narcotics, loansharking, and prostitution); (2) the illegal control and sponsorship of legal activities and legitimate businesses (e.g., loans, owning and operating resort casinos and hotels, investment in and control over real estate development and firms and federal reserve banks); and (3) the illegal operation of numerous "rackets" (e.g., labor union racketeering and extortion from legitimate businesses).

5. Estimates of the annual revenues and profits of organized criminal enterprises in the United States indicate that organized crime is one of our largest "industries."

6. Neither traditional sociological nor interactionist theories are well suited to explaining organized crime. Both are focused on the crimes of individuals, not on the crimes of organizations. Furthermore, traditional sociological perspectives have emphasized the role factors in the "immediate social environment" play in the generation of crime. These factors—like poverty, broken homes, deteriorating schools, and so on—are not the factors associated with an organized crime that often is a part of the most politically powerful and wealthy sectors of society. The interactionist perspective is also inadequate because it leads to a rather exclusive concern with those crimes and criminals that are labeled and stigmatized as such—labels that organized crime has been able to escape with some ease even though its activities are no less criminal than those of street criminals less able to escape this stigmatization. Radical criminology is the best explanation of organized crime because it is most able to explain crimes that (1) are economic in nature, (2) are organized, and (3) are an integrated part of American political and economic institutions and thus escape significant criminalization.

7. An adequate theory of organized crime must recognize "the myth of the Mafia": that organized crime represents a "national crime network" of criminal, business, and political interests, not a small number of Italian or Sicilian

"families" that can easily be scapegoated for our "crime problem." It must also recognize the extent to which organized criminal interests are integrated into the legitimate and legal economy; the way in which the economic productivity of organized crime serves ruling interests in society, assisting in the social control of a growing surplus population by providing a "parallel opportunity structure" and by "mystifying" the sources of this population's exploitation; and the ways in which organized crime's continued existence and profitability are dependent on the corruption of police, government, and foreign policy.

8. Political and economic obstacles to policing and punishing organized crime include the corruption of governments and their law enforcement agencies, the way in which organized criminal enterprise is integrated with legal business activity and institutions, the fact that organized crime tends to be "orderly" crime that contributes to the social order and stability that serves the interests of established institutions and those who benefit most from them, and the further entanglement of local and state governments with organized criminal interests as they legalize previously illegal activities (e.g., gambling) to help resolve their budgetary crises.

9 Corporate Crime

**CHAPTER
OUTLINE**

Conceptual Clarity

    Unit of analysis
    What organizational behaviors are "criminal"?

The Extent of Corporate Crime

    Edwin Sutherland's study: prior to 1944
    Fortune's study: 1970 to 1979
    The Clinard Report: 1975 to 1976

The Categories of Corporate Crime

    Crimes against employees
    Crimes against consumers
    Collective jeopardy: pollution of the environment
    Human jeopardy: international dimensions

The Punishment of Corporate Crime
Explanations for Corporate Crime

    Criminogenic social conditions
    The interactionist perspective
    The radical perspective

KEY TERMS

    Corporate crime
    Corporate dumping
    Monopoly
    Monopoly capitalism
    Price fixing
    Price gouging
    Shared monopoly

Over 40 years ago Edwin Sutherland, the esteemed criminologist, tried with minimal success to direct the attention of his colleagues away from street criminals and toward what he termed "white-collar" crimes—those crimes committed by "respectable" persons.[1] He combined in this category crimes by individuals and crimes by organizations. Chapter 6 focused on these crimes by individuals, such as fraud and embezzlement. This chapter is devoted to the second segment of Sutherland's concept—those crimes by economic organizations.

These crimes by corporations have much greater economic and social consequences in American society than any other type of crime—at an annual cost of $200 billion in inflated prices; poisoned air, land, and water; corruption of government officials, and evaded taxes (Kelly and Gest, 1982, p. 25). Ironically, though, there is no centralized official reporting system to provide data on such momentous crimes as antitrust violations, pollution and environmental degradation, corporate bribery, unsafe products, and hazardous working conditions for employees. The lack of an official accounting system for corporate crime is coupled with a failure of the criminal justice system to mount an effective campaign against the perpetrators of these dangerous activities. In fact, both the Carter and Reagan administrations actually reduced the already meager funds for research and action projects involving corporate crimes. As Geis and Stotland have stated, this neglect "suggests something about the state of our priorities" (Geis, 1980, p. 10).

CONCEPTUAL CLARITY

There are two issues we must address at the beginning of this analysis of corporate crime: (1) the unit of analysis and (2) the definition and scope of "crime" in this context.

The Unit of Analysis

Attention in the analysis of corporate crime is directed toward large organizations rather than individuals who make up those organizations. Although it is difficult, the analyst must consider the organizations as acting units, even though individuals within it actually make the decisions that harm (Ermann and Lundman, 1982, pp. 3–7). The individuals in these organizations can be ignored because large organizations are not collections of people but collections of positions occupied by replaceable people. These replaceable people are constrained by the positions they occupy. The occupants of these positions are trained to act in certain ways and to advance the interests of the organization. A major study of when managers in corporations are fired found, for example, that the most important standard by which they were judged was profit. This implies, according to the researchers, that "if managers who fail to bring in high earnings are fired, they cannot be

---

[1] From 1939, when Sutherland called for research on white-collar crime, to 1972 some 3700 articles or books were cited in the *Criminology Index*, yet only 92 (2.5 percent) dealt with economic crime (Wheeler, 1978, p. 5).

expected to put social responsibility before profitability'' (James and Soref, 1981, p. 16). Whoever the managers are, the profit imperative constrains them to reduce costs which may, in turn, lead to pollution, unsafe working conditions, antitrust violations, and unsafe products. This implies further that while individuals within an organization may engage in criminal acts, the organization itself can be criminal. Clinard and Quinney have forcefully made this point:

> The nation's leading corporations are committing destructive acts against man and nature. Specifically, all of this is being done systematically and repeatedly, rather than randomly and occasionally. The crimes are being committeed as a standard operating procedure. In order to insure profits at a minimum of expense, these corporations are willfully engaging in crime. The corporations themselves as legal entities, as well as some of the corporate officials who make specific decisions, are criminal. And what is most frightening is that once these systematic crimes become normal operating procedure, they are not the responsibility of any one individual in the corporation. Rather they are corporate crimes, in the sense that the corporation itself is criminal. (Clinard and Quinney, 1973, p. 212)

What Organizational Behaviors are "Criminal"?

Ronald Kramer has defined corporate crime broadly and appropriately. For him, it refers to the ''illegal and/or socially harmful behaviors that result from deliberate decision making by corporate executives in accordance with the operative goals of their organizations'' (Kramer, 1982, p. 75). This definition includes those illegal acts by corporations punished by administrative, civil, or criminal law, thus broadening the definition beyond just the criminal law (Clinard and Yeager, 1980, p. 16). It also differs from other crimes in that the perpetrator is not a person but an organization. This means that the perpetrator cannot be jailed but only fined and/or ordered to refrain from further violations. Also the police and courts are typically not involved in apprehending and punishing corporate lawbreakers since these responsibilities are handled by quasi-judicial regulatory agencies of the government such as the Federal Trade Commission, the Environmental Protection Agency, the Securities and Exchange Commission, and the Food and Drug Administration. This is an important difference from other types of crimes explaining in part the low level of law enforcement. The fundamental reason is that these agencies tend to be sympathetic with the interests of business (and anti-labor, consumer, and environment). This is seen most blatantly in the composition of these governmental agencies. The members are appointed by the administration in power and typically are highly placed corporate executives who intend to return to the corporate world following their stint as the regulators of business.

The definition of corporate crime used here is extremely broad because it goes beyond the laws. In our view some corporate acts are crimes whether there are laws prohibiting them or not. The key is whether the acts do serious physical, social, or economic harm to employees, consumers or the public at large (Schrager and Short, 1978, p. 407). The reason to go beyond the law is that the statutes on corporate behavior ignore many harmful acts. This is because the laws (or the lack of specific laws) show the influence of corporate power on legislation (Clinard and Yeager, 1980, p. 21). As Ralph Nader has stated, "willful and knowing violations of auto, tire, radiation, and gas pipeline safety standards are *not* considered crimes under the relevant statutes even if lives are lost as a result" (Nader in Mintz and Cohen, 1971, p. xiii). Using this definition the following examples of legal corporate behavior are considered crimes even though not specified as such by the law:

- The automobile industry has resisted successfully the efforts by Congress to mandate air bags. Had all cars manufactured in 1975, for example, been equipped with air bags, 9500 persons would have died in car crashes in that year instead of the 27,200 who did. Moreover, 104,000 serious injuries would have been prevented (*Dollars and Sense,* 1978, p. 7).

- Asbestos companies continue to expose workers to that substance despite the scientific evidence over the past 30 years that prolonged exposure has fatal effects (Reasons et al., 1982, p. 56).

- When the government makes it illegal to sell a proven dangerous product (drug, pesticide, or food product) within the United States, some corporations will sell these products overseas where no law prohibits such an act.

Are these legal activities by corporations crimes? As T. R. Young has argued, "If [these] are not crime[s], the concept has no meaning"(1982, p. 19).

THE EXTENT OF CORPORATE CRIME

Just how guilty are American corporations of lawless and otherwise socially harmful behaviors? The answer is impossible to know for several reasons. First, as we have seen, the government does not compile statistics of these kinds of corporate acts. As Ralph Nader has noted "there is no list of the 10 most wanted corporations" (in Mintz and Cohen, 1971, p. xiii). Second, the government, either by willful negligence or inadequate staff does not vigorously prosecute known corporate violators of pollution control laws, offshore drilling regulations, or mining safety to name a few. Third, politicians and the media tend to direct public attention to crimes in the streets rather than crimes in the suites. Fourth, the style of violence perpetuated by corporations is difficult to measure.

Unsafely designed automobiles, pollution, harmful food additives, and other contaminants embody a silent kind of violence with indeterminate, unpredictable incidences per victim. That impact does not provoke immediate response of pain or anguish directed at the source of the harm. (Nader in Mintz and Cohen, 1971, p. xiv)

Workers in an asbestos plant may not develop cancer until 20 years of exposure and then it is not clear whether the conditions of the workplace are responsible.

Similarly, it is not easy to ascertain whether a car crash is the result of driver error or a defect. Is an oil spill in the Gulf of Mexico the responsibility of the oil company or a hurricane? In short, corporate culpability is often quite difficult to assess.

Recognizing that we can just identify part of the problem, let's look at the results of the three major studies focusing on the magnitude of corporate law-breaking.

Edwin Sutherland's Study: Prior to 1944

Sutherland (1949) examined the life history—an average of 45 years—of 70 of the largest manufacturing, mining, and mercantile corporations in the United States. His sources were the official records of violations of laws governing restraint of trade; misrepresentation in advertising; infringement of patents, trademarks, and copyrights; unfair labor practices; rebates, financial fraud, and violations of war regulations. Sutherland's methodology minimized the actual incidence of socially harmful acts by corporations because it (1) limited the analysis to a narrow range of crimes; (2) only considered violations of the law thus ignoring many legal but nevertheless harmful acts; (3) used official records, which omit the approximately 50 percent of cases that are settled out of court; (4) focused on a period during which some of the laws that were violated were not enacted (some were not enacted until the 1930s); and (5) it was not until 1932 that the government began a relatively vigorous prosecution of corporations.

Despite these limitations, which grossly understate the actual extent of corporate criminality, Sutherland's findings show that criminal behavior by large corporations is "normal." In most states, for example, persons with four convictions are "habitual criminals." If that standard were applied to the corporations in Sutherland's sample, 41 companies (59 percent) would be so designated. In addition to actual convictions there were a total of 980 negative decisions against the 70 corporations, an average of 14 against each, with one company receiving 50.

Sutherland (1949, pp. 217–233) drew a number of conclusions from his analysis that continue to be pertinent:

1. The criminality of corporations, like that of professional thieves, is persistent. The data showed that 97 percent of the 70 largest corporations in the United States were recidivists (having two or more adverse decisions).
2. Corporate illegal behavior is much more extensive than the data indicate. According to Sutherland, many of the violations are industry wide (i.e., practically all firms in the industry violate the law).
3. The corporate officials who violate the laws on behalf of their companies do not lose status among their business associates. In effect, a violation of the legal code is not necessarily a violation of the business code. "Prestige is lost by violations of the business code but not by violation of the legal code except when the legal code coincides with the business code" (Sutherland, 1942, pp. 219–220).

4. Corporate officials, like professional thieves, customarily feel contempt for the law and the government because they impede profitable behaviors.
5. Corporate crime is not only deliberate but also organized. There are corporate networks among "competitors" to fix prices, control labor, and influence legislation.
6. Corporate officials employ experts in law, public relations, and advertising to build up and maintain the corporation's public image as law-abiding and community-oriented entities. This public posture of good citizenship conceals the criminal activities common in the business world.

Fortune's Study: 1970 to 1979

Fortune magazine, clearly a pro-business advocate, compiled a list of major corporations found guilty of crimes over the decade of the 1970s (Ross, 1980). The crimes were domestic bribery, fraud, illegal political contributions, tax evasion, and antitrust violations. This study, which minimizes the extent of crime even more than Sutherland's earlier study did, has the advantage of examining 1043 corporations. *Fortune* found that 11 percent of these corporations had been involved in at least one major crime in the 10-year period. Of the 163 separate crimes recorded 60 percent were for antitrust violations. Some companies were multiple offenders with Gulf Oil leading the way with four, two for illegal political contributions, one for bribing an Internal Revenue Service agent, and one for fixing the price of uranium. International Paper was convicted three times for major antitrust violations involving paper labels, folding cartons, and corrugated containers. In a commendable show of honesty, *Fortune* even noted that a subsidiary of Time, Inc., the publisher of *Fortune,* was 1 of 22 companies convicted in the folding-carton antitrust case.

The author of the *Fortune* study, Irwin Ross (1980, p. 58; 62–63) noted four reasons for corporate crimes:

1. The common perception within the business community is that activities such as fixing prices are *not* crimes.
2. Within certain industries (e.g., trucking, construction, and on the loading docks), it is customary to bribe in order to achieve competitive advantage.
3. In regulated industries companies sometimes violate the law by doing acts that are legal in other industries. In the beer industry, for example, the federal and state governments prohibit some otherwise normal sales techniques such as discounts and rebates.
4. There are extensive pressures on corporate executives to "produce or perish." The competitive climate, then, drives some individuals outside the law for an edge.

Conspicuously missing from this list of possible reasons for corporate crime is that it is the strategy of some corporations to circumvent the law to take advantage of clients, the government, and the public.

The Clinard Report: 1975 to 1976

Marshall Clinard and his associates, in a study financed by the Law Enforcement Assistance Administration, investigated the illegal behavior of the 582 largest publicly owned corporations in the United States (Clinard and Yeager, 1980; Clinard et al., 1979). The data covered all enforcement actions by 24 federal agencies directed at these corporations over a two year period. This study is the most thorough to date, significantly widening the scope of crimes included. The findings show a remarkable pattern of corporate criminal activity:

- More than 60 percent of the corporations had at least one legal action instituted against them. The average for these firms with one or more violations was 4.2.
- Among the 300 manufacturing corporations, there was an average of 4.8 actions against each during the two year period.
- The larger the corporation, the greater the likelihood of being involved in a violation. Corporations with annual sales exceeding $1 billion had twice the expected number of violations (given their number in the sample). They also were more likely to commit the more serious offenses.[2]
- The automobile, oil refining, and drug industries accounted for almost one half of all violations. About 90 percent of the corporations in these industries violated the law at least once.

As strong and compelling as these findings are, they still greatly understate the actual incidence and magnitude of corporate crime in America (Young, 1981). This study only considered government enforcement actions, which are weak at best when aimed at the business sector. The study did not include large corporations in banking, insurance, transportation, communication, or utilities. There are over two million corporations in the United States but this study only looked at 582. And the Clinard Report did not consider those corporate acts that do harm but that are legal. We must not forget that corporate capital greatly influences (some would say controls) the legislative process and in so doing affects what is and what is not defined as legal activity.

But despite these criticisms, the Clinard Report is the best barometer of corporate illegality that we have. The limitations of the study should force us to understand that the basic finding of the report—that crime is endemic to corporate capitalism—is even stronger than Clinard has suggested. The next section will reinforce this by showing the range of socially harmful corporate activities and how these activities have occurred throughout American history.

---

[2]This research finding is an extremely significant point for those interested in a more democratic and decentralized economy.

THE CATEGORIES OF CORPORATE CRIME

The three major studies of corporate crime just considered limited their analyses to a narrow range of behaviors that were legally defined as crimes. Absent from these studies are such crimes as disregard for employee safety, the marketing of unsafe products, and pollution of the environment. These must be included because they jeopardize the health and safety of us all (Nader in Mintz and Cohen, 1971, pp. xv–xvi). We will include them along with the standard ones considered by Sutherland, *Fortune,* and Clinard. The types considered are divided according to the victims: (1) crimes against employees; (2) crimes against consumers; and (3) collective human jeopardy.

Crimes against Employees

The discussion here involves three types of crimes where employers confront employees with dangers in the workplace—union busting, occupational health hazards, and discrimination against females and minorities.

Violence against Unions

America industrialized rapidly after the Civil War as immigrants came to the United States and as people left farms and small towns for work in the factories, mills, and mines. The number of wage earners grew from slightly less than 1 million in 1849 to more than 2 million in 1869 and 6.6 million in 1909 (Davis, 1940, p. 18).

Prior to the Industrial Revolution families tended to own some land, raise at least part of their food, do their own spinning and weaving, and if they worked in industry, they derived only part of their living from it. The factory system, on the other hand, demanded full-time workers who lived near work. Workers left their farms and became completely dependent on their work for their livelihoods. The ready supply of workers kept wages low. Employers also were not motivated to keep their factories, mines, or mills clean or safe because these costs would reduce profits. Job security was minimal because immigrants and migrants were often willing to work for lower wages. Also in economic downturns employment or severely reduced wages hurt employers further. Employees in these settings had few, if any, fringe benefits. Sick leave, unemployment insurance, medical insurance, retirement pensions, and the like were not available through government or employers during the early Industrial Revolution in the United States.

Not only were wages low but the work day was very long. Carl Sandburg described the situation in a New England cotton mill about 1840:

> They spent fourteen hours a day at the factory. Bells rang at the break of day in some factory towns, the workers tumbled out of sleep, crept into their clothes and reported at the factory gates in fifteen minutes, when the gates were closed. . . . At Paterson, New Jersey, women and children began the day's work

at 4:30 in the morning. Overseers in some textile mills cracked the cowhide whips over women and children. (Sandburg, 1926, pp. 125–126)

In this setting of worker abuse—inadequate wages, long hours, unsafe working conditions, and job insecurity—the union movement gathered momentum as workers sought collective power in their efforts to bargain with employers. Although there were sporadic efforts at unionizing even in the late 1700s, the union movement began having some national power only around 1880. This was a period of industrial strife. In 1886, for example, there were over 1500 strikes, the most famous the strike of McCormick Harvester Company. In 1892 there was the bitterly fought Homestead strike in the steel industry and in the next year the famous Pullman strike.

These strikes were bitter confrontations between employers and employees. Employers resisted union activities because they were financially harmful. But the economic issue was not the only one, perhaps not even the most important reason for employer resistance. The main issue for many was power. The unions intruded on the heretofore sacred right of employers in a free enterprise system to set wages, hire and fire, and determine working conditions. The workers collectively sought to change the system and in so doing limited the employer's freedom. The employers hired strikebreakers, blacklisted employees who went on strike, used the lockout, used spies, hired thugs to terrorize strikers and their families, and employed armed guards to safeguard their property, which often led to violent confrontations with pickets. The employers also enlisted the aid of local governments, the police, and the state militia to assist them in breaking strikes (Stein, 1940, pp. 509–545).

Although these battles between organized labor and employers have tended to be in the distant past, the struggles still occur, especially in the South, and between agricultural workers and farmers. The economic downturn in the early 1980s presented employers with a new weapon to reduce the benefits to workers—the real threat of unemployment.

Dangers in the Workplace[3]

The union movement in the United States has been modestly successful in raising the wages for workers, adding fringe benefits, and making the conditions of work safer. But the owners were slow to change and worker safety was, and continues to be, one of the most difficult areas. Many owners of mills, mines, and factories continue to consider the safety of their workers a low-priority item, presumably because of the high cost. The mining industry provides an excellent example of this neglect. Coal-mining firms, for example, have generally refused to comply with state and federal safety regulations. ABC News found, for instance, that the mining companies, when fined for violating safety regulations, not only refused to make the mines safer but also declined to pay the fines; in 1974 there were some 91,000 unpaid fines worth some $20 million (ABC News, 1976). In 1981 an explo-

---

[3] This section is largely dependent on Simon and Eitzen (1982, pp. 109–113).

PANEL 9-1

The Antiunion Actions of the Ford Motor Company

After General Motors became unionized in 1937, Ford was the last major holdout in the automobile industry. The company had a massive security force employed specifically to keep order in the plants through terror and repression. The man in charge was Harry Herbert Bennett, second only to Henry Ford in the corporation. Bennett's main responsibility was to discourage labor organizers. His strategy was the use of violence and he had as many as 8,000 ex-prisoners on the payroll for this purpose (Ford claimed credit as a social crusader for hiring released prisoners but the goal was not to give these people jobs but to create an army of toughs). This security force used several tactics to keep the workers in line. They beat up workers who dared complain about working conditions. They infiltrated the plant and the community to determine who were prounion. These people were then the objects of harassment. When Walter Reuther and other United Auto Workers distributed leaflets at a Ford plant in 1937 they were brutally beaten by Ford's security force. One member of the security force later testified before the National Labor Relations Board that he had been instructed to "beat up" anyone he saw passing out leaflets. Another tack by Bennett was to weaken the United Auto Workers by financing rival unions. And, they had links with organized crime to help keep labor "peace." At one point a "vote of confidence" in the policies of Henry Ford was circulated through its River Rouge plant. Those refusing to sign had their badge numbers taken. The Company then publicized the vote as an endorsement of its labor policies and a rejection of the U.A.W.

Source: Frank Browning and John Gerassi, The American Way of Crime, *New York: Putnam, 1980, pp. 393–405. See also, the decision of the National Labor Relations Board (December 24, 1937), cited in Stein (1940, pp. 524–525).*

sion in a Colorado coal mine killed 15 workers. That mine had received 1133 citations and 57 orders for immediate correction of known dangers from federal inspectors since 1978 (Seigel, 1981). It has been estimated that approximately 39 percent of job injuries in the United States are due to illegal working conditions (Ashford, 1976, pp. 107–115).

Despite the owners' reluctance to make industry safer, there have been some improvements. The probabilities of cave-ins, fires, and other plant disasters are much less now than in the days before unionization. This does not mean, however, that occupational dangers have been significantly reduced. The dangers today are invisible contaminants such as nuclear radiation, chemical compounds, dust, and asbestos fibers in the air. These dangers from invisible contaminants are increasing because the production of synthetic chemicals has increased so dramatically—from 1.3 billion pounds in 1940 to 306.6 billion pounds in 1977 (*U.S. News*

& World Report, 1979, p. 39). The magnitude of this problem is underscored by the fact that more than 20 million Americans work with one or more of the chemicals known to be neurotoxic, that is, to do damage to the human nervous system (Anderson, 1982).

The extent of job-induced illnesses is impossible to ascertain exactly, primarily because for some diseases it takes many years of exposure to affect the skin, lungs, blood chemistry, nervous system, or various organs. The government estimates that about 100,000 Americans die and 390,000 are disabled annually because of occupational diseases. They also estimate that at least 20 percent of all cancer cases are linked to the workplace (Lens, 1979).

The following are examples of the specific risks of continued exposure in certain industries:

Item   Workers in the dyestuffs industry (working with aromatic hydrocarbons) have about 30 times the risk of the general population of dying from bladder cancer (Cole and Goldman, 1975, p. 171).

Item   The wives of men who work with vinyl chloride are twice as likely as other women to have miscarriages or stillbirths (McGhee, 1977).

Item   In 1978, Occidental Chemical Company workers handling a pesticide DBCP were found to be sterile as a result of the exposure, substantiating a 1961 study by Dow Chemical that indicated that DBCP caused sterility in rats (Ben-Horin, 1979).

Item   A 1976 government study determined that if 129,000 workers were exposed to the current *legal* level of cotton-dust exposure, over a period of time 23,497 would likely become byssinotics (victims of "brown lung") (Schinto, 1977, p. 29). (See Panel 9-2).

Item   Starting with 632 asbestos workers in 1943, one researcher determined each of their fates after twenty years of employment. By 1973, 444 were dead, a rate 50 percent greater than for the average white male. The rate for lung cancer was 700 percent greater than expected and the rate for all types of cancers was four times as great (reported in Epstein, 1978, pp. 84–86). (For a detailed account of the asbestos threat to employees see Ermann and Lundman, 1982, pp. 59–80.)

Item   Karen Silkwood, a plutonium-plant worker, charged that the plant where she worked, owned by Kerr-McGee Corporation was unsafe and that she was contaminated. After her death in a car crash, her family sued Kerr-McGee.

This last case illustrates the disregard of industry for the safety of their employees. During the trial employees testified that they were provided little or no training on the health hazards involved in handling plutonium. They were never told that radiation exposure could induce cancer. Attorneys for Kerr-McGee argued in court, however, that there had been no documented case of plutonium cancer in humans. This was countered by the testimony of Dr. John Gofman, one of the first physicians to isolate plutonium, who said that Ms. Silkwood had an instant "guarantee of cancer based on her exposure" (*Newsweek,* 1979).

The record of industry has often been one of ignoring the scientific data or stalling through court actions rather than making their plants safer. The example of vinyl chloride forcefully makes this point.

In 1970 an Italian toxicologist reported that long-term intermittent exposure of rats to vinyl chloride in air resulted in the production of several types of cancers (Epstein, 1978, pp. 100–112). This was the first test on the possible carcinogenicity in the plastics industry. In 1972, the earlier findings were confirmed by a major study supported by British, Belgian, and French firms. Cancers were found at the lowest level tested, fifty parts per million (at the time the permissive exposure level for U.S. workers was 500 ppm). Representatives of U.S. industry were given the full details of these studies in January 1973 but entered into an agreement with the European consortium not to disclose the information without prior consent. The U.S. organization involved in this agreement, the Manufacturing Chemists Association, failed to disclose the dangers of vinyl chloride despite a request from a government agency for all available data on the toxic effects of vinyl chloride. The data were finally revealed to the government fifteen months later when three workers exposed to vinyl chloride at a B. F. Goodrich plant died of angiosarcoma of the liver. According to a special committee report of the American Association for the Advancement of Science, the Manufacturing Chemists Association had deliberately deceived the government and "because of the suppression of these data, tens of thousands of workers were exposed without warning, for perhaps some two years, to toxic concentrations of vinyl chloride" (cited in Epstein, 1978, pp. 103–104).

The lack of concern for the safety of workers in the plastics industry is typical of other industries as well. Safety regulations for cotton dust have been fought by the textile industry. As usual the claims were that it would cost billions to clean up the mills, jobs would be lost, and prices to consumers would rise dramatically. Similarly, the copper refiners have resisted rigorous safety regulations. For example, a study of mortality among Tacoma smelter workers found the death rate from lung cancer to be between three and four times as high as normal, and ten times as high for workers exposed to the highest toxic concentrations. Moreover, a study found that children within a half mile of the smelter had absorbed as much arsenic as the workers themselves (Williams, 1979). Despite these findings, the owner of the smelter in Tacoma, ASARCO, led an industrywide campaign against the government's new standards. Again, the company offered the familiar argument that the costs of compliance would be $100 million, adding 15 cents to the now 72 cents needed to produce a pound of copper.

This raises the critical question—at what point are profits more important than human life? Speaking of the cotton industry, which is representative of the other industries, one observer has argued

In a society in which profits did not take precedence over people . . . the finer points of byssinosis [brown lung disease] would have been considered tangential long ago and the road to its prevention would now be clear: Better air filtration systems would have been installed and other capital expenditures made. But in the United States, where society is tuned to a different chord, the

PANEL 9-2

Worker Health versus Corporate Profits: The Cotton Industry

A debate that divides liberals and conservatives, workers, and owners, is the degree to which government should mandate safety levels in the workplace. A significant plank in Ronald Reagan's winning platform in 1980 was to reduce the regulatory burden on business. A 1981 Supreme Court ruling affecting the cotton industry is of special importance in this context.

Government studies estimate that at least 20 percent of America's textile workers get byssinosis (brown lung) from inhaling microscopic particles from the raw cotton fiber processed in the mills. OSHA (the Occupational Safety and Health Administration) ruled that cotton mills must reduce cotton-dust levels to no more than 200 micrograms per cubic meter of air. The American Textile Manufacturers Institute and 13 major companies argued before the Court that this standard imposed unreasonable costs on manufacturers and might drive small companies out of business. In their view the benefits of health regulation should bear a reasonable relationship to the cost of compliance. This was a case that did not meet the test in the view of the companies. The laborers, on the other hand, argued that the health of employees must be paramount. The Supreme Court in a 5–3 decision ruled for the workers—worker health is more important than all other considerations.

Some corporations place profits before the welfare of their employees. Here an effort is waged by workers to boycott a textile manufacture for its resistance to curb brown lung disease among its employees.

present delay over preventive measures, like the oblivion which preceded it, is rooted not in science and technology but in economics and politics—in the callous traditions of the cotton industry and in government's compromising ways. (Schinto, 1977, p. 28)

Discrimination in the Workplace

Women and minorities have long been the objects of discrimination in American industry. Currently (and we have progressed mightily) approximately 50,000 charges of discrimination by organizations are filed annually with the U.S. Equal Opportunity Commission. The charges now and in the past have centered on hiring policies, seniority rights, restricted job placement, limited opportunities for advancement, and lower pay for equal work. A number of recent court suits (and those settled out of court) illustrate the discriminatory policies that have been common among corporations (Kalette, 1983; Lienert, 1983):

- A court has awarded $52 million in back pay to Northwest Airlines flight attendants for previous policies regarding maternity and pay.

- In 1974 the Justice Department ruled that the steel industry was discriminatory against women (only 3 percent of employees were women and their pay averaged only slightly more than 50 percent of men) and blacks who earned only 90 percent of what whites did for comparable jobs. The Justice Department demanded that 45,000 employees receive $31 million in back pay and set up procedures to monitor future practices in hiring, training, and promotions in the industry.

- In 1973 AT & T was judged in court to owe $45 million to previously discriminated employees.

- In 1981 a Labor Department judge ruled that 1800 women employees of Harris Bank in Chicago were owed $12.2 million in back wages to make restitution for their disproportionately low wages in the past.

- In 1983 General Motors, after a 10-year court battle, settled out of court agreeing to spend $42.5 million over 5 years to increase the representation of women and minorities at all levels in the company.

Crimes against Consumers

Excessive Costs

Consumers overpay for the goods and services they purchase because of four characteristics of the corporate economy—monopoly, price fixing, price gouging, and deceptive advertising. These corporate strategies are crimes because they take unfair advantage of powerless consumers.

Monopoly. The United States has moved from competitive capitalism to a stage of monopoly capitalism. Karl Marx (1967), well over 100 years ago, correctly predicted this current stage. Free enterprise, he argued, will result in some firms

PANEL 9-3

Corporate Attempts to Blame the Victims for Work-related Cancer

With cancer, as with much else that we fear and cannot fully explain, we develop popular mythologies to explain what science has not. Unfortunately, some are dangerously misleading, and may be preventing us from avoiding unnecessary cancers.

One such current myth, propagated through the unlikely and unwilling partnership of holistic health advocates and the nation's chemical industries, holds that the causes of virtually all cancers are rooted in life styles. The implication is that if you contract cancer it is essentially your fault.

As with all myths, this one contains a germ of truth. Smoking, for example, is clearly a life-style choice that contributes heavily to our high rate of lung cancers.

But while holistic health practitioners stress the positive aspects of the importance of life style—their point is that we are at least to some extent responsible for our own health—U.S. chemical industries are making deliberate use of the argument in an attempt to escape responsibility for the cancers caused by their own products.

Fearing increased federal regulation, industry-sponsored physicians and scientists have manipulated statistics, withheld critical information and, in several cases, misrepresented data in studies produced for industry lobbying efforts. One recent report, produced by the American Industrial Health Council—an organization created by the chemical industry to fight regulation of carcinogens in the workplace—claims that cancer is actually on

the decline, that all recent increases in cancer mortality rates are due to smoking and that industrial chemicals are responsible for no more than 5% of all cancers in the United States.

Examination of recent evidence, however, shows that, although life-style factors are important contributors to cancer mortality, the role of occupational and environmental carcinogens has been grossly underrated. Moreover, industry and industry-funded consultants are greatly exaggerating the role of even such clearly dangerous life-style factors as smoking in their attempt to divert public attention from the occupational causes of lung and other cancers.

Thus, the mining and textile industries have for many years pointed to smoking as the primary culprit in the high rates of black- and brown-lung cases, respectively, among their work forces, even though more likely causes are coal dust and cotton fibers.

Contrary to industry claims that all increases in cancer mortality have been due to smoking, the lung-cancer rates for nonsmokers approximately doubled between 1958 and 1969, and have continued to rise. Of the approximately 100,000 annual lung-cancer deaths in the United States today, about 20% involve nonsmokers.

Further challenges to the dominant role ascribed to smoking are provided by studies of specific occupational groups. For example, lung-cancer rates among American Indian uranium miners, Swedish zinc-

Panel 9-3 (Continued)

lead miners and others exposed to a wide range of industrial carcinogens are about as high in non-smokers as smokers.

Certain ethnic groups have higher risks of lung cancer, not because they smoke more but because they are concentrated in certain types of occupations. Topside coke-oven workers, for example, with five or more years on the job, have a lung-cancer rate up to 10 times that of steel workers in general. Roughly 75% of the topside workers are non-white, whereas only about 12% of the non-topside workers are non-white.

The relative risks of lung cancer for smokers versus non-smokers have been grossly overestimated because of a failure to consider the effect of non-voluntary exposures to carcinogens in the environment. Variations in smoking, for example, do not account for the significant excess of lung cancers in both men and women living in communities adjacent to petrochemical and other industrial plants. A large number of studies have found sharp increases in lung cancer in areas with heavy air pollution.

Evidence continues to grow that involuntary exposures may have a much larger role in causing other types of cancer as well.

During the seven years between 1969 and 1976, U.S. cancer mortality climbed more than 5%, a rate of increase similar to that of the preceding 35 years. The overall probability of a person born today getting cancer by age 85 is calculated to be about 27%, in contrast to 1950, when it was only 19%.

It is not mere coincidence that increases in cancer mortality follow the growth of our chemical industries. Recent cancer rates reflect exposures to carcinogens 20 to 30 years ago. The production of synthetic organic chemicals, which include many known and suspected carcinogens, was only about 1 billion pounds in 1935, but rose to 30 billion by 1950 and 300 billion by 1975.

The five states with the highest cancer rates are found in the Northeast, where the nation's heavy industry is located. By contrast, the states with the lowest cancer rates are in predominantly rural Western and Southern states, where there is relatively little industry.

Higher production levels of industrial chemicals have increased the exposures not only of industrial workers, but of the general public as well. Prior to the passage of the 1976 Toxic Substances Act, which the chemical industries stalled for years, there were no requirements for testing chemicals before use. Thus, the overwhelming majority of the thousands of chemicals now in use have never even been tested for carcinogenic effects. To make matters worse, the chemical industries refuse to disclose the identity of many chemicals to which workers are exposed, claiming that the need for trade secrecy prevents such disclosure.

It is clear that industry consultants have no basis at all, other than self-serving and wishful thinking, for their "guess" that the industry's products are responsible for only 5% of the cancers contracted each year.

A recent study by a committee of internationally recognized experts from three federal agencies arrived at a completely different conclusion. This study, based on

Panel 9-3 (Continued)

a review of more than 5000 workplaces, estimates that up to 38% of total cancer mortality over the next 30 years will be associated with past exposure to asbestos and five other major industrial carcinogens. This estimate, it should be noted, does not even include the effects of radiation and a very wide range of other occupational carcinogens.

Many cancers are preventable—simply through removal or control of the cancer-causing agent. This will require not only individuals' dropping certain habits such as smoking, but also greater regulation of carcinogens in the environment and the workplace. The chemical industry's efforts to escape regulation by clouding the issues so far have been quite successful. But they also have cost many lives, and will claim still more until the industry's self-serving arguments are exposed for what they are.

Source: Samuel Epstein, "Cancer: Twisting the Statistics About Its Causes," Los Angeles Times (May 19, 1981), Part II, p. 5. This article was originally written for Pacific News Service.

becoming bigger and bigger as they eliminate their opposition or absorb small competing firms. The ultimate result of this process is the existence of a monopoly in each of the various sectors of the economy. Monopolies, of course, are antithetical to the free-enterprise system because they, not supply and demand, determine the price and the quality of the products. This, as we will see, increases the benefits for the few at the expense of the many.

For the most part, American society upholds Marx's prediction. Although there are a few corporations that are virtual monopolies, most sectors of the American economy are dominated by "shared monopolies." Instead of a single corporation controlling an industry, the situation is one in which a small number of large firms dominate an industry.

> When four or fewer firms supply 50 percent or more of a particular market, a shared monopoly results, one which performs much as a monopoly or cartel would. Most economists agree that above this level of concentration—a four-firm ratio of 50 percent—the economic costs of shared monopoly are most manifest. (Green et al., 1972, p. 7)

Currently the industries where shared monopolies occur are motor vehicles (where the four largest firms control 93 percent); light bulbs (90 percent); breakfast cereals (89 percent); turbines and generators (86 percent); primary aluminum (76 percent); chocolate and cocoa (73 percent); photo equipment (72 percent); brewing (64 percent); guided missiles and spacecraft (64 percent); and roasted coffee (61 percent) (*U.S. News & World Report*, August 24, 1981, p. 69).

The concentration of American industry has accelerated in the early 1980s with massive mergers and corporate takeovers. This trend toward fewer and larger firms has a number of negative consequences. Some of these are greater influence over government policy, greater power to resist organized labor, inflationary pressures in the economy, and greater unemployment. For our purposes, the significant result of corporate concentration is overpricing. A study by the Federal Trade Commission has estimated that if industries with the four largest firms were reduced in control from 50 to 40 percent of sales, prices would fall by at least 25 percent. When industries are so concentrated that four or fewer firms account for 70 percent of sales, they are found to have profits 50 percent higher than the lesser concentrated industries (Green et al., 1972, p. 14). To amplify this point, the Agriculture Department reported that American consumers paid more than $16 billion a year in overcharges on food because of industry concentration (Associated Press, 1980).

Price Fixing.   When consumers are overcharged for goods because of collusion among "competitors," this is a crime. This form of corporate stealing costs consumers about $60 billion a year (Kelly and Gest, 1982, p. 25). The *sine qua non* of capitalism is competition.[4] As we have seen, though, the tendency toward concentration makes a mockery of the claim that the American version of capitalism is competitive. The existence of shared monopolies allow the few corporations that control an industry to eliminate price wars by parallel pricing and product homogeneity. The former depicts the practice where tacit collusion by "competitors" achieves a common price, whereas the latter means that prices are going to be roughly equal because the "competitors" produce products with similar specifications. Both practices are common and have the consequence of equal prices regardless of whether the leading companies in an industry conspire to do so or not.

Prices are also manipulated to maximize profits through collusive activities of the companies supposedly in competition with each other. This practice is called *price fixing*. It refers to the explicit agreement among "competitors" to keep prices artifically high to maximize profits. Price fixing is illegal and complaints are monitored and brought to court by the Antitrust Division of the Justice Department. The illegality of price fixing, however, has not deterred competing companies from conspiring to make abnormal profits through this practice. One review of cases where price fixing was proved from 1963 to 1972 revealed that the practice occurred among companies producing and marketing the following: steel wheels, pipe, bed springs, metal shelving, steel casting, self-locking nuts, liquefied petroleum gas delivery, refuse collection, linoleum installation, swimsuits, structural steel, carbon steel, baking flour, fertilizer, railroads, welding electrodes, acoustical ceiling materials, hydraulic hose, beer, gasoline, asphalt, book matches, concrete pipe, drill bushings, linen, school construction, plumbing fixtures, dairy products, fuel oil, auto repair, brass fittings, plumbing contracting, bread, athletic equipment, maple floors, vending machines, ready-mix concrete, industrial chemicals, rendering, shoes, garage doors, automobile glass, and wholesale meat (Hay and Kelley, 1974). Examining these and other cases, the

---

[4]This section is taken largely from Simon and Eitzen (1982, pp. 78–82).

researchers tried to determine if there was a pattern associated with price fixing. They concluded that "conspiracy among competitors may arise in any number of situations but it is most likely to occur and endure when numbers are small [few companies involved], concentration is high [when four or fewer firms control fifty percent or more of the market], and the product is homogeneous" (Hay and Kelley, 1974, pp. 26–27).

Price Gouging.[5]   Because private corporations are entirely profit oriented, they take whatever advantage they can to sell products or services at the highest possible prices. In this section, we want to describe yet another manifestation of profit-maximizing behavior—price gouging. This term refers to the practice of taking extraordinary advantage of consumers because of the bias of the law, monopoly of the market, or because of contrived or real shortages.

Low-income consumers are the victims of price gouging from a variety of merchants, banks and finance companies, landlords, and the like. Some plausible reasons why the poor pay more might include higher rates of street crimes in the neighborhoods, which raise the cost of doing business, and the economic marginality of the poor, making their credit especially risky. But even when these rationales are accounted for, the poor are the victims of unusually high prices, which of course tend to perpetuate their poverty. Many food chains find that it costs 2 or 3 percent more to operate in poor neighborhoods, yet low-income consumers pay between 5 and 10 percent more for their groceries than would those living in middle-income areas (Cross, 1976, p. 119). Perhaps the best example of price gouging by ghetto stores is that they tend to raise prices on the first and the fifteenth of each month because these are the days when welfare checks are received. Similarly, there is evidence that grocers in the Mississippi Delta raised prices when food stamps were introduced (Cross, 1976, p. 124).

Banks and other financial organizations also take advantage of the poor. Because they are not affluent and therefore have inadequate collateral or credit reference, the poor must pay higher interest rates or may be forced to deal with loan sharks because they are denied resources through the legitimate financial outlets.

The sharp entrepreneur is always looking for the special events that might lead to spectacular profits. For example, when California passed Proposition 13 in 1978, local property taxes were dramatically reduced by $7 billion. This event was used by some people to increase profits substantially. The California-based corporations made an instant additional profit of $2 billion, yet did not lower prices on their products.

A few years ago a worldwide shortage of sugar caused the price to increase rapidly for U.S. consumers. This caused a concomitant rise in a number of products using sugar. The cost of candy bars increased while their size dwindled (the price tripled while the size shrunk to one third its former size). The cost of soda also increased markedly during this period. Canned soda from vending machines went from 15 to 25 cents a can. Interestingly, and revealing of the tendency of

---

[5]This section is taken from Simon and Eitzen (1982, pp. 82–86).

corporations to gouge whenever possible, the cost of diet soda (which, of course, contained no sugar) went up in price to 25 cents as well. Moreover, when the sugar shortage subsided, the cost of soda stayed at the shortage-created level. Also, all major soda companies had the same pricing strategy—a form of parallel pricing or price fixing.

But the best example of using a crisis to one's economic advantage, and the one that has had the greatest impact on the American consumer, is the price gouging by the oil companies following the oil boycott of the OPEC countries in 1973 to 1974 and the shortages caused by the upheavals in Iran in 1979.

Price gouging also occurs because of deception. One classic example of this occurred when General Motors placed several hundred thousand Chevrolet engines in higher-priced Oldsmobiles. Another example of this tactic of putting lower-priced goods in higher-priced categories occurred when the MGM-Grand Hotel in Reno violated federal liquor laws by refilling 16,000 bottles with cheaper liquor over a 14-month period. For a much wider used scheme to deceive consumers, let's examine the pharmaceutical industry.

The sale of prescription and nonprescription drugs is a large industry, representing 10 percent of all medical costs in the United States (approximately $1.2 billion annually). About half of all prescription drugs come in two forms—under a brand name or under the generic name. Although a drug is identical chemically, if marketed under a brand name it is very much more expensive—and therefore profitable.

The ABC Newsmagazine "20/20" visited the Mylan Pharmaceutical Company and found one machine producing erythromycin tablets. Some of the tablets were then dyed pink, others were dyed yellow, while still others were dyed orange. The only difference among the three sets of tablets was the color, yet the three would be priced very differently. The pink version is the generic and sells for $6.20; the yellow pills are marketed by Smith-Kline and sell for $9.20; and the orange ones are called Bristamycin and are marketed for $14.00. Similarly, at the Phillips-Roxanne Laboratories, 60-mg cidamenphene-todene tablets are placed in a Smith-Kline bottle to be sold wholesale for $13.20/100, but when they are put in a Phillips-Roxanne package, they sell for $10.80. Again, the products are precisely identical—even manufactured at the same place (ABC, 1978).

To counteract the problem, the Department of Health, Education, and Welfare published in 1978 a *Guide to Drug Prices* to provide information for consumers, pharmacists, and doctors. Former HEW Secretary Joseph A. Califano, Jr., has said that "if one of five physicians uses this *Guide* to cut the costs of prescriptions by 10 percent, that would save consumers $120 million a year in prescription drug costs" (Steif, 1978, p. 13).

As a final example of price gouging there is the case of corporate suppliers to the defense industry. The military places some 30 million orders for parts each year and these often are purchased for reasonable prices through competitive bids. But these procedures are time consuming and often avoided. Contractors sometimes charge what they believe they can get away with because the military is in a hurry. This has resulted in such celebrated inflationary costs as (Kelly, 1983; *Rocky Mountain News*, 1983): $112 for a microcircuit available for $2.37 elsewhere; $44

PANEL 9-4

Boeing's Greed Shakes Faith in System

The story of the Boeing Co. and the plastic stool cap is an ugly story, but it is a factual story and the facts add up to outrage. The facts come from *The Washington Post,* which published them a week ago. The outrage is my own.

The *Post*'s expose, by staff writer Barton Gellman, ran to 2000 words. It was a model piece of straightforward reporting. Let me summarize.

In the cockpit of the giant AWACS radar plane is a small blue and gray stool. Ordinarily the stool is folded into a bulkhead. The stool is provided for the plane's navigator to stand on if he has to reach a periscope to check his bearings. This rarely happens.

The legs of the stool have plastic caps on the bottom. The caps, fabricated of white nylon, are intended to keep the stool from wobbling on those rare occasions when the stool is put to use. A matchbook, a well-folded handkerchief or a borrowed billfold would serve as well.

One day this past January a crew chief at Tinker Air Force Base in Oklahoma, Charles R. Kessler Jr., noticed that caps were missing on two stools in planes under his care. He requisitioned replacements. His order went routinely through the Pentagon's purchasing system. The system's computers reported the item could be supplied only by the Boeing Co. Confirmation of the order went back to Oklahoma. Kessler happened to see the paperwork. He hit the ceiling.

The plastic caps were priced at $1,118.26. Each.

Kessler went to his superiors. His superiors went to their superiors. A considerable flap ensued. The Department of Defense insisted the incident was a fluke. A spokesman for Boeing said the company "felt chagrined," for the price was "obviously too high." Kessler got a commendation and a bonus. A mechanic put the caps on the stools. End of story.

But not end of story. The *Post*'s man dug out a statement Boeing had prepared in 1981 to justify its bill for providing three of the plastic caps at that time. The material costs were 78 cents, or 26 cents for each for the nylon cubes. According to Boeing, it took nearly 50 hours of "production labor" to manufacture the three caps. Another eight hours of labor were required for "inspection." Fringe benefits, tools, overhead, state and local taxes, and a "profit fee of 15 percent" ran the total to $2,749.65, or $916.55 each. By 1983, owing to internal surcharges added by the defense supply system, the price had swollen to the $1,118.26 that caught Kessler's eye.

The failure of the Defense Department to detect this highway robbery can be explained. Items are ordered not by physical description but by number.

Boeing's conduct also can be explained, but it cannot be excused. The explanation lies in greed, sheer greed. Knowing it was dealing with Uncle Sucker, the company designed a fancy cap that would have been needlessly expensive at $2 each. Let us be generous, and throw in all the proportionate costs of overhead, use of tools and fringe benefits, and call it $10 per cap.

I do not use the word "outrageous"

Panel 9-4 (Continued)

more than three or four times a year, but the word applies here. For Boeing to have inflated the price of this item to more than $900—by its own 1981 statement—is flatly outrageous.

As editor and columnist, I have spent a good part of the past 30 years defending capitalism, the marketplace, the free enterprise system and the integrity of American business and industry. The case of the plastic stool cap shakes a man's faith. If Boeing could get away with so gross a swindle, what are we to surmise of other companies on other contracts? Let us sound applause for the Sergeant Kesslers of this world, but for the Boeing Co. let us cry shame.

Source: James Kilpatrick, "Boeing's Greed Shakes Faith in System," from a syndicated column appearing in the Fort Collin's Coloradoan, *September 2, 1983, p. A6.*

for a lamp bulb available for 17 cents; $110 for a 4-cent diode; and $435 for a claw hammer.

Deceptive Advertising.[6]   Another tenet of capitalism is expansion. Each corporation wishes to produce an increasing amount so that profits likewise will inflate. The problem, of course, is that the public must be convinced to consume this ever-larger surplus (Freeman, 1977). One way to create demand is through advertising.

Although a legitimate tool of business, advertising can be used to deceive—to sell a product even through the use of lies. As a retired advertising executive has said, the cardinal principle is

Don't worry whether it's true or not. Will it sell? . . . The American people . . . are now being had from every bewildering direction. All the way from trying to persuade us to put dubious drug products and questionable foods into our stomachs to urging young men to lay down their lives in Indochina, the key will-it-sell principle and the employed techniques are the same. *Caveat emptor* has never had more profound significance than today, whether someone is trying to sell us war, God, anti-Communism or a new improved deodorant. Deceit is the accepted order of the hour. (Cohane, 1972)

Several examples will show the ways advertising can be outright false:

Item   An analysis of news items appearing in *The New York Times* during 1974 revealed court cases of FTC rulings concerning deceptive advertising for the

[6]Simon and Eitzen (1982, pp. 86–88).

following: Air France, Fram Oil Filters, Ford, GM, Chrysler, American Cynamid, Clorox, Calgon, Listerine, Lysol, A&P, Sterling Drug, Kayser Pantyhose, Hardees, Carte Blanche, California Milk Producers, Skippy Peanut Butter, Sugar Associate, Viceroy Cigarettes, and Jack LaLanne Health Spas (Barlow, 1978, pp. 252–253).

Item   When Libby-Owens-Ford Glass Company wanted to demonstrate the superiority of its automobile safety glass, it smeared a competing brand with streaks of vaseline to create distortion, then photographed it at oblique camera angles to enhance the effect. The distortion free marvels of the company's own glass were "shown" by taking photographs of a car with the windows rolled down (Preston, 1975, p. 235).

Item   The nation's largest toymaker CPG Products, a subsidiary of General Mills, was found guilty in 1979 of two deceptive acts: (1) use of a television commercial that showed a toy horse being able to stand on its own (when in fact it could not) through the use of special camera techniques and film editing and (2) using oversized boxes in model airplane kits that gave the misleading impression of the size of the contents.

Unsafe Products

Commonly, the concern over violence in society is directed toward murder, rape, child abuse, and riots. We do not include in the context of violence the harm inflicted on people by unsafe products (Simon and Eitzen, 1982, pp. 97–101). The National Commission on Product Safety has revealed that 20 million Americans are injured annually in the home as a result of incidents connected with consumer products. "Of the total, 110,000 are permanently disabled and 30,000 killed. According to the National Commission on Product Safety, a significant number could have been spared if more attention had been paid to hazard reduction" (Aaker and Day, 1974).

Considerable evidence points to unsafe products from clothing to toys to tires, but nowhere has the poor corporate safety record been more visible than in the automobile industry and we will therefore concentrate on it. The indictment against this industry involves two basic charges: (1) faulty design and (2) working against governmental and consumer efforts to add safety devices as basic equipment.

In 1929, the president of DuPont tried to induce the president of General Motors to use safety glass in Chevrolets, as Ford was already doing. The president of GM felt that this addition was too costly and would therefore hinder sales. In his reply to DuPont, he said

I would very much rather spend the same amount of money in improving our car in other ways because I think, from the standpoint of selfish business, it would be a very much better investment. You can say, perhaps, that I am selfish, but business is selfish. We are not a charitable institution—we are trying to make a profit for our stockholders. (Mintz and Cohen, 1971, p. 260)

This example shows how the profit motive superseded the possibility of preventing deaths and serious injuries. It is not an isolated instance in this industry. Let's consider one case in some detail, the infamous Ford Pinto (the following is taken primarily from Dowie, 1979).

From its beginning the Pinto was flawed by a fuel system that ruptured easily in a rear-end collision. Preproduction crash tests established this problem, but since the assembly-line machinery was already tooled, Ford decided to manufacture the car as it was—*"even though Ford owned the patent on a much safer gas tank"* (Dowie, 1979, p. 24).

This decision was made partly because the Pinto was on a tight production schedule. Ford was trying to enter the lucrative subcompact market dominated by Volkswagen as quickly as possible. The time span from the conception of the Pinto to production was targeted at 25 months, when the normal time for a new car was 43 months. Also involved in the decision to go with the original gas tank were styling considerations and the effort to maximize trunk space.

The profits-over-human considerations is clearly evident in the reluctance of Ford to change the design of the Pinto as fatalities and injuries occurred because of the faulty gas tank. Although the company calculated that $11 per car would make the car safe, it decided that this *was too costly*. They reasoned that 180 burn deaths and 180 serious burn injuries and 2100 burned vehicles would cost $49.5 million (each death was figured at $200,000) but that a recall of all Pintos and the $11 repair would amount to $137 million (Dowie, 1979, p. 24). (See Table 9-1.) In addition to the decision to leave the Pinto alone, Ford lobbied in Washington to convince government regulatory agencies and Congress that:

Auto accidents are caused not by *cars,* but by (1) people and (2) highway conditions. This philosophy is rather like blaming a robbery on the victim. Well, what did you expect? You were carrying money, weren't you? It is an extraordinary experience to hear automotive "safety engineers" talk for hours without

TABLE 9-1

$11 versus a Burn Death (Benefits and Costs Relating to Fuel Leakage Associated with the Static Rollover Test Portion of FMVSS 208)

Benefits

    Savings: 180 burn deaths, 180 serious burn injuries, 2100 burned vehicles.

    Unit Cost: $200,000 per death, $67,000 per injury, $700 per vehicle.

    Total Benefit: 180 × ($200,000) + 180 × (67,000) + 2100 × ($700) = $49.5 million

Costs

    Sales: 11 million cars, 1.5 million light trucks.

    Unit Cost: $11 per car, $11 per truck.

    Total Cost: 11,000,000 × ($11) + 1,500,000 × ($11) = $137 million.

SOURCE: Ford Motor Company internal memorandum, "Fatalities Associated with Crash-Induced Fuel Leakage and Fires," cited in Mark Dowie, "Pinto Madness," *Mother Jones,* September/October 1977, p. 24. © *Mother Jones.* Used by permission.

ever mentioning cars. They will advocate spending billions educating young-sters, punishing drunks, and redesigning street signs. Listening to them, you can momentarily begin to think that it is easier to control 100 million drivers than a handful of manufacturers. They show movies about guardrail design and advocate the clear-cutting of trees 100 feet back from every highway in the nation. If a car is unsafe, they argue, it is because its owner doesn't properly drive it. Or, perhaps, maintain it. (Dowie, 1979, p. 30)

Meanwhile, fiery crashes involving Pintos were occurring with some regularity. Liability suits against Ford increased, with judgments routinely found against Ford. In 1978 a jury in California awarded $127.8—including $125 million in punitive damages—to a teenager badly burned when his 1972 Pinto burst into flame after being hit in the rear by a car traveling 35 miles per hour. At that time up to 50 Pinto-related civil suits were pending in various courts.

In that same year, 10 years after the government had begun investigating the Pinto problem, the Department of Transportation finally announced that its tests showed conclusively that the Pinto was unsafe and ordered a recall of all 1971 to 1976 Pintos. One critic of Ford's outright defiance of human considerations made this telling observation: "One wonders how long Ford Motor Company would continue to market lethal cars were Henry Ford II and Lee Iacocca [the top Ford officials] serving 20-year terms in Leavenworth for consumer homicide" (Dowie, 1979, p. 39).

The infamous Pinto case occurred in the past and the automobile industry learned its lesson, or so we ought to assume. However, internal company docu-ments at General Motors have revealed that the company was warned repeatedly by its test drivers before the cars went into production that the 1980 X-body automobiles had serious brake locking problems. The cars were produced anyway without correction. The government filed suit against General Motors in 1982 arguing that it had received more than 1700 complaints about brakes locking on these cars, with 15 deaths occurring when the cars went into dangerous spins (Herbert, 1983).

Dangerous Nutrition[7]

The food industry, in its search for more profits, often disregards the health of consumers. We will explore three areas in which human considerations are often secondary to profit: (1) the sale of adulterated products and (2) the extensive use of chemical additives.

Adulterated Products.   We will use the meat industry as an illustration of blatant disregard for the health of consumers. Upton Sinclair's exposé of the Chicago stockyards and meat-packing houses around 1900 showed how spoiled meat was sold, how dangerous ingredients were in sausage (such as rats and dung), and how rats overran piles of meat stored under leaking roofs (Sinclair, 1960). President

[7]Simon and Eitzen (1982, pp. 101–103).

Theodore Roosevelt commissioned an investigation of Chicago meat packers and, as a result, the Meat Inspection Act of 1906 required that meat sold in interstate commerce had to be inspected according to federal standards. However, meat processed and sold within a state was not subject to the law (omitting as late as 1967 nearly 15 percent of the meat slaughtered and 25 percent of all the meat processed in the U.S.). As a result:

Surveys of packing houses in Delaware, Virginia, and North Carolina found the following tidbits in the meat: animal hair, sawdust, flies, abscessed pork livers, and snuff spit out by the meat workers. To add even further flavoring, packing houses whose meat did not cross state lines could use 4-D meat (dead, dying, diseased, and disabled) and chemical additives that would not pass federal inspection. Such plants were not all minor operations; some were run by the giants—Armour, Swift, and Wilson. (McCaghy, 1976, p. 215)

At the end of 1967, the Wholesome Meat Act was passed, specifying that state inspection standards must at least match federal standards. This was accomplished in 1971 but there have been continuing violations. One problem is "Number 2" meat—meat returned by a retailer to a packer as unsatisfactory, which is then resold as Number 2 meat to another customer if it meets standards of wholesomeness. As an example of how this can be abused, consider the following occurrence in a Los Angeles Hormel plant:

When the original customers returned the meat to Hormel, they used the following terms to describe it: "moldy liverloaf, sour party hams, leaking bologna, discolored bacon, off-conditioned hams, and slick and slimy spareribs." Hormel renewed these products with cosmetic measures (reconditioning, trimming, and washing). Spareribs returned for slimness, discoloration, and stickiness were rejuvenated through curing and smoking, renamed Windsor Loins, and sold in ghetto stores for more than fresh pork chops. (Wellford, 1972, p. 69)

The Extensive Use of Additives in Food. The profits from the food industry come mainly from the processing of farm goods through fortifying, enriching, and reformulating them into products that look appealing, have the right taste and aroma, and will not spoil (Gussow, 1980). In 1977, there were more than 1300 food additives approved as flavors, colors, thickeners, preservatives, and other agents for controlling the properties of food.

There is a great deal of controversy among scientists about the results of these additives in our diet. "Altogether, laboratory tests have produced evidence that some 1400 substances—drugs, food additives, pesticides, industrial chemicals, cosmetics—might cause cancer. But there are only a few chemicals that *all* the experts see as linked to human cancer (Miller, 1976). Typically, government scientists disagree with the scientists hired by industry. Several considerations, though, should cause us to be cautious about what we eat. First, many of the additives are poisons. The quantities in food are minute, but just what is the tolerance level? Is any poison, in any amount, appropriate in a food? Is there the possibility of a residue buildup in vital organs?

A second caution flag is signaled in what happened to laboratory animals fed relatively large quantities of these additives. They are poisoned; they do get cancer; and they do suffer from other maladies induced by the additives.

Finally, there is the serious question of what happens with the interaction of these additives on humans. Scientists may be able to test the effects of a few chemicals but what about the hundreds of thouands of possible combinations? In a slice of bread, for example, there can be as many as 93 possible different additives. The danger is that it takes years—maybe 20 or 30—of a particular diet for an individual to develop cancer. Since most of the additives are of recent origin, we do not know the eventual outcome. We do know that the average American has increased his/her yearly intake of food additives from three pounds in 1965 to about 5 pounds in 1977. Also known is that the cancer rate continues to rise.

Why, then, do the food companies insist on adding these potentially harmful chemicals to our food? One possibility is that consumers demand more variety and convenience. But more important, the food industry has found that the processing of synthetic foods is *very* profitable. As one food marketer has remarked: "The profit margin on food additives is fantastically good, much better than the profit margins on basic, traditional foods (Zwerdling, 1978, p. 20).

Collective Jeopardy: Pollution of the Environment[8]

In a capitalist system companies make decisions based on making profit. This places the environment in jeopardy. Best and Connolly have shown how corporate decision makers choose alternatives that have negative impacts on the ecology. They describe the logic of capitalism in the following:

> Under such circumstances [capitalism] it is quite irrational for any individual producer or consumer to accept the higher costs involved in curtailing various assaults on the environment. Thus a company that purified the water used in production before disposing it into streams would add to its own costs, fail to benefit from the purified procedures. Since it is reasonable to assume that other companies in a market system will not voluntarily weaken their position in this way, it is irrational for any single company to choose to do so. . . . Thus a range of practices which are desirable from the vantage point of the public are irrational from the vantage point of any particular consumer or producer. And a range of policies which are rational from the vantage point of individual consumers and producers are destructive of the collective interests in preserving nonrenewable productive resources and in maintaining the environment's capacity to assimilate wastes. (Best and Connolly, 1978, p. 419)

Why, for example, does the United States depend on an irrational transportation system? If mass transit for commuting replaced the automobile in our urban

[8] Simon and Eitzen (1982, pp. 121–123).

Corporations have tended to resist government and citizen efforts to curb their pollution of the environment because pollution control reduces profits.

centers, 50 percent of the fuel now consumed by cars would be saved and pollution reduced significantly. The evidence is clear that the automobile industry intervened to suppress a viable mass transit alternative. Three facts buttress this argument. First, in the middle twenties, General Motors, sometimes with Standard Oil and Firestone, purchased control of electric trolley and transit systems in 44 urban areas. After purchase, the electric-rail systems were dismantled and replaced by diesel-powered bus systems (supplied by General Motors). When the systems were subsequently sold, part of the contract stated that no new equipment could be purchased that used a fuel other than gas. GM favored the diesel bus because its life was 28 percent shorter than its electric counterpart (resulting in more profit for the company). Standard Oil and Firestone obviously benefitted from such an arrangement (Kwitny, 1981). The result is well known. We are dependent on gasoline for transportation and our cities are smothered in toxic emissions of carbon monoxide, lead, and other deadly chemical combinations from internal-combustion engines.

Other examples come from the substitution of synthetic for organic materials. Decisions by industry displaced soap with synthetic detergents because the profit margin increased from 30 percent of sales to 52 percent (Commoner, 1979, p. 285). The decision was not made by consumers but by management. These decisions and others (e.g., the change from wool and cotton to synthetic fibers; plastics substituted for leather, rubber, and wood; and synthetic fertilizers replacing organic fertilizers) have often been incompatible with good ecology because the new chemicals are sometimes toxic and/or nonbiodegradable. Remember, citizens as voters and consumers were not involved in these decisions to shift from organic to synthetic products. Rather the decisions were made for them—and, it turns out, against their long-term interests—by companies searching for more lucrative profits. Barry Commoner has claimed that these new technologies have invariably been more polluting, but were introduced nonetheless because they yielded higher profits than the older, less polluting, displaced technologies. Moreover, the costs to the consumers are borne in the increased health hazards and in the cost for cleaning up the environment.

> Environmental pollution is connected to the economics of the private enterprise system in two ways. First, pollution tends to become intensified by the displacement of older productive techniques by new ecologically faulty, but more profitable technologies. Thus, in these cases, pollution is an unintended concomitant of the natural drive of the economic system to introduce new technologies that increase productivity. Second, the costs of environmental degradation are chiefly borne not by the producer, but by society as a whole, in the form of "externalities." A business enterprise that pollutes the environment is therefore being subsidized by society; to this extent, the enterprise, though free, is not wholly private. (Commoner, 1979, p. 291)

Human Jeopardy: International Dimensions

A number of corporate practices have harmful effects on the peoples in other countries. Some of these are: arms sales that heighten world tensions, colonial relationships (extracting natural resources and cheap labor from dependent nations), and the intervention in the affairs of other governments. For illustrative purposes we will concentrate only on one form—international corporate sales that endanger life (see Simon and Eitzen, 1982, pp. 156–158).

There is a relatively common practice called corporate dumping, which refers to the exporting of goods that have either been banned or not approved for sale in the United States because they are dangerous. Most often the greatest market for such unsafe products is among the poor in the Third World. This is because these countries often do not bar hazardous products and because many of the poor are illiterate and therefore tend to be unaware of the hazards involved with the use of such products. Corporate dumping, then, is the sale of products known to be dangerous to the unsuspecting for profit.

Examples of the products involved in corporate dumping are growing at a rapid pace. The following are some of these examples:

> An undisclosed number of farmers and over 1000 water buffalos died suddenly in Egypt after being exposed to leptophos, a chemical pesticide which was never registered for domestic use by the Environmental Protection Agency (EPA) but was exported to at least 30 countries.
>
> After the Dalkon Shield intrauterine device killed at least 17 women in the United States, the manufacturer withdrew it from the domestic market. It was sold overseas after the American recall and is still in common use in some countries.

No one knows how many children may develop cancer since several million children's garments treated with a carcinogenic fire retardant called Tris were shipped overseas after being forced off the domestic market by the Consumer Product Safety Commission (CPSC).

Lomotil, an effective anti-diarrhea medicine sold only by prescription in the United States because it is fatal in amounts just slightly over the recommended doses, was sold over the counter in Sudan, in packages proclaiming it was "used by astronauts during Gemini and Apollo space flights" and recommended for use by children as young as 12 months. (Dowie, 1979b)

As a final example, let's look at a recent celebrated case—the advertising and marketing of powdered baby formula as a substitute for mother's milk in the Third World. Baby formula is not a health hazard if used properly. But when used improperly it can lead to infant malnutrition and death. In the Third World infant formula can have disastrous consequences because the powder can be mixed with contaminated water, bottles and nipples are rarely sterilized before use, and after water is added storage must be at correct temperatures or bacteria flourish. The cost is high to purchase the formula (as much as 20 to 50 percent of a family's income) so many mothers stretch their supply by diluting it but in the process malnourishing the child.

In these circumstances the use of baby formula instead of breastfeeding is inadvisable. Yet the declining birth rate in the industrialized nations makes the Third World, where fertility is high, an important source for sales in this industry with $2 billion in worldwide sales. The companies (Swiss-based Nestlé and the U.S. companies of Abbott, American Home Products, and Bristol–Myers) have used all their marketing skills (appealing posters, radio jingles, free samples given to new mothers while still in the hospital, employees dressed as medical personnel going from village to village to promote the products) (*Time,* 1981).

Because of the health hazard of infant formula use in the Third World the World Health Organization in 1981 considered the adoption of an international code of conduct restricting the advertising and marketing of baby formula. The final vote was 118 to 1 in favor of such a code. The only dissenting vote came from the United States on orders from President Reagan, who felt that the code restricted free speech and free trade by regulating how private businesses promote their products. It is also important to note that the three U.S. formula makers and the Grocery Manufacturers of America lobbied the government to have the United States vote no or at least abstain on this code. Once again, in the eyes of the critics of the free enterprise economy, business needs seem to supersede human and humane concerns.

THE PUNISHMENT OF CORPORATE CRIME

Although it is impossible to know the exact monetary and social costs of corporate crime, it should be clear that these costs are not only enormous but far exceed the costs of all other types of crime. In addition to the huge costs from overpricing, the merchandizing of faulty goods, the loss of federal revenues through the unreported profits, and the like, there are the actual hazards to life. As Clinard and Yeager (1980, p. 9) have pointed out,

> This includes losses due to sickness and even death resulting from air and water pollution and the sale of unsafe foods and drugs, defective autos, tires, and appliances, and hazardous clothing and other products. It also includes the numerous disabilities that result from injuries to plant workers, including contamination by chemicals that could have been used with adequate safeguards and the potentially dangerous effects of other work-related exposures. Far more persons are killed through corporate criminal activities than by individual criminal homicides: even if death is an indirect result, the person has died.

Despite the enormity of these costs to individuals and society, corporations and corporate executives have gone relatively unpunished. Clinard's research, for example, found that in only 1.5 percent of all enforcement actions was a corporate officer convicted for a crime (Clinard and Yeager, 1980, p. 272). And of those convicted, 63 percent received probation, 21 percent had their sentences suspended, and only 29 percent were incarcerated (Clinard and Yeager, 1980, p. 287).

In a study of Canadian corporations that compared the disposition of cases involving theft by individuals with those involving misleading advertising by corporations over a two-year period, Snider (1982, p. 251) found that in the 56,699 theft cases prosecuted, 11,608 (20 percent) of the perpetrators were sent to prison while of the 126 misleading advertising cases prosecuted not a single person was sentenced to prison.

Clinard found that of the 1860 violations of federal law committed by the largest 582 corporations in 1975 and 1976 only 328 (18 percent) resulted in fines. Over 80 percent of these fines were for less than $5000 and less than 4 percent exceeded $50,000 (Clinard and Yeager, 1980, p. 125). The fining of companies is not much of a deterrent. The $437,500 imposed on General Electric in the electric equipment price-fixing conspiracy has been likened to a parking fine for the average person (Geis, 1973, p. 196). When Chevron paid a $1 million fine in 1972 for violation of offshore antipollution laws, the fine amounted to about 0.03 percent of the company's gross income (about the same as a $10 traffic ticket for a person making $25,000 a year) (Clinard and Yeager, 1980, p. 125). Put another way, if a $300 million company pays a $100,000 fine, a rare occurrence, it would be the equivalent of a person who makes $15,000 a year paying a fine of less than a half-dollar (Ermann and Lundman, 1982, p. 234).

A primary deterrent to a strong government effort to punish corporate crimes is that the law is weak and often ambiguous. The law is explicit and punitive toward offenses by individuals such as theft, possession of stolen goods, burglary, and vehicle theft. But this is not the case for selling defective products, deceptive packaging, or price fixing. Snider has described how in Canada (and the generalization holds for the United States) the courts have much greater latitude in dealing with corporate crimes than with traditional ones. The maximum terms for imprisonment are lighter and the written sanctions much less punitive (Snider, 1982).

The Coddling of Criminal Executives

A serious problem with corporate crime is that often the highly placed executives who directed the harmful corporate acts are rewarded by their corporations. As an example, consider the treatment of two convicted felons from the Fruehauf Corporation (a $2 billion in sales truck manufacturer). In 1975, a judge found the corporation guilty of evading $12.3 million in excise taxes by using deceptive invoices and a false wholesale price. The judge ruled that the president and chief executive officer, Robert Rowan, and the chairman of the board, William Grace, be fined $10,000 and sentenced to six months in jail.

The company clearly did not treat these men as criminals. While Rowan and Grace appealed the verdict, Fruehauf continued to pay Rowan his annual salary of $500,000 and to pay for all court expenses. When the appeal lost, Fruehauf accepted their resignations but continued to pay Rowan as a $100-an-hour consultant. The judge in the meantime suspended their jail sentences and ordered them to do community service while under supervised probation. Following this sentence, Fruehauf's shareholders reelected Rowan and Grace to the board of directors and reinstated Rowan as the chief executive officer.

Source: Nathan (1980).

More important, many corporate crimes, while harmful, are legally defined as noncriminal. According to Snider (1982, p. 237),

> The continuing noncriminal legal status of [upperworld offenses] reflects not their lack of harmfulness but, rather, the superior resources of upperworld criminals and corporations. They have been successful in defining their own acquisitive acts as noncriminal and even harmless, despite the reams of data that have documented the heavy dollar losses and even heavier loss of life and limb they cause.

Either because of the lack of a mandate or the political clout of corporations, the federal government has not pursued corporate crimes with much vigor. A 1979 survey of the Department of Justice by the *New York Times* revealed that the Department lacked the personnel, expertise, and in some cases, the motivation to conduct successful criminal investigations and prosecutions against major corporations or their top executives (Taubman, 1979). The evidence is clear that government efforts to fight ''crime in the suites'' have been reduced even further during the Reagan administration (Braithwaite and Geis, 1982). Such conscious restriction of corporate crime prosecution may be the result of a philosophical stance, for example, the policy of laissez faire, which opposes government interference in business activities. Or it may result from the fear of corporate reprisals, such as withholding of votes and campaign contributions.

A significant obstacle to the prosecution of corporate crime is the legal protection that limits the government's ability to control corporate behavior. A corporation is considered as a person separate and distinct from the individuals who make decisions within it. This means that, although considered a person, a corporation cannot be jailed or executed. Moreover, corporate executives are rarely held responsible for the corporate activities under their control.

Unlike the case with most traditional crimes, the offenses by corporations are less readily apparent. When someone is murdered there is a corpse and a weapon but when a miner dies of lung disease do we know with certainty that it is the result of corporate murder. People who pay more for a product because of price fixing are usually unaware that they are the victims of crime. Similarly, shareholders when given a falsified balance sheet are not likely to realize that they have been defrauded. This relative invisibility of many corporate crimes severely hampers its control (Braithwaite and Geis, 1982, pp. 294–296).

Related to the above impediment to the prosecution of corporate crime is the difficulty in proving guilt. There are several facets to this complication. One is the question of who in the corporation is responsible? Is it the board, chief executive officer, some vice-president, or other employee? Another problem involves motive. Did the company willfully produce and market a dangerous product? When 51 Research-Cottrell workers were killed when the scaffolding for a water tower collapsed, the violation of OSHA regulations was clear, but were these violations due to willful neglect by the company (Braithwaite and Geis, 1982, p. 299)? Also, how can one prove beyond a reasonable doubt that working in a cotton mill "caused" brown lung? After all, about 80 percent of workers in mills do not get that disease. Lawyers for the corporations, and they can afford the best, will argue that an "observed correlations between *a* and *b* is explained by an unknown third variable, *c*. The scientist can never eliminate all the possible third variables" (Braithwaite and Geis, 1982, p. 299).

The difficulty in proving guilt in occupational and environmental-related diseases is based on the legal justifications call the "year-and-a-day rule."

> What [this rule] says is that if the defendant pollutes his victim's water supply or poisons his cattle feed or exposes his lungs to cotton dust or buries high-level radioactive waste in his community and the victim does not die within a year and a day after exposure, then no one can be held criminally liable for any deaths that result at some indeterminate time in the future. (Savoy, 1981, p. 763)

When it takes years of constant exposure for cancer, brown lung, and black lung to develop, the perpetrators will be assumed innocent under the "year-and-a-day" rule.

In the final analysis, corporate crimes are not vigorously pursued by the authorities for two fundamental reasons: (1) the corporate elite use their power over the law-making machinery to either emasculate the law or to see that the law overlooks certain corporate activities and (2) because those corporate activities, even those we consider "crimes," are fundamental to the way capitalism in American society works. This last point is especially important. Precisely because corporate crimes maintain the economy and the political status quo, they go relatively unpoliced.

EXPLANATIONS FOR CORPORATE CRIME

Criminogenic Social Conditions

The traditional sociological explanations commonly given for street crimes such as poverty and social disorganization are inappropriate for understanding corporate crime. The guilty individuals in corporations whose decisions harm workers, pollute the air, and deceive the public are not driven to these deviant acts by their poverty or the poverty of their corporations. To the contrary, these decision makers are the most powerful individuals in the most powerful organizations in society.

Sutherland, the pioneer in studying American corporate crime, believed that corporate leaders were driven to their harmful behaviors by their association with colleagues who advocated such behaviors and an absence of people advocating opposite actions.

> Criminal behavior is learned in association with those who define such behavior favorably and in isolation from those who define it unfavorably, and that a person in an appropriate situation engages in such criminal behavior if, and only if, the weight of favorable definitions exceeds the weight of the unfavorable definitions. (Sutherland, 1949, p. 234)

It is important to note that the climate in some industries and corporations appears to be more unethical than in others. In some industries pollution is the norm while in others there is more social responsibility. In some industries worker safety is especially jeopardized while in others more money is spent to promote safe working conditions. There are also corporate variations within these industries. Several factors may account for this variance such as union strength, the clout of consumer or environmental protection groups, and the ethical standards imposed by the corporate leadership. Stone has argued that a particular corporation, like a political administration, appears to have a culture that promotes or retards illegal/unethical behaviors. He has referred to this as the "culture of a corporation"—the entire constellation of attitudes and forces, some of which contribute to illegal behaviors. The factors contributing to illegal behaviors include:

> a desire for profits, expansion, power; desire for security (at corporate as well as individual levels); the fear of failure (particularly in connection with short-comings in corporate innovativeness); group loyalty identification (particularly

in connection with citizenship violations and the various failures to "come forward" with internal information); feelings of omniscience (in connection with adequate testing); organizational diffusion of responsibility (in connection with the buffering of public criticism); corporate ethnocentrism (in connection with limits in concern for the public's wants and desires) (Stone, 1975, p. 236).

The Interactionist Perspective

Interactionists argue that deviance is not inherent in any act but is a property conferred on the act by others. In other words, an act is deviant (or criminal) only when it is defined as such. This insight aids in the understanding of why the corporate behaviors labeled here as crimes are not always considered as crimes by the perpetrators or the public. This is because there is a lack of consensus in society about whether pollution, monopoly, and corporate dumping overseas are deviant acts (Ermann and Lundman, 1982, pp. 227–230). This indecision is the result of several factors: (1) the sharp contrast in how radicals, liberals, and conservatives view the social responsibilities of corporations; (2) the government's mild treatment of violators; (3) the relative lack of information on the questionable activities of corporations found in the media; and (4) the corporations' active efforts to defend and redefine their actions before the public. This last point is significant. Corporations exert their enormous powers to deflect and diffuse potential negative images of them. These powers include their influence over the lawmaking and law-enforcing processes of government (Domhoff, 1978), the giving or withholding of advertising to the media, and massive public relations efforts. The interactionists, however, do not focus on the political and economic resources of the corporations, which translate into the power to define what is criminal and what is not. Therefore, their insights should be combined with those of the radicals for a more adequate understanding.

The Radical Perspective

In the radical view the assumptions and workings of the capitalist economy promote corporate crime (Young, 1982). The rational pursuit of profit leads to bribery, fraud, the marketing of dangerous products, the neglect of workers, the conspiracy to fix prices, and the pollution of the environment.

One tendency of capitalism, the ever greater concentration of assets in fewer and fewer firms, is related to criminal behavior. Conklin (1977), for example, has reported that there is a greater likelihood of price fixing and deceptive advertising in those industries where there is a shared monopoly.

The radical perspective recognizes that the relationship between business and government is most significant. The evidence is clear that throughout American history government policies tend to serve the interests of big business (Balkan et al., 1980, Chap. 9). This relationship is not coincidental. The leadership in the corporations realizes that the policies of government can be used to maximize profits. Profits are maximized when workers are not unionized or, if unionized, their ability to strike is weakened by the law or by government police actions. Profits are maximized when the laws against certain corporate practices such as pollution are weak or nonexistent. And, most significantly, profits are maximized when the regulation of business is not viewed as a legitimate function of government—as is the case under President Reagan and his dismantling of the "regulatory state."

The radical theorist focuses on the capitalist economy, which itself is criminal. As Quinney (1979, pp. 202–203) has argued:

> As capitalism continues to develop, corporations must accumulate more capital and expand, raising profits by whatever means in order to survive. A consequence is increasing use of criminal operations—against the pollution, as well as against other corporations, the government, and the society. The capitalist economy becomes criminal in itself.

In sum, the radical perspective considers corporate executives, the corporations, the economy, and the society guilty when they promote profits over human and humane considerations. Joel Swartz (1975, p. 18) has argued, for example, that occupation-related deaths should be considered murders:

> By any legitimate criteria corporate executives who willfully make a decision to expose workers to a dangerous substance which eventually causes the death of some of the workers, should be considered murderers. Yet no executive has ever served even a day in jail for such a practice, and most probably are well rewarded for having saved the company money. The regulatory apparatus that is complicit with such practices should of course be considered an accomplice.

But the guilt does not stop with corporate executives, as Swartz goes on to argue:

> In the long run it is not the outright deception, dishonesty and cunning of corporate executives, doctors and bureaucrats which is responsible for the problem. Rather, the general functioning of the system is at the heart of the problem . . . the tremendous toll in occupational illnesses results from the oppression of one class by another. The people who own corporations try to exact as much wealth as they can from the workers. Improvements in working conditions to eliminate health hazards would eat into the profits that could be exacted. . . . In particular the asbestos industry would rather spend millions of dollars trying to prove that asbestos is safe, than spend the money necessary to eliminate exposures. In oil refineries many of the exposures to chemicals result from inadequate maintenance of plant equipment. Maintenance costs come to 15 percent of total refinery costs, but these costs are considered controllable. In other words, skipping on maintenance is a good way to cut costs. Only the worker suffers. Another reason that the system causes occupational illnesses is the pressure it applies for expansion, especially in certain industries such as

chemicals and plastics. The chemical industry, especially, is able to reap high profits by rapidly introducing new chemicals. . . . Thus demands that chemicals be adequately tested before use, and the possibilities that new chemicals found to be dangerous might be banned, constitute a tremendous threat to the industry. . . . The ultimate reason for the problem is the drive of corporations to extract as much profit as possible from the workers. But to continue to function this system requires constant efforts by people from corporate executives to scientists to bureaucrats. These efforts result in a staggering toll in death and disease which should qualify the perpetrators as criminals by any reasonable human standards. But the system, functioning the way it is, rewards certain criminals very handsomely. The ultimate success in the battle to improve health and safety conditions will require getting rid of these criminals, and the system which enables them to operate. (Swartz, 1975, pp. 19–20)

Swartz directs attention to the heart of the radical's interpretation of corporate crime. Corporate crime is *not* the result of the sins of corporate executives. Corporate crime is the logical consequence of the structure of capitalist society. The corporate owners and managers are part of the ruling class, which maintains its power and gains materially by oppressing the powerless (workers and consumers). This buttresses the point made at the beginning of the chapter—individuals in corporations make decisions to advance the interests of the corporation. It does not matter who these individuals are. Corporate executives in American society are replaceable people constrained by the positions they occupy. Their decisions will inevitably be to increase corporate profits and such decisions often have inhumane consequences (thus, they are corporate crimes). The solution to the problem of corporate crime, then, is not to change the attitudes of corporate executives but to change the political-economic structure of society.

CHAPTER REVIEW

1. Corporate crimes are deliberate acts by large business enterprises that do physical or economic harm to the environment, employees, or to customers. These corporate acts are crimes whether there are laws prohibiting them or not. The unit of analysis is the corporation not the individuals within it because large organizations are not collections of people but collections of positions occupied by replaceable people under similar constraints.
2. The major studies on corporate crime by Sutherland, *Fortune,* and Clinard, although actually understating the incidence and magnitude of corporate crime, reveal that these crimes are endemic to American society.
3. A major category of corporate crime is crimes against employees, which is typically manifested in violence against unions, dangerous working conditions, and discriminatory labor practices.
4. Corporations employ several strategies to extract excessive prices for their products—monopoly, price fixing, price gouging, and deceptive advertising.

5. Corporations commit crimes when they produce and distribute unsafe products whether they be flawed automobiles or unhealthy foods.

6. Corporations in the rational pursuit of maximum profit do harm to the environment by promoting products that pollute, and by not curbing the pollutants from their plants that negatively impact the land, water, and air.

7. Corporate policies also endanger people outside the United States through the sale of arms, colonial relationships, the intervention in the affairs of foreign governments, and corporate dumping.

8. Corporate crimes are rarely punished because (a) sometimes there are no laws governing the harmful activities; (b) there is a lack of consensus in society as to what constitutes corporate crime; (c) they are often difficult to detect; and (d) many of them are fundamental to the way capitalism works in American society.

9. The traditional sociological explanations for crime and the interactionist perspective are not particularly relevant to understanding corporate crime. The radical perspective, on the other hand, centers corporate crime in the capitalist economy where profit is promoted over human and humane considerations.

10 Political Crime

**CHAPTER
OUTLINE**

Political Crimes against the Government
Crimes by the Government

The overt basis of government
Government lawlessness

Sociological Theories and Political Crime

Traditional sociological approaches
The interactionist perspective
The radical perspective

KEY TERMS

Ecocide
Genocide
Political crime
Unjust law
War crimes

Political crime is conceptualized as crime by individuals and groups against the government, and crime by the government against the people.[1] Criminologists interested in political crimes have traditionally concentrated on crimes against the government—acts of dissent and violence to change the existing order. These are violations of the law and are perceived by the authorities as detrimental to the state and therefore are suppressed (Roebuck and Weeber, 1978, p. iv). While these political acts are important to understand, the exclusive focus on them ignores acts by the state that are detrimental to the people. Crimes by the government against the people include such acts as official lawlessness by government agencies, war crimes, suppression of individual rights, secrecy, and deceit. Since the politically powerful also make the laws, the law itself can be biased, as we saw in Chapter 3. Therefore, the definition of political crime goes beyond the purely legal boundaries (Galliher and McCartney, 1977). We will examine government policies that do legal violence to certain categories of people; we will see how the law is biased toward the propertied over the propertyless, toward the owner over labor, and toward the majority over racial/ethnic minorities.

The view of political crime that includes the acts of government runs counter to that of most citizens. The typical conception is that political crimes are acts by deviant individuals and organizations. This one-sided view assumes that the government is somehow immune from criminality. Clinard and Quinney (1973, p. 158) have shown that even criminologists have tended to adopt this standard toward political crime. To counteract this neglect, we will emphasize the crimes by government. But before turning to the deviance of the government, let's first consider political crimes by dissidents.

POLITICAL CRIMES AGAINST THE GOVERNMENT

Political crimes against the state are violations of the law by individuals and groups that are motivated by political intent (Minor, 1975, p. 390). Generally, three kinds of activities are included: (1) illegal acts undertaken in an attempt to change the existing structure of political power; (2) illegal efforts to seize power; and (3) the refusal to obey the law because of political or ideological beliefs (Sykes, 1980, p. 48).

Political criminals differ from other criminals. They are driven to challenge the existing political structure because they accept a belief system that supersedes the one that prevails in society. They do not seek monetary gains but political change toward a better world. They are willing to go to jail or even to die for the cause. They assume that many laws serve the interests of those with the power to make and enforce them. The law is considered a tool by which the powerful retain their advantage and therefore must be disobeyed (see Panel 10-1). From the perspective of the political criminal, the system and its agents are the criminals and the enemy.

Although political criminals and other criminals may both pose a threat, the

---

[1]Not included here as political crimes are crimes by politicians for personal monetary gain, such as corruption, which are more appropriately considered white-collar crimes.

Political dissidents challenge the existing political order because they consider its actions illegitimate.

former are considered a direct threat to established political power and therefore are subject to stern punishment.

> If the members of a ruling elite believe a particular individual or group to be imminently hostile to the prevailing pattern of value distribution, and if they activate the criminal process against him (or them) for that reason, what results is a political trial. Additionally, if members of the ruling elite feel someone seriously intends to alter the *way* in which the government distributes those values, and if the elite activates the criminal process against them for that reason—that, too, constitutes a political trial. (Becker, 1971, pp. xi–xiii)

Throughout American history groups that were oppressed resorted to various illegitimate means to secure the rights and privileges that they believed were rightfully theirs. The revolutionary colonists used acts of civil disobedience and finally eight years of war to accomplish their goals. Native Americans have sought the intrusions of white settlers and systematic suppression by the U.S. government. Other groups such as farmers, slaveholders, WASP supremacists, ethnic and racial minorities, and laborers have at times broken the law in efforts to

PANEL 10-1

Just and Unjust Laws

Martin Luther King, Jr., was jailed many times for his political activities. He led the civil rights movement in the South to break the segregationist customs and laws, which met with great resistance from the authorities. His tactics, although nonviolent, were questioned even by many who sympathized with the movement's goals. Among the critics were religious leaders who, among other things, expressed their disdain for King's willingness to break laws. What follows is part of his response to these clergymen in his famous "Letter from the Birmingham Jail."

You express a great deal of anxiety over our willingness to break laws. This is certainly a legitimate concern. Since we so diligently urge people to obey the Supreme Court's decision of 1954 outlawing segregation in the public schools, at first glance it may seem rather paradoxical for us consciously to break laws. One may well ask, "How can you advocate breaking some laws and obeying others?" The answer lies in the fact that there are two types of laws: just and unjust. I agree with St. Augustine that "an unjust law is no law at all."

Now what is the difference between the two? How does one determine whether a law is just or unjust? A just law is a man made code that squares with the moral law or law of God. An unjust law is a code that is out of harmony with the moral law. To put it in the terms of St. Thomas Aquinas, an unjust law is a human law that is not rooted in eternal law and natural law. Any law that uplifts human personality is just. Any law that degrades human personality is unjust. All segregation statutes are unjust because segregation distorts the soul and damages the personality. It gives the segregator a false sense of superiority and the segregated a false sense of inferiority. Segregation, to use the terminology of the Jewish philosopher Martin Buber, substitutes an "I-it" relationship for an "I-thou" relationship and ends up relegating persons to the status of things. Hence segregation is not only politically, economically and sociologically unsound, it is morally wrong and sinful. Paul Tillich has said that sin is separation. Is not segregation an existential expression of man's tragic separation, his awful

change what they considered an unfair system. While these are extremely important, we will concentrate here on the efforts by dissenters during the Vietnam War to change the government's course, and the governmental efforts to silence these critics.

The Vietnam War was never formally declared by Congress. It escalated from presidential decisions and commitments that were camouflaged from the public.

Panel 10-1 (Continued)

estrangement, his terrible sinfulness? Thus it is that I can urge men to obey the 1954 decision of the Supreme Court, for it is morally right; and I can urge them to disobey segregation ordinances, for they are morally wrong.

Let us consider a more concrete example of just and unjust laws. An unjust law is a code that a numerical or power majority group compels a minority group to obey but does not make binding on itself. This is *difference* made legal. By the same token, a just law is a code that a majority compels a minority to follow and that it is willing to follow itself. This is *sameness* made legal.

Let me give another explanation. A law is unjust if it is inflicted on a minority that, as a result of being denied the right to vote, had no part in enacting or devising the law. Who can say that the legislature of Alabama which set up that state's segregation laws was democratically elected? Throughout Alabama all sorts of devious methods are used to prevent Negroes from becoming registered voters, and there are some counties in which, even though Negroes constitute a majority of the population, not a single Negro is registered. Can any law enacted under such circumstances be considered democratically structured?

Sometimes a law is just on its face and unjust in its application. For instance, I have been arrested on a charge of parading without a permit. Now, there is nothing wrong in having an ordinance which requires a permit for a parade. But such an ordinance becomes unjust when it is used to maintain segregation and to deny citizens the First-Amendment privilege of peaceful assembly and protest.

I hope you are able to see the distinction I am trying to point out. In no sense do I advocate evading or defying the law, as would the rabid segregationist. That would lead to anarchy. One who breaks an unjust law must do so openly, lovingly, and with a willingness to accept the penalty. I submit that an individual who breaks a law that conscience tells him is unjust, and who willingly accepts the penalty of imprisonment in order to arouse the conscience of the community over its unjustice, is in reality expressing the highest respect for law.

Source: Martin Luther King, Jr., "Letter from the Birmingham Jail," Why We Can't Wait, New York: Harper & Row, 1963, pp. 84–86.

In effect, the United States had taken a side in an Asian civil war without the consent of the people or, if they had consented as we now know, it was done through the manipulation of events and information by our leaders. Because of the uniqueness of our involvement in this war, many young men refused to serve. Some became fugitives from the law by hiding in the United States or by fleeing to other countries. Others accepted imprisonment. Some 20,000 Americans of all ages refused to pay all or a part of their taxes because the money would support a war they considered illegal, immoral, and unjust. As a result, they risked harassment by the Internal Revenue Service and possible imprisonment.

At one demonstration before the Oakland induction center in 1965, one David Miller set fire to his draft card saying, "I believe the napalming of villages to be an immoral act. I hope this will be a significant political act, so here goes" (cited in Goodell, 1973, p. 130). He was arrested and later sentenced to two and one half years in prison. This started a rash of similar protests that the establishment considered a threat to its power. At one rally, the Reverend William Sloane Coffin, Dr. Benjamin Spock, and two others announced that they would henceforth counsel young men to refuse to serve in the armed forces as long as the Vietnam War continued. They were arrested and convicted for conspiracy and sentenced to two years imprisonment.

One of the most infamous political trials of this era involved the Chicago Eight. In 1968, a time of ghetto riots and the assassinations of Martin Luther King, Jr., and Robert Kennedy, Congress passed the "Rap Brown Amendment" (Brown was chairperson of the Student Nonviolent Coordinating Committee, SNCC, at the time), which nearly outlawed interstate travel by political activists. In the summer of that year, the Democratic National Convention convened in Chicago. Because Hubert Humphrey, a hawk on Vietnam, was the leading nominee, thousands of youths flooded Chicago bent on protesting the war and venting their anger against what they perceived as an unresponsive political leadership. They protested and the police reacted violently, adding to the volatility of the situation.

Months later, when Richard Nixon took office and John Mitchell became attorney general, the federal government issued indictments against individuals felt to be the leaders of the Chicago riots—David Dellinger, Rennie Davis, Tom Hayden, Abbie Hoffman, Jerry Rubin, Lee Weiner, John Froines, and Bobby Seales—soon to be known collectively as the Chicago Eight. These persons were charged with conspiracy to cross state lines with intent to cause a riot (violating the Rap Brown law). These men represented various kinds of dissent such as radical pacifism, the New Left, political hippies, academic dissent, and black militance. The case was heard in the U.S. District Court in Chicago, with Judge Julius Hoffman presiding.

Many knowledgeable observers, including Ramsey Clark, the predecessor of John Mitchell, felt that the trial was a political gesture by the new Nixon administration to demonstrate a no-nonsense policy against dissent. The conspiracy charge made little sense because the actions of the defendants and their constituencies were uncoordinated. Moreover, Bobby Seales, an alleged co-conspirator, knew only one of the other defendants.

This trial was a symbolic showcase for the defendants as well. Because of their disrespect for the system, the defendants refused to accept the traditional role. Instead of allowing the system to keep them quiet while the long judicial process wound down, the defendants behaved in such a way that their actions would be headline news. Thus, they continually challenged the judiciary's legitimacy. As Sternberg has characterized their rationale:

The argument that the court is illegitimate rests on the defendant's analysis and condemnation of the existing situation in the United States. They see themselves as political prisoners trapped by a power structure of laws created by societal groups hostile to their interests. The court is both an agent for these groups and institutions—most significantly, monopoly capitalism, racism, colonialism, the military-industrial complex, and incipient fascism—and also an oppressive power group in its own right. Although defendants may vary somewhat in the rank or order of their targets, all are in agreement that the criminal court's allegiances are squarely with the oppressor groups and directly hostile to the powerless classes in American society. (Sternberg, 1974, p. 281)

As a result of their disrespectful behavior toward the court, Judge Hoffman judged the defendants and their lawyers guilty of 159 contempt citations and sentenced them to jail for terms ranging from 68 days to four years and 13 days. In addition, each defendant was found guilty of inciting a riot, receiving a sentence of five years in prison and a $5000 fine. All were acquitted of conspiracy charges. Before the sentences were passed, each defendant was allowed to make a final statement. The speech by Tom Hayden captured the essence of the problem from the perspective of the accused:

Our intention in coming to Chicago was not to incite a riot. . . . [It] was to see to it that certain things, that is, the right of every human being, the right to assemble, the right to protest, can be carried out even where the Government chooses to suspend those rights. It was because we chose to exercise those rights in Chicago . . . that we are here today. . . . We would hardly be notorious characters if they had left us alone in the streets of Chicago last year. . . . It would have been testimony to our failure as organizers. But instead we became the architects, the master minds, and the geniuses of a conspiracy to overthrow the government. We were invented. We were chosen by the government to serve as scapegoats for all that they wanted to prevent happening in the 1970s. (quoted in Danelski, 1971, p. 177)

In speaking of his concern for the direction of the government, Daniel Berrigan, himself a political prisoner, has spoken eloquently of the need for dissent:

Indeed it cannot be thought that men and women like ourselves will continue, as though we were automated heroes, to rush for redress from the King of the Blind. The King will have to listen to other voices, over which neither he nor we will indefinitely have control: voices of public violence and chaos. For you cannot set up a court in the Kingdom of the Blind, to condemn those who see; a court presided over by those who would pluck out the eyes of men and call it rehabilitation. (Berrigan, 1970, pp. x–xii)

Political dissent is not limited to the past. It is as recent as today's newspaper headlines where protests of various kinds are likely to be found, for example, against taxes (too much or too supportive of the military), against some domestic policy such as the farm program, against the draft, opposition to the deployment of an antimissile defense system, against the building and use of nuclear reactors for energy, against some segment of the foreign policy such as an intervention in Latin America, or in favor of the nuclear freeze. Some of these protests are peaceful and within the existing law, whereas others are not. As an example of the latter, a group known as the Plowshares Eight broke into a General Electric plant in 1980 and desecrated nuclear warhead cones with hammers and blood. This illegal act was done to bring attention to the government's nuclear deterrent policy, which the protestors regarded as sheer folly. In the words of one of these protestors, Philip Berrigan:

> Two convictions support our civilly disobedient attitude toward the law: First, the State has perverted law to the point of legalizing its nuclear psychosis. Second, the State is invincible unless such legalizing is rendered null and void by non-violent civil disobedience. We cannot leave the State invincible in its determination to initiate (or provoke) nuclear war.
>
> Who expects politicians, generals, and bomb makers to disarm? People must disarm the bombs. That's the only way it will happen. (Berrigan, 1981, p. 51)

The source of individual political crime is a society perceived as unjust and immoral. The overt and covert acts of government, which we consider political crimes, especially serve as a catalyst for the formation and maintenance of dissident groups. These acts are the subject matter of the next section.

CRIMES BY THE GOVERNMENT

There are two basic types of crimes by the government against its citizens. There are the overt governmental decisions that benefit the powerful and do harm to the powerless, and there are the actual acts of government lawlessness. The first type is not criminal in the legal sense because the acts reflect our heritage and are considered appropriate by most citizens because they involve the normal activities and decisions of government. The second category involves criminal behavior, but, ironically, these activities are typically not considered inappropriate by the citizenry.

The Overt Bias of Government

Who benefits from government policies? At times, most everyone does, but whenever the interests of the advantaged clash with those of the less advantaged, the decisions of government tend to benefit the former. As examples, examine carefully how the president and Congress deal with the problems of energy shortages, inflation, or deflation. Who is asked to make the sacrifices? Where is the budget cut—for military expenditures or funds for food stamps? When the Congress considers tax reform, after the clouds of rhetoric recede, which groups benefit by the new legislation or by the laws that are left alone? When a corporation is found guilty of fraud, violation of antitrust laws, bribery, or whatever, what are the penalties? How do they compare with the penalties for crimes committed by poor individuals such as "welfare chiselers" and thieves? When there is an oil spill or other ecological disaster caused by huge enterprise, what are the penalties? Who pays for the cleanup and the restoration of nature? The answers to these questions are obvious—the wealthy benefit at the expense of the less well-to-do.

This bias has been present throughout American history. The writers of the Constitution, who represented wealth and property, were concerned about the potential power of the masses (Beard, 1919). They were opposed to representative democracy. Their attitude was stated well in the following statement by Alexander Hamilton:

> All communities divide themselves into the few and the many. The first are the rich and the well born, the other the mass of the people. The voice of the people has been said to be the voice of God; and however generally this maxim has been quoted and believed, it is not true in fact. The people are turbulent and changing; they seldom judge or determine right. Give therefore to the first class a distinct, permanent share in the government. They will check the unsteadiness of the second and as they cannot receive any advantage by a change, they therefore will ever maintain good government. (Ferrand, quoted in Parenti, 1980, p. 53)

Even more blatant was the statement by Governor Morris at the Constitutional Convention:

> The time is not distant when this Country will abound with mechanics and manufacturers [industrial workers] who will receive their bread from their employers. Will such men be the secure and faithful Guardians of liberty? . . . Children do not vote. Why? Because they want prudence, because they have no will of their own. The ignorant and the dependent can be as little trusted with the public interest. (quoted in Parenti, 1980, p. 57)

As a result of this type of thinking, which by the way was characteristic of the complaints by intellectuals throughout history until the last 100 years or so, the Constitution was designed to retain the power among the propertied few, while utilizing seemingly democratic principles. The appearance of democracy actually had the effect of fragmenting the power of the masses.

> By separating the executive, legislative and judiciary functions and then providing a system of checks and balances among the various branches, including staggered elections, executive veto, Senate confirmation of appointments and ratification of treaties, and a two-house legislature, they [the Founding Fathers] hoped to dilute the impact of popular sentiments. To the extent that it existed at all, the majoritarian principle was tightly locked into a system of minority

vetoes, making swift and sweeping popular actions nearly impossible. (Parenti, 1980, p. 56)

The blatant disregard for the masses, as determined by the Constitution, is seen in the following (Parenti, 1980, pp. 57–58):

Item   The senators from each state were to be elected by their respective state legislatures (the 17th Amendment, adopted in 1913, finally provided for the direct election of senators).

Item   The election of the president was on the surface to be decided by the voters, but in reality the president was to be selected by an electoral college composed of political leaders. This procedure allowed the upper classes to control the presidential vote regardless of the popular vote. Each state had as many electors as it had senators and representatives. Each political party would select a slate of electors, who would vote for president if their party's candidate carried the state. Interestingly, and indicative of the contempt for the masses, some states allowed their electors to vote for anyone, not necessarily the presidential candidate of their party (five states still retain that right).

Item   The Supreme Court justices were to be nonelected. They were appointed to life tenure by the president and confirmed by the Senate.

Item   The matter of who was allowed to vote was left to the individual states. This meant, in effect, the disenfranchisement of many voters. All the states disallowed women from voting (changed in 1919 by the passage of the 19th Amendment). All the states denied voting to those held in bondage (changed following the Civil War by the passage of the 14th Amendment). In various states it was common to require that voters own certain amounts and kinds of property.

Other nondemocratic practices occurred throughout the states early in our history, some continuing into the present. One was the limiting of political candidates to the wealthy—candidates had to pass steep property qualifications for holding office. This meant that most voters could not qualify as candidates. "The result was that the gentry, merchants, and professionals monopolized the important offices" (Parenti, 1980, p. 51).

A common practice throughout American history has been for the majority in legislatures (at all levels) to revise political boundaries for their advantage. This tactic, known as "gerrymandering," occurs when the party in power designs the political boundaries to negate the power of the opposition. Assume, for instance, that the Democrats control the state legislature. The boundary lines can be redrawn in order to take Republican strongholds from problematic districts, placing them in nearby strong Democratic districts. The Democratic district is strong enough to absorb the Republicans without losing their advantage, and in the former Republican district, the Democrats have a better chance of gaining control.

These practices to minimize, neutralize, or negate the voting privileges of the relatively powerless are most evident in the efforts of the dominant whites to neutralize the votes of blacks.

Although the 14th Amendment to the Constitution gave blacks the right to vote following the Civil War, the white majority in the southern states used a variety of tactics to keep them from voting. Most effective was the strategy of intimidation. Blacks who tried to assert their right to vote were often subject to beatings, destruction of property, or even lynching. The more subtle approach, however, was quite effective in eliminating the black vote in the southern states. Through legal means, laws were passed to achieve illegal discrimination. One tactic was the white primary that excluded blacks from the party primary (Key, 1949, Chap. 25). The Constitution prohibited the states from denying the vote on the basis of race. A political party, however, since it was a private association, *could* discriminate. The Democratic Party throughout most of the south chose the option of limiting the primary to whites. Blacks could legally vote in the general election but only for the candidates already selected by whites. And since the Democratic party in the South was supreme, whoever was selected in the primary would be the victor in the general election. This practice was nullified by the Supreme Court in 1944.

Other legal obstacles for blacks in the South were the literacy test and the poll tax, which also have been ruled illegal by the Supreme Court, but only after many decades of denying blacks the right to vote. Both obstacles were designed as two southern suffrage requirements to admit whites to the electorate and exclude blacks (without mentioning race). Let's look briefly at the literacy test because it and the related requirements were so blatantly racist (Key, 1949, Chap. 26).

The object of the literacy test was to allow all adult white males to vote and exclude all blacks. The problem with this test was that many whites would also be excluded because they were also illiterate. The legislators in the various southern states contrived alternatives to the literacy requirements that would allow the illiterate whites to vote. One loophole to accomplish this was the "grandfather clause, which, using Louisiana law as the example, exempted persons from the literacy test who were registered voters in any state on January 1, 1867, or prior thereto, the sons and grandsons of such persons, and male persons of foreign birth naturalized before January 1, 1898."

Another alternative designed to allow illiterate whites to vote was the "understanding" clause. In such an instance a person who could not read any section of the Constitution would qualify as an elector if he could "understand" and give "a reasonable interpretation" of what was read to him. This procedure gave registrars the latitude to decide who could vote, and thus they had the ability to discriminate, which they did uniformly. A similar law in some states authorized registration of illiterates if they were "of good character" and could "understand the duties of obligations of citizenship under a republican form of government."

Racial minorities have also been severely disadvantaged by official government policies throughout American history. The government supported slavery. The government took land forcibly from the Indians, and for a time had an official policy of exterminating them. During World War II, Japanese-Americans were relocated in detention camps causing great loss of property for them. The law itself has helped to do violence to minority groups (Burns, 1978). A study of sentences for rape in Florida between 1940 and 1964, for example, found that none of the whites found guilty of raping a black woman was sentenced to death, but 54 percent of the blacks found guilty of raping white women were.

The government has had a continuing bias in favor of the business community, especially big business, throughout American history. As local business shifted to large scale manufacturing during the last half of the 19th century, governmental support of the business sector increased. Business was protected from competition by protective tariffs, public subsidies, price regulation, patents, and trademarks. Throughout that century when there was unrest by troubled miners, farmers, and laborers, the government inevitably took the side of the strong against the weak. The militia and federal troops were used to crush the railroad strikes. Antitrust laws, which were not used to stop the monopolistic practices of business, were invoked against labor unions. President Cleveland's Attorney General, Richard Olney, a millionaire owner of railroad stocks:

> used antitrust laws, court injunctions, mass arrests, labor spies, deputy marshals and federal troops against workers and their unions. From the local sheriff and magistrate to the President and the Supreme Court, the forces of "law and order" were utilized to suppress the "conspiracy" of labor unions and serve "the defensive needs of large capitalist enterprises." (Parenti, 1980, p. 67)

During this time, approximately 1 billion acres of land in the public domain (almost one half of the present size of the United States) was given to private individuals and corporations. The railroads in particular were given huge tracts of land as a subsidy. These lands were and continue to be very rich in timber and natural resources.

This active intervention of the government in the nation's economy during the 19th century was almost solely on the behalf of business. "The federal government did exercise a kind of laissez-faire in certain other areas: little attention was given to unemployment, poverty, education, the spread of urban slums, and the spoliation of natural resources" (Parenti, 1980, p. 68).

The early 20th century was a time of great governmental activity in the economy, which gave the appearance of restraining big business. However, the actual result of federal regulation of business was to increase the power of the largest corporations. The Interstate Commerce Commission, for instance, helped the railroads by establishing common rates instead of ruinous competition. The federal regulations in meat packing, drugs, banking, and mining weeded out the weaker cost-cutting competitors, leaving a few to control the markets at higher prices and higher profits.

World War I intensified the governmental bias toward business. Industry was converted to war production. Corporate interests became more actively involved in the councils of government. Governmental actions clearly favored business in labor disputes. The police and military were used against rebellious workers because strikes were treated as efforts to weaken the war effort and were therefore treasonous.

The New Deal is typically assumed to be a time when the needs of those impoverished by the Great Depression were paramount in government policies. But "the central dedication of the Franklin Roosevelt administration was to *business recovery* rather than *social reform*" (Parenti, 1980, p. 71). Business was subsidized by credits, price supports, bank guarantees, stimulation of the housing industry, and the like. Welfare programs were instituted to prevent widespread starvation but even these humanitarian programs also worked to the benefit of the big business community. The government provided jobs, minimum wages, unemployment compensation, and retirement benefits, which obviously aided those in dire economic straits. But these programs were actually promoted by the business community because of benefits to them. The government and business favored social programs at this time not because millions were in misery but because of the threat of violent political and social unrest. Two social scientists, Piven and Cloward (1971), after a historical assessment of government welfare programs, have determined that the government institutes massive aid to the poor *only* when the poor constitute a threat. When large numbers of people are suddenly barred from their traditional occupations, the legitimacy of the system itself may be questioned. Crimes, riots, looting, and social movement bent on changing the existing social, political, and economic arrangements become more widespread. Under this threat, relief programs are initiated or expanded by the government to diffuse the social unrest. During the Great Depression, Piven and Cloward contend, the government remained aloof from the needs of the unemployed until there was a surge of political disorder. Added proof for Piven and Cloward's thesis is the contraction or even abolishment of public assistance programs when stability is restored.

The historical trend for government to favor business over the less powerful interests continues in current public policy. This bias is perhaps best seen in the aphorism once enunciated by President Calvin Coolidge and since repeated by President Reagan: "The business of America is business."

Subsidies to Big Business

There is a general principle that applies to the government's relationship to big business: business can conduct its affairs either undisturbed by or encouraged by government, whichever is of greater benefit to the business community. The following are some illustrative cases of where governmental decisions were beneficial to business:

Item   In 1979, the Chrysler Corporation, after sustaining losses of $207 million in the previous year, appealed to the government and received $1.5 billion in loan guarantees. The government's aid to Chrysler is typical—if the company is big enough. Penn Central received $125 million when it faced bankruptcy and the government guaranteed Lockheed $250 million in new bank loans. The irony, of course, is that the big companies receive emergency help while the government does very little to aid the approximately 10,000 small business and 300,000 individuals going bankrupt annually.

Item   From 1965 to 1967, several major petroleum companies leased acreage in Alaska for oil exploration, paying a sum of $12 million for leases worth upward of $2 billion. In a subsequent oil lease auction, the companies paid the government $900 million for lands that are expected to be worth some $50 billion within a decade (Parenti, 1980, p. 70). In 1979, during the midst of an oil shortage crisis, the government leased 33,749 acres of land surrounding an area of active wells *without competitive bids* for $1 per acre to the Texas Oil and Gas Corporation. The value of the leases was estimated at $10 million.

Item   The government develops new technologies at public expense and then turns them over to private corporations for their profit. Using the case of nuclear energy, Ralph Nader has said:

> Nuclear power would never have existed if it weren't for the government. The government funded the basic research, funded the technology, gave the designs to the utilities gratis, enriched the uranium, protected the utilities from liability under the Price-Anderson Act, and has now decided to pay the costs for nuclear wastes. From start to finish, it's a classic case of an industry that has been sponsored, shielded, and protected by the government. (quoted in *Public Opinion,* 1979, pp. 12–13)

The government's bias toward the business community does harm to segments of the society in three important ways. First, a relaxation in government regulation can do harm to workers. Historically, businesses, if left to self-regulation, opt for profits over worker safety. Yet, under President Reagan, the safety regulations of the work place were reduced as were the number of inspectors. For example, the federal Mine Safety and Health Administration reduced its activities significantly from 1980 to 1981 resulting in a 27 percent decrease in fines by mine operators, a 16 percent decline in citations for safety violations, and a 9 percent drop in orders to close mines or correct hazards. Concomitant with these indicators of federal laxity in monitoring and correcting mine hazards was the highest death rate in mining accidents in six years—153 miners killed in 1981 (McCarthy, 1982, p. 11A).

Second, the federal government under President Reagan reduced its efforts to regulate the advertising, manufacture, and sale of consumer goods. The argument is that business should move toward self-regulation. But, as we observed in the preceding chapter, the evidence from history and the contemporary scene is that if left unsupervised business will tend to place profits above consumer interests. As Michael Pertschuk (1982, p. 84), former chairman of the Federal Trade Commission has argued "civilization has never flowed spontaneously from American business, and the lack of it is an inevitable by-product of vigorous, profit-maximizing behavior. Consequently, we have looked to government as the civilizing force." Corporate greed, even when regulated by the federal government, has often resulted in unsafe products, distorted advertising, excessively processed goods, and the promotion of dangerous nutritional practices. Clearly, consumers need a strong monitoring of the business community.

The government's strong business ties has another detrimental effect on the less powerful segments of society: the less powerful subsidize the powerful in significant ways. These costs are outlined in the following section.

"Trickle-Down" Solutions

Periodically, the government is faced with the problem of finding a way to stimu-late the economy during an economic downturn. One way to accomplish this goal is to spend federal monies through unemployment insurance, government jobs, and housing subsidies. In this way the funds go directly to those most hurt by shortages, unemployment, inadequate housing, and the like. Opponents of such plans advocate that the subsidies should go directly to business, which would help the economy by encouraging companies to hire more workers, add to their inven-tories, and build new plants. Thus, by subsidizing business in this way, the advo-cates argue, everyone benefits. To provide subsidies to businesses rather than directly to needy individuals is based on the assumption that private profit max-imizes the public good.

There are two possible reasons why government officials tend to opt for these "trickle-down" solutions. First, because they tend to come from the business class, government officials believe in the conservative ideology that says what is good for business is good for America. The second reason for the pro-business choice is that government officials are more likely to hear the arguments from the powerful. Since the weak, by definition, are not organized, their voice is not heard or, if heard, not taken seriously, in decision-making circles.

President Reagan instituted a number of trickle-down programs to stimulate business profits, which, in turn, were assumed to promote business investment and create more jobs. The tax policies initiated by the Reagan administration and passed by Congress provide an excellent example of how the business community and the affluent were to be helped: the rate of equipment depreciation was in-creased, tax credits for new investment were expanded, the windfalls profits tax on newly discovered oil was reduced, and corporate tax rates were reduced. The degree to which individuals were helped by the new tax laws depended on how affluent they were. Investors were aided by a cut in the rates for capital gains taxes and increased amounts of dividends excluded from taxes; heirs benefitted as estates up to $600,000 in value were scheduled to escape all federal estate taxes; gift taxes, which were attached to gifts over $3000, were now limited to gifts in excess of $10,000; Americans employed abroad were exempted from federal in-come taxes on the first $75,000 in foreign earnings; and executives who exercise stock options to buy their companies' share at below-market prices were provided favorable tax rules. Budget and tax changes from 1981 to 1984 resulted in annual *losses* of $390 for households with annual income of less than $10,000 and an average *gain* of $8,270 for households with incomes of more than $80,000.

Although the government most often opts for trickle-down solutions, such plans are not very effective in fulfilling the promise to trickle down the benefits to the poor. The higher corporate profits generated by tax credits and other tax incen-tives do *not* necessarily mean that the companies will increase wages or hire more workers. What is more likely is that the corporations will increase dividends to the stockholders, which exacerbates further the existing problem of maldistribution of resources. Job creation is also not guaranteed since the companies may use their

PANEL 10-2

The New Class War

Two social scientists, Frances Fox Piven and Richard Cloward, have argued in their book, *The New Class War,* that the Reagan Administration has initiated an assault on the unemployed, the unemployable, and the working poor *for the benefit of the business community.* The strategy is twofold: (1) to increase the profits of business through trickle-down policies and reduced government regulation of business, and (2) to cut or eliminate programs that provide low income people with cash, food, health care, and low-cost housing.

This business-oriented plan reverses a pattern of government welfare programs to the needy begun during the Great Depression. But why would the business community support such a plan? The reason, argue Piven and Cloward, is economic: reducing welfare increases the profits of business. When unemployment is high and welfare opportunities low, economic insecurity drives wages down.

Large numbers of unemployed people exert a downward pressure on wages because people searching for work are forced to underbid the wages of those currently working. A mass of unemployed also inhibits workers from making other work place demands; workers are less militant when there is a long line of job applicants outside the factory gates. Because the unemployed exert a downward pressure on wages and other labor costs, the existence of a large pool of unemployed tends to maintain and enlarge profits. (Piven and Cloward, 1982, pp. 19–20)

The twin fears of unemployment and low welfare makes the labor force insecure.

When people fear for their subsistence, they accept onerous and dangerous working conditions. They work harder, and they work longer. They more readily accept discipline, follow orders, and submit to humiliation. An insecure labor force is thus a more productive labor force and a cheaper one. (Piven and Cloward, 1982, p. 28)

Source: Frances Fox Piven and Richard A. Cloward, The New Class War: Reagan's Attack on the Welfare State and Its Consequences, *New York: Pantheon, 1982.*

newly acquired wealth to purchase labor-saving devices. If so, then the government programs will have actually widened the gulf between the "haves" and the "have nots."

The Powerless Bear the Burden

Robert Hutchens, in his critique of American government policy, characterized the basic principle guiding internal affairs: "Domestic policy is conducted according to one infallible rule: the costs and burdens of whatever is done must be borne by those least able to bear them" (1976, p. 4). Let's review several examples of this.

When threatened by war, the draft system is instituted by government. A careful analysis of the draft reveals that it is in reality a "tax on the poor" (Ognibene, 1979, p. 12). During the Vietnam War, for instance, the chances of getting killed while in the service were about three times greater for the less educated than for the college educated (Zeitlin, Lutterman, and Russell, 1977). Even more blatant was the practice that occurred legally during the Civil War. The law at that time allowed the affluent who were drafted to hire someone to take their place in the service.

The poor, being powerless, can be made to absorb the costs of societal changes. In the 19th century, the poor did the back-breaking work that built the railroads and the cities. Today they are the ones pushed out of their homes by urban renewal, the building of expressways, parks, and stadiums (Gans, 1971).

The government's attempts to solve economic problems generally obey this principle that the poor must bear the burden. A common "solution" for runaway inflation, for example, is to increase the amount of unemployment. Of course, the poor are disproportionately laid off work, especially the minorities (whose rate of unemployment consistently is twice the rate for whites), since they are the ones to make the sacrifice for the economy. This "solution," aside from being socially cruel, is economically ineffective because it ignores the real sources of inflation—excessive military spending, excessive profits by energy companies (foreign and domestic), and administered prices set by shared monopolies, which, contrary to classical economic theory, do not decline during economic downturns (Harrington, 1979).

More fundamentally, a certain level of unemployment is maintained continuously, not just during economic downturns. Genuine full employment for all job seekers is a myth. But why, since all political candidates extol the work ethic, and it is declared national policy to have full employment? Economist Robert Lekachman (1979) has argued that it is no accident that we tolerate millions of unemployed persons. The reason is that a "moderate" unemployment rate is beneficial to the affluent. Among these benefits are (1) there are people willing to work at humble tasks for low wages; (2) the unemployed swell the armed forces allowing the children of the middle upper classes to avoid the draft; (3) the unions are less demanding; (4) workers are less likely to demand costly safety equipment; (5) corporations do not have to pay their share of taxes because local and state governments give them concessions to lure them to or keep them in their area; and

(6) it retains the existing wide differentials between white males and the various powerless categories such as females, teenagers, Hispanics, and blacks.

When in the early 1980s the United States was faced with the important and related economic problems of inflation, high interest rates, and a huge national debt, there was a general consensus among the experts that these problems could be alleviated through fiscal restraint by the government. President Reagan and the conservative Congress decided to curtail government spending sharply on those programs aimed at providing benefits to the poor while simultaneously expanding military spending dramatically (a commitment of $1.5 trillion over five years) and, as we have seen, providing increased tax breaks to the business community and affluent individuals. This is a clear case of the poor being asked to be the inflation fighters while the powerful benefit. Let's look at some of the social programs cut or eliminated by the probusiness/antipoor policies called "Reaganomics."

- Reduced Medicaid payments by $1 billion over three years.
- Medicare patients must pay a larger share of their doctor and hospital costs.
- An estimated 400,000 families once on welfare became ineligible under the new rules, and 285,000 families had their benefits reduced.
- The Food Stamp program, which helps to feed some 22 million low-income persons, was cut by $6 billion over a three-year period as payments were reduced, and 1 million people once eligible were no longer so.
- Congress slashed $1.5 billion from school lunch subsidies.
- The program of public service jobs and training (CETA) was abolished with 300,000 persons losing their jobs.
- The Legal Services Corporation, a program providing legal services to the poor, was abolished.
- Housing subsidy funds were cut by $500 million.

Government Lawlessness

This section considers five forms of government lawlessness. We will consider three domestic crimes: (1) secrecy, lying, and deception; (2) the abuse of power by government agencies, especially the FBI and the CIA; and (3) the use of citizens as unwilling and unknowing guinea pigs. At the international level, we will consider (4) American intervention in the domestic affairs of other nations; and (5) war crimes.

Secrecy, Lying, and Deception

The hallmark of any democracy is consent of the governed based on a reliable flow of information from the government. There are a number of mechanisms by which this principle is thwarted in American society. A common technique to withhold information is the use of "executive privilege" by the president to keep things secret from Congress and the courts. The doctrine of executive privilege is the constitutionally questionable belief that the president and his staff cannot be forced to testify and that presidential documents cannot be examined without the president's permission. The argument given for such immunity is that such information might compromise national security. Some examples of how this doctrine has been used are (Dorsen and Shattuck, 1974)

Item   President Truman refused to turn over to the House UnAmerican Activities Committee an FBI report on a government scientist.

Item   General Maxwell Taylor declined to appear before the House Subcommittee on Defense Appropriations in 1963 to discuss the Bay of Pigs invasion.

Item   In 1972, the Securities Exchange Commission refused to give certain information to the House Interstate and Foreign Commerce Subcommittee concerning its investigation of ITT.

Item   In 1973, President Nixon refused to surrender the White House tape recordings to Special Prosecutor Archibald Cox.

Another method used to "stonewall" is to designate information as "classified." The classification of documents is based on the necessity of safeguarding sensitive military and foreign-policy information in the national interest. One problem with classifying documents as "secret" is defining the category: even while some material is warranted as classified, too much ends up as secret. Describing the magnitude of this problem, the Chairman of the House Foreign Operations and Government Information Subcommittee said in 1972:

> There are 55,000 arms pumping up and down in Government offices stamping "confidential" on stacks of Government documents; more than 18,000 Government employees are wielding "secret" stamps, and a censorship elite of nearly 3,000 bureaucrats have authority to stamp "top secret" on public records.
>
> These are not wild estimates. These numbers were provided by the Government agencies, themselves. But even this huge number of Government censors is just the top of the secrecy iceberg. (Phillips, 1974, p. 71)

The classification of sensitive materials can also be used as a ploy to hide materials embarrassing to government officials. An apt example is the attempt by the White House to suppress publication of the Pentagon Papers, which revealed how American involvement in Vietnam had been shaped during several administrations while being shielded from the public. In early 1965, before President Johnson had sent combat troops to Vietnam, the goals of the United States, as stated in a secret memorandum from the Assistant Secretary of Defense Daniel McNaughton to Secretary Robert McNamara were:

> 70 percent to avoid a humiliating U.S. defeat (to our reputation as a guarantor),
> 20 percent to keep South Vietnam (and the adjacent territory) from Chinese hands,
> 10 percent to permit the people of South Vietnam a better, freer way of life.
> (cited in McCloskey, 1972, p. 54)

Had the people and Congress been aware of these goals:

> Would Congress have authorized a major war and more than 50,000 U.S. combat deaths for these goals? Would the American people have supported a war for these goals? And if not, was an American President justified in going to war for them anyway? More importantly, was an American President justified in concealing these goals and our own acts of provocation while he was, in fact, making a unilateral decision to go to war? (McCloskey, 1972, p. 54)

Precisely because the people would not have supported the war if they had known about the government's goals, President Nixon, who broadened the war from Johnson's policies, attempted to suppress publication of the Pentagon Papers, which would have revealed our true intentions and behaviors. In addition, the weight of the government's force was brought to the prosecution of those who had leaked the Pentagon Papers (Daniel Ellsberg and Anthony Russo). The government even went so far as to offer the judge in that case the directorship of the FBI, while the case was being heard (Parenti, 1980, p. 157).

Although all of the above tactics work to deceive the public, none is more onerous than outright lying by government officials. Examples of this strategy from recent American history are (Wise, 1973):

Item   In 1954, Secretary of State John Foster Dulles said that Americans were not involved in the coup in Guatemala to depose the regime of leftist President Guzman, even though the operation was financed, organized, and run by the CIA.

Item   In 1960, a spy plane, flown by a CIA pilot, was shot down over Russia. Although the United States had been using U-2 planes to spy on Russia for the preceding four years, our officials denied the incident, saying we had not violated Russian air space.

Item   In 1961, the CIA, under President Kennedy, organized an invasion of Cuba at the Bay of Pigs. Yet when the Cubans charged in the United Nations that the United States was behind the operation, Ambassador Adlai Stevenson responded that no U.S. personnel or government planes were involved.

Item   In 1963, the United States supported, but officially denied its involvement in, the coup against South Vietnam President Ngo Dinh Diem.

Item   In 1964, President Johnson used an incident where American ships were allegedly shot at in the Tonkin Gulf to give him a free hand to escalate the war in Vietnam. Congress was deliberately misled by the official representation of the facts.

Item   President Johnson praised our Asian allies for sending "volunteers" to fight in Vietnam when actually our government had paid Thailand and the Philippines $200 million each for making this gesture.

Item   President Nixon and his advisors told the American public that the neutrality of Cambodia had not been violated, when we had already conducted 3600 bombing missions in a five-year period in that country. To carry out this deception, the death certificates of Americans who died in Cambodia were falsified by our government to read that they had died elsewhere.

CASE STUDY: WATERGATE

The Watergate-related crimes, committed by officials of the government, represent acts of official secrecy and deception taken to the extreme. They demonstrate forcefully and fearfully just how far away from the Democratic ideal the American political system had moved at the time and how close it was to approaching totalitarianism. In the words of David Wise:

Watergate revealed that under President Nixon a kind of totalitarianism had already come to America, creeping in, not like Carl Sandburg's fog, on little cat feet, but in button-down shirts, worn by handsome young advertising and public relations men carrying neat attaché cases crammed with $100 bills. Men were

The irony of Watergate is that the government prosecuted all of the known perpetrators *except* the one ultimately responsible.

willing to perjure themselves to stay on the team, to serve their leader. It came in the guise of "national security," a blanket term used to justify the most appalling criminal acts by men determined to preserve their own political power at any cost. It came in the form of the ladder against the bedroom window, miniature transmitters in the ceiling, wiretaps, burglaries, enemies lists, tax audits, and psychiatric profiles.

It is not easy to write the word totalitarian when reporting about America, but if the word jars, or seems overstated, consider the dictionary definition: "Of or pertaining to a centralized government in which those in control grant neither recognition nor tolerance to parties of differing opinion."

And that is very close to what happened, for, as we learned from the Watergate investigation, the enormous power of the government of the United States, including the police power and secret intelligence apparatus, had been turned loose against the people of the United States, at least against those who held differing opinions, against the opposition political party, and the press. (Wise, 1973, pp. x–xi)

The Watergate investigation revealed a number of criminal and undemocratic actions by President Nixon and his closest advisors. These activities demonstrate how far the United States had moved in the direction of a totalitarian government. A partial list of these acts includes:

Item   Burglars, financed by funds from the Committee to Reelect the President, broke into and bugged the headquarters of the Democratic party (in the Watergate apartment complex).

Item   These burglars were paid hush money and promised executive clemency to protect the president and his advisors.

Item   Burglars also broke into the office of the psychiatrist of Daniel Ellsberg; Ellsberg was the person who leaked the Pentagon Papers to the press. These papers, of course, were instrumental in showing the public how they had been systematically deceived by a series of presidents during the long Vietnam war.

Item   The White House offered the judge in the Ellsberg case, while the trial was in session, the possibility of his being named director of the FBI.

Item   President Nixon's personal attorney solicited money for an illegally formed campaign committee and offered an ambassadorship in return for a campaign contribution.

Item   Money gathered from contributions, some illegally, was systematically laundered (to conceal the donors). Much of this money was kept in cash so when payoffs occurred, the money could not be traced.

Item   President Nixon ordered secret wiretapping of his own aides, several journalists, and even his brother. Additionally, he had secret microphones planted in his offices to record clandestinely every conversation.

Item   The director of the FBI destroyed vital legal evidence at the suggestion of the president's aides.

Item The attorney general of the United States, John Mitchell, participated in the preliminary discussions about bugging the Democratic headquarters. He even suggested that one means of gaining information about the Democrats was to establish a floating bordello at the Miami convention of the Democrats.

Item The president's men participated in a campaign of "dirty tricks" to discredit the various potential Democratic nominees for president. These "tricks" included the publication and distribution of letters, purporting to come from Senator Muskie, claiming that Senator Jackson was a homosexual.

Item The White House requested tax audits of administration opponents.

Item The White House used the CIA in an effort to halt the FBI investigation of Watergate.

Item President Nixon offered aides Robert Halderman and John Erlichman as much as $300,000 from a secret "slush fund" for their legal fees after they were forced to resign.

Item The president and his advisor, using the cloak of "national security," strongly resisted attempts by the special prosecutor, the courts, and Congress to get the facts in the case.

Item Various administration officials were found guilty of perjury and withholding information.

Item When the president, under duress, did provide transcripts of the tapes or other materials, they were edited.

Item The president, on television and in press releases, lied to the American public over and over again.

This infamous list of indiscretions comprises a tangled web of activities that posed a significant threat to the United States' democratic political system. All of the efforts were directed at subverting the political process so that the administration in power would stay in power, regardless of the means. There was a systematic effort to discredit enemies of the administration, to weaken the two-party system, and to control the flow of information to citizens.

Although the Nixon administration was guilty of these heinous acts, we should not assume that President Nixon was the first American president to be involved in such chicanery. Watergate was no sudden aberration but rather was the end result of practices of government that have been with us in significant ways throughout our history.

Abuse of Power by Government Agencies

Watergate revealed to Americans that their highest leaders had conspired, among other things, to win an election by using such illegal means as dirty tricks, burglary of opponents, and soliciting of campaign funds by threats and bribes. These White House transgressions are only one expression of illicit government intervention. In this section we will focus on the deviant actions of government agencies in several key areas.

Many government abuses have occurred under the guise of internal security. Domestic surveillance is one example. Government agencies have a long history of surveillance of its citizens. The pace quickened in the 1930s and increased further with the perceived communist threat in the 1950s. Surveillance reached its peak during the height of the antiwar and civil-rights protests of the late 1960s and early 1970s. The FBI's concern with internal security, for example, dates back to 1936 when President Roosevelt asked Director J. Edgar Hoover to investigate domestic communist and fascist organizations in the United States (Harris, 1977, pp. 30–42). In 1939, as World War II began in Europe, President Roosevelt issued a proclamation that the FBI would be in charge of investigating subversive activities, espionage, sabotage, and that all law-enforcement offices should give the FBI any relevant information on suspected activities. These directives began a pattern followed by the FBI under the administrations of Presidents Truman, Eisenhower, Kennedy, Johnson, Nixon, Ford, Carter, and Reagan.

The scope of these abuses by the FBI and other government agencies, such as the CIA, the National Security Agency, and the Internal Revenue Service, is incredible. In the name of ''national security'' the following have occurred against American citizens:

Item From 1967 to 1973 the NSA (National Security Agency) monitored the overseas telephone calls and cables of approximately 1650 U.S. citizens and organizations, as well as almost 6000 foreign nationals and groups.

Item The CIA opened and photographed nearly 250,000 first-class letters in the United States between 1953 and 1973.

Item As director of the CIA, William Colby acknowledged to Congress that his organization had opened the mail of private citizens and accumulated secret files on more than 10,000 Americans.

Item The FBI, over the years, conducted about 1500 break-ins of foreign embassies and missions, mob hangouts, and the headquarters of such organizations as the Ku Klux Klan and the American Communist Party.

Item The FBI confessed to the Senate Intelligence Committee that it had committed 238 burglaries against 14 domestic organizations during a 26-year period ending in 1968.

Item The FBI collected over 500,000 dossiers between 1959 and 1971 on communists, black leaders, student radicals, and feminists.

Item The husband of an officer in ACTION, a St. Louis civil rights organization, received a handwritten note that said: ''Look man, I guess your old lady doesn't get enough at home or she wouldn't be shucking and jiving with our black men in ACTION, you dig? Like, all she wants to integrate is the bedroom and we black sisters ain't gonna take no second best from our men. So lay it on her man or get her the hell off Newstead [Street].'' The couple soon separated and the local

FBI officer wrote to headquarters: "This matrimonial stress and strain should cause her to function much less effectively in ACTION."

Item   In 1972 the FBI paid 7402 "ghetto informants" to provide information about racial extremists.

Item   In 1970, actress Jean Seberg helped raise money for a militant organization, the Black Panthers. According to documents released by the FBI after the suicide of Ms. Seberg in 1979, the FBI tried to discredit the actress by planting the rumor that the father of her baby was a prominent Black Panther leader. This false story led to a miscarriage and psychotic behavior, and possibly her suicide (see Panel 10-3).

Item   "The FBI had turned its arsenal of surveillance and disruption techniques on Martin Luther King and the civil rights movement. It was concerned not with Soviet agents nor with criminal activity, but with the political and personal activities of a man and a movement committed to nonviolence and democracy. King was not the first such target nor the last. In the end we are all victims, as our political life is distorted and constricted by the FBI, a law enforcement agency now policing politics (from Halperin, Berman, Borosage, and Marwick, 1976, p. 89).

Another example of an FBI vendetta against a nonexistent threat involved the Socialist Workers Party (SWP), a small, peaceful, and legal political party. This party became the target of FBI abuses because it supported Castro's Cuba and worked for racial integration in the South. For these transgressions, the FBI kept the SWP under surveillance for 34 years. FBI documents have revealed that in one 6½-year period in the early 1960s the agency burglarized the offices of the party in 94 raids, often with the complicity of the New York City police department. Over this period, FBI agents photographed 8700 pages of party files and compiled dossiers totaling 8 million pages.

The FBI tried to destroy the party by sending anonymous letters to members' employers, working to keep the party's candidates off the ballot, and by otherwise sabotaging political campaigns. Informants were also used to collect information about the political views of the organization.

Several points need to be made about these activities of the FBI to neutralize or destroy the SWP. Obviously, they were a thorough waste of time and money. As one observer put it: "If they had devoted tens of thousands of man-hours to pursuing true criminals—say, those involved in organized crime—they might have served the public interest as they were meant to" (Harris, 1977, p. 40). Most important, the FBI's tactics were not illegal but were directed at an organization that was working legally *within* the system.

Just as the FBI's illegal assumption of the authority to investigate subversive activities led to illegal methods, the failure of those methods to produce evidence that could be used to take legal action against radical and liberal political movements led to further lawlessness: active efforts to destroy them. In Octo-

PANEL 10-3

A Challenge to American Justice

Amnesty International, the London-based human-rights organization, has recommended that the U.S. government undertake an inquiry into the FBI's counter-intelligence operations in the early 1970s. Amnesty is right on target; there has never been, in this nation's history, a program as infamous as the FBI's COINTELPRO, which was deliberately designed to use false information to discredit, jail, and "neutralize" individuals in political movements regarded as evil by FBI Director J. Edgar Hoover in his declining years.

In the case of the Black Panthers, for example, FBI tactics included

- Using false letters and other material to foster a violent split among Panther leaders.
- Targeting celebrity supporters of the Panthers, such as actress Jean Seberg, whose eventual suicide has been blamed on FBI rumor that she had become pregnant by a black man.
- Unlawfully using informants to eavesdrop on discussions between defendants and their attorneys.
- Seeking to estrange defendants from potential witnesses on their behalf.

The FBI has never been willing to divulge to the public, to former "targets" of COINTELPRO, or even to Congress, the complete facts of COINTELPRO activity.

The agency's reluctance is understandable. To the extent that any of its agents may have conspired to deny any individual his constitutional right of fair trial, those agents were guilty of a federal crime.

Honorable FBI agents today are ashamed of COINTELPRO. Well they might be. As a special Senate committee headed by then Senator Frank Church pointed out in 1976, "in COINTELPRO, the bureau secretly took the law into its own hands . . . COINTELPRO involved specific violations of law" and the program evolved into "attempts to interfere with the judicial process."

In its 140-page report released last week, Amnesty International cited the case of a Los Angeles Black Panther leader, Elmer (Geronimo) Pratt, as one in which COINTELPRO may very well have violated the Helsinki human rights treaty by failing to protect Pratt's right to a fair trial. Amnesty has asked for an independent federal investigation because California state courts have been unwilling to demand full disclosure by the FBI of its involvement in the Pratt case.

A target of COINTELPRO from at least 1969 to 1972, Pratt was arrested, tried, convicted, and sentenced to life imprisonment without ever knowing that the FBI was secretly manipulating the whole process.

While the FBI to this day refuses to disclose fully what its agents actually said and did during the years in which Pratt was a target, a number of facts about what the agency *tried* to do have been painfully extracted from FBI records through Freedom of Information Act procedures and congressional inquiry.

The known facts are these.

Elmer (Geronimo) Pratt enlisted in the Army in 1965 at the age of 17. He took airborne training and served two tours of

Panel 10-3 (Continued)

duty in Vietnam, earning several commendations, including the Purple Heart. He was honorably discharged as a sergeant in May, 1968, and moved to Los Angeles. While enrolled in UCLA's high-performance program, he became involved in the Black Panther movement.

On the evening of Dec. 18, 1968, two black men robbed and shot a couple preparing to play tennis on a public court in Santa Monica. The woman died.

Two years later, Pratt was arrested and charged with the crime, primarily on the testimony of Julius Butler, a Black Panther who had secretly become an FBI informant. Pratt's defense was based on his claim that on the evening of Dec. 18, 1968, he was attending a meeting of Black Panther leaders in Oakland, 400 miles away.

What was not known at the trial, what has been learned only from the Church inquiry and extracted grudgingly from the FBI over the years, is the following:

On Nov. 26, 1968, a few days before the "tennis court murder," FBI Director Hoover ordered his Los Angeles and San Francisco field offices, among others, to submit "imaginative and hard-hitting counterintelligence measures aimed at crippling the Black Panther Party." A later Hoover directive made it clear that false information was to be used; it was "immaterial whether facts exist to substantiate the charge."

An FBI wiretap on Dec. 20, 1968, indicated that an unidentified Panther leader had been met at Oakland Airport early in the evening of Dec. 18, and that Pratt was in Oakland on the day of the wiretap.

On Aug. 14, 1969, FBI agents contacted Butler, who, while out on bail, admitted possession of a machine gun, for which he could have been sentenced to a long jail term. Butler expressed fear of Pratt and said he had written a letter, then in a friend's possession, which could send some Panther leaders "to the gas chamber."

The FBI continued to meet with Butler, and on Nov. 4, 1969, he agreed "to provide information to the FBI on a confidential basis." FBI records show that Butler met with FBI agents on at least 19 separate occasions between July 31, 1970, and April 28, 1972, and on each occasion the FBI agent noted Butler's status as a "probationary racial informant." The last meeting with Butler was just prior to Pratt's trial.

In December, 1969, a month after Butler agreed to become an informant, the Los Angeles FBI office issued a memo stating that the FBI was "furnishing on a daily basis information to . . . the Los Angeles Police Department . . . concerning the activities of the black national group and the anticipation that such information might lead to the arrest of these militants."

On Jan. 28, 1970, the FBI Los Angeles office asked Washington for approval of the "creation of an anonymous 'paper' underground to attack, expose, and ridicule the image of the BPP (Black Panther Party) and to foment mistrust and suspicion amongst the current and past membership. . . . Operation No. 1 is designed to challenge the legitimacy of the authority exercised by . . ." Pratt, the party's defense minister.

In June, 1970, an FBI Los Angeles memo said: "Constant consideration is given to the possibility of the utilization of counterintelligence measures with efforts being directed toward neutralizing Pratt as an effective BPP functionary."

The "friend" holding Butler's letter for

Panel 10-3 (Continued)

safekeeping was a Los Angeles police officer, Swayne Rice. He has stated that two FBI agents demanded that he surrender the letter or face prosecution for obstruction of justice. In the letter, Butler alleged that Pratt had "confessed" the tennis-court murder to him.

The male victim identified Pratt as his assailant after viewing a police lineup in which Pratt was the only person wearing the type of clothing that had been worn by the tennis-court killer. Neither the defense nor the jury was told that the victim had identified another man in an earlier lineup as the killer. Years later, a deputy public defender testified to being present when the earlier identification was made, but the "witness slip" was never produced by the LAPD, and could not be used in cross-examination by Pratt's lawyer.

Even after Pratt's arrest, COINTEL-PRO continued operations against him. It fabricated a letter to Kathleen Cleaver, then in North Africa, designed to intimidate her from returning to the United States and possibly testifying in support of Pratt's alibi.

The FBI also used information to infiltrate Pratt's defense team and report on conversations between Pratt and his lawyers.

In January, 1971, the Panthers expelled Pratt, and the party's newspaper printed a denunciation that was remarkably similar in wording to an "anonymous" statement proposed earlier by the FBI.

On March 29, 1971, the FBI discovered information pertaining to the identity of a second suspect in the tennis-court killing, and claims it passed this information on to the LAPD. This information was not passed on to the defense, as the law requires.

Pratt went to trial in June, 1972, and at no time were he, his attorney, the court, jury or prosecutor ever advised of the facts noted above. Clearly, COINTEL-PRO could have engineered all the pretrial events within the purview of its secret instructions to "neutralize" the Panther leader.

But this speculation pales into insignificance when compared with the FBI's silence at the trial itself, when Julius Butler, called as the prosecution's chief witness, testified under oath that he had never worked for the FBI. If not perjury—there is no evidence that he was on the FBI payroll—this was at least misleading the court. The FBI, as part of the Department of Justice and an officer of the court, would ordinarily have felt an obligation to

ber, 1961, for example, the FBI put into operation its "S.W.P. Disruption Program." The grounds for this program, as a confidential Bureau memorandum described them, were that the Socialist Workers Party had been "openly espousing its line on a local and national basis through running candidates for public office. . . ." The memorandum is astonishingly revealing about the political sophistication of the FBI. If these Socialists were openly espousing their line by running candidates for public office, including the Presidency, these activities obviously weren't illegal. And if their support for the civil-rights

Panel 10-3 (Continued)

prevent the court from being misled in this manner. Yet the FBI, which monitored the trial, remained silent, neither advising the court of Butler's relationship with the agency, nor mentioning the existence of the wiretap evidence, the second suspect, or any part of its COINTELPRO activities.

Pratt's lawyer, Johnnie L. Cochran Jr., later to become a respected deputy district attorney for Los Angeles County, believes that his former client is innocent and should have a new trial.

Obviously, Cochran would have conducted the defense far differently had he known the facts concealed by the FBI. The prosecutor rested his whole case on Butler's allegation that Pratt had confessed the crime to him. Had the jury known that Butler was an informant, had it known of the FBI's program to use false information, would it have convicted Pratt? Would Pratt have spent the last nine years in jail?

Should any American be tried for murder by one law-enforcement authority without knowing that another was working secretly to accomplish his "neutralization" through the use of false information?

When a federal agency willfully withholds key evidence from a state court, shouldn't the federal government be under an obligation to review the matter thoroughly?

Amnesty International so recommends.

Amnesty International earned the 1977 Nobel Peace Prize because of its impartiality and fairness in unmasking injustice in dozens of countries, communist, fascist and ostensibly democratic. Their recommendation that the United States owes an obligation to investigate its own conduct as a possible violation of international law deserves our serious consideration.

We owe Amnesty International a great deal for prodding our consciences on a possible injustice of incredible proportions. The Pratt case should be investigated by one, of not all three branches of the federal government. Only when the FBI is forced to make a full disclosure will we finally clear the air on a sordid chapter in American history.

Source: Paul N. McCloskey, Jr., "A Challenge to American Justice," Los Angeles Times, *October 20, 1981, Part II, p. 5.*

movement was subversive, then so was that of many millions of Americans. (Harris, 1977, p. 40)

Although these incidents are extremely important, the exclusive focus on these highly publicized crimes by government agencies diverts attention from the pervasive and systematic nature of political surveillance and intimidation in the United States (Thomas, 1981). Prominent individuals and groups with divergent political goals are targets for surveillance but so, too, are millions of Americans. In 1977, for example, the Internal Revenue Service had files on 11,000 individuals and groups chosen for their political activities; the CIA had an index of over 300,000 names of those opposed to the Vietnam War; the CIA had a computerized index of 1.5 million names of potentially "problem" individuals; and the FBI had a list of 500,000 persons in its domestic intelligence file (Borosage, 1977). At another level, the amount of information available to the government on the financial, medical, political, and personal life of most Americans is staggering—an average of 15 files for each American. For example, the main government data banks in 1980 were the Department of Health, Education, and Welfare, which had 1.03 billion personal records on recipients of various government programs; the Treasury Department, which had 780 million records on taxpayers; the Justice Department, which had 201 million records on criminals and criminal suspects; the Defense Department, which had 334 million records on service personnel; and the Department of Transportation, which had 24 million records including all motorists whose licenses had been suspended or revoked by any state (Gest, 1982, p. 35; see also Bacon and Kelly, 1978, p. 45).

Also, it is important to recognize that these acts of government that violated the rights of individuals were not just an aberration of the Nixon years. These have been ongoing activities by the government, especially since the 1920s. Considering just illegal activity—the FBI's use of telephone wiretaps and microphone buggings without authorization by a court warrant—the use was highest in the Roosevelt and Truman administrations, and the Kennedy/Johnson years were actually higher than either the Eisenhower or Nixon years in the White House (*U.S. News & World Report,* 1976).

The Use of Citizens as Unwilling and Unknowing Guinea Pigs

Nazi Germany is often cited as a horrible example of a government's disregard for human life. Among the crimes of the Nazis was medical experimentation on human subjects. The United States also has a history of using unwilling and unknowing subjects in potentially dangerous medical experiments. One case that clearly rivals Nazi Germany for its contempt for the human subjects was conducted by the U.S. Public Health Service. Beginning in 1932, doctors under the auspices of the Public Health Service began observing 400 black men in Macon County, Alabama, who had syphilis. The subjects did not know they had syphilis but were told rather that they had "bad blood." The purpose of the study was to assess the consequences of *not* treating the disease. As a result, during the 40 years of the experiment the men were not treated; their pain was not alleviated; when their wives contracted the disease, the project did nothing; and when their children were born with congenital syphilis, they also were untreated (Jones, 1981).

Between 250,000 and 300,000 American soldiers and civilians were exposed to radiation during the 192 nuclear bomb tests from 1946 to 1963. Among the tests conducted by the Army was one to assess the psychological effects on soldiers who observed an atomic blast four times the size of the bomb dropped on Hiroshima from a distance of two miles. The Army wanted to determine whether soldiers could perform battlefield assignments after being exposed to such an explosion. The men so exposed suffered severe long-term negative effects from this experiment yet the government has been unwilling to accept the blame for the higher-than-usual incidence of leukemia and cancer among them. They have tried to suppress scientific research findings linking low-level radiation exposure to medical problems. There has also been an unusual disappearance of many medical records of the men exposed (Rosenberg, 1976; Melanson, 1983).

A recent declassification of government documents revealed that the American people had been subjects in 239 open-air bacteriological tests conducted by the Army between 1949 and 1969. On one of these tests, San Francisco was blanketed with poisonous bacteria known as serratia, which causes a type of pneumonia that can be fatal. One hospital treated 12 persons for serratia pneumonia and one victim died. The objectives of this and other tests were to investigate the offensive possibilities of biological warfare, to understand the magnitude of defensing against biological warfare, and to gain data on the behavior of biological agents as they are borne downwind (Cousins, 1979).

Another example of the exposure of Americans to potentially dangerous chemicals without their knowledge or consent was the behavioral-control experiments conducted by the government (Bowart, 1978). For 35 years various agencies of the government have used tens of thousands of individuals to test several techniques of mind control: hypnosis, electronic brain stimulation, aversive and other behavior-modification therapies, and drugs. Many of the subjects in these experiments were volunteers but many were not. Our interest is in the use of subjects without their consent. We will focus our attention on the government agency that is well known for disregarding the rights of citizens in its quest for national security—the CIA.

Item   Documents revealed under the Freedom of Information Act show that during the height of the cold war, the CIA developed knockout substances and incapacitating agents. The pool of subjects used to develop these compounds consisted of terminal cancer patients who had no idea they were being used as guinea pigs (M. Lee, 1982).

Item   In 1953, a CIA scientist slipped LSD into the after-dinner drinks of scientists from the Army Chemical Corps. The drug had an especially adverse effect on one of these persons; he experienced psychotic confusion and two days later leapt to his death from a hotel window. The CIA kept the facts from the victim's family for 22 years (Bowart, 1978, pp. 87–91).

Item   The CIA hired prostitutes in San Francisco to give their customers drugs. The behavior of the victims was then observed through two-way mirrors and heard through hidden microphones (Marks, 1979).

Item   The CIA administered LSD to the borderline underworld—"prostitutes, drug addicts, and other small timers who would be powerless to seek any sort of revenge if they ever found out what the CIA had done to them" (Marks, 1979, p. 14). Agents working on the project would randomly choose a victim at a bar or off the street and, with no prior consent or medical prescreening, would take the individual back to a safe house and administer the drug. For many of the unsuspecting victims, the result was days or even weeks of hospitalization and mental stress (Halperin et al., 1976, p. 52).

These examples demonstrate the arrogance of an agency of government that is willing to victimize some of its citizens to gain an edge in its battle against the country's enemies. Some would argue that this behavior, so contrary to life in a free society, makes them the enemy. The present policy, at least overtly, is not to use human subjects. The risk is always present, however, that this may occur again. It is important to note in this regard that President Reagan's 1983 budget for chemical and biological warfare was just over half a billion dollars—up from $157 million in 1980.

Crimes by the government are not limited to those directed at its citizens. War is an obvious example of the willful attempt by a government to harm citizens of another country. Other acts by government short of war are also harmful to others, acts such as trade embargoes, arms sales, colonial arrangements, and the like. In this section we will discuss two other types of crimes perpetrated by the American government against others: intervention in their domestic affairs and war crimes.

American Intervention in the Domestic Affairs of Other Nations

What would be the response of our political leaders and citizens if foreigners assassinated the president? Foreign agents tried to influence the outcome of an election? If foreign power supported one side in a domestic dispute with money and weapons? Obviously we would not tolerate these attempts by outsiders to affect our domestic affairs. Such acts would be interpreted as imperialistic acts of war. The irony, of course, is that we have and continue to perpetrate such acts on other countries as part of our foreign policy.

The number of clandestine acts of intervention by the U.S. government is legion. Evidence from Senate investigating committees has shown, for example, that over a 20-year period, one government agency—the CIA—was involved in over 900 foreign interventions, including paramilitary operations, surreptitious manipulation of foreign governments, and assassinations (Roebuck and Weeber, 1978, p. 82). We will limit our discussion here to several of the more well-known cases of CIA involvement in the domestic affairs of other nations.

1.   *Chile*.   The United States, primarily through the CIA, has been actively involved in orchestrating the internal politics of Chile for a number of years. The government's concern was to protect American business interests, primarily those of ITT. ITT feared the rise of revolutionary parties because they would likely expropriate foreign holdings. In 1966, an election was held and the United States gave the moderate candidate Eduardo Frei $20 million in direct campaign contributions. After Frei's victory, Chile expanded its telephone system, giving the contract to ITT even though a Swedish company had a lower bid.

In the 1970 elections, the CIA and ITT feared the election of the socialist candidate Salvador Allende because he had pledged to seize the company's $150 million Chilean property. The CIA spent some $13 million to block Allende's election, including $350,000 to bribe members of the Chilean Congress, who cast electoral votes, to vote against Allende.[2] Despite these efforts Allende was elected. After Allende's victory, the CIA plotted his overthrow. The strategy was to create economic chaos in the country, which would lead the Chilean army to stage a coup. Some of these efforts were (1) the CIA spent $8 million on economic sabotage; (2) U.S. banks boycotted Chile; (3) rumors were spread that Chile's copper supplies were far greater than they were in reality in a deliberate campaign to weaken the price of copper, Chile's major product; (4) U.S. companies refused to supply repair parts for machines; and (5) the United States played an important role in the creation of an extensive black market in goods and dollars. These efforts were successful. Allende was assassinated in 1973 amidst right-wing violence and a military takeover.

The ruling military regime that followed Allende completely changed domestic and foreign policy. Most important to ITT and the United States was the adoption of a program of unconditional support for U.S. policies and business interests in Chile.

2. *Iran*. The United States has had a long-term special interest in Iran because of that country's vast supplies of oil and its proximity to Russia. United States involvement in the internal affairs of Iran began in the early 1950s when Prime Minister Mohammed Mossadegh moved to nationalize U.S. oil companies. The CIA engineered a coup that ousted Mossadegh and restored the Shah to power. Over the next 25 years, despite the Shah's rule becoming increasingly tyrannical, the United States supported the Shah's government, especially with military aid. The Shah in turn was a trusted ally faithfully supporting U.S. interests in the Persian Gulf area, supplying oil, and remaining staunchly anti-communist.

3. *CIA murder plots*. In 1975, the Senate Select Committee on Intelligence reported on the activities of the CIA over a 13-year period. The publication of this report occurred over the objections of President Ford and CIA Director William Colby. The reason for their fears was obvious: the government was embarrassed for citizens to find out that the CIA was actively involved in assassination plots and coups against foreign governments (*U.S. News & World Report*, 1975; Powers, 1979).

Item   Between 1960 and 1965, the CIA initiated at least eight plots to assassinate Fidel Castro, Prime Minister of Cuba. The unsuccessful attempts included applying instantly lethal botulinium toxin to a box of Castro's cigars, hiring the Mafia to poison him, and presenting him a gift of a wet suit (for skin diving) treated with a fungus.

Item   The committee found strong evidence that CIA officials had planned the assassination of Congolese (Zaire) leader Patrice Lumumba and that President Eisenhower had ordered his death.

[2]The extent of ITT's involvement in the 1970 election has not been made public because the government has refused to prosecute for fear that such a trial would expose CIA secrets.

Item   The United States was implicated in the assassinations of Dominican dictator Rafael Trujillo, South Vietnam's President Ngo Dinh Diem, and General Rene Schneider of Chile.

The CIA's actions are contrary to American principles in fundamental ways. Aside from supporting regimes notorious for their violation of human rights, the United States, which achieved its independence claiming the people's right to self-determination, is now actively involved in manipulating foreign governments to achieve its will. The infusion of money in foreign elections, and the use of propaganda, assassination attempts, and the like are all contrary to the guiding principle of the Monroe Doctrine—the self-determination of peoples—which we invoke readily when nations intrude in the affairs of state of any Western Hemisphere nation.

War Crimes

There are three interpretations of war crimes. One is that crimes in war are illogical—war is hell and anything goes. The only crime, from this position, is to lose. A second view is that war crimes are acts for which the victors punish the losers. The winners denounce the atrocities committed by the enemy while justifying their own conduct. Thus, the Germans and Japanese were tried for war crimes at the conclusion of World War II, but the United States was not, even though it had used atomic bombs to destroy two cities and most of their inhabitants. (Even if one assumes that the bombing of Hiroshima was necessary to bring an early end to the war, a debatable assumption, the bombing of Nagasaki two days later was clearly an unnecessary waste of life.)

A third view of war crimes is one that applies a standard of morality to war that is applicable to winners and losers alike. As the chief U.S. prosecutor at Nuremberg, Robert Jackson, said:

If certain acts in violation of treaties are crimes, they are crimes whether the United States does them or whether Germany does them, and we are not prepared to lay down a rule of criminal conduct against others, which we would be unwilling to have invoked against us. (cited in Knoll and McFadden, 1970, p. 1)

We will apply this last approach to our understanding of war crimes. As we use the concept, nations throughout history have been guilty of war crimes, including the United States (in our case, some examples are the conquering of the Indians, and our 1900 counter-insurgency campaign in the Philippines). Since the government, the media, and the schools always point out the heinous acts of our enemies throughout history, we will focus on the war crimes perpetrated by the United States, limiting the discussion to the Vietnam experience. The principle we will apply is the definition of war crimes established by the Nuremberg tribunal (Principle VI, b):

Violations of the laws or customs of war which include, but are not limited to, murder, ill-treatment or deportation to slave-labor or for any other purpose of civilian population of or in occupied territory, murder or ill-treatment of prisoners of war or persons on the seas, killing of hostages, plunder of public or private property, wanton destruction of cities, towns, or villages, or devastation not justified by military necessity. (cited in Knoll and McFadden, 1970, p. 183)

The Vietnam War provides many examples of American actions in violation of this principle.

1. *Indiscriminate shelling and bombing of civilians.* The National Liberation Front was difficult to fight because they were everywhere. We often could not distinguish allies from enemies. Thus, in strategic terms, the entire geographical area of Vietnam was the enemy. As Roebuck and Weeber have observed: "In order to 'save' Vietnam from Communism, it was therefore necessary to destroy the entire country" (Roebuck and Weeber, 1978, p. 70). Thus, civilian villages were bombed in the enemy region of North Vietnam and in South Vietnam as well. The amount of firepower was unparalled in history, according to Gabriel Kolko:

From 315,000 tons of air ordnance dropped in Southeast Asia in 1965, the quantity by January-October, 1969, the peak year of the war, reached 1,388,000 tons. Over that period 4,580,000 tons were dropped on Southeast Asia, or six and one-half times that employed in Korea. To this we must add ground munitions, which rose from 577,000 tons in 1966 to 1,278,000 tons in the first 11 months of 1969. (cited in Knoll and McFadden, 1970, p. 57)

A most significant bomb used by the United States was napalm. This is a jellylike, inflammable mixture packed into canisters and dropped from aircraft. The mixture of benzene, gasoline, and polystyrene is a highly incendiary fluid that clings. It is an antipersonnel weapon that causes deep and persistent burning. George Wald, a nobel-winning scientist has described it:

Napalm is probably the most horrible anti-personnel weapon ever invented. The point of a weapon in war is to put an enemy out of action, and that is most readily and permanently accomplished by killing him; but civilized nations have tried not to induce more suffering than is necessary to accomplish this end. Napalm, in its means of action, in its capacity to maim permanently and to induce slow death, is a particularly horrifying weapon. That its use in Vietnam has involved many civilians—peasant families in undefended villages—has magnified the horror. (cited in Knoll and McFadden, 1970, p. 73)

2. *Ground attacks on villages and civilians.* The most celebrated and infamous incident of the war was the March 1968 massacre at Song My (also known as My Lai). Under orders from their superiors, American soldiers slaughtered over 500 civilians (Taylor, 1971, pp. 122–153). The troops had been told to destroy all structures and render the place uninhabitable. They killed every inhabitant, regardless of age or sex, and despite this no opposition or hostile behavior was encountered.

In Operation Cedar Falls, 30,000 American troops were assigned the task of destroying all villages in a 40-square-mile area. In this and other operations, groups of soldiers, known as "Zippo squads" burned village after village.

> The intensely cultivated flat lands south of the Vaico Oriental River about 20 miles from Saigon are prime "scorched earth" targets. U.S. paratroopers from the 173rd Airborne Brigade began operating there last weekend.
>
> They burned to the ground every hut they saw. Sampans were sunk and bullock carts were smashed. The 173rd laid their base camp among the blackened frames of burned houses. Within two miles of the camp not a house was left standing. . . . .
>
> Every house found by the 173rd was burned to the ground. Every cooking utensil was smashed, every banana tree severed, every mattress slashed. . . . Thousands of ducks and chickens were slaughtered. . . . Dozens of pigs, water buffalo and cows were destroyed. A 20-mile stretch along the Vaico Oriental was left scorched and barren. (cited in Herman, 1970, p. 84)

A variation on the "scorched earth" policy just noted was the use of anticrop chemicals. The Air Force sprayed defoliants on 100,000 acres in 1964 and 1.5 million acres in 1969. Herbicides were used to destroy foliage that hid the enemy and crops that fed the Vietcong soldiers and their civilian supporters. The results of this campaign were devastating in a number of ways: (1) timber, a major crop in South Vietnam, was destroyed and replaced by bamboo, generally considered a nuisance; (2) the mangroves in swamplands were killed, negatively affecting shellfish and migratory fish, major sources of protein for the Vietnamese; (3) vast areas of soil eroded; and (4) toxic substances such as 2,4,5T were ingested by humans and animals, which may lead to birth abnormalities. Gaston has summarized this catastrophe of American strategy as follows:

> After the end of World War II, and as a result of the Nuremberg trials, we justly condemned the willful destruction of an entire people and its culture, calling this crime against humanity *genocide*. It seems to me that the willful and permanent destruction of environment in which a people can live in a manner of their own choosing ought similarly to be designated as a crime against humanity, to be designated by the term *ecocide*. . . . At the present time, the United States stands alone as possibly having committed ecocide against another country, Vietnam, through its massive use of chemical defoliants and herbicides. (cited in Knoll and McFadden, 1970, p. 71)

In addition to ecocide, the American conduct in Vietnam killed a sizeable portion of the population. The population of entire villages was killed. Thousands were killed in bombings. The enormity of this is seen in data supplied by the Senate Subcommittee on Refugees. It estimated that from 1965 to 1969 over a million refugees were killed and 2 million were wounded by the U.S. Armed Services (Roebuck and Weeber, 1978, p. 71).

In sum, America's strategy in the Vietnam civil war shattered the whole society from its ecology to village life, and to life itself. Daniel Ellsberg has called this violent destruction of a patterned society sociocide (quoted in Knoll and McFadden, 1970, p. 82). Most certainly that qualified as the ultimate war crime.

SOCIOLOGICAL THEORIES AND POLITICAL CRIME

Traditional Sociological Approaches

The theories involving criminal behaviors from this perspective do not pertain to political crimes. For example, considering political dissent, the individual dissenters are generally involved because of a commitment to a cause, not because of some underlying socially-induced pathology. As Sykes has argued, the "traumas of childhood, personality defects, the breakdown of primary groups—all may be less important than the individual's perception of the faults of society and a consciously chosen strategy of involvement in social action" (1980, p. 5).

The political radical is unlike street criminals since he or she has consciously chosen to be a nonconformist. As Merton has observed (1976, pp. 29–32), the nonconformist publicly challenges the legitimacy of the accepted norms and conforms rather to what is claimed to be the deepest values of the society. The goal of sociological research should be to answer the question, Under what conditions do individuals reject society's dominant values and seek to change the political system? In the 1960s and early 1970s political dissent was common. The possible reasons for this surge in political nonconformity were the U.S. involvement in an unpopular war, the draft, the age structure (the members of the baby boom generation were adolescents and young adults), the rising hopes of the oppressed (minorities and women), and the repression of nonconformists by government agents and agencies. Other conditions may lead to a return to the political violence of the 1960s or even surpass it (Sykes, 1980, pp. 51–52): military conflict, a prolonged economic depression, a loss of faith in the actions of government, a belief that the gap is widening between the advantaged and the disadvantaged, and a crisis such as a nuclear plant meltdown. Sykes has argued that these factors plus others lead to the heightened possibility of increased political dissent in the future.

The powerful example of the confrontations of the late 1960s, the radicalism that is far from vanished even though somewhat underground, the unresolved problems of poverty and racism that continue to breed bitterness and resentment—all make it likely that political protest in the immediate future will not remain confined to orderly disagreement. (Sykes, 1980, p. 52)

Interactionist Perspective

One emphasis of the interactionists is on the positive side of negative identities in political conflicts (Osborne, 1974). Political deviants accept their negative labels because they deny the legitimacy of the social order. They do not seek social acceptance from the dominant society. The efforts of political authorities to stigmatize them is viewed by the dissidents as positive because they hold to a higher set of values (Goffman, 1963, p. 146). Indeed, they want society's negative label because they feel that it (the negative label) should be the legitimate one:

> Examples abound of individuals and groups undercutting existing value orientations by aggressively seeking to win acceptance for their views of reality as expressed in the labels they attempt to legitimate: colonists who dumped tea into Boston Harbor, failed to pay taxes, and asserted their independence; slaves who conspired to rebel and flee and the whites who sheltered them, the Confederacy that sought to dissolve the Union; the early years of labor organizing and conflict; pacifists throughout American history who were brought to trial and jailed; the numerous phases of the black struggle for civil rights; women's efforts to win suffrage; the battle by Communists to gain the right to free speech and the right to hold public office; the conflicts surrounding atheists who refused to pray and science teachers who neglected Genesis. (Schervish, 1973, p. 53)

The efforts of the dissidents in these and other cases were directed at challenges to the legitimacy of the government. Government leaders when threatened in this way attempt to convince the public that the acts of government were indeed legitimate and those of the dissenters illegitimate (Archer and Gartner, 1978). Typically, the government wins in these battles for the public's perception of "reality" because the members of society are socialized to accept the legitimacy of government and because there is a massive tendency for the mass media to support the status quo.

The Radical Perspective

One assumption of liberal democratic theory is that the government cannot be guilty of lawlessness. After all, the government is sovereign over the people; it makes the law. The radical conception of government, on the other hand, is that the government can be criminal. Governments can do violence. Governments, which are supposed to guarantee civil liberties, may be the very violators of those rights (Clinard and Quinney, 1973, pp. 158–159).

The liberal democratic theory assumes that all groups in society help determine government policy, either through direct efforts or through their elected representatives. But as Clinard and Quinney, presenting the radical perspective, have argued, this assumption is not based on fact.

Instead many individuals and groups are either excluded from the traditional processes or are unsuccessful in being represented in the policy decisions. And when the traditional processes fail, the only recourse may be to engage in non-traditional procedures. The use of these procedures may easily result in criminal behavior. That is to say, those in power will define as criminal those who resort to illegitimate politics. (Clinard and Quinney, 1973, p. 166)

The liberal democratic conception of government assumes a consensus among the populace on societal values. This common sharing of the dominant values results in a common perception of the political system as legitimate. This view, radicals argue, disregards those who hold different values, such as atheism, pacifism, or socialism. Groups that hold to different values are likely to question the legitimacy of the system and to engage in political behaviors that are viewed by the majority as "extremist" and therefore criminal. Moreover, very often political dissidents choose to attack society because they are victims of the system's oppression. The public, however, blames them rather than the true source of their dissidence.

Finally, radicals are intrigued by the inconsistency of the government's actions, which tends to criminalize legal behavior and decriminalize illegal behavior. The government (agents of social control) police those actions (legal or illegal) that threaten the system and ignore those actions (legal or illegal) that maintain it. In the case of political crimes, the government actually squelches the constitutionally legitimate actions of some when these acts are perceived as threatening to the existing power structure or "the American way of life." Thus, legal acts are treated as crimes. Illegal acts by the government such as police brutality or war, on the other hand, are usually accepted as legitimate because they are seen as necessary for maintaining and enhancing the current economic and political systems.

CHAPTER REVIEW

1. Political crime is either a criminal act by individuals or groups against the government or a criminal act by the government against the people.
2. Political crimes against the state include illegal acts (a) to change the existing structure of power, (b) seize power, and (c) of refusing to obey the law for political or ideological reasons.
3. When government decisions systematically favor the powerful in society and do harm to the powerless, they constitute collectively political crimes. This bias takes several forms: (a) favors to big business in subsidies, tax breaks, and protective legislation; (b) the choice of "trickle-down" solutions to stimulate the economy; and (c) the poor disproportionately bearing the burden in war, inflation, and deflation.
4. There are five forms of government lawlessness: (a) secrecy, lying, and deceit; (b) the abuse of power by government agencies; (c) the use of citizens as

unknowing guinea pigs; (d) American intervention in the domestic affairs of other nations; and (e) war crimes.

5. The traditional sociological approach to crimes are not applicable to political crime.

6. Interactionists have noted that political dissidents, unlike the case of other criminals, accept their negative labels because they deny the legitimacy of the political order. Indeed, the negative label for the dissident is the legitimate one.

7. A fundamental contribution of the radical perspective is that governments can be guilty of lawlessness. Governments, however, are generally perceived by the public as legitimate regardless of their acts and they use their powers to squelch dissidents.

THE CRIMINAL JUSTICE SYSTEM

We now turn to those institutions in American society—known collectively as the criminal justice system—most directly charged with the responsibility for preventing and controlling crime.

The American criminal justice system has its foundation in the criminal law. Violations of the law can result in the other components of the criminal justice system becoming involved: the police, who investigate reported crimes, make arrests, and book those arrested; the criminal court, that formally charges individuals, determines their guilt or innocence, and sentences them; and the correctional system, that punishes, supervises, or attempts to reform or rehabilitate the convicted offender.

In a very real sense, the American system of criminal justice is a "filtering or funneling" system: there are more reported crimes than arrests, more arrests than charges filed, more charges filed than convictions, and more convictions than sentences to prison (imprisonment representing the most severe punishment normally meted out by the criminal justice system). The diagram on page 364 identifies the key components in the criminal justice system and their official functions. These components and their functions will be described in detail in this section of the text.

The chapters in this section will not just describe the official organization, operation, and purpose of the criminal justice system, however. The reality of American criminal justice has often diverged significantly from the ideal. For example, as we describe the processing of those reported as perpetrators of criminal acts and arrested, we will begin to see that the "filtering" that our justice system does is not random or arbitrary. The filtering process is in reality a "homogenization process" (see Shelden, 1982; Newton, Shelden, and Jenkins, 1975) that reflects the bias of the criminal justice system. The "homogenization process" ensures that only certain kinds of people in American society are processed through the entire system and receive its most severe sanctions. We will also see why some have taken the ongoing crises and failures of American criminal justice to mean that it is less a crime control system than it is a "nonsystem" (see Moore, 1981).

The Criminal Justice Funnel

CRIMES REPORTED TO THE POLICE

POLICE
1. Investigate
2. Arrest
3. Book

CRIMINAL COURT
1. Arraign and charge
2. Set bail or bond/ grant pretrial release
3. Determine guilt or innocence/plea bargaining or trial
4. Sentence

CORRECTIONS
1. Probation
2. Community corrections
3. Prison
4. Parole

11 Policing

**CHAPTER
OUTLINE**

The Historical Origins and Development of the Municipal Police Force

    The modern police force: repression or reconciliation?

The Police Subculture and Police Discretion
The Social Organization of the Police Bureaucracy

    Bureaucratic constraints to crime control
    Bureaucratically induced social control
    Police department "styles"
    Police professionalization, unionization, and Taylorization
    The contradictions of contemporary policing

Police Criminality, Brutality, and the Use of Deadly Force
Improving Law Enforcement

KEY TERMS

    Clearance rates
    Legalistic-style policing
    Order maintenance
    Police discretion
    Police professionalization
    Police subculture
    Proactive policing
    Reactive policing
    Service-style policing
    Taylorization of police work
    Watch-style policing

NEW YORK, N.Y. (AP) New York City's police force has dwindled to its smallest size in 17 years, while the crime rate continues to climb, police figures show.

As of Nov. 19, the department says, 22,170 officers, detectives, supervisors and recruits were on the force. That figure includes 1,000 rookies in the Police Academy and due to graduate Dec. 14.

The force reached its peak in 1970, with 31,797 members. In 1980, 710,153 major crimes—the most ever—were recorded in the city.[1]

How large is the American police force? Are there enough police in American society to control crime effectively? What are the police really doing, anyway? Is it different from what they say they are doing? If so, how? This chapter answers these questions in some detail. But before getting more specific, we will indicate the general direction of our answers here.

First of all, it appears as though the American police force is a large one. At present, there are approximately 700,000 legally sworn police officers working for approximately 19,500 county or city police departments. These agencies are spending more than $11 billion per year (Gibbons, 1982). This does *not* include the activities and expenditures of other local police such as county sheriff departments (often quite large in major metropolitan areas); state police, for example, state highway patrols and state troopers, as well as tax-enforcement organizations, liquor control commissions, and game wardens; federal domestic policing agencies like the Federal Bureau of Investigation, the Drug Enforcement Administration, the Secret Service, and the military police among others; and over 800,000 private police—private security personnel, Pinkertons, Burns Detectives, and so on—at work in the United States.[2]

Washington, D.C., for example, has eight police agencies (excluding the Secret Service and military police) patrolling its streets. This works out to one federal or city police officer for every eight District of Columbia residents (Stein, 1981). As one commentator has put it, if more police were the answer to a growing crime problem, "surely a night-time stroll six blocks north of the White House would, by now, be as safe as a noontime schuss down the Swiss Alps" (Stein, 1981, p. 14).

Asking you to keep in mind *all* of the various kinds of police work going on in American society, this chapter concentrates on the municipal police. The great majority of crimes in American society are criminalized by state law, and it is the municipal police department who is charged with the primary responsibility of enforcing this law. Therefore, it is the city police who spend the most time making

---

[1] *Source:* The Associated Press, "Crime Rises, Police Dwindle," December 8, 1981.
[2] The recent rise of private policing in the United States will be discussed at length in Chapter 15.

the most arrests for the crimes that are most often policed in our society—street crimes. In this chapter we will only consider other police forces when they seem to impact directly the activity of the city police: as when, for example, the policies and practices involved in the FBI's enforcement of federal law have influenced local police in their efforts to enforce municipal and state criminal law.

Turning to another issue, we want to ask questions (and provide answers) that have to do with the relationship between the police and the incidence of crime or crime rates. Do more police necessarily mean better crime control? Do fewer police mean more crime or less? The Associated Press clipping that appears at the beginning of this chapter seems to imply that in New York City cuts in police protection have led to increases in crime. Panel 11-1, on the other hand, presents information from another urban center that suggests the opposite may actually be true: that those cities with the smallest police presence have the lowest crime rates and those with the largest police forces have the highest reported incidence of crime. This may very well be the case since more police may find and report more crime and fewer police may find and report fewer crimes.[3]

Also in this chapter, we will attempt to make the character of police work less mysterious. That is to say, we are interested in the real effects of "the cop on the beat" doing what the police bureaucracy requires of him or her. What have the municipal police department and the police officer accomplished historically? What are they accomplishing at present? Was the municipal police force originally a response to a growing and rising criminality? Is this its primary function at present? Is the primary function of the police, as they claim, to control serious crime?

While the prevention of felonious acts and the protection of the community from acts of interpersonal violence is usually assumed to be the reason for the development and maintenance of modern criminal law, the modern police, and corrections systems, we now know that *most* modern police activity has been, and is, concerned with other kinds of criminal behavior, namely, criminal misdemeanors (Manning 1977; Timmer, 1978).[4]

Another basic fact of municipal police work is that it is *reactive,* not *proactive.* Typically, the police patrol reacts and responds to a citizen's complaint or call "after-the-fact," that is, after a crime or noncriminal disturbance has taken place. Only now and then do the police act and initiate their own activity:

> Somewhere in the neighborhood of 90 percent of police contacts with citizens are in response to calls initiated by citizens, rather than the result of the police drumming up business through detection of offenses. Drawing on data from studies in several American cities, Albert Reiss observed that: "Our observational studies of police activity in high-crime-rate areas of these cities show that

---

[3] The relationship between the police presence and crime rates will be explored in more detail in the section "The Organization of the Police Bureaucracy." It should be noted here that the relationship between the actual incidence of crime and crime that is reported, that is, the crime rate, makes the relationship between police presence and the actual incidence of crime extremely hard to establish (see Chapter 4).

[4] This characteristic of police work in the United States will be discussed further in the next section.

PANEL 11-1

HIGHER POLICE RATIO DOESN'T ASSURE LESS CRIME: DENVER AND ITS SUBURBS

Will putting more police on the street reduce crime? Probably not.

Consider: The three cities with the highest concentrations of police manpower in the metropolitan Denver area also are the cities with the highest crime rates.

And the city with the lowest crime rate in the metro area has the lowest number of officers per resident.

Those statistics, from the FBI's 1980 Uniform Crime Report, support police officials' conclusions that hiring more policemen is not always the best way to fight increasing crime. More important than sheer numbers, they say, is the way in which those officers are used.

"I can give you a policeman on every block and it won't stop crime," noted Art Dill, chief of the Denver Police Department. The Denver force is the region's largest at 1,690 employees in 1980. Included in that number were 1,393 sworn officers; the rest were civilians.

"Police don't have much to do with the

City	Population	Index Crimes	Crime Rate Per 100,000	Personnel	Personnel Per 1,000
Arvada	84,576	3,792	4,483.5	148	1.75
Aurora	158,588	12,089	7,622.9	349	2.2
Boulder	76,685	6,354	8,285.8	145	1.89
Broomfield	20,730	1,469	7,086.3	42	2.0
Commerce City	16,234	1,718	10,582.7	52	3.2
Denver	491,396	58,782	11,962.2	1,690	3.4
Englewood	30,021	4,121	13,727.0	94	3.1
Golden	12,237	838	6,848.0	31	2.5
Lakewood	112,848	9,033	8,004.6	284	2.5
Littleton	28,631	1,994	6,964.5	64	2.2
Longmont	42,942	3,456	8,048.1	75	1.7
Northglenn	29,847	2,382	7,980.7	55	1.8
Thornton	40,343	2,990	7,411.4	74	1.8
Westminster	50,211	3,917	7,801.1	105	2.09
Wheat Ridge	30,293	2,415	7,972.1	66	2.17

Chart shows crime rates and police manpower levels for the 15 largest cities in (the Denver) metropolitan area in 1980. Number of index crimes includes murders, rapes, robberies, aggravated assaults, burglaries, thefts and auto thefts. Personnel totals include all police department employees. National average crime rate in 1980 was 5,899.9 per 100,000 population. Colorado's rate in 1980 was 7,333.5. Figures from Uniform Crime Report published by the FBI.

Panel 11-1 (Continued)

crime rate," agreed Jim O'Dell, assistant chief of the Lakewood Police Department, the area's third largest.

For instance:

- The suburban city of Englewood, which has the area's highest rate of serious crime based on population, has 3.1 police employees for every 1,000 residents, according to computations based on figures in the FBI report. That compares with a national average of 2.5 employees per 1,000 population, and an average in Colorado of 2.3.

  Denver, with the area's second-highest crime rate, has 3.4 police employees per 1,000 population, the highest concentration of officers. And Commerce City, with the third-highest crime rate, has 3.2 employees per 1,000 people.

- By contrast, the city of Arvada, a community of 84,576, has the lowest crime rate of the major cities in the five-county area, despite having only 1.75 police employees per 1,000. When civilian employees are discounted, Arvada has only 1.28 officers on the streets for every 1,000 people in town. That's the lowest manpower ratio in the metropolitan area.

  Arvada Police Chief William Koleszar says his motto is "Work smarter, not harder."

  Koleszar said many factors contribute to a community's crime rate, and the number of police officers is only a part of it. Other police officials agreed that hiring more officers not only will not guarantee a reduced crime rate; it could even cause an increase in the rate simply because more officers generate more police work. . . .

In some cases, tight budgets have forced administrators to live with fewer officers than they would like. So they have tried to reorganize duties to make more efficient use of each officer's time.

Koleszar said Arvada has been "tailoring back" some duties to civilian employees so sworn officers have more time on the streets. About 80 percent of traffic investigation, he said, is done by civilians.

"There are so many positions you don't need a sworn officer to do," he said.

87 percent of all patrol mobilizations were initiated by citizens. Officers initiated (both in the field and on view) only 13 percent. . . ." (Gibbons, 1982, p. 399)

But in order to refine further our answer to the question, "What are the police really doing, anyway?", we need to examine the historical origins and development of the U.S. municipal police. With the aid of the perspective of radical criminology—"the political economy of policing"—we will now turn to that history.

Panel 11-1 (Continued)

While Koleszar claimed the efficiency of his department plays a part in Arvada's low crime rate, he also noted the nature of the community has a large role.

He said a recent municipal study showed 85 percent of working adults in Arvada are employed outside that city, reducing the regular population.

By contrast, the 30,021-resident population of Englewood is more than tripled during the day by an influx of shoppers, professionals and clients doing business there, according to Englewood Police Chief Robert Holmes.

Large crowds of people in small areas attract crime, police say.

In response, Holmes has urged his officers to be more visible in the community. He denied the officers have quotas for such things as traffic citations, but they are supposed to take some type of positive action as often as possible so people see those red flashing lights.

"If you see a police car, you tend to slow down and remember it for three blocks," said Holmes. "If you see a police car with its lights flashing and taking some enforcement action, you might remember that for 10 blocks."

That will also help give the town the reputation of being tough on criminals, he said.

"There's no question if you've got additional people and they're used wisely, it will help," noted Dill. "But additional police officers will not deter crime with random patrol."

Dill said increased police paperwork and down-time due to court appearances have sapped patrol strength over the past decade.

"The only way you can get a reduction (in crime) is through increased community awareness and participation," said Dill. And Denver has a two-year-old program called Block Watch that encourages such participation.

"People have just gotten to the point in the last two years that they're sick and tired of crime," he said.

Source: Kevin Flynn, "Study: Higher Police Ratio Doesn't Assure Less Crime," Rocky Mountain News, *November 8, 1981, pp. 7 and 18.*

THE HISTORICAL ORIGINS AND DEVELOPMENT OF THE MUNICIPAL POLICE FORCE: RADICAL CRIMINOLOGY

The municipal police are clearly a modern social institution. The first police department, in London, was not founded until 1829. Sir Robert Peel's London department then became the model for the earliest American forces. In the United States, Boston's police originated in 1838, New York City's in 1845, and Washington, D.C., was without a municipal police department until 1861 (Lundman, 1980).

From the 1830s and on through the 1880s, more and more large cities in the United States began to turn to what may be called "modern police." Unlike earlier policing arrangements, these modern police forces may be defined as public and bureaucratic: they were increasingly characterized by persons having full-time police responsibilities, continuity in office and procedures, and accountability to a central government authority, that is, the state (Lundman, 1980). Until this time, policing in Europe and the United States (including Colonial America) had been primarily informal and communal or private and run for profit. Spitzer (1979) has described these premodern policing "systems" in rich and concrete terms—the "Frankpledge" in England, the "watch," "big-stick," and "private" constable in the United States—and has noted that these forms of premodern policing were found in precapitalist societies.

Why, then, the emergence of the modern municipal police force at this juncture in history? After all, as late as 1785, a bill introduced in the English Parliament to create a modern police force was rejected as "a dangerous innovation and an encroachment on the rights and security of the people" (quoted in Critchley, 1967, p. 37). Research directed toward answering this question has consistently identified a societal elite's interest in social and public *order*.[5] Lundman, for example, has directly attributed the *rise* of the modern public police to elite interests:

> The . . . factor responsible for the formal organization of municipal police was elite interest and involvement. Persons of power, wealth and prestige overcame the historic reluctance surrounding the police idea. Their motivation was purely economic—elites used their influence to create police who would protect and promote their vested interests (1980, p. 15).

Spitzer and Scull (1977) have defined these "elite interests" as those that correspond to a developing market economy. The elite interest is in the social control required by the system of capitalist production and distribution. According to these authors, the private and profit-oriented crime control system of the feudal landed aristocracy in England was unsuitable for the crime control needs of the rising commercial class—the bourgeoisie. Further, they contend, the market economy requires (more than any other economy in history) a stable and orderly environment, and the costs of this "collective good,"[6] this order and stability, must be transferred to the public sector, that is, to the government. In other words, why should one part of the commercial private sector, one business, finance this crime control system that would obviously benefit other private businesses and interests? Hence the development of the public municipal police.

Silver (1967), too, has suggested that municipal police departments in England and the United States originated from the need for a tranquil domestic population

[5]This consistent research finding concerns the historical origins and development of municipal police forces; it does *not* represent a consensus on the police function in contemporary capitalist, advanced capitalist, communal, socialist, or communist societies.
[6]For a clarification of this concept, see Olsen (1965).

and socially pacified communities dictated by the expansion of the market economy, industrialization, and urbanization, not to prevent crime per se. Capitalist industrialization and growth in the 19th century required *social control, not crime control.* The process of capitalist industrialization led to increasing economic inequality and exploitation and class stratification. Rioting became an essential political strategy of an underclass (a surplus population) and a working class suffering this increasing economic deprivation. The modern system of policing evolved to control this riotous situation. And through the control mechanism of the modern public police, the ruling economic and political elites were able to separate "constitutional authority" from their own social and economic dominance—their own class dominance. It began to appear as though laws, not men and women, ruled. Finally, the police, not the military, emerged as the visible everyday presence representing the central political authority in society.

In the years immediately preceding the rise of municipal police departments in London and large U.S. cities, members of the rising middle classes and the elite generally came to attribute crime, public demonstrations and protests, rioting, and public drunkenness[7] to members of the "dangerous classes." "The image was that of a convulsively and possibly biologically criminal, riotous, and intemperate group of persons located at the base of society" (Lundman, 1980, p. 29). From this class location, it appeared as though the actions of the "dangerous class" were ruinous of social order and stability. In the United States, this class was easily identified, consisting primarily of poor foreign immigrants and blacks beginning to infiltrate the major cities. An excerpt from the Boston Debates of 1863 (the Argument of Charles M. Ellis, Esq., in Favor of the Metropolitan Police Bill, Wednesday, March 18, 1863) illustrates, for example, the view held by Boston's white Protestant elite:

> In cities there are large bodies who are amongst us, but not of us, whose sentiments and principles do not harmonize with those of the State; who have influence, though they not have rightful influence; or, if citizens, have not the same influence as the great body of citizens—a foreign, floating population— those controlled by extraneous, alien influences, trade, criminal, or other. You have amongst you those elements of society called . . . the dangerous classes. [In short, the] . . . establishment of professional police came to be seen as a possible solution to the problem of public disorder. Transitional police (temporary, unstable, part-time, 'private-public mix' policing arrangements typical of early industrializing England and America) proved ineffective in the face of riots and the military was frequently called in to suppress them. (Lundman, 1980, p. 26, parentheses added)

Rioting, be it criminal or not, needed to be socially controlled. Certain crimes could be tolerated if they were not directly threatening to social order and control.

---

[7] Alcoholic drink was at this time (and still is in some circles) generally believed to be a primary cause of crime and public riot. Ironically, public drunkenness was unknown until the emerging market economy encouraged the commercial sale of alcohol. When this occurred, drinking was torn from communal and family-oriented mealtime use. Alcohol became a commodity for private consumption.

What was evolving was a system of social, not crime control. Richardson has written:

> As much as moralists objected to commercialized vice . . . their most serious fears arose from the threat riots posed to property and public order. And riots were frequent. . . . There were so many in 1834 alone that it was long remembered in New York history as the year of the riots (1970, p. 27).

What must be emphasized here is that the interest in social control described above has historically been *class specific*. As Quinney has put it, "definitions of crime are composed of behaviors that conflict with the interest of the dominant class" (1975, p. 38). In effect, during the late 19th and early 20th centuries, this class took control of the law creation and law enforcement machinery of the state when it perceived the actions of powerless segments in society threatening its interests and position. By declaring certain actions illegal and then creating special agencies to enforce the law, these powerless groups or classes were brought under the state's control. According to Parks,

> The history of social control in the United States is the history of transition from "constabulary" to "police society" . . . which . . . was not essentially for the protection of the "general welfare" of society but was for the protection of the interests and life-styles of but one segment of society—those holding positions of wealth, "respectability," and power (1976, p. 129).

The historical origins of the New York City Police Department are a case in point: the public police were instituted, by and large, to control an "organizing labor force."[8] In fact, as Reiman (1979) has pointed out, the historical period that brought the development of the municipal public police is also the period of growth of the industrial working class in the cities of England and the United States. This was more than coincidental: the public police were repeatedly used to impede efforts at labor and union organization and even to break strikes.

> Throughout the formative years of the American labor movement, public police forces, private police such as the Pinkertons, the National Guard, and regular army troops were repeatedly used to protect the interests of capital against the attempts of labor to organize in defense of its interests. (Reiman, 1979, p. 165)

The municipal police, then, did play a significant role in the bloody and violent labor history of the industrializing United States (see Taft and Ross, 1969). Although the police were normally employed as an arm of big capital in these management-labor conflicts and struggles, this was not exclusively the case. As Johnson (1976) has pointed out, there are historical instances of the municipal police force—particularly in Chicago and New York City—intervening in strike

---

[8]For a detailed history of this particular situation, see the Center for Research on Criminal Justice (1975).

situations, not on behalf of industry, but in support of striking workers. The reason for this occasional "turn-around" are related, for the most part, to the social position of the police officers themselves—they were (and are) primarily working-class individuals.[9]

The origins of police forces in Denver, Buffalo, and Texas also attest to the influence of the dominant class and ruling elites. Bordua and Reiss have summarized studies done on the origins of various U.S. municipal police departments and underscored the argument made here:

> The paramilitary form of early police bureaucracy was a response not only, or even primarily, to crime per se, but to the possibility of riotous disorder. Not crime and danger but the "criminal" and "dangerous classes" as part of the urban social structure led to the formation of uniformed and military organized police. Such organizations intervened between the propertied elites and propertyless masses who were regarded as politically dangerous as a class (1967, p. 283).[9]

The Modern Police Force: Repression or Reconciliation?

The classic French sociologist Emile Durkheim writing at the turn of the 20th century developed his theory of penal evolution. This theory held that the punitive practices of non-industrialized societies relied on harsh and repressive measures whereas industrialized societies were more likely to utilize punishments that were less severe. In industrial societies, Durkheim contended, reconciliation and restitution between offender and victim would be the norm. As Montesquieu had put it, "As freedom advances, the severity of the penal law decreases" (quoted in Walker, 1980). Others since, however, have suggested that Durkheim confused the issue and that the opposite may indeed be true. It appears more likely that complex, industrial, technological, and highly stratified societies rely on repressive and more severe criminal justice practices, whereas less technologically sophisticated and economically stratified societies tend to practice reconciliation and restitution (see, for example, Chambliss and Seidman, 1971). At least two cross-cultural studies of over 50 societies, ranging from non-industrial to highly industrialized, have confirmed this refutation of Durkheim's theory (see Schwartz and Miller, 1964; Spitzer, 1975b). And, even more important for purposes of this chapter, both studies concluded that *the police are found only in industrial societies with a well-developed division of labor* (specialization). The police are unknown in the more conciliatory and less severe pre-industrial environment. Schwartz and Miller have summarized their study:

> Superficially at least, these findings seem directly contradictory to Durkheim's major thesis in *The Division of Labor in Society*. He hypothesized that penal law—the effort of the organized society to punish offenses against itself—

---

[9]The first part of this section is taken in large part from Timmer (1981).

occurs in societies with the simplest division of labor. As indicated, however, our data show that police are found only in association with a substantial division of labor. Even the practice of governmental punishment for wrongs against the society . . . does not appear in simpler societies. By contrast, restitutive sanctions—damages and mediation—which Durkheim believed to be associated with an increasing division of labor, are found in many societies that lack even rudimentary specialization. Thus Durkheim's hypothesis seems the reverse of an empirical situation in the range of societies studied here (1964, p. 166).

And the modern municipal police force in the United States has not escaped the effects of the repressive crime control system that it has helped institutionalize and maintain. The city police have been impacted by a *militarization* of their operations that gradually turned the public image of police work almost exclusively toward the use of "crime-fighting technologies." As it turns out, however, this public image has never been an accurate one.

In 1924, when he was appointed director, J. Edgar Hoover began to militarize the FBI and create a "crime-fighter" image for American law enforcement. For Hoover, police work meant the science and technology of "fingerprints and firearms." And since this man headed up the leading law enforcement agency in the country, his influence on the municipal police was strong.

More and more technology was introduced into local police departments. The automobile, telephone, and two-way radio replaced "the cop on the beat." Citizen relations with the police became more formal and impersonal. Traffic laws and their enforcement meant that for the first time significant numbers of middle- and upper-class people had contact with the police. In this way, the police function expanded beyond the control of the "dangerous classes" and served to make even larger segments of the population suspicious of, and hostile toward the police.

But the introduction of communications technology—the telephone and the "two-way" in particular—had another unanticipated effect on police work. These two technologies allowed the individual citizen to summon the police and see them arrive in a very short time. Many police departments began to advertise the assistance they could provide, and the public began to call upon the police for a wider and wider range of services, often relating to non-criminal matters. In fact, by the 1960s, as much as 80 percent of American municipal police work was consumed by those noncriminal matters (Walker, 1980).

This led to an important contradiction still evident in American policing: even while Hoover and the FBI were busy militarizing the nation's law enforcement agencies and furthering the image of the "crime fighters," the police were increasingly doing another kind of work—misdemeanant and noncriminal social-service work. The measure for evaluating police work, the Uniform Crime Report, that Hoover and the FBI devised, was consistent with the image of the police the agency created, no matter how far this measure diverged from the social reality of police work:

While day-to-day police work increasingly involved non-criminal activities, the crime-fighter image continued to grow. The advent of the UCR in 1930 contributed to this development. Simply because it was the only available set of statistics (and no one thought to devise a different one), it became the standard measure of police work. "Success" in policing was defined by the fluctuations of the official crime rate and the percentage of crimes cleared. This drew attention even further away from the non-criminal, social-service aspects of policing. (Walker, 1980, p. 191)

There has developed, then, an image or ideology of police work in American society that bears little resemblance to the actual character and activity of the contemporary police force. This will become even more evident later in this chapter.

Theory

An examination of the historical origins and development of the municipal police force in the United States indicates that the perspective of radical criminology—the political economy of policing—is a most useful one. As the above history makes clear, the city police have historically engaged in social control efforts that have enforced a social order, an order that has benefitted some elite and class interests in society but not others. Crime control per se, has not been the only, or the primary, police activity. Contrary to more traditional sociological accounts of modern police systems, the historical record does *not* indicate that either the origins or further development of U.S. law enforcement is characterized by the pursuit of criminal activities defined by a consensual criminal law that reflects the interests of all parts of a community and is enforced in the interests of that entire community.

Focusing on the question, "What is policed and what is not?", radical criminology's answer is that those activities that threaten a class-biased social order have been and will be policed. These policed activities and behaviors may be illegal but need not be if they are sufficiently disruptive to the ongoing social order. Panel 11-2 illustrates the lengths to which—often illegal themselves—the police may go in their effort to control *legal* activities that are perceived by some part of society and/or the police bureaucracy as potential sources of public disorder.

THE POLICE SUBCULTURE AND POLICE DISCRETION: INTERACTIONIST CRIMINOLOGY

The police in American society form a distinct subculture with a distinct view and knowledge of crime and the criminal. Police work is also characterized by a high degree of discretion. A long tradition of sociological studies of the police have focused on the impact of police discretion on American law enforcement. Donald Black's (1980) police studies, for example, lead one to the conclusion that whether or not a police-encountered activity is illegal or legal is not in itself a very good predictor of police behavior. Other variables are more important in determining

PANEL 11-2

Policing Public Disorder: Illegal Spying

Los Angeles For more than two years, activists in the Santa Monica-Venice chapter of the anti-nuclear Alliance for Survival knew Richard Gibbey as a soft-spoken member who regularly attended meetings, rallies, and forums and frequently volunteered to help with security at Alliance events.

What Alliance members did not now was that Gibbey was also a Los Angeles police officer assigned to the department's Public Disorder Intelligence Division—the modern version of the city's old "Red Squad." As a result, Gibbey is now a defendant in a lawsuit filed in July by the American Civil Liberties Union (ACLU), charging the Los Angeles Police Department with spying on lawful political groups.

The lawsuit brings to nine the number of Los Angeles police officers accused of spying in suits filed over the past three years.

The extent of the department's political spying became clear in 1978, when the Citizens' Commission on Police Repression, a Los Angeles-based watchdog group, released a list it had obtained of 200 organizations the police had under surveillance. Included were local chapters of the National Organization for Women, the National Council of Churches, Southern Christian Leadership Conference, Gay Community Services Center, United Farm Workers, and the National Women's Political Caucus. Later, it was found that the police had also spied on members of the city council and the board of education.

Evidence is mounting that other local law-enforcement agencies may be involved in spying as well. Last June, the ACLU filed suit against the Los Angeles school district, charging that a special school security agent had infiltrated a group formed to conduct public education about the murders of black children in Atlanta. At a meeting of more than thirty persons, the undercover officer got up and, according to sworn affidavits filed in the case, said, "I think that the only way we can stop the murdering of children in Atlanta is for us to go out and kill white babies."

Los Angeles is one of dozen of cities around the country with long histories of police spying. After several years in the courts, suits against spying in New York and Chicago have recently been settled, although the merits of the settlements are being hotly debated. Critics have argued that the court-sanctioned guidelines are still too vague to curtail surveillance. In the Los Angeles cases, which will probably be combined in one major trial that may not be held for at least two more years, the Citizens' Commission and the ACLU are seeking a permanent ban on spying with criminal penalties for violations. Only one city in the nation—Seattle—currently has such an ordinance on the books.

With case after case of police surveillance surfacing in Los Angeles, Police Chief Daryl Gates's stock reply to critics has been, "I don't know what police spying is." He ought to put down the binoculars and pick up a mirror.

Source: Michael Balter, "Peering Cops," The Progressive, September 1981, p. 18.

how the police will act in a given situation. These variables are all extremely susceptible to the influences of the police subculture and police discretion. Black has identified the variables that best predict police behavior as the seriousness of the incident, the preference of the complainant, the social distance between the complainant and the suspect, and the deference shown police officers.

Although not at all historical in its approach, the interactionist perspective provides significant insights into the twin phenomenon of police subculture and police discretion. This perspective focuses on the social psychology of law enforcement: the face-to-face interaction and encounter between those being policed and those doing the policing. Rather than conceptualizing police behavior as the more or less rational, formal, and mechanical application of law enforcement authority, as more traditional sociological approaches have done, the interactionist perspective has emphasized the ways in which the very actions of the police may facilitate, amplify, escalate, and *create* crime and deviance (see G. Marx, 1981, for example).

Returning to our question, "What is policed and what is not?" the interactionist reply revolves not around the idea of a rational, formal, and mechanical application of the criminal law to illegal acts, but around the notion of *arbitrary* enforcement. Panel 11-3 reports one instance of this kind of discretionary and arbitrary use of police authority. Police subculture, the police "working knowledge" of crime and criminals, and police discretion all ensure the arbitrary use of police authority. A groundswell of interactionist research has confirmed the reality of this aspect of police work.

There are, of course, known drunks, cars, and burglars that are constantly under the police eye. But the police have developed a much more elaborate scheme for identifying social and criminal types. Just as Sudnow (1965) found public defenders to have developed notions of "normal crimes," the police have notions of "normal criminals." Manning has found that:

What occurs in a given incident cannot be understood by simply counting behavioral outcomes. One must give attention to what is "out of sight" or the "pre-constituted typifications" of normal and routine encounters employed by the police. . . . The police thus create by their own definitions of "crime" and "criminals" a system of typifications and assumptions that might be called an "occupational culture" . . . . (1974a, p. 23)

What Manning calls the occupational culture comprises, in effect, what could be called the police officer's "work world" or "the situational contingencies of policing." Others have identified it as "a secondary reality" (Young, 1971), or more typically, as the police subculture (for example, Shearing, 1979).

Police officers also have their own theories of crime causation and policing. The police possess a "lay social theory which serves to direct working policemen in their selection of candidates for criminalization and in their use of the law to initiate this process" (Shearing, 1979).

Our own research indicates, for example, that the police "know" that there

PANEL 11-3

Police Discretion and the Political Bumpersticker

A series of violent, bloody encounters between police and Black Panther Party members punctuated the early summer days of 1969. Soon after, a group of black students I teach at California State College, Los Angeles, who were members of the Panther Party, began to complain of continuous harassment by law enforcement officers. Among their many grievances, they complained about receiving so many traffic citations that some were in danger of losing their driving privileges. During one lengthy discussion, we realized that all of them drove automobiles with Panther Party signs glued to their bumpers. This is a report of a study that I undertook to assess the seriousness of their charges and to determine whether we were hearing the voice of paranoia or reality.

Recruitment advertising for subjects to participate in the research elicited 45 possible subjects from the student body. Careful screening thinned the ranks to 15—five black, five white, and five of Mexican descent. Each group included three males and two females. Although the college enrolls more than 20,000 students (largest minority group numbers on the west coast), it provides no residential facilities; all participants, of necessity then, traveled to campus daily on freeways or surface streets. The average round trip was roughly ten miles, but some drove as far as 18 miles. Eleven of the 15 had part-time jobs which involved driving to and from work after class as well.

All participants in the study had exemplary driving records, attested to by a sworn statement that each driver had received no "moving" traffic violations in the preceding twelve months. In addition, each promised to continue to drive in accordance with all in-force Department of Motor Vehicles regulations. Each student signed another statement, to the effect that he would do nothing to "attract the attention" of either police, sheriff's deputies or highway patrolmen—all of whom survey traffic in Los Angeles county. The participants declared that their cars, which ranged from a "flower child" hippie van to standard American makes of all types, had no defective equipment. Lights, horns, brakes and tires were duly inspected and pronounced satisfactory.

The appearance of the drivers was varied. There were three blacks with processed hair and two with exaggerated naturals, two white-shirt-and-necktie, straight caucasians and a shoulder-length-maned hippie, and two mustache-and-sideburn-sporting Mexican-Americans. All wore typical campus dress, with the exception of the resident hippie and the militant blacks, who sometimes wore dashikis.

A fund of $500 was obtained from a private source to pay fines for any citations received by the driving pool and students were briefed on the purposes of the

Panel 11-3 (Continued)

study. After a review of lawful operation of motor vehicles, all agreed on the seriousness of receiving excessive moving traffic violations. In California, four citations within a twelve-month period precipitates automatic examination of driving records, with a year of probation likely, or, depending on the seriousness of the offenses, suspension of the driver's license for varying lengths of time. Probation or suspension is usually accompanied by commensurate increases in insurance premiums. Thus, the students knew they were accepting considerable personal jeopardy as a condition of involvement in the study.

Bumper stickers in lurid day-glo orange and black, depicting a menacing panther with large BLACK PANTHER lettering were attached to the rear bumper of each subject car and the study began. The first student received a ticket for making an "incorrect lane change" on the freeway less than two hours after heading home in the rush hour traffic. Five more tickets were received by others on the second day for "following too closely," "failing to yield the right of way," "driving too slowly in the high-speed lane of the freeway," "failure to make a proper signal before turning right at an intersection," and "failure to observe proper safety of pedestrians using a crosswalk." On day three, students were cited for "excessive speed," "making unsafe lane changes" and "driving erratically." And so it went every day.

One student was forced to drop out of the study by day four, because he had already received three citations. Three others reached what we had agreed was the maximum limit—three citations—within the first week. Altogether, the participants received 33 citations in 17 days, and the violations fund was exhausted.

Drivers reported that their encounters with the intercepting officers ranged from affable and "standard polite" to surly, accompanied by search of the vehicle. Five cars were thoroughly gone over and their drivers were shaken down. One white girl, a striking blonde and a member of a leading campus sorority, was questioned at length about her reasons for supporting the "criminal activity" of the Black Panther Party. This was the only time that an actual reference to the bumper stickers was made during any of the ticketings. Students, by prior agreement, made no effort to dissuade officers from giving citations, once the vehicle had been halted.

Pledges to Drive Safely   Students received citations equally, regardless of race or sex or ethnicity or personal appearance. Being in jeopardy made them "nervous" and "edgy" and they reported being very uncomfortable whenever they were in their automobile. After the first few days, black students stopped saying "I told you so," and showed a sober, demoralized air of futility. Continuous pledges to safe driving were made daily, and all expressed increasing incredulity as the totals

Panel 11-3 (Continued)

mounted. They paid their fines in person immediately after receiving a citation. One student received his second ticket on the way to pay his fine for the first one.

No student requested a court appearance to protest a citation, regardless of the circumstances surrounding a ticketing incident. When the investigator announced the end of the study on the eighteenth day, the remaining drivers expressed relief, and went straight to their cars to remove the stickers. . . .

No More Stickers   It is possible, of course, that the subject's bias influenced his driving, making it less circumspect than usual. But it is statistically unlikely that this number of previously "safe" drivers could amass such a collection of tickets without assuming real bias by police against drivers with Black Panther bumper stickers.

The reactions of the traffic officers might have been influenced, and we hypothesize that they were, by the recent deaths of police in collision with Black Panther Party members. But whatever the provocation, unwarranted traffic citations are a clear violation of the civil rights of citizens, and cannot be tolerated. . . .

As a footnote to this study, I should mention that Black Panther bumper stickers are not seen in Los Angeles these days, although the party has considerable local strength. Apparently members discovered for themselves the danger of blatantly announcing their politics on their bumpers, and have long since removed the "incriminating" evidence.

Source: F. K. Heussenstamm, "Bumper Stickers and the Cops," Trans-Action (Society) 8, February 1971, pp. 32 and 33.

really are criminal persons and that they can be further differentiated into—in their own words:[10]

1. *Fresh meat*   Those police-encountered persons who have no previous formal or informal record of contact with the police.
2. *Shrods and dirt bags*   Continual petty troublemakers, petty thieves, "fighters," and so on. "They are dirty people, they look dirty, they act dirty." "But they wouldn't hurt or kill a cop."
3. *Pukes*   "Hard core." "Have done time for burglary, armed robbery, manslaughter. . . ." Given the "right circumstances," they would hurt or kill a cop.

[10] Much of what follows is drawn from original field research which appears in a slightly different form in Timmer (1981). For the most part, this research merely serves to confirm the interactionist perspective employed in other recent field observations of the police and referred to throughout this section. Also, all quoted material in this section, unless otherwise noted, is taken from patrol officers we encountered as they went about their day-to-day police work.

4. *Lower-than-lifes* "Animals." They have no ethics or morals. Even without the "right circumstances," they would hurt or kill a cop or anyone else.[11]

As mentioned above, police officers also have their own theories of crime causation. One theory can be identified as having to do with "distorted perceptions." The notion here is that criminals do not understand right and wrong. They do not understand that others have rights and how they, the criminals, may violate those rights.

Other officers put stock in the "there-is-no-free-lunch" theory. In other words, criminals represent that sector of society that is looking for a "deal," something for nothing, "a free lunch." They do not understand that they live in a society organized around the idea that there is no "free lunch." Panel 11-4 describes yet another police theory of crime and criminals: the "rotten-apple" perspective.

There is the recognition on the part of some officers of a "sociological" theory of the causes of crime. For certain types of crime in certain parts of the city, it may indeed be the case that social conditions are seen as the culprit. In the officer's consciousness, the "shrod crime" of the ghetto or the barrio, for example, is often related to poverty and unemployment.

Police officers also often point to the importance of ringleaders in the situations they encounter. Ringleaders always seem to emerge in domestic, bar, and neighborhood disturbances. The police believe that control of ringleaders is indispensable in attempting to control these situations. Therefore, it is sometimes important to the police to either have "come from" or to have developed personal and trusting relationships in these bars and neighborhoods. In this regard, police officers also spend time attempting to establish relationships with on-the-street informants such as bartenders or particular juveniles who know "who's hanging around." The police are convinced of the utility of informal, personal, and trusting relationships in securing social control, in helping to "keep things under control."

An overriding resentment resides in the police officer's relationship to criminal due process and the courts. Because the officer purportedly encounters the illegal activity itself and witnesses guilt before making an official arrest, he or she "knows" who is guilty before court procedures begin. When the police "know" who is guilty, innocence founded on the technicalities of criminal due process is difficult to understand or respect.

The data also indicate that police officers tend to create opportunities for social control. The symbols constructed for and used on those to be controlled, for example, "fresh meat," "shrods," "dirt bags," "pukes," and "lower-than-lifes/ animals," facilitate this process. This symbolism further suggests an image of those to be controlled that is reminiscent of the "dangerous class." In the United States this "dangerous class" that is disproportionately singled out by the police for criminal processing by the criminal justice system tends to be extremely visible, as if it is victimized by social, political, and economic inequities: it is the

---

[11] A former Detroit police officer has indicated to us that categories similar to these, with ample local variation, of course, can be found in most city police departments in the country.

PANEL 11-4

Police Social Theory: "Rotten Apples"

What is the foundation of the police view? On the basis of our interviews with police and a systematic study of police publications, we have found that a significant underpinning is what can best be described as a "rotten apple" theory of human nature. Such a theory of human nature is hardly confined to the police, of course. It is widely shared in our society. Many of those to whom the police are responsible hold the "rotten apple" theory, and this complicates the problem in many ways.

Under this doctrine, crime and disorder are attributable mainly to the intentions of evil individuals; human behavior transcends past experience, culture, society, and other external forces and should be understood in terms of wrong choices, deliberately made. Significantly—and contrary to the teachings of all the behavioral sciences—social factors such as poverty, discrimination, inadequate housing, and the like are excluded from the analysis. As one policeman put it simply, "Poverty doesn't cause crime; people do."

The "rotten apple" view of human nature puts the policeman at odds with the goals and aspirations of many of the groups he is called upon to police. For example, police often relegate social reforms to the category of "coddling criminals" or, in the case of recent ghetto programs, to "selling out" to troublemakers. Moreover, while denying that social factors may contribute to the causes of criminal behavior, police and police publications, somewhat inconsistently, denounce welfare programs not as irrelevant but as harmful because they destroy human initiative. This negative view of the goals of policed communities can only make the situation of both police and policed more difficult and explosive. Thus, the black community sees the police not only as representing an alien white society but also as advocating positions fundamentally at odds with its own aspirations. A report by the Group for Research on Social Policy at Johns Hopkins University (commissioned by the National Advisory Commission on Civil Disorders) summarizes the police view of the black community:

The police have wound up face to face with the social consequences of the problems in the ghetto created by the failure of other white institutions—though, as has been observed, they themselves have contributed to those problems in no small degree. The distant and gentlemanly white racism of employers, the discrimination of white parents who object to having their children go to school with Negroes, the disgruntlement of white taxpayers who deride the present welfare system as a sinkhole of public funds but are unwilling to see it replaced by anything more effective—the consequences of these and other

Panel 11-4 (Continued)

forms of white racism have confronted the police with a massive control problem of the kind most evident in the riots.

In our survey, we found that the police were inclined to see the riots as the long range result of faults in the Negro community—disrespect for law, crime, broken families, etc.—rather than as responses to the stance of the white community. Indeed, nearly one-third of the white police saw the riots as the result of what they considered the basic violence and disrespect of Negroes in general, while only one-fourth attributed the riots to the failure of white institutions. More than three-fourths also regarded the riots as the immediate result of agitators and criminals—a suggestion contradicted by all the evidence accumulated by the riot commission. The police, then, share with the other groups—excepting the black politicians—a tendency to emphasize perceived defects in the black community as an explanation for the difficulties that they encounter in the ghetto.

Several less central theories often accompany the "rotten apple" view. These theories, too, are widely shared in our society. First, the police widely blame the current rise in crime on a turn away from traditional religiousness, and they fear an impending moral breakdown. Yet the best recent evidence shows that people's religious beliefs and attendance neither reduce nor increase their propensity toward crime.

But perhaps the main target of current police thinking is permissive child-rearing, which many policemen interviewed by our task force view as having led to a generation "that thinks it can get what it yells for." Indeed, one officer interviewed justified the use of physical force on offenders as a corrective for lack of childhood discipline. "If their folks had beat 'em when they were kids, they'd be straight now. As it is, we have to shape 'em up."

The police also tend to view perfectly legal social deviance, such as long hair worn by men, not only with extreme distaste but as a ladder to potential criminality.

Nonconformity comes to be viewed with nearly as much suspicion as actual law violation; correspondingly, the police value the familiar, the ordinary, the status quo, rather than social change. These views both put the police at odds with the dissident communities with whom they have frequent contact and detract from their capacity to appreciate the reasons for dissent, change, or any form of innovative social behavior.

Source: Jerome H. Skolnick, The Politics of Protest, A Report Submitted to the Task Force on the Violent Aspects of Protest and Confrontation of the National Commission on the Causes and Prevention of Violence, *Washington, D.C., U.S. Government Printing Office, 1969, pp. 259–262.*

One source of resentment among blacks is the overwhelming white presence on the police force and throughout the criminal justice system.

poor, the unemployed, and minorities. The "criminal-types" that comprise this "class" were referred to in general by police officers in Toronto as "scum" (Shearing, 1979).

Further evidence that the police are significantly involved in a "nonlegalistic" social control is indicated by their estimation that 90 to 95 percent of their policing contact is with "fresh meat," "shrods," "dirt bags," "first contacts," "petty troublemakers," "dirty people"—not serious criminal offenders.

The police come to know what they know by "creating" circumstances that will confirm their view of what is going on. Through the self-fulfilling prophecy (see Merton, 1968) the police become convinced that their knowledge and beliefs about their work world are indeed "correct" or "accurate." Panel 11-5 illustrates the way in which the "lay social theory" of the police is self-fulfilling and serves to verify and confirm what the police hold to be true in regard to crime and criminals.

The police are aware of the extent to which the abilities, skills, rules, and methods that are required to get the police job adequately done emerge from the concrete policing situations that they encounter. These rules and methods—we will call them "folk methods"—are developed by the police themselves as they engage in policing. They are situationally created, not dictated exclusively by the formal organization of the police department or other special factors or conditions in the community. They emerge primarily because they "work" for the police in the concrete situations they encounter.

Often, the rules and methods employed by the working police officer can directly contradict the formal rules and methods required by the law and the police department. For instance, an out-of-state licensed vehicle can be less likely to receive a ticket for, say, running a red light, than an in-state vehicle. This is

PANEL 11-5

The Self-fulfilling Prophecy: How Police Knowledge and Beliefs about Crime and Criminals Are Confirmed

A police officer assigned to the downtown area stops to make a bar check (designed simply to make the police visible) at the "rough" bar. "This bar is so rough that you never find any women in it. . . ." Upon entering, the police officer and I are encountered by two young white males standing at the end of the bar—obviously "dirt bags"—who have long since passed the initial stages of drunkenness. They begin by expressing their resentment toward the Chicanos at the back of the bar who are supposedly monopolizing the pool table. They check our skin to make sure we are white and then attempt to solicit our support vis-a-vis the Chicanos. When the police officer does not cooperate with their plan they begin to grow agitated. They begin to point accusing fingers at our chests (calling the patrol officer a "pig," and the observer a "lawyer"). Pretty soon, their hands are on our chests. The patrol officer slowly and gracefully excuses us from the situation. Upon leaving the bar, the police officer says, "Within an hour we'll be called to respond to a fight in this bar. . . ." Within half an hour three police cars answer a call at that bar. A fight is in progress. One of the "dirt bags" we encountered initially is unconscious under the pool table. A Chicano had responded to a derogatory remark with a pool cue to his temple. The police officer's knowledge of what kinds of people, involved in what kinds of circumstances, engage in criminal behavior, is confirmed. He "knows" he's "right". . . .

Source: Doug A. Timmer, Organizational and Phenomenological Determinants of Local Crime Control: The Historical Selectivity of Municipal Policing, *unpublished dissertation, Fort Collins: Colorado State University, 1981.*

particularly true, where an out-of-state party must be bonded, creating a just-as-soon-avoided piece of dreaded paperwork for the officer on the street. The folk methods of the working officer supersede the formal requirements of the law.

The police production of folk methods is not something that is accomplished at one point in time and then mechanically applied whenever the appropriate circumstances arise. For instance, the recent proliferation of reported sexual assaults, rapes, obscene phone calls, threats on women's lives and sexuality, and other sexually motivated episodes vis-a-vis females have increasingly put the police in what they feel is a relatively helpless and hapless situation. Officers have only recently begun to create methods that offer the "practical" solution to the problem of somehow telling a victimized woman that her victimization is a serious matter that should be reported to the police, and at the same time letting her know that there is very little they can or will do about it.

Another example: folk methods emerge for a slow shift "when there's nothing going on." Generally, either the patrol car is parked and the ever-present burden of paperwork is caught up on, or there is the very conscious attempt to create conditions that need to be controlled. As a ready and reliable instrument to assist in this creation, each patrol officer carries a radar gun. Consciously, the police resort to radar on a "slow Sunday night." "You can always get a speeder, anytime you want one. . . ."

When confronted with it, the reality of police folk methods often makes sense to the police officer. He/she cannot generally articulate them, however. To a significant extent, the police officer believes that he/she is the only person who "knows" how policing is done, that no one can really instruct the police, tell them how to police.

Scrutiny of the folk methods employed by patrol officers to accomplish police work reveals that formal law enforcement training is often overshadowed by control strategies and survival techniques learned "on the beat." Many officers, for example, tend to regard "backing up"—providing assistance to an officer initially called to answer a complaint—as more preferable police-work than actually confronting a situation requiring the invocation and application of legal authority (i.e., requiring the use of police power and making an arrest). "Backing up" is used not only to provide protection and security to other officers; it is also used to create the dramatic impression of real involvement in direct policing when it may actually not be occurring.

Folk methods also include policing techniques that are not necessarily legal. The utilization of legal and law enforcement authority can be determined by individual officer "profit-motivation": for example, travel (all expenses paid court appearances in desirous geographic and climatic regions) and income ("pin money" for the officer via the collection of municipal court fines). Also, policing is routinely interrupted by the unwanted paperwork that particular arrests would entail and, as mentioned above, law enforcement activity is subject to the arbitrary control inherent in "slow-shift folk methods."

Finally, it is clear that police officer folk methods constantly change, adapt, and evolve. The changing requirements for social control in society require constant renegotiation and reconstruction of the police officer folk methods for accomplishing police work.[12]

Conclusion

If anything at all emerges from the interactionist analysis of policing, it is that a great amount of police discretion occurs, in terms of any kind of application of the law, to behaviors that are "objectively" illegal. That is to say, sometimes the police legally sanction illegal behaviors; sometimes they do not.

---

[12] The findings presented in this chapter are not intended to criticize or chastise the individual police officer. There is a need in criminology and sociology to begin to understand the police as part of the working class—as workers with a unique relationship to the ruling class' "means of social control." (For efforts in this direction see Rainwater, 1967; Johnson, 1976; Robinson, 1978.)

The social reality of the police subculture and police discretion suggests that the police are actually involved in social control, even though official law enforcement policy in the United States espouses crime control. The notion that the police are practicing social control, not crime control, is thus derived from both radical criminology's analysis of the historical origins and development of law enforcement agencies in the United States, and the interactionist approach to understanding the social psychology of policing, the police subculture, and police discretion.

The law is but one instrument or resource available to the police in controlling a situation or community. Police officers believe they "control situations"; not that they "mechanically apply the law." "We keep the community the way it is. . . ."

In many policing situations the law is not technically involved at all. Questions of "order maintenance"—domestic disputes, the public use of streets, neighborhood conflicts, labor disputes and strikes—illustrate this point (see Manning, 1974a; Bittner, 1967). "The police rarely deal with 'crime' and 'criminals'; they deal for the most part with requests for service that are not imbedded in a legal context" (Manning, 1974a, p. 24).

The law will most likely be invoked—mechanically applied to the police-encountered situation—if its end purpose is social control. If this end is not served, utilization of legal authority, that is, the law, is often notably absent (see Mehan and Wood, 1975, p. 86–91). This suggests two possibilities, both referred to in our earlier discussion of the failure of U.S. law enforcement efforts in the area of "organized" crimes: organized, corporate, and political crime. One, that control of social situations is as important a variable in explaining police behavior as is whether or not legal or illegal activity is encountered. And, two, that illegal activities often go "unpoliced" because of their contribution to social order, stability, and control.

The police consistently maintain that "circumstances" must always be weighed against the mechanical application of the law when considering an arrest. (The police officer is normally quite conscious of this process in his or her behavior.) For example, few arrests are made for domestic and neighborhood fights and disturbances. "It would probably only make the situation worse in the future. . . ."[13]

Police folk methods attempt to approach the optimum in social control. The police officer must learn the proper use and combination of tickets and arrests vis-a-vis verbal and written warnings. In many ways, this "balance" represents the most efficient and effective control of the situation and/or the community. Too many tickets and arrests may result in citizen resentment and thus increasing problems of social control.[14] Not enough tickets and arrests, on the other hand, may lead to the deterioration of police authority, where "there is nothing behind our threats to enforce the law. . . ." Generally, it appears as though the police normally attempt to write as few tickets and make as few arrests as possible, but still maintain their respect, authority, and ability to control situations, neighborhoods, and communities.

[13] Again, all quotes, unless otherwise noted, are from police officers themselves.
[14] It is interesting to hear "older" officers discuss the "newer" officers' inevitable fear of writing tickets and making arrests, that is, the initial fear of confronting people with police authority.

THE SOCIAL ORGANIZATION OF THE POLICE BUREAUCRACY

Continuing with our consideration of the question, "What is policed and what is not?", we now examine the organization and operations of the typical municipal police department. Specifically, we begin to delineate the ways in which the police bureaucracy itself determines what types of crime, under what conditions, tend to be policed.

Bureaucratic Constraints to Crime Control

Compared with other formal organizations (see, e.g., Blau and Scott, 1962; Haas and Drabek, 1973; Hall, 1977; Perrow, 1979), police departments possess at least one very unique characteristic: the lowest-level members of the police hierarchy—patrol officers working the street—have a great deal of latitude in doing their work (cf. Bittner, 1970). Police officer discretion is high. "To a great extent, the work of the patrol officer is unsupervised, and to a lesser extent it is unsupervisable" (Lundman, 1980, p. 53). For most of his/her eight-hour shift, a patrol officer is out on the street. Hence, police supervisors have no reliable method for determining what their officers are doing.[15]

To rectify this problem in the police hierarchy, municipal police departments have devised an alternate system for assessing police officer accountability and efficiency. Again, however, a paradox emerges: this alternate system of supervision leads police activity away from crime control and toward more arbitrary forms of social control.

1. *Organizational accountability: paperwork and crime control.* Municipal police officers are literally overwhelmed with paperwork. Since sergeants, lieutenants, and captains cannot be physically present, the police officer's shift behavior is monitored and evaluated by his/her written account of nearly anything and everything that transpires in that eight-hour period. Patrol officers must document when they go on duty and when they leave, when they go to the toilet, when they take a coffee break, weather conditions, radio calls when they were assigned, mileage driven during their shift, and the traffic citations they issue. There are also forms to be filled out for criminal incidents, accident reports, arrest reports; special forms are required if the officer is involved in an accident him/herself, uses physical force, or fires a gun. This incessant documentation and paperwork overload is a real determinant of police activity and behavior. Police officers actually begin to make decisions about whether or not to invoke legal authority—to police—based on the extent to which paperwork is already backlogged or on the amount of additional paperwork intervention in a particular situation would require.

2. *Organizational effectiveness: "statistical performance records" and crime control.* Does this kind of alternate system of police officer accountability and supervision lead to any sort of effective attainment of the police organization's stated goal and

---

[15] Recently, many large metropolitan area police departments have begun to attempt to rectify this situation by "Taylorizing" police work. See the discussion below.

purpose: crime prevention and control? Recent research findings answer this question with a fairly unequivocal "no!"

Labor negotiations that have ended in police strikes have ironically made clear what the police must otherwise attempt to make invisible: contemporary municipal police departments often do little or nothing to prevent or control crime. Police strikes have seldom resulted in even minimal increases in crime rates:

> In the case of crime, factors like the birth rate, unemployment, the sense of community that exists in a given neighborhood, and even the weather probably have much more to do with the incidence of crime than do the police. (Goldstein, 1977, p. 14)

National clearance rates[16] published in the FBI's Uniform Crime Reports suggest that investigative police-work is extremely ineffective. In 1977, for example, the national clearance rate for homicide in the United States was 75 percent, for aggravated assault, 62 percent; for rape, 51 percent; for robbery, 27 percent; 20 percent for larceny; 16 percent for burglary; and 15 percent for auto theft. A U.S. Department of Justice-Rand Corporation study (Greenwood, Chaiken, Petersilia, and Prusoff, 1975) of the criminal investigative process leads to the same conclusion. This study analyzed mailed questionnaires returned by 153 detective bureaus, and follow-up visits to 25 police departments. They found that detectives spend most of their time involved in dead-end interviews with victims. The researchers also found that most cleared cases are the result of offender identification at the time the offense is reported to the police. For cases without this immediate offender identification, clerical tasks like checking mug shots and *modus operandi* files were found to produce a large majority of additional clearances. The study concluded that at least one half of the officers assigned to detective bureaus could be dismissed or reassigned without altering existing clearance rates.

Through these rates, police bureaucracies are made accountable to their funding sources—municipal, state, and federal governments. Rates become, in turn, extremely political creatures (see Chapter 4). Rates must prove the police effective; the police department must at least be perpetuated at present levels. But rates must not convey the impression of an overly effective police department; it must appear as though the crime problem is still not under control and increased funding and bureaucratic expansion are necessary. In short, these rates are often manipulated for political and bureaucratic purposes.

Municipal police departments routinely rely on two related procedures for constructing "satisfactory" statistical rates: unfounding and defounding. Unfounding refers to the process of "statistically declaring" that particular unsolved crimes

---

[16] Clearance rate simply refers to the percent of reported crimes solved through patrol and investigative police work.

were never crimes committed in the first place. Defounding involves "statistically lessening" unsolved felonies to misdemeanors. Both procedures, of course, effectively raise clearance rates.

In this way, the organized crime control efforts of the police most often lower crime rates, not levels of crime itself.

The Nixon administration's early-1970s "law and order" rhetoric led to the establishment of a "national crime control laboratory" in Washington, D.C. Given the necessary financial resources and police personnel, the city was to become a model in efficient and effective crime control. Crime statistics—rates— were used to measure the success of this program. Crime rates did fall, particularly burglary and larceny. Crime did not fall because of increased police activity and resources, however; they fell because of defounding. Seidman and Couzens have concluded that:

> at least part of the decline in crime statistics for the District of Columbia is attributable to increased downgrading of larcenies and, to a lesser extent, of burglaries. This appears to be a pure case of the reactivity of a social indicator: the fact that the statistic is used as a measure of performance affects the statistic itself. The political importance of crime apparently caused pressures, subtle or otherwise, to be felt by those who record crime—pressures, which have led to the downgrading of crimes. (1974, p. 476)

A decrease in New York City's crime rate provides another illustration of this process. In a recent year, the city's crime rate decreased and the clearance rate increased, both at very significant levels. This occurred when both of these rates in all other large American cities were proceeding in the opposite direction. When a reform police administration finally brought unfounding and defounding under control, the effects on crime in New York City were astounding: within one month's time both robbery and assault increased by 200 percent, larceny by 300 percent and burglary by 500 percent (Lundman, 1980, pp. 65–66).

Yet another example of the lack of a relationship between the municipal police bureaucracy and actual crime control is the Kansas City Preventive Patrol Experiment (Kelling, Pate, Dieckman, and Brown, 1974). In this experiment, three demographically similar areas of Kansas City were assigned differential police presence and activity. One area received regular patrol; a second, double patrol; and the third, no patrol (police entered this area only when its residents requested their presence to make an arrest). The researchers reported at the end of the experimental period that no differences existed between the three areas in terms of crime rates. And, as Lundman has added, "On the basis of their own experiences, most precinct administrators and patrol officers know that the findings of the Kansas City Experiment are essentially correct" (1980, p. 66).

This profound inability to control crime effectively is important to the extent that it turns municipal police bureaucracies toward something they can provide with much more efficiency and effectiveness—a more arbitrary social control.

Bureaucratically Induced Social Control

Since police administrators are aware that the policing of felony crimes and making felony arrests is largely out of their control and that superior administration and extra patrol officer efforts in this area will not significantly better department statistical performance records, police resources and personnel are deployed to areas where they *can* control their own performance: meter, parking, and traffic violations; public drunkenness; domestic disturbances; and the like. To help ensure that these activities under the control of the police administration yield acceptable statistical performance records, ingenious methods of arbitrary control are employed. Lundman has reported:

> A sergeant short of parking or meter citations will assign a silent car—one that dispatch does not know is out on the street—to do nothing but write citations. I once rode with a patrol officer in a silent car who wrote 32 parking citations in eight hours. The officer took only a short lunch break and was exhausted when finished. The officer's sergeant and colleagues, however, were most pleased (1980, p. 67).

And he further documents the arbitrary character of this police work:

> A sergeant in need of moving violations will also put a silent car out and may give the officer the privilege of leaving early provided a certain number of citations have been issued. In this circumstance, the officer typically goes to a location known to be productive of traffic law violations. In most cities, there are intersections with short yellow lights. Large numbers of motorists regularly go through on the red, thereby providing officers with a nearly inexhaustible source of moving violations (Lundman, 1980, 67).

Petersen's (1971, pp. 358–359) study of police officers' reactions to traffic law violations has confirmed Lundman's observations. In a police department emphasizing traffic law enforcement, police officers were under pressure to issue traffic citations. To ease this pressure, patrol officers developed an informal quota system of around 40 traffic citations per month per officer. Patrol officers were encouraged by their peers not to deviate too far from this subcultural norm. Officers were free, however, to determine how and when they produced their citations: some worked traffic regularly, others only toward the end of the month, still others worked traffic aggressively early in the month and became lax later on. Petersen has reported that:

> On one occasion an officer and the writer sat in an immobile patrol car in a deserted parking lot in the city for more than three hours. "I'm a little tired tonight," the officer explained. "Besides I've got thirty (citations) already this month, and it's only July 11th." (1971, pp. 358–359)

In sum, for bureaucratic and organizational reasons—the formalization of work performance, organizational effectiveness, and accountability (see Price, 1968)—police personnel who might otherwise be involved in other activities, like crime control, spend their time and resources producing "good numbers," numbers that ensure the police department's survival.[17]

Police Department "Styles"

Although the internal organizational operation of the police bureaucracy is a real determinant of police behavior, it is clearly not its only determinant. The wider community context within which municipal policing occurs can be so influential in this regard that distinct styles of police work may emerge. James Q. Wilson (1968) has identified three such styles:[18]

1. *Watch-style policing.* This tends to predominate in very large, old cities that have large minority and poor populations. Machine politics usually control both the police department and the city in general. Chicago under Mayor Daley and Philadelphia under Mayor Frank Rizzo typified the city political machine replete with a watch-style police department.

Avoidance characterizes the approach of the watch-style police: traffic violations, many juvenile offenses, domestic disputes, and many other misdemeanors are simply ignored. Policing in the minority and poor neighborhoods is minimal as long as residents prey upon and victimize each other. Victimless crimes are not policed in the face of community tolerance and even the encouragement of city hall. In short, order maintenance, not technical law enforcement is the primary orientation of these departments. And although the police often follow the path of least resistance and are inclined to render an informal "street justice" in many situations, they are notoriously hard-nosed and tough when in a more serious circumstance that they believe requires it.

Generally, watch-style policing is said to be highly discretionary and discriminatory: minorities, the poor, the unemployed, the young and defiant tend to be singled out and receive an undue amount of police attention. "Curbside justice" often means the frequent use of unnecessary force—on occasion, even the use of deadly force. Crimes without victims, on the other hand, often go unpoliced because the police have been paid to protect the interests of organized crime. Thus, police corruption tends to be widespread in watch-style departments.

2. *The legalistic style of policing.* This tends to occur in cities demographically similar to the "watch-style metropolis" that have experienced the decay of a political machine and are in the political control of a reform city government and police department.

The legalistic-style police department also is usually located in a newer and more affluent city than the watch-style department, many times administered by

---

[17] Much of the first part of this section has been taken from Timmer (1981).
[18] The discussion of police styles that follows is taken primarily from Lundman (1980, pp. 45–51).

Watch-style policing is characterized by tough treatment of minorities, the poor, the unemployed, the young, and the defiant.

professional city managers. This style of policing aims to be professional but unobtrusive.

According to Wilson, enforcement is the dominant characteristic of police work in these settings. All juvenile offenses, domestic problems, traffic violations, public drunkenness, and participation in the so-called vices are seen as situations requiring formal police intervention. Therefore, the legalistic-style department generates large numbers of traffic citations and arrests.

3. *Service-style policing.* This takes place most frequently in the affluent suburbs surrounding large cities. These suburbs are almost exclusively white and middle and upper class.

Service-style departments are prone to take all calls for police assistance and intervention seriously and are more "proactive" than the watch and legalistic departments. Yet, according to Wilson, leniency is what characterizes this style of police work. Police intervention is frequent but informal and leisurely. Troublesome juveniles, traffic offenders, and those who are drunk and/or disorderly are counseled and warned, not arrested or ticketed. Domestic disputes are normally handled with "crisis intervention" counseling or referred to an appropriate social service agency. And a positive police-community relations orientation pervades the active service-style department.

Of course, the potential for police corruption in these affluent suburbs is insignificant as compared with the watch-style department since organized crime and vice is normally located in the core or central city. The unnecessary use of police force is also diminished in this context as its usual victims—members of the minority and poor underclass—are not present and therefore do not present the perceived threat to community order and stability.

Since they are found in relatively wealthy and homogeneous communities, service-oriented police departments are provided with the economic means that make this kind of policing possible. They are asked to provide this sort of law enforcement service because of the relative lack of culture, race, and class conflict. Most of those policed by the service-style department share the same cultural traditions and aspirations, the same life-styles and values, as do the police themselves. Community consensus concerning the role of law enforcement is evident. Limited police budgets and resources and high levels of economic inequality and racial and class conflict, by contrast, are more typical of the old urban centers with large minority and poor populations, where watch-style policing is more the norm.

The watch and service styles are further contrasted (indeed, they seem to be the polar extremes or opposites in Wilson's discussion of the three styles of policing) when the influence of organized crime on the political institutions at work in their respective communities is examined:

> The political orientation of elected officials in the communities served by watch departments contributes to this style of policing. In these communities, elected officials often represent privatized or special interests. The interests of the community's elite are almost always represented, but frequently the interests of those who provide illegal but widely demanded services—gambling, prostitution, drugs, and pornographic materials—are among those considered important by elected officials. Often this is the case because elected officials are illegally paid to represent these interests. . . . A police department in such a community generally has little choice but to offer a watch style of policing, one that ignores the criminal actions of persons protected by elected officials. . . . (Lundman, 1980, p. 50)

Police Professionalization, Unionization, and Taylorization

The police are workers in American society, workers facing the same problems that other public employees and many workers in the private sector encounter. These problems—adequate wages, health and safety, retirement pensions, and job security—became extremely critical for the police beginning in the first two decades of the 20th century. As Panel 11-6 indicates, these problems still confront the police as workers.

From the Boston police strike of 1919 onward, one of the primary responses of the rank-and-file police to help ensure better wages, benefits, and security has been efforts at unionization for purposes of collective bargaining with city and police administrations. But, as Panel 11-6 indicates, these efforts have not always been successful, at least not initially. By 1920, the first wave of police unionization had by and large been discredited and police officers in most cities found themselves without an effective voice in the administration of their departments. As a result, the police tended to retreat to their "Benevolent," "Protective," and "Fraternal" orders, associations, and organizations. These groups, for the most part, shied away from any attempts at labor organization or collective bargaining. In fact, they were not politically involved in much of any way.

The defeat of these first attempts at police unionism aided in the development of the police subculture discussed earlier in this chapter. Without an established procedure for expressing their grievances in the police bureaucracy, much police anger, hostility, suspicion, frustration, and alienation were displaced and turned on the public, the communities, and the neighborhoods they policed. In this way, the police rank and file became isolated from the community and reinforced this isolation and estrangement by tending to associate only with other members of the subculture, both on and off the job. To this day, police officers tend to limit their interaction to other police officers, not only in the workplace, but in their private, personal, and social life as well (Walker, 1980).

Perhaps a more significant occurrence in the local police department accompanied the defeat of rank-and-file unionization in the 1920s: police executives and administrators found their position and control strengthened. Indeed, internally at least, American municipal police departments became increasingly authoritarian over the next 40 years. Only a second wave of police unionization and racial turmoil in large American cities, both beginning in the 1960s, would challenge this severe management.

Confounding police work still further in the 1960s was a federal government-assisted thrust toward "police professionalization." Police professionalization had been advocated, without much success, by all sorts of police reformers for over 50 years. In 1967, the President's Commission on Law Enforcement and the Administration of Justice reported that municipal police departments in the United States were badly in need of reform. As a former director of the federal government's National Institute of Justice put it, the nation's 17,000 local police departments were found to be "essentially unsophisticated, lethargic, erratic and inefficient" (quoted in Lewin, 1982, p. 4).

Police professionalization over the next 15 years was characterized basically by an enormous federal expenditure (primarily through the Law Enforcement Assistance Administration) on police training, education, and research. Whereas, "years ago, a young man could be made a cop by barely being literate" (according to Patrick Murphy, Director of the Police Foundation in Washington, D.C.; quoted in Lewin, 1982, p. 4), today, after some 15 to 20 years of federal tuition grants and loans, it may be that more than half of all U.S. police officers have some college credit and many of them have earned undergraduate and even graduate degrees.

Police professionalization, however, did not turn out to be the successful reform it was touted to be. It created at least as many problems as it solved, perhaps more. Most significantly, it aggravated both police-community relations and relations within the department.

PANEL 11-6

Police as Workers: The Boston Police Strike: Then* and Now[†]

Then . . .

The strike by the Boston police in September 1919 is perhaps the most famous event in the history of American policing. Coming in the midst of nationwide racial turmoil, the Red Scare, and bitter strikes in other major industries, it galvanized public fears of a breakdown in law and order. President Woodrow Wilson called it a "crime against civilization," and Massachusetts governor Calvin Coolidge built his own national political reputation on the basis of his statement that "there is no right to strike against the public safety by anybody, anywhere, at any time."

The immediate cause of the strike was the inflation produced by the wartime economy. The cost of living doubled between 1915 and 1920, while salaries for the police and most other public employees remained the same. In addition to the basic necessities of life, Boston police officers had to purchase their own uniforms, and the price of these doubled during the war. Police officers also felt bitter and alienated because their status had dropped relative to that of other working people. During the nineteenth century, police salaries had far exceeded the earnings of factory workers and skilled craftsmen. But as unionism spread among these other occupations, the police lost their traditional advantage. . . .

Prounion sentiment among the police spread rapidly across the country in 1917. It was a spontaneous, grass-roots movement, for police officers were impressed by the gains made by unions in the private sector. The movement caught organized labor off guard. The American Federation of Labor had serious reservations about attempting to organize the police. In June 1919, however, grassroots pressure forced the AFL to change its position. It endorsed unionism and in the next two months issued charters to thirty-three of the sixty-five locals that applied for recognition. . . .

Events took a very different turn in Boston. The officers' fraternal group, the Boston Social Club, began seeking a $200 a year raise in late 1917. After negotiations produced nothing for a year and a half, the club voted to become a union and affiliate with the AFL. The question of affiliation became the principal obstacle to a settlement. Police Commissioner Edwin U. Curtis, an arrogant and inflexible person, ordered his officers to disaffiliate. When they refused Curtis took disciplinary action against the leaders of the Boston Social Club. The firing of nineteen officers precipitated the strike. . . .

Panel 11-6 (Continued)

On Tuesday afternoon, September 9, 1919, a total of 1,117 police officers walked off their jobs, leaving only 427 officers available for duty. Disorder erupted in the city. In addition to looting and vandalism, citizens attacked both striking and non-striking officers. Prominent members of the community, including many from Harvard University, organized a volunteer force to help preserve order. After much confusion and delay, Governor Coolidge mobilized the state militia, which took control of the city by Thursday afternoon. Compared with the recent race riots, the disorders were rather limited. But newspapers across the country painted a lurid and exaggerated picture of "anarchy" in Boston.

Public opinion turned against the police, and the strike soon collapsed. All the striking officers were fired and replaced by new recruits. Meanwhile, police unionism in other cities quickly subsided, and by 1920 the movement was completely dead. The Boston police strike discredited police unionism for decades. . . .

and now . . .

TERRE HAUTE, Ind. (AP) Policemen here went on strike Wednesday after rejecting a pay raise proposal, leaving the city's protection to the department chief and about a dozen officers.

The policemen voted Tuesday night to reject the City Council's offer of a $200-per-year, across-the-board pay raise. Some 110 of the 122 officers struck. Members of the Fraternal Order of Police are seeking a 15 percent pay raise. . . .

Some of the striking policemen, along with spouses and children, camped in front of City Hall Tuesday night and Wednesday.

Police Chief Gerald Loudermilk spent Tuesday night at headquarters along with an assistant chief and a civilian radio operator. Officials said two patrol cars were touring Terre Haute streets. "I thought that I would have more people," Loudermilk said.

Mayor Pete Chalos said his administration is "willing to meet with these people anytime if they want to bring somebody in to look at the books." Chalos said the city would need nearly $700,000 to meet pay raise requests from the police and firemen.

The mayor blamed the city's budget problems on reduction in federal funds, increased utility costs and a freeze on property taxes.

First-year or probationary officers in this city of 63,800 receive $9,230 annually. After the first year, an officer receives a base pay of $11,131, the patrolman's wage committee said. The raise sought by the policemen would boost that annual base pay to $12,800.65.

*Source: Samuel Walker, Popular Justice: A History of American Criminal Justice, New York: Oxford University Press, 1980, pp. 166–169.
†Source: The Associated Press, "Terre Haute Policemen Reject Pact, Stage Walkout," July 16, 1981.

The Kerner Commission, studying the causes of the race riots that besieged many large American cities in the 1960s, reported on the aggravating influence of professionalization: "many of the serious disturbances took place in cities whose police are among the best led, best organized, best trained, and most professional in the country" (quoted in Walker, 1980, p. 240). But the professional departments' "aggressive stop-and-frisk tactics" purported to be required for effective crime control only served to arouse the resentment of those who were most often its target: young, poor, un- and underemployed blacks in the inner cities. Here, police professionalization came to mean police repression and it seems plausible that "a half century of professionalization had created police departments that were vast bureaucracies, inward-looking, isolated from the public, and defensive in the face of any criticism" (Walker, 1980, p. 240).

Professionalization also failed to correct a long history of racist hiring practices in big-city police departments. In the 1970s and on into the 1980s, the proportion of black police officers continued to lag behind the proportion of the total black population in almost all urban centers.[19] And, even though a recent Police Foundation study in Washington, D.C. found women patrol officers as effective as men, no large police department is even remotely close to having a female presence that is proportional to the general population.

Inside the police bureaucracy, police professionalization meant an emphasis on managerial efficiency and effectiveness. To accomplish this, the police administration centralized authority and tightened the chain of command. The rank-and-file officers were to carry out their duties "by the book." Police discretion was to be reduced, and perhaps, some of it was. But in the meantime, the individual police officer was subjected to the whims of a highly authoritarian police bureaucracy and a cold and calculated internal discipline. Because of this, those in the police subculture gradually came to feel the same way about the police administration as they did about the public or community in which they worked; hostility and suspicion became divisive factors in the police department. Increasingly, the police rank and file—the police subculture—came into conflict with both the public and the local police administration.

By the mid-1960s then, a second wave of police unionism shook American cities. The police rank and file quickly organized to resist deteriorating wages and benefits, authoritarian police department organization and procedure; charges of police corruption, brutality, and other misconduct (particularly in the black ghetto), and various efforts by liberal mayors (in New York, Boston, Cleveland, and Detroit, for example) to improve police-community and black-white relations. (This latter situation often, paradoxically enough, pitted liberal but antiunion mayors against conservative but prounion police.) Rank-and-file militance, as well as courts that were growing more sympathetic to all kinds of public employee unions, ensured that this outburst of police unionism would be widespread and successful. By the early 1970s, nearly every large city police department in the

---

[19] The Detroit Police Department may be an exception here. By the late 1970s, black officers comprised at least 40 percent of its force.

United States had unionized and was engaged in collective bargaining[20] (Walker, 1980).

Police strikes were common in the 1970s: New York City officers went out on strike in 1971, Baltimore officers in 1974, and the San Francisco police in 1975. Alternatives to actual strikes also were used by the unions. These job actions included "sick-ins," "blue-flu" epidemics, and work slowdowns and speed-ups, where officers would either write very few tickets and make very few arrests or would produce an enormous number of each.

But strikes and other job actions were not the only effects of this resurgent tide of police unionism. A significant decentralization of administrative power and authority in the police bureaucracy took place. "Police chiefs accustomed to exercising virtually unlimited power suddenly found that almost every administrative decision was subject to negotiation" (Walker, 1980, pp. 241–242). The police rank-and-file had gained some voice in the administration of their departments. This was most evident in the approaches several departments took in regard to police reform. Reforms like "team policing" and "the task force approach to innovation," for example, recognized the need for the direct participation of the police rank and file in police administration (Walker, 1980).

Many of these gains, made by police unions in the 1960s and early and middle 1970s, however, would not survive the late 1970s and early 1980s. The continued flight of affluent whites and business from the central cities, leaving the centers of metropolitan areas (particularly in the Northeast and Midwest) with a greatly reduced tax base, combined with the prolonged and severe economic recession (a depression in many large U.S. cities) to bring many municipal governments to the edges of bankruptcy. The cities' budgetary and fiscal crises meant layoffs, cutbacks, and wage and benefit concessions for the police, as it did for many other workers in both the public and private sectors.

In many circles, an extremely simplistic and conservative response to the city's fiscal crises was to blame public employee unions (including police unions) for it, the premise being that the unions had pushed the costs of city government too high. Sidney Harring (1981) has offered an alternative explanation for the fate of the police in the late 1970s and early 1980s—what he calls the "Taylorization of police work." We will examine his argument in some detail here.

According to Harring, the kinds of studies noted throughout this chapter indicating that the degree of police presence has little to do with effective crime control, as reflected in official crime rates, combined with this fiscal crisis to provide a rationale for reducing the size of the police force by eliminating rank-and-file officers. In addition to those studies mentioned earlier, others showed that one-person cars were as effective as two-person cars and were no more dangerous and that police "response time" (the time required by the police to get to the place where they've been called) was not an important factor in solving crimes.

In addition to these cutbacks that began in the mid- and late 1970s and so adversely effected the police rank and file, other changes were occurring in the

---

[20] No single union was able to dominate, however, and efforts at establishing national unions met with very limited success.

nature of police work itself. These changes that have begun to undo the inroads police unions had made into police administration in the preceding decade that Harring refers to as Taylorization.[21]

Taylorization means that the division of labor in the police department is increased (police work is broken down into more and more highly specialized tasks), patrol work becomes more "reactive" and more dangerous, and technology is used to reconcentrate authority and control in the hands of the police administration:

> The general and interesting work of a police officer increasingly is being broken down into single function tasks, with specialists hired in specific task lines. While an officer might previously have done 911 emergency telephone work, traffic work, desk work, and night patrol over a few years of a 20 year career, now all those tasks except night patrol increasingly are outside of the police role. This not only sets up isolated and alienating low pay "careers" for civilians (who take on each of the various functions done previously by the police); it has the same effect on the police officer. He is left simply a "patrolman." But even his patrol work has been modified; the level of autonomy is reduced as the independent patrol is succeeded by a "response" type of patrol, not entirely unlike the work of the fire department. Instead of going from fire to fire, the patrolman will go from felony crime to felony crime: highly dangerous work, much more tightly controlled by a dispatcher and senior officer . . . there also is no question that . . . computerization (of police-work) leads to increased management control over the police labor process. (Harring, 1981, pp. 28–29, parentheses added)

Harring goes on to argue that since "Taylorization" separates and isolates police officers from the police administration (and from "specialized" civilian workers who begin to perform duties formerly belonging to the police), we can expect a decline in the effectiveness of the police department taken as a whole. This, in turn, will cause city and police administrators to speed up the Taylorization process in hopes of making up the difference. Taylorization becomes the solution to the problem of Taylorization.

Professionalization has also been impacted by the Taylorization of police work. Cutbacks, layoffs, wage and benefit reductions, coupled with declining and limited promotional opportunities, have undermined the notions of police work being a "career" or a "profession" for many of the police rank and file:

> Virtually all of the police officers attending John Jay College, a bastion of the ideal of police "professionalism," are officers with 10 to 15 years of service, *who are getting degrees in order to get off the police force as 15 or 20 year retirement time approaches. They explicitly are not getting their degrees to*

---

[21] Taylorization refers to the "scientific management" practices advocated by Frederick Taylor beginning in the 1880s. These practices in American industry had, and have, an almost exclusive focus on the technical aspects of job specialization, efficiency, and effectiveness.

further "professional" ideals or advance their careers. (Harring, 1981, p. 31, italics added)

In sum, throughout the 1970s, changes in the organization of police work itself—what Harring calls its Taylorization—have meant fewer police complaints about the "lack of public support" and more complaints about the "lack of police department support." More and more, the police rank and file, the police subculture, police unions, have found the source of their anger, hostility, suspicion, frustration, and alienation in the organization and administration of the local police department.

Many of the problems presently rampant in the police bureaucracy are the result of a fundamental contradiction inherent in contemporary police work: although the police are workers, although they normally come from and help make up the working class, their function in American society is, to a significant extent, to enforce a social order and control that primarily serves the interests of ruling groups, elites, and classes. In other words, the police themselves are working class but the police institution is not.

This is not the only contradiction that currently plagues American police work. We will conclude this section by at least mentioning some others.

The Contradictions of Contemporary Policing

Accompanying the racial and student unrest of the 1960s was a cry from many segments of society for "law and order." But at the same time some groups "were also far more conscious of the legal aspects of police work and not reluctant to bring suit or file complaints where they felt unjustly treated" by the police (Walker, 1980, p. 251). The police were trapped between those who advocated order at any cost and those who were committed to the preservation of civil liberties and rights. Making police work still more prone to incapacitating tension, conflict, and contradiction were the increasing requests by community members for police intervention in an ever-widening array of noncriminal matters. How could the police be reasonably expected to control serious crime when 80 to 90 percent of their time was spent on other matters? It is no doubt true that this contradiction continues to burden municipal police work at present.

Things worsened in the late 1970s and on into the 1980s. Taxpayers revolted against the ever-increasing costs of city government. As explained earlier, more and more cities found themselves in a budgetary crisis confounded by a prolonged period of economic decline, while recession, depression, and high levels of unemployment helped ensure a healthy and growing crime rate. The calls for reducing the crime rate, ensuring public order and stability, and providing some measure of personal and public safety increasingly fell upon local police departments not up to the task. Diminished budgets and forces, along with internal division precipitated by the processes of Taylorization, had left a weakened police presence and weakened ability to control crime precisely when many in society sensed that a need for greater police strength had emerged.

POLICE DISCRETION REVISITED: CRIMINALITY, BRUTALITY, AND THE USE OF DEADLY FORCE

Police discretion, joined with the historical and contemporary concern with enforcing order (rather than a primary concern with controlling crime) has helped to produce the dark side of American policing. In carrying out their function in society, the police have all too often been criminal themselves; indeed, even brutal and murderous.

Police Criminality and Corruption

Generally, corruption takes place whenever and wherever money, goods and/or services are accepted to ignore activities that are illegal and should be policed, or when these things are accepted by the police to do what they should be doing anyway (Lundman, 1980). More specifically, police corruption and criminality include these activities on the part of the police:

1. Acceptance of free or discount meals and personal services.
2. Acceptance of kickbacks for referrals to "favorite" services such as towing companies, funeral homes, attorneys, and so on.
3. Opportunistic theft from defenseless and helpless persons and unsecured premises.
4. "Shakedowns" of individuals and small businesses (threatening to enforce a normally unenforced law unless payments are made to the police).
5. Providing protection (for a price) for illegal activities (usually those known as organized crime).
6. Fixing cases (again, for the right price).
7. Direct involvement in planned theft.
8. Department assignment and promotion based on "payoffs" inside the police bureaucracy (this list is adapted from Barker and Roebuck, 1973).

Panel 11-7 discusses another kind of police corruption that may be emerging at present. The legality of "entrapment"-type law enforcement methods has not been firmly established even though the FBI's famed ABSCAM operation involving law enforcement efforts to bribe U.S. Congress persons has resulted in criminal convictions and an expulsion from the U.S. Senate.

Reports of police corruption always abound in the mass media:

Item   In Chicago, in the 1960s, most residents knew how to avoid traffic citations and kept a $5 or $10 bill wrapped around their drivers license. Officers routinely took the money and gave the motorist a verbal warning only.

Item   A two-year investigation of Chicago police ended in a 114-page indictment with 67 criminal charges against 10 officers (known as the "Marquette Ten"). The officers were charged with violating federal narcotic, civil rights, racketeering, and extortion laws. Officers were said to accept bribes in return for failing to

PANEL 11-7

Police Entrapment: Crime or Crime Control?

GALVESTON, TEXAS (AP) Deputies investigating what they thought was a drug smuggling operation instead broke up an FBI bribery "sting" and took a federal agent into custody, sheriff's officials say.

"The sting got stung," said Galveston County Deputy Sheriff J.D. Irwin after the capture Thursday of an undercover FBI agent who offered bribes to three county officials.

The agent was released after proving his identity, officials said.

An FBI spokesman in Houston confirmed the events, in part.

"We were involved down there and the sheriff's office did, indeed, take in one of our people," said Johnie Joyce.

Joyce said an operation under way there "was interrupted and we did at that time terminate the situation." Beyond that, said Joyce, he could not comment.

But Sheriff Joe Max Taylor was happy to comment.

According to the sheriff, his investigators marshaled a full-scale undercover operation two months ago aimed at trapping what they believed to be drug suspects offering bribes to local officials to look the other way.

Thirty officers were working on the case with videotape and audio recording equipment borrowed from a Houston TV station. District Judge Don Morgan was re-

cruited to act as a crooked judge, and meetings, under the eye of a hidden camera, were arranged.

As it turned out, said Irwin, "it was spy versus spy. We did a better job than they did."

The FBI agent arranged to meet with two of the sheriff's spies at the plush Galvez Hotel on the Galveston Island beach front.

The federal agent offered to pay $25,000 in bribe money to each law enforcement officer or judge involved in assuring the safe delivery to Galveston of drug shipments, the sheriff said.

The sheriff's men took the agent into custody. Another agent, also part of the federal undercover scheme, fled.

Taylor said the FBI operation had apparently been under way for some time. Local authorities became suspicious, he said, "because of some of the things [the agents] were doing."

The sheriff's officers didn't release the undercover FBI agent until they were assured he was, in fact, with the FBI. That required a long meeting Thursday between Galveston County officials and representatives of the Houston FBI office.

FBI agent Joyce refused to give any details of the meeting but insisted, "It's not because we're embarrassed" but because of Justice Department policy.

Source: The Associated Press, "FBI Gets Stung During a 'Sting,' " June 12, 1982.

enforce narcotics laws and failing to arrest drug dealers. They also were charged with arranging the dismissal of various charges against certain known narcotics figures and with the theft of narcotics seized during arrests that were then sold to other drug dealers. The indictment also alleged that the police officers warned some narcotics dealers of investigations and raids that the police department had planned for them.

Item A federal grand jury indicted nine Miami homicide detectives for stealing over $400,000 in cash and drugs from homicide scenes. The detectives were also charged with aiding Miami's flourishing cocaine trade by working as "inside tipsters" for cocaine racketeer Mario Escandar—who referred to the detectives as his "young men of iron." All in all, prosecutors said the nine detectives were involved in "bribery, extortion, narcotics trafficking, and accepting bribes of money, gifts and cocaine" (United Press International, July 16, 1981).

Item Two Miami police officers were charged with kidnapping and holding for ransom several wealthy Miami area residents (some of them influential drug dealers). The victims were reportedly stopped for routine traffic violations, blindfolded and bound, and then held for "$1 million or their lives." The extent to which police officers were involved in these schemes is not known since, according to the Miami Police Department, some persons paid the ransom and did not report the crime.

Item Fourteen Chicago police officers and two of their wives were arrested in June of 1982. The state attorney's office said the officers were charged with 68 counts of possession and delivery of heroin, cocaine, and marijuana and official misconduct. Some of those indicted had actually sold drugs from their squad cars to police undercover agents (Associated Press, June 12, 1982).

Employing a sociological perspective, we cannot simply attribute police corruption and criminality to the flawed morality or character of the individual police officer (just as we have seen, from a sociological point of view, we cannot blame the biology, psychology, or character of the individual criminal for crime in general). Rather, we must begin to understand how social and organizational factors and processes are at the center of police corruption. The individual police officer who engages in crime and corruption is not necessarily a pathological individual; this dark side of police work may have more to do with the crime and deviance of the police bureaucracy, the police department itself (i.e., with organizational crime and deviance) (see Ermann and Lundman, 1981).

Police corruption does not "stay or go away" simply as a function of the kinds of officers who fill the police role in the police organization. A department of "exemplary" officers does not guarantee the absence of corruption and criminality. Conversely, a department of "morally tainted" officers does not ensure a corrupt department. In many ways, the police role is bigger than the individual officer who fills and "plays" it. When the corrupt officer goes, corruption may stay. The police organization may expect, teach, and require corruption. Corruption in the police role is indeed often "in conformity with internal operating norms, and supported by socialization, peers, and the administrative personnel of the department" (Lundman, 1980, p. 141).

It is not exaggeration to claim that for police corruption to be most "effective," it must be organizational not individual. Lundman has offered this concrete illustration of the organizational character of police corruption that serves to protect the interests of organized crime:

Provision of illegal but widely demanded services such as gambling and narcotics are lucrative enterprises in contemporary society. They also can be risky, since police organizations are charged with the arrest of persons who offer these services. The solution is to pay police to ignore these actions. But it is not sufficient to purchase arrest immunity from a single officer or even a small group of officers. Any unpaid officer can then disrupt these activities. Equally, new police officers may stumble upon such operations or members of the dominant administrative coalition may order that arrests be made. Meaningful arrest immunity only occurs when an entire department is deviant. (1980, pp. 141–142)

Of course the acts of police crime and corruption are carried out by individuals. But it is also true that police corruption could not exist, or at least could not be so "successful," if it did not find its source and vital support in the deviant organization or department.

Police Brutality and Deadly Force

By the 1920s it was apparent that police brutality was widespread in the United States. A national crime commission—the Wickersham Commission—had revealed frequent police use of the "third degree," "the inflicting of pain, physical or mental, to extract confessions or statements." Furthermore, this Commission noted:

cases where the police had suspended criminal suspects by their ankles out of second-story windows and subjected them to beatings and even sexual indignities in an effort to extract confessions. The Detroit police took suspects "around the loop," moving from one station house to another to isolate them from family, friends and legal counsel. The chief of the Buffalo, New York police expressed open contempt for guarantees of individual rights in the U.S. Constitution. (Walker, 1980, p. 174)

But even though police brutality continued to be a problem in the 1930s, 1940s, and 1950s, it was not until the 1960s that it reemerged as a controversial issue in American society. At this time, the civil rights movement exposed the reality of racist and brutal police practices in the black community, as well as the way in which those practices victimized civil rights protesters themselves.

Police brutality may be defined generally as the police use of unnecessary force that is both severe and illegal. Police work has often included the use of violence and brutality most often used in making an arrest.

Item A study in New York City found that the police were making arrests to cover up assaults they had committed against suspects. In this way, the police attempted to conceal their own violence by arresting and charging citizens with some offense (Chevigny, 1969).

Item A deputy sheriff in Los Angeles shot and killed a 17-year-old youth after the youth had reportedly tried to "ram" the patrol car with his car.

Item   Los Angeles police shot and killed a 92-year-old woman involved in a dispute over the payment of her gas bill; 12 shots were fired at her.

Item   Four police officers in Bridgeport, Connecticut were indicted by a federal grand jury for assaulting two teenagers.

Item   After a family member told police in Fairfax County, Virginia that he had seen an officer speeding in a patrol car, four members of his white, middle-class family were assaulted in their own front yard by the police.

Item   On August 13, 1979, the U.S. Justice Department filed a civil rights suit against the Philadelphia Police Department, charging widespread brutality. The suit followed national television's coverage of a confrontation involving Philadelphia police and a local radical, black political organization. Footage showed close-ups of police officers hitting and kicking protesters. Among the charges filed against the Police of Department in the "City of Brotherly Love":

- Shooting nonviolent suspects when deadly force was not required to make an arrest.
- Physically abusing handcuffed suspects.
- Stopping pedestrians and motorists without probable cause and then abusing them if they resisted or protested their being stopped.

The Justice Department said that the Philadelphia police shoot approximately 75 people per year and that citizens file in the neighborhood of 1100 police brutality complaints each year. However, federal officials also said that most of these brutality complaints are dropped because department protection of the officers involved undermines federal attempts to investigate and prosecute. Mayor Frank Rizzo and 19 other top police and city officials were named and charged in the suit. The federal government asked that a court order forbid the police to engage in the brutal practices charged in the suit and also threatened to cut federal funds to the Philadelphia Police Department (the last five "items" reported in *U.S. News and World Report,* August 27, 1979).

Item   After four white police officers in Miami were charged with beating black insurance salesman Arthur McDuffie to death (see Chapter 5), there were widespread reports that the police were operating a "points system" for the violence officers handed out to suspects. The beating and eventual death of McDuffie was said to have rated a police department score of 29 out of a possible 30 (Wright, 1980).

Item   On May 17, 1980, the New Orleans City Council voted to establish a new agency to investigate alleged misconduct of all city employees. The agency was created in response to a series of police shootings of blacks earlier in the year. However, a state grand jury decided not to indict any of the 14 police officers involved in the series of incidents that included the fatal shooting of four blacks.

Cities like Mobile, Memphis, and Houston, in addition to those mentioned above, have also recently seen their police departments officially charged with police brutality.

As is made clear from several of the examples just cited, police brutality can entail the use of not only brutal force, but deadly force as well. Beginning in the late 1950s, and continuing to the present, there have been at least 300 and as many as 600 persons killed by the police each year. These figures mean that between 2 and 4 percent of all U.S. homicides in a given year are the result of police shootings. These shootings are not color-blind. They reflect racist social arrangements and practices in the municipal police department, the entire criminal justice system, and American society in general: about 50 percent of all victims of police shootings are black (Binder and Scharf, 1982).

There are some indications that the late 1970s and early 1980s have seen an increase in police brutality and police use of deadly force. According to a spokesperson for the National Urban League, there have been "increasing incidents of police brutality . . . particularly in the use of deadly force" (quoted in Mouat, 1979, p. 69).

Corroborating this view is a U.S. Commission on Civil Rights study—"Who is Guarding the Guardians?"—released in the autumn of 1981. The three-year investigation of several major U.S. cities concluded that "the volume of complaints of police abuse received by the commission has increased each year, and the nature of alleged abuse has become more serious" (Associated Press, October 17, 1981). The commission also said that "individual citizens have no effective protection from growing police misconduct" and called for "local civilian review procedures and tougher federal laws against police brutality" (Associated Press, October 17, 1981).

Data that would allow us to generalize about the frequency of police brutality are extremely difficult to find. At least part of this difficulty is due to police departments' and administrations' unwillingness to either discuss or recognize police brutality as a significant problem. One study that used civilian observers in patrol cars in Chicago, Boston, and Washington, D.C., found that at least 3 percent of suspects encountered by the police were victimized by unnecessary police force (Reiss, 1976).

Perhaps ironically, perhaps not, police brutality does not usually occur in response to serious crime or serious threats to police officers' safety. Several studies done over the past 40 years (see Westley, 1970; Rubenstein, 1973; Reiss, 1976, for examples) have again and again pointed to defiance of police authority and exceptionally deviant (from the police point of view) behavior on the part of suspects as the primary factors precipitating the excessive, or deadly, use of police force. Reiss' research has indicated that nearly half of all unjustified uses of police force takes place when suspects openly defy police authority. Another third of the instances of police brutality occurred during encounters with those living deviant life-styles: drunken, drug-using, or gay persons.

As with police corruption, police brutality could, in a nonsociological fashion, be attributed to, or blamed on, a few "sick" or "sadistic" individual police officers. "However, the importance of defiance and deviance in precipitating such

PANEL 11-8

Police Brutality: An Interview with Criminologist Paul Takagi

Q Mr. Takagi, will the new concern over brutality hurt police morale and hamper law enforcement?

A No. Criticism of police has been going on for quite some time. Many police officers become very defensive about it—and understandably so—but it's my view that the criticisms will have absolutely no impact on the effectiveness of law enforcement.

There's no evidence that police require the abuse of authority to be able to carry out their jobs. Informed officers will agree.

Q Will increased scrutiny of police work discourage people from entering the field?

A I doubt it. More of a threat to police is the Proposition 13 mentality that is trimming the budgets of police departments. Another factor discouraging police candidates is the trend toward using civilians for jobs once performed by officers—a development that results from overemphasis of management principles. That gets in the way of police work.

Q Just how widespread is police brutality?

A It has gradually increased over the years and ranges all the way from minor abuses of authority to the improper use of firearms. It is hard to get data on the subject without the cooperation of police departments.

However, public health services around the country do track instances of shootings by police that lead to death. These statistics show a gradual rise over the years in the number of civilians who have been killed by police.

Q Where are problems most likely to occur?

A Instances of abuse occur almost everywhere. Southern states rank high on the list of problem areas, but so does California. Philadelphia, Miami, Boston and Chicago have had substantial numbers of people killed by police. And in rural areas of Colorado, New Mexico and Arizona, Chicanos have suffered particular abuse.

Q Who usually are the victims of excessive force by police?

A In terms of shootings, the pattern statistically is that the killing of blacks and Chicanos by police is 10 to 13 times higher per 100,000 population than it has been for whites.

Police abuse of authority has led to all sorts of complaints from the black community. It's a very, very explosive situation.

Q Are you saying that brutality is often racially motivated?

A It seems that way. But it's very important to make the distinction between a situation in which a person has allegedly been physically abused by police and one in which a suspect is in a shoot-out with officers. No one, I think, questions the latter situation.

Panel 11-8 (Continued)

What concerns people, however, are cases in which blacks and other minorities are shot with little provocation. In a recent Los Angeles case, two officers emptied their guns on a black woman who had no firearm. In another recent instance in Oakland, a black youth was shot in the back five times.

A close examination shows that many killings by police do not necessarily result when serious crimes are committed. Shootings might follow from a routine traffic violation or at the scene of a domestic quarrel.

Q Why are minorities more often the target of abuse?

A For one thing, they are arrested at a much higher rate than are whites. There's also the hypothesis—one that I'm beginning to support more—that many white police officers have a fundamental fear of blacks. That accounts for much of the hostility and confrontations that occur.

Q Aren't police under more pressure today?

A Yes. The crime rate has increased enormously in this country in the last 10 to 15 years. The police have a very, very frustrating job, and the public expects them to do more than they realistically can.

Budget cuts in many cities have made police less visible by replacing traffic officers with "meter maids" and using only one man in a patrol car instead of two. We live in a society, too, that is losing its feeling of neighborliness—which means that police are being called on to solve every little problem, including retrieving the cat from someone's roof.

Q What can be done to reduce the chances for brutality?

A One step would be for police to follow the policy of the Federal Bureau of Investigation, which directs its agents not to use weapons unless their lives or someone else's is in imminent danger.

Better training and screening of police candidates is also needed. One police chief told me he knows the kind of officer who is apt to get into trouble. He's the person who is always cleaning and polishing his gun and acting like a cowboy. The Law Enforcement Assistance Administration might well fund more studies into personality types that are unsuitable for police work.

Q Can police community-relations programs help?

A Absolutely. Cities that have hired more black officers also have eased tensions, particularly within the minority community. In general, police departments need to be more open and more accountable to the public.

Beyond that, society must address problems that breed crime and violence, such as the high unemployment rate among black youths. Disrespect for law and authority often results when a person's social consciousness is disrupted because he can't find work.

Source: U.S. News and World Report, *"Abuse of Authority is a Very Explosive Situation"* (Interview with Paul Takagi), August 27, 1979, p. 29.

force and the relatively large numbers of victims each year suggest that it might be useful to provide an alternative image'' (Lundman, 1980, p. 161). In other words, there is a need to understand police brutality as socially organized deviance—as organizational deviance, not as individual pathology.

Indeed, all of the social and organizational factors and processes that contribute to the existence of police corruption and criminality (as outlined above) can and do apply to the origin and persistence of police brutality and the use of deadly force. In addition, other sociological factors such as an extremely isolated police subculture emphasizing secrecy and solidarity, a community with a large minority and poor underclass (a large surplus population) sharply divided along racial and class lines, and watch-style policing in a watch-style department may also increase the frequency and severity of police brutality in specific communities.

IMPROVING LAW ENFORCEMENT: TECHNOLOGY OR COMMUNITY?

In bringing our discussion of policing to a close we would like to raise a very basic and fundamental question: What is law enforcement? What is crime control? How is it best accomplished?

The theoretical perspectives on crime and its control that we have utilized throughout this book tend to provide quite distinct answers to this question.

What we have called *pre- and nonsociological perspectives* come the closest to understanding policing and law enforcement in a purely technical sense. Crime control from the point of view of these theories consists primarily of police technology and procedures. Improved law enforcement simply means improved technology and technique. In this view, more sophisticated communication systems, weaponry (like the Taser gun that immobilizes suspects with a 50,000-volt dart and is now used by over 300 police departments), illicit drug detection equipment, and television monitoring devices ensure more and better crime control.

Turning to sociological accounts of crime and crime control, it is apparent that the *traditional sociological perspectives* we have discussed are not as technologically oriented in their view of law enforcement as the pre- and non-sociological perspectives are. Nevertheless, policing is still conceptualized basically as the techniques and methods that control the criminal individual, that adjust the criminal individual to society. The human dimension is introduced in this view of policing, however, since improved crime control efforts must include the humane and just application of improved law enforcement methods and technologies.

The *interactionist perspective* on policing focuses on social processes and social interaction, particularly on those processes and interaction between the police and the policed. The technology of law enforcement is only significant to the extent that it contributes to the normally ''unjust'' labeling and stigmatization of the policed by those doing the policing. From this point of view the ultimate social paradox is that efforts to control crime are actually responsible for its production. Following the logic of this theoretical approach, if current crime control efforts actually contribute to the social construction of crime, then improved law enforcement would necessarily mean not only more human policing (less severe criminal labeling and stigmatization) but significantly *less* policing as well. And this is

PANEL 11-9

Crime Control: More Technology?

MIAMI BEACH, FLA. (AP) In an effort to deter rising crime and quell fears, the city of Miami Beach is installing television cameras to monitor its streets.

Workers began last week to mount 112 camera boxes on 25-foot-high traffic signal poles along a three-mile stretch of streets.

Many of the hooded, futuristic-looking boxes will hold portable television cameras. Others will be empty dummies. Both should undermine the confidence of killers, rapists, muggers, purse-snatchers and shoplifters who plague merchants and residents, according to police Maj. Fred Woolridge.

A command post, complete with television monitors and direct telephone lines to police dispatchers, is quartered in a neighborhood housing project. Police officers and citizen volunteers will staff the center.

Preying on Paranoia

"[The system] preys on the paranoia of the criminal," Woolridge said. "He's not really sure where he stands, whether he's being watched or he isn't."

The FBI's recent annual statistical report said Miami—just across Biscayne Bay from Miami Beach—had more crimes per capita last year than any other city in the nation. Five other Florida cities appeared on the FBI's list of the top 10 cities in crime.

In a sampling of opinion taken by the Miami News, residents were pleased about the TV camera project. Store manager Olga Perez said on her block, "we get 10 shoplifters a day. We run after them, but I hope the cameras can help catch them. I really think we need something that lets thieves know someone is watching them."

Erma Shoneberg, 72, said, "They can watch me all they want. What I want them to see is the kook stealing my pocketbook."

Not One Complaint

Woolridge, who is in charge of the project, said he hasn't heard a single complaint.

"People are demanding that they be turned on now," he said. "When we were laying out locations, merchants came and said, 'Please put a camera in front of my store.' "

Miami Beach's federally funded, $230,-000 pilot program was scheduled to begin last summer. It was delayed, however, when City Attorney John Ritter expressed fears that it might invade the privacy of citizens.

"We had some strong feelings in my office," Ritter said. "We asked ourselves if we were sanctioning government intrusion into people's privacy."

He asked state Attorney General Jim Smith for a decision. In a legal opinion issued this month, Smith said there was no violation of privacy laws.

Sidewalks Not Private

He said the cameras would see nothing more private than would be seen by anyone on the sidewalks. "The public wants desperately to be served by such an intrusion," said Smith.

Asked if the cameras will be perceived as "Big Brother," as in George Orwell's novel, "1984," about a totalitarian state, Woolridge said, "In '1984,' we are talking about an oppressive government watching everything. In this case, the public is demanding a relief from the oppression of criminals."

Times change, he said. "Twenty years ago, I'd have been run off the beach for trying something like this."

Source: The Associated Press, "Miami Beach Turns Big Eye on Crime," November 16, 1981.

PANEL 11-10

Crime Control: More Community?

NEW YORK (UPI) Students faked car burglaries to see if New Yorkers would intervene.

But unlike residents of Phoenix and San Francisco, only a few challenged the "thieves." Some New Yorkers even offered to help the criminals.

A study showed that out of about 8,000 people who passed by 250 "break-ins" into parked cars in New York, only 12 tried to stop the "robbers."

Prof. Harold Takooshian, a social psychologist at Fordham University, conducted the New York study, published in the New York magazine. Students pretended to burglarize their cars and then surveyed passersby for their reactions.

The study said that 40 passersby offered to help the "thieves" and five witnesses to the break-ins demanded part of the loot for their assistance.

The survey said most of those who offered to help the "criminals"—including several police officers—were "naive Samaritans" who did not know a theft was in progress.

The rest of the passersby simply did not notice or ignored the break-ins.

The magazine said another similar study showed residents of other cities were even less inclined to notice. In Baltimore, Buffalo, N.Y., Toledo, Ohio, Miami and Ottawa, the intervention rate was zero.

The rate was 20 percent in San Francisco and 25 percent in the Phoenix area.

The daytime car break-ins were staged in midtown Manhattan from October 1977 to September 1980 with student volunteers using coat hangers to break into the vehicles in most cases.

The magazine said to test the possibility that the passersby feared being harmed for intervening, Takooshian placed a uniformed police officer 50 feet from some of the cars broken into.

He said the majority of passersby did not inform the officer and in two cases they warned the "thief" that a policeman was nearby.

To determine if passersby believed the cars being broken into belonged to the students, several "more convincing" break-ins were staged.

They included smashing a car window to gain entry and the simultaneous break-in of two cars. Takooshian said the pedestrians remained uninvolved.

He said interviews with some passersby disclosed that they were upset by what they saw but "didn't know what to do."

Source: United Press International, "Few Intervene to Prevent Staged Car Burglaries," November 17, 1981.

---

exactly what interactionists like Edwin Schur have proposed in the name of things like "radical nonintervention" (see Schur, 1973). In short, from the perspective controlling crime entails adjustments in social processes and interaction, not in technology.

Finally, *radical criminology* challenges both the technological views of law enforcement and the interactionist notion that crime can be controlled best by controlling it less. From this perspective, crime is a real and serious problem that needs to be controlled in all race and class-divided cities, states, and nations. It can, however, only be controlled with *community,* not *technology.* Only the sense and reality of genuine community, and the authentic, intimate, and concerned social relations and relationships it breeds, can begin to control crime. Without this, all of the technological reforms in law enforcement imaginable will not lead to a less criminal society. Panel 11-10 reports on a study that discovered the impact of the lack of community sentiment and involvement on controlling street crime in several large American cities.

Since crime reflects unjust economic and political conditions and arrangements in society, how, ask radical criminologists, can we expect reforms in law enforcement only to improve crime control efforts. It is society that needs reform. If crime is to be controlled we must live in stable, neighborly, egalitarian communities:

> Crime and criminals, as many United States police officials have noted, can never be detected and apprehended adequately by police. But if crimes are committed in real neighborhoods and communities, neighbors respond and capture the criminals. (You cannot steal your neighbor's bicycle when everyone knows it is his or her bicycle. You cannot go to another neighborhood and steal easily, since you would be recognized as an outsider.) In stable communities, crimes and criminals are detected fairly easily. (Liazos, 1982, p. 336)

Evidence can be found that the failure to control crime may have more to do with the social, political, and economic inequalities and alienation that prevent the emergence and development of genuine communities than it has to do with the formal law enforcement activities of the police. There is some indication, for example, that neighborhood crime prevention programs with high degrees of citizen participation have used a sense of community to combat high levels of street crime (see Viviano's, 1981, discussion of some of these efforts in Detroit). Also, at least a few societies have, in the course of overcoming past inequalities and class divisions, experimented with community justice systems that have claimed some success in controlling crime (see, for example, Liazos', 1982, Chap. 12, discussion of attempts at socialist justice in China and Cuba).

CHAPTER REVIEW

1. A few general facts about the police in American society are: (1) there are approximately 700,000 legally sworn police officers working for approximately 19,500 county or city police departments; (2) although there are many different kinds of police in our society (including county sheriffs, various state and federal police agencies, private police, etc.), it is the city police that do the bulk of the policing of the crimes that are most often policed in the United States—street crimes (usually criminalized by state law); (3) it is *not* the case that more police necessarily lead to lower crime rates or less crime; (4) most municipal police activity is concerned with criminal misdemeanors, not with more serious violent and felonious criminal threats to the community; and (5) most municipal police work is reactive, not proactive.

2.   Municipal police forces developed in the 19th century in the United States as a response to the "dangerous-classes"—the urban underclass and the industrial working class—and the public disorder they created in response to their increasing economic inequality and exploitation brought on by the advance of an industrial market-economy. Municipal police forces did not emerge primarily to provide crime control; their primary function was to ensure social control—social order and stability.

3.   Contrary to the theory of penal evolution stated by the classic French sociologist Emile Durkheim, it appears that non-industrialized, non-technological societies with a low division of labor, have tended to practice conciliatory and restitutive punishment for criminal offenders, while highly technological, industrial societies with a high division of labor have tended to use more severe and repressive punishment practices. The police, for example, are only known in this latter kind of society.

4.   Although the militarization of American police work (that began in the 1920s) has led to the public image of the police as technological "crime fighters," the reality of police work in our society is something quite different: as much as 80 percent of police time and resources may be spent on non-criminal matters.

5.   The perspective of radical criminology is better suited than more traditional sociological perspectives to explain the origins and further development of the municipal police force in the United States. The historical record does not indicate that law enforcement agencies are characterized primarily by the pursuit of criminal activities defined by a consensual criminal law that reflects the interests of all parts of the community and enforced in the interests of that entire community. Rather, history confirms, to a significant extent, radical criminology's view that the municipal police force was a response to social disorder and instability that threatened elite interests in society.

6.   A long tradition of studies of the police done from the interactionist perspective have confirmed the importance of the police subculture and police discretion in determining what is policed and what is not policed in American society. Important elements of the police subculture include the "lay social theory" of the police made up of their notions about who is criminal and what causes crime, and the folk methods that working officers develop to get their job done. Through the mechanism of the "self-fulfilling prophecy," police definitions of crime, criminals, and causes of crime tend to be confirmed as "true" and "accurate." The interactionist examination of police discretion indicates that the police are not involved primarily in the formal and mechanical application of the law to illegal acts. Rather, the law, legal authority, and police power tend to be used only when they contribute to the social control of a situation, neighborhood, or community. As radical criminology found with the historical origins and development of the municipal police, interactionist analysis finds with contemporary police work: policing has more to do with providing social control than it has to do with controlling crime per se.

7. The police bureaucracy finds it very difficult to supervise those who are most responsible for policing in our society—the police officers on the street. This contributes to high levels of police officer discretion and negatively impacts crime control efforts, as does the system the police bureaucracy has relied on to make its officers and operations more accountable and effective—paperwork reporting, statistical performance records, and crime rates. Since police administrations ultimately recognize their departments' inability to police and make arrests for serious crime, they turn police attention, resources, and personnel to those activities they can control—parking, traffic, public drunkenness and disorder, domestic and neighborhood disturbances, and so on—thereby contributing to the maintenance of social order and control.

8. Distinct styles of policing can be found in American cities. Watch-style policing tends to be found in older metropolitan areas under the control of political machines, with large minority and poor populations, and high levels of culture, race, and class conflict. This type of police department tends to avoid and ignore a lot of ''less serious'' crime but often uses its power in harsh and severe ways when it deems a situation ''serious.'' Legalistic-style policing can be found in newer and more affluent cities than the watch-style department (or in a city once under the influence of a machine but now governed by a ''reform'' government). Legalistic police departments aim to be professional and attempt to intervene as often as they can in a wide variety of illegal activities. They tend to generate large numbers of traffic citations and arrests. Service-style departments are most likely to be found in affluent and homogenous suburban areas. These departments are more ''proactive'' than watch or legalistic departments, taking all calls for police assistance seriously and intervening as often as they can. Their intervention, however, is normally as informal, leisurely, and lenient as the situation will allow.

9. There have been two ''waves'' of police unionism in the United States: one in the 1920s and one beginning in the mid-1960s. By the early 1970s, nearly every U.S. big-city police department had unionized.

10. Recently, layoffs and cutbacks, coupled with the ''Taylorization of police work,'' have begun to undo many of the inroads police unions had made into police administration during the past 10 to 15 years.

11. The Taylorization of police work refers to changes in the nature of police work itself: increasing division of labor in the police department, more reactive and dangerous patrol work, and the increasing use of technology to reconcentrate authority and control in the hands of police administrators.

12. Although the cumulative effect of drives toward police professionalism may include some increase in police department efficiency, more trained and educated officers, and some control of police discretion, it has also contributed to (1) aggravated police-community relations, (2) deteriorated labor-management relations within police departments, and (3) heighted police isolation and alienation in the police subculture.

13. At least three contradictions of policing affect contemporary police-work. The police find themselves between demands for law and order and the protection of civil rights and liberties, between demands to intervene in noncriminal matters and to control serious crime, and being called upon to control crime set in motion by a prolonged period of economic decline that has also left their forces depleted and weakened.

14. Police discretion, an isolated police subculture, racism, class bias, and the police force's historical and contemporary concern with insuring social order have combined to help produce the dark side of American policing: police corruption and criminality, police brutality, and the unnecessary use of deadly force. It is important to remember that these criminal and deviant acts are not the product of individual pathological or morally flawed police officers but of criminal or deviant police organizations.

15. Different theoretical perspectives point to very diverse ways of improving law enforcement and crime control. Pre- and nonsociological theories focus on technological improvements. Traditional sociological views have added a concern that these technological changes in policing be applied in a humane and just fashion. The interactionist perspective has argued that improved crime control entails adjustments in social processes and social interaction, not in technology. Radical criminologists generally contend that meaningful crime control comes only with the development of genuine human community.

12 The Criminal Courts

CHAPTER
OUTLINE

The Court System: An Overview
The Pretrial Process

Pretrial hearing
Pretrial maneuvering: prosecutor discretion
The defense attorney and the adversary system
Plea bargaining: negotiated guilt

The Trial

Trial by judge or jury
The presentation of evidence: procedures and protocol
Sentencing: judicial discretion
An alternative: determinate sentencing

Theoretical Interpretations of the American Criminal Court Process

The perspective of traditional sociology
The interactionist perspective
The radical perspective

KEY TERMS

Adversary system
Bail
Civil cases
Criminal cases
Determinate sentence
Double jeopardy
Due process
Exclusionary rule
Grand jury
Habeus corpus
Hung jury
Indeterminate sentence
Indictment
Information
Mandatory sentence
Nolle prosequi
Parole
Plea bargaining
Pretrial hearing
Probation
Voir dire

The administration of justice through the courts is based, by definition, on principles that guarantee fairness. Judaic-Christian premises dictate what we in American society consider fair. But, as Gwynn Nettler (1979) has pointed out, these premises result in some fundamental contradictions: between retribution and love; between right procedure (due process) and right consequences; between equity and equality; and between treating people as individuals and treating them uniformly. These tensions result in standards of justice that are inconsistently applied and often perceived as blatantly unfair. For some the system is too rigid; for others it has too many loopholes. For some the system is too oriented toward protecting the rights of the accused while for others it is clearly too one-sided for the prosecution. The purpose of this chapter is to describe the decision-making process in American criminal courts. The essential questions addressed are (1) How does the court system really work? and (2) Are some kinds of people advantaged and others disadvantaged in this process? The answers to these questions reveal how the court system acts and reacts to the contradictory pressures of what is considered fair.

THE COURT SYSTEM: AN OVERVIEW

The U.S. court system is really 52 systems—one for each state and the District of Columbia, and a federal system. Within each of these systems there are trial courts where cases are first heard. There are also appellate courts where decisions from the trial courts are reviewed. In each of the state and federal systems there is a supreme court that has ultimate power. The U.S. Supreme Court does not interfere in state law unless there is a violation of federal law.

There are about 1400 federal judges and 8000 judges in the state systems, and 18,600 municipal judges, which are under the jurisdiction of the state (*U.S. News & World Report,* November 1, 1982, p. 36). The federal judges are nominated by the president and must be confirmed by the Senate. When a federal vacancy occurs (in all but the Supreme Court), the senators from that state recommend a candidate. In practice, the senator from the president's political party has what amounts to a veto over all nominees. Once selected, a federal judge cannot be removed except by impeachment and conviction (which has not happened since 1936). Supreme Court justices are nominated by the president and must be approved by the Senate. As with the federal judges, Supreme Court justices are appointed for life and may only be removed by impeachment and conviction or by voluntary retirement. The rationale for life appointments is that it removes judges from political pressures.

The states vary in the procedures for the selection, retention, and removal of judges. In about two thirds of the states, judges are elected and in the remainder they are appointed. In many states the judges must periodically go before the electorate for a retain/remove vote. There are procedures in all states for the removal of incompetent or misbehaving judges, but actual removal is difficult to achieve (*U.S. News & World Report,* November 1, 1982, p. 46).

At every level—municipal, state, and federal—the courts are incredibly over-burdened. The accused in some jurisdictions must wait as long as 18 months before trial because there is such a backlog of cases. This situation runs counter to the constitutional guarantee of the right to a speedy trial.

Item   In Colorado's 18th Judicial District, the average annual caseload per judge rose from 655 in 1961 to 1350 in 1981 (Hurtt, 1981, p. 63).

Item   The number of cases filed in U.S. Courts of Appeal rose from 14,535 in 1972 to 26,362 in 1981 (up 81 percent) (*U.S. News & World Report,* February 22, 1982, p. 39).

Item   The U.S. Supreme Court examined 5311 cases in 1981, up from 1312 in 1953 (United Press International, 1982).

The reasons for the congested courts, which appear to be clogging at an ever accelerated pace, are many. An obvious reason is that the number of courts have remained stable while the population continues to grow. The state legislatures and Congress enact new criminal legislation at every session, adding whole new areas of heretofore noncriminal activity into the criminal category. Another reason is that many of the cases before the courts probably do not belong there. Chief Justice Burger of the U.S. Supreme Court has argued that a number of cases should be removed from the courts and handled by arbitrators, paralegals, or some other mechanism (such as in cases involving personal injury, the adoption of children, divorce and child custody, and probate proceedings where there is no contest, *U.S. News & World Report,* February 22, 1982).[1] Burger also hinted that a source of the burgeoning case loads may be that there are too many lawyers in the country. The United States has one lawyer for every 400 people, the highest rate in the world (3 times as many lawyers per capita as Great Britain and 21 times as many as Japan), and this may increase the likelihood of litigation.

An overwhelming source of the crowded court dockets is the criminalization of consensual acts contrary to the morality of the powerful. These so-called vic-timless crimes of gambling, prostitution, drunkenness, and drug use preoccupy the criminal justice system.

The statistics concerning victimless crimes are sobering: it is generally accepted that *half* of all arrests made by policemen through the nation are for victimless crimes, and that *half* of all the people in jail are being held in connection with such crimes. If all this business were removed from the courts, it is argued, then

---

[1] The courts are clogged because of two kinds of cases—civil and criminal. Civil cases involve actions by one party against another. One party may, for example, bring suit against another for violation of privacy, for defamation of character, for the custody of children in divorce, for halting the construction of a building that blocks a view, or for the contesting of the will of the deceased. In these cases, the court acts as an arbiter trying to assess fair compensation to victims or to determine an equitable compromise between the conflicting parties. These civil cases are a major reason for the overburdened courts and for this reason Justice Burger has argued for their being handled, for the most part, outside the formal courts. In criminal proceedings, the topic of this chapter, the law has purportedly been violated and the objectives of the court are to determine guilt or innocence, and if guilt is established, to set a fair punishment.

the problems of congestion and misuse of police and judicial manpower would be dramatically affected. (Seymour, 1973, p. 82)

A clear reason for overcrowded courts is that the justice process in many cases is too deliberate. This process, as we will see in this chapter, is slow basically for the protection of the accused. The process almost grinds to a halt when a wealthy defendant hires lawyers who prolong the case with every imaginable legal ploy. For example, John Hinckley, who shot four people in front of television cameras in his attempt to assassinate President Reagan, pled innocent by reason of insanity. Hinckley, the son of a wealthy oil entrepreneur, hired lawyers who developed the most elaborate insanity case ever devised: 13 months of pretrial maneuvering over procedures and admissible evidence, thousands of pages of legal arguments, eight weeks in court, and more than $1 million in fees for lawyers and expert witnesses (one psychiatrist received $122,742.91 in fees and expenses) (Taylor, 1982, pp. 56–57).

When some cases take unusual court time, such as the Hinckley trial, the ever-growing backlog of cases increases the pressure on other cases, resulting in cases being disposed of too quickly. As Downie has characterized it:

> Judge, prosecutor, defense attorney, policeman, and clerk are working partners struggling to keep their heads above water as the flood of cases rises. Is it not natural that, for them, expediency should take precedence over justice, eventually becoming one and the same in the minds of bureaucrats? (Downie, 1971, p. 33)

The overriding consequence of the overcrowding of the courts, then, is a bias against the poor who cannot afford shrewd and expensive lawyers who know how to manipulate the system for their client's benefit. The poor, instead, tend to receive a rapid disposition of their cases in a bargain-counter, assembly-line system of justice (Blumberg, 1967, p. 5), which often is not just. This bias against the poor is found throughout the court procedures, as we will document in this chapter.

THE PRETRIAL PROCESS

Before the actual trial begins there are several important phases that are of ultimate importance to the state and the accused: the pretrial hearing where the judge determines whether the defendant will be released or not, the formal charge, and the initial combat between the attorneys for both sides in the preliminary hearing and during plea bargaining. Since about 90 percent of criminal cases never reach the trial stage, the decisions regarding guilt and the sanctions to be imposed are generally made in these crucial pretrial proceedings. And, when these pretrial maneuverings are compared with formal trial procedures, they are found to be much less fair and more open to judicial discretion and the power of the prosecuting attorney. The court's procedures during trial tend to be guided by due process and relative impartiality but these constitutional guarantees are less likely to occur in the pretrial stages.

Pretrial Hearing

The accused first appears before the judge at the pretrial hearing. At this time the judge examines the facts of the case, the previous record of the accused, and the potential threat to the community if the accused is released, to determine whether he or she should be released or confined before the trial. The judge has at least four options: release on own recognizance, pretrial release with services such as medical or community corrections, release on bail, or detention in jail.

Pretrial release, whether on recognizance or by bail, is an extremely important right of the accused. The first Congress realized this in 1789 by passing a law declaring that suspects have a right to pretrial release except when accused of crimes punishable by death. Foremost, pretrial release reaffirms the principle that the accused is legally innocent since guilt has not yet been formally established. The accused, if freed, may continue working, make an income, and spend time gathering evidence to support his/her case. Most important, the individual, who may be innocent, escapes the degradation of being in jail. As the President's Crime Commission has argued:

> We doubt whether any innocent person (as all before trial are presumed to be) can remain unscarred by detention under such a degree of security. . . . The indignities of repeated physical search, regimented living, crowded cells, utter isolation from the outside world, unsympathetic surveillance, outrageous visitors' facilities, Fort Knox-like security measures, are surely so searing that one unwarranted day in jail itself can be a major social injustice. (President's Commission, 1967, p. 25)

Most important, there is evidence that defendants who are jailed rather than released prior to trial, are more likely to be convicted and receive longer sentences (Rankin, cited in Reid, 1982, p. 363).

Release on Own Recognizance

At the judge's discretion, the accused may be released after signing a statement under oath that she or he will appear for trial. A variation of this is a "signature bond," the release on the promise in writing to pay the court a defined amount if one fails to appear for the trial. Unquestionably, the strength of these methods is that the poor have the same chances for escaping jail as the wealthy. The potential disadvantage of these methods (and bail) is that those released may commit crimes. In one celebrated case, for example, a Nebraska man accused of rape was released by the judge and three days later raped and killed an elderly woman. An outraged Nebraska legislature passed—and the state's voters endorsed—a constitutional amendment allowing judges to deny bail to accused rapists when the evidence against them is strong (Gest, 1981).

Bail

The traditional purpose of bail is to ensure the presence of defendants at trials. There is an implied constitutional right to bail as well as an explicit prohibition against excessive bail. In practice, the granting of bail tends to undermine the ideal of treating all people fairly. To begin, judges have great powers with regard to bail. They may deny bail or if bail is allowed, they determine what the level will be for each defendant. A high level of bail can be set to "teach the accused a lesson" or to "protect the community." This has often been the case when the defendants have been political protestors or minority group members. The setting of an extremely high bail to protect the community, for example, is inherently discriminatory. As Altman and Cunningham have argued, "If the dangerous defendant can raise the bail sum, he goes free. By its nature, therefore, the system succeeds in retaining only the 'dangerous poor.' 'The dangerous rich' post bond and are released" (cited in Barlow, 1981, p. 393).

The setting of bail by the judge is also unfair because judges tend to determine the amount of bail by the type of crime alleged instead of the accused's ability to pay. A flat $10,000 for everyone accused of a felony, for instance, would result in a greater likelihood of the poor staying in jail while the more affluent go free.

The obvious result of the system of setting bail is that the poor remain in jail and the wealthy are released. This occurs because the well-to-do have their own money for bail, or because bail bondsmen consider them better risks. This highlights another problem with bail: the power of bail bondsmen to decide whom they will bond and whom they will not. Of course, the poor are considered more risky. Moreover, bondsmen may refuse to grant bail as a "favor" to the police.

But the biggest problem with bail, to reiterate, is that it tends to imprison the poor, and the amount of time spent in jail before trial does not count toward whatever sentence may be imposed if the defendant is convicted. Time spent in jail before trial varies by locality and the backlog of cases before the court. The extreme is in New York City where defendants who cannot make bail spend as much as 18 months in jail waiting for their day in court. Clearly, this violates the spirit of the "innocent until proven guilty" dictim since it provides punishment before conviction. The difference then between those who languish in jail before their trial and those who are free is money. The unfairness of this system is forcefully described by former Attorney General Ramsey Clark:

> The bail system is worse than senseless—it discriminates for no reason against the poor. Bail diverts the criminal justice system from what matters—the individual—to what doesn't—his money. Rather than asking does he need treatment, has he violated parole, should be be supervised, might he leave the country, or is he dangerous, bail asks only—does he have $500? (Clark, 1971, p. 303)

Pretrial Detention

We have seen that the setting of bail often obscures the real intent of the judge: to keep certain persons (the presumed dangerous) and categories (the politically deviant and the poor) in jail rather than in the community. Judges, if their goal is to imprison the accused until trial, have a more honest option, which is to refuse bail. This is often avoided, however, because of the defendant's right to bail except in extreme cases. This reluctance is decried by conservatives who feel that criminals have too many rights. President Reagan and the Justice Department have endorsed "preventive detention." So, too, did the American Bar Association Task Force on Crime, which recommended in 1982 that judges be allowed to use preventive detention to keep potentially dangerous criminals in jail while awaiting trial. The committee argued that this no-bail procedure would be preferable to the current practice of setting unrealistically high bail, but that it should be used sparingly and with strict safeguards. Bail should be denied, according to this proposal, only in cases when the suspect is accused of a crime of violence and when at least one of three factors apply: (1) the accused's pattern of behavior indicates that there is no condition of release that will reasonably insure the safety of the community; (2) the alleged crime was committed while the suspect was on bail, probation, or parole for a previous crime of violence; and (3) the accused had been convicted of another crime within the previous 10 years (*Denver Post,* 1982). Proponents of this proposal fear that defendants will commit further crimes if given their freedom before the trial. As evidence for this fear, they might cite a study funded by the Law Enforcement Assistance Administration, which found that in a total of 3500 cases in eight cities, 7.8 percent of the defendants were convicted of crimes and 1.9 percent were convicted of serious crimes while out on bail (cited in *Rocky Mountain News,* 1982).

Opponents of preventive detention argue that other research finds that less than 1 percent of all those accused and awaiting trial commit another crime within 60 days of their original arrest. From this perspective, therefore, the constitutionally guaranteed speedy trial is the best criminal justice reform in this area.

Organizations such as the American Civil Liberties Union are wary of prevention detention because it denies the rights of defendants, most fundamentally, the presumption of innocence. The civil libertarians view the small percentage of defendants who while free on bail commit a serious crime as a small price to protect the rights of the accused, many of whom will eventually be judged innocent, yet under preventive detention would be jailed for weeks or even months.

The accused who await trial in custody are usually detained in jails. A jail is a facility used to incarcerate unconvicted persons as well as those convicted of minor offenses. The number of people who have served time in jails in a given year is nearly 500,000, considerably more than the number found in state and federal prisons (Press, 1980). There is a high rate of turnover in jail populations and the inmates are typically poor, black or Hispanic, and serving sentences for disorderly conduct, public drunkenness, and prostitution, and awaiting court dates for a variety of street crime charges.

Jails are warehouses, places where drunk drivers and petty thieves serve short sentences next to criminal defendants held because they can't make cash bail. The young and old, innocent and convicted, predatory and passive, middle-class and poor, men and women are hurled together into the criminal justice system's Cuisinart where they are intermingled, spun about—and rarely emerge as they were. (Press, 1980, p. 74)

The conditions in local jails are generally appalling. They are commonly crowded, filthy, poorly ventilated, and have inadequate plumbing. When contrasted with state and federal prisons, jails are clearly less humane. The following is a description of an Atlanta jail, which is typical:

> The jail was far worse than the state prisons I have just seen. Inside a relatively modern exterior in a modest, busy part of town was a cramped, dark, dank interior. Large, four-sided cages each held sixteen men, with disheveled beds and an open toilet. Inmates were kept inside these cages twenty-four hours a day throughout their often prolonged stays at the Atlanta jail. There is no privacy and no activity at all, artificial air and light, and nothing to do day and night. A dismal atmosphere, a constant din and a wretched stench pervaded the place. (Goldfarb, 1975, pp. 5–6)

In 1984 the Supreme Court made a significant step toward upholding the principle of preventive detention. By a 6-3 vote the Court ruled that juveniles can be incarcerated before they are tried if they present a "serious risk" of committing another offense before trial. The Court did not rule on adult criminal defendants who appear to be a "danger to the community."

Pretrial Maneuvering: Prosecutor Discretion

Before the criminal trial, the police provide their evidence to the district attorney and his/her assistants. The initial task of this public prosecutor is to determine if the evidence is sufficient to convince a jury of guilt "beyond a reasonable doubt." They may enter a *nolle prosequi* ("I refuse to prosecute") if there is not enough evidence, or if the case is believed to be relatively unimportant. In this latter situation, the prosecutor may feel that the courts are already hopelessly overcrowded and the district attorney's office could spend its limited time more wisely by prosecuting more important cases. The main procedural reasons for the prosecutor dismissing a case involve problems with weak evidence. There may be a lack of physical evidence, such as the weapon or the stolen property, or there may be insufficient testimony from witnesses.

Prosecutors, ideally, have the duty to seek justice, not merely convict. They should weigh the evidence dispassionately and use their important discretionary powers wisely and fairly. There are constraints on prosecutors, however, that work contrary to this ideal. District attorneys are usually elected officials and their visibility often makes their position a stepping-stone for higher political office. As a result, district attorneys are especially sensitive to public opinion. They may, therefore, decide to prosecute or not prosecute a case because of political pressures rather than the objective facts.

When prosecutors decide to take the case to trial in some states they file an *information* with the court stating the charges. In the other states serious criminal accusations are presented to a *grand jury*. The grand jury varies in size from 6 to 23 members and meets in closed sessions to consider whether there is enough evidence to warrant going to trial. The grand jury only hears the prosecutor's side and if convinced, issues an *indictment* (a formal accusation). The grand jury was originally intended to be an independent check of the prosecutor's power but in practice it follows the recommendations of the prosecutor. In the words of the famous defense lawyer F. Lee Bailey, the grand jury is "a flock of sheep led by the prosecutor across the meadows to the finding he wants" (cited in Sykes, 1978, p. 357).

The filing of an information or a grand jury's indictment is a significant stage between arrest and trial. The prosecutor specifies the violations in the law that it will seek to prove. The formal accusation also informs the defendant of the crime with which he or she is charged. This right of the defendant to know the exact charges is required by the Sixth Amendment to the Constitution.

The Defense Attorney and The Adversary System

In principle, the innocence or guilt of the accused is established in the courts through a contest between adversaries. One side is the state, represented by the prosecuting attorney's office, and the other is the accused, represented by legal counsel. Each side uses all of its powers to present the strongest case to the jury. The referee in the ensuing legal battle is the judge who acts impartially to protect the legal rights of both sides.

There is a wide gulf, however, between the ideal just described and the reality of how the courts actually function. For this fundamental principle of the American system of justice to work, the adversaries must be relatively equal in ability, incentive, and resources. The state has enormous resources (e.g., the police, crime laboratories, detectives, and information retrieval systems) from which to build its case. The accused, perhaps even if wealthy, cannot match the resources and expertise of the state.

Poor defendants are especially disadvantaged in the adversary system. They must accept a court-appointed lawyer or public defender and remain in jail if they cannot make bail. Obviously, they cannot pay for the detective work and other things necessary to build their court cases. As Chesterfield Smith said when he was president of the American Bar Association:

One problem is our adversary system—a great system when the adversaries are equal. But it's like putting a championship tennis player in against a beginner when one man has all the chips. You've got somebody with the best lawyer and all the resources litigated against somebody who doesn't have the resources. (quoted in Star, 1974, p. 21)

This unequal situation is the rule rather than the exception. About 60 percent of all felony defendants cannot afford to hire a private attorney so they must rely on court-appointed public defenders. Public defenders are in the anomalous position of being employed by the state to defend clients who are being tried by the state. They have a tremendous disadvantage because, typically, they are overworked and relatively inexperienced. Often they are but a few years out of law school and may have to grapple with as many as 400 cases a year (*U.S. News & World Report,* November 1, 1982, p. 37). The huge caseload means that they cannot spend adequate time in preparing for a trial. The result is that public defenders must choose a few cases to give their attention to, while giving their minimal attention to others. They also feel constrained to have their clients plead guilty, since that drastically reduces the time demands on them.

The degree of unfairness for the poor varies by the monies spent. Alaska and California spend the most money defending the poor—in 1980–1981, $8.18 and $3.94, respectively, for each state resident. The lowest amounts spent were 45 cents per person in Alabama and 48 cents per person in Mississippi (Associated Press, July 5, 1982). The current economic crisis has caused many state legislatures to cut back money the already meager monies for legal aid and President Reagan has made drastic cuts at the federal level, threatening further the constitutional right to legal counsel.

The adversary system in principle assumes two sides equal in power. This system is also supposed to protect the accused against any violation of his or her constitutional rights. This principle is often upheld in the trial:

> It is in the courtroom, at the trial itself, that the majestic rights enshrined in the Constitution are upheld; it is there that evidence illegitimately obtained will be suppressed; it is there that the prosecution will be required to keep the high standards to which it is held; and it is there that the presence of counsel and judge will prevent oppression or overreaching by police or prosecutor, however weak, humble, or lowly the accused may be.
>
> In fact, these things do happen in many, probably most, cases that actually reach adversary, public hearings. But in the United States, it is an abnormal criminal proceeding that ends up in public hearings. *At least ninety percent of all criminal prosecutions result in guilty pleas,* most of them after negotiations between the accused (or his counsel) and the prosecuting attorney. (Chambliss and Seidman, 1971, pp. 398–399)

Plea Bargaining: Negotiated Guilt

Less than one tenth of those charged with crimes ever go to trial. The thousands of cases that bypass the trial process do so because either the charges are dropped or the accused pleads guilty to the original or lesser charges. The latter case is called *plea bargaining* since the defendants bargain away their right to a trial in return for their guilty plea and a more lenient punishment than if they were found guilty of the original charge (see Pious, 1971; Feder, 1974; Heumann, 1978). In other words, plea bargaining has become the rule, not the exception, in the disposition of criminal cases in the United States.[2]

There are many pressures on defendants, lawyers, prosecutors, and judges to encourage plea bargaining. The foremost is the overwhelming caseload facing the

[2]The most famous plea bargaining case of recent years involved Spiro Agnew while he was vice-president. Agnew agreed to plead "no contest" to one charge of tax evasion rather than stand trial for tax evasion, bribery, and extortion. He was to resign from office, be fined $10,000, and receive a three-year suspended sentence.

police, prosecutors, and judges. Without guilty pleas to speed defendants through the system, the criminal justice process could not function because of the crowded courts. One obvious solution is for judges to encourage guilty pleas by implementing the agreements negotiated by prosecutors and defense counsel. Similarly, the prosecutor encourages plea bargaining because of his or her large caseload. In addition, it is important for prosecutors to have a high conviction rate and plea bargaining achieves this goal at relatively little expense (Pious, 1971, p. 26).

Defendants are pressured to plea bargain in several ways as well. People who are assigned counsel are typically encouraged by their lawyers to "cop a plea." One reason for this is because assigned counsel receives little compensation and they would rather return quickly to their private and more lucrative practice. Counsel may also feel that it is in the best interests of the client to plea bargain since to do so will reduce time spent in jail awaiting trial. Plea bargaining is also often forced on defendants because DAs charge them with more serious crimes (carrying heavier penalties) to encourage them to plea bargain and lessen caseloads. If a defendant refuses, he or she then faces the possibility of more "serious time." Public defenders also encourage plea bargaining because of their large case loads and small investigative staffs. They would rather concentrate their efforts on capital crimes.

A strong argument for defendants giving up their constitutionally guaranteed right to a trial is the fact that it increases the likelihood of stern punishment. A 1971 study of U.S. District Court trials revealed that those who insisted on a jury trial and were convicted (73 percent ended in convictions) were likely to receive a sentence three times more severe than those who pleaded guilty at arraignment (Feder, 1974, p. 400). Two possible reasons for this disparity are (1) those who plead guilty appear to be conscience stricken and (2) those who plead innocent but are found guilty are penalized for taking up the court's time.

There are special pressures on defendants who are poor or of moderate means to plead guilty. They will be unable to bear the expense of a lengthy trial. Moreover, those unable to make bail must await trial in jail. These factors deter poor defendants from insisting on their rights.

Although it may be a necessity given the overcrowded courts, plea bargaining subverts the basic foundations of the system of criminal justice. Contrary to the Bill of Rights, the practice operates on an implicit assumption of guilt. It fails to distinguish between innocent and guilty, thus penalizing the innocent and rewarding the guilty. The procedure, as we have pointed out, especially discriminates against the poor. The poor defendant is pressured to bargain from a relatively low power base. He or she is in jail already with lawyers who are court appointed. The last point is crucial because the defendants in a plea bargaining situation must have competent and conscientious counsel. Obviously a lawyer receiving a handsome fee will tend to be more interested in a client's welfare than an overburdened and undercompensated court-appointed one.

The reduction of sentence through plea bargaining may actually be a sham. One study found that some prosecutors file excessive charges on the assumption that they will be reduced. Thus, some defendants are not getting a bargain at all (cited in *LEAA Newsletter,* 1977, p. 7).

The widespread use of plea bargaining arrangements can lessen considerably the power of judges.

Finally, we should note once again the awesome power of the prosecutor. As we have seen, throughout the pretrial maneuverings the prosecutor decides to proceed with the case or not, determines the formal charges (including manipulating the grand jury), and with plea bargaining, the prosecutor in effect sentences the accused. All of these functions make the prosecutor the most powerful person in the criminal justice system. This power far surpasses the power of judges since 90 percent of criminal convictions are based on guilty pleas adjudicated *without* a trial, although the judge does do the actual sentencing.

THE TRIAL

The Sixth Amendment to the Constitution guarantees "In all prosecutions, the accused shall enjoy the right to a speedy and public trial, by an impartial jury." The clogged courts, despite the huge number of negotiated pleas, mean that most cases do not go to trial quickly, as the Constitution demands. A survey of 32 metropolitan areas by the National Center for State Courts showed that the median time from the filing of charges to trial ranged from 42 days in Portland, Oregon, to a year in Buffalo, New York (cited in *U.S. News & World Report,* November 1, p. 38). The other elements of the Sixth Amendment proscription are

A jury trial in process. In general, it is to the advantage of the accused to have a jury trial.

met—a public trial before a jury. The following description of the trial process includes jury selection and composition, the presentation of evidence, and the role of the judge, especially in sentencing.

Trial by Judge or Jury

A major decision prior to trial is whether the trial will be conducted before a judge alone or before a judge and jury. State law may dictate that certain crimes must be decided only by a judge. In most felony cases, however, the defendant has the choice.

The defense lawyer will likely advise his or her client to waive a jury trial under certain conditions (Stuckey, 1976, p. 91). The record of the trial judge assigned to the case may be perceived as favorable to the accused. The crime may be so well publicized that an unbiased jury would be virtually impossible. The previous criminal record of the accused may prejudice the jury, or the accused may be black, Chicano, or native American and local feeling may make an impartial jury problematic.

In general, though, it is definitely to the advantage of the accused to have the decision made by a jury rather than a judge. Some judges are biased, eccentric, or even senile. Most important, research suggests that juries tend to be more lenient than judges. In one study of 3576 cases, investigators compared actual jury verdicts with the hypothetical verdicts of the judges involved in the cases. The judge and jury agreed in about 80 percent of the cases. In cases where there was disagreement, the juries were more lenient than the judges in 17 percent of the cases and less lenient in 2 percent of the cases (Kalven and Ziesel, 1966, pp. 55–56).

Jury Composition

Fundamental to a fair system of criminal justice is the right to a trial by jury. The assumption is that a defendant should be tried by a representative body of citizens. In practice, however, certain categories of persons are underrepresented on juries: occupational groups low in prestige, minorities, people not registered to vote, and students. The result is that the poor, especially the poor from minority groups, are not judged by a jury of their peers. Three examples will suffice to show this bias (Overby, 1970).

Item In Lownes County, Mississippi, no blacks were on the jury list from 1900 to 1961.

Item In a Colorado county of 17,000 inhabitants, 719 people had Spanish surnames but not one served on any jury during an eight-year period.

Item In one Alabama county, blacks comprised 80 percent of the population, yet from 1953 to 1965 only seven blacks appeared on the jury lists.

These examples of the underrepresentation of blacks on juries has been and continues to be the case for other racial minorities as well. So, too, have women been omitted from juries. For most of American history they were not allowed on juries at all. As late as 1966 this was still the case in Alabama until the law barring women as jurors was finally declared unconstitutional. A recent study has found that nonwhites, young people, and women were underrepresented on juries (Kairys, Kadane, and Lehorsky, 1977). In one locality, for example, blacks constituted 30 percent of the population but only 17 percent of the jury wheel. In another jurisdiction, women comprised 53 percent of the population but only 17 percent of the jury list.

The failure of juries to reflect communities is significant because the people least represented are those most apt to challenge community norms. This puts a special burden on defendants accused of political crimes (e.g., civil rights protest, antiwar protest).

Selecting the jury is perhaps the most critical point in a trial and as a consequence the process may take longer than the trial itself. Many assume that the jury members are selected because they are fair and open-minded but lawyers for both sides choose jurors whom they believe will favor their side. As New York attorney Herald Price Fahringer has said, "I don't want an impartial jury. I want a jury that is compatible to my client's cause" (quoted in Friedrich, 1981, p. 47).

The selection process is called the *voir dire* ("to tell the truth") where potential jurors are questioned by the lawyers and the judge. They may be excluded with cause if their answers indicate that they are biased or otherwise unfit to try the case. Each lawyer can also ban a juror by exercising a preemptory challenge. Each side is given a limited number of these challenges, which allows them to exclude people without cause (the number of preemptory challenges allowed varies by state). In making these decisions the lawyers may use stereotypes. Sociologist Rita Simon's research has shown that prosecutors tend to favor men,

Republicans, the affluent, bankers, engineers, and accountants, whereas defense attorneys favor women, Democrats, poorer people, social scientists, and minorities (Simon, 1980). Chicago prosecutor William Kunkle has said that he feels that self-employed business people, home owners, and those with strong religious convictions are most likely to accept the state's arguments. He would challenge, however, "anyone who has had one psychology course or *one sociology course in college*" (quoted in Friedrich, 1981, p. 47; emphasis added).

The selection process tends to be unfair. Once again the state has an enormous advantage because of the investigatory and financial resources at its disposal. The government may use the police and the FBI to investigate minute details about each prospective juror. Unless the accused is very wealthy, the defense usually decides on the basis of intuition and superficial data.

In recent years, the defense in some political trials has used social science techniques successfully in the jury selection process. Sociologist Jay Schulman and social psychologist Richard Christie volunteered their expertise in the defense of the Harrisburg conspiracy trial, the Camden 28 trial, the Gainesville Eight trial, the trial of the Attica defendants, and the trial of Indian militants Dennis Banks and Russell Means. The most important procedure employed was to conduct a survey of a random sample of registered voters in the community (Schulman, 1973). The respondents were asked their attitudes (depending on the case) toward minority groups, the police and other symbols of political authority, U.S. participation in the Vietnam War, and the like. The results were then divided into categories to establish how certain social categories from the community might be expected to react as jurors. Their survey of Harrisburg revealed that women, working-class Lutherans, Catholics, and Brethren would be most sympathetic to political protestors. In Gainesville, Schulman and Christie found that men, high-status Episcopalians, and Presbyterian professionals would be most likely to react positively to the arguments presented by the defense (*Time*, 1974). In addition to obtaining a sociological profile of the community, the social scientists enlisted volunteers to investigate the backgrounds of each member of the jury panel (usually about 200 persons). And while the *voir dire* was in progress, the defense had experts (psychologists and body language specialists) scrutinize each prospective juror.

The trials where the defense employed these social scientists have all resulted in either hung juries or acquittals. Of the 36 jurors selected in the Harrisburg, Camden, and Gainesville trials, the jury selection experts picked 34 who voted for acquittal. Moreover, in each case, they successfully predicted who the jury would select as its foreperson.

The proponents of the use of social science techniques in jury selection argue forcefully that the state has an enormous edge over the defense. The exclusive use of registered voters for potential jurors makes the jury finally selected predominantly white, middle, and working class. As defenders of elite-enforced norms, they are unlikely to be sympathetic with political deviants or persons with deviant life-styles. As relatively successful people, they will not likely identify with those who are poor and minorities. Moreover, the state has the resources (money and

PANEL 12-1

Some Facts About Juries

- Of all the criminal jury trials in the world, some 80 percent occur in the United States.
- More than 90 percent of all cases in the United States never come before a jury.
- Some 300,000 cases a year come before a jury.
- About 3 million citizens are called to jury duty every year, and 40 percent never get on a jury at all.
- Jurors serve an average of 10 days.
- For their services, the nation's jurors are paid $20 million a year (a high of $45 a day in Kewaunee County, Wisconsin, to a low of $5 a day in San Francisco) and their absence from work costs their employers an estimated $1 billion.
- A study of 3000 jurors in 1976 found that 90 percent had a favorable reaction to jury duty.
- About 80 percent of the time judge and jury agree on the verdict.
- When they disagree in a criminal case, the jury is six times more likely to acquit than the judge.

Source: Selected from Otto Friedrich, "We, the Jury, Find the . . ." Time, September 28, 1981, pp. 44–56.

personnel) to investigate the backgrounds of prospective jurors whereas the defense usually does not.

In answering their critics, Schulman and his associates argued:

Our contribution to the defense effort was within the law; we did no "jury tampering". We spoke with none of the prospective jurors before their appearance in the courtroom. And we agreed before the trial that if anyone from our survey sample was called as a prospective juror, we would not provide defense lawyers with specific information about that person. If our behavior was improper, the impropriety was an ethical, not a legal matter.

Is it ethical, for instance, for social scientists to take sides in a dispute, in negotiations, or in any social interaction? The question has already been answered positively by market researchers, military and industrial psychologists, private political pollsters, and many other social scientists engaged in applied research. . . .

In the Harrisburg trial, we believed strongly that the defendants' rights to presumption of innocence was seriously threatened. The Government chose a conservative location of the trial. J. Edgar Hoover proclaimed the defendants' guilt long before the trial began. William Lynch [the prosecutor] made public some of the controversial Berrigan-McAlister letters. As in most criminal and political trials, the investigatory and financial resources of the Government far outweighed those of the defendants. And the trial raised a host of constitutional questions, from wire-tapping to conspiracy law. For these reasons we believed, and still believe, that our partisanship was proper. (Schulman et al., 1973, p. 84)

Opponents are especially skeptical of the application of social science techniques in jury selection because the interest is not to eliminate bias but to create it. The method is designed to stack the jury in favor of the defendant, and therefore, an unconstitutional manipulation of the criminal justice system. As Sykes has argued:

That jury stacking is a common practice among trial lawyers does not justify further abuse of the system with techniques of the social sciences. The liberal causes that have motivated social scientists to engage in this work have tended to obscure the fact that they are attempting to create biased rather than impartial juries—which is tampering with the jury. (Sykes, 1978, p. 426)

The Presentation of Evidence: Procedures and Protocol

After the jury is selected the trial begins. The prosecution opens the case by explaining to the jury the charge against the defendant and the case that the state will build to establish his or her guilt. After the prosecutor's opening statement, the attorney for the defendant makes an opening statement outlining the strategy for establishing the innocence of the accused. Although the opening statements by both sides are relatively wide open, several limitations exist: statements by both lawyers are not to be portrayed as evidence, neither side can refer to evidence they know is inadmissible, and prosecutors cannot refer to any prior criminal record[3] of the accused.

The prosecution presents its case first. Witnesses are called and questioned under oath. After each witness, the lawyer for the defendant has the right to cross-examine. This interrogation is fundamental to the adversary system. The object is to attack the credibility of the witness and to add new information.

At the completion of the prosecution's efforts, the defense calls its witnesses. As before, the witnesses are questioned by the defense attorney and cross-examined by the prosecutor.

The judge acts as a referee in the trial insuring that the rights of the accused are

---

[3] Unless they are being tried under "habitual criminal" statutes.

protected and that proper procedures are followed in the interrogation of witnesses and the presentation of evidence. Foremost, the judge must guarantee that the rules of evidence (from the English common law) are followed. These rules prohibit certain types of evidence because they either obscure the truth or violate somebody's legal rights. (The following is taken largely from Sykes, 1978, pp. 426–429.)

First, with few exceptions, hearsay evidence is not acceptable in court. Hearsay evidence refers to a statement that a witness obtained indirectly or from someone else. A witness can only testify to what she or he saw or heard not to what somebody told them they saw or heard. The reason why hearsay evidence is usually not permitted is that there is no opportunity to cross-examine the actual witness. An exception may be a statement of a dying person made to the testifying witness.

A second rule of evidence is that privileged communications are usually excluded. The privacy of communications between wife and husband, lawyer and client, psychiatrist and patient, and priest and parishioner are protected. The reasons why these communications are exempt are that the integrity of such relationships require protection and the testimony, if allowed, would be difficult to verify.

A third rule concerning admissible and inadmissible evidence is the controversial exclusionary rule. This rule, stemming from the Supreme Court's 1961 interpretation of the Fourth Amendment, forbids federal and state governments from using evidence in violation of constitutional guarantees against unreasonable search and seizure. In short, evidence gathered illegally cannot be used against suspects in court. The intent of the exclusionary rule is to prevent police excesses, which in their zeal to apprehend criminals violate civil rights. Proponents argue that if the police were allowed to use illegally obtained evidence, then the integrity of law enforcement would be diminished. Opponents argue that the exclusionary rule makes a mockery of the criminal justice system since it allows people to go free on a technicality, even though there is evidence of their guilt.

The Reagan administration sought to modify the exclusionary rule with a "reasonable good-faith" exception. This proposal would permit evidence to be admitted in a trial if police officers had acted in "good faith," not knowing that they had violated the law. There are three major problems with this compromise. First, it invites a flood of litigation defining what "good" and "bad" faith is. Second, judges will vary in their interpretations of what police behaviors are considered in "good faith" thus inviting court appeals and further clogging the courts. And, third, the proposal encourages law enforcement officials to feign ignorance or to be ignorant of the law (*Forbes,* 1983).

Jerome Skolnick, a law professor and avowed liberal, has argued that the Reagan proposal is a timely, moderate, and sensible one, affirming police fidelity to the law (Skolnick, 1982). He feels that the proposal is moderate because it does not call for the repeal of the exclusionary rule. Second, the police must still act prudently enough to convince the court that the mistakes were objectively reasonable. Third, the police cannot argue, in good faith, that they made the same mistake more than once. And, finally, if we get rid of the results of the exclusionary rule that most offend common sense, then public pressures to reduce the civil rights of the accused should decline.

In 1984 the Supreme Court made two decisions that undercut the exclusionary rule considerably. In the first instance (*Nix v. Williams*) the Court allowed evidence obtained illegally to be used if "it probably would have been found legally." In the second case (*New York v. Quarles*) the Court ruled that the police can ask questions of a suspect *without* first giving Miranda warnings if their questions are "prompted by a concern for public safety."

A fourth important rule of evidence is the defendant's protection, by the Constitution's Fifth Amendment, from self-incrimination. This means that the accused may choose not to testify. If he or she does not testify, the prosecution cannot introduce testimony concerning past crimes of the defendant. If the defendant does take the stand, he or she is treated as any other witness, subject to cross-examination, and may not refuse to answer any proper question.

When the defense rests its case, the prosecution has the opportunity to rebut any points made by the defense. This choice may not be taken because new witnesses or evidence cannot be introduced.

The attorneys for both sides sum up their positions in their closing arguments. The prosecutor presents the state's case first, followed by the defense, and a rebuttal by the prosecution. Each side summarizes its case and tries to combine everything in a logical manner for the jury. The prosecutor is more constrained than the defense in these closing arguments because his or her misconduct is subject to appeal while misconduct by the defense attorney is not appealable if the defendant is acquitted (Stuckey, 1976, p. 188). Because the prosecution is under a threat of committing a prejudicial error, he/she is less likely than the defense attorney to appeal to the emotions of the jury in these closing statements.

The next step is for the judge to instruct the jury as to the relevant laws in the case. Most significant, the judge instructs the jury on the doctrine of "beyond a reasonable doubt," which assumes the accused innocent unless there is strong evidence of his/her guilt.

The jury retires to the jury room to reach a verdict. While the members deliberate, they are prohibited from communicating with anyone other than a court bailiff or the trial judge. They are also not allowed to read newspapers or watch television accounts of the trial.

Occasionally, a jury cannot reach a decision, which results in a hung jury. The judge then declares a mistrial and the prosecutor is faced with the decision to retry the case, plea bargain for reduced charges, or to drop the charges.

Nearly three fourths of all trials end in guilty verdicts. If acquitted, the defendant goes free and cannot be tried again for the same crime (under the Constitutional guarantee of no double jeopardy). If guilty, the defendant may appeal. The defense may ask for a mistrial if it believes the judge acted prejudicially or if the jury was compromised by outside information, bribes, or threats. The case may be appealed to an appellate court. These courts may choose not to hear a case (in effect, agreeing with the original decision). If they consider the case, the record of the lower court is reviewed carefully to determine the legality of the proceedings. Only about one fifth of those cases that are heard by appellate courts are reversed, and the majority of these result in reconvictions after retrial (Hunt, 1972, p. 380). While a case is being appealed, the defendant is usually allowed to be free.

Under the dual court system, the state and federal courts are separate. Violators of state laws are tried in state courts and appeals are limited to the appellate courts within that state. The only state cases that may be appealed to the federal level are those involving the alleged violation of federal law or constitutional rights.

An important guarantee provided persons found guilty of state laws is the writ of habeas corpus. Prisoners who believe that they have been unconstitutionally convicted in state court, and the state's appellate courts have refused to redress the wrongs, have a final appeal outside the state courts—the federal *habeas corpus* petition. If accepted, the federal district courts and federal appeals courts can judge whether constitutional guarantees have been denied in the state courts. The Reagan administration proposed to limit *habeas corpus* by barring those petitions of persons who fail to begin the petitioning process within one year after all state appeals have failed. The administration's justification for this dilution of a constitutional protection is that *habeas corpus* petitions have flooded the courts. Judd Burstein, a lawyer, has made two important arguments against the Reagan proposal. First, the inundation of the courts with *habeas corpus* petitions has not been the case. In fiscal 1981, for example, each of the federal district courts have an average of only 13 such petitions. Second, and more important, it is fairness, not convenience, that must characterize the judicial system.

> Constitutional rights, by their very nature, are inconvenient. They stand as a buffer between the state and the citizen, assuring the citizen of fair prosecution. Undoubtedly, life for the judges and court aides would be easier if they did not have to be so concerned about a defendant's constitutional rights. Indeed, it is true that most habeas-corpus petitions are without merit, for most state prisoners have received fair treatment. But what of those relatively few prisoners . . . whose rights are grievously violated? Do we allow them to slip through the cracks of the justice system? Can we justify, for example, a refusal to overturn a conviction based upon prosecutorial pandering to racial prejudice simply because a state court already has rejected an appeal or because the defendant, perhaps through ignorance, did not present his constitutional claim to the federal courts until a year and a day after it had been rejected by the state court? Does the passage of time or an erroneous decision by a state court make this violation of the right to due process any more tolerable? (Burstein, 1982, p. 72)

Sentencing: Judicial Discretion

We have seen that throughout the criminal justice process—from the initial police contact to the various options open to prosecutors—there is considerable latitude in the choices open to authorities. The process tightens up during the actual trial with a number of safeguards to protect the rights of the accused. But once the accused is found guilty by a jury (or more commonly pleads guilty without going to trial), the judge is given sweeping powers to sentence the offender. Marvin

Frankel, a federal appellate judge, has argued that "the almost wholly unchecked and sweeping powers we give judges in the fashioning of sentences are terrifying and intolerable for a society that professes devotion to the rule of law." (1973, p. 5)

Probation

A major sentencing decision of judges is whether to send the offender to prison or to place him or her on probation. The choice, about 60 percent of the time, is probation. Probation permits the offender to live in the community under supervision and under conditions imposed by the judge. Probation, although clearly a more lenient punishment than incarceration is nevertheless, a degrading penalty.

> When placed on supervised probation (the usual case) the probationer is often required to fulfill a variety of demeaning stipulations or conditions. The conditions of probation are often left to the discretion of courts and probation services, though they have in some cases been legislated and thus made part of the official criminal code. The degradations lie in these conditions. Probationers have been told they must attend church; must not marry without permission; must not drive a car, even if needed for work; must spend their evenings and days in ways dictated by probation officers; must spend their earnings only in certain ways; must not travel certain distances, or to certain places; must dress in ways that conform to community standards; or must not smoke or drink. (Barlow, 1981, p. 414; see Imlay and Glasheen, 1971; Czajkoski, 1973)

The American Bar Association (1970, p. 1) argued that probation is a desirable disposition in appropriate cases because:

1. It maximizes the liberty of the individual while at the same time vindicating the authority of the law and effectively protecting the public from further violations of the law.
2. It affirmatively promotes the rehabilitation of the offender by continuing normal community contacts.
3. It voids the negative and frequently stultifying effects of confinement, which often severely and unnecessarily complicate the reintegration of the offender into the community.
4. It greatly reduces the financial costs to the public treasury of an effective correctional system.
5. It minimizes the impact of the conviction upon innocent dependents of the offender.

There are some general guidelines for when probation is permissible. Generally excluded from this sentence are offenders of serious crimes and repeat offenders of felonies. Beyond these restrictions judges are left wide discretion. They pre-

TABLE 12-1

Percentage of Probations Adjudicated Guilty by Selected Social Characteristics

Variable	Percentage Adjudicated Guilty
Race	
Whites	28.3
Blacks	41.1
Age	
Under 21	21.4
21–25	32.8
26–35	41.3
36 and over	48.3
Education	
0–6 years	49.6
7–9 years	38.2
10–11 years	28.3
High school graduate	25.6
Some college	21.7
Type of attorney	
Court appointed	39.3
Private	28.2
Type of plea	
Not guilty	47.1
Guilty	33.7
Nolo contendere	19.9

SOURCE: Adapted from Theodore G. Chiricos, Phillip D. Jackson, and Gordon P. Waldo, "Inequality in the Imposition of a Criminal Label," *Social Problems* 19, Spring, 1972, pp. 558, 561.

sumably decide whether to place on probation or imprison, based on a careful study of the offender's criminal background and potential for success. Unfortunately, when judges review the case, their decisions often reflect stereotypes common in the rest of society. Their judgments are often based on such questions as what type of person is a safer risk, a black or white? an uneducated or educated person? a white-collar worker or a chronically unemployed, unskilled person? One study of the social characteristics of 2419 consecutive felony probation cases in Florida reveals that judges tend to be biased against certain kinds of people (Chiricos, Jackson, and Waldo, 1972). Florida law, as is typical in most states, has two forms of probation. The judge has the option of withholding adjudication of guilt from defendants who are placed on probation. For persons accused of a felony, this step allows them to escape the stigma associated with the status of "convicted" felon. Others are given probation but formally adjudicated as guilty. The findings indicate a bias by judges against blacks, the poor, the poorly educated, and those who are defended by court-appointed attorneys (see Table 12-1).

Evidence of Judicial Capriciousness in Sentencing

For the most part, we have had a system of individualized justice. In other words, the judge can take into account the peculiar factors of the case in his/her decision. Although this is a worthy ideal, the procedure does give judges the right to make arbitrary decisions. As Frankel has argued:

> Everyone with the least training in law would be prompt to denounce a statute that merely said the penalty for crimes "shall be any term the judge sees fit to impose." A regime of such arbitrary fiat would be intolerable in a supposedly free society, to say nothing of being invalid under our due-process clause. But the fact is that we have accepted unthinkingly a criminal code creating in effect precisely that degree of unbridled power. (1973, p. 8)

The discretionary power of judges has resulted in a sort of courtroom roulette. Let's look at some examples of the disparities in sentencing among judges.

Item   Two persons guilty of embezzling about the same amount of money, both with previously clean records, served time in the federal penitentiary in Atlanta. They had appeared before different judges; one received a sentence of 117 days, whereas the other got 20 years (Mapes, 1970).

Item   Violators of federal forgery laws received an average jail term of 22 months in New York, 45 months in California, and 70 months in Kansas (Mapes, 1970).

Item   In 1983, a Denver judge sentenced a man to four years in prison for murdering his wife. In that same year, the Supreme Court considered the case of a South Dakota man who was sentenced to life imprisonment for writing a $100 "no account" check.

Item   In an experiment, 50 federal judges in the East were presented with a number of hypothetical cases to ascertain the range of sentences they would impose. For a cab driver convicted of selling heroin, the sentences ranged from 1 to 10 years. A businessman convicted of tax evasion received anywhere from three months and a $5000 fine to 3 years and a $5000 fine. A 26-year-old with no prior record convicted of theft from an interstate shipment received anywhere from 4 years probation to $7\frac{1}{2}$ years in prison (Malloy, 1974, p. 5).

These examples clearly show that judges have varied widely in their sentencing. These sentences, moreover, are not subject to review by a higher court. The conviction can be appealed, but the sentence stands unless it is cruel or blatantly bizarre. The argument for granting judges this power is that the sentence should fit the criminal not just the crime.

These examples of inconsistent sentences indicate the judges' wide latitude. There are a number of factors that account for these disparities. An obvious one is the variation in the demands by state legislatures. Drug laws during the 1970s present a clear example of variation by jurisdiction. In New York, for example, the possession of one eighth of an ounce of marijuana meant an indeterminate sentence of eight years to life, whereas in Oregon, possession of less than an ounce meant probation and a fine not to exceed $100.

Most fundamental to the judicial variation in sentencing is the principle that each individual case deserves to be judged on its own merits. No two cases are precisely alike and this requires individualized evaluation. The judge must consider the type of crime, the circumstances surrounding the crime, the age of the defendant, and his or her previous criminal record.

There is also the possibility of judicial bias. The majority of judges are particularly harsh on political dissidents because these persons challenge the foundations of the system judges are sworn to protect. The gender of the offender is another potential source of judicial bias. Some judges are sexist as they are more punitive to males (or females) because of their assumptions about the differences between the sexes behaviors and motivations.

The social class of the offender is another extra-legal characteristic that makes a clear difference in judicial sentencing. We have noted throughout this book that upper-class criminals receive relatively light sentences for corporate crimes, fraud, embezzlement, and the like compared with the sentence given to those guilty of predominantly lower-class crimes such as robbery, burglary, and assault. For example, a man pleaded guilty to the illegal trading of $20 million with Swiss banks. He received a $30,000 fine and a suspended sentence. A few days later the same judge heard the case of an unemployed black who pleaded guilty to stealing a television set worth $100; the judge sentenced him to one year in jail (Mapes, 1970). Unfortunately, such an example is not an aberration. There is a clear bias against crimes committed by the poor, minorities, and the working class, and favorable to criminals from the upper strata of society.

Race has been and continues to be another relevant factor in the sentencing process. Let's examine some evidence for this assertion.

Item A study of 787 misdemeanor cases in Detroit found that black defendants, even when represented by a lawyer, received jail terms twice as often as whites (Mapes, 1970).

Item A study of sentences for rape in Florida between 1940 and 1964 found that none of the whites found guilty of raping a black woman was sentenced to death but 54 percent of the blacks found guilty of raping a white woman were (Florida Civil Liberties Union, 1964).

Item A 1980 Rand Corporation study sponsored by the Department of Justice found that California courts typically imposed sentences six and a half months longer for Hispanics and one and a half months longer for blacks than for whites; in Michigan, sentences averaged more than seven months longer for blacks than for whites; and in Texas the average was three and a half months longer for blacks and two months longer for Hispanics than was the case for whites (*Justice Assistance News,* 1983).

Item A study of males found that blacks were 20 percent more likely to be sentenced to prison than whites, even when the type of offense, prior record, and other variables were controlled (Spohn, Grul, and Welch, 1981).

TABLE 12-2

Average Length of Sentence (Months) for Federal Prisoners by Offense and Race, 1979

Offense	Race	
	White	**All Other**
Assault	96.5	108.4
Burglary	88.4	80.1
Drug laws	80.8	101.3
Embezzlement	42.1	44.6
Robbery	176.7	172.5
Kidnapping	353.7	414.5
Juvenile delinquency	25.6	67.4
Income tax	26.1	47.8
Military court martial	262.1	286.5

SOURCE: Timothy J. Flanagan, David J. van Alstyne, and Michael R. Gottfredson (eds.), *Sourcebook of Criminal Justice Statistics—1981,* Washington, D.C.: U.S. Department of Justice, 1982, p. 490.

Item   The data on federal prisons for 1979 reveal that the average sentence for a white inmate was 98.9 months compared with 130.2 months (over two and a half years more) for the average nonwhite inmate (see Table 12-2).

Item   Unnever, Frazier, and Henretla (1980) found that whites have an 18 percent greater chance of receiving probation than blacks.

These examples show clearly that blacks (and one could find the same differences for Indians, Chicanos, and other minority racial groups, as well) are discriminated against in sentences by judges.

One could argue that these sentencing disparities were part of our racist past but that this is no longer the case, but there is considerable evidence that racism as a factor in sentencing persists. In 1977 there were 114 men on death row in Florida prisons and 94 percent of them had killed a white victim, 2 percent had killed white and black victims, and 4 percent had killed only blacks (Zeisel, 1981). These data suggest that the victim's race may have a conscious or unconscious effect on the sentencing judge—killing a white person is a more serious crime than killing a black one. Zeisel found this bias and also discovered that it was strengthened further when the race of the offender was added to the equation.

Forty-seven percent of the black defendants arrested for murdering a white victim were sent to Florida's death row; only twenty-four percent of the white defendants arrested for murdering a white victim received the same sentence. When both the victim and offender were black, the ratio sank to one percent. There were no white persons on death row for killing only a black person; there had never been such a person on Florida's death row in living memory. (Zeisel, 1981, p. 460)

A reevaluation of research on racial bias in criminal sentencing in capital cases from 1930 to 1978 reveals that racial bias in death sentences and/or executions is present only in the South (Kleck, 1981). But this apparent nonbias in the non-South may be a consequence of the devalued status of black crime victims. As Zeisel noted above, black offenders are not punished as much as white offenders because their victims are usually black and, as pointed out in Chapter 5, most street crime victimization in the United States is intraracial. The research of two sociologists, William Bowers and Glenn Pierce, determined this in their analysis of data from Florida, Texas, Georgia, and Ohio. In Texas, for example, the statistical probability of a death sentence is 18 times greater if the victim is white rather than black (cited in Associated Press, 1979).

A major reason why there is such a wide discrepancy in sentencing is the common practice of the use of the indeterminate sentence—for example, a sentence of 5 to 15 years. The rationale for this form of sentencing is that once prisoners have been rehabilitated they should be released. Since judges at sentencing cannot predict accurately how long this will take, they vary in the maximum sentence imposed. The net effect of these indeterminate sentences is that prison officials and the parole board decide the actual length of sentence.

The problems with indeterminate sentencing are many. Foremost, the discretionary power of the judge is shifted to the parole board. This board may make decisions based on whether the prison is overcrowded or not. Since parole board members are typically appointed, they may have been chosen for their liberalism or more likely, their conservatism, and thus the political composition of the board will affect their decision making.

Since indeterminate sentences are based on the presumed rehabilitation of imprisoned criminals, there is the problem of knowing when a prisoner is "rehabilitated." There are no guidelines, rules, or standards, which results often in a lack of uniformity in parole decisions.

In addition to the demoralizing effects of inconsistent parole decisions on prisoners, they are further frustrated psychologically by not knowing when their release will occur. They only know the data when they may first apply for parole. This and subsequent applications for parole that are rejected have a devastating effect on the morale of individual prisoners. And, if rage and alienation are the consequence, then rehabilitation will continue to be an elusive goal of our penal institutions.

An Alternative: Determinate Sentences

The wide disparity in sentencing and the further differences in actual time spent in prison leads to the obvious charge of injustice. One consequence of this is a feeling of alienation among prisoners who see that their sentences are unjust and unreasonable compared with others. At the other extreme are members of the public and politicians who voice their displeasure with what they feel are relatively light sentences to some felons. Thus, there have been some alternatives to permitting judges such freedom in sentencing.

In 1977, California was the first[4] state to replace indeterminate sentences with

---

[4]By 1983, nine states—California, Connecticut, Minnesota, New Mexico, North Carolina, Maine, Indiana, Illinois, and Colorado—enacted determinate sentencing laws, thus eliminating the discretionary power of parole boards to release prisoners.

determinate sentences. This change reflected a shift in philosophy—from the rehabilitation of prisoners to their punishment (Brewer, Beckett, and Holt, 1981). This was acceptable because many legislators, penologists, and others had become disillusioned with the apparent lack of rehabilitation taking place in prisons. For example, a review of 231 studies by Lipton, Martinson, and Wilkes (1975) led to Martinson's (1974, p. 25) conclusion that "with few and isolated exceptions, the rehabilitative efforts that have been reported so far have had no appreciable effect on recidivism" (this will be elaborated further in Chapter 13).

The provisions of the California plan are (Brewer et al., 1981, pp. 204–205):

1. Judges retain the discretion to choose between probation and prison for all but the most serious crimes.
2. For each crime, judges are empowered to choose between one of three sentences. For example, for second-degree murder, the judge must choose a sentence of five, six, or seven years. It is assumed that the judge will assign the middle sentence unless aggravating or mitigating circumstances are found.
3. If more than one crime is charged, the judge selects the sentence for the more serious as the base and decides whether the others will result in concurrent or consecutive terms. If the terms are consecutive, one third of the middle sentence of the crime committed is added to the base term.
4. Every year of the prisoner's term may be reduced by three months for good conduct and one month for participation in a work program.
5. There is a standard one-year parole period for all but lifers, who have a three-year parole period.
6. Retroactive provisions provide for the recalculation of sentences for persons imprisoned under indeterminate sentences.

A Variation of Determinate Sentencing: Mandatory Sentences

Some argue that even determinate sentences, while more punitive than indeterminate sentences, are still too lenient. The judges still can give probation in many cases and can opt for relatively light sentences, and the prisoners can reduce their sentences through good behavior. Consequently, there has been a trend toward mandatory sentences, which provide for an absolute sentence with no provision for probation or parole. As of 1983, some 43 states had enacted laws requiring mandatory sentences for people convicted of violent crime; 30 states had mandatory sentences for repeat offenders; and 37 states had set mandatory prison terms for violations of gun laws (Galvin, 1983).

Clearly, the discretionary powers of judges are reduced significantly if such a plan is implemented. The main arguments are directed, however, at the certainty of punishment and the reduction of crime. The proponents of mandatory sentences make three arguments for their position. First, crowded courts and shrinking budgets combine to create a system of "stopwatch justice on overloaded assembly lines" (Kennedy, 1976), with the result that crime pays (see Figure 12-1). Second, defense lawyers, prosecutors, and judges are pressured to plea bargain, which allows offenders to receive relatively light sentences. If they are

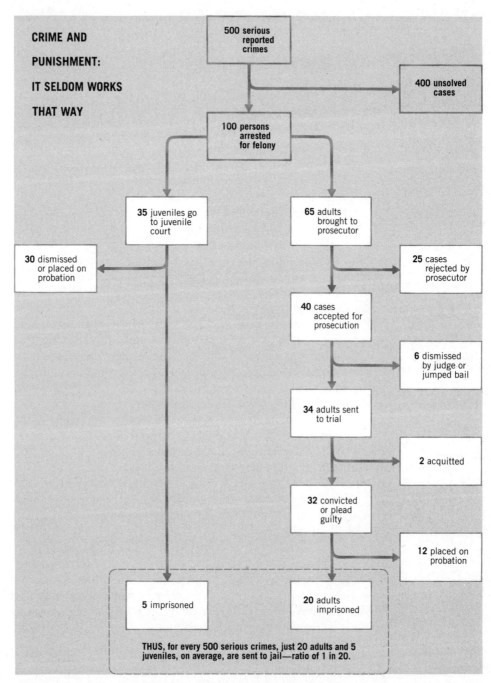

CRIME AND PUNISHMENT: IT SELDOM WORKS THAT WAY

- 500 serious reported crimes
- 400 unsolved cases
- 100 persons arrested for felony
- 35 juveniles go to juvenile court
- 65 adults brought to prosecutor
- 30 dismissed or placed on probation
- 25 cases rejected by prosecutor
- 40 cases accepted for prosecution
- 6 dismissed by judge or jumped bail
- 34 adults sent to trial
- 2 acquitted
- 32 convicted or plead guilty
- 12 placed on probation
- 5 imprisoned
- 20 adults imprisoned

THUS, for every 500 serious crimes, just 20 adults and 5 juveniles, on average, are sent to jail—ratio of 1 in 20.

Figure 12-1 For every 500 serious crimes, just 20 adults and five juveniles, on average, are sent to jail—a ratio of 1 in 20 (USN&WA—Basic data: INSLAW, Inc.).

SOURCE: *U.S. News & World Report,* Nov. 1, 1982, p. 41.

PANEL 12-2

The Case for Mandatory Sentencing

Edward M. Kennedy, Senator

Today I introduce bipartisan legislation calling for the imposition of mandatory minimum sentences in certain cases of violent street crime—the crime which troubles our citizens the most. This legislation provides that a mandatory minimum sentence of 2 years imprisonment—without the possibility of probation or parole—be imposed: First, in cases involving burglary or aggravated assault under the assimilated crime statute; second, murder in the second degree; third, crimes in which a handgun or other dangerous weapon is used; fourth, rape; fifth, robbery where the victim suffers serious bodily injury; and sixth, trafficking in heroin. In addition, a 4-year minimum term would be imposed if the convicted defendant were a repeat offender who had committed one of the above enumerated crimes for a second time.

An exception to the imposition of a mandatory sentence would be permitted only if the defendant were under 18 years of age, suffering from a mental disease, acted under duress or was merely an accomplice and not the principal offender. A post-trial hearing would be held to resolve such situations.

This legislation is designed to deal with the spreading plague of violent street crime which has risen by over 57 per cent since 1968 and by some 18 per cent the first 6 months of this year. This proliferation of violent street crime must be dealt with firmly. It is intolerable when the Nation's citizens must walk their own neighborhood streets in fear of being mugged or robbed. Recent surveys show that almost one-half of our population is afraid to venture out of their homes at night. In addition, the statistics demonstrate that one out of every three homes in our inner cities is the target of a burglary during a one-year period. More often than not, the victims of these street crimes are the poor and the minority groups who live in the inner cities. Direct, immediate action is needed now to stem this wave of violent crime.

What I introduce today is not touted as the final solution to our soaring crime problem. The problem of crime is elusive and complex; it defies simple analysis. The major first step for all of us to take in fighting crime is to recognize and acknowledge candidly that there is no easy panacea, no magic formula for reducing the Nation's crime rate. Certainly, slogans like "law and order" or the more subtle euphemism "domestic tranquility" are not the answer to rising crime. Tough talk without action avails us nothing.

But we must not counter the "law and order" syndrome with arguments that crime can only be controlled by eliminating poverty and discrimination and providing decent health care and education to our citizens. These are, of course, noble goals which all citizens of conscience must steadfastly pursue. Our heritage requires no less.

Panel 12-2 (Continued)

But firm, immediate action must be taken now to deal with crime; we must all fight a more practical, less ideological war on crime.

The bill that I am introducing is a modest step in the right direction. It deals with the very heart of our criminal justice system—the sentencing process. It is there that we must concentrate our efforts.

We must make punishment and imprisonment of the violent offender a certainty. Our existing criminal justice system—beset with expanding dockets, court congestion, and overcrowding—does not persuade the criminal offender that if he is caught, the chances are high that he will be swiftly and surely punished. The result, in all too many cases, is that crime does indeed pay. During an 8-month period in 1974, a special Boston police anticrime unit made 636 individual arrests for violent street crimes. Yet only 7 per cent of those arrested received a jail sentence of any duration. In New York City, 97 per cent of all adults arrested for a felony are filtered out of the system and escape a prison term. Simply stated, swift, certain punishment of the offender has all too often become the exception rather than the rule.

By imposing mandatory minimum sentences, this bill makes certainty of punishment more of a reality. The bill is not based on any vindictive desire to punish. Rather, it arises out of the need to deter potential offenders from criminal conduct while, at the same time, keeping the violent offender in jail and off the street.

In applying the mandatory minimum sentence we must also make sure that it is applied even handedly to all offenders, regardless of social class. Just as the poor suffer the most as victims of crime, so too do they often pay a heavier price for crime than others in society. We must end that shameful double standard and assure that mandatory sentences be applied with an equal hand.

I am aware that the Federal Government's role in this area is limited. Most street crime occurs in local neighborhoods and is purely a local problem. Nevertheless, Federal crime legislation incorporating mandatory minimum sentences can be a model for governments in confronting their criminal justice problems and the problems of sentencing.

To call for such sentences, however, without providing the courts with the financial resources and technical assistance necessary to meet the challenge of increased case loads would be self-defeating. Certainty of punishment must be coupled with swift justice. The Congress must increase financial aid and assistance to the courts if the concept of mandatory minimum sentences is to be truly effective.

Source: Edward M. Kennedy, from a statement presented on the floor of the U.S. Senate on November 20, 1975, on the occasion of his co-introducing S. 2698. Reprinted in American Bar Association, Congressional Digest 55, August/September 1976, pp. 204, 206, 208.

placed on probation, receive suspended sentences, or short jail sentences, they are soon back on the streets to again commit crimes. Third, mandatory sentences would, according to its champions, demand certain punishment, which is the greatest deterrent, and would reduce crime (see Panel 12-2).

The arguments against mandatory sentencing are convincing. The American Bar Association through its Project on Standards for Criminal Justice has argued that the imposition of mandatory sentences does not distinguish between offenders who do and offenders who do not deserve the harsh treatment demanded.

> . . . [I]t is at most only some offenders from whom the public needs . . . protection, and the legislature is not in a position to identify the precise individuals who pose the feared risk. It is perfectly apparent that *every* robber and *every* mugger, and indeed *every* murderer does not pose the same type of future danger to the community. (American Bar Association, 1976, p. 205)

The absolute imposition of mandatory sentences may be unjust to some offenders. A classic example is that of William James Rummel who was sentenced to life in Texas for thefts totaling $229.11 (Goetz, 1980). In 1964, Rummel used someone else's credit card to buy tires worth $80; in 1969 he forged a check for $28.36; and in 1972 he accepted a check for $120.75 to repair an air conditioner but never did the work. Texas law was clear: anyone convicted of three noncapital felonies is an habitual criminal and must automatically serve a life sentence. He began his life sentence in 1973, while appealing the case to the Supreme Court. His argument before the court was that this punishment was unconstitutionally cruel and unusual since it was so disproportionate to his crimes. The court ruled, in 1980, by a 5 to 4 margin *against* Rummel. Writing for the majority, Justice William Rehnquist argued that states have the right to set sentences in what are their interests. The Constitution does not demand uniformity in sentences because this would be against states' rights. The Supreme court reversed itself, however, in 1983 when, by a 5 to 4 decision, it ruled for the first time in history that a prison sentence can be struck down because it was too harsh for the crime committed. In this case, a South Dakota judge had sentenced Jerry B. Hein to life imprisonment without parole as a repeat offender. Hein had a history of seven nonviolent felony crimes (burglary, writing bad checks, and driving while intoxicated). Justice Powell, writing for the majority, argued that a jail term must be proportionate to the crime and this was clearly not the case in the sentence given Hein in South Dakota. Chief Justice Burger, in his dissent, argued that the Supreme Court should not meddle in the business of the states. Meanwhile, William Rummel in Texas was unaffected by the ruling in the Hein case because he did have the possibility of parole after 12 years.

A third objection to mandatory sentences is a practical one: it increases the size of the already crowded prison population dramatically. In a study sponsored by the LEAA of the Justice Department, criminologists Joan Petersilia and Peter Greenwood found that mandatory sentences reduce the crime rate but at a cost of boosting prison populations. Among their findings (cited in *Human Behavior,* 1979):

1. Violent felonies would be reduced by 15.8 percent if each offender who had a previous conviction were sentenced to five years. Such a plan would increase the prison population by 190 percent.

2. If all offenders convicted of *any* felony were automatically sentenced to five years, the crime rate would be reduced by 31 percent but the number of prisoners would rise by 450 percent as a result.

3. The optimum situation—the highest crime reduction at the least cost—would be to imprison all felons for 1.2 years. This would reduce the crime rate by 20 percent and increase the prison population by 85 percent.

The recent trend is for legislatures to enact legislation requiring mandatory sentences for certain crimes. One result was that the prison population has increased dramatically, as we will see in Chapter 14.

A final objection to mandatory sentences is that they may have an opposite effect from the one intended. The goal of mandatory sentences is to have a relatively harsh and certain punishment. Legislatures have sometimes passed mandatory sentencing laws too quickly and without adequate study. For example, the Massachusetts legislature in 1975 passed a law requiring a judge to impose a one-year sentence for carrying a gun. Similarly, the New York legislature in 1973 passed a law requiring extremely harsh sentences for drug offenders. Such laws may backfire if they are perceived by police, prosecutors, juries, and judges as too extreme. Consequently, these upholders of the laws may be reluctant to seek the arrest and conviction of suspects. A study by the National Institute of Justice found that in both New York and Massachusetts the actual number of offenders affected by the harsher penalties demanded by the law was much smaller than expected (cited in Allen, 1982). A Detroit judge, speaking of the 20-year minimum sentence applicable upon conviction of the sale of narcotics said:

> This is a ridiculous law, passed in the heat of passion without any thought of its real consequences. I absolutely refuse to send to prison for twenty years a young boy who had done nothing more than sell a single marijuana cigarette to a buddy. The law was not intended for such cases. I have been accused of usurping commutation and pardon powers. This is not true. I simply will not give excessive sentences and where the legislature leaves me no alternative, I will lower the charge or dismiss altogether. (quoted in American Bar Association, 1976, p. 207)

Thus, the mandatory sentences may backfire and the discretionary powers of the judge, supposedly curtailed, are used to circumvent the intent of the legislature.

THEORETICAL INTERPRETATIONS OF THE AMERICAN CRIMINAL COURT PROCESS

The principle guiding the American legal system is best summed up in the inscription on the U.S. Supreme Court building: "Equal Justice Under Law." Is the process followed by the United States and state courts programmed to ensure that this goal of equal justice actually occurs? Are individuals regardless of social position, wealth, race, and ethnicity recipients of equal treatment in the courts? Do we, as Willis (1981, p. 11) has asked, "have a single system of justice applied equally to all, or do we have a dual system of justice?" The traditional sociological approach has assumed, incorrectly, that the United States has a single system of justice. Interactionists and radicals agree on the contrary position that the United States has a skewed system of justice, which is therefore unjust.

The Perspective of Traditional Sociology

The traditional assumption has been the acceptance of the system as basically just. The laws are based on consensus. Violations of the laws require punishment since the "collective conscience" has been violated and the moral boundaries of society must be maintained. Thus, the courts serve to preserve the social order.

Traditional sociologists further posit that in the processing of alleged criminals, offense-related factors (such as prior record, the offense charged, and the circumstances accompanying the criminal incident) are more influential in the case's disposition than offender-related factors such as age, sex, race, and occupation (Hagan et al., 1979). Adherents of this approach are not bothered by the data that show the lower classes are more likely than the middle and upper classes to be found guilty and punished more severely because these people are less likely to share the values and behaviors of the successful in society. These persons, from this perspective, are simply more likely to commit criminal acts and therefore it is logical that they are overrepresented in the courts and in the prisons.

The fundamental problem of the courts from the traditional perspective is not the process (which critics argue is biased) but that the process is often stymied by being overloaded. The answer is more judges, more prosecutors and assistants, more court personnel, and more prisons. More repressive measures may also be necessary: mandatory and uniform sentencing, preventive detention before trial, and reform of the exclusionary rule and other civil rights that (it is argued) overly protect the accused. These harsh measures are required to reduce the crime rate by removing criminals from the streets and by deterring potential criminals from yielding to temptation.

The Interactionist Perspective

The interactionists argue that the criminal justice process is biased. Unlike the traditional sociologists who posit the preeminence of offense-related factors in determining the fate of the accused, interactionists argue that offender characteristics such as race and social class, and offender behaviors such as demeanor, speech patterns, and dress explain why the decisions of the powerful (prosecutors, judges, and juries) are biased. These decision makers are guided by their perceptions and definitions of the situation formed in interaction with the accused. The degree to which the suspect is perceived by control agents as cooperative, respectful, and remorseful has positive consequences. Hagan's research on presentence investigations found, for example, a link between the probation officer's perception of the offender's demeanor . . . [an] following evaluation (definition) of the offender's prospects for success on probation. This sequence is in turn linked to recommendations offered by probation officers, and the final dispositions imposed. (Hagan, 1975, p. 635)

The interactionists also assert that the label of "criminal" increases the likelihood of a criminal identity and career (secondary crime). The courts, of course, are responsible for the imposition of this negative label. The problem is that this negative labeling tends to be more frequently applied to certain kinds of people. The key reason for this, from an interactionist perspective, is the difference in values and behaviors, between those responding to the deviant and the deviant (Bernstein, Kick, Leung, and Schulz, 1977, p. 363). Prosecutors, judges, and juries represent the middle and upper classes. They are overwhelmingly white. They represent and uphold the dominant values of society. Therefore, they are less likely to understand the values, behavior, and demeanor of those who are different—the black or Chicano, the poor, and the poorly educated. The result is that these people disproportionately receive the formal designation of "criminal." As Chiricos, Jackson, and Waldo have argued:

The tendency to favor white over black, educated over uneducated, comes as little surprise to those who contend . . . that the least powerful among us are the most likely to be "criminalized." Inasmuch as the least powerful are also more likely to be observed, arrested, and prosecuted . . . it is entirely in character with our system of justice that such persons also will be more likely to receive a formal convict label. . . . Assuming that a criminal label increases one's chances of developing a criminal identity and career, then it appears that our manner of dispensing justice somewhat insures that such identities will be concentrated in specific segments of our population. That is, we generally expect blacks, the poorly educated, and the indigent to be the most criminal among us, and we manage to affix criminal labels, in such a way that a "self-fulfilling prophecy" makes it so. (Chiricos et al., 1972, p. 571)

The Radical Perspective

The radical perspective is similar to that of the interactionists except that the bias is attributed to the power relations inherent in a class society (Chiricos and Waldo, 1975). The thrust of this perspective is that the criminal justice system, of which the court system is the heart, is biased systematically to weed out the middle and ruling classes "so that indeed by the time we reach *the end of the road in prison,* the vast majority of those we find there come from the lower classes" (Reiman, 1979, p. 96). The bias begins with the law (by excluding certain ruling class behaviors that do enormous harm, such as corporate pollution and the selling of dangerous products) and continues at every level of the criminal justice system. As Reiman has summarized:

For the same criminal behavior, the poor are more likely to be arrested; if arrested, they are more likely to be charged; if charged, more likely to be convicted; if convicted, more likely to be sentenced to prison; and if sentenced, more likely to be given longer prison terms than members of the middle and upper classes. In other words, the image of the criminal population one sees in our nation's jails and prisons is an image distorted by the shape of the criminal justice system itself. (Reiman, 1979, p. 97)

But let's concentrate here just on the role of the courts in this systematic bias, using the argument supplied by Reiman (1979, pp. 110–123).

Money is the crucial variable that often determines guilt or innocence. The accused, if poor, may not be able to afford bail, which means jail. This means that they are punished while still legally innocent because they are poor. But beyond this obvious ugliness, the poor are denied active participation in their own defense by being handicapped in seeking out witnesses and evidence. Furthermore, by spending time in jail prior to trial they are more susceptible to plea bargaining even if innocent; an admission of guilt may be, at least, a way out of jail.

Money also is crucial to determining guilt or innocence because it governs the type of lawyer the defendant will have. Research shows that privately retained counsel is considerably more likely to get defendants favorable treatment in the courts (cases dismissed, favorable plea bargains, and acquittals) than are public defenders and court-appointed counsel.

What this means in simple terms is that regardless of actual innocence or guilt, one's chances of beating the rap increase as one's income increases. Regardless of what fraction of crimes are committed by the poor, the criminal justice system is distorted so that an even greater fraction of those convicted will be poor. (Reiman, 1979, p. 114)

The system is doubly biased against the poor when it comes to sentencing. First, there is the class bias concerning crimes. The crimes of the poor carry harsher penalties than do white-collar and corporate crimes. And, second, "for *all* crimes, the poor receive less probation and more years of confinement than the better-heeled defendants *convicted of the same offense,* assuring us once again that the vast majority of those who are put behind bars are from the lowest social and economic classes in the nation" (Reiman, 1979, p. 115).

Blacks and other exploited racial and ethnic groups are disproportionately poor in American society and therefore are the recipients of a double bias in the courts. When blacks commit the same crimes as whites, they receive longer sentences (except for murder and rape when the victim is also black). When they plead guilty, they receive harsher sentences than whites who do.

Summarizing the radical interpretation of the way American criminal courts operate, Reiman has said:

I have tried to argue . . . that this is not a simple process of selecting the dangerous and the criminal from among the peace-loving and the law-abiding. It is also a process of *weeding* out the *wealthy* at every stage, so that the final picture . . . is not a true reflection of the real dangers in our society but a distorted image. . . . My point is that people who are equally or more dangerous, equally or more criminal, are not there [in prison]; that the criminal justice system works systematically, not to punish and confine the dangerous and the criminal, *but to punish and confine the poor who are dangerous and criminal.* (Reiman, 1979, p. 126)

For Reiman and other radicals the criminal justice system is systematically class biased. The system serves the interests of the rich and powerful in American society by (1) ignoring the dangerous acts of the affluent and focusing rather on the crimes of the poor, (2) conveying the image that the real threats are from the poor, and (3) promising the ideology that the crime problem is the fault of pathological individuals rather than a symptom of social and economic injustice. The resulting unjust system continues because those victimized by it are powerless to change it while those with the power to change it have no incentive to do so (Reiman, 1979, pp. 138–141).

CHAPTER REVIEW

1. The U.S. court system is really 52 systems—one from each state and the District of Columbia, and a federal system. Each of these systems is overburdened with too many cases. The major consequence of the congested courts is a bias against the poor, a bias that is found throughout the court procedures.

2. Ninety percent of criminal cases are determined without going to trial. The pretrial maneuverings are much less fair and more open to the discretion of the prosecuting attorney and judge than the formal trial. Decisions are made concerning whether to continue or not (i.e., is the evidence sufficient and the case important enough to warrant the time and cost of proceeding), whether to hold the accused without bail, and if bail is deemed appropriate, how much will it be. The poorer the defendants, the less justice they will receive in these decisions.

3. The courts are organized around the adversary system in which the state represented by the prosecuting attorney and the accused's attorney engage in "combat" before a neutral judge. In reality, though, the system favors the state. Especially disadvantaged are poor defendants who must use court-appointed attorneys and who remain in jail because they cannot afford bail.

4. Plea bargaining, where defendants bargain away their right to a trial in return for their guilty plea and a more lenient punishment, is the rule, not the exception in the disposition of criminal cases.

5. Trial by jury is a right guranteed by the Constitution. The assumption is that the accused should be tried by a representative body of citizens. In practice, however, certain types of people are underrepresented on juries—the poor, the young, and minorities—resulting in some defendants not being judged by a jury of their peers.

6. Certain rules of evidence govern the conduct of trials: (a) hearsay evidence is not acceptable, (b) privileged communications are excluded, (c) evidence cannot be presented if obtained illegally (the exclusionary rule), and (d) defendants do not have to testify, protected as they are against self-incrimination.

7. Nearly three fourths of all trials end in guilty verdicts. When found guilty, it is up to the judge to determine the punishment. Judges, for the most part, have considerable latitude in their sentencing decisions. These discretionary powers have been curbed recently by the trend for legislatures to set mandatory and determinate sentences.

8. Mandatory sentences, while curbing the capriciousness of judicial sentencing and making punishment certain and therefore a better deterrent, have several problems: (a) by definition, they do not distinguish between offenders who do and those who do not deserve punishment; (b) they may be unfairly imposed; (c) they increase the size of the already crowded prisons dramatically; and (d) they may have the opposite of the intended effect if the rules are perceived by police, prosecutors, juries, and judges as too extreme.

9. Traditional sociologists are not bothered by the data that show the lower classes are more likely than the more affluent to be found guilty and punished because they assume that the poor are least likely to share the appropriate values and behaviors of society.

10. Interactionists argue that the criminal justice process is biased as offender characteristics such as race, social class, and behaviors affect the decisions of the powerful. The criminal justice process is really the formal labeling process whereby the less powerful in society disproportionately are labeled "criminal," which in turn increases their likelihood of a criminal identity and career, thus fulfilling society's prophecy.

11. Radicals, too, focus on the bias of the system but view it more clearly in terms of the power relations in a class society. Money is the crucial variable that often determines guilt or innocence. Not only are the poor disadvantaged at every stage in the criminal justice system, but the wealthy are weeded out. The system works systematically not to punish and confine the dangerous and criminal but to punish and confine *the poor* who are dangerous and criminal.

13 Punishment

CHAPTER OUTLINE

Protection of Society
Retribution

    Capital punishment as retribution

Rehabilitation
Deterrence

    Specific (special) deterrence
    General deterrence
    A Case Study: Capital Punishment and General Deterrence

Summary

KEY TERMS

Capital punishment
General deterrence
Just desserts
Medical model
Probation
Recidivism
Rehabilitation
Retribution
Specific deterrence

The vilest deeds like poison weeds/Bloom well in prison air:/It is only what is good in Man/ That wastes and withers there.

Oscar Wilde (1854–1900)

Penology . . . has become torture and foolishness, a waste of money and a cause of crime . . . a blotting out of sight and heightening of social anxiety.

Paul Goodman

Prisons don't rehabilitate, they don't punish, they don't protect, so what the hell do they do?

Governor Jerry Brown

Our emotions cry for vengeance in the wake of a horrible crime, but we know that killing the criminal cannot undo the crime, will not prevent similar crimes by others, does not benefit the victim, destroys human life, and brutalizes society. If we are to still violence, we must cherish life.

Ramsey Clark

The process of criminal justice ends with the punishment of those judged to be guilty of crimes. The forms of punishment vary from a fine to death, depending on the assumed severity of the crime, although we know that the bias of the system allows some crimes with severe consequences (white-collar, corporate, and political crimes) to go relatively unpunished.

The mildest form of punishment is to impose a monetary fine. In 1980, some 14 percent of the defendants sentenced in U.S. District Courts received this penalty as their exclusive punishment (Flanagan, van Alstyne and Gottfredson, 1982, pp. 410–411). This is the typical punishment assessed to criminal corporations or governmental agencies since it is difficult to isolate guilty individuals within them. There are at least three problems with this mode of punishment: (1) a fine may be too mild a punishment, not fitting the gravity of the offense; (2) fines disproportionately favor the wealthy and punish the poor; and (3) for poor persons assessed a fine, it must be paid from family resources, thus punishing not only the offenders but their families as well (Thomas and Hepburn, 1983, p. 440).

The most frequently imposed sentence is probation. In 1980, 39 percent of those found guilty in federal courts received this sanction (Flanagan et al., 1982, pp. 410–411). To be "placed on probation" means that the offender must obey a set of rules imposed by the court, such as no excessive use of intoxicants, isolation from disreputable persons, and maintenance of steady employment. Those on probation are also under the supervision of a probation officer. Although technically imposed by a judge, probation is most frequently the decision of the prosecutor through plea bargaining. The bias of the criminal justice system is seen vividly when we consider who is placed on probation rather than sent to prison. As Shelden has summarized:

First, probation is almost a matter of routine for white-collar and corporate offenders, in addition to high status persons who commit felonies. Second, young and inexperienced offenders, those with steady jobs, those with the highest level of education, and those out on bail are more likely to be given probation, even when we consider the seriousness of the offense. (Shelden, 1982, p. 385)

The two most extreme forms of punishment—imprisonment and capital punishment—are reserved disproportionately for the poor, the uneducated, and minorities. The rationales for imposing these severe sanctions on anyone are the topics of this chapter, focusing particularly on imprisonment. In essence, we ask: What are prisons for?

There are four major justifications for imprisoning criminals: protection, revenge, deterrence, and rehabilitation. The effectiveness of prisons in accomplishing these aims are evaluated below.

THE PROTECTION OF SOCIETY

Supposedly, there is a major benefit from punishing offenders by placing them in prison: while incarcerated they cannot harm the public. This use of isolating potentially harmful people is effective for, in the short run, the goal is accomplished. The argument is compelling because everyone wants to remove dangerous persons from circulation. Two advocates of this rationale for punishment, Sherman and Hawkins (1982), have argued that the criminal justice system should only imprison those who are dangerous to society. Since this number is significantly smaller than the present prison population, society would have the added benefit of reducing the number of prisoners and the need for increased expenditures for prison construction. Prisoners would benefit by the elimination of overcrowded conditions (see Panel 13-1).

While apparently effective, there are some major problems with imprisonment for protection. First, there is the question of whom to send to prison. Do the courts use mandatory sentences imprisoning everyone committing a particular act for a specified time? If so, then both the dangerous and those who pose no future threat are imprisoned. Second, if the courts want to imprison only the dangerous, what criteria should be used—past behavior, psychological tests, the testimony of psychological experts? In this regard, the American Psychiatric Association declared in a brief before the Supreme Court that "there are no reliable criteria for psychiatric predictions of long-term future criminal behavior" (quoted in Hughes, 1982, p. 40; see also Pfahl, 1980). A third, and related, difficulty is determining how long dangerous people need to be separated from society. A mandatory sentence is, by definition, arbitrary and will not suit everyone. Indeterminate sentences leave the decision to parole boards and how accurate will their decisions be? A fourth problem with the prison-as-protection approach is a moral one. Imprisonment in these circumstances involves punishment not only for what one has done but for what a person might do (Hughes, 1982, p. 40). Not only, as just noted, are predictions of future behaviors unreliable, but do the courts have the right to keep someone in prison for something they have not yet done (and perhaps never will)?

A major flaw with this approach is that for the most part it is a short-term solution. Some 95 percent of prisoners eventually are released (about 360 persons leave American prisons each day). If these people are dangerous, the threat is only delayed until they are set free. Moreover, the prison experience itself, as we will see in the next chapter, may increase the probability of further criminal behaviors by exconvicts.

Finally, this belief that incarceration incapacitates the criminal element and thereby frees the public from the fear of crime is a fallacious one. As noted in an earlier chapter, data from 1981 show that for every 500 serious reported crimes, there are 100 persons arrested, of whom 32 are convicted, and 25 are eventually imprisoned—a rate of only one imprisonment for every 20 serious crimes (*U.S. News & World Report,* November 1, 1982, p. 41). Data like these have led criminologist Hans Mattick to conclude that "if the prisons were opened tomorrow, it wouldn't make any difference" (quoted in Fangmeier, 1980, p. 324). As Fangmeier has concluded: "The awareness that only a miniscule number of law violators go to prison at least raises serious questions about the prevailing mythology that we are significantly safer because several hundred thousand people are behind bars" (Fangmeier, 1980, p. 324).

RETRIBUTION

There are many citizens, scholars, and professional law enforcement personnel who believe that the prison's essential function is to punish persons for their heinous acts. There is a common assumption that wrongdoers owe a debt of suffering to the victim and society (Gross, 1979, p. 393). This approach is often called "just desserts," which means the perpetrator of a crime receives a punishment he or she deserves. Ernest van den Haag (1975, p. 183), a prominent criminologist, has argued that the avoidance of punishment is a miscarriage of justice—"punishment must be inflicted for the sake of justice because it is deserved" (see also Wilson, 1975; Fogel, 1975). The benefit of imprisonment from this perspective is again not to the criminal, but to the society. By such punishment, society defines the boundaries of permissible behavior (Durkheim, 1947).

Reid (1982, p. 479) has observed that retribution (deserved punishment) is the major reason for punishment today. It clearly fits with the trend toward determinate and mandatory sentencing, where the punishment is predetermined in relation to the gravity of the crime.

A major problem with this position is determining fair punishment. Is the amputation of a thief's hand, as is practiced in Muslim countries, fair (see Panel 13-2)? Is two years in prison twice as severe as one year? What is a just punishment for a bank thief who uses a gun? Is it the same for a bank embezzler using a computer? You may argue the position of the courts and prosecutors that the use of violence or potential violence makes the former a more dreadful act deserving of more

PANEL 13-1

A Proposal to Isolate Criminals from Society

Tom J. Farer, distinguished professor of law at Rutgers University, is concerned with our present prison system: (1) prison makes people more vicious so when they are freed they will present an even greater danger to society than when they entered prison; (2) prisons are costly to build as is the maintenance for each prisoner ($20,000 or so per prisoner annually); and (3) the character of prison life is nightmarish with its hopelessness, unspeakable humiliations, and its deadly violence. Farer offers as an alternative to our penal system, penal colonies to isolate the most dangerous criminals from society.

One of the most innovative means of reducing the fiscal and moral costs of long-term imprisonment, worthy of testing, stems from the British experiment with exporting criminals to colonial territories, such as Australia. In its essence, this is a *proposal for self-governing penal colonies*. The colonies would be located in places with an easily guarded periphery. Because all the guards would be on the outside, there would be none of the corrupting relationship between effectively omnipotent keepers and helpless prisoners.

The prison would be treated as if it were a classic colony or trust territory being prepared for self-determination. It would be guaranteed a very modest standard of living, but given the opportunity to apply for technical and capital assistance that, if properly used, would allow the prisoners to manage a progressive increase in their standard of living. Periodically, supervised democratic elections would be held. Elected officials would be responsible for all political, administrative, and judicial functions, subject to outside intervention only in case of grave abuse. The commission of such abuses would be punished by returning the delinquents to a traditional maximum-security prison.

punishment. But how, then, does one explain the disparity in sentences between nonviolent embezzlers and nonviolent automobile thieves? What we have now is a situation in which less than one fifth of embezzlers go to prison while over two thirds of car thieves do (Fangmeier, 1980, p. 325). This raises the important question, not raised by the proponents of retribution, of what "just desserts" means when crimes of the powerful—white-collar, organized, corporate, and political crimes—receive little if any punishment for the harms done to their victims (Schrag, 1977, p. 570).

Another problem with retribution is that because of the sustained stigmatization resulting from the labels of "criminal" and "ex-con," the debt is never repaid—a point emphasized by interactionists. Ideally, the receipt of punishment equal to the crime should restore the individual to the ranks of respectable community

Panel 13-1 (Continued)

On the face of it, such colonies would cost far less than ordinary prisons. The citizens of a less developed country like Sri Lanka manage a decent life on an annual income of a few hundred dollars a year. With an initial capital investment of about $25,000 per prisoner for building materials, farm equipment, irrigation facilities, training, etc., the experience of developing countries implies that prisoners could maintain an acceptable standard of living, perhaps a quite comfortable one—depending on effort and organizational abilities—if they were extended financial assistance in the range of $1,000 per capita, one twentieth of what it takes in today's prisons.

The success of such a scheme would depend on who is right: those who say that violent criminals are too sick, too emotionally and psychologically crippled to perform necessary social functions, or those who claim that many violent criminals are among the most energetic and potentially intelligent and effective members of our underclass. If the latter are right, then this opportunity to experience self-government and to acquire administrative and technical skills could have those rehabilitative consequences that we have sought for over a century without conspicuous success. And we would then have a real basis for determining who could be returned to society.

Given the problems that beset our existing system, this is an approach worth testing. Several states could join together to develop such a test in conjunction with the federal government. Perhaps we could work together with one or more foreign governments. For example, the government of Panama operates an almost self-supporting prison on the Island of Coiba, which, according to one expert, has fertile land sufficient to maintain a very much larger population.

Source: Tom J. Farer, "Innovating Policies," Society 19, July/August 1982, pp. 10–12. For critiques of Farer's plan, see the five articles that follow in that issue of Society.

citizens, but the punishment never ends because of the continuing stigma and suspicion (Gross, 1979, p. 391). Panel 13-3 describes one attempt to overcome this problem.

Finally, retributive justice does not address the sources of crime or the inequities in the criminal justice system. As Greenberg and Humphries have noted:

a just desserts philosophy focuses attention on the individual perpetrator alone. If I lose my job because the economy is in a state of contraction and then steal to support myself and my family—or if I am a juvenile and steal because the state has passed child labor legislation—or if I strike out in rage because the color of my skin subjects me to discrimination that reduces my opportunities—

PANEL 13-2

Retributive Justice in the Muslim World

The Prophet Muhammad revealed in the *Koran* the following principle for determining punishment: "As for the thief, both male and female, cut off their hands. It is the reward of their own deeds, an exemplary punishment from Allah. Allah is mighty, wise." Although the *Koran* was written some 1300 years ago, many predominantly Muslim countries base their laws on its precepts. The result is a harsh eye-for-an-eye justice, as the following examples show:

- An American couple in Saudi Arabia caught their Pakistani houseboy stealing one day and ordered him to report to the police. They were astonished when he returned home minus one hand. It had been chopped off and the stub of his arm plunged into boiling tallow to disinfect it.

- In 1977, four men were convicted of rape in Saudi Arabia's Al-Hasa province and sentenced to death. One, a bachelor, was beheaded. The other three were married and guilty of adultery as well as rape. They were buried up to their waists in sand and stoned to death by a mob that used small rocks instead of boulders to prolong their agony.

- In North Yemen, a convicted thief is required to pick up his chopped-off hand and raise it to his forehead in a salute to the presiding judge.

Source: Excerpts from "Crime or Punishment?" Time, July 25, 1977, p. 38.

the just desserts model simply indicates that I should be punished for my wrongful act, though perhaps not as severely as I would be at present. One need not deny individual responsibility altogether in such cases to see that, in placing my culpability and the punishment I should receive at the center of attention, other topics are pushed to the periphery: the dynamics of the capitalist economy; the manner in which it allocates benefits and injuries among classes, races, and sexes—and in so doing generates the structural conditions to which members of the society respond when they violate the law; and the way class interests are represented in or excluded from the law. All these are neglected in favor of an abstract moral preoccupation with the conduct of the individual offender. (Greenberg and Humphries, 1981, p. 375)

Capital Punishment as Retribution

The death penalty is a good example of retribution: the state kills the perpetrator of some horrible act because it is deserved. The death penalty has been part of American justice since colonial days. The highest rates in American history took place during the Great Depression when about 200 persons were killed annually. The rate gradually declined from the 1930s until the 1960s when there were fewer than 50 executions a year.

In 1972, the Supreme Court ruled in *Furman v. Georgia* that the death penalty was "cruel and unusual punishment" in violation of the Eighth Amendment. This ruling invalidated all U.S. death penalty laws and commuted the death sentences of the 600 inmates on death rows in the various state and federal prisons to life imprisonment (including mass murderer Charles Manson and Robert Kennedy's assassin, Sirhan Sirhan). In 1976, the court upheld the constitutionality of capital punishment but required that the laws provide suitable standards to be followed by judges and juries for deciding who should be put to death and who should live. As a result, a number of states have revised their laws or passed new ones to conform with the court's dictates.

The 1980s have seen a renewed interest by the public and state and federal governments in capital punishment. By the end of 1983 some 38 states permitted executions. And, since Gary Gilmore was executed in Utah in 1977, the first since the moratorium in 1967, another five had been killed and 1255 men and 13 women were on death row awaiting execution.

The Supreme Court's 1976 decision in *Gregg* v. *Georgia* recognized retribution as an appropriate basis for capital punishment. Five years later Supreme Court Justice William Rehnquist decried the fact that in the years since the death penalty was reinstated hundreds of juries had sentenced people to death but only a handful had actually been put to death. His argument for capital punishment is based on the principle of retribution:

> One principal purpose of capital punishment is retribution. The testimony of Lord Justice Denning, then master of the roles of the Court of Appeal in England . . . answers those who insist that respect for the "sanctity of life" compels the end of the death sentence for any crime, no matter how heinous. As Denning explained, "Punishment is the way in which society expresses its denunciation of wrongdoing; and, in order to maintain respect for law, it is essential that the punishment inflicted for grave crimes should adequately reflect the revulsion felt by the great majority of citizens for them. It is a mistake to consider the objects of punishment as being deterrent or reformative or preventive and nothing else. . . . The truth is that some crimes are so outrageous that society insists on adequate punishment, because the wrongdoer deserves it, irrespective of whether it is a deterrent or not." There can be little doubt that delay in the enforcement of capital punishment frustrates the purpose of retribution. As Justice Potter Stewart stated for the court in 1976, "When people begin to believe that organized society is unwilling or unable to impose upon criminal offenders the punishment they 'deserve,' then there are sown the seeds of anarchy—of self-help, vigilante justice, and lynch law." (Rehnquist, 1981)

The most telling argument against capital punishment as retribution is that it is administered selectively to certain kinds of people—most notably, the poor and minorities. From 1930 to 1979 there were 3862 executions conducted under civil

PANEL 13-3

Punishment and Restoration

Connecticut's Department of Correction has adopted a statement of mission (see below) that recognizes *the administration of punishment as a primary reason for its existence*. As a rationale for correctional activity, punishment differs from rehabilitation and incapacitation in a number of respects.

The most important of these is that punishment alone explains why the people in whose lives the State intervenes, by means of the criminal justice system, must be liable to account for a criminal act. We must admit that punishment necessarily involves suffering, which is partially justified by a double moral judgment: the act to which we respond must be one for which the individual is responsible and the act must be wrongful. A system of State-administered punishment serves several important social purposes. Together with the influence of families and schools, the threat of punishment may encourage people to abide by the law and the administration of punishment by the State may be necessary as an alternative to private vengeance.

In my view, however, the prevention of criminal acts by others—including vigilante activity—does not by itself justify the infliction of suffering on any particular individual. The judgment that a person is responsible for a criminal act carries with it a recognition that he or she is a rational human being whose dignity is violated if we treat him or her simply as a means to an end. In attempting to justify the punishment of particular individuals, I find myself resorting to the metaphor of a balance which the offender has upset by victimizing others. He or she has incurred a serious debt which can only be expiated by means of suffering. The suffering, however, must then have a meaning for the offender. It must enable him or her to recognize the moral values that he or she has violated.

Offenders are benefitted by punishment in that by restoring their social credit it allows them to participate in a community where relationships can be governed by mutual trust and respect. It should go without saying (though it is far easier said than done) that in punishing offenders we must live up to the moral principles that we are punishing them for breaking.

I have been speaking so far in ideal terms, which make it appear that the act of punishment by itself accomplishes a Good that justifies the suffering involved. As a practical matter, however, we must recognize that the individuals in our prisons

Panel 13-3 (Continued)

and jails are often the victims of personal and social handicaps that limit but do not eradicate responsibility for their actions. In addition, our standard method of punishment—the prison—is not well known for its ennobling effects on inmates. Finally, communities are reluctant to accept punished offenders as people who have squared their accounts.

In my view, these facts count against the legitimacy of our current practices rather than against the ideals I have described, which are the only ones that can provide an institution of punishment with legitimate purposes. Consequently, the offering of education, counseling and work activities to offenders is vital, but not as a reason for punishment.

These services are necessary measures to lessen the debilitating effects of imprisonment, which generally involves suffering far in excess of the temporary deprivation of liberty to which the offender has been sentenced. The services are necessary also as ways of awakening or reviving the punished individual's sense of personal responsibility, in the absence of which his or her restoration to the community is bound to fail. In order to achieve these vital purposes, treatment programs should be fully voluntary and should probably be run by neutral outside contractors rather than by employees of the correctional establishment. If the conditions I have described were met, our institutions of punishment would have a chance of living up to the twin values of punishment and restoration. And it is only by carrying out these twin values that the deliberate imposition of suffering on particular individuals can be legitimate.

Statement of Mission Membership in a free community requires that we respect the dignity, rights and liberties of other members of society. It is the responsibility of the criminal justice system to promote and enforce such respect by administering predictable, proportionate, fair and humane punishment upon those who violate the law. Punishment in this context means only that an individual has been found accountable for a criminal offense and must pay a penalty in order to regain the right to full participation in a community of free citizens. By requiring the offender to pay his or her debt to society, punishment aims to restore a responsible relationship between the offender and the society whose laws he or she has broken.

Source: David Lovell, "Punishment and Restoration," The Key (Newsletter of the Section on Criminal Justice Administration, American Society for Public Administration) 9, Fall 1983, pp. 2–3, 6.

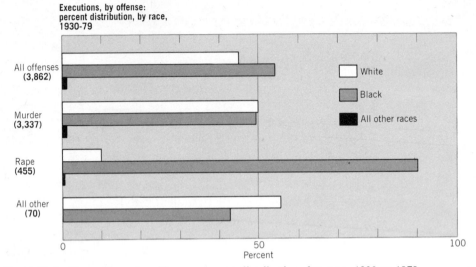

**Executions, by offense:
percent distribution, by race,
1930-79**

All offenses
(3,862)

Murder
(3,337)

Rape
(455)

All other
(70)

White

Black

All other races

0   50   100
Percent

Figure 13-1 Executions, by offense; percent distribution, by race, 1930 to 1979.
SOURCE: U.S. Department of Justice, *Capital Punishment 1979,* Washington, D.C.: U.S. Government Printing Office, 1980, p. 9.

authority in the United States and of this total, 54 percent were blacks, 45 percent were whites (Hispanics were included in the white category until 1977), and 1 percent were other races (U.S. Department of Justice, 1980, p. 9). Most notably, 89 percent of all prisoners put to death for rape were black (see Table 13-1).

The bias against blacks is not just a vestige of past racism; it continues, although somewhat lessened. In late 1982 there were 1058 inmates on death rows across the nation and 42 percent were black (Watson, 1982). The overrepresentation of blacks on death row (350 percent greater than their proportion in the larger population) leads to the obvious conclusion that blacks are singled out for the ultimate retribution of the state, unless it is established that they are disproportionately guilty of capital crimes.

So, too, are those from the low rungs of the social stratification system. Government data provide one indicator of this: the relationship between the amount of education received and receiving the death penalty. Of the people sentenced to death in 1979, for example, 63 percent had never graduated from high school and one fourth had an eighth-grade education or less (U.S. Department of Justice, 1980, p. 30). This inverse relationship between educational level and the imposition of the death sentence shows that either judges and juries are biased against the undereducated or the undereducated, because they are also poor, do not have the resources to reduce the sentences in the courts.

In sum, the principle of retribution is one where the criminal justice system punishes lawbreakers to "get even" for the harm caused to the victim(s) and society. The application of the ultimate form of retribution—the taking of life—is seriously flawed, however, because it disproportionately disadvantages the members of disadvantaged groups in society. Capital punishment is also seriously flawed for a number of political, religious, and ethical reasons (see Leiser, 1979, pp. 236–297).

Group counseling in prisons is based on the "medical model," which assumes that inmates are sick and must be changed.

REHABILITATION

Prisons are called correctional institutions and prison guards "correctional officers" because prisons have been assumed to "correct" wrong behavior. Central to this goal of prisoner rehabilitation is the medical model, which MacNamara has characterized as follows:

> In its simplest (perhaps oversimplified) terms, the medical model as applied to corrections assumed the offender to be "sick" (physically, mentally, and/or socially); his offense to be a manifestation or symptom of his illness, a cry for help. Obviously, then, early and accurate diagnosis, followed by prompt and effective therapeutic intervention, assured an affirmative prognosis— rehabilitation. . . . Basic to the medical model, although rather surprisingly denied by many of its proponents, is that the criminogenic factors are indigenous to the individual offender and that it is by doing "something" for, to, or with him that rehabilitation can be effected. (MacNamara, 1983, p. 237)

The medical model implies that inmates must be treated with therapeutic interventions such as behavior modification, drugs, or counseling. Related to this is the belief by many that offenders are morally sick and need religion to change their lives.[3]

---

[3]This is the guiding assumption of the organization called "Prison Fellowship" founded by Charles Colson, former aide to Richard Nixon, and because of his complicity in Watergate, a former prisoner.

Interactionists vehemently oppose the medical model upon which the goal of rehabilitation rests. They argue that prisoners are not all that different from non-prisoners. While crime is found in all segments of society, prisons are used to house, punish, and change those at the bottom. They are singled out for the devalued status and associated stigma of "criminal" and, according to the re-habilitation model, are those who need treatment for their "illness." From this perspective, the criminal justice system does not incarcerate the sick but the weak (the poor and minorities).

The assumptions of the medical model have dominated the criminal justice system as evidenced by the widespread use of indeterminate sentences. This type of sentence, as noted in the previous chapter, gives parole boards the right to free a prisoner when they feel he/she is a good prospect for readjusting into society. Typically, this decision is based on the premise that the prisoner has been re-habilitated through the educational, vocational, and therapeutic programs in the prison. The recent trend toward determinate sentences and even the elimination of parole in several states indicate that rehabilitation is less the goal of imprison-ment than it once was.

The question is how successful is imprisonment in the rehabilitation of wrong-doers. There are successes—individuals who leave prison and lead relatively normal lives. There are people who are changed dramatically. Others employ the skills and education they received in prison to become useful members of society. But, for the most part, the prisons do not rehabilitate. The arguments behind this assertion are several.

First, involuntary confinement, especially when inmates realize they have been singled out for punishment while many equally deserving others go free, makes people angry and anger is not a condition conducive to rehabilitation. As an inmate in the Stateville Correctional Center in Illinois said "Rehabilitate? What is rehabilitate? *You* can't rehabilitate *me* if I don't want to" (quoted in Anderson, 1982, p. 38).

A prison is a place of punishment. Many politicians, prison administrators, and prison guards believe that it must be a place of suffering—of deliberate harm. A spokesperson for this extreme view, the Reverend Sydney Smith, said in 1822 that a prison should be "a place of punishment, from which men recoil with horror—a place of real suffering painful to the memory, terrible to the imagination . . . a place of sorrow and wailing, which should be entered with horror and quitted with earnest resolution never to return to such misery" (quoted in Tullock, 1974, p. 110). If pain and suffering are the goals of imprisonment, deterrence may result (probably not, as we will see) but rehabilitation will surely not. As some critics have asked:

Can a person be "corrected" in a cage? Can humanization occur in a de-humanizing atmosphere? Can a patient be involuntarily "cured"? Prison is a totalitarian institution; it controls every aspect of daily life, and thus it creates either utter dependency or radical revolt. (Morris, 1975, p. 47)

Perhaps the major flaw in the assumption that imprisonment will "straighten the crooked" is that for many inmates imprisonment has the opposite effect. Typically, the prison experience is one in which one learns that the powerful prey on the weak (guards vs. inmates; inmates vs. inmates), and an environment of intimidation and fear is not conducive to the building of positive character traits.

A major difficulty with the rehabilitation model is that it assumes the indeterminate sentence. Inmates are not released until they have convinced the authorities that they have changed. This creates three problems. First, since the offenders must stay in until they are "cured," their sentences may exceed the prison terms of those sentenced under determinate sentences. Second, how is change to be measured—by attitudes, behaviors, the observations of professionals, or a battery of tests? Clearly, the present state of the behavioral sciences, at least, has not provided the sophisticated tools required to make accurate judgments about future behaviors. And, third, since adequate methods for measuring change are missing, parole boards must base their decisions on the judgments of prison employees and on the interviews with inmates before the board. Under these conditions, inmates are forced to contrive their behaviors and answers to "con" their keepers into believing that genuine change has occurred when it has not. These inauthentic behaviors are the only way out. Thus, the goal of rehabilitation actually promotes deceit.

What kind of rehabilitation do prisons seek? Critics argue that the goal of "rehabilitation" in prison is really control. "The key to successful rehabilitation is conformity—nothing more, nothing less. When the 'deviant' no longer deviates from the values of the dominant class, s/he is 'rehabilitated' " (Morris, 1975, p. 47). As Jessica Mitford has said:

> For the prison administrator, whether she/he be warden, sociologist, or psychiatrist, "individualized treatment" is primarily a device for breaking the convict's will to resist and hounding him into compliance with institution demands, and is thus a means of exerting maximum control over the convict population. The cure will be deemed effective to the degree that the poor/young/brown/black captive appears to have capitulated to his middle class/white/middle-aged captor, and to have adopted the virtues of subservience to authority, industry, cleanliness, docility. (Mitford, 1973, pp. 116–117)

The key question to ask of prison rehabilitation proponents is, Does it work? Probably the best evidence would be to assess various rehabilitation programs as to their effect on recidivism (reinvolvement in crime after being released from prison). In essence, does participation in the rehabilitative efforts of prisons reduce the chances of returning to prison? Robert Martinson, a sociologist, examined carefully the methodology and results of 231 studies investigating this question and concluded: "With few and isolated exceptions, the rehabilitative efforts that have been reported so far have had no appreciable effect on recidivism." (1974, p. 25) This generalization is true regardless of the treatment—education, vocational training, individual or group counseling, institutional environment, or medical treatment.[4] There are, Martinson noted, a few instances of success or

---

[4]The one exception is the almost complete elimination of sex crimes after castration. A Danish study of sex offenders found that 29.6 percent of those treated with hormones continued to commit sex crimes but only 3.5 percent of those who had been castrated did (reported in Martinson, 1974, pp. 35–36).

Inmates at the Santa Fe, New Mexico prison receiving college degrees. The assumption guiding prison education programs is that such efforts decrease the recidivism rate.

partial success, but there is "no clear pattern to indicate the efficacy of any particular method of treatment." (1974, p. 49) Martinson (1979) later moderated his extreme pessimism by recognizing that there appear to be some conditions where rehabilitation efforts have a chance. A survey of current research by Palmer (1983) also provides some cautious optimism concerning the effectiveness of rehabilitation but Martinson's original dreary conclusion is still widely held by experts. The question, then, still rages: Should prisons abandon the ideal of rehabilitation or not? Charles Tittle (1974, p. 393) has argued that prisons should abandon the rehabilitative mission and perform what they are suited for—punitive detention for implementing vengeance, generating deterrence, or reinforcing moral imperatives. Rehabilitation, in his view, ought to be provided, not in prison, but by community-based institutions that serve anybody in need—including released convicts.

On the other side, arguing for the retention of the rehabilitative ideal for prisons are people like Francis Allen (1981). Allen has argued that even though rehabilitation programs are often ill conceived and imperfect, the commitment to that ideal makes prisons less barbarous places. We should not abandon the noble goal to repair broken lives. If that goal is abandoned, then prisons become strictly places of punishment.

Finally, the absolute contrast between traditional sociologists and radicals provides insight as to why prisons fail to rehabilitate. Rehabilitation is central to the traditional sociologist because problem individuals must be changed to adapt to society. Radicals argue that this goal is misguided and is precisely why recidivism is so high. The traditional approach is doomed to failure because it focuses on the problem individual and ignores the structure of society that coerces some persons toward criminal behavior. From the radical perspective, efforts to rehabilitate must be directed at changing a problem society rather than problem individuals.

DETERRENCE

Punishment has long been considered a means to repress crime. By inflicting harm on criminals, it is assumed that they will not engage in further crimes because they fear more punishment (specific deterrence). The general public also will be afraid to violate the law because they know that criminals are punished (general deterrence). The belief in deterrence is based on the assumption that individuals rationally calculate potential costs and benefits prior to action and regulate their behaviors accordingly. Thus, it is held that undesirable acts will not occur if enough costs are attached to them and if the amount of pain is made knowable to all.

Specific (Special) Deterrence

Specific deterrence is the goal of most punishment. Parents and teachers, for example, punish children so that they will not violate a rule again; so, too, are criminals punished. The object is to make the punishment more painful than the pleasure derived from the illegal act, which will prevent further crimes by the offenders. For specific deterrence to work, then, punishment must vary according to the type of crime and the situation of the offender. This means that specific deterrence can contribute to the social class bias evident in the sentencing disparities noted in the previous chapter. By the logic of this, a prison sentence is more likely to be imposed on the poor than on a white-collar criminal or guilty corporate executive. A bank teller who embezzles is likely to be deterred from future crimes if fired while the unemployed robber must be imprisoned to deter repetition, at least this may be the case following the logic of specific deterrence (von Hirsch, 1964, p. 147).

The goal of specific deterrence—prevention of future crime by a former perpetrator—is accomplished, of course, when a criminal is killed by the state. The goal is also accomplished in the short run since imprisonment does not permit offenders to commit crimes against the public. However, what about the 95 percent of inmates who eventually leave prison? Does the fear of additional punishment constrain their behaviors or do they return to criminal activities knowing the consequences if caught? The answers to these questions require that we examine recidivism in some detail.

Recidivism in its broadest sense means reinvolvement in criminal behavior. Because so much crime goes unsolved, the facts are unknown concerning the actual amount of criminal behavior by people previously found guilty of crime (Barlow, 1981, pp. 461–462). A study of former inmates that reports the proportion who have not been arrested does *not* inform us if these persons actually have refrained from criminal activity since their release from prison. Typically, recidi-

PANEL 13-4

The Presumption of Innocence Takes Holiday

Jimmy Jay Michalek has a family. He also has a prison record. And when his roles as family man and ex-convict collide, life for Jimmy Jay Michalek gets very difficult.

"I was standing talking to my friend next door while his kid and my little boy was out there playing," Michalek recently recalled. "And the cops come up. They told me straight out, 'Punk, you ain't got no rights.'

"And my little boy, he's 8 years old, and he asked me, 'Daddy, how come he called you a punk and said you ain't got no rights?' And I told him, 'It's because I been in prison.' But, you know, I really didn't know how to explain it all to him."

Jimmy Jay Michalek, 32, is a special target. He and seven other Minneapolis residents, all repeat offenders, have been singled out by the Minneapolis police for intense surveillance. They are being followed and watched under a new program called Target 8. It puts every policeman in the city on a 24-hour lookout for them, whether or not they break the law.

Target 8 in Minneapolis is one of the nation's newest targeting programs—and perhaps its most systematic. The Min-

neapolis police refuse to disclose who their targets are—except to the targets themselves, and only if they ask. But The Los Angeles Times obtained the contents of a secret notebook issued to police officers naming and picturing the targets and sketching their criminal backgrounds. Those who agreed to be interviewed were surprised to learn that they were targets.

Most said they had noticed that they were attracting new attention from the police. All said they thought the targeting program violated their civil rights. Some asked not to be identified for fear the police would harm them if officers learned they had spoken to a reporter.

Michalek, who agreed to the use of his name, recalled noticing that officers had been following him. "I wondered why I been seeing them around my house so much," he said. "They been sneaking around the alleys, and certain ones been popping up at certain places I've been. I have wondered why they been harassing me."

Michalek, a 200-pounder with a beard and shoulder-length hair, concedes serving 10½ years in prison for a variety of convictions, including armed robbery. But

vism studies attempt to eliminate this problem by taking as their measure of criminal behavior reentry into prison. This, too, may lead to inaccurate conclusions because so much crime goes undetected. Also, former inmates, if on parole, are often returned to prison for technical violations of their parole, offenses that are not forbidden to the general public. Also, probation officers and police personnel closely watch exprisoners and often assume criminal behavior of these persons regardless of their demeanor. This surveillance and harassment of exprisoners may lead to situations that fulfill the prophecy, as Panel 13-4 indicates. Thus,

Panel 13-4 (Continued)

he said he has been out for five years—and deserves to be left alone. Target 8, he said, shows that the police are "sick" people."

Michalek laughed uneasily.

"They've told me before, 'If we don't nail you on something, we'll just open our files and reach in there and get something and put it on you,' " he said. "Now this makes me think that's what they're trying to do."

Minneapolis Police Chief Anthony Bouza says Target 8 violates no one's rights. He says a Rand Corp. study that proposes using a person's criminal history to predict his future behavior "really describes the philosophy" behind Target 8—but Bouza claims the Minneapolis program was his own idea. Putting the program together fell to Deputy Chief Bernard Jablonski.

Using meticulous criteria, a committee headed by a captain in the Organized Crime Division selects those who become the eight targets from a basic pool of nominees provided by policemen.

Only eight are chosen, Jablonski said, because of the costs of targeting.

Once the eight are selected, their names and what the police know about them are placed in large, three-ring binders with red targets on the covers. The binders go to every precinct and division. They contain color photographs of the targets and their names, addresses, descriptions, dates of birth, past criminal activity, known associates, descriptions of vehicles they have access to, their Minneapolis police numbers and their FBI numbers.

Synopses and smaller photographs go into blue pocket notebooks which are issued to every one of the 750 police officers on the Minneapolis force.

Officers are instructed to watch for the targets. They note whom the targets meet—and might photograph the meetings if they are important to cases. They check the ownership of vehicles the targets use. They follow the targets, and they might radio ahead to have them followed in adjoining precincts. They are encouraged to check the targets' homes to note whether they are present.

The police report what they learn to a special telephone that feeds a large-capacity tape recording system at police headquarters. An officer monitors the tapes, and the Organized Crime Division analyzes the information.

Source: Richard E. Meyer, "Presumption of Innocence Takes Holiday," Denver Post, *December 19, 1982, p. D-1. Reprinted from the* Los Angeles Times.

the recidivism rate is artifically inflated. With these caveats in mind, let's look at prisons and recidivism to determine as best we can the deterrence effect of prisons.

Presumably the prison experience deters further criminal activity either because the former inmate has been rehabilitated or because they fear further punishment. However, one has only to look at the number of repeat inmates in prisons to see that previous punishment in prison did not deter subsequent crime for a significant number.

Officially, the FBI estimates the recidivism rate at about 70 percent. Daniel Glaser (1964, p. 14) has argued that official government data grossly overstate the case because they are based on faulty research methods. When the prison backgrounds of inmates are examined at any one time, recidivism rates will be inflated, because repeat offenders get longer sentences and are less likely to be paroled when compared with first offenders. The result is that a prison population is disproportionately composed of recidivists. Much more accurate studies follow a cohort of offenders after prison to determine what proportion eventually return to prison. When this is done, and the number of studies so designed are few, the recidivism rate appears to be about one third—which means about two thirds of ex-convicts manage to evade prison (Glaser, 1964, pp. 15–35).

General Deterrence

The assumption of general deterrence is that the punishment of offenders will keep other potential offenders from committing the heinous act. To maximize effectiveness, it is argued, there must be certain and severe punishment. Advocates favor toughening the laws with mandatory and longer sentences. Most important, potential offenders must be aware of the costs of criminal acts. Presumably they will then weigh these costs against the benefits and, if the costs clearly exceed the benefits, they will refrain from crime (Austin and Krisberg, 1981, p. 178).

There is some evidence that stricter laws for certain crimes have a deterrent effect. In 1982, a number of states passed laws with stringent and mandatory penalties for drunken driving. The early evidence appears to indicate that these laws are changing some behaviors as arrests for driving while intoxicated are down and automobile accidents involving drinking are lower than before the passage of these laws. This supports the finding from an earlier study in England. The Road Safety Act was passed in 1967 making driving while intoxicated a crime and calling for the revocation of the offender's license and a stiff fine. As a result, seemingly, the rate of traffic fatalities declined significantly. As Ross summarized the findings:

> In Britain it was shown that a significant drop in motor-vehicle casualties occurred precisely at the time of introduction of the new legislation. Furthermore, the drop in casualties was greatest on weekend nights, when alcohol is usually heavily involved in serious crashes, and not present during weekday commuting hours, when alcohol is less often a cause of such crashes. (Ross, 1982, p. 310)

In a study of the effects of a dramatic increase in the severity and certainty of punishment for parking violations on a college campus, Chambliss (1977) found a deterrence effect. He concluded, though, that one cannot generalize to other crimes because parking violations, unlike murder, is a conscious act done deliberately without passion. As with speeding, parking violators can usually determine whether they will get caught and can weigh the risks and benefits of committing the crime.

The argument for general deterrence is logical enough but impossible to prove with certainty. The only measure of general deterrence is to compare crime rates with punishment rates. We know that crime rates are suspect, though (see Chapter 4), and that punishment is not fairly distributed.

In addition to problems of measurement, there are other problems with the principle of general deterrence. Foremost, it obviously does not work completely since if it did, there would be no crime at all (Andenaes, 1952). Also, general deterrence assumes that the causes of crime center on the choices of individuals.

A number of criminals in various categories are not affected by the fear of punishment. Some of these are professional thieves, members of organized crime, drug traffickers, underage drinkers, prostitutes, income tax evaders, and political criminals. There is evidence that the sexual crimes of exhibitionism, rape, and incest, as well, are not much affected by the penalties for these behaviors. Andenaes (1952) reported that in response to an increase in sex offenses, Norway in 1927 increased the punishment for such crimes. During the next five years, a period when other crimes remained constant, sex crimes actually rose by 68 percent, when compared with the five years prior to change. The rise might be explained not by the actual increase in the crimes, but by public awareness, police zeal, and more rigorous reporting. But the law clearly did *not* have the intended general deterrence effect.

The results from other studies call into question the general deterrence effects of stiff sentences for criminal behavior. In 1961, California, for example, significantly increased the penalties for attacking police. A follow-up study found that by 1966 police were about twice as likely to be attacked as before the law (cited in Mitford, 1973, pp. 306–307). Also in 1973, New York State passed one of the most severe laws on illegal drug sales and possession to be found anywhere in the United States. The avowed purposes of this tough law were to frighten drug users out of their habit and drug dealers out of their trade. The Association of the Bar of New York (1977) and the Drug Abuse Council compared the rates before the passage of the law with those in 1976. They found that heroin use was as widespread after the law as before, supplies were not constricted, and that the use of so-called soft drugs (stimulants, barbiturates, tranquilizers, sedatives, and cocaine) was more widespread in 1976 than in 1973.

A CASE STUDY: CAPITAL PUNISHMENT AND GENERAL DETERRENCE

Does the threat of death intimidate potential murderers? In a word, no! Research indicates that the existence of the death penalty does not have the deterrent power argued by its proponents. For example, Schuessler's study of capital punishment effects from 1925 to 1949 shows that the death penalty had no effect on homicide rates (1971; see also Sellin, 1959; Passell, 1975). Schuessler's assertion is based on the following facts:

● States without capital punishment have lower homicide rates than states with the death penalty. This relationship also holds when the abolitionist states are compared with neighboring states with capital punishment.

- The homicide rate varies by age, social class, ethnic background, community size, and season "but in no instance can these differences be ascribed to corresponding differences in the application of the death penalty" (Schuessler, 1971, p. 192).
- The death penalty is hardly ever used with women in the United States, yet the murder rate by women is lower than for men.

Data from other countries—Canada, Great Britain, New Zealand, Australia, Denmark, Sweden, Norway, the Netherlands, Italy, and Austria—support the contention that capital punishment has little effect on the number of murders committed (Bowers, 1974).

A penalty cannot have much of a deterrent effect if it is rarely or inconsistently applied. This is clearly the case in the United States, where few murderers and rapists receive the death penalty and even for those who receive it, only a small proportion actually are killed.[5] From 1977 to the beginning of 1983, only six persons were killed. If the rate were increased to 100 executions a year, "a killer's chances of getting caught, convicted, and executed would for him still be comfortably low: 250 to 1" (Anderson, 1983, p. 35). Clearly, this is not a situation in which people are going to be deterred because of the likelihood of getting caught and being punished.

As a final argument against general deterrence, there is a serious moral question: Does society have the right to punish one person in order to deter another (Morris, 1976, p. 45)? General deterrence requires the inflicting of pain on some individuals for the benefit of others. This is the same criticism leveled against specific deterrence where an individual is imprisoned for a long period because of his or her assumed future lawlessness. In both cases, such punishment is unjust.

The moral questions raised by both forms of deterrence and the lack of research support for their positive effects, have not deterred state and federal governments from instituting legislation that implements mandatory sentences, capital punishment, and other manifestations of a get-tough crime control philosophy. Again, radical theory argues that increased repressive measures are responses to an economic depression that increases the surplus population in society (Bowers, 1974, p. 165). "Today's concern for reinstating the death penalty appears to be a repressive response during the current period of economic crisis. Capital punishment appears to be related less to the facts of a particular case than to the political economy of the times" (Balkan et al., 1980, p. 124).

SUMMARY

This chapter has provided an overview of the practical and philosophical considerations concerning the punishment of offenders. There is general agreement, except perhaps by extreme interactionists, that some offenders should be pun-

---

[5]The present trend is for an increase in death sentences and executions but the generalization still holds—relatively few guilty of capital crimes will actually be executed.

ished. The consensus breaks down, however, on what the goal of that punishment should be. Should the goal be to protect society, retribution, rehabilitation, or deterrence? Traditional sociologists tend to favor the rehabilitation model because it focuses on changing problem individuals. Radicals oppose this approach because it misdirects our attention away from problem institutions, including the criminal justice system. To focus on problem people is to blame the victim, who is assumed to be flawed, when the system is really to blame and in need of fundamental change.

CHAPTER REVIEW

1. Offenders, when found guilty by the courts, are punished. The forms of punishment vary in severity from fines, to probation, imprisonment, and death.

2. A major justification for imprisonment is to protect society from threatening individuals. The problems with this rationale are (a) the inability to judge accurately who should and who should not be isolated from society; (b) the solution is a short-term one because 95 percent of offenders eventually return to society; and (c) to accept that we are safe with the prisons full is a myth because only about 5 percent of the perpetrators of serious crimes are imprisoned.

3. Retribution—punishment in relation to the crime—is the major justification for imprisonment today. Determinate and mandatory sentences are congruent with the goal of retribution.

4. The death penalty is imposed on the perpetrators of the most heinous acts and thus is an example of retribution. There is a renewed interest by the public and legislatures in the death penalty. This ultimate punishment is not uniformly applied, however. Most significantly, the race and social class of capital offenders makes a difference in whether they are sentenced to die or not—with blacks and the lower classes vastly overrepresented.

5. Rehabilitation is another goal of punishment. This goal is based on the medical model—that offenders are physically, emotionally, or socially "sick" and with the proper therapeutic intervention (such as behavior modification, drugs, or counseling) they can become law-abiding citizens. The indeterminate sentence is based on the assumption that prisoners should not be released from prison until they are good prospects for readjusting into society. The evidence supporting rehabilitation is meager and inconsistent.

6. The final justification for imprisonment is deterrence, which takes two forms. The desired effect of specific deterrence is that the person punished will not do the criminal act again for fear of further punishment. The assumption of general deterrence is that the punishment of offenders will keep other potential offenders from committing crimes. Research indicates that general deterrence works in some instances (e.g., drunken driving, parking violations) but is ineffective for capital crimes.

14 Prisons

CHAPTER OUTLINE

The Growth and Composition of American Prisons

   Incarceration rates
   Demographic characteristics

Historical Patterns
The Latent Functions of Prison

   Latent functions that reinforce the status quo
   Latent functions that work against the expressed goals of prisons

The Social Organization of the Prison

   Prison management
   The inmate social system
   Inmate violence
   Prison riots

   Conclusion

KEY TERMS

   Auburn plan
   Formal Social system
   Incarceration
   Informal social system
   Jails
   Latent consequences
   Less eligibility
   Philadelphia plan
   Politization of prisoners
   Prisonization
   Prisons
   Regulatory violence
   Resocialization
   Total institution

The degree of civilization in a society can be judged by entering its prisons.

Feodor Dostoevsky (1821–1881)

I asked a man in prison once how he happened to be there, and he said he had stolen a pair of shoes. I told him if he had stolen a railroad, he would be a United States Senator.

Mary Harris "Mother Jones" (1900)

About 1 of every 600 Americans is in prison—not jail[1] or reform school—but in a state or federal prison (Anderson, 1982, p. 38). The annual growth rate in 1981 and again in 1982 was 12 percent (which, if continued, means the prison population will double in six years). Of the industrialized nations of the world only the Soviet Union and the Union of South Africa have a higher percentage of their populations in prison. Many politicians and citizens are calling for an even larger prison population to accommodate the criminals they believe are deserving of such punishment.

This chapter examines several topics related to prisons and punishment. The introductory section provides the background information on the growth and composition of the prison population. Examined next is the history of American prisons, focusing on the relationship of penal practices and economic conditions in society. Third, the consequences of prison that are not intended but occur nonetheless are elaborated. Finally, the social organization of the prison is described.

THE GROWTH AND COMPOSITION OF AMERICAN PRISONS

Incarceration Rates

The historical analysis of prison incarceration reveals, with some fluctuations, a steady trend upward. In 1880, there were 61.1 state and federal prison inmates per 100,000. In 1977 the rate was 135 per 100,000 (Cahalan, 1979, p. 14). By the end of 1982, the rate had risen even higher to 170 per 100,000 (see Table 14-1). It is important to note that while the U.S. rate continues to rise, it is declining in other western nations. The rates in other countries are incredibly lower than in the United States, for example, 32 per 100,000 in Sweden, 28 per 100,000 in Denmark, and 18 per 100,000 in the Netherlands.

Cahalan's (1979) historical examination reveals several interesting patterns. First, there is a positive relationship between unemployment rates and prison rates. When unemployment is high there is a heightening of punitiveness in the criminal justice system resulting in a higher incarceration rate (this supports the

---

[1]Jails, it should be remembered, are local lockups for persons awaiting trial and unable to make bail, or serving short sentences for relatively minor crimes. Approximately 500,000 persons spend time in jails during an average year. Prisons, on the other hand, are run by the states and the federal government and are reserved for offenders of serious crimes.

TABLE 14-1

The Prison Profile at Year-end, 1982

States with 10,000 or More Prisoners		States with Increases of 20 Percent or more Since 1981		States with Increases of 1000 or More Since 1981		States with In-carceration Rates of 200 or More per 100,000 U.S. Population	
Texas	36,282	North Dakota	28.2	California	5257	Nevada	301
California	34,459	Alaska	27.7	Texas	4780	South Carolina	270
New York	27,910	Nevada	25.4	Florida	4241	Florida	261
Florida	27,830	New Mexico	23.0	Ohio	2349	North Carolina	255
Ohio	17,317	Oklahoma	21.0	New York	2311	Louisiana	251
North Carolina	16,578	Delaware	20.6	Georgia	1876	Delaware	250
Michigan	14,737			Maryland	1677	Georgia	247
Georgia	14,320			Louisiana	1520	Maryland	244
Illinois	13,875			Pennsylvania	1157	Texas	237
Maryland	11,012			New Jersey	1115	Alabama	215
Louisiana	10,935			Oklahoma	1109	Mississippi	210
Pennsylvania	10,522			Alabama	1030	Arizona	209
Virginia	10,079					Oklahoma	201

SOURCE: *Justice Assistance News* 4, May 1983, p. 11.

Note: The District of Columbia, as a wholly urban area, is excluded from the list of States with high incarceration rates.

Rusche theory, explained at length in the next section). Second, despite these fluctuations, there is a marked willingness to rely more and more upon imprisonment. Third, since the 1800s, the proportion of persons confined in prison for nonviolent crimes has remained relatively constant—about 60 percent.[2] And, fourth, since the 1800s, the proportion of minorities in prison has ranged between 40 and 50 percent. Earlier, recent immigrants were prominent in the prison population but their numbers have decreased significantly in the intervening years. This decline has been offset by the increase in the proportion of black and Hispanic inmates.

The present prison population is experiencing a surge in growth. By the end of 1982, the population in state and federal prisons was 412,303, with estimates that the size will reach 500,000 before the end of 1984. About 7 percent of the inmates are in federal prisons at present and the remainder are in state facilities. The prison population at the state level is increasing twice as rapidly as at the federal level.

The reasons for the sharp increase in prison inmates is attributed to the recent changes in sentencing laws and sentencing practices by the states. From 1977 to 1982, 37 states passed mandatory sentencing laws and 11 states passed determi-

[2]This past trend may no longer be the case. The recent increases in prison populations are due primarily to the increasing proportion of property rather than violent offenders incarcerated.

nate sentencing. In addition, five states (Illinois, Indiana, Minnesota, Maine, and New Mexico) actually outlawed parole. Judges, too, have become more punitive, granting less probation and imposing harsher sentences. As an example of this trend toward increased judicial vindictiveness, the average federal prison sentence has steadily risen from 17.5 months in 1950, to 29.6 months in 1960, 41.1 months in 1970, 45.5 months in 1975, 51.9 months in 1980, and 58.6 months in 1982 (Administrative Office of the U.S. Courts, 1983, p. 14).

These practices and policies have combined to create a crisis in most prisons— overcrowding. For example, Texas, the largest state system, has 32,000 inmates (230 percent above capacity) and New York's prisons are 110 percent above the limit (Mianowany, 1982). Prison officials have employed several strategies to cope with overcrowded conditions. A common practice has been to keep new prisoners temporarily in county jails until there is room; unfortunately, the jails are also overcrowded. Another coping device has been to doublebunk inmates in cells designed for one. The American Correctional Association has set the minimum size for an individual's prison cell at 60 square feet (about the size of the average bathroom). However, because of overcrowding and doublebunking only about one fifth of U.S. inmates have cells that meet this standard (Anderson, 1982, p. 39). In 1981, by an 8 to 1 margin, the Supreme Court upheld the right of states to house two inmates in cells of 63 square feet (which was the case in the Ohio prison under review by the court). The justices observed that the Constitution does not guarantee ''comfortable prisons'' for persons convicted of serious crimes. In 1984 the Supreme Court reaffirmed that prisoners do not have the right to comfortable living conditions.

Demographic Characteristics

The prison population is disproportionately young, male, black, poor, and under-educated. That the poor and racial minorities are overrepresented is not surprising given the bias throughout the criminal justice system toward certain kinds of crime (street crimes) and against certain kinds of people (the powerless).

Age.   Forty percent of the prison population is under 24 years of age. This is because most street crimes tend to be committed by adolescents or postadolescents.

Sex.   Women comprise 4.4 percent of the state and federal prison population. This translates into 17,839 female inmates (as of September 1982). What is of interest is that the number is rising at a rate about twice that of males. This shift is not so much the reflection of the changing criminal behavior of women but rather the increase results from a tougher stance toward female criminals by judges and parole boards than was the case previously.

A study of Michigan prisons found the number of women prisoners increased 500 percent from 1968 to 1978 and that the women inmates tended to be unskilled, poor, and with little formal education. Nearly one half were single parents. And, most significantly, their crimes were typically neither serious nor violent (usually larceny, forgery, and drug offenses) (*ISR Newsletter,* 1981).

TABLE 14-2

Inmates in State Prisons by Selected Demographic Characteristics, 1979

Characteristics	Percentage of Inmates
Sex	
Male	96.0
Female	4.0
Age	
Under 30	63.0
30 years and older	37.0
Race	
White	49.6
Black	47.8
Other	2.5
Level of educational attainment	
Less than 12 years	58.0
12 years or more	42.0
Employment status (year prior to arrest)	
Full-time employment	60.3
Part-time employment	9.9
Unemployed	29.5
Personal income (year prior to arrest)	
Without income	22.2
Less than $3000	19.2
$3000–9999	30.2
$10,000 or more	24.9

SOURCE: Timothy J. Flanagan, David J. van Alstyne, and Michael R. Gottfredson (eds.), *Sourcebook of Criminal Justice Statistics—1981*, Washington, D.C.: U.S. Government Printing Office, 1982, p. 485.

Race.　Although whites constitute 51 percent of the prison population, blacks, Hispanics, and Native Americans are vastly overrepresented when compared with their proportion in the larger population. Blacks in 1981 comprised 45 percent of the inmates in federal and state prisons yet they were only 12 percent of the total U.S. population. Not only is the prison population disproportionately black, but as the prisons have grown rapidly, they have also gotten blacker. Data from 1973 and 1979 reveal that the incarceration rate for whites rose from 46.3 per 100,000 to 65.1 during this period while the black incarceration rate increased from 368 to 544.1 per 100,000 (Christianson, 1981, p. 365).

Although his data are dated and therefore understate the case as it is now, Erik Olin Wright has shown, in dramatic fashion, the disproportionate probabilities of being incarcerated if black in American society. On an average day in 1960, 1 of every 26 black men between the ages of 25 and 34 was either in jail or prison compared with 1 out of 163 white men in the same age category. In California on an average day in 1970, approximately 1 out of 7 black men between 20 and 24 was in prison or jail, on parole or probation, compared with 1 in 30 white men (Wright, 1973, p. 33).

Data from 1970 show that the ratio of the representation by race in prison was markedly skewed in favor of whites (a ratio of 1.0 would mean a percentage in prison equal to the proportion in the entire population). Reasons (1974, p. 5) found the ratios to be whites, 0.6; blacks, 3.7; native Americans, 3.4; and Hispanics, 1.8.

Socioeconomic characteristics. The inmate population is mostly comprised of low income, unemployed or underemployed, and undereducated persons. Data from 1981 reveal that 61 percent had never finished high school, 43 percent were unemployed at the time their crime was committed, and 46 percent had pre-arrest annual incomes of less than $3000 (*U.S. News & World Report,* November 1, 1982).

HISTORICAL PATTERNS

The first jail in the colonies was established in 1635. The early jails were local lockups to hold criminals temporarily before and during trials. Sentences throughout colonial history involved corporal and capital punishment, banishment, flogging, stocks, and branding rather than confinement in prison. Imprisonment was not used as punishment then for several reasons. The jails were small and could not hold many prisoners. Second, the colonists wanted to avoid the costs of maintaining prisoners. And, third, many criminals were laborers and servants who, if imprisoned, would deprive their masters of their cheap labor (a bias not lost on contemporary radical criminologists) (Takagi, 1980).

The success of the colonists in the Revolutionary War changed thinking concerning incarceration and punishment. The state and federal officials were now anxious about protecting and preserving order. State and federal prisons became one of the ways of centralizing the powers of the state (Takagi, 1980). Also instrumental in changing penal philosophy were Quaker leaders in Pennsylvania who favored a more humane and civilized form of punishment than the colonial methods. At the home of Benjamin Franklin on March 9, 1787, several Quaker leaders formed the Pennsylvania Prison Society. Their efforts led to the creation of the Walnut Street Jail of Philadelphia in 1789 and the passing of a law by the Pennsylvania legislature that provided for any felon sentenced to 12 months or more to be confined in the Walnut Street facility if the county were willing to help defray expenses.

The Quakers were successful in having the prison organized to replace punishment with rehabilitative treatment—in the form of prolonged solitary confinement (Goldfarb, 1974). The trend of sentencing offenders to confinement in prisons spread rapidly throughout the states in the early 19th century. These new prisons were organized in one of two ways. The "separate" system, as established by the Quakers in Philadelphia (known as the "Philadelphia system") placed prisoners in solitary confinement where they would have time to reflect on their crime, become penitent (hence, the term *penitentiary*), and converted. To encourage conversion, the only reading material allowed was the Bible. The other organizing principle for prisons was the "congregate" system, which was first practiced in Auburn, New York, in 1821. This plan emphasized common activities, external discipline, hard labor, and forced rehabilitation (Quinney and Wildeman, 1977, pp. 136–137).

The Philadelphia system did not work as planned. The assumption of the Quakers that criminals, if left alone, would repent for their sins, be saved, and become good citizens, was naive. Some, doubtless, did change their ways, but many others went mad or even died because of the extreme deprivation of extended solitary confinement. The experiment was generally abandoned by mid-19th century and was supplanted by the "congregate-hard labor" system. This "Auburn Plan" has continued to serve as the basic model for prisons of today.

The "congregate-hard labor" plan was, like the "separate" plan, intended to reform the criminal. But instead of solitary soul-searching, the reform of the criminal was to occur through extreme regimentation. This emphasis on obedience, order, and rigidity that pervaded all of prison life was, according to Rothman, also intended to provide a model for the whole of society.

> The functioning of the penitentiary—convicts passing their sentences in physically imposing and highly regimented settings, moving in lockstep from bare and solitary cells to workshops, clothed in common dress, and forced into standard routines—was designed to carry a message to the community. . . . By demonstrating how regularity and discipline transformed the most corrupt persons, it would reawaken the public to these virtues. The penitentiary would promote a new respect for order and authority. (Rothman, 1971, p. 107)

Although the adoption of the Auburn Plan by 1850 and its use through today implies stability in how prisoners have been treated, the degree of punitiveness directed at them has varied considerably.

Traditionally, criminologists have argued that variations in incarceration rates, sentence lengths, and physical punishment occurred in response to the actual amount of crime in society. As crime rates rise the agents in the criminal justice system tend to become more punitive as a way to deter criminals and potential criminals and thus curb the criminal trend. Radical criminologists believe that the historical analysis of imprisonment forms and the structure of punishment reveals that the variations are related to political and economic circumstances rather than crime rates. This radical interpretation, summarized in this section, comes primarily from the works of Georg Rusche (1933), Rusche and Kirchheimer (1939), and Sellin (1944).

Rusche (1933) noted three periods in European history when the form of punishment varied. In the early Middle Ages practically the only forms of punishment were penance and monetary fines. In the late Middle Ages, however, the punishment system was characterized by cruel torture and death sentences. This changed in the 17th century with the norm being prison sentences. These shifts were directly related to social conditions. The early period when fines and penance were the rule corresponded to the needs of a thinly populated peasant economy. Land was relatively plentiful and property crimes few. The situation in the late Middle Ages was quite different, with property now more in demand than people. The land was settled and crowded. Now large numbers were poor and propertyless. Under these conditions, there was a rapid increase in property crimes by hordes of beggars, thieves, and robbers.

As a result, the sphere of action of criminal justice had to be completely altered. If in the Middle Ages fines were preferred over corporal punishment, now the traditional system of monetary fines had outlived its usefulness because these criminals had no possessions with which they could pay. Gradually, traditional punitive methods were replaced by whippings, mutilation, and killing, at first still redeemable through money, later the universal means of punishment of and protection against the criminality of the gathering crowds of have-nots. The most gruesome imagination is hardly sufficient to visualize the justice of that time. (Rusche, 1933, p. 14)

Around 1600, the third epoch emerged as the conditions of the labor market changed. The supply of labor became relatively scarce because of the expansion of trade and new markets, the influx of gold and silver from the New World, and wars and plagues. Workers were scarce and valuable. Now it did not make sense to harm criminals physically or kill them when their labor in prisons earned many times their keep.

But this "humanitarian" system was brief. The Industrial Revolution in the 18th and 19th centuries, which replaced workers with machines, made labor cheap.

The lower classes sank into misery, underbid each other on the labor market, and compulsory measures lost their meaning. Prisons were no longer profitable. When wages were high, they had brought high gains; but when workers voluntarily offered their labor for a minimum existence, it was no longer worth it to come up with the cost for confinement and supervision. . . . Penal punishment remained a leftover from a previous and quite different epoch, but adjusted by necessity to changing needs. Institutions of forced labor, penitentiaries became places of pure torture, suitable to deter even the most wretched. Prisoners were insufficiently clothed and were cramped together. Work, having become unprofitable, served as torture: loads of stone had to be lugged without purpose from one place to another by the prisoners; they had to work waterpumps which let the water flow back again, or treadmills which were not used for any purpose. The discipline of this routine was reenforced by the deterrent effect of beatings. (Rusche, 1933, pp. 14–15)

Rusche's examination of these historical patterns led him to an economic theory of punishment. He hypothesized that imprisonment is related to the principle of "less eligibility," which is that prison conditions must always be worse than those of the working poor. Otherwise, the working poor would not be encouraged to remain in the work force. Thus, the conditions of prisons and the forms of punishment will vary with the conditions of the working class. And, as Rusche demonstrated, whenever there was a labor shortage and wages were relatively high, penal institutions were relatively humane. Conversely, when there was a worker surplus and the life conditions of the working class worsened, punishment of criminals became brutal and repressive.

Rusche's theory that changes in forms of punishment reflect changes in economic and political institutions in the larger society has been applied by Shelden (1981) to penal changes following the Civil War in the South. His data make a strong case that as the southern states changed from a slave economy to a capitalist one after the Civil War, the prison system made changes to accommodate the new economic forms.

Prior to the Civil War, the southern prisons were predominantly white. The prisons were organized on the Auburn plan with strong discipline and convict labor to make profits for each of the states. Following defeat in the war, the South faced three critical problems: (1) the rebuilding of its railroads, factories, and farms; (2) finding a cheap source of labor to replace slavery; and (3) controlling the ex-slaves. The criminal justice system adjusted to meet these problems. Blacks were controlled by passing Jim Crow laws, which perpetuated social segregation, and Black Codes, which permitted the authorities to arrest blacks for vagrancy, "suspicious behavior," or for looking at white women the "wrong" way. As a result, the prisons shifted from predominantly white to predominantly black (e.g., the Nashville prison shifted from 33 percent black in 1865 to 67 percent black in 1877). Following the war, the prisons began to lease convicts to private businesses. This policy benefitted capitalists by providing them with an abundant and steady source of cheap and forced labor.

> Under leasing, convicts were released from prison during the day to work outside the prison walls for a particular company. At night they were returned to their cells, in some cases after working 10 to 12 hours under grueling conditions (deaths, attempted escapes, and escapes were quite common). In return, the corporation paid the state a certain fee. For instance, one lease in Georgia involved a hundred black convicts who worked on the Georgia and Alabama railroad for one year, for which the state was paid $2,500. In some cases leases were signed for longer periods, thus insuring a steady supply of cheap labor and keeping convicts in bondage, as under slavery. (Shelden, 1981, pp. 362–363)

The Rusche theory has been demonstrated for societies with pre-capitalist and early capitalist economies but does it hold for the late capitalism that characterizes contemporary American society? Unlike 100 or 200 years ago, there now are trade unions, welfare systems, child labor laws, dual worker families, and other factors that affect the conditions of the labor market. The question is, Under the conditions of late capitalism, does the level of labor scarcity affect imprisonment rates and the conditions within prisons? The available research supports the hypothesized relationship. David Greenberg (1977) examined the relationship between unemployment (his indicator of the state of the business cycle) and prison admissions. He found that in the United States from 1945 to 1959 the correlation between per capita admissions to prison and the proportion of the labor force unemployed was an extremely high 0.92. Similarly, for the period 1960 to 1972, the correlation was 0.91 for first admissions to federal prison and 0.86 for first admissions to state prison. Supporting the Rusche hypothesis, Greenberg found that during the late 1960s, a period of economic expansion, crime rates and arrest rates rose, yet prison admissions declined. Just the opposite occurred in the recession of the early 1970s—crime rates continued to rise, and prison admissions rose dramatically. Greenberg is skeptical, however, of the Rusche explanation:

> [The Rusche proposal] seems implausible for the period under consideration, for it requires that we assume that Canadian and American judges, almost without exception, orient their sentencing policies to the requirements of the labor market and that they agree on how this can best be done. For the present period, this assumption is farfetched. Perhaps the absolute monarchs of seventeenth century Europe could instruct judges to commute sentences in order to obtain galley slaves, but neither the prime minister of Canada nor the president of the United States exercises comparable authority over sentencing. For the present era, it is more plausible to assume that judges are less willing to grant probation to offenders when they are unemployed, or that unemployment affects levels of community tolerance toward offenders, to which judges respond in sentencing. (Greenberg, 1977, p. 650)

Ivan Jankovic (1977) found support for the Rusche hypothesis when he found that state prison inmate levels between 1926 and 1974 rose and fell with annual unemployment rates in the United States.

Further confirmation of the Rusche hypothesis is found in the sophisticated research of Don Wallace (1981). He looked for the relationship between labor force participation rates and allocation of expenditures for prisons, parole rates, and imprisonment rates. He found that the fiscal activities of the states during the early 1970s was largely attributable to labor force fluctuations. "States in which the labor force participation rate declined (indicative of a labor surplus) were those states in which imprisonment expenditures increased" (Wallace, 1981, p. 61). Moreover, "prison expenditures are paralleled by welfare expenditures; states AFDC [Aid to Families with Dependent Children] benefit levels *increase* as do prison expenditures. Overall, the combination of labor force decreases and welfare expenditure increases is highly predictive of increased fiscal allocations for adult segregative control [prisons], with the further revelation that welfare functions as a social control mechanism in tandem with prison expenditures" (Wallace, 1981, p. 61).

Regarding parole, Wallace found that there is a relationship between the willingness to grant parole and the demand for cheap labor. Whenever the labor supply is short and welfare benefits low, the states tend to increase the probation of prisoners released early. In short, the parole system serves to regulate low-wage labor. Wallace also found direct evidence that changes in labor force participation are related to the rate of incarceration of adult prisoners in state institutions. He found that states with increases in their prison populations had labor surpluses.

The conditions of contemporary American society also appear to confirm the Rusche hypothesis. In early 1983, unemployment rates were the highest since the Great Depression. Approximately 50 million Americans were close to or below the official poverty line (which understates the actual numbers in poverty, see Eitzen, 1983). There was clearly a labor surplus and a relatively low standard of living for the working class. As this marginal surplus population increases, there is less need for labor, and, as Rusche would predict, punishment of criminals will become more retributive. This prediction is verified in several ways: (1) incarceration rates are rising rapidly; (2) prisons are severely overcrowded; (3) states are passing legislation instituting mandatory sentences; (4) capital punishment is clearly on the rise and strongly supported by public opinion; and (5) President Reagan and other conservative politicians are calling for tougher laws, stricter sentencing, and more prisons. For example, the 1984 budget proposal of the Reagan administration called for huge increases in federal spending on both state and federal prison expansion.

THE LATENT FUNCTIONS OF PRISON

The preceding chapter examined the reasons for imprisonment—to protect society, to punish offenders, to rehabilitate them, to deter them, and to reduce the crime rate. These manifest consequences of prisons are fulfilled, as we have seen, in small and varying degrees. The prisons also have latent consequences, that is, the unintended and generally unrecognized consequences of social arrangements. It is important to identify the latent functions of prisons because they inform us of how these organizations really work. Most important they reveal two significant patterns that help to explain (1) why prisons are so difficult to reform and (2) why prisons often accomplish the opposite of their formal objectives.[3]

Latent Functions That Reinforce the Status Quo

Traditional sociologists, known as functionalists, believe that a social arrangement such as prison exists because it has positive consequences for certain segments of society and that many of these functions may either not be served or ill-served by alternatives to prison. Clearly, society—or at least part of it—is served, in the short term, when dangerous persons are locked up. Society or some segment of it is served if criminals are reformed and potential criminals are deterred from crime. Although research demonstrates that these functions are only minimally served by prisons in the United States, many groups in American society believe they are served significantly and when coupled with retribution, may feel that prisons are not only necessary but reasonably successful.

There are also specific interest groups that are served by the latent functions of prisons as they are organized at present. For example, in 1982 there were almost 300,000 prison guards, probation and parole officers, and other prison personnel (*U.S. News & World Report,* November 1, 1982, p. 36). Reasons and Kaplan

[3]The following discussion is largely dependent on the insights of Reasons and Kaplan (1974).

(1974, pp. 9–10) have argued that prison is a place where marginal professionals are employed. Often they have minimal degrees with some qualifications but not enough to practice in other, more professional contexts. The custody staff (guards), in particular, have relatively low educational attainment and lack skilled training so the labor market is especially tenuous for them. Prisons, then, function to employ hundreds of thousands of individuals who might otherwise have difficulty in finding employment. Opportunities and jobs are also created for contractors who build prison facilities and suppliers of goods to prisons.

Prisons serve another latent function—scientific research—which creates other constituencies interested in preserving the status quo. Inmates are an important source of subjects for various groups requiring human subjects for testing. This captive population is a rich source of data for medical, psychological, and sociological testing. Inmates may be divided into different groups receiving different kinds of treatments, such as behavior modification, psychotherapy, or drug therapy, to see which is most effective. Most important, inmates are the major source of "human guinea pigs" for medical research. Drug companies rely on them to test new products. Jessica Mitford (1973) found that prisons furnish virtually all the subjects for the testing of new drug compounds for effectiveness and possible toxic properties. The prisoners in these experiments are not always motivated by humanitarian reasons but the hope of early parole. The prison system thus provides "willing" experimental subjects, the availability of which increases the profits of drug companies, among other interests.

The third latent function—slave labor—serves the state and private industry (see Miller, 1974). Prisoners produce products for the state, such as license plates, furniture, and agricultural goods, for extremely low wages—from a low of $2\frac{1}{2}$ cents an hour at Angola, Louisiana's maximum security prison, to 35 to 50 cents an hour elsewhere. "If the penitentiary did not exist, the state would be forced to turn to the open market and hire labor at competitive wages, rather than slave labor. It is, therefore, understandable why attempts to institute minimum wage laws in prison are not looked upon kindly by state officials and prison administrators" (Reasons and Kaplan, 1974, p. 11).

The Justice Department of the federal government has a corporation called Unicor, which organizes prison labor to make products for public sales. In 1980, Unicor had more than $110 million in sales and profits of $12.7 million (Martin, 1982).

Prison labor also serves private enterprise. Prisons rent out inmates to private businesses and farmers at low cost. There are also some unique experiments whereby private industry contracts with the state for prison labor (Ackland, 1981). For example, some inmates at the state prison in Stillwater, Minnesota, work at a computer parts assembly plant. A sheet metal plant in Leavenworth, Kansas, hires prisoners for its labor force. And the Arizona Department of Corrections and the Arizona Pork Producers operate a meat packing plant as a joint venture.

Private industry is also served by the low wage pool of ex-convicts. A common condition of parole is that an inmate must have a job waiting. The prospective employer knows that the inmate has few options and will take very low wages. The stigma of being an ex-convict continues to make job security tenuous for them, resulting in a reluctance to ask for higher wages and better working conditions.

Latent Functions That Work Against the Expressed Goals of Prisons

Prisons are supposedly designed to protect society, deter crime, and rehabilitate criminals, but they fail. They do not, as we have seen, reduce or prevent crime. In fact, the prisons actually work to maintain and encourage a visible "class of criminals."[4]

The prisons are designed to fail because the way they are organized accomplishes three latent consequences. The first is that the prison experience tends to provide inmates with a criminal identity. Individuals are stripped of their identity and dignity. In this context the inmate social system develops its own organization and stratification system (see the next section). By accepting and being accepted in this system, the self-esteem and prestige of inmates is enhanced. But prestige in this system depends generally on toughness, rejection of the straight world, and loyalty to inmates. A criminal identity is also promoted by society. Ex-offenders carry the label forever. As Reiman has characterized it:

> Ex-offenders . . . can never pay their debt to society . . . they [are] always different from "decent citizens". . . . They [are] deprived for the rest of their lives of rights, such as the right to vote. They [are] harassed by police as "likely suspects" and [are] subject to the whims of parole officers who can at any time threaten to send them back to prison for things no ordinary citizens could be arrested for, such as going out of town or drinking or fraternizing with the "wrong people." (Reiman, 1979, p. 4)

The second latent function that works against the avowed objectives of the prison is that the prison is a crime school. Prison is a learning experience and the behaviors and values transmitted and reinforced support criminal behavior. Sutherland's theory of differential association (1974) applies here—criminal behavior is learned from peers in intimate personal groups, and that one becomes criminal if there is an excess of definitions favorable to the violation of law as compared with the definitions unfavorable to law breaking. Clearly, the prison promotes this kind of differential association as inmates interact on a status and prestige-producing basis only with other inmates.

The third latent function of prisons that promotes goals contrary to the objectives of reducing crime and rehabilitating criminals is politization. Prisoners have enormous amounts of time for reflection and contemplation. One issue they consider individually and collectively is the unfairness of the criminal justice system. There is a strong tendency to believe that they have been arbitrarily singled out for unjust punishment and, as we have seen, this is an essentially accurate assess-

[4]This is the insightful thesis of Reiman (1979). This section depends largely on his persuasive arguments.

ment. They know that white-collar criminals are much less likely to be imprisoned. They know of persons committing crimes similar to their's who, because of shrewd lawyers or the wide latitude given prosecutors and judges, were punished much less severely. And, if a member of a racial minority, these feelings of injustice and rage are often multiplied (see Reasons, 1974). As Angela Davis has observed:

> Prisoners—especially blacks, Chicanos, and Puerto Ricans—are increasingly advancing the proposition that they are political prisoners. They contend that they are political prisoners in the sense that they are largely victims of an oppressive politico-economic order, swiftly becoming conscious of the causes underlying their victimization. (Davis, 1971, p. 37)

To the degree that inmates feel they are unfairly confined, they will reject the social order and act in "anti-social" ways rather than have remorse for their past misdeeds (Reiman, 1979, p. 3).

But why would society tolerate a prison system that is structured to fail? Reiman, in his radical critique of the criminal justice system, asserts provocatively that the actual goal of our criminal justice policy is to maintain crime rather than reduce it. The prisons, disproportionately comprised of the members of the underclass—the unemployed and underemployed, undereducated, the poor, and minorities—fail to deter, rehabilitate, and to protect society. This reinforces the belief that the ultimate threat to society comes from the underclass.

> *The criminal justice system fails to reduce crime while making it look like crime is the work of the poor.* And it does this in a way that conveys the image that the real danger to decent, law-abiding Americans comes from below them, rather than from above them, on the economic ladder. This image sanctifies the status quo with its disparities of wealth, privilege, and opportunity and thus serves the interests of the rich and powerful in America—the very ones who could change criminal justice policy if they were really unhappy with it. (Reiman, 1979, p. 5)

THE SOCIAL ORGANIZATION OF THE PRISON

There is considerable variation among prisons. Some are for adults, others for juveniles. There are male prisons and others for women. Some prisons are designed for maximum security, whereas others have no walls. In the description that follows, we will focus on adult male maximum security prisons. But this focus should not hide the characteristics that all types of prisons and prisoners share. Many of these commonalities result from the properties that prisons have in common with other total institutions such as mental hospitals, nursing homes, monasteries and convents, military academies, and military boot camps.

Erving Goffman's (1961) research on mental hospitals led him to the concept of "total institution," which provides many insights for understanding how prisons are organized formally and informally. A prison is a total institution, a place where inmates are confined in an all-encompassing social environment. They are under

Prisons are total institutions where inmates are regimented and dehumanized.

the absolute control of a hierarchy of officials. Most important, the inmates are stripped of their former identities and resocialized. Most of their personal possessions are confiscated; they are stripped, searched, disinfected, issued institutional clothing, assigned living quarters, and given a number. Inmates are dehumanized in prison by the loss of privacy. They are further dehumanized by the loss of adulthood, since they are now placed in situations of enforced childhood with no control over their time or actions (Reiman, 1979, p. 3).

A total institution is a miniature society with its own structure and culture. Inmates must be resocialized, that is, they must learn and incorporate the rules and roles expected in the new setting because the old ones are no longer relevant. This requires that prisoners learn both the formal and informal social systems. The formal system involves the explicit rules provided and enforced by the prison authorities. But there is also an informal system that inmates must learn. These are the unwritten rules for what are appropriate and inappropriate behaviors in interacting with guards and other inmates.

These insights of Goffman on total institutions guide the following description of the social organization of the prison. The discussion is divided into two parts: (1) the administration of the prison and (2) the inmates' social world.

Prison Management

Prisons are organized as bureaucracies. Authority is arranged hierarchically in a clear chain of command. Rules are standardized and they are enforced with force or the threat of force.

The prison bureaucracy is organized to control its "clients." The objective is to minimize trouble and process the prisoners according to the dictates of the courts. The prevailing assumption of prison officials is that inmates must be tightly controlled for fear that otherwise they will be violent to authorities and to themselves, and without control they will escape to terrorize the community. Thus, in an authoritarian way, social order is imposed on the inmates. The inmates are continually observed and searched. Their lives are completely regimented. They are constantly demeaned and dehumanized by the demands of the authorities. The emphasis is on maintaining the routine through control. And this routine is perceived by inmates as for the good of the institution rather than their welfare.

Regulatory Violence

The main goal of prison administrators is control of the inmates. This control is accomplished primarily through the threat or use of violence. Beatings occur in the name of discipline. Although torture such as floggings, thumbscrews, and the rack were ruled out some 150 years ago, it continues in other forms. In the 1960s, for example, it was revealed that the Arkansas state prison used the "Tucker Telephone," an electrical device wired to the genitals as a means to punish inmates. Deprivation is a common form of violence administered by prison authorities as inmates are placed in solitary confinement, food or heat withheld, and the like. In the Marion federal penitentiary in Illinois, for example, there is a Controlled Unit Treatment Program. Problem inmates are placed in solitary confinement. The inmates placed there have alleged that while in this unit they have been beaten, drugged without their consent, given an inadequate diet, and denied physical exercise (Miller, 1977).

Drugs are used to control problem inmates in two ways. One is to give prisoners powerful tranquilizers that will pacify them—make them sleepy, sluggish, and nonviolent (see Spieglman, 1980). Drugs are also used in aversion therapy to inflict terror as a way of modifying behavior. The drug Anectine has been used on inmates for this purpose.

> According to Dr. Arthur Nugent, chief psychiatrist at Vacaville [California] and an enthusiast for the drug, it induces "sensations of suffocation and drowning." The subject experiences feelings of deep horror and terror, "as though he were on the brink of death." While he is in this condition a therapist scolds him for his misdeeds and tells him to shape up or expect more of the same. Candidates for Anectine treatment were selected for a range of offenses: "frequent fights, verbal threatening, deviant sexual behavior, stealing, unresponsiveness to the group therapy programs." Dr. Nugent told the *San Francisco Chronicle,* "Even the toughest inmates have come to fear and hate the drug." (Mitford, 1971, p. 142)

The Compromising of Official Authority: The Informal System

The social organization of a prison, or any other organization, does not correspond exactly to the formal rules of the bureaucratic blueprint. Informal systems emerge that compromise and at times even negate the formal system. In the case

AN ELECTRIC 'PACIFIER' FOR INMATES

MOUNDSVILLE, W.VA. (AP) A good shot of about 50,000 volts of electricity will make even the most rambunctious prisoner gentle as a kitten, says a West Virginia warden who uses a hand-held device called a Taser gun to keep inmates in line.

West Virginia Penitentiary Warden Donald Bordenkircher keeps the plastic, flashlight-sized weapon plugged into a wall socket, where its battery pack is charged with electricity.

The Taser gun shoots darts, connected to wires, that deliver a shock.

Bordenkircher said his guards have used the gun twice—most recently last month—to subdue unruly inmates. Since then the prison's population has been fairly quiet, Bordenkircher said.

"It's absolutely the most humane weapon I've seen used," he said. "There are absolutely no after effects. No one gets hurt."

Bordenkircher is not alone in his views, according to Taser Systems Inc. of City of Industry, Calif., which started producing the guns in 1975.

Elaine Taylor, a spokeswoman for the company, said the devices now are being used by 300 law-enforcement agencies and nine prisons around the country, including police departments in Los Angeles, Calif.; Nashville, Tenn.; and Akron, Ohio. The guns also are being used by the Florida Highway Patrol, she said.

Taylor said more than 5,000 have been sold.

Bordenkircher said the device is not used in his prison without permission from him or his deputy.

"When an inmate becomes terribly violent and vicious and has to be controlled," Bordenkircher said, the Taser is disconnected from the socket and carried by guards to the scene of the disturbance.

"You push a button and two little darts shoot out of it that have two little strings attached to the power pack, and that's it. It totally immobilizes you."

The darts are connected to 20-foot-long wires that run to the battery pack.

"If you have a knife in your hand and try to attack me and I use the Taser, you cannot move," the warden said.

Bordenkircher said brochures from the weapon's manufacturer claim that the Taser delivers 50,000 volts, but no amperes. The absence of amperes is what makes it safe, the brochures contend.

But according to Wils Colley, professor of electrical engineering at West Virginia University, an absence of amperes would mean an absence of shock.

"You wouldn't feel anything unless there was some flow of current," Cooley said. "The word 'no' cannot be taken literally. They probably mean negligible or extremely small."

With low amperage, however, a shock of 50,000 volts would not be fatal, he said.

"If you walk across your carpet and touch the doorknob and get a shock, you're getting about 20,000" volts, Cooley said.

The warden said the weapon has been praised even by the inmates who have felt its sting.

"One of the inmates told me and the other told a doctor that it was one of the most effective rehabilitation programs they've had administered," Bordenkircher said.

"That's their cute way of saying they have had enough of that. They don't want any more of it."

Source: Associated Press release, "An Electric 'Pacifier' for Inmates," June 26, 1982, p. 12.

of a prison, two informal systems are salient—one among the prison custodians and the other among the inmates.

Gersham Sykes (1958) and others (see McCorkle, 1970) have directed attention to how the dominance of the administrative staff and guards is less than total. The staff cannot, for instance, use too much force since this may precipitate inmate violence. Realizing that inmates are not going to obey because of loyalty to the organization, there is a general willingness on the part of guards to overlook relatively trivial inmate infractions provided that inmates comply with the more important rules. Guards are evaluated, promoted, and given pay increases based on the behavior of the inmates in their charge. By ignoring minor rule violations such as drug trafficking, guards can achieve some cooperation from inmates, which works to the advantage of both (Colvin, 1981, 1982). Guards may also fail to enforce regulations because they are friends with the inmates or because they have accepted bribes. The smuggling of contraband is common in prisons and guards are the usual source. Finally, most prisons permit some inmates to do a number of jobs that are supposed to be done by those in authority, such as distributing mail and supplies and taking inventory. Thus, inmates come to control more of prison life than is commonly acknowledged. As Sykes has summarized:

> In examining the social structure of the custodial institution, then, it is important to realize that officials do *not* reign as unquestioned dictators enforcing every rule. . . . In almost all custodial institutions, however varied though they are, a basic sociological principle can usually be seen at work. If it is true that power corrupts and absolute power corrupts absolutely, it is also true that the maxim has another meaning: Power—even total power—is apt to be corrupted as it is exercised. No social organization corresponds exactly to the blueprint of the ruling few. The custodial institution is apt to be marked by an informal social system in the making of which the prisoners have a large hand. (Sykes, 1978, p. 519)

The Inmate Social System

When inmates enter a prison they are degraded, deprived, and dehumanized. Inmates react to this difficult situation differently. Some withdraw and react passively. Others rebel and fight the system at every turn. Still others accommodate to the system trying to make the best of a bad situation. But regardless of the individual response to incarceration, inmates go through a process called "prisonization" (Clemmer, 1940), where they learn and internalize the culture of the inmate prison system.

Within this system there are norms for what behaviors are appropriate and these normals are enforced by various social control devices. The prison society also reflects cleavages found in the larger society with cliques forming commonly along racial lines. Also the prison population is often divided against itself, with the strong dominating the weak. Predatory behaviors are often encouraged by prison administrators as a means of social control within the prison. The more that the prison population is divided, the less likely inmates will unite to threaten the official control of the prison. Also, troublesome inmates can be controlled by threats to move them into a situation unsafe for them.

Inmate Violence

The existence of an inmate social system should not imply that it always operates as a smooth-functioning unit. The degree of inmate solidarity varies from prison to prison and within a prison over time. In the history of a single prison there may be times of strong cohesion among the inmates while at other times the inmate social structure may be fragmented into small, warring cliques. Most significantly, regardless of the degree of inmate cohesion, there is always a strong undercurrent of fear and tension that threatens to erupt into episodes of violence.

The targets of inmate violence are three: the self, other inmates, and prison authorities. We will not focus on self-destructive acts by inmates, leaving that to psychologists, except to report that the suicide rate of prisoners is twice as high as found in the general population (Sylvester, Reed, and Nelson, 1977, p. xxii).

Inmate-inmate violence takes several forms including verbal abuse, physical threats, homosexual rape, beatings, torture, and homicide. The incidence of prison violence is much higher than found outside the prison for obvious reasons. The prison population is, after all, composed disproportionately of persons who have histories of aggressive and predatory behaviors. The prison experience increases their rage and frustration because of the overcrowding, lack of privacy, being the objects of abuse by prison guards, the belief that they are political prisoners, the tedium of prison life, the lack of sexual outlets, the lack of meaningful work, and the realization that even when they are released they have little hope of success.

The violence may be by individual predators who systematically terrorize weaker inmates or more spontaneously by individuals overcome by rage because of some precipitating incident. The aggression against inmates may also be by multiple assailants who plan and commit violence against an individual as punishment for violation of the inmate code, most commonly directed at suspected "snitches." There are also gang conflicts, which are often racially motivated; some prisons are plagued by power struggles among blacks, whites, and Hispanics (Castro, 1982). The result of these various forms of inmate-inmate violence is that the average prisoner has a 1 in 3300 chance of being killed during a year's stay in prison. As an extreme example, among the 2900 inmates in one prison, San Quentin, the 1981 toll was seven murders and 54 inmates stabbed, clubbed, or beaten by fellow inmates (Anderson, 1982).

Inmate violence directed at guards occurs in isolated instances of retaliation or in full-scale prison riots. Before we discuss prison riots, we need to understand the bases for the animosity that inmates tend to feel toward those who keep them captive. Hostility between these two groups develops in several ways. First, the inmates are at the mercy of the guards who may use unwarranted force on them. Second, guards work in an extremely tense setting where some inmates, if given the opportunity, may try to escape, take them as hostages, or otherwise harm them. Third, guards symbolize the unfair authority of the system to politicized prisoners, and inmates are viewed by the guards as convicted criminals deserving of punishment. Fourth, guards and inmates come from different social worlds. The guards live near prisons, typically located in rural areas. The prisoners, on the other hand, are disproportionately from urban settings. Also leading to misunderstandings between members of these two groups is that the guards tend to be white and the inmates are disproportionately black and Hispanic.

Prison Riots

Violent rebellions of prisoners against authorities have been numerous throughout American history. There were at least 400 known prison uprisings from 1855 to 1955. These uprisings are either spontaneous or organized and their causes varied. The most common riots occur to dramatize prisoner demands for reform: better food and medical attention, more recreational facilities, productive work, relief from overcrowding, improved sanitation, increased educational opportunities, restoration of basic human rights, and more humane treatment by guards (see Panel 14-2).

In the 1960s and early 1970s, corresponding with the heightened political activity of deprived groups in the larger society, prisoners became more political. Black leaders such as Eldridge Cleaver, George Jackson, and Malcolm X emerged in prison settings and raised the political consciousness of black inmates. They argued that black convicts were the "most abused victims of an unrighteous order" (Jackson, 1970, p. 35). They made convincing arguments that blacks were in prison because the politicoeconomic system denied racial minorities equal opportunities and because the criminal justice system was racist in its unequal punishment of blacks.

The politization of inmates is not confined to racial minorities. Whites also understand the class oppression in society and how it was reflected in the criminal justice system. As a result, in a variety of prison disturbances, most notably in three California prisons—San Quentin, Soledad, and Folsom—in 1970, white and black inmates joined to fight the system (Balkan et al., 1980, pp. 140–141).

The most famous politically motivated prison rebellion occurred at Attica, New York (Wicker, 1975). In May 1971, the Attica Liberation Front organized and presented 29 demands, which centered on prisoners' rights to organize politically and economically and on living and working conditions. A negotiating committee met with officials concerning these demands but nothing happened. Four months later, on September 9, inmates seized 43 guards as hostages, and 1500 prisoners controlled the prison yard. Most significantly, the leaders represented a coalition of whites and blacks unified against a common enemy. Two additional demands were added to the original list: transportation to a non-imperialist country for those who wished it and total amnesty for participants in the insurrection. The negotiations, which lasted four days, focused on only two very political demands of the 31: amnesty and the resignation of the prison warden. These two demands were too much for the state officials to accept because "they would have established the precedents that prisoners have a right to participation (if not control) in the process of choosing who rules them, and that they have a right to rebel without

PANEL 14-2

A Bill of Rights for Prisoners

This is a composite bill of rights for prisoners assembled from various state prisoners' demands:

- Right to organize prisoner unions.
- Right to adequate diet, clothing and health care.
- Right to vote and end second-class citizenship.
- Right to furloughs or institutional accommodations to maintain social, sexual and familial ties.
- Right to noncensorship of mail, literature and law books.
- Right to access to the press and media.
- Right to procedural and substantive due process to guarantee rights.
- Right to personality; resistance to coercive attempts by ''correctional'' staff to change behavior thru brain surgery, electric stimulation of brain, aversion therapy, hormones or modification techniques.
- Right to properly trained counsel.
- Right to be free from racial, ethnic and sexist discrimination.
- Right to freedom from mental and physical brutality.
- Right to have the community come into the prison.
- Right to have surveillance teams in prisons to monitor rights, protect prisoners' due process and see that they have access to their own files.
- Right to make restitution in lieu of further incarceration.
- Right to know their release date at time of entry to the prison.

Source: Mark Morris (ed.), Instead of Prisons: A Handbook for Abolitionists, *Syracuse, N.Y.: Prison Research Education Action Project, 1976, p. 175.*

fear of punishment'' (Pallas and Barber, 1980, p. 152). Governor Rockefeller refused to negotiate and ordered a full-scale assault by the State Police, which resulted in 43 deaths (including 10 of the hostages, all of whom were killed by police gunfire).

The New Mexico prison riot of 1980 was a completely different riot from Attica, reflecting a major difference in the inmate cultures of the two prisons. It was just as deadly (33 inmates killed) but the disturbance at Santa Fe was unorganized and not politically motivated. And, the violence was inflicted by the inmates on other

Aftermath of the Santa Fe, New Mexico prison riot in 1980.

inmates rather than by the authorities. As Mark Colvin has compared the two: "political apathy and infighting had replaced the politization and solidarity of a decade earlier" (1982, p. 449). When the prisoners took over the New Mexico state prison, many of the inmates went on a violent rampage. They beat and sodomized their hostages. Certain inmates were tortured and killed ("snitches," a child rapist, and the "mentally disturbed" were the targets) apparently because they were vulnerable and their deaths would not be revenged. The killings were unusually brutal and appear to be a reflection of the major criterion for status in that prison—toughness. As Colvin has observed:

> The riot was clearly an occasion to enhance or build reputations for violence and represents an escalation of the relations that had evolved in the inmate social structure prior to the riot. The building of a reputation for violence as the prevalent source of inmate power involved not just a quantitative competition (how many you kill) but also a qualitative competition (how you kill) that engendered the extremes of torture and humiliation during the riot. (Colvin, 1982, p. 459)

The result was the most violence by inmates in U.S. penal history. The New Mexico riot ended differently from the Attica riot as well. Apparently the orgy of violence and drug taking (the prison pharmacy was an early target of the inmates) exhausted the rioters and they gave up without resistance after 36 hours.

The New Mexico-style riot with its lack of inmate unity and its inward-directed violence is much more prevalent now than the Attica-style riot. Violence seems to be the norm in prisons with or without actual riots (in the Jackson, Michigan, prison, for example, there were 51 reported stabbings in the first four months of 1981). The increased violence appears to be the consequence of several related factors, such as overcrowding, idleness, unequal treatment by authorities, and the like, combined with the get-tough, punitive philosophy that dominates the current political climate. The primary objective of prison administrations has always been control of the inmates. But this has been accomplished traditionally, as we have seen, not only by force but by overlooking some infractions, such as drug trafficking and the making of alcohol, in return for overall order.

In effect, the prison achieves order by tolerating disorder. This contradiction creates a situation where eventually the indulgences become viewed as too tolerant. The prison authority then cracks down, disrupting the social relationships, roles, and structure within the inmate social structure. This removes important opportunity structures within the inmate society as well as important sources of inmate power (Colvin, 1981, 1982). Other mechanisms to wrest control from inmates are to increase the use of solitary confinement, break up cliques by transferring inmates, and more security searches. As the old sources of power within the inmate community are removed, the resulting power vacuum triggers "a struggle for power among the inmates. Power [becomes] increasingly based on violence as alternative sources of nonviolent power are diminished" (Colvin, 1982, p. 455). Describing the situation at New Mexico prior to the riot, Colvin has said:

> The competition to establish a violent reputation in turn generated more violence. Inmates found a willingness and ability to engage in violence as the best protection against other inmates. A reputation for violence became a necessary requisite for survival—and especially protection from sexual assault. . . . The only alternatives were submission or seeking the protection of officials; these two alternatives, most inmates agreed, contained worse consequences than fighting and forming self-protection cliques with other inmates. (Colvin, 1982, p. 455)

The result is a climate of violence within the prison whether there is a riot or not. As one inmate at the state prison in Jackson, Michigan, characterized the situation: "In here, not having a knife is a death sentence" (Magnuson, 1981, p. 18).

CONCLUSION

President Reagan and the conservative allies of his administration argued that the present criminal justice system and especially the prisons are impotent in the battle to reduce rising crime rates. What is required, they inform us, is a no-nonsense stance by the courts so that criminals receive a just and certain punishment. Also needed are more prisons to house all the criminals. This get-tough, lock-'em-up philosophy is based on the assumption that crime will be reduced if the "costs" of crime—punishment through imprisonment—are increased (Currie, 1982a, p. 28).

Interactionist and radical criminologists obviously disagree with this conservative approach. Rather than a buildup of the criminal justice system, radicals argue for its reduction and/or a buildup of the social justice system, through the democratic reformation and transformation of crime-producing social, political, and economic institutions and policies. Interactionists want only the most antisocial individuals to receive the labels "criminal" and "ex-con," which would be accomplished through the decriminalization of some crimes and more generous probation policies. The prisons as presently organized increase rather than decrease crime (Goldfarb, 1974; Reiman, 1979). We need fewer rather than more prisons. Prisons are needed only for the truly dangerous, not for all offenders. Therefore, there must be alternatives to prison for the vast majority who do not need to be behind walls. The next chapter investigates some of these alternatives.

CHAPTER REVIEW

1. Of the industrialized nations of the world only the Soviet Union and the Union of South Africa have higher percentages of their population in prison than the United States. The U.S. rate is rising rapidly because of the trend toward mandatory and determinate sentences and more punitive decisions by judges. The result of these policies is serious prison overcrowding.

2. The prison population is disproportionately young, male, black, poor, and undereducated.

3. Historically, American prisons were organized in one of two ways. The Philadelphia system, which was short-lived, used universal solitary confinement to provide the offenders with time to reflect and repent for their sins. The Auburn plan remains the model today. This plan emphasized common activities, external discipline, hard labor, and forced rehabilitation.

4. An issue that divides traditional criminologists from radicals is the source of variations in incarceration rates, sentence lengths, and the punitiveness of prison. Traditional criminologists argue that these vary in response to the actual amount of crime occurring in society. Radicals, on the other hand, provide evidence that these variations are related to political and economic circumstances rather than crime rates.

5. The latent functions—those unintended and generally unrecognized consequences—of prisons reinforce the status quo by providing marginal professionals with jobs, providing human subjects for scientific and commercial research, and slave labor to the state and private industry.

6. The prisons fail to protect society, deter crime, and rehabilitate criminals. They have these opposite effects of their stated goals because they work to maintain and encourage a visible class of criminals. Prisons fail because the way they are organized accomplishes three latent consequences: (a) the inmate social system encourages criminal identities, (b) the prison is a crime school, and (c) the prison experience politicizes prisoners so that they will tend to reject society.

7. Prisons are total institutions—places where inmates are confined in an all-encompassing social environment. Prisoners are under the absolute control of a hierarchy of officials. They are stripped of their former identities and resocialized. They are dehumanized by the loss of privacy and the loss of adulthood.

8. The prison bureaucracy is organized to control the inmates. The assumption is that inmates must be tightly controlled, so social order is imposed in an authoritarian manner. Control is accomplished primarily through the fear of force or force itself. The control of inmates is not total, though, as an informal system develops between guards and inmates.

9. Inmates develop their own social system with rules, roles, stratification, and methods of social control. This does not mean that the system always functions smoothly. Violence is common in prisons and takes three forms: self-destructive acts, inmate-inmate, and inmate-guard. These last two types of violence prevail in prison riots.

15 The Crisis in Criminal Justice

**CHAPTER
OUTLINE**

The Crisis of Incarceration
The Crisis of Decarceration

Community corrections defined
Community corrections: reduced imprisonment?
Community corrections: reduced recidivism?
Community corrections: more humane?
Community corrections: less costly?
A theory of decarceration
The demise of community corrections

The Crisis of Deviant Ghettoization
The Crisis of Private Justice

Private security and policing: policing for profit
Private corrections: treating and correcting for profit

The Crisis of Popular Justice

The progressive side of popular justice
The repressive side of popular justice

KEY TERMS

Community service
Decarceration
Deviant ghettoization
Diversion programs
Halfway houses
Popular justice
Presentence investigation
Pretrial release
Private justice
Probation/parole revocation
Residential treatment
Restitution
Work-release

Since the early 1960s, the American criminal justice system has been plagued by a prolonged period of change and crisis. This has been particularly evident in law enforcement, criminal courts, and corrections. This chapter focuses on five separate, "smaller" crises that have contributed to the overall crisis in criminal justice: the crises of incarceration, decarceration, "deviant ghettoization," "private justice," and "popular justice."

Adding to the development of these problems in criminal justice are two fundamental crises of contemporary American society. The first is the ever-increasing surplus population composed of those persons who are either not needed by, or cannot be accommodated in, the system of economic production and consumption such as the unemployed, underemployed, the poor, the working poor, street criminals, and deviants of all sorts. The structure of American society and the organization and operation of the American economy that marginalizes more and more of these persons increases their potential for criminal activity. Thus, there has been a push toward an expansion of, and greater effectiveness of, the various mechanisms of social control, including the criminal justice system. This pressure underlies all of the crises discussed in this chapter.

The second societal crisis, exacerbating the first, is that at the very time the criminal justice system is asked to expand and be more effective, the means to finance such proposals are receding. The fiscal crisis of local, state, and federal governments, as we will see, has limited the responses of a criminal justice system that is called upon to be "bigger and better."

Before turning directly to the crisis of criminal justice, a word on the organization of this chapter is in order. Rather than a specific section of the chapter being devoted to the "historical origin and development" of the phenomenon under consideration (as has been done in many of the preceding chapters), here we consider the "historical origin and development" of each of the five crises, one by one, as we move through the chapter. "Alternative explanations" for the origins and development of each of the crises in criminal justice—be they *traditional, interactionist,* or *radical*—are used whenever and wherever they are relevant and useful. Any conclusions drawn concerning the origins, causes, or possible solutions of any of the crises under discussion will also be identified in terms of the three perspectives on crime and crime control that we have used throughout the book.

THE CRISIS OF INCARCERATION

The professed goal of corrections throughout American history has been to "correct" criminal activity so as to prevent its recurrence. Thus, the primary criterion for evaluating correctional effectiveness has been and still is the reduction of criminal recidivism. But, beginning nearly two decades ago, it became increasingly apparent that the traditional imprisonment of criminal offenders was not serving this goal. Extensive surveys of correctional effectiveness studies would later declare U.S. prisons almost uniformly ineffective (see, for example, Lipton,

Martinson, and Wilkes, 1975). Prison reform became an issue and "the politics of contemporary corrections" were born.

Also beginning about this time, a number of criminologists and sociologists expressed skepticism about the possibility of any kind of effective rehabilitative efforts behind prison walls. There seemed to be a fundamental contradiction between the rehabilitative goals and the custodial or security functions of prisons. Some, particularly those using an interactionist perspective, were concerned that socialization into the inmate subculture would deter rehabilitation by increasing the commitment to a criminal career. From this perspective, it was also suggested that the societal stigmatization of incarcerated "convicts," and even "ex-convicts," would prevent any return to a "straight" or non-criminal life-style. Generally, correctional alternatives less stigmatizing for the offender seemed appropriate.

Still others, following more traditional sociological perspectives, pointed to the illogic involved in taking offenders who had presumably turned to crime out of weak ties to family, neighborhood, school, occupation, and community, and "correcting" them with a punishment that severed completely those already fragile ties. Perhaps, from this perspective, correctional alternatives that kept the individual in the community and aided in strengthening these ties would "reintegrate" and rehabilitate the offender much more effectively.

Many of these criminologists and sociologists, as well as liberal politicians, reformers, and activists argued, therefore, that it was both feasible and desirable to experiment with and establish new and innovative treatment programs for inmates. Federal commissions, the American Bar Association, the American Correctional Association, the National Council on Crime and Delinquency, all called for the development and use of community-based alternatives to incarceration (Austin and Krisberg, 1982). Ultimately, beginning in the mid- and late 1960s, a host of correctional programs, thought of primarily as alternatives to traditional incarceration, appeared. In short, what was to become known as community-based corrections became a reality.[1]

But the increased rehabilitative or therapeutic potential of community corrections (as compared with the traditional prison) was not, according to its proponents, the only advantage that "decarceration" or "deinstitutionalization" offered. It was not just that community-based corrections would reduce recidivism, and to some extent, by implication, crime rates. At least three other arguments were put forth.

First, it was argued that community corrections—even if they did not result in decreased recidivism rates—were desirable because of their more humanistic or humane response to the offender. The unnecessarily harsh and severe aspects of the large centralized prison could be circumvented. Second, advocates of community-based corrections contended that some of the harshest and severest aspects of prison life—those resulting from prison overcrowding—could also be lessened by channeling the offender back into the community. Decreased reliance on im-

---

[1] The first part of this section is taken primarily from Timmer (1980).

PANEL 15-1

The Costs of Correction: Prison and Community Alternatives

The cost of maintaining each inmate in Iowa's prison system averages nearly $49 a day, or $17,782 annually, according to the Iowa Department of Social Services.

The most expensive correctional institution to operate is the Iowa Security and Medical Facility at Oakdale, which costs $102 per inmate daily. The Oakdale facility mainly treats prisoners referred for diagnosis and treatment of psychological problems, or those referred by courts for pre-trial or pre-sentence evaluations.

The least costly prison is the Iowa Men's Reformatory at Anamosa, which costs $27 per inmate daily.

Average daily costs at other institutions, based on January statistics, are: Correctional Treatment Unit at Clarinda, $51; Iowa State Penitentiary at Fort Madison, $45; Riverview Release Center at Newton, $39; Women's Reformatory at Rockwell City (since moved to Mitchellville), $38; Medium-Security Unit at Mount Pleasant, $36.

According to a Department of Social Services report, the state saves large amounts of money when it uses community corrections programs such as pre-trial release, probation, residential facilities, work release and parole.

For example, while the average daily cost of keeping someone in prison is nearly $49, the average cost per day for each probationer is slightly more than $1. The average daily cost for pre-trial release clients is less than $2.

"These cost savings . . . do not include the benefits society realizes when an offender remains in the community, retains a job and pays taxes, supports his or her family and makes restitution to the victim of his crime," says the report.

As of May, Iowa had 14,452 criminal offenders under supervision. This figure includes 19 percent who were imprisoned and 81 percent in some type of community program.

The current annual budget for state adult corrections is more than $57 million. This includes nearly $44 million for prisons and almost all of the remainder for community and parole programs.

Source: William Petroski, "Each Inmate's Cost Averages $49 Per Day," Des Moines Register and Tribune, August 23, 1982, p. 3a.

prisonment through the increased use of community correctional programs would surely take pressure off growing institutional populations. And third, and this was without question the most appealing argument to state legislators, bureaucrats, and correctional administrators, community corrections would be less costly than imprisonment (see Panel 15-1). Imprisonment is, and always has been, the most expensive correctional alternative. By lowering both the rate and absolute number of persons incarcerated, community corrections would aid in bringing skyrocketing criminal justice costs into line.

In sum, the "crisis of incarceration" meant that state and federal prisons in the United States had become too ineffective, too inhumane, too overcrowded and too costly. The way out of this crisis was to be the development of alternatives to incarceration: community corrections.

THE CRISIS OF DECARCERATION: THE RISE AND DEMISE OF COMMUNITY CORRECTIONS

Beginning in the mid-1960s then, in spite of conservative opposition that argued for the continued reliance on the deterrent and punitive functions of prison, a proliferation of community-based alternatives to prison emerged in many states. Today, an overwhelming majority of convicted offenders under the supervision of the criminal justice system are not incarcerated; instead, they are under the control of one or another community corrections program. In this section we will (1) Define briefly community corrections: (2) Examine the evidence generated between 1965 and the present that answers the following questions: Have community correctional alternatives reduced imprisonment and recidivism? been more humane than traditional corrections? been less costly than incarceration? (3) Explain the rise and reality of community corrections in a way that challenges those explanations offered by its advocates and proponents; and (4) Suggest the pending and current failure and demise of community-based corrections.

Community Corrections Defined

Community corrections, as they have developed and expanded over the past 15 years, include, in most localities, some or all of the following alternatives to incarceration:[2]

Pretrial release and diversion programs. These programs were designed to either "divert" persons away from the criminal justice system—to more appropriate rehabilitative services such as psychiatric and mental health treatment, family counseling, drug and alcohol treatment, job and vocational training, educational institutions, and so on—or if retained in the justice system, to release them from any confinement before going to trial. This conditional release was, and is, often coupled with involvement in one or another of the services just mentioned.

Presentence investigation. Many community corrections programs have made these rather detailed queries into the background (criminal and otherwise) of convicted offenders available to the criminal court before sentencing. The objective of this consideration of the individual's specific background and circumstances is to increase the likelihood that he/she can reasonably be sentenced to a community program rather than prison.

---

[2] Initially at least, these local communities were encouraged by the availability of federal and state funds to develop these community-based programs.

Probation.   Although probation as such was not new to the criminal justice system, community corrections expanded its use and introduced a variable intensity of supervision for different kinds or classifications of offenders in order to keep more convicted persons in the community.

Residential treatment.   For those whom the criminal court was not willing to put on street probation, community residential facilities offered some minimum security and confinement, but in a small, decentralized setting in the local community. The emphasis in this setting was to be on rehabilitative activities—psychotherapy, family therapy, drug and alcohol treatment, vocational or educational training, and work.

Other sentencing alternatives: restitution and community service.   Restitution and community service sentences have been used in varying degrees across the country. Restitution refers to offenders, under court order, repaying their victims for the crimes they have committed. Community service sentences normally entail the offender being ordered to volunteer a specified number of hours, days, weeks, or months for work in some community or public organization or agency.

Post-release alternatives: parole, work-release, and halfway houses.   Like probation, parole is much older than the advent of community corrections. But, again, like probation, community corrections encouraged an expanded use of parole from prison. Here too, the intensity of parole supervision was to be adjusted to the needs of the person released to the community. Early release from prison was also made easier with the development of parole halfway houses, work-release houses, reentry centers, and pre-release centers. These facilities were to provide the same kinds of services to those released from prison as residential treatment facilities were to provide for persons convicted but not sent to prison.

With these community corrections programs more or less in place, new questions began to emerge. To what extent could these correctional alternatives be more fully developed? To what extent would they be utilized by the criminal justice system? To what purpose would they be put? And most important, would community corrections do what its supporters promised?

Community Corrections: Reduced Imprisonment?

Between 1965 and 1979 the number of persons imprisoned in the United States increased by approximately 30 percent—from around 363,600 to nearly 472,400. All of this increase came during a period of intense development and use of community corrections programs.

Also during this same period, the number of adult offenders on probation or parole increased in the neighborhood of 145 percent, from over 573,200 to approximately 1,387,600. These increases—in both the numbers of persons incarcerated and on probation or parole in the community—came at a time when the adult arrest rate was rising by roughly 65 percent (from 2830 to 4660 arrests per 100,000 adult population) and the 18 years of age and older population in the United States was increasing by 27.2 percent.[3] Also during the time when community-based alternatives were being used more and more, a National Council on Crime and Delinquency (1980) study of California's prison system between 1975 and 1979 found that while prison commitments increased by 32.7 percent, reported crimes increased by only 10.9 percent, and felony arrests and felony convictions actually decreased, by 3.5 and 7.7 percent, respectively.

In 1980, the American Correctional Association reported that each of the previous five years had witnessed an all-time high in the number of persons imprisoned in the United States. In fact, between 1970 and 1979, while there was a 10 percent increase in the U.S. population, there was a 58 percent increase in incarceration (U.S. Bureau of the Census 1979, reported in Hylton, 1982). This kind of increase continued through 1983 (see Panel 15-2, which also documents more recent increases in the numbers of persons under probation or parole supervision).

Specific community programs, such as restitution and community service, for example, have failed to reduce imprisonment. Restitution has been used generally on minor property offenders with few convictions, misdemeanants, traffic offenders, and in place of fines. Further, it is normally used in combination with probation or parole supervision, thus extending, rather than limiting, the social control of the offender by the criminal justice system. In these ways, restitution has been used for offenders who would not have been sentenced to prison anyway. Much the same can be said for the way in which community service sentences have been utilized (Austin and Krisberg, 1982).

Neither is there any evidence that post-release community alternatives have reduced imprisonment. Again, these programs have almost always been used to supplement traditional parole from prison, increasing, not decreasing, control over offenders who would be paroled anyway. Also, alternative post-release programs with high rates of rule violations and escapes may have the ironic consequence of increasing rates and length of incarceration (Austin and Krisberg, 1982).

It could be argued that those states that have enacted community corrections "acts" or legislation represent the strongest effort or commitment to reduce incarceration. There is convincing evidence, however, that even here, community corrections have failed (Austin and Krisberg, 1982).

California's legislated Probation Subsidy Act entailed state encouragement for local counties and communities to keep convicted and sentenced offenders in their communities by subsidizing local jurisdictions that held down the numbers of persons sentenced to state institutions (i.e., to prison). This money could then be used to supervise these offenders in community corrections programs. Studies indicate, nevertheless, that not only did this act increase the proportion of all state

[3]These are U.S. Department of Justice, President's Commission·on Law Enforcement and Administration of Justice, and National Council on Crime and Delinquency figures cited in Austin and Krisberg (1982). These authors point out that these sources most probably represent conservative counts, particularly those having to do with the numbers of persons incarcerated: "there are serious limitations in these aggregate figures . . . the data on incarceration refer to persons "on hand," not the volume of offenders moving through the institutions. If average prison terms have declined (as indicated by several studies in California), the use of imprisonment is more pronounced than these one-day counts would suggest" (Austin and Krisberg, 1982, p. 376, f.3).

PANEL 15-2

Recent Rates of Imprisonment and Probation and Parole Supervision

WASHINGTON, D.C. (AP) Approximately 2 million adults in the United States were behind bars or on probation or parole at the end of last year, the Justice Department said Sunday.

That number, which has continued to grow, accounts for about 1 out of every 83 people over age 18.

More than 1.2 million adults were on either state or federal probation, while nearly 223,800 were on parole from state or federal correctional institutions, according to the latest government figures.

The Justice Department has already reported there were 369,000 adults in prison at the end of last year, while the most recent jail figures show a population of nearly 157,000.

In addition to the 1,971,800 behind bars or on state or federal parole or probation, there were several thousand adults on locally operated parole programs.

Bradford Smith of the National Council on Crime and Delinquency says there may be another 5,000 to 20,000 adults on county or city-run parole. The crime council supplied the Justice Department's Bureau of Justice Statistics with much of the data for its latest report.*

WASHINGTON, D.C. (AP) One of every 200 adult Americans was on probation in 1982, the Justice Department said Sunday.

The number of adults on probation increased by 9 percent during the year to reach a total of 1,335,359.

During the same year, the number of adults on parole nationwide rose by 8 percent to 243,880. Georgia headed the list because of "special releases" that were granted to lessen the load on overcrowded prisons.

The Department of Justice, which issued these statistics, said the number of paroles and people on probation have increased steadily for years. Between 1979 and 1982 the rise in the probation population was 25 percent and in paroles 12 percent.

That, however, was substantially below the 42 percent increase in the prison population in the same period.

Only Illinois, South Carolina and the District of Columbia did not report probation increases last year, and the situation in Illinois may have come about because of changes in reporting procedures.

In Georgia, there was an 86 percent increase in parolees. In Iowa, state officials reported that parole board actions to reduce prison populations increased the number of parolees by 34 percent.†

*Source: The Associated Press, "2 Million Adults Jailed or on Probation, Parole in '81," August 16, 1982.
†Source: The Associated Press, "Probation, Parole Numbers on the Rise," September 19, 1983.

residents under the control of the criminal justice system, but it also increased incarceration—this time at the local, not the state, level (Lemert and Dill, 1978; Lerman, 1975; Miller, 1980):

> Where adult commitment rates were reduced, the strategies employed by local counties frequently involved increased use of other forms of incarceration available to local officials . . . (1) split sentences (jail plus probation), (2) civil commitments of narcotic addicts to the residential California Rehabilitation Center, and (3) pre-sentence ninety-day diagnostic commitment of offenders to the California Department of Corrections. . . . All three dispositions could be used without being counted as prison commitments under the state's probation subsidy formula. The increased use of alternative forms of incarceration compensated for reductions in prison commitments and actually increased both the number and rate of admissions to the state prison system. (Austin and Krisberg, 1982, pp. 394–395)

Local jurisdictions restrained their use of state prisons, benefitted from the subsidy provided by the act, and incarcerated offenders at the county level.

Researchers have also reported that the impact of the Minnesota Community Corrections Act on incarceration was similar: residential centers typically confined those who would have been sentenced to probation, not to prison, and beginning the year after the implementation of this legislation, the state prison population began to increase dramatically. Parole practices became more conservative with the advent of this act as well. Fewer and fewer paroles were granted, more and more of individual sentences were actually served, and this caused a rise in the prison population. Some observers have argued that what happened here is a "natural" effect of community corrections: prison and corrections officials come to regard those in prison—as opposed to those who remain in community programs—as the worst of all offenders, requiring longer and more severe periods of imprisonment (see, for example, Lerman, 1975). Finally, the Minnesota Department of Corrections (1981) concluded that many times the state's resources were being used in local community corrections programs in ways that were totally unrelated to their expressed goal of reducing imprisonment (Austin and Krisberg, 1982).

Austin and Krisberg have identified the continued deterioration and overcrowding of the U.S. correctional system with increases in the rate of incarceration and the number of persons incarcerated, recent declines in new prison construction, and the movement toward more conservative sentencing practices—more determinate and mandatory sentences:

> [T]he United States prison population is reaching unprecedented levels . . . . From 1972 to 1978, the total number of persons confined in prisons and jails rose by 54 percent. The rate of incarceration climbed from 164 per 100,000 population to 297 per 100,000 population. . . . During this same period, prison construction, or remodeling to increase capacity, met less than one third of the new required bed space. Already straining correctional systems were pushed be-

yond their limits. The most obvious symptom of this dilemma has been a wave of litigation, in which federal courts have declared crowded correctional facilities in violation of the Eighth Amendment. Some observers predict that the current movement toward determinate sentencing, harsher criminal penalties, and presumptive prison sentences may produce even larger prison populations. (Austin and Krisberg, 1982, p. 375)

In effect, it is clear that even in the face of developing community correctional alternatives, the rate of incarceration has not declined nor has the absolute number of persons imprisoned. Far from community corrections keeping its promise of reducing prison populations, over the past 15 to 20 years, the proportion of the U.S. population in prison has actually grown. Hylton has quoted the conclusions of several leading students of American corrections, all with different perspectives on crime and its control, but all drawing essentially the same conclusion (1982, pp. 343–346):

. . . the prison shows no signs of disappearing anywhere in the world . . . .

Morris, 1974, p. 12

. . . our jail and prison population has once again increased (to record levels), overcrowding is rife, and old, discarded buildings are being reopened and crammed with prisoners . . . .

Scull, 1982, p. 107

. . . it is by no means clear, in regard to crime and delinquency at least, that decarceration has been taking place as rapidly as the ideology would have us believe . . . .

Cohen, 1979, p. 343

. . . for all the novelty and popularity of this (community treatment) perspective, for all the unanimity in calling for a moratorium on the construction of new institutions and for a reduction in the number of inmates and patients, there is little cause to believe that our long and grim history of incarceration is nearing its end . . . .

Rothman, 1975, p. 22.

In sum, the data presented here indicate, in spite of the declining proportion of guilty persons receiving prison sentences (see Scull, 1977), that the rise and consequent development of community-based corrections has been accompanied by:

1. A rise in the absolute number of prison inmates.
2. An increase in the proportion of the total U.S. population incarcerated.
3. A rise in the absolute number of persons in the community who are under the supervision of the criminal justice system.

4.   An increase in the proportion of the total U.S. population under the supervision of the criminal justice system.

Rather than reducing imprisonment, community corrections seem to have resulted in simply putting more of the total population under the control and supervision of the criminal justice system. The implications of this will be discussed later in this chapter.

Community Corrections: Reduced Recidivism?

We need to ask: Have community correctional programs reduced criminal recidivism? The best answer, based on research spanning the last two decades, is, *no*. Major surveys of correctional effectiveness evaluation studies (see Greenberg, 1977, for example), of both prison and community corrections programs, have indicated that neither significantly reduces recidivism rates. As Greenberg has said, "The blanket assertion that 'nothing works' is an exaggeration, but not by very much" (1977, p. 141).

In effect, there is no evidence that community corrections have been any more successful than penal institutions in preventing offenders from returning to criminal activity and more contact with the criminal justice system. This conclusion is based primarily upon the comparison of recidivism rates for incarcerated offenders and those offenders diverted to community programs. Specific studies of restitution, community service, intensive community treatment, and a wide variety of post-release correctional alternatives have all confirmed this failure of community corrections (Austin and Krisberg, 1982).

Another way to measure the correctional effectiveness of community corrections (rather than examining recidivism rates) would be to assess changes in overall crime rates themselves. This approach is no more encouraging. All countries—the United States, Canada, England, and other European nations—that have developed community corrections alternatives in the past 15 to 20 years also have reported substantial *increases* in their official crime rates (Hylton, 1982). In sum, "it has not been established that any community alternative is more effective in reducing crime (through preventing recidivism) than traditional imprisonment" (Cohen, 1979, p. 343).

The promise of community corrections appears unmet again. The inescapable conclusion is that "there is no evidence that the widespread adoption of community programs has reduced crime rates or the use of correctional institutions . . . [or] . . . that community programs, by lowering recidivism rates, help to reduce pressure on the correctional system to expand" (Hylton, 1982, pp. 348–349).

An important offshoot of these "negative findings" for community corrections departments and programs with a vested interest in their own survival, may be a changing of the criterion of correctional effectiveness itself, for both traditional and community corrections. If the goal of reduction of offender recidivism cannot be met, the goal itself might be changed. It may be asserted that the rationale for corrections is that incarceration and community-based alternatives alike are simply systems of control and surveillance for persons troublesome or "surplus" to the community (Ward and Kassebaum, 1972). The pretense of rehabilitation may simply be dropped.

Theory and the Failure of Community Corrections to Reduce Recidivism

To the extent that community corrections have not fulfilled their promise to reduce criminal recidivism, traditional sociological and interactionist perspectives are called into question. Although the former maintain that keeping the offender in the community increases his or her ties with those networks of meaningful family, community, and workplace relationships that could prevent a return to crime, and the latter concludes that community corrections are not as quick to label, and thereby, stigmatize the criminal offender thereby lessening his or her recidivist potential, the evidence suggests that these assumption are not correct. A third perspective, radical criminology, offers a better explanation for the failures in community corrections.

The uniformity of research results in regard to the failure of community-based corrections suggests that explanations for it probably are not to be found in the details of particular community programs. In other words, the failure appears to have something to do with the theoretical and practical assumptions of community corrections programming in general (Timmer, 1980). Greenberg has written:

> I never thought it likely that most of these programs would succeed in preventing much return to crime. Where the theoretical assumptions of programs are made explicit, they tend to border on the preposterous. More often they are never made explicit, and we should be little surprised if hit-or-miss efforts fail. (Greenberg, 1977, p. 41)

An adequate explanation of correctional failure—both in the prison and the community—necessitates a turn from theories that focus upon the individual offender and his or her individual adjustment, readjustment, or rehabilitation to the requirements of the social order in which he or she lives. More than anything else, studies of correctional effectiveness—again, both in prison and the community—have shown the inherent limitations of an individualistic approach to the elimination of crime (Timmer, 1980).

Quinney (1977) has argued against individualistic conceptions of crime and its control. In his analysis, these two phenomena are not only part of the same dialectical social process (see Chapter 2), but are inherently structural and historical. Similarly, Chambliss (1978) has maintained that crime be understood as a critical foundation for, and part of, the ongoing institutional functioning of the political economy in capitalist-democratic societies (see Chapter 8). If this kind of criminological theory represents assumptions more in line with the social reality of contemporary crime and efforts at its control, then the failure of both tradition and innovation in corrections during the past two decades is made more readily understandable. How do you eliminate crime through efforts at individual adjustment when crime is generated structurally? The implication is clear: if crime is not primarily a result of individual deviance and pathology and is, instead, structurally-induced, then its effective control must be structural also. Crime control may become truly effective only in those societies that undergo the structural and historical changes necessary to eliminate those social conditions that generate crime (Timmer, 1980).

Community Corrections: More Humane?[4]

A common assumption is that community-based corrections are more humane than large and overcrowded state institutions. However, observers have argued that in some instances they are even less humane. The problem is that the community program has often duplicated the negative aspects of imprisonment in the local community. This has often been the case with residential treatment facilities and halfway houses, for example. Rather than truly decarcerating offenders, these programs often represent alternative institutions that are very prisonlike:

> residential treatment centers in which offenders eat, sleep, often work, may receive educational instruction and other "betterment" lessons (from grooming to encounter therapies), and so on. Control mechanisms may include curfew and grounds restrictions, daily schedules, and behavior modification procedures with specific rewards for approved behaviors and negative sanctions for disapproved behaviors. (Klein, Teilmann, Styles, Lincoln, and Labin-Rosensweig, 1976, p. 112, quoted in Hylton, 1982, p. 350)

In other words, these kinds of community-based programs are more of an "alternative form of incarceration" than they are an "alternative to incarceration." And even when offenders are diverted away from the criminal justice system itself, they may find themselves experiencing—in the community—the institutional controls of medical, mental health, or welfare bureaucracies.

One of the reasons so much of community corrections has taken on an institutional character is the opposition of many local communities to the very idea of community-based correctional alternatives. In order to make their programs acceptable to local communities and individual neighborhoods, correctional administrators have had to give up "treatment" for supervision, security, and control. Community or neighborhood fear of offenders has in this way made many community corrections programs more institutional and prison-like—the opposite of the stated philosophy of community corrections to integrate the offender with his or her local community.

The prison-like setting that comes with institutional community corrections programs which emphasize custody and control is reinforced by another failure that has often accompanied efforts to provide community-based alternatives. Many times these programs provide little or nothing in the way of rehabilitative services to their clients. Consider this description of the probation services—

---

[4]This section is taken in large part from Hylton (1982).

perhaps the most heavily used component of community-based corrections—most offenders receive:

> The 1967 President's Commission found that over 76 percent of misdemeanants and 67 percent of felons placed on probation were handled by officers with case loads of 100 or more. In such instances, probationers received a ten- or fifteen-minute interview once or twice monthly. (Hylton, 1982, p. 355)

We will discuss this lack of services and its implications for the future of social control in our society when we consider "The Crisis of Deviant Ghettoization." Suffice it to say at this point that the "humane alternative" to the inhumane American prison has not always been so humane.

An examination of the legal rights of offenders in community corrections programs also reveals circumstances and situations that may be less than humane. Community corrections programs have tended to "divert" offenders at three different points in the criminal justice process: at the pre-trial stage before a decision has ever been made to prosecute, between prosecution and conviction, and after conviction. Diversion to community programs at the pre-trial or pre-conviction phase may result in a significant loss of due process rights for the offender. In effect, diversion in these cases may actually represent "sentencing" without a finding of guilt.

Throughout this text we have discussed the use and abuse of discretionary power in the criminal justice system. Police, prosecutors, prison officials, and probation and parole officers all use, and often abuse, this power. Community corrections have also been characterized by high levels of discretionary power over offenders (or in the cases where community corrections programs are utilized before a finding of guilt, "alleged offenders"), often limiting their legal rights. Messinger (1973), for example, has pointed out how the decision to "lock-up" or "detain" clients in community programs is most often simply a staff decision, whereby the offender is denied the right to a legal hearing that would accompany a traditional parole revocation seeking to "detain" him or her in prison. Messinger has even suggested that perhaps the avoidance of these due process hearings is one of the primary reasons for the development of community "alternatives" to prison.

Also, the criminal justice system often transfers its control over offenders in the local community to medical, mental health, or other welfare bureaucracies. Addicts, alcoholics, and those deemed psychologically unfit are frequently dealt with in this manner. These bureaucracies are not accountable to the criminal justice system, and their decisions concerning the fate of the individual offender may not be subject to legal scrutiny and the safeguarding of due process rights. By labeling what is at first recognized to be a criminal justice problem, a psychological or drug or alcohol abuse problem, and assigning the person to a medical or welfare bureaucracy, "such encumbrances as a trial, the right to appeal, and the right to legal representation are circumvented" (Hylton, 1982, p. 359).

In sum, much of the operation of community corrections can be characterized as informal and discretionary. Decision making becomes arbitrary and unclear.

The result is a weakening of both the constraints on the power of corrections officials and the legal rights of offenders.

Those who are not diverted by community "alternatives" and are sentenced to prison may also experience an institution that has grown more inhumane because of the existence of "alternative" programs in the local community. If more and more "less serious" offenders are kept in the community, more and more of the prison population will be made up of "dangerous" or "more serious" offenders. Since the prison population is perceived to be more dangerous, it may also be perceived to require more control and security. The prison may become even more inclined to give up on its rehabilitative goals and rely more exclusively on the containment and discipline of supposedly "hard to control and manage" inmates. Some observers are already convinced that prisons in American society have turned into this sort of "human garbage heap" where ever more sophisticated strategies and electronic technologies of social control are used to make the monitoring and surveillance of prisoners more efficient.

Finally, community corrections represent a new strategy for social control that often extends, rather than limits, the inhumane aspects of the older and more traditional correctional system. Proponents of community corrections, as we have seen, have argued that community control should replace institutional control, thereby limiting the state's unnecessary intervention—via its criminal justice system—into the lives of individuals. The evidence suggests, however, that community control has not replaced or even limited institutional control; it has supplemented it. Instead of a more humane and less intrusive criminal justice system, community corrections have given rise to an expanded social control apparatus in American society. Social control is no longer limited to the limited number of persons who can be accommodated in large centralized prisons. Increasingly, persons are subject to official control and supervision in the community. The social control "net" has grown "wider and stronger" and often, less humane (Austin and Krisberg, 1982):

> Persons who were not subjected to control previously may now be controlled under the guise of community treatment. . . . Once the institution is no longer the receptacle for those society cannot tolerate, the community becomes an appropriate forum for supervision, control, and punishment. (Hylton, 1982, pp. 362–363)

Radical criminological thinkers like Michel Foucault (1979) and Stanley Cohen (1979) have warned that ultimately community corrections have the potential to turn the community we live in into a "punitive city."

Community Corrections: Less Costly?

On the surface, it does appear as though community corrections are cheaper than traditional imprisonment. In 1975, for example, even though there were three to four times as many persons under some form of community supervision (e.g., probation or parole) as there were persons incarcerated, individual states spent

$1.55 billion on prisons and only $.27 billion on community programs. The states employed 98,983 prison workers and only 19,731 persons in all community corrections programs (National Criminal Justice Information and Statistics Service, 1977). Studies that have compared the "costs per offender" in the institution with those of the offender under community control have generally concluded that community corrections are the cheaper alternative (see, for example, Panel 15-1).

These figures, however, may be deceptive for at least three reasons. First, many community programs provide little or nothing in the way of rehabilitative services for offenders. Doing little or nothing, of course, costs little or nothing. In these situations, community programs are not necessarily cost-efficient. They simply are not making the expenditures necessary to fulfill the promise of counseling, educational, vocational, and employment services made to their clients. In order to survive, however, community corrections have had to appear cost-efficient in the eyes of their funding sources and they have accomplished this by providing minimal services to large numbers of clients[5] (Hylton, 1982).

Second, the community programs that tend to do more than "little or nothing" are precisely those programs that have been most institution- or prison-like. Residential treatment facilities and halfway houses have not only been most like "community-based prisons" but they have cost roughly the same as imprisonment. In other words, those community programs that have had higher costs because they actually do provide some "service" have usually been institutional programs. And the costs of these programs have been similar to the costs of state prisons. These institutional programs in the community have not represented a substantial cost savings or efficiency (Hylton, 1982).

Third, there is no evidence that any state, county, or city has reduced criminal justice expenditures by and through the development of community-based corrections. This is the case primarily because community corrections have been used to supplement, rather than replace, the use of prisons. In terms of the language used above, community corrections have not so much been a "different social control net" as they have contributed to a "wider and stronger social control net." Hylton (1982, p. 366) has explained how community corrections have either failed to reduce, or have actually increased, costs incurred by the jurisdictions using them:

> The costs of using community correction to supplement rather than replace traditional programs have . . . been assessed. . . . In a review of eleven California diversion projects . . . half the diverted clients would normally have moved farther into the justice system if they had not been diverted, while the processing of the other half would have been terminated at an earlier point if they had not been diverted. If only the former are considered, then financial savings can be demonstrated. But because the processing of half the clients was extended by diversion, the expenses incurred by the projects exceeded by over one-third the costs of traditional processing. . . .

---

[5] Again, the relationship of a lack of genuine services made available in community corrections programs to the process of "deviant ghettoization" will be discussed below.

Since community corrections have subjected more, not fewer, persons to the supervision and control of the criminal justice system, they have tended to increase, not decrease, the overall costs of corrections in the United States.

In sum, it appears as though community-based corrections has failed significantly in its attempt to fulfill its promise. Imprisonment and criminal recidivism have not been markedly reduced. Crime itself has not undergone any significant decline; indeed it appears to have grown right alongside community programs. And neither have community "alternatives" always been more humane and less costly than prison.

In the light of all of this evidence we must say to the advocates and proponents of community corrections, "Why has this enterprise failed to meet its objectives?" More than any other perspective, radical criminology has attempted to answer this question. We will examine that response here. It is a response that challenges the usual explanations of the rise and reality of community corrections.

A Theory of Decarceration

The perspective on the rise of community corrections described here is that of radical criminologist Andrew Scull in his book *Decarceration: Community Treatment and the Deviant* (1977).

Scull, true to the traditions of radical criminology, has maintained that an adequate understanding of the origin and subsequent development of community-based corrections must be *historical* and *structural*. Scull's analysis has pointed out how in 19th-century America the market-economy penetrated society and began to deteriorate and destroy community and family networks that had previously served as effective and informal social control mechanisms. When crime and deviance could no longer be controlled in this manner, however, a formal, modern, institutional, and bureaucratic response to the need for control developed—incarceration.

According to Scull, the political ideology behind the movement to decarcerate offenders, beginning in the 1960s, was the same as that used by all earlier "reform" movements interested in the control and treatment of deviant and criminal populations: "It's cheaper and more humane at the same time." A rather full-scale decarceration of offenders did begin in the United States in the 1960s and early 1970s. But, as we have argued above, Scull has made it clear that decarceration has not replaced incarceration; that even with an increasing rate of decarceration, more people are presently in prison (both in terms of absolute numbers and as a proportion of the total population) than ever before.

Scull dismisses two popular and conventional explanations for the advent of community treatment for criminal offenders (see Scull, 1977, Chaps. 5 and 6). One of these accounts attributes community programs to the development of psychotropic drugs that purportedly allow certain persons to function in the community, who without the drug therapy would need to be institutionalized. Scull's survey of the research literature on this topic, however, reveals that "drugged" patients or offenders in the community are no more likely to "adjust" to their setting than are persons who are, or have been, institutionalized. A second explanation of the origins of community treatment for the criminal and deviant cites the work of social scientists. Here, it is argued that the devastating negative critique of the effects of prison and other "total institutions" on offenders and other deviants, and the demonstrated superiority of community alternatives, both provided by social scientists, fueled the growth of community corrections. This, Scull has contended, is highly unlikely since the same critique of "total institutions" in the 19th century failed to decarcerate anyone.

But the 20th-century story is different. Contradictions in the economies of advanced capitalist societies like the United States have grown more and more severe in the latter part of this century. For example, since economic production in the United States is increasingly technological in character, machines and raw materials assume an ever-expanding role. Labor itself becomes less and less important in this process and more and more workers join the surplus population, posing more and more of a threat to the smooth functioning of the capitalist system of production and consumption. An expanding surplus population, coupled with the way in which capitalism has eroded and made ineffective previously "controlling and socializing" institutions like the family, neighborhood, and community, means that the state must intervene, and provide social control.

The state intervenes here to "socialize" the costs involved in the process of private economic production for purposes of private profit. The primary cost is the cost of supporting and controlling the population that naturally grows surplus in a capitalist economy. The costs, however, are the burden of the public (through the government), not the burden of those who privately create the population and the cost and in the process profit from it. So, the welfare state and the criminal justice system are expanded to support and control the surplus population. But in the meantime, the state drains its resources and experiences budgetary problems; it begins to go broke. A *fiscal crisis* is born.

Enter decarceration. According to Scull, a policy of decarceration is adopted because it can supposedly allow a cheaper and more efficient (as compared with incarceration) control of an ever-increasing surplus population. But, as we have already seen, community corrections have not always turned out to be cheaper. The cost savings have not often been realized.

The Demise of Community Corrections

There is some evidence that both the philosophy and practice of genuine community corrections programs are currently on the decline. This is due in part to these community programs not having to prove themselves cheaper than institutional programs as they are used to expand, rather than shrink, the criminal justice and social control apparatus. It is also due in part to the return to a conservative ideology of crime control in the United States, one that emphasizes isolation and punishment rather than treatment and rehabilitation. The continued growth of the criminal, deviant, and surplus population in the United States has not slowed, however, and the state's fiscal crisis has intensified. The search for yet less expensive forms of social control has led to another crisis in the practice of American criminal justice. It is to that crisis that we now turn.

THE CRISIS OF DEVIANT GHETTOIZATION

As we have seen, those community corrections programs that are inadequately funded and staffed are less expensive than imprisonment. In turn, it has been discovered that only one thing is cheaper than a "bad" community program: *no program at all*. This raises the specter of *deviant* ghettos.

Many local communities have used many tactics to ensure that community-based programs are confined to those areas where the poor and minorities reside. This has been accomplished via zoning laws, city ordinances, neighborhood organizations applying political pressure, and bureaucratic whim, among other strategies. In this way, rather than being reintegrated with the community, offenders are segregated and excluded from it. This community resistance to community corrections, along with the tendency of many community programs to provide little or nothing in the way of services to offenders, has produced a growing population, particularly in the inner cities of our largest metropolitan areas, that is geographically isolated from the rest of the community and formally under the supervision of the criminal justice system. To the extent that this is taking place, some criminologists have argued that we are witnessing the development of criminal and deviant ghettos in many U.S. cities. Although the criminal justice system is officially charged with the supervision and control of this criminal and deviant population, it does not necessarily mean that it occurs. As noted legal scholar Norval Morris has commented in regard to one aspect of community corrections, probation: "One important latent purpose of probation is to allow a judge to give the appearance of doing something while in fact doing nothing" (quoted in Hylton, 1982, p. 355).

In other words, when community corrections programs are not well-funded and are relegated to the "back wards" of the city, we may simply be allowing the surplus, criminal, and deviant population to wander the streets, oft times without job, shelter or food, not to mention any kind of rehabilitative services. As long as those in this population only victimize others from this same population and not from other parts of the community, the police, indeed the whole of the criminal justice system, need not intervene. Social control of this population is achieved and at a considerable cost savings, but another cost is incurred: we are throwing an ever-increasing number of persons in our society to the wind, persons who have already been victimized by a long line of economic, political, and social institutions and practices in American society.

The economic policies of the Reagan administration only worsened the situation. The 10 to 15 million Americans presently unemployed, are, potentially at least, members of this population "left out in the cold." The dismantling of social welfare programs has had the same effect, with approximately 700,000 families losing all or part of their benefits from the Aid to Families with Dependent Children (AFDC) program.

A recent study of homeless adults in New York City has concluded that "the routes to homelessness are many" but that the impact of three significant "social and economic developments" can clearly be seen: (1) rises in unemployment, (2) decreases in the availability of low-cost housing, and (3) the deinstitutionalization of mental patients, many of whom may have been originally diverted from the criminal justice system to the mental health system (reported in McCarthy, 1981). Indeed, "America has a permanent refugee class, people driven into the streets . . . from pressures created only recently" (McCarthy, 1981, p. 7a).

The relationship of these kinds of developments in American society to crime and crime control are more direct than they might first appear. For example, rising unemployment and cuts in social welfare programs represent definite criminogenic conditions to all three of the theoretical perspectives dealt with throughout this book: the traditional, interactionist, and radical perspectives. They are seen alternatively as either "a deterioration in the immediate social environment," "increasing the susceptibility to criminal stigmatization," or "a thrust into the surplus population" for the individuals affected. From the point of view of these perspectives, when these things happen, we witness an increase in that part of the population that is potentially criminal and/or deviant. When this, in turn, causes increases in the proportion of the population that is to be controlled, we can expect that the American criminal justice system will be driven to seek out those methods of control that cost and do the least, but control the most—social control processes like "deviant ghettoization."

There are more than 1 million decarcerated mental patients living in squalor in private nursing homes, boarding houses, and flophouses (National Institute of Mental Health and U.S. House Committee on Aging figures, reported in McGarrah and Kusnet, 1981). Add to this the undetermined number of criminal offenders who have been dumped onto the street in similar fashion by the criminal justice system—without meaningful supervision or service—and the beginnings of full-fledged deviant ghettoization become clear. These ghettos can already be seen in places like Chicago's Uptown and Manhattan's Harlem. As corrupt "total" institutions and prisons were the scandal of the 1960s, deviant ghettos may well become the scandal of the 1980s (McGarrah and Kusnet, 1981).

Ironically, as criminologist Paul Rock has pointed out, social control in American society seems to be taking on certain characteristics that were a part of the 17th-century Acts of Settlement in England:

Those acts were designed to enforce immobility upon the poor. People were barred from travel, work, or alien residence. As a kind of shadow parish, sanctuaries and bastard sanctuaries housed the criminal, the debtor, the bankrupt, the pauper, and the eccentric in relatively unpoliced and autonomous areas of geographical and social space. [So too, in the present,] a growing resort to zoning regulation, defensive alliances among residents, the tendency to provide welfare and other provisions in centralized locations, and the economics of housing have worked together to create new sanctuaries. In effect there has been a limited restoration of neo-feudal styles of control. It is unlikely that the new deviant ghettoes will be rigorously patrolled unless their populations

PANEL 15-3

Work Camps: A Step toward Deviant Ghettoization?

NEW YORK, N.Y. (AP) Work camps will be set up on two East River islands for shoplifters, vandals and other petty criminals whom judges are reluctant to sentence to prison, Mayor Edward Koch said Wednesday.

Koch said he believes most of those sentenced to the camps will be teen-agers. He said they will be paid 50 cents a day and the average sentence will be about five days.

The camps will be ready by the end of summer, he said, and work on the islands will include general cleaning, rehabilitating buildings and making concrete blocks. The camps will house 124 male inmates each day initially and up to 275 prisoners daily after work is completed on the facilities.

Quality of Life

"The work camps will demonstrate that we are serious in our efforts to improve the quality of life in our city," Koch said at a City Hall news conference.

Koch, a candidate for the Democratic gubernatorial nomination, first proposed the work camp idea before declaring his candidacy.

The mayor's plan was criticized by the New York Civil Liberties Union and groups specializing in criminal justice. They said it was too costly and did not address the causes of crime.

The top administrative judge for New York City courts, Betty Weinberg Ellerin, called the proposal "a positive step."

The mayor said judges would be given a tour of the facilities to try to persuade them to send chronic offenders there.

"Beautiful Place"

Correction Commissioner Benjamin Ward said he was confident criminals would voluntarily do the work and that they would not try to escape. He said a work camp was "a beautiful place" compared to a city jail.

When Koch was asked what kind of security would be provided, he replied: "The suggestion was we would bring in alligators."

The mayor, who once suggested wolves be used to protect subway yards from vandals, hastened to add that he was kidding.

Richard Emery, staff counsel of the New York Civil Liberties Union, called the mayor's plan "half right," in that work was desirable for petty criminals but prison was not. "The camps are prison, no matter what you call them," Emery said.

One work camp will be on Hart Island off the Bronx shore. The other will be on Rikers Island, between the Bronx and Queens. Work camp prisoners will be segregated from inmates in the city jail on Rikers Island.

Source: The Associated Press, "Petty Criminals to Spend a Few Days in Work Camps," May 13, 1982.

swamp out over their borders. The inhabitants of black and inner-city areas are more often the victims of crime and least often the recipients of police support. When those areas also become new reservations for the deviant, policing is likely to become even more token. (Rock, personal communication with Scull, 1977, p. 153)

This situation could grow even more desperate in the large industrial cities of the Northeast and Midwest. While suburbanization in the 1950s and 1960s increased the proportion of the poor, minority and surplus population in the central cities, the present migration to the Sun Belt is doing this on a national scale. As industry—capital and technology—escapes organized labor and settles in the Southwest and Southeast, those who are able and qualified follow, leaving the surplus, unemployed, poor, deviant, derelict, and criminal population behind in the decaying inner cities of decaying industrial centers. These "old" cities of the Northeast and Midwest may well become "custodial reservations" for those the American economy has left behind (Bender, 1981).[6] One class and one race of Americans will follow the sun and the economy. Another class, another race, may well be out in the dark, and surplus to their society, many becoming residents of a deviant ghetto in a dying city.

THE CRISIS OF PRIVATE JUSTICE

An ever-growing deviant and criminal population coupled with the budgetary crisis of local, state, and national governments has made, as we have already seen, the inefficiency and ineffectiveness of the criminal justice system more and more visible. Accompanying the public sector's inability to finance and operate an efficient and effective criminal justice system in the light of these trends in American society has been the emergence of private sector alternatives. For those able to afford it, private justice services—primarily private policing and private corrections—have become alternatives that are increasingly employed as substitutes for the public criminal justice system. Here, policing and corrections are transformed from public services to "policing and correcting for profit." And, as we shall see below, criminal justice in the private sector has without question emerged as an economically productive and profitable enterprise in recent times. The rise of private justice, however, has given birth to yet another crisis in the organization and practice of criminal justice in our society.

Private Security and Policing: Policing for Profit[7]

It has been estimated that the private security industry in the United States generates at least $5 billion in revenue per year (O'Toole, 1978). Some estimates range as high as $10 to $15 billion per year. The bulk of this private policing occurs

---

[6]This actually represents, for example, the urban policy contained in the Carter Administration's President's Commission for a National Agenda for the Eighties report—*Urban America in the Eighties*.
[7]Throughout this discussion we have relied on the article by Michael T. Klare (1975).

through private interests purchasing police services for protection of their private interests and property. The private security firms and police in American society stand outside of the criminal justice system in significant ways and, as we will attempt to make clear below, "whether [they work] for Macy's or the Mafia is less significant than the fact that they do not work for the voters and taxpayers" (O'Toole, 1978, p. 18).

While many of America's largest private security firms—for example, the Pinkerton's and Burns Detective Agency—were founded more than 50 or 60 years ago, only in the past 10 to 15 years have they become a widespread and common feature of everyday life. Today, the private police seem to be everywhere: in apartment buildings, shops, department stores, office buildings, factories, museums, schools, universities, hospitals, theaters, stadiums, buses, and subways. It now appears as though, "for the average person . . . if someone is following him, watching him, investigating him, protecting his safety or guarding his treasures, it is far more likely to be a private policeman than the CIA, the FBI or the county sheriff" (from the *San Francisco Examiner,* quoted in Klare, 1975, p. 487).

Earlier on, a number of today's private security firms had developed in order to provide private detective and other investigative services to the federal government. The public Federal Bureau of Investigation was not organized until 1908, and until that time local police departments could only purchase or contract out for the services of private detective and investigative agencies (see Walker, 1980; Weiss, 1981). Later, these private firms began to branch out into other kinds of private security and police work. By the 1930s, for example, some of them (including the Pinkerton's) had developed significant anti-labor and anti-union reputations, as companies purchased the services of private guards to disrupt and suppress the organization of labor unions (see Klare, 1975; Spitzer and Scull, 1978). Oftentimes, in fact, company towns provided their own private police force—accountable to literally nothing or no one on the outside—to keep order in their own self-contained communities[8] (see, for example, Couch, 1981).

Much of the anti-labor and anti-union character of early private security work and policing has spilled over into the present. In the 1970s, an annual report of one of the largest private security companies in the country—Burns—extolled the virtues of the uses of undercover agents in American industry. These private agents, Burns claimed, could, by holding an actual job, working full-time, and drawing a regular paycheck so as to prevent arousing any suspicion among employees, aid in solving many of management's problems. Further, this could be done without running any of the risks of bad publicity that could go along with a regular public police investigation. Intelligence gathering among employees resulting in regular and secret reports to industrial managers could help prevent and control, according to the report, employee "crimes" like:

---

[8]Researchers report evidence that this type of private policing is again occurring in the energy "boom towns" of the Rocky Mountain West. Large energy conglomerates, for instance, are presently engaged in this kind of self policing in these types of communities in Wyoming (Davidson and Massey, 1982).

inventory losses	willful neglect of machinery
pilferage	waste of time and materials
theft	theft of tools
fraud	unreported absenteeism
falsification of records	supervisory incompetence
forgery	inadequate surveillance

(quoted in Klare, 1975, p. 488)

But some involved in the private security business have gone (and continue to go) a step farther. Undercover private police work also has the potential to glean information from employees that may be useful to the managers of industry, even though it may have absolutely nothing to do with any criminal activity on the part of workers. Things like:

- The effectiveness of new employee indoctrination.
- The effect of company "cliques" on new employees.
- The extent of excessive loitering.
- Whether or not production breakdowns are intentionally caused by employees.
- The general nature of employee attitudes and morale. (Klare, 1975)

Of course, just as much as the earlier and more direct intervention of the private police in American industry had been anti-labor and anti-union, determining "the general nature of employee attitudes and morale" can certainly include intrusions into the political and union beliefs and activities of employees. In short, the historical and contemporary uses of private security in American industry suggest yet another crisis in the American justice system—the crisis of private justice.

The Size, Organization, and Characteristics of the Private Police Force

With basically only one systematic study of the size, organization, and characteristics of the private police having been completed to date, the data on this aspect of the private practice of criminal justice in the United States are, in the main, few and far between.[9] Nevertheless, enough is known to paint a picture of the private police force in broad strokes.

There are at present probably somewhere in the neighborhood of 800,000 private police personnel at work. This compares with roughly 700,000 legally sworn public police.[10] It is apparently the case that the numbers of private police have surpassed those of the public force since the mid-1970s.

Spending on private policing services has been increasing faster than spending on public law enforcement. Most of this expense has been shouldered by working and middle-income people as large corporations pass the price of their purchased

---

[9] This study was first commissioned by the National Institute of Law Enforcement and Criminal Justice and undertaken by the Rand Corporation (see Kakalik and Wildhorn, 1971, revised in 1977).
[10] See Chapter 11.

police protection on to consumers via higher prices for basic goods and services (Klare, 1975).

The increased spending on private policing has served to concentrate a growing share of the large and expanding revenues in the largest security firms providing the police services that have come to be required by many of our institutions. The "Big Four" in the private policing industry—Pinkerton's, Burns, Walter Kidde and Company, and Wackenhut Corporation—saw their revenues more than triple between 1963 and 1969 and then nearly double again in the next five years (Klare, 1975).

In general, it appears as though the private police are increasingly being relied upon to provide a wide array of police services in American society. This, together with the increasing division of labor in the municipal police bureaucracy that has led to more and more specialized police functions, is likely to culminate in the private police performing many of the former duties of the public force. ". . . as public law-enforcement agencies devote more and more time to complex urban problems like narcotics abuse, riot control, VIP protection, etc., rent-a-cops will increasingly replace public policemen as the 'cop on the beat'" (Klare, 1975, p. 487). At minimum it is clear that we should not ignore the profound impacts that private security and policing have begun to have on our system of social control and criminal justice (Shearing and Stenning, 1983).

There are basically two kinds of private police: "in-house" and "contract." "In-house" police are security employees who work for the individuals, company, or public institution they are protecting. "Contract" police work for private security firms who sell their services—protection, investigation, and so on—to an individual, a company, or a public institution willing to rent or purchase their service. There are at least 500,000 arrests made by "in-house" police alone in the United States each year (Lipson, 1975). These arrests are taken directly to the criminal justice system without any public or official law enforcement intervention (the negative implications of this will be discussed below).

Most of the employees of private security firms, probably close to 90 percent, are guards. The "elite" or highly skilled in this industry—private detectives and investigators—are few. Seventy percent of these private police or guards (as they are usually referred to) are "in-house" employees. The remainder work for private, "rent-a-cop" firms (Lipson, 1975). A Rand Corporation study (1971) concluded that the typical private guard was a middle-aged or older white male, poorly educated, unskilled, and poorly paid. Testimony before a Select Committee of the Pennsylvania House of Representatives in the mid-1970s confirmed this description of the typical guard, with one exception. At least in the largest cities in Pennsylvania, many private police, if not a majority, were black (reported in Lipson, 1975).

The private security guard, as late as the mid-1970s, was among the most unskilled and underpaid of all American workers. The irony here, of course, is that those from the very bottom of society are charged with protecting the wealth and assets of the most powerful and affluent corporations and individuals in the world.

In effect, those unskilled workers lacking the qualifications for almost any other kind of employment have gravitated toward a private security industry that is without minimum physical, mental, educational, literacy, or in some cases even age and citizenship requirements. Furthermore, one of the causes of the extremely high turnover rate in the security industry is the criminal activities of the private police themselves (roughly 10 percent of the guard turnover results from dismissals for criminal involvement). For instance, "the Board of Education of the City of New York was rudely shaken when some of its security guards were picked up in the act of committing crimes, and turned out to have long prison records" (Lipson, 1975, p. 87).

An assistant manager of a Philadelphia "contract" security agency summed up the employment situation in his industry, and its impact on the quality of police services, in this way:

> It might be interesting to note that 90 percent, maybe more, of your security members in this City [Philadelphia] do this kind of work as a second job, as a pension, and because some of them, many of them, I would say, cannot do physical labor, cannot do intelligent labor, so they go into the security field, in order to make a living wage. If these guys are only doing this, they work some terrific number of hours for $1.75 to $2.00 an hour, you'll find men working sixty, seventy, or eighty hours weekly to take home some kind of decent pay. No one stops to think that after forty hours a week, this guy—or after nine or ten hours a day—this guy is not effective as a security guard, which he should be. (testimony before the Pennsylvania House of Representatives on October 26, 1973, quoted in Lipson, 1975, p. 83)

Nor have these private security firms attempted to upgrade the skills of the private police force with any kind of job training, even though the need for training is readily apparent. The Rand Corporation has reported that 97 percent of the private security officers it studied were unable to pass a simple examination testing their knowledge of the basic legal procedures and requirements involved in their work. Fifty percent of all private police have been armed, yet only one fifth of these officers have received any training in the use of firearms (Lipson, 1975; Klare, 1975). The same assistant manager of a private security firm quoted above, testified in this regard:

> Today, gentlemen, the hiring practices of many of the security agencies in the City of Philadelphia are a joke. They only ask you to be 21 years of age, no police record, have a home phone, and an automobile. You go into this agency and get an application; they will fingerprint you; and on the application it states, "Do you have a police record?" You put, "No," you could go to work that night. You are hired and you are ready for a uniform. You get a shirt, a hat, a jacket, a pair of trousers, along with two badges of the security company. You are given a location to work. And all you know when you leave the agency is that you are to report to such and such a location. . . .

I went on such a location, told the man who I was. I was in uniform. He handed me a .38 pistol, one of the old jobs, with a 6-inch barrel, and told me I was to stand on the platform of the place and just watch for troublemakers.

I was new at this thing. I didn't know what this guy meant by "troublemakers." Boy, this is bad! He has given me a gun, and what am I supposed to do with it? I know what a gun is; I know what a gun can do; my training in the Marine Corps taught me this. (in Lipson, 1975, p. 84)

Part of the crisis of private justice is made clear here. Since private policing is done for the purpose of accumulating private profit, training is seen as an unnecessary expense that may cut into a firm's profit margin and these firms are not inclined to pass up opportunities for profit because they are without a trained force. Another executive of a large private security firm has commented on the lack of training given the private police:

They're (the private security firms) not going to pass up a job because they don't have trained men; they're not going to do it. They're going to use these men, and give them the basic requirements, if they give them that. . . . In the guard service business, they hire men, put a gun on them and send them out. (quoted in Lipson, 1975, p. 88; parentheses added)

More recently, however, the training and skill level of the private police force has been upgraded significantly. Unfortunately, this has not occurred without contributing to a new set of problems resulting from our society's increasing reliance on the private justice system. More and more, public, municipal police officers are going to work for private policing agencies. In addition to their regular work week on the municipal force, these officers "moonlight" as private police. In some ways, it appears as though the distinction between public and private police in American society is beginning to break down.

The police in Denver, Colorado, for example, are allowed to work up to 32 hours per week as private police (over and beyond their regular work week for the police department). About 60 percent of the city's 1370 legally sworn officers moonlight as private security police and/or investigators. The Denver Police Department has conceded that this private policing sometimes includes the use of public Police Department equipment, even the use of department patrol cars. The department has also conceded that officers' work schedules are often manipulated to accommodate the private agencies' needs. Further, the form a Denver police officer must complete to secure the department's authorization to work as a private police officer does not require the disclosure of the private employer's identity. Finally, in spite of the fact that the Police Department keeps a list of officers who have been "violence-prone" and have been more likely than other officers to use unnecessary force against citizens in the past, the list is not consulted when authorizations to do private police work are approved (Green, 1982, p. 1).

Thus, even though the use of public police officers by agencies policing for profit has upgraded the quality of the private police workforce, it has created other problems. Denver Police Chief Art Dill has identified some of these problems, that often run contrary to the public interest:

- Policemen working at sites where there may be contraband.
- Policemen receiving money from drug users or other persons of ill-repute or bad character.
- Policemen working for persons suspected of criminal activity.
- Policemen working for attorneys who represent persons charged with violating criminal laws.
- Work or actions that could result in a damage claim against the city (Green, 1982, p. 10).

But most importantly, public police working as private police could lead to police work performed for a profit that actually goes against the goals, purposes, objectives, and procedures of public law enforcement agencies.

The Legal Status of the Private Police

The crisis created by the use of private police in American society is apparent when the legal status of this private force is examined. Private police actions touch many lives in many ways. Often, these actions are not legal ones. For example, we know that millions of private conversations between American citizens are tapped each year without legal authorization.

Private policing represents a more serious threat to civil liberties than public policing, primarily because the actions of the private police force are not subject to governmental or judicial review. The private police are not legally accountable to governments, the courts, or the public. In a very fundamental way, therefore, the activities of private law enforcement agencies and officers, undertaken as they are by an unregulated—and untrained, as we have seen above—police force, calls into question the very concept of justice and the guarantees of due process that are presumed to be the essence of the American legal system (Rojek, 1979).

Legally, the private police have no special powers. With the exception of a "citizen's arrest" that everyone has the right to make, they cannot arrest anyone. However, neither are they subject to the many laws that attempt to regulate the behavior of the public police. They are not subject to laws governing evidence, like the exclusionary rule. The laws of search and seizure do not apply to them. The 1966 Supreme Court Miranda decision, which prevents the public police from introducing as evidence confessions obtained before, or without, advising an alleged offender of his or her rights to silence and legal counsel, does not apply to the activities of private police. In short, by side-stepping the exclusionary rule and other rules of search and seizure and evidence gathering, as well as the Miranda decision, the private police are freer to do their job and violate the civil liberties of American citizens.

Moreover, the legality of certain routine private police "services" is highly

PANEL 15-4

The Virtues of Private-Enterprise Law Enforcement: A Conservative's View

A great debate is about to get under way this year on the role of handguns in American society.

Two major trends seem about to converge. On one hand, a major effort is being made to get anti-handgun proposals enacted into law. In California, an outfit called Californians Against Street Crime and Concealed Weapons is trying to get a far-reaching anti-handgun initiative on the November ballot.

On the other hand, the biggest trend in pistols and revolvers is their increasing sale to ordinary citizens who want protection against the growing national crime rate. Fifteen years of promises by politicians haven't done a thing to solve the problem. The courts are overcrowded, the legal system is bogging down and the police are all too often helpless—so people are buying guns to defend themselves.

And this is the irony. Handgun sales are getting out of hand. Too many are being sold. Too many are in circulation.

But is this a cause of crime or a reflection of crime? If a jurisdiction should pass a far-reaching anti-handgun law now, would it just be helping the criminals, who already have guns or can get them, while taking away the means of self-defense for ordinary citizens and householders?

In early March, I read a fascinating article in the Sunday Philadelphia Inquirer magazine on "The Rearming of Philadelphia." It seems that growing street crime is turning the City of Brotherly Love into a city of brotherly suspicion. Women who, 10 years ago, were going to peace vigils and civil-rights rallies now are going to target practice. Handgun sales are soaring.

Most important, the FBI's Uniform Crime Statistics are beginning to show a fascinating pattern. In the few metropolitan areas in which figures are kept on the number of criminals killed by private citizens, that number is two or three times as high as the number of criminals being killed by the police. In other words, private citizens are using their guns—mostly handguns—to kill many more criminals than the police are managing to gun down.

I'm not certain this is a compelling argument for a continued policy of easy citizen access to handguns. But before we pass any new handgun restrictions, I'd like to know exactly how, in full details and with real numbers, the police and the courts are going to use new restrictions to nail the criminals now being put out of business by private enterprise.

Source: Kevin Phillips, "Private-Enterprise Law Enforcement," The Des Moines Register, *April 24, 1982, p. 4a.*

questionable. Many of these services would appear to be illegal if performed routinely and without a court's authorization by public law enforcement agencies. The potential is great for the illegal invasion of privacy in private security services like "pre-employment investigations and personal security checks, including polygraph examinations; financial responsibility investigations; surveillance of business and residential premises, hotels and employees; fingerprint and document analysis and shopping tests of all kinds to determine the honesty of employees and dealers'' (from a Burns advertisement, quoted in Klare, 1975, p. 89).

The routine performance of some of these services has resulted in the creation of dossiers on individual citizens. Private security firms, of course, limit access to these confidential files to those who are able to pay the price to see them. Normally, the subject of the file is not only unaware of those who pay to see it, but is probably even unaware of the existence of the file. The Rand Corporation study (1971) reported that there were at least 3 to 4 million of these files in the hands of the largest security firms in the country.

On occasion, the illegality of the activities of the private police are made public:

[T]he pursuit of background data on job applicants has led to the arrest and prosecution of officials of several prominent security firms: in 1971, six security executives, including officers of Pinkerton's, Burns and Wackenhut, pleaded guilty to charges that they had bribed New York City police officers to obtain confidential police records on prospective employees of American Airlines and Trans-Caribbean Airlines. (The defendants pleaded guilty to the misdemeanor charge of ''giving an unlawful gratuity to a public servant'' rather than face trial for bribery and conspiracy.) (Klare, 1975, p. 489)

And Panel 15-5 describes yet another source of private police corruption. This raises the question of the extent to which the private police may, in certain instances, actually represent organized criminal interests.

Abuses of private police authority and power have been, and are, widespread. And even if the abuses of the private police are no more numerous than those of the public police force, there is still cause for alarm. The often untrained and unregulated private police force's use of improper search, seizure, and surveillance and unnecessary force—even deadly force[11]—will no doubt continue, to be even more difficult to control than the abuses of public police.

Explaining the Rise of the Private Police

Why have we witnessed such a tremendous increase in the numbers and use of the private police in the United States, particularly since the mid-1960s? Several factors appear to be involved.

The political activity, sometimes violent, of the antiwar movement and minority communities in the late 1960s and early 1970s was perceived by many threatened institutions as requiring added police protection. During this time, banks, corporations, and colleges and universities clamored for more private security services with many of them doubling or even tripling their expenditures in this area.

In addition, the U.S. business community has, for at least a decade, grown more convinced that shoplifting and other crimes against business have been

---

[11] All major American cities have, by this time, witnessed the use of lethal and even deadly force by armed security guards.

PANEL 15-5

Private Justice: Who Will Police the Police?

The mob seems to have found a new growth industry. With the city's private security businesses booming, authorities are compiling evidence that mobsters have taken over several local security-guard firms and a few of the guard unions.

Though most guard companies and unions are legitimate, well-placed hoods in the security business have engineered the assignment of friendly guards to aid in moving contraband, including drugs, through airport security networks, according to investigators. With their handpicked guards on the lookout, the mob has stolen truckloads of produce from the food markets, swiped shiploads of shellfish from the piers, and arranged burglaries to clean out shopping centers and warehouses.

"We found one guard company working out of midtown that was run by the Colombo crime family," said a federal agent with the Organized Crime Strike Force. "They'd send one team over to put in a burglar alarm and another team over to wipe you out."

What's more, even as they pressure security guards to look the other way during heists, mobsters have also moved in on the guards' unions. Hoods are suspected of having siphoned hundreds of thousands of dollars from guard-union pension and welfare funds, often with the collusion of the employers, who get sweetheart contracts for their cooperation. The hoods have also managed to drain union coffers by paying themselves hefty salaries and writing off new cars, restaurant bills, and travel expenses to the locals.

The security mobsters are also suspected of using their connections with other mob-run unions and private carting firms to keep legitimate unions from organizing employees, especially at some of the city's fast-food restaurants.

"These fast-food franchises sign up with one of the mob unions, and they not only get their places guarded, but the garbage gets picked up without a hassle and they get their windows cleaned instead of broken," said an investigator for the United States Department of Labor.

Some of the guard unions being investigated are independent locals with no national affiliations, no charters, no executive boards, and no minutes. They're all part of a crazy quilt of unions that at one time or another have represented thousands of security guards at construction sites, retail stores, wholesale markets, warehouses, piers, airports, hospitals, and methadone centers throughout the metropolitan area. Recently, investigators have even found mob-tainted unions representing guards at military installations and atomic power plants.

The independent locals have spread because of a federal labor-law ruling barring guards from membership in the same unions as the employees they're supposed to be patrolling. The rule is designed to prevent collusion between the

Panel 15-5 (Continued)

watchdog and his charges, but it's kept investigators busy trying to unravel connections.

"These guard unions tend to collapse and reappear like circus tents," said Queens District Attorney John Santucci. "But they're always run by the same cast of characters."

An excess of guards apparently does not guarantee labor peace, however. In Rochdale Village, Queens, a recent battle between rival guards at the housing complex erupted into shootings, sniper fire, arson, vandalism, and assaults. Things got so bad at the 25,000-resident complex that Alfred Mossman, the co-op president, asked Governor Carey to send in the National Guard.

With the security-guard business exploding far beyond the abilities of its regulators to keep up, the industry has turned into an ideal target for organized crime. According to the federal Department of Labor, security guards are now the third-fastest-growing occupation in the country, behind public employees and hospital workers. . . .

The business has grown so fast that none of the agencies assigned to regulate it has been able to handle the paperwork, let alone monitor the system. . . .

"There's been such a tremendous boom in the security field, with companies and union locals springing up everywhere, that, until now, no one has really been watching the supposed watchdogs," said Santucci.

Though the majority of security-guard firms and their employees are untainted, the mob's infiltration of the industry has authorities worried. Acting on complaints from disgruntled union members, security firms, and client companies, both federal and state agencies have started investigations. . . .

Recently, the teamsters have become very active in security-guard work. Not long ago, Teamster Local 282, whose president, John Cody, has been described by the feds as a close associate of the late crime boss Carlo Gambino, shut down

rising steadily. Many businesses have responded to this situation by purchasing millions and billions of dollars worth of private guard services. Even some small businesses—the corner grocery and tavern—have felt compelled to make these policing expenditures. To the extent that it can help cut losses, private policing is perceived as a good investment by the business community.

Whether or not violent and property street crimes have increased in the past 15 years is debatable; but the increase in the fear of these kinds of crime is not. As a result, we have found some scared citizens banning together to form neighborhood or block associations that collectively purchase the services of private street guards. Merchants too, particularly in the inner cities, have organized to contract for private patrol services that will presumably make their neighborhoods and

Panel 15-5 (Continued)

construction jobs throughout the city, Nassau, and Suffolk after complaining that employees had been endangered by a brawl involving affirmative-action demonstrators at a midtown construction site.

"It was a very suspect brawl," said one federal agent looking into the incident. "The affirmative-action demonstrators always call the contractor in advance, arrive on a bus, demonstrate for the press, and go home. This time, no one knew any of the thugs who showed up at the scene, and there were fistfights and a stabbing or two."

The Teamsters refused to return to their jobs until they could station an armed Teamster security guard on every floor of every building going up and at the entry of every construction site. The construction companies said Cody's plan would cost $130,000 a day.

"It's the difference between paying a guard $15,000 a year and a Teamster guard $35,000 a year," one midtown contractor said. "Right now we're trying to negotiate with them about a guard on every other floor and every other entrance."

If the prospect of mob-influenced guards patrolling warehouses, stores, and street corners is frightening enough, the most recent development promises even more trouble.

"Federal arsenals and even Andrews Air Force Base have been taking their security work away from the traditional military police and turning it over to private companies because it is cheaper," a federal investigator said. . . . We have private guards taking over at the government's arsenal in upstate Plattsburg and at Andrews Air Force Base, in Washington.

"Things have gotten so bad today," the agent continued, "that we've got men running some of the security-guard unions today who couldn't qualify as guards."

Source: Nicholas Pileggi, "The Godfather and the Guards," New York, April 27, 1981, pp. 34–35 and 37.

---

shops safer for them and their customers. Public institutions such as schools, hospitals, and museums, have also increased their budgets for private security to ward off crime on their premises and assure their patrons that they are providing a safe environment.[12]

The recent economic recession-depression in the United States has also contributed to the increased use of private policing services by private business and industry. Many large corporations facing economic uncertainty (even bankruptcy in some cases) and declining profit margins, also face—because of the economic

---

[12]The first part of this section relies on the analysis in *The Iron Fist and the Velvet Glove* by The Institute for the Study of Labor and Economic Crisis (1982).

downturn—greater threats to their property, inventory, and profitability because of the increased likelihood of theft, vandalism, and sabotage. The use of private police services is presumed to lessen some of this threat.

Spitzer and Scull (1977) have employed a radical criminological analysis to point to yet another factor related to the recent rise of private policing. These criminologists have examined the changes in the political economy of the United States and how these changes are related to the increasing corporate reliance on private, rather than public, police services. They have argued that in advanced capitalist societies like the United States, the nature of economic production undergoes significant changes. Economic production under a system of corporate capitalism grows more and more technologically intense. Machinery and "high technology" replace the skills of the labor force. The production process grows more and more systematic, scientific, and rational, and less human. But this increasingly technological and rational production process also becomes more and more vulnerable to breakdown as each aspect of production grows more and more interdependent.[13] To prevent this kind of breakdown and disorder, the capitalist class—the class that owns and controls corporate production—must extend its control over labor and this more technical and rational system of production. One way in which this extension of control has been accomplished is through the intense policing of the corporation, the increased policing of the labor or production process itself. This policing has been, and continues to be, primarily private policing.

Finally, a host of more isolated events have also led to an increased demand for private policing services. Events like airline hijackings and "executive kidnappings" have been met with the purchase of private security services. "Executive protection services" have also contributed to the coffers of private security agencies (Klare, 1975).

It is clear, then, that there has been a vastly increased demand for police services by private industry, businesses, and individuals, as well as by many public institutions, during the past 10 to 15 years. But why has this demand not been met by the criminal justice system—the municipal police and other public law enforcement agencies? To be sure, some of it has been met by the public sector. However, due to budget limitations—the fiscal crisis, again—local, state, and federal governments have not been able to finance and provide the quantity and quality of police protection that has come to be required by many private, and some public, institutions.[14]

Fiscal crisis or not, many large, private corporations have come to recognize the many advantages—from their point of view—of private police services.

---

[13] The recent rise of so-called computer crimes is evidence of this point.

[14] Although it is quite clear that attempts at private justice are to a large extent a response to the inability of government at all levels—local, state, and federal—to finance the expansion of the criminal justice system, it is not nearly as clear that increased government expenditures on criminal justice have actually contributed to the fiscal and budgetary problems of these governments. Criminal justice expenditures, although they have at least doubled since the mid-1950s, still represent a very small percentage of both the Gross National Product and total government expenditures, and include less than 10 percent of what governments spend on social welfare programs. For further analysis of this problem, see Wenger and Bonomo (1978).

Whereas public law enforcement agencies have many duties, obligations, and responsibilities, the private police can, and do, devote their full attention and responsibility to those who have purchased their services. Also, the private police remove any risk that public police investigative work could uncover irregularities or illegalities on the part of the corporation itself. These irregularities or illegalities could lead to prosecution in the public criminal justice system, a system, of course, to which public law enforcement agencies are to report, at least in principle, any and all illegal activities. Corporations have been attracted as well to the ease with which they can hire and fire private police in response to their changing security needs. The public police have had a greater potential to protect themselves from such corporate whim by utilizing civil service and/or union protections to maintain their jobs. Perhaps the most attractive aspect of private policing to the corporation is the price. Private security has simply been much less expensive than the provision of public services. "In general, private guards are employed when a firm wants plentiful, cheap, flexible and personalized protection" (Klare 1975, p. 488).

Other Consequences of the Rise of the Private Police

The "crisis of private justice" manifest in private policing is not unrelated to the crisis of "deviant ghettoization" discussed in the previous section. As early as 1969, the National Commission on the Causes and Prevention of Violence described the future of America's major metropolitan areas in the following terms:

Central business districts in the heart of the city, surrounded by mixed areas of accelerating deterioration, will be . . . largely deserted except for police patrols during nighttime hours.

High-rise apartment buildings and residential compounds protected by private guards and security devices will be fortified cells for upper-middle and high-income populations. High speed, patrolled expressways will be sanitized corridors connecting safe areas [while] armed guards will "ride shotgun" on all forms of public transportation. (quoted in Klare, 1975, p. 490)

Three factors stand out here. First, there is the prominent role played by the private police in the division of urban areas into secure areas for the affluent and the enterprises they engage in, on the one hand, and less secure areas, "areas of accelerating deterioration"—deviant ghettos?—on the other. Second, the extent to which this "prediction" appears to have been a good one. Those living in a large city in the United States today can readily see their city developing along the lines of the pattern described by the Commission. Third, if our urban centers are indeed developing in this direction, the implications for successful crime control are disturbing. The racial and class separation and exploitation that contribute in both direct and indirect ways to criminal acts is only likely to grow more severe in cities where the white middle and upper class live in "fortified cells," isolated from the poor and minorities—the surplus population—who are relegated to unsafe and rundown neighborhoods of their own.

Another potential negative consequence of the rise of private policing, in addition to its relationship to the process of deviant ghettoization, is the way in which it may actually contribute to a more fearful, not a more safe and secure, society:

> The expansion of private security operations is only a symptom of a larger process of urban decay, yet one must ask whether the proliferation of armed guards will enhance rather than lessen the "culture of fear" in American cities. What is the psychological effect (especially on children and adolescents) of repeated encounters with armed guards in apartment buildings, schools, subways, stores, restaurants, parks and other public facilities? It requires no extensive research to determine that a ubiquitous guard presence can contribute to the climate of fear and alienation in inner-city neighborhoods—even if it does discourage some forms of crime. (Klare 1975, p. 490)

Finally, there is no reason to believe that as a greater and greater proportion of all policing done in American society is carried out by a private police force, it will not commit the same class-biased and racist acts committed by the agents of public law enforcement. Initial indications are that the private police, too, tend to single out the crimes of the poor, unemployed, minorities and otherwise "surplus" citizens for arrest and prosecution.

Private Corrections: Treating and Correcting for Profit

Policing is not the only area where attempts to replace the public justice system with a private system have arisen. Corrections has also witnessed the development of private alternatives.

As we have seen, beginning in the mid-1960s and continuing on until the present, the development of community-based corrections has meant that more and more persons have come under the supervision of the criminal justice system in general, and community corrections programs in particular. Many of these persons retained in the community have, as a condition of their remaining in the community, participation in some kind of treatment or rehabilitation program. In some instances, these offenders are sentenced to programs (often institutional programs) run by community corrections departments themselves. Others are diverted from the criminal justice system to some part of the mental health or social welfare system. In these cases, community corrections programs often contract from private agencies for services they are not able or willing to provide. To the extent that this has happened, community corrections has contributed to the crisis of private justice via the "privatization" of corrections. Alcohol and drug abuse services, as well as psychiatric treatment (both in settings ranging from in-patient clinics to residential centers legally designated as minimum or medium security jails or prisons), are purchased, for example, from private agencies who provide these services while attempting to make private gain. Although this arrangement obviously includes the public subsidization of private business, this type of "contracted" treatment or therapy is said to be cheaper than providing the service publicly, as a component of the criminal justice system itself. And cheaper it is; particularly since the criminal court may decide not to pay for the private service if the offender, his/her insurance company, or some other public mental health or welfare fund is unable or unwilling to foot the bill. In our own work in the criminal justice system we have witnessed the denial of treatment or other services to offenders for precisely this reason, no one can or wants to pay for it. In this way, the inability to finance the services that are a court-ordered condition of an offender staying in the community can actually result in that offender being sent to prison.

The private sector has also made inroads into state prison systems. In Iowa and other states, prison medical and psychiatric care is purchased from private firms. More recently it has been suggested that state governments get out of the prison business altogether. As prison costs and populations soar, state governments find it increasingly difficult to finance, operate and manage their penal systems. The head of the Rand Corporation's criminal justice research program has suggested that the solution to this problem is to have the state "contract out" its inmate population to prisons run by private enterprise, for purposes of private profit (Greenwood, 1981). This is reminiscent of the penal system in pre-industrial Europe where the state paid private individuals to confine criminals and other deviants and derelicts, and also permitted and encouraged the private use of their labor. The state of Colorado, for instance, has proposed the development of private correctional facilities in lieu of building another $35 million prison because "these facilities can be run at one half the cost of state-run facilities."

The crisis in private corrections then, although probably not as widespread at this moment, matches the crisis in private policing: here a public correctional system that is publicly regulated, accountable, and at least minimally staffed and trained, is replaced by an untrained, unaccountable and unregulated private, run-for-profit system. How a society ensures that those who fall under the supervision and authority of private corrections have their legal rights safeguarded is not yet clear. And, early indications are that private providers of correctional services cannot always resist the temptation to increase profits by lowering the quality of the services offered. In the most extreme cases, private corrections have meant little more than boarding houses or flophouses (what some critics have called "cockroach capitalism"), that fail to meet minimum health and safety requirements, let alone provide any rehabilitative services (see McGarrah and Kusnet, 1981). When this happens, the relationship between the crisis of private corrections and the crisis of deviant ghettoization becomes clear.

The Booming Security Industry

In light of the readily visible failures of the American criminal justice system, the economic profitability of private justice has led to an enormous expansion of other areas of the private security industry. Among them, private international intelligence agencies—private CIAs, if you will—have sprung up recently to offer espionage services to multinational corporations doing business in Third World countries where political and economic instability, as well as organized political opposition, could threaten, disrupt, or even nationalize their operations. These

The widespread need for home security has spawned a number of entrepreneurial efforts—in the instance, the sale and training of guard dogs.

corporate clients are willing to pay a big price for this political intelligence and the international private police are providing it for a good profit. Many of these "private CIAs" are organized and run by former government employees—former employees of the Justice Department, CIA, FBI, IRS, NSA, and SEC—and may still retain at least informal access to classified and confidential government intelligence information.

The home security industry may currently be the fastest growing industry in America. As individual homeowners, and on occasion entire developments, attempt to protect themselves with guards, guns, dogs, fence, moats, locks, barred windows, hair-trigger burglar alarms, television monitors, and around-the-clock electronic surveillance systems (that, with the press of one button alerts a private security firm that, in turn, notifies the police), the private profit accumulates (see Nagy, 1981).

Record handgun and tear gas canister sales, along with record enrollment in gun and tear gas training "schools," represent other contemporary and successful attempts to turn citizen fear and insecurity into private gain.

It is increasingly apparent that no profitable sale of "security and protection" has been wasted on the private security industry. As mentioned in Chapter 5, one can now buy mugging insurance in the United States. Another example of this phenomenon is the design and sale of "crime-proof" clothing and fashions.

The crisis in criminal justice has led to the rise of a "private justice system" where "justice" (or "safety" and "protection") is sold for a profit, and delivered only to those who can pay the price. The practice of private justice in American society is not the practice of justice at all. It represents a class-biased "justice system" that provides justice, safety, and protection only to the affluent and powerful in society. Those less fortunate and less powerful are left to depend on the often inadequate justice and protection of the public criminal justice system.

THE CRISIS OF POPULAR JUSTICE

Americans have a long history of "taking the law into their own hands." The westward expansion, "settling" the American frontier, included not only violence and lawlessness, but also efforts to contain and resolve the conflicts that led to this violence with informal or unofficial mechanisms of criminal justice. A formalized, official, criminal justice system was absent. This same kind of conflict, violence, and lawlessness, and the same kind of informal, unofficial, and often, vigilante practice of "justice," accompanied many other late 19th and early 20th century developments in American society: disorder in the cities resulting from rapid industrialization and immigration; struggles between labor and management, as workers attempted to organize and unionize to protect themselves from the insecurity and brutality of the capitalist factory; religious intolerance—primarily anti-Catholicism and anti-Semitism—in growing urban centers; racist efforts to maintain an illegal system of slavery, a tradition of vigilante justice that survives until today in the likes of the Ku Klux Klan, among others (Walker, 1980).

Recently—beginning in the late 1970s—there has been a resurgence of these efforts to practice informal, unofficial, or popular justice. As compared to the formal and official criminal justice system, these efforts at "popular" justice are less bureaucratic; more decentralized; not set apart, as distant and remote, from the other institutions of everyday life; and depend less on the expertise of legal or criminal justice professionals. Furthermore, popular justice efforts can include a deep distrust of official law and the official criminal justice system, and attempt to practice a law that is "vague, unwritten, commonsensical, flexible, ad hoc, and particularistic" (Abel, 1982, p. 2).

The recent growth in the practice of informal or popular justice in the United States has included two different sorts of "unofficial" efforts. Some of these practices—like Neighborhood Watches where neighborhood residents cooperate and voluntarily watch or police each other and each other's property—are sponsored by and work with the official justice system (in this case the local police). Others arise more spontaneously, without any support or assistance from the official justice system (often, in hostile opposition to this system). Neighborhood justice as practiced in neighborhood courts, outside of the purview of the official criminal court, is an example of this kind of popular justice. "Community Boards" are presently dispensing justice and resolving disputes—in both civil and

Two members of the Guardian Angels assume their self-appointed task of protecting subway riders in New York City.

less serious, normally not felony, criminal cases—independent of the official justice system. "Community Boards" are probably most well developed in the San Francisco Bay area but are spreading all over the country—in Anchorage, Alaska; Cambridge, Massachusetts; New Haven, Connecticut; Cleveland, Ohio; and Eugene, Oregon; among others (Peirce, 1982). Neighborhood police patrols, where neighborhood residents do their own policing, are another example of this sort of popular justice. Some popular justice groups and activities alternate between receiving the support or the hostile opposition of the official criminal justice system. The Guardian Angels—described in Panel 15-6—are, perhaps, the best known example.

The question that arises here is, "Why has popular justice resurfaced at this time?" Although our answer must necessarily be tentative at this point, given the newness of the phenomenon, at least two things appear to be involved.

First, there is a growing rejection of the formal and official legal system in American society. More and more individuals, groups, neighborhoods, and communities are less and less convinced that state and federal governments are capable of making the changes that would lead to an effective and efficient criminal justice system. Increasingly, the perception is that the American system of justice is too bureaucratic, too institutional, too concerned with due process and the rights of offenders, too unconcerned with the rights of victims, too involved with professional therapy and rehabilitation, not concerned enough with punishment and deterrence, and generally incapable of ensuring public and private safety. Because of this, many groups, organizations, associations, neighborhoods, and

PANEL 15-6

The Guardian Angels: Community Control or Vigilantism?

NEW YORK   The flashing lights, pulsating music and parade of top politicians were a far cry from the perilous world of lonely streets, dimly lit subway platforms and graffiti-covered trains.

The scene was Magique, a chic discotheque on Manhattan's East Side. As cast members from such shows as "A Chorus Line" and "Sugar Babies" looked on, New York Lt. Gov. Mario Cuomo and Carol Bellamay, president of the New York City Council, led festivities honoring the Guardian Angels. Designers Bill Blass and Oscar de la Renta, many of whose clients normally spurn subways, contributed clothes to a fund-raising auction for the group and pop artists provided posters and prints.

While the evening afforded youngsters from tenements and people from plush cooperative apartments a chance for entertainment, it also provided a valuable clue to something more—just how far the Guardian Angels have come in gaining legitimacy in New York in just two years.

The Guardian Angels are distinctively dressed volunteers, mostly in their teens from ghetto neighborhoods, who patrol the city's worst trouble spots—subways, parks and streets. Their red and white T-shirts and red berets have become a common sight in a city that worries about crime.

The Angels always patrol in groups of at least eight. They spread through subway trains, one to a car and are careful to stand near the door that connects the cars. Each patrol member memorizes an elaborate set of signals to quickly summon help. The SOS signals can range from a member waving his beret or stopping to comb his hair. When the Guardian Angels walk the streets, there is always a car with a two-man backup within two blocks of the main group.

On many trains, the Angels, who receive some martial arts training, are applauded by subway riders. Grateful residents give them meals when they guard some streets. In two years their membership has grown from 13 original volunteers who named themselves the "Magnificent 13" to 1,000, including 28 women.

Branches of the Guardian Angels have spread to Jersey City, Hoboken, Elizabeth and Newark in New Jersey to Hartford, Conn., the suburbs of New York City and most recently Los Angeles.

For many of the teen-agers, the New York Guardian Angels provides some of the first real discipline and community encouragement they have ever received.

"These kids are creating a patrol presence in places where no one else is going. They have caught the imagination of the city," a high-ranking New York City police official said.

Police Commissioner Robert J. McGuire has announced his intention to give the group some training and to register its members. Under current plans that still are being negotiated and that still have to be formally approved by Mayor Edward I. Koch, the Guardian Angels would receive identification cards. They would be given lectures in the legal guidelines for making arrests without warrants, first-aid training and, on a selective basis, courses in cardiopulmonary resuscitation.

More than 100 organizations already provide civilian patrols in the city. These include cab drivers instructed to report

Panel 15-6 (Continued)

crimes over their two-way radios and residents of some neighborhoods who ride the streets in radio-equipped private cars. But the Guardian Angels is the only citizens unit that attempts to fight crime in the subways.

"Clearly, you have a large group of kids from poorly educated and low socioeconomic families who on the face of it are committed to doing something good in a volunteer way," Robert G.M. Keating, the mayor's criminal justice coordinator, said.

However, Koch has been ambivalent about the Angels, first labeling them "vigilantes" and later withdrawing the charge. He has spurned requests from the Guardian Angels for a mayoral commendation. That has brought anger from Curtis Lee Sliwa, 23, the group's founder.

"One problem we have is the mayor," he said. "He is not our biggest fan and a man who has been known to bear personal grudges. Remember, I have been banging away at him every since he first started calling us vigilantes and paramilitaries."

According to Sliwa, 65 percent of the Angels in New York attend the 10 most violent high schools in the city; 80 percent

live in the 10 worst crime areas. Latinos and blacks make up 85 percent of the volunteer patrol's membership.

"They tend to come from the lower economic order of society," Sliwa said, adding that many become local heroes.

"When they are in their communities, people go overboard for the Guardian Angels. The respect is just unbelievable. You get a pat on the back, a handshake. People go out of their way to thank you, come up to you, kiss you, hug you, give you that moral support that is so necessary."

The Guardian Angels' leader believes a secondary benefit is the example the group sets for younger children.

"When we walk through the streets while on patrol, we like to see the reaction of younger children. We're talking about the 8-year-olds, the 6-year-olds. At that stage of their lives they are not getting all calloused. It's the time when they really believe in the super heroes like Batman and Robin and Superman, in doing good and in helping older people."

Sliwa claims his group has made 128 citizen's arrests, a figure the police department says it has not sought to document.

communities have decided to develop their own "system," an alternate system of justice.

Second, the underlying fiscal crisis along with an expanding deviant, criminal and surplus population, that has contributed to each of the particular crises in criminal justice discussed in this chapter has also been related to the rise of popular justice. Citizens feel less safe and secure, but the courts and prisons are overflowing and the state is broke. The cost of expanding the official criminal justice system is prohibitive and popular justice presents a less expensive alternative to, or expansion of, society's social control system. In like manner, as we have already seen, community corrections, deviant ghettoization, and private justice are thought to present this same advantage. To some extent then, the rise

Panel 15-6 (Continued)

According to Sliwa, members of the Guardian Angels must be at least 16 years old and must be recommended by a member of the group. There is a three-month probationary period. Sliwa says before they can go out on patrol all new Angels must be able to defend themselves against sticks, knives and must be judged on how they react to being shoved or hit, deliberately or inadvertently.

"The purpose of the physical training isn't to determine if you're a physical incarnation of Bruce Lee," he said. "It's important how you react to being hit, which is going to occur at some point . . . We don't want anyone who is going to become outraged and is going to want to kill."

Patrol leaders must be Angels for at least eight months. The flunk-out rate is high. According to Sliwa, 166 members of the group have been thrown out for a variety of offenses: missing patrol (an eight-hour a week requirement), smoking in subway bathrooms, kidding around, becoming loud and offensive, not following instructions from a group leader.

"You have a group of eight or more people depending on you to be there. There are no guns, there are no weapons," Sliwa said. "The only thing we can depend on is people power. And if you are not there you are hurting the organization."

The Guardian Angels have no formal manual of procedures. Sliwa says instructions are drilled into members during weekly rap sessions.

The organization stresses that it is not an investigative agency and does not serve as an informant for the police. Guardian Angels do not make drug arrests or attempt to detain people with illegal handguns unless the weapon is being used in a crime. The patrols will stop the harassment of women, intervene in cases of attempted rape, try to prevent vandalism and graffiti.

"We are primarily a deterrrent, but in the case of a crime being committed, we are there to make the arrest. But we are not trying to play cops. We are not informers for the cops," he said.

Source: John J. Goldman, "Guardian Angels: A Godsend for New Yorkers," The Collegian, Fort Collins, Colo., February 18, 1981.

of popular justice represents an admission by at least some in society—primarily ruling and dominant groups and interests—that we can no longer afford official and formal justice and due process for *all* in society. And presently, with its reliance on primarily volunteer labor, with only a few minimally paid staff members, popular justice is cheaper than official justice. In San Francisco, for example:

Last year . . . volunteers handled 500 cases and brought about 100 to a full hearing. But consider, in contrast, the performance of a municipal court like San Francisco's. In 1980, with a $73 million budget, it received 11,500 criminal cases. But by the time the lawyers had finished their summary dismissals and plea bargaining, an incredibly meager 120 cases reached actual jury trial. (Peirce, 1982, p. 7a)

The Progressive Side of Popular Justice

Some early analysts of the recent rise of popular justice contend that it is to be understood essentially as a positive and progressive development in American society. It is said that this is the case because popular justice:

- Contributes to a more democratic and thorough recognition and airing of conflict and controversy.
- Contributes to increased democratic participation on the part of disputants who resolve their own conflict.
- Reduces passive dependence on criminal justice professionals and the criminal justice bureaucracy.
- Helps to rebuild the neighborhood solidarity of an earlier era.

But most important in this regard, it has been argued that the organization and practice of popular justice is similar to other community and neighborhood groups organized to work toward progressive social reform and change (organizations working for tenant rights, rent control, improved city services, utility rate reduction, etc.) in that it leads to higher levels of democratic participation that may ultimately help to ensure the democratic self-control of local communities. In other words, popular justice may not only assist in controlling crime, but may be part of a larger social movement, moving toward greater social justice.

Evidence that some uses of popular justice in American society threaten the status quo with their potential for progressive change is reflected in the attempts by dominant classes and interests to suppress or coopt certain popular justice efforts—both in the past (for a discussion of the fate of the Knights of Labor, see, for example, Garlock, 1982), and in the present (as has happened to the practice of neighborhood justice in some cities, see Abel, 1982). However, if there is a side of popular justice that is potentially positive and progressive, there is also a side that is potentially negative and repressive. On this side lies the real crisis of popular justice.

The Repressive Side of Popular Justice[15]

Among the actual and potential problems that have accompanied the recent rise of popular justice in the United States are:

1. Popular justice does not guarantee the procedural protections and due process that are part of the constitutional and legal rights of citizens in the same way that the official justice system does. In this sense, popular justice is by definition, as is

---

[15] Most of the ideas presented in this section are taken from Abel (1982).

the case with private justice, an unaccountable and unregulated "system of justice." And whenever this is the case, the dangers of unchecked vigilantism are present. The rather infamous "law and order" efforts of Tony Imperiale's North Ward Citizen's Committee in Newark, New Jersey are a case in point. This community "justice system" has done anything and everything that is required to maintain neighborhood "law and order"—including the illegal and sometimes violent exclusion of blacks and "other radicals" from the community (see Goldberger, 1971).

2.   Popular justice may actually represent an extension of the state's social control system—creating "a wider and stronger" criminal justice system "net." Popular justice, much like community corrections, allows social control to leave isolated, segregated, coercive institutions (like the prison) and permeate the entire community. Social control is decentralized and more readily dispersed (see Cohen, 1979). With popular justice, the criminal justice system may become more all-encompassing and add to the kinds of behaviors that are subject to control by diversifying and individualizing the practice of criminal justice, expanding the limited punishment repertoire of fine, probation, jail, or prison used by the traditional criminal justice system (Abel, 1982). And this extension of the criminal justice system is relatively inexpensive, a requirement in an era of fiscal crisis.

Popular justice bears other similarities to community corrections. Initial evidence seems to indicate that a majority of cases dealt with by the practice of popular justice may simply not have been dealt with at all if this "alternative system" did not exist. In other words, as was also indicated in our analysis of community corrections, popular justice may be an alternate "system of justice" that supplements—but does not replace—the official and traditional practice of criminal justice in American society. To the extent that this is true, popular justice expands, rather than contracts, the system of coercive social control.

3.   Whereas the official criminal justice system is primarily passive and reactive, popular justice may be more aggressive and active, breaking down, as it penetrates every aspect of community life, the distinction between public and private behavior, and what is acceptable and unacceptable behavior.

4.   Even though popular justice may be coercive, it is usually careful to cultivate a non-coercive image. As this "non-coercive" control expands in the community, institutional and penal control necessarily becomes more severe and brutal (as evidence suggests it is doing at present in our society) as it is reserved for those who are thought to be the worst of all offenders, the most dangerous and violent.

5.   Evidence that popular justice extends the control of the official criminal justice system is found in the way in which it often integrates itself with this system. Officially sponsored popular justice, like Neighborhood Watches, for example, refer most of their cases to the official justice system. Popular justice also may replicate the class-bias of the official justice system: the poor, the unemployed, the working-class and minorities may be disproportionately policed here as well; policed in the interest of those who have the most to protect in the present social, economic, and political order, in the interest of some ruling group or class.

6.   Popular justice, like the official criminal justice system, tends to individualize conflict and offer individualistic solutions to it. Crime is treated as if it is caused

solely by the individual criminal and can be controlled by punishing the individual offender. Most recent attempts at popular justice in the United States have not recognized, and consequently have not operated on the premise (like the official justice system), that conflict and crime may be collective phenomena that are generated by the structure of American social and economic institutions, and that therefore, the reduction and/or elimination of crime may require collective and structural solutions such as the democratic reform of society.

7. Some analysts have concluded that we have popular justice because people *want* it. Evidence suggests, however, that people prefer the authority and formality of the official justice system that necessarily has more ability to uphold and enforce their rights. In this regard, it has been found that those attempts at popular justice that are most powerless in terms of official legal authority, are the most unused mechanisms of informal justice (Abel, 1982). It is perhaps, then, in the interests of the dominant classes in society to have dominated groups use popular justice whenever possible—thus, freeing the official system for their use in those cases that presumably require expert and professional attention and the full authority of the official legal and judicial system.

8. When dominant groups, classes or interests in society impose popular justice on other parts of society—as when officially supported and assisted Neighborhood Watches are organized or when private corporations and foundations finance neighborhood justice centers (as in the case of the San Francisco Community Boards mentioned above, see Peirce, 1982)—it seems quite likely that the end result could be an extension of the control of the official criminal justice system. As we have seen, this official system has not been very democratic.

9. And finally, if it is true that popular justice contributes to neighborhood and community solidarity, we must be careful to assess exactly what kind of community it helps to foster. If popular justice aids in the development of elitist, racist, sexist or religiously intolerant local communities, then we can hardly applaud its progressive character. And to the extent that popular justice contributes to the non-democratic features of American communities, it can be said to be different than the official criminal justice system in style and cost only—not in substance.

In conclusion then, it appears that all five of the crises in criminal justice discussed in this chapter represent efforts—both formal and informal, official and unofficial—to resolve a wider and more fundamental crisis in American society: the contradiction between the fiscal crisis of the state and the need for an expanded social control apparatus for an increasing deviant, criminal, and surplus population.

CHAPTER REVIEW

1. Since the early 1960s, the American criminal justice system has gone through a series of crises: the crises of incarceration, decarceration, "deviant ghettoization," "private justice," and "popular justice."

2. The "crisis of incarceration" that occurred in the mid- and late 1960s meant that state and federal prisons were increasingly recognized as ineffective, inhumane, overcrowded, and too expensive. The way out of this crisis was said to be the development of alternatives to imprisonment—the development of community-based corrections.

3. Community corrections, as they have developed and expanded over the past 15 years, include, in most localities, some or all of the following alternatives to incarceration: pre-trial release and diversion programs, pre-sentence investigation, residential treatment, restitution, community service, increased use of probation and parole, and work-release and halfway houses.

4. Today, an overwhelming majority of convicted offenders under the supervision of the criminal justice system are not incarcerated, but under the supervision of some community corrections program.

5. The development of community corrections has not reduced the number of persons incarcerated, or the rate of imprisonment, over the past 20 years. Rather, community corrections seem to have resulted in simply putting more of the total population under the control and supervision of the criminal justice system.

6. Community corrections have so far proved no more effective in reducing criminal recidivism and crime rates than traditional imprisonment. Traditional sociological and interactionist perspectives would lead us to expect that community corrections would be more effective in this regard. The former has suggested that increased social ties and bonds in the community would make the offender less likely to return to crime, while the latter has argued that the same result should follow the less severe labeling and stigmatization of community correction programs. Radical criminology, on the other hand, would suggest that this failure of community corrections to reduce recidivism and crime rates could be expected; since crime itself is structurally produced, any and all correctional efforts that are based on the adjustment or rehabilitation of individual offenders are bound to fail to control crime.

7. Prison-like programs in the community, lack of adequate rehabilitative services, the subversion of due process involved in diversion programs, and the fact that community control of offenders has supplemented (more than replaced or reduced) institutional control, all suggest that community corrections may not be significantly more humane than prison.

8. Because community corrections programs often do "little or nothing" for offenders, are often as expensive as prisons (particularly the more "institutional" community programs), and supplement (rather than replace) imprisonment, they are not necessarily cheaper or more cost-efficient than incarceration.

9. There is some evidence that community corrections programs are currently on the decline. Contributing to this is the failure of community-based corrections to lower criminal justice costs and a return to an extremely conservative ideology of crime control in the United States—one that emphasizes isolation and punishment, not treatment and rehabilitation. The growth of the criminal, deviant, and surplus population in the United States has not slowed, however, and the state's fiscal crisis has worsened. The search for newer and even less expensive forms of social control has led to another crisis in American criminal justice: the crisis of deviant ghettoization.

10. Deviant ghettoization refers to what may be the criminal justice system's least expensive method of social control: segregating all sorts of criminals, deviants, and other members of the surplus population in decaying inner city areas where they can be left to victimize each other, without having to be supervised or policed by the criminal justice system in any way.

11. Private justice—selling policing and corrections for a profit—has emerged in the past two decades as a significant and growing alternative to the inefficiency and ineffectiveness of the official public criminal justice system.

12. There are now probably more private than public police in the United States. Private security and policing are at least a $5 billion per year industry (maybe as high as a $10 to $15 billion per year industry). Historically, American industry has been the primary employer for private police, often putting them to anti-labor, anti-union uses. However, at present, as the private police make inroads into areas formerly handled by the public police, the presence of the private security force is more and more pervasive: in apartment buildings, shops, department stores, office buildings, factories, museums, schools, universities, hospitals, theaters, stadiums, buses, and subways.

13. Private security and policing are related to the "crisis of private justice" in the following way: there are virtually no employment standards in the private police industry; the private police have tended to be untrained, unskilled, and poorly paid; there is a high rate of turnover in the private security industry; a high rate of crime exists among private security employees themselves; "moonlighting" public police often make up an overworked and fatigued private police force; private and public law enforcement may often contradict each other and work at cross-purposes; the private police force is legally accountable to no one and represents a serious threat to the civil liberties of American citizens.

14. All of the following have contributed to the rapid rise of private policing in the past two decades: perceived threats to social institutions resulting from antiwar and minority political activity; perceived increases in crimes against business; increased citizen fear of crime in neighborhoods and public institutions; the increased likelihood of theft, vandalism and sabotage of private business during periods of economic downturn; more vulnerable corporations due to a more technological, rational and interdependent system of economic production; and a host of more isolated occurrences like airline hijackings and executive kidnappings.

15. Large corporations in particular have been attracted to the "advantages" that private police have for them when compared with public police. Private policing is more plentiful, flexible, inexpensive, and personalized protection, while avoiding the risks of uncovering the corporation's own "irregularities and illegalities."

16. The growth of private justice is also evident in the criminal justice system's purchase of correctional treatment and rehabilitative services from private sources (leading to the same kind of lack of regulation and legal accountability as surrounds private policing), the rise of the international private police, and the tremendous growth in the home and personal security industries.

17.   The crisis in criminal justice has led to the rise of the "private justice system" where "justice" (or "safety" and "protection") is sold for a profit, and delivered only to those who can pay the price. The practice of private justice in American society is not the practice of justice at all. It represents a class-biased justice system that provides justice, safety, and protection only to the affluent and powerful in society. Those less fortunate and less powerful are left to depend on the often inadequate justice and protection of the public criminal justice system.

18.   Another response to the failures of the official criminal justice system has been the recent developments in popular justice. Popular justice refers to attempts by local neighborhoods and communities to develop informal and non-bureaucratic alternatives to the official justice system. Some of these efforts have been officially sponsored by the criminal justice system itself—like "Neighborhood Watch" programs—while others have resulted in unofficial neighborhood or community courts (e.g., "Community Boards") and police patrols (e.g., the Guardian Angels).

19.   Although some early analysts of the recent rise of popular justice in the United States have argued that it has positive and progressive effects on society, others have contended that it has negative and repressive consequences for the social control system in society, and therefore, contributes to the crisis in criminal justice.

20.   All five of the "crises in criminal justice" discussed in this chapter represent efforts—both formal and informal, official and unofficial—to resolve a wider and more fundamental crisis in American society: the contradiction between the fiscal crisis of the state and the need for an expanded social control apparatus for an increasing deviant, criminal, and surplus population.

PART 4 CONCLUSION

16 Controlling Crime in the 1980s

SOCIOLOGICAL THEORIES OF CRIME AND CRIME CONTROL: POLITICAL AND POLICY IMPLICATIONS

In contemporary sociological criminology three broad theoretical orientations or perspectives predominate. Most of the sociological literature in American criminology, in one way or another, is derived from theoretical assumptions and perspectives that can be identified as either traditional, interactionist or radical. These theoretical perspectives imply distinct political orientations and public policy recommendations. In this sense, traditional, interactionist and radical theories suggest alternative routes for both understanding and *controlling crime* in American society.

Traditional Theories and Conservative-Liberal Politics and Policy

Traditional theories of crime emphasize the role of factors in the immediate social environment—unemployment, poverty, broken homes, deteriorating schools, subcultural or peer group influences, lack of adequate job or vocational training, drugs, drinking—that lead the offender to criminal behavior. Furthermore, traditional theories have tended to neglect organized, corporate, and political crimes and preferred to take the street crimes of the poor, minorities, and the working class as synonymous with crime itself. But in spite of their apparent emphasis on the social sources of crime and the occasional advocacy by many proponents of these perspectives of social programs that would purportedly lessen the impact of criminogenic social conditions on individual offenders, they ultimately tend to "blame the victim." The individual offender is perceived as the "carrier" of crime. When this view is coupled with a "functional" or "consensual" analysis of law and criminal justice, one that emphasizes the role these systems play in enforcing and ensuring an order in society that is in *everyone's* interest to preserve and protect, the relatively conservative nature of this sociological perspective begins to emerge. From this vantage point, it is in the whole society's interest— the public interest—to control and resocialize the individual offender to the social order. According to these traditional accounts, criminal behavior and offenders, although affected by social factors, are instances of individual pathology and deviance that must be controlled and reconciled to society's requirements.

Thus, when it comes to policy, traditional sociological theories often lead to appeals for "technological innovation" in the criminal justice system that is supposed to control, adapt, and reconcile the individual offender. Crime control, from this perspective, is often a problem of technique. Improved techniques in policing, the criminal court, and corrections will better control, adjust, and rehabilitate the individual offender. In extreme instances, for example, these techniques may be nothing more than technology itself, as in some behavioral control and modification programs, the use of lie detectors, new forms of eavesdropping, and video tape surveillance and "sting" operations.[1]

---

[1] "Sting" operations range from "luring" criminals with money in the wallets of sleeping winos (who are actually police "plants") to the famed "Abscam" operation where federal agents posed as wealthy

Historically, both political conservatives and liberals have approached crime and criminal justice from this sociological point of view.

Interactionist Theory and the Liberal Politics of Reform

Interactionist criminology generally contends that the crux of the crime problem in American society is "secondary crime," not the original or "primary" violation of legal statutes themselves. Secondary crime, from this perspective, is crime that is generated when the criminal justice system applies a stigmatizing label to the "offender" and then comes to expect the behavior that is associated with the criminal label. Sooner or later, the argument goes, the offender is likely to take on this stigmatized or "marked" criminal identity as his or her own, and may even commit him/herself to a criminal career. Since the criminal justice system in particular, or the society or community in general, makes it very difficult for the offender to free him/herself from this criminal definition or label, he/she will begin to respond to this "branding" or "exclusion" from the noncriminal community by living up to the identity that has been imposed "from above." The ultimate irony or paradox here, of course, is that the system that is supposedly there to control crime may actually be contributing to its development by, inadvertently perhaps, committing offenders to more of it.

Therefore, to decrease crime in society, the interactionist perspective suggests that we reduce secondary crime. This can be done by following through on policy recommendations that make an arbitrary, stigmatizing, dehumanizing criminal justice system less severe and more humane. The criminal justice system should intrude in the lives of law violators less often and less brutally. It should be more careful with, and use less often, criminal labels that may "mark" a person for life and commit that person to more crime, that is, to secondary crime. Liberal reforms that "humanize" the criminal justice system logically follow the tenets of interactionist criminology and have been supported by its adherents. Examples of such reforms would be replacing adult penal institutions with community correctional programs or following a program of "radical nonintervention" vis-a-vis juvenile delinquents (Schur, 1973).

The political and policy implications of interactionist views can and have sometimes been stretched beyond "the liberal politics of reform." Taken to an extreme, the interactionist perspective may give rise to libertarian politics or policy. Here, a laissez-faire social policy is suggested. The criminal justice system that controls, labels, and stigmatizes the least, is the best. Crime may be best controlled by ignoring it or "defining it away"; by instituting a hands-off social policy that is hesitant to criminalize any behavior. At the very least, a sweeping decriminalization of victimless crime is called for.

Saudis willing to corrupt U.S. congressmen and senators. Ironically, these operations may not only create crime and criminals where there were none before, but may also create the impression of crime control. This serves the ideological function of legitimatizing to the public an otherwise ineffective and beleaguered criminal justice system. This function is particularly well served where local television stations film and telecast successful "sting" operations (as has been done in many large cities).

Radical Criminology and the Progressive Politics of Social Change

Radical criminology holds that crime is a *structural* phenomenon. It focuses primarily on how crime is generated by and through the social structure of advanced-capitalist societies. It holds that the political economy of these societies—societies like the United States—is, in the final analysis, most responsible for crime, as well as for the failure of organized and official attempts to control it. For example, the organization and operation of the American capitalist economy begins and ends with a class and racist society. Because of this, some in society are systematically excluded from meaningful participation in economic (and therefore political, social, and cultural) production and therefore are unable to participate in the processes of economic distribution and consumption. This excluded and "surplus population" grows frustrated and alienated from society and increasingly responds with that set of behaviors called "street crime." But the criminal activity of this excluded class in a class society—of the poor, unemployed, and disenfranchised minorities—is not effectively controlled by a law enforcement and criminal justice system that is structured to fail (Reiman, 1979). The system is structured to fail because it helps to maintain a large and visible, poor and minority, criminal class that deflects attention away from the problems that originate at the "top of society."

From the point of view of radical criminology, the problems emanating from the top of society include white-collar, organized, corporate, and political crime. These are crimes that generally have escaped the analyses of traditional sociological and interactionist criminologists but are the most harmful and costly crimes in American society. Many of these acts are not even crimes in the legal sense. Powerful interests have been successful in limiting the creation and enforcement of laws to those that tend to strengthen and maintain their position of power and privilege in society. Much of this kind of criminality is a response to what some radical criminologists have called the "criminal-legal" foundation of an advanced-capitalist econony (Chambliss, 1978). This economy, in its present stage of organization and operation could not continue to function without considerable integration with illegal activities. Thus, there is a structural invitation and encouragement to all sorts of organized and corporate crimes perpetrated by various economic and political elites.

The political and policy implications of radical criminology are quite clear: if crime is produced structurally, then its control is to be found in transforming that structure. Progressive politics oriented toward the wholesale change of the social, economic, and political structure of American society is needed if we are really serious about controlling and reducing crime. Liberal and liberal-reform politics, recommendations, programs and adjustments in society do not, in the end, go far enough. If crime is to go away, democratic control over a corporate-dominated economy and an elite-run and financed political and governmental process and system must be established. To a large extent, the democratization of the economy and political, social, and cultural life must begin outside of the established and non-democratic political process and system. From the grassroots—

neighborhoods and local communities—to the national level, those in the working class and the surplus population—workers, the unemployed, the poor, minorities of all colors, women—must organize and agitate for this democratization, for the structural changes that can remove criminogenic social and economic conditions.[2] Only when a genuinely democratic community comes about can we expect crime to subside permanently.

THE RETURN TO A PRE- AND NONSOCIOLOGICAL PERSPECTIVE ON CRIME AND ITS CONTROL: THE PRESENT ERA

... wicked people exist ... nothing avails but to set them apart from innocent people ...

> James Q. Wilson,
> *Thinking about Crime*

Some men are prone to evil, and society has a right to be protected from them.

> **Ronald Reagan, speech before the International Association of Chiefs of Police, New Orleans, September 1981**

The theory of crime and crime control presently endorsed, propagated and influencing criminal justice policy at the highest levels of government in the United States represents a return to a pre- and nonsociological perspective. At least 60 years of sociological theory and research on crime and its control are being dismissed out of hand. Indeed, in the speech quoted above, President Ronald Reagan explicitly denied the relevance of *any* sociological perspective for explaining crime in American society. (Sociology, try as it may, has, for example, according to this president, been unable to show any link between unemployment and crime.) This return, in the 1980s, to pre- and nonsociological accounts of crime and their always conservative political and policy implications, may strike those in the liberal, progressive, and sociological communities as a bit ironic. However, the irony disappears when the national government's approach to crime and criminal justice is placed in the context of its generally conservative political ideologies and programs. Conservative presidential administrations will not be convinced in the near future that cross-national variations in crime alone undermine pre- and nonsociological theories of crime, as well as the conservative crime control policy they encourage.

Again, pre- and nonsociological theories of crime are similar in their contention that there is something "inside" criminals that "predisposes" them to criminal acts (e.g., physiology, chemistry, genes, abnormal psychology, and nutrition). Furthermore, in the recent Reagan administration's version of this perspective, crime ultimately reflects a nasty, evil, and brutish human nature that must be controlled if we are to avoid social breakdown and collapse.

---

[2]There is evidence that mere involvement in this "organization and agitation" process reduces crime in working-class and "surplus" areas and communities. This will be discussed in more detail below.

A "social" version of this "human nature-crime connection" has been advocated by academicians such as James Q. Wilson and Edward Banfield who have advised and counseled the Reagan Administration on crime and crime control policy. They have argued that "bad culture" causes crime. For them, it is the "culture of criminals" that causes crime.

It should be noted here that any and all theories that take social factors or social structure as the primary cause of crime (be they traditional, interactionist, or radical), even when they lead us to an individualistic view of crime (as in the case of most traditional views), are at least liberal in their political and policy implications. Some sort of adjustments are to be made in society and social institutions if crime is to be reduced. On the other hand, theories of social problems like crime and poverty—the "culture of poverty" argument is probably the most illustrative here[3]—that take culture to be the primary cause of the problematic behavior, tend to be conservative in their political and policy implications. The "Banfield-Wilson-Reagan formulation," for instance, may begin by blaming culture for individual criminal behavior, but this necessarily ends in blaming the person, that is, the criminal, for crime. This belief that "bad culture" causes crime really means that "bad people" cause crime. For to be afflicted by this criminal culture is to possess the cultural traits and attributes that *predispose* the *individual* to crime. In the words of one proponent of this "culturological" perspective: "The United States may have relatively high levels of criminality because it is inhabited by Americans" (David Bayley, quoted in Currie, 1982a, p. 31). In this way, the individualistic and conservative nature of this kind of "cultural perspective" is made plain: crime control means changing the individual offender, not the community or society.

Of course, if crime is the result of the particular culturally-induced character traits and attributes of particular individuals that arise from the tendency toward evil, toward a brutish human nature, then crime control is not to be realized following the policy recommendations of traditional, interactionist, or radical sociological criminology. Rather, a more severe, harsh and punitive criminal justice system is believed to be the only hope for controlling all those who have "lost control."

The Recent Reagan Crime Control Program

When rejecting any sociological perspective on crime, it is not surprising that federal criminal justice policy ignores the sociology of crime control as well. Instead, crime control is to become more effective as legal restraints on law enforcement are curtailed, legal and constitutional guarantees of due process before the law are sidestepped, and punishments are made more severe by an increasing reliance on imprisonment.

Elliott Currie reporting on a recent article in *Atlantic Monthly* (1982) by James Q. Wilson and George Kelling, called "Broken Windows," captures the essence of this approach to crime control:

[3] See, for example, Oscar Lewis (1971).

Wilson and Kelling . . . argue that the police can . . . play an important role in insuring public "order" in neighborhoods, where "order" is defined as protecting the "community" against infractions against "civility" by insolent youth, drunks, or other sundry undesirables. To achieve this, they argue, the police ought to be free to do what they probably do best—establish control over the streets by rousting drunks and suspicious strangers and "kicking ass" with gang youth. All of this, Wilson and Kelling conclude, may mean playing somewhat fast and loose with hard-won legal restraints on police conduct—but that's probably a small price to pay for the return of civility to the community. Nothing is said about why there are so many drunks or beggars or unruly youth in these communities in the first place, nor about where they might go once sternly sent on their way by the sturdy guardians of the local sensibility. (Currie, 1982b, p. 24)

The recent Reagan administration crime control program taken as a whole represents an attack on the individual rights and civil liberties of both the accused and nonaccused, the criminal and noncriminal.[4] Senate bill 1630 and a number of other "incremental" bills that have been pending before both the U.S. Senate and House would:

- Eliminate the exclusionary rule
- Establish preventive detention
- Limit the right of persons convicted in state courts to appeal their conviction through habeas corpus proceedings in federal courts
- Reinstate the federal death penalty
- Raise maximum penalties for most offenses
- Eliminate federal parole
- Limit good-time release from prison
- Require mandatory minimum sentences
- Establish a determinate sentencing system
- Strengthen the federal obscenity law
- Apply federal extortion laws to labor organizing activities and strikes
- Expand the Anti-Riot Act
- Expand the federal criminal courts jurisdiction to include particular anti-nuclear organizing activities and demonstrations
- Facilitate the use of Defense Department resources—both personnel and technology—by local police, the FBI, and the CIA . . . among other things (see Petti, 1982).

---

[4]The chief justice of the U.S. Supreme Court, Warren Burger, as evidenced in a series of speeches (among them an address before the American Bar Association in February 1981), has endorsed the thrust of this Reagan-sponsored program (Burger, 1981). Several Supreme Court decisions in 1984 have begun the implementation of this conservative anti-crime agenda.

No organized liberal or progressive opposition to this kind of legislation has emerged on Capitol Hill and its passage seems probable. Oddly enough, the only visible opposition has come from the political right: "In recent months, the Moral Majority and big-business troops have come out to lobby against the criminal code revision measure [Senate bill 1630] because they feel it does not go far enough towards their goal of restricting diversity and dissent in American life and curtailing the exercise of civil rights and constitutional liberties" (Petti, 1982, p. 83).

Beyond this legislative package, the Reagan administration's crime control program was fortified by the president's executive order that now governs the intelligence community. This order frees the CIA to infiltrate certain kinds of domestic groups and organizations, and expands its powers to conduct surveillance and collect and disseminate information on Americans, both at home and abroad.

Paradoxically, yet predictably, this kind of repressive crime control program, which is intent on criminalizing and punishing as much of the behavior of the less powerful and affluent in society as it can, acts simultaneously to decriminalize as much of the activity of the powerful and affluent who own and manage a corporate-dominated economy as it can. The U.S. Justice Department was "asked" by the Reagan administration to curtail its already meager efforts to prosecute corporate crime so that its resources could be focused more precisely on violent street crime. This has included dropping pending charges against some high-placed corporate executives. No one described this better than sociologist Bertram Gross:

> Reagan has personally launched the most audacious decriminalization program in American history. His people are punching holes in—or refusing to enforce—existing laws against "murder in the workplace," consumer fraud, environmental pollution, product safety, tax evasion, bribery, monopoly, price-fixing and employment discrimination. (Gross, 1981, p. 13)

Gross concluded of Reagan and his crime control strategy:

> Above all, he sends out the message—loud and increasingly clear—that the poor and the middle-income people shall be robbed to nourish the truly rich. (1981, p. 13)

The centerpiece of this conservative criminal justice policy is an increased reliance on prison: the increasing use of bigger, better, and more punitive prisons is said to be the best antidote for the increasing crime and violence in our streets. Indeed, the recent formula for a more effective criminal justice system in America is really quite a simple one: more police/more prisons, the age-old conservative response.

With the exceptions of the repressive regimes in South Africa and the Soviet Union, the United States has the highest incarceration rate in the world. In the industrialized West, the United States clearly leads all other nations in rate of imprisonment and the number of persons imprisoned (according to the U.S. Justice Department, at the time of this writing, there were 175 persons incarcerated for every 100,000 in population). Since 1973, the U.S. prison population has more than doubled while the overall population has grown by only 10 percent (Martin, 1982). Between 1975 and 1981, the incarceration rate in state and federal prisons increased by more than one third (Currie, 1982a). Under the Reagan administration, this trend, incredible as it seems, worsened: between 1980 and 1981 the number of persons imprisoned in the United States rose by 12.1 percent and in California, the largest state, the number imprisoned rose by 19 percent during this same period (Mitford, 1982). More and longer prison sentences, more mandatory and mandatory-minimum sentences—during the past several years, 37 states have passed mandatory and/or determinate sentencing laws requiring fixed prison terms and 10 states have eliminated parole—left nearly 700,000 Americans in state and federal prisons and local jails by the end of 1981 (Martin, 1982).

In 1982, the number of inmates in state and federal prisons grew by a record 42,915 and reached an all-time high of 412,303. This increase was the largest in absolute numbers of new inmates in one year since the federal government began keeping these statistics in 1925. In 1982, there was also an 11.6 percent rise in the state and federal prison population, second only to the 12.1 percent increase in 1981. And the number of state prison inmates kept in local jails to relieve prison overcrowding rose by 20 percent (or 8217 inmates) in 1982 (U.S. Justice Department in the Associated Press, April 25, 1983). These phenomenal increases in imprisonment in the United States have led to state inmates being housed two and three in a cell, or in tents, sheds, and military stockades. 31 states are presently under court orders to reduce prison overcrowding, while 9 others are in court over the issue.

These trends continued into the first three months of 1983, when there was an additional increase of 13,288 inmates to the state and federal prison population, rising to 425,678 (figures from the U.S. Department of Justice in the Associated Press, August 9, 1983). In Illinois, another large state, the prison population in mid-1983 was twice the size it had been in 1974 (Illinois Criminal Justice Investigation Authority in the Associated Press, July 31, 1983).

Of course, if more and more persons are incarcerated, more and more prisons must be built. With the support of the Reagan Administration and a conservative Congress, prison construction budgets have grown. As this text goes to press, almost $1 billion is being spent on new state and federal prisons; at least 20 states have appropriated another $1 billion for additional prison space and 33 states are debating another $1.5 billion worth of prison construction. As if this were not enough, Republican Senator Robert Dole introduced legislation (the Criminal Justice Construction Reform Act, Senate Bill 186) that would provide states with up to $6.5 billion in federal monies to improve their prison facilities, and the Reagan Administration asked Congress for $94 million to build new federal prisons—the largest one-year funding request for new prisons in U.S. history (Martin, 1982; Associated Press, April 25, 1983).

As more and more persons are incarcerated for longer and longer periods, the ideological rationale for prisons and imprisonment has changed. Rehabilitation and even deterrence have all but disappeared as justifications for penal institutions. Increasingly, imprisonment is rationalized, without apology or embarrass-

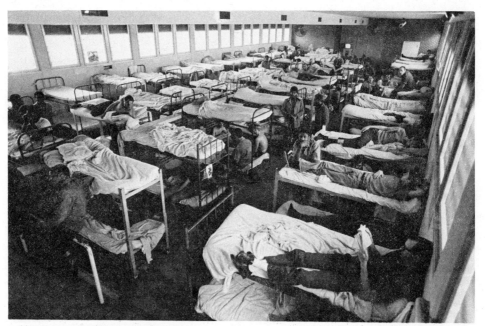

Main prison dormitory, Kilby Prison, Mt. Meigs, Alabama. Prison overcrowding is a major problem in the United States.

ment, as nothing more than protection and/or retributive punishment. Thus, as the number of persons incarcerated has increased, the number of dollars spent on the rehabilitation and reform of offenders has decreased.

The changes in criminal justice policy and procedures the Reagan Administration and other conservatives have recently advocated have been steadily adopted at the state, as well as the federal level. This was evident in the fall 1982 elections, where voters in a number of states passed conservative crime control measures:

- Massachusetts restored the death penalty.
- Colorado denied bail to persons accused of capital crimes.
- Arizona prohibited bail to those considered a danger to society.
- Virginia rejected a constitutional amendment that would have given the legislature the authority to restore felons' civil rights.
- New Jersey approved a $170 million bond for new prison construction.
- New Hampshire reaffirmed a constitutional amendment supporting the right to bear arms.
- California rejected Proposition 15, a proposal for strict handgun control.

Earlier in 1982, Californians had voted in favor of Proposition 8, which further institutionalized the conservative more police/more prisons approach to crime control by:

- Relaxing rules about what kind of evidence could be legally considered.
- Restricting bail.
- Implementing preventive detention.
- Abolishing plea bargaining.
- Restricting the criminal insanity defense.
- Making youthful serious felony offenders ineligible for commitment to youth penal facilities.
- Increasing the likelihood of prison, as opposed to probation, sentences.

And these measures were passed after the state had shown its first decline in reported crime in a decade. It was not as though Proposition 8 represented a turn away from a "soft on crime" policy:

> In fact, so tough had California already become on crime that the state was sending more than twice the proportion of people to prison than it did 10 years ago: 99 for every 100,000 citizens last year [1981] as compared with 49 in 1971. (Leary, 1982, p. 9a)

A Critique of the Conservative Crime Control Program

Although conservative crime control policy, like most traditional and interactionist sociological perspectives, is incomplete because it focuses almost exclusively on street crime, we will criticize it here, for the most part, on its own terms. In other words, we will assess it in terms of its effectiveness in preventing, reducing, and controlling conventional street crimes and not, in the main, for its inability to recognize and control those other kinds of crime in American society that radical criminology has pointed to as the most injurious and harmful—white-collar, organized, corporate, and political crime. This will also have the added benefit of focusing the attention of radical criminology on the victims of street crime, which is often overlooked because of it's emphasis on the crimes of political and economic organizations.

The approach to crime control that has recently been advocated and implemented is not a new one. Again and again the conservative "more police/more prisons formula" for controlling crime has had significant impact on American criminal justice policy. The repressive nature of this crime control program, the way in which it threatens democratic, civil, and individual rights and liberties, should be challenged on political and moral grounds. But beyond this, the evidence is irrefutable that such a crime control program simply does not work. The conservative approach has not effectively controlled crime in the United States in the past, nor does it at present. Even if evaluated on their own terms, overwhelming evidence suggests that conservative crime control methods create more crime than they control or prevent. Conservative crime control policy and practices do not work because they do not take account of the sociology of crime and its control; they do not take account of the social and economic conditions and conflicts in American society that lead to crime in the first place.

How, for example, can the following conservative proposals possibly curtail crime? The limiting of the appeal process so that those convicted in state courts could not have their convictions reviewed by federal courts will not "unclog" the criminal court and lead to a more efficient and effective justice system since it involves such a small number of cases in the first place. Likewise, repealing the exclusionary rule and accepting what is now illegally obtained evidence and/or confessions has implications for only the infinitesimally small number of all criminal cases that are thrown out of court each year for violating this rule. What good is a program of preventive detention that punishes those who are still innocent before the law when we know that no more than 1 percent of those who are released before trial commit, within 60 days of their initial release, another offense? There is some evidence that the large majority of crimes committed by persons out on bail comes more than six months after arrest. If this is the case, speedier trials appear to be a much more effective—and less repressive—criminal justice reform in this area. How can limitations on plea bargaining that will only increase the inefficiency of the criminal court lead to a justice system that offenders and non-offenders alike are prone to perceive as legitimate and just and therefore likely to "think twice" before transgressing? And the ludicrousness of limiting the insanity defense to make the justice system more effective is even more pronounced: less than 1 percent of all offenders use this defense and less than 2 percent of this 1 percent use it successfully.

Fundamental to the conservative attack on crime is the notion that imprisonment works. The evidence to the contrary is beyond question: the prison does little to reduce, control, or prevent crime. Incredibly high recidivism rates, in all kinds of prisons all over the country, rule out both deterrence and rehabilitation as prudent justifications for, and accurate descriptions of, the function of American prisons. The longer offenders stay in prison, the more likely they will become recidivists. It appears as though sentences longer than six months markedly increase the probability of recidivism and the severity of the recidivist's crime (McCarthy, 1981). Those who have described prison as "crime factories" or "crime schools" have not been given to hyperbole. Nor is protection a viable rationale for imprisonment. The facts are otherwise. According to the U.S. Bureau of Prisons, more than 95 percent of those who go to prison will one day be released; each day more than 360, each year more than 130,000 persons are released from American penal institutions—a majority of whom will be recidivists (McCarthy, 1981). Increasing the number of prison inmates will, in the end, only increase the number of offenders returning to society. Where is the protection in all of this?

But, in spite of all of the evidence, conservatives continue to argue that the "more police/more prisons formula" is the most effective crime control program. Prison overcrowding and the general deterioration of prison conditions have proceeded until a full-scale penal crisis now exists in the United States, replete with periodic, brutalizing prison riots. This crisis has been heightened significantly through tremendous increases in the number of property, not violent, offenders imprisoned, many of whom (expert estimates range from 40 to 60 percent of all persons incarcerated) could just as readily and safely be "sanctioned" in the local community (Currie, 1982a).

Apparently, it does not appear curious to the architects of conservative and repressive crime control measures that the nation with one of the highest incarceration rates (as measured by the number of persons incarcerated and the proportion of its total population incarcerated) also has the highest violent crime rate in the "advanced" industrial world. How do advocates of conservative crime control policies explain, for example, the Georgia Department of Offender Rehabilitation's conclusion that Georgia's incarceration rate—430 inmates for every 100,000 persons in the state—which is the highest rate of any state in the United States and probably the highest rate in the world, has absolutely no effect on its crime rate?

Yet, the conservative agenda calls for more prisons. Prisons that are not only expensive and fail to alleviate crime, but also fail to relieve prison overcrowding and create better and more humane conditions "on the inside." The latter occurs because new prisons reach their capacity (and often, more) almost immediately. If more prison space is available, more persons are sent to prison. The more police/ more prison formula ensures that prisons are filled almost as fast as they are built. A Standing Committee on Legal Services for Prisoners of the California State Bar has concluded that "building more institutions may simply mean incarcerating an even greater share of the population" (quoted in Mitford, 1982, p. 426) and cited a report prepared by ABT Associates in Boston for the U.S. Justice Department that "gathered data on every new prison opened in the U.S. between 1955 and 1976 . . . [and indicated] . . . New prisons generally reached rated capacity by only the second year after opening" (quoted in Mitford, 1982, p. 426).

In sum, what we have in the United States today is a "crime-prone society" and an "upside-down criminal justice system." Unchecked and unregulated criminogenic social and economic forces make American society "crime-prone," and a criminal justice system that does more to create and maintain a relatively large, extremely visible, permanent criminal class, than to control and reduce it, is obviously "upside-down" (see Reiman, 1979). The ultimate paradox here is that the conservative, "law and order," more police/more prisons approach to controlling crime actually promotes it. Conservative social and economic policies fail to protect those most vulnerable to the free workings of the market place with social programs and other state intervention in, and regulation of, the private sector of the economy. In this way, these policies encourage criminogenic forces in society. However, contemporary conservatives, like those conservatives before them who "have successfully posed as the guardians of domestic tranquility for decades" typically promote the social and economic policies "that bear a large part of the responsibility for the level of crime and violence we suffer today" (Currie, 1982b, p. 25).

TOWARD PROGRESSIVE PROPOSALS FOR CONTROLLING CRIME: NOBODY SHOULD BE MUGGED

The sociological perspectives on crime and its control that held sway in criminology during the 1960s and early 1970s were the traditional ones. These approaches were quite consistent with, underscored, and contributed to, the development of a liberal approach to crime control. A plethora of social programs—educational, vocational, job, treatment, and community correctional programs—were designed and implemented by federal, state, and local governments to remove the social and economic disadvantage that was believed to be the cause of the individual offender's inability to adjust to society's "mainstream." But these programs had little, if any, effect on crime rates. More and more of the political elite, academic criminologists, and the citizenry in general became convinced that most programs to rehabilitate offenders were failures. By the early 1970s, traditional sociological perspectives on crime control had grown considerably less credible and informed less and less of official criminal justice and crime control policy.

Interactionist criminology generally failed in its attempt to provide an alternative to traditional perspectives, and in doing so, generally failed to contribute to the reform of the American criminal justice system. Although a few attempts to decentralize and humanize a brutalizing and stigmatizing criminal justice system—one that interactionists believed to be the key contributor in the social processes that generated crime—were made in the late 1960s, throughout the 1970s, and even into the 1980s, interactionists' tenets on effective crime control were never taken very seriously in Washington or state capitols. Particularly to those who perceived American cities to be violent crime "jungles," the interactionists' reforms—all in some way or another "noninterventionist"—seemed idealistic, naive, and foolhardy. Real criminal victimization could not be ignored by either the political right or left (since most victims of street crimes are poor and/or minorities) and the interactionist influence on crime control waned before it waxed.

Since the mid-1970s, conservative crime control policy and strategy have slipped into this political and policy void. Today, the more police/more prisons formula that has been common throughout American criminal justice history, has again grown stronger and stronger. However, as we have seen, there is a problem with this formula: it does not work. And curiously enough, even though the strategy fails to reduce, prevent, or control crime, there is an on-going conservative clamor for more and more of it.

From any and all sociological perspectives on crime and its control, it is clear that the conservative approach must fail. Sociologically, it represents an "after-the-fact" crime control strategy. It addresses itself to the consequences of crime only; it intervenes to reduce, prevent, or control crime after it has occurred. Nowhere is this illustrated any better than in the focal point of the recent Reagan crime control program: build more prisons and use them more often for longer periods of time.[5] From a sociological point of view, prison represents the "remotest" point in an overall "after-the-fact" American criminal justice system and strategy. Prison is even a more "after-the-fact" intervention than the police or criminal court. Probably less than 1 percent of all criminal offenders in the United

---

[5]The folly of this approach is made even more clear when the recommendation of Attorney General William French Smith's Task Force on Violent Crime is seriously examined. The Task Force proposed spending 2 billion federal dollars on expanding the role of federal and state prisons in controlling crime when the National Institute of Justice has determined that it would take $8 to 10 billion (in 1978 dollars) to provide more humane and less overcrowded—as required by law—prison facilities for the present state prison population.

States end up in prison, yet conservatives maintain that prison has something to do with controlling crime. If it does, its connection is so far removed as to be insignificant. Most of the rest of the industrial world understands this. Nations as diverse as Japan, Great Britain, and Sweden, who share violent and property crime rates markedly lower than those found in the United States, rely considerably less on imprisonment. Although these nations have continued to incarcerate those for whom other alternatives do not appear feasible, they do not rely on incarceration as a strategy for controlling, reducing, or preventing crime as we do in the United States:

> None of this argues that we should close all prisons, or denies that there are substantial numbers of people who need to be locked up, some for a very long time. But recognizing that, and coming to terms with the need for prisons, is not the same as believing that building more of them will markedly reduce crime. The first is a necessary, if sobering, recognition. The second is magical thinking. It's a form of magical thinking, too, that has been largely abandoned in most other advanced industrial societies. Again, many of them are still looking for ways to *decrease* their reliance on prison even further. Most have adopted the position that it may be both practically and morally necessary to lock up dangerous people who hurt others—but they are under no illusion that doing so will do much about the crime rate. (The other difference between those countries and ours is that you can often walk around at night in their cities.) (Currie, 1982a, p. 35)

What is urgently needed is a progressive alternative to the illogic of the conservative plan. This requires a recognition that crime control is sociological; that it is not simply a matter of the appropriate technology or technique being applied by a beleaguered criminal justice system that cannot possibly do what it is being asked to do—to control crime "after the fact." A progressive sociological perspective holds that crime can only be controlled "before the fact." If crime is to be controlled, its *causes* must be removed. The social and economic conditions that generate crime must be transformed. A criminogenic society must be transformed, rearranged, to become non-criminogenic. This progressive alternative must learn not only from the mistakes of conservative approaches but also from liberal and reform errors, that is, the errors of both traditional sociological and interactionist perspectives. Unlike the interactionist view, this alternative must recognize that crime in American society represents serious alienation, exploitation, and victimization and that extensive intervention in political, economic, and social institutions is required if it is to be reduced significantly. Unlike traditional perspectives, a progressive approach must appreciate the basic contention of radical criminology: that more than minor adjustments and repairs in the American political economy may be necessary if crime is to go away; that the structure of American society, the structure of an advanced-capitalist industrial society, is itself criminogenic and its wholesale change is ultimately required.[6] But this pro-

---

[6]To be fair to these traditional perspectives, it should be noted that not all of the failures of social and rehabilitation programs in the late 1960s and early 1970s can be attributed to not taking the impact of

Progressive efforts to reduce street crime are aimed at the social and economic conditions that generate crime.

gressive proposal for controlling crime cannot afford to become too visionary or utopian. Crime is an immediate problem and the full democratization of American society is not immediately forthcoming. The mass-based political coalition that could begin to accomplish this has not yet formed. Therefore, in the meantime, progressive crime control strategies must be practical, within reach, meaningful and effective in the here and now. We cannot afford to wait on some hypothesized revolution.

A progressive proposal for controlling crime in the United States has its foundation in what we already know about the sociology of crime. Contrary to the pronouncements of conservatives, we do know something sociological about what causes crime. Among these causes are:

Poverty. Recent evidence confirms what many sociological criminologists have been suspicious of for sometime: potential offenders, offenders, and ex-offenders who gain some legal means to escape poverty are much less likely to turn or return to street crime than those who remain poor and without a legal livelihood (see the study by Berk, Lenihan, and Rossi, 1980, for instance).

Unemployment. The typical American community or city that experiences increases in unemployment will also experience increases in street crime. Harvey Brenner's (1976) classic studies of the impact of unemployment on American

---

the ''wider structural forces'' that generate crime into account—and focusing, by contrast, on the ''more immediate social environment''—since this ''rehabilitative approach'' was never more than half-heartedly supported, funded, and implemented.

cities, for example, found that a 1 percent increase in unemployment was invariably followed by 4 to 6 percent increases in a variety of street crimes.[7]

Income inequality. We know that those advanced industrial nations with the highest degrees of income inequality have the highest violent and property crime rates—the United States is included here—while those with the lowest degrees of income inequality experience the lowest rate of both of these types of crime (see, for example, Braithwaite, 1979; Shelley, 1981).

Dual labor market. Historically, street crime in American society has tended to come from a particular segment of the labor force, a labor force that responds to a "dual" or "divided" labor market (see Bonacich, 1976). There is a segment of the labor market that requires skills, training, and educational attainment; it offers in return meaningful jobs, job security, promotions, careers, and good wages. This part of the labor market is populated primarily by white males. The other side of the labor market offers unskilled, alienating, insecure, menial, dirty, and poor-paying jobs to marginally working-class whites and ghettoized blacks, Hispanics, and other members of the American surplus population. Members of this segment of the labor market have been disproportionately involved in street crime.

With this kind of sociological knowledge—knowledge of relationships and factors that are clearly capable of being politically and socially manipulated—a progressive proposal for controlling crime begins to emerge. Instead of the conservative "more police/more prisons formula" for crime control, the following progressive proposal for controlling crime is suggested. It is a proposal that is admittedly preliminary and incomplete, but nonetheless is a necessary beginning.[8]

1. *Community organization.* Local communities must begin to organize and assert political pressure and power to resist and mobilize against any and all victimizations that their members suffer. The weak—the working class, the poor, minorities, women—must become empowered (see Gross, 1981) to protect themselves against not only criminal victimization (that results from street crime, as well as white-collar, organized, political, and corporate crime) but other related victimizations as well: poverty, unemployment, income inequality, alienating and menial jobs, the oppressive effects of racism and sexism, lack of adequate public services such as affordable utilities, schools, transportation, housing, and health care, and so on.

There is already ample evidence that communities, classes, or racial and ethnic minorities that organize and agitate for social and economic justice are able to reduce crime. The struggle for social and economic justice is one of the most effective crime control mechanisms available. When communities unite against the sources of their oppression, they tend to stop criminally victimizing each other. All members of the community now have a stake in it, and it is a community

---

[7] Ironically, as we have seen, a majority of Americans responding to a variety of survey opinion polls identify unemployment as one of the leading causes of crime—consistent with sociological research—while the Reagan administration rejected this established empirical relationship.
[8] Much of what follows here is similar to proposals recently made by Elliott Currie (1982a, 1982b), Bertram Gross (1981, 1982), and Frank Browning (1982).

that has the potential to become a better, fairer, more just place to live. The most impressive examples of crime control through organizing for social and economic justice in American history are the reductions in crime that accompanied progressive political and labor organizing in the Great Depression and the civil rights movement in the early and mid-1960s (see Browning, 1982; Solomon, Walker, O'Connor, and Fishman, 1980).

2. *Full employment.* If crime is to be significantly reduced in the United States every American must be guaranteed a meaningful, well-paid job. Local, state, and national governments must protect all their citizens from the whims of the free-market, and the dual labor market, and implement and make good on a full employment policy. Decent jobs not only reduce unemployment but can also begin to lessen income inequality, both of which should lead to reductions in violent and property crime. Indeed, all advanced industrial nations that have instituted a full employment policy and program have lowered their violent and property crime rates well below those of the United States.

3. *Controlling all crime.* The American criminal justice system must be reformed to criminalize, police, prosecute, and punish all harmful acts in society, not just street crime. White-collar crime, organized crime, the crimes of governments and corporations, all victimize more persons each year and cost Americans more lives and dollars than street crime. If no one should be mugged on the streets of U.S. cities, neither should anyone be "mugged" by an American corporation or by their government. The American criminal justice system must be rid of the class and race bias that keeps it focused on "crime in the streets" so that it can begin to address itself to "crime in the suites."

4. *Victim programs.* Even if the above proposals immediately became reality in American society, all of the causes and consequences of crime would not go away overnight. In light of this, it is significant that the one "after-the-fact" component of a generally "after-the-fact" criminal justice system that has been ignored is the crime victim. Local, state, and federal governments should develop and maintain programs that provide crime victims with insurance, income protection, counseling, medical services, and restitution. Victims should also be protected by programs that offer monetary and social support to witnesses.

In sum, until a progressive sociological approach is taken, crime will not be reduced significantly. Lest we stay the course and continue with the conservative more police/more prisons strategy, we should reflect on these words of sociologist Alfred McClung Lee:

> As I look at the deprivation in such places as Newark and the Bronx, all I can think about is how poor conditions force the building of more prisons. Why do we not spend more money attacking the causes of crime, the stimulants of criminal behavior? Why must we throw more and more people into "finishing schools for criminals," our prisons? (1982, p. 546)

Bibliography

Abel, R. L. (1982) "Introduction." In R. L. Abel (ed.), *The Politics of Informal Justice,* Vol. 1. New York: Academic Press, pp. 1–13.

Ackland, L. (1981) "Prison-Industry Marriage Called Union-Busting Affair," *Chicago Tribune* (August 23):5, Section 1.

Administrative Office of the U.S. Courts (1983) *Federal Offenders in United States District Courts 1982.* Washington, D.C.: U.S. Government Printing Office.

Albrecht, W. S. (1979) "Surprising Profile of the White Collar Crook," *U.S. News & World Report* (July 23):61.

Alcohol, Drug Abuse and Mental Health Administration News (1981) "Studies Link Addiction and Crime," *Alcohol, Drug Abuse and Mental Health Administration News* (March 20):2.

Allen, F. A. (1981) *The Decline of the Rehabilitative Ideal: Penal Policy and Social Purpose.* New Haven, Conn.: Yale University Press.

Allen, I. A. (1982) "Study Says Mandatory Sentencing Laws Backfiring," *Denver Post* (August 9):B4.

Allen, S. (1979) *Ripoff: The Corruption That Plagues America.* Secaucus, N.J.: Stuart.

Alter, J. (1983) "Why Crime Is on the Decline," *Newsweek* (September 26):37–38.

Altheide, D. L., P. A. Adler, P. Adler, and D. A. Altheide (1978) "The Social Meanings of Employee Theft." In M. Johnson and J. D. Douglas (eds.), *Crime at the Top: Deviance in Business and the Professions.* Philadelphia: Lippincott, pp. 90–124.

Altman, J. R., and R. O. Cunningham (1967) "Preventive Detention," *George Washington University Law Review* **36.**

American Bar Association (1970) *Standards Relating to Probation.* Washington D.C.: American Bar Association.

American Bar Association (1976) "Is Expanded Use of Mandatory Sentences a Social Approach to Reducing Crime?" *Congressional Digest* **55**(August-September): 203,205,207,209.

American Broadcasting Company (1976) "West Virginia: Life, Liberty, and the Pursuit of Coal" (telecast). American Broadcasting Company, "20/20" (November 30).

American Friends Service Committee (1971) *Struggle for Justice.* New York: Hill & Wang.

Andenaes, J. (1952) "General Prevention—Illusion or Reality?" *The Journal of Criminal Law, Criminology and Police Science* **43**(July–August):176–198.

Anderson, J. (1980) "The Mob's New Racket." United Features Syndicate. *Rocky Mountain News* (November 17):51.

Anderson, K. (1982) "What Are Prisons for?" *Time* (September 13):38–41.

Anderson, K. (1983) "An Eye for an Eye," *Time* (January 24):28–39.

Anderson, P. (1981) *High in America: The True Story behind NORML and the Politics of Marijuana.* New York: Viking.

Archer, D., and R. Gartner (1978) "Legal Homicide and Its Consequences." In I. L. Kutash, S. B. Kutash, and L. B. Schlesinger (eds.), *Violence: Perspectives on Murder and Aggression.* San Francisco: Jossey-Bass, pp. 219–232.

Ashford, N. (1976) *Crisis in the Workplace: Occupational Disease and Injury.* Cambridge, Mass.: MIT Press.

Associated Press (1979) "Death Penalty Found Most Likely if Victim White," (March 18).

Associated Press (1979) (May 7).

Associated Press (1980) "Monopolies in Food Industry Hit" (May 6).

Associated Press (1980) (October 3).

Associated Press (1981) "Mob Linked to Growth of Garment Sweatshops" (February 27).

Associated Press (1981) "3-Generation Cycle of Crime Revealed in Routine Arrest" (March 27).

Associated Press (1981) "Tennessee Bookies Pay Tax on $1 Million in Bets" (July 1).

Associated Press (1981) "Terra Haute Policemen Reject Pact, Stage Walkout" (July 16).

Associated Press (1981) "Juveniles Blamed for 23% of Violent Crime in U.S." (August 17).

Associated Press (1981) "More Cop Brutality, Commission Finds" (October 17).

Associated Press (1981) "Miami Beach Turns Big Eye on Crime" (November 16).

Associated Press (1981) "Crime Rises, Police Dwindle" (December 8).

Associated Press (1982) "IRS Says Tax-Cheating Toll Has Tripled Since 1973" (March 23).

Associated Press (1982) "Business Boom in Car Thefts Costs $4 Billion a Year" (March 25).

Associated Press (1982) "Petty Criminals to Spend a Few Days in Work Camps" (May 13).

Associated Press (1982) "FBI Gets Stung During a 'Sting' " (June 12).

Associated Press (1982) "14 More Police Officers Arrested in Drug Case" (June 12).

Associated Press (1982) "Cuts Hurt Poor's Defense" (July 25).

Associated Press (1982) "2 Million Adults Jailed or on Probation, Parole in '81" (August 16).

Associated Press (1982) "Reported Crime's Dip 5%: First Drop in 4 Years" (October 20).

Associated Press (1983) "Record Growth Lifts Prison Population to All-Time High" (April 25).

Associated Press (1983) "25 Million Households Hit by Crime" (June 13).

Associated Press (1983) "Report Finds Illinois Prison Population Doubles" (July 31).

Associated Press (1983) "Prison Population Reaches Record 425,678 Inmates" (August 9).

Associated Press (1983) "Probation, Parole Numbers on the Rise" (September 19).

Associated Press (1983) "25 Million Households Hit by Crime" (October 20).

Association of the Bar of the City of New York and Drug Abuse Council, Inc. (1977) *The Nation's Toughest Drug Law: Evaluating the New York Experience.* Washington, D.C.: U.S. Department of Justice.

Austin, J., and B. Krisberg (1981) "Wider, Stronger, and Different Nets: The Dialectics of Criminal Justice Reform," *Journal of Research in Crime and Delinquency* **18**(January):165–196.

Austin, J., and B. Krisberg (1982) "The Unmet Promise of Alternatives to Incarceration," *Crime and Delinquency* **28**(3):374–409.

Babbie, E. R. (1980) "The Saints and the Roughnecks." In *Sociology: An Introduction.* Belmont, Calif.: Wadsworth, p. 159.

Bacon, D. C., and O. Kelly (1978) "Uncle Sam's Computer Has Got You," *U.S. News & World Report* (April 10):44–48.

Bailey, W. C. (1982) "Capital Punishment and Lethal Assaults against Police," *Criminology* **19**(February):608–625.

Balkan, S., R. J. Berger, and J. Schmidt (1980) *Crime and Deviance in America: A Critical Approach.* Belmont, Calif.: Wadsworth.

Balter, M. (1981) "Peering Cops," *The Progressive* (September):18.

Baridon, P. C. (1976) *Addiction, Crime, and Social Policy.* Lexington, Mass.: Lexington Books.

Barker, T., and J. Roebuck (1973) *An Empirical Typology of Police Corruption: A Study in Organizational Deviance.* Springfield, Ill.: Charles C Thomas.

Barlow, H. D. (1981) *Introduction to Criminology,* 2nd ed. Boston: Little, Brown.

Beard, C. (1919) *An Economic Interpretation of the Constitution.* New York: Macmillan.

Becker, H. S. (1963) *Outsiders: Studies in the Sociology of Deviance.* New York: Free Press.

Becker, T. (ed.) (1971) *Political Trials.* Indianapolis, Ind.: Bobbs-Merrill.

Beire, P. (1979) "Empiricism and the Critique of Marxism on Law and Crime," *Social Problems* **26**:273–285.

Bender, T. (1981) "The Carter Urban Report: A Nation of Immigrants to the Sun Belt," *Nation* (March 28):359–361.

Ben-Horin, D. (1979) "The Sterility Scandal," *Mother Jones* 4(May):51–63.

Bentham, J. (1823) *An Introduction to the Principles of Morals and Legislation.* New York: Hafner.

Bequai, A. (1978) *White-Collar Crime: A 20th-Century Crisis.* Lexington, Mass.: Lexington Books.

Berk, R. A., K. J. Lenihan, and P. H. Rossi (1980) "Crime and Poverty: Some Experimental Evidence from Ex-offenders," *American Sociological Review* 45 (October):766–786.

Bernstein, I. N., E. Kick, J. T. Leung, and B. Schulz (1977) "Charge Reduction: An Intermediary Stage in the Process of Labeling Criminal Defendants," *Social Forces* 56(December):362–384.

Berrigan, D. (1970) *The Trial of the Catonsville Nine.* Boston: Beacon Press.

Berrigan, P. (1981) "Why We Seized the Hammer," *The Progressive* 45(May): 50–51.

Best, M. H., and W. E. Connally (1978) "Nature and Its Largest Parasite." In R. C. Edwards, M. Reich, and T. E. Weisskopf (eds.) *The Capitalist System,* 2nd ed. Englewood Cliffs, N.J.: Prentice-Hall, pp. 418–425.

Binder, A. and P. Scharf (1982) "Deadly Force in Law Enforcement," *Crime and Delinquency* (January):1–23.

Bittner, E. (1967) "The Police on Skid Row," *American Sociological Review* 32(April):239–258.

Bittner, E. (1970) *The Function of the Police in Modern Society.* Washington, D.C.: U.S. Government Printing Office.

Black, D. J. (1970) "Production of Crime Rates," *American Sociological Review* 35(August):733–748.

Black, D. J. (1976) *The Behavior of Law.* New York: Academic Press.

Black, D. J. (1980) *The Manners and Customs of the Police.* New York: Academic Press.

Blau, J. R., and P. M. Blau (1982) "The Cost of Inequality: Metropolitan Structure and Violent Crime," *American Sociological Review* 47(February):114–129.

Blau, P. M., and W. R. Scott (1962) *Formal Organizations.* San Francisco: Chandler.

Block, A. A., and W. J. Chambliss (1981) *Organizing Crime.* New York: Elsevier.

Blumberg, A. S. (1967) *Criminal Justice.* Chicago: Quadrangle.

Blumdell, W. E. (1976) "Equity Funding: I Did It for the Jollies." In D. Moffett (ed.), *Swindled.* New York: Dow-Jones Books, pp. 42–89.

Blumstein, A., J. Cohen, and D. Nagin (eds.) (1978) *Deterrence and Incapacitation: Estimating the Effects of Criminal Sanctions on Crime Rates.* Washington, D.C.: National Academy of Science.

Bonacich, E. (1976) "Advanced Capitalism and Black-White Relations in the United States: A Split Labor Market Interpretation," *American Sociological Review* 41(February):33–48.

Bonger, W. (1916) *Criminality and Economic Conditions.* Trans. by Henry P. Horton. Boston: Little, Brown.

Bonnie, R. J., and C. Whitebread II (1974) *The Marijuana Conviction*. Charlottesville: University Press of Virginia.

Booth, A., D. R. Johnson, and H. M. Choldin (1977) "Correlates of City Crime Rates: Victimization Survey Versus Official Statistics," *Social Problems* **25**(December):187–197.

Borosage, R. L. (1977) "What to Do with the Intelligence Agencies," *Working Papers* **4**(Winter):37–45.

Bordua, D. J., and A. J. Reiss, Jr. (1967) "Law Enforcement." In P. F. Lazarsfeld, W. H. Sewell, and H. L. Wilensky (eds.), *The Uses of Sociology*. New York: Basic Books, pp. 275–303.

Bowart, W. H. (1978) *Operation Mind Control: Our Government's War Against Its Own People*. New York: Dell.

Bowers, W. (1974) *Executions in America*. Lexington, Mass.: Heath.

Braithwaite, J. (1979) *Inequality, Crime, and Public Policy*. London: Routledge & Kegan Paul.

Braithwaite, J., and G. Geis (1982) "On Theory and Action for Corporate Crime Control," *Crime and Delinquency* **28**(January):292–313.

Brenner, H. M. (1976) "Estimating the Social Costs of National Economic Policy: Implications for Mental and Physical Health and Criminal Aggression." Prepared for the Joint Economic Committee, U.S. Congress. Paper No. 5. Washington, D.C.: U.S. Government Printing Office.

Brewer, D., G. E. Beckett, and N. Holt (1981) "Determinate Sentencing in California: The First Year's Experience," *Journal of Research in Crime and Delinquency* **18**(July):200–229.

Britton, H. (1981) "The Serious Threat of White Collar Crime," *Vital Speeches* **47** (June 1):485–488.

Brom, T. (1980) "America's 'Outlaw' Economy . . . Jobs for Many, Protection for None," *Pacific News Service* (December 10).

Browning, F. (1981) "Life on the Margin: Atlanta Is Not the Only City Where Black Children Are Dying," *The Progressive* **45**(September):34–37.

Browning, F. (1982) "Nobody's Soft on Crime Anymore: Rethinking America's Impossible Problem," *Mother Jones* **7**(August):25–31,40–41.

Browning, F., and J. Gerassi (1980) *The American Way of Crime*. New York: Putnam.

Buckley, W. F., Jr. (1981) "Don't Jail the Non-Violent Criminal," *Rocky Mountain News* (March 27):73.

Bunker, E. (1976) "The Phony Opium War: Washington Can't Kick the Habit," *The Nation* (May 15):595–596.

Bureau of Domestic Commerce (1974) *The Cost of Crimes Against Business*. Washington, D.C.: U.S. Department of Commerce.

Burger, W. (1981) "Crime: 'Are We Not Hostages within Borders of Our Own Self-styled Civilization?' " *Rocky Mountain News* (February 15):77–78.

Burns, H. (1978) "Black People and the Tyranny of American Law." In C. E. Reasons, and R. M. Rich (eds.), *The Sociology of Law: A Conflict Perspective*. Toronto: Butterworth, pp. 353–365.

Burstein, J. (1982) "Habeas Corpus 'Reform' That Would Exalt Efficiency over Fairness," *Des Moines Register* (April 14):72.

Cahalan, M. (1979) "Trends in Incarceration in the United States Since 1880," *Crime and Delinquency* **25**(January):9–41.

Calvin, A. D. (1981) "Unemployment Among Black Youths, Demographics and Crime," *Crime and Delinquency* **27**(April):234–244.

Carmichael, S., and C. V. Hamilton (1967) *Black Power: The Politics of Liberation in America*. New York: Random House.

Carroll, L., and P. I. Jackson (1983) "Inequality, Opportunity, and Crime Rates in Central Cities," *Criminology* **21**(May):178–194.

Cartwright, J., and J. Patterson (1974) *Been Taken Lately?* Wayzata, Minn.: Ralph Turtinen Publishing Co.

Castro, A. L. (1982) "Hispanics in Prison: Reform . . . or Riots," *Civil Rights Quarterly Perspectives* **14**(Spring):8–11.

Census Bureau (1979) *Statistical Abstract of the U.S.: 1979*. Washington, D.C.: Government Printing Office.

Census Bureau (1980) *Social Indicators III*. Washington, D.C.: U.S. Government Printing Office.

Center for Research on Criminal Justice (1975) *The Iron Fist and the Velvet Glove*. Berkeley, Calif.: Center for Research on Criminal Justice.

Chambliss, W. J. (1964) "A Sociological Analysis of the Law of Vagrancy," *Social Problems* **12**(Summer):67–77.

Chambliss, W. J. (1969) *Crime and the Legal Process*. New York: McGraw-Hill.

Chambliss, W. J. (1971) "The Deterrent Influence of Punishment." In S. E. Grupp (ed.), *Theories of Punishment*. Bloomington: University of Indiana Press, pp. 196–204.

Chambliss, W. J. (1976) "Functional and Conflict Theories of Crime: The Heritage of Emile Durkheim and Karl Marx." In W. J. Chambliss and M. Mankoff (eds.), *Whose Law? What Order?* New York: Wiley, pp. 1–28.

Chambliss, W. J. (1977) "Markets, Profits, Labor and Smack," *Contemporary Crises* **1**:53–76.

Chambliss, W. J. (1978) *On the Take: From Petty Crooks to Presidents*. Bloomington: Indiana University Press.

Chambliss, W. J. (1978) "Toward a Political Economy of Crime," In C. Reasons and R. Rich (eds.), *The Sociology of Law*. pp. 191–211.

Chambliss, W. J., and M. Mankoff (eds.) (1976) *Whose Law? What Order? A Conflict Approach to Criminology*. New York: Wiley.

Chambliss, W. J., and R. F. Seidman (1971) *Law, Order, and Power*. Reading, Mass.: Addison-Wesley.

Chambliss, W. J., and R. F. Seidman (1982) *Law, Order, and Power,* 2nd ed. Reading, Mass.: Addison-Wesley.

Changing Times (1980) "White Collar Crooks," *Changing Times* **34**(December):10.

Chapman, J. (1980) *Economic Realities and the Female Offender*. Lexington, Mass.: Lexington Books.

Charleston Courier Journal (1981) Editorial (January 14).

Chevigny, P. (1969) *Police Power*. New York: Pantheon.

Chicago Tribune Wire Services (1981) "Miami Abductions Laid to Policemen," *Chicago Tribune* (April 11):4.

Chiricos, T. G., P. D. Jackson, and G. P. Waldo (1972) "Inequality in the Imposition of a Criminal Label," *Social Problems* **20**(Spring):553–572.

Chiricos, T. G., and G. P. Waldo (1975) "Socioeconomic Status and Criminal Sentencing: An Empirical Assessment of a Conflict Proposition," *American Sociological Review* **40**(December):753–772.

Christiansen, K. O. (1968) "Threshold of Tolerance in Various Population Groups Illustrated by Results from the Danish Criminologic Twin Study." In A.V.S. de Reuck and R. Porter (eds.), *The Mentally Abnormal Offender.* Boston: Little, Brown.

Christianson, S. (1981) "Our Black Prisons," *Crime and Delinquency* **27** (July):364–375.

Claiborne, R. (1978) "The Great Health Care Rip-Off," *Saturday Review* (January 7):10–16,50.

Clark, R. (1971) *Crime in America.* New York: Simon & Schuster.

Clemmer, D. (1940) *The Prison Community.* New York: Holt, Rinehart, & Winston.

Clinard, M., and R. Quinney (1973) *Criminal Behavior Systems: A Typology,* 2nd ed. New York: Holt, Rinehart, & Winston.

Clinard, M. B., and P. C. Yeager (1980) *Corporate Crime.* New York: The Free Press.

Clinard, M. B., P. C. Yeager, J. Brissette, D. Petrashek, and E. Harris (1979) *Illegal Corporate Behavior.* Washington, D.C.: U.S. Government Printing Office.

Cloward, R. A., and L. E. Ohlin (1980) "Differential Opportunity and Delinquent Subcultures." In D. H. Kelly (ed.), *Criminal Behavior: Readings in Criminology.* New York: St. Martin's Press, pp. 205–216.

Cohan, J. P. (1972) "The American Predicament: Truth No Longer Counts," *Los Angeles Times* (October 1). In M. R. Haskell and L. Yablonsky (eds.), *Criminology: Crime and Criminality,* 2nd ed. Chicago: Rand McNally, 1978, p. 172.

Cohen, A. (1966) *Deviance and Control.* Englewood Cliffs, N.J.: Prentice-Hall.

Cohen, S. (1979) "The Punitive City: Notes on the Dispersal of Social Control," *Contemporary Crises* **3**(October):339–363.

Cole, P., and M. B. Goldman (1975) "Occupation," In J. F. Fraumeni, Jr. (ed.), *Persons at High Risk of Cancer.* New York: Academic Press.

Colvin, M. (1981) "The Contradictions of Control: Prisons in Class Society," *The Insurgent Sociologist* **11**(Fall):33–45.

Colvin, M. (1982) "The 1980 New Mexico Prison Riot," *Social Problems* **29**(June):449–463.

Committee of Concerned Asian Scholars (CCAS) (1972) *The Opium Trial: Heroin and Imperialism.* Boston: New England Free Press.

Committee for the Study of Handgun Misuse (1983) *Handgun Violence Fact Sheet* (June).

Commoner, B. (1979) "The Economic Meaning of Ecology." In J. Skolnick and E. Currie (eds.), *Crisis in American Institutions.* Boston: Little, Brown.

Conklin, J. E. (1977) *Illegal but Not Criminal: Business Crime in America.* Englewood Cliffs, N.J.: Prentice-Hall.

Conrad, P. (1980) "Implications of Changing Social Policy for the Medicalization of Deviance," *Contemporary Crisis* **4**(February):195–205.

Conrad, P., and J. W. Schneider (1980) *Deviance and Medicalization: From Badness to Sickness*. St. Louis, Mo.: Mosby.

Cook, J. (1980) "The Invisible Enterprise," *Forbes* (September 29):60–71.

Cook, J. (1980) "The Invisible Enterprise: Part 3, Casino Gambling: Changing Character or Changing Fronts?" *Forbes* (October 27):89–104.

Cook, J. (1980) "The Invisible Enterprise: Part 4, The Most Abused, Misused Pension Fund in America," *Forbes* (November 10):69–82.

Cook, J., and J. Carmichael (1980) "The Invisible Enterprise: Part 5, The Mob's Legitimate Connections," *Forbes* (November 24):145–158.

Couch, S. R. (1981) "Selling and Reclaiming State Sovereignty: The Case of Coal and Iron Police," *The Insurgent Sociologist* **10**(4)–**11**(1):85–91.

Cousins, N. (1976) "Malpractice—With or Without Insurance," *Saturday Review* (March 20):4.

Cousins, N. (1979) "How the U.S. Used Its Citizens as Guinea Pigs," *Saturday Review* (November 10):10.

Cressey, D. R. (1953) *Other People's Money*. New York: The Free Press.

Cressey, D. R. (1965) "The Respectable Criminal." *Trans-action* **3**(March/April).

Cressey, D. R. (1969) *Theft of a Nation*. New York: Harper & Row.

Cressey, D. R. (1982) "Warehousing Criminals," *Society* **19**(July/August):19–22.

Critchley, T. A. (1967) *A History of Police in England and Wales, 900–1966*. London: Constable.

Cross, J. (1976) *The Supermarket Trap,* revised ed. Bloomington: University of Indiana Press.

Currie, E. (1977) "Crime: The Pervasive American Syndrome," In *These Times* **1**(7):5–11.

Currie, E. (1978) "Is Image of Violence-Prone Urban Youth a Bum Rap?" Pacific News Service. In *Des Moines Register* (March 7) OP/ED page.

Currie, E. (1982a) "Crime and Ideology," *Working Papers* **9**(May/June):26–35.

Currie, E. (1982b) "Fighting Crime," *Working Papers* **9**(July/August):16–25.

Curvin, R., and B. Porter (1979) "Blackout Looting!" *Society* **16**(May–June):68–76.

Czajkoski, E. H. (1973) "Exposing the Quasi-Judicial Role of the Probation Office," *Federal Probation* **37**:9–13.

Dahrendorf, R. (1958) "Toward a Theory of Social Conflict," *Journal of Conflict Resolution* **2**:170–183.

Danelski, D. J. (1971) "The Chicago Conspiracy Trial." In T. Becker (ed.), *Political Trials*. Indianapolis, Ind.: Bobbs-Merrill, pp. 134–180.

Davidson, R., and G. Massey (1982) Personal Communication (October 1).

Davis, A. Y. (1971) *If They Come in the Morning*. New York: The New American Library.

Davis, J. (1940) "Workers' Problems and Modern Industry." In E. Stein and J. Davis (eds.), *Labor Problems in America*. New York: Farrer & Rinehart, pp. 3–140.

De Crow, K. (1975) *Sexist Justice*. New York: Random House.

Denver Post (1982) "Preventive Detention" *Denver Post* (January 4):2B.

Des Moines Register (1982) "Who's 'Soft on Crime'?" (April 10): Opinion Page.

De Wolf, L. H. (1975) *Crime and Justice in America: A Paradox of Conscience.* New York: Harper & Row.

Diggs, J. F. (1982) " 'Tis the Season to Be Wary of Crooks," *U.S. News & Report* (December 6):78–79.

Dirks, R. L., and L. Gross (1974) *The Great Wall Street Scandal.* New York: McGraw-Hill.

Dod, S., T. Platt, H. Schwendinger, G. Shank, and P. Takagi (1976) "The Politics of Street Crime," *Crime and Social Justice* **5**(Spring/Summer):1–4.

Doe, J. (1982) "On a Warm Night Last August, I was Raped . . . ," New York Times News Services, *Des Moines Register* (September 6):7a.

Doleschal, E. (1979) "Crime—Some Popular Beliefs," *Crime and Delinquency* **25**(January):1–8.

Doleschal, E., and N. Klapmuts (1974) "We Need Criminals," *Intellectual Digest* **4**(May):15–17.

Dollars and Sense (1978) "Detroit Fights Airbags," *Dollars and Sense* **38**(July/August):6–7.

Domhoff, G. W. (1978) *The Powers That Be.* New York: Random House.

Donner, F. (1982) "The New F.B.I. Guidelines: Rounding Up the Usual Suspects," *The Nation* **97**(August 7–14):110–116.

Dorsen, N., and J. H. F. Shattuck (1974) "Executive Privilege: The President Won't Tell." In N. Dorsen, and S. Gillers (eds.), *None of Your Business: Government Secrecy in America.* New York: Viking, pp. 27–60.

Dowie, M. (1979a) "Pinto Madness." In J. H. Skolnick and E. Currie (eds.), *Crisis in American Institutions,* 4th ed. Boston: Little, Brown, pp. 23–40.

Dowie, M. (1979b) "The Corporate Crime of the Century," *Mother Jones* **9** (November):24–25.

Downie, L., Jr. (1971) *Justice Denied: The Case for the Reform of the Courts.* Baltimore, Md.: Penguin.

Durkheim, E. (1949) *The Division of Labor in Society.* Trans. by G. Simpson. New York: Free Press. (Originally published in 1893.)

Duster, T. (1970) *The Legislation of Morality: Law, Drugs and Moral Judgment.* New York: The Free Press.

Edelhertz, H. (1970) *The Nature, Impact, and Prosecution of White-Collar Crime.* Washington, D.C.: U.S. Government Printing Office.

Editorial Research Reports (1981) "Violent Crime's Return to Prominence," *Congressional Quarterly* (March 13):191–208.

Eitzen, D. S. (1978) *In Conflict and Order: Understanding Society,* Boston: Allyn & Bacon.

Eitzen, D. S. (1980) *Social Problems.* Boston: Allyn & Bacon.

Eitzen, D. S. (1982) *In Conflict and Order: Understanding Society,* 2nd ed. Boston: Allyn & Bacon.

Eitzen, D. S. (1983) *Social Problems,* 2nd ed. Boston: Allyn & Bacon.

Elsasser, G. (1981) "Violent-Crime Report Urges War on Gangs," *Chicago Tribune* (August 23):1.

Epstein, S. S. (1978) *The Politics of Cancer.* San Francisco: Sierra Club Books.

Epstein, S. (1981) "Cancer: Twisting the Statistics About Its Causes," *The Los Angeles Times* (May 19):Part II,5.

Erickson, K. (1964) "Notes on the Sociology of Deviance." In H. S. Becker (ed.), *The Other Side*. New York: Free Press.

Erickson, K. (1966) *Wayward Puritans: A Study in the Sociology of Deviance*. New York: Wiley.

Ermann, M. D., and R. J. Lundman (1981) *Organizational Deviance*. New York: Holt, Rinehart & Winston.

Ermann, M. D., and R. J. Lundman (1982) *Corporate and Governmental Deviance: Problems of Organizational Behavior in Contemporary Society*, 2nd ed. New York: Oxford University Press.

Etzioni, A. (1973) "Grass, Greed and the Slow Gain of Social Progress," *Human Behavior* **2**(February):4–5.

Fangmeier, R. A. (1980) "Myths and Realities about Prison and Jails," *The Christian Century* (March 19):323–325.

Feder, B. (1974) "Plea Bargaining: The Used-Car Lot of Justice," *The Nation* **219**(October 26):398–403.

Federal Bureau of Investigation (1983) *Uniform Crime Reports, Crime in the United States, 1982*. Washington, D.C.: U.S. Government Printing Office.

Ferdinand, T. N. (1967) "The Criminal Patterns of Boston Since 1849," *American Journal of Sociology* **72**(July):84–99.

Ferrand, M. (ed.) (1927) *Records of the Federal Convention*. New Haven, Conn.: Yale University Press.

Ferri, E. (1917) *Criminal Sociology*. Boston: Little, Brown.

Figgie International (1982) *The Figgie Report on Fear of Crime*. New York: Research & Forecasts.

Fishman, M. (1978) "Crime Waves as Ideology," *Social Problems* **25**(June):531–543.

Flanagan, T., D. van Alystyne, and M. Gottfredson (1982) *Sourcebook of Criminal Justice Statistics—1981*. Washington, D.C.: U.S. Department of Justice.

Fleetwood, B., and A. Lubow (1975) "America's Most Coddled Criminals," *New Times* (September 19):27–36.

Florida Civil Liberties Union (1964) *Rape: Selective Electrocution Based on Race*. Miami: Florida Civil Liberties Union.

Flynn, K. (1981) "Study: Higher Police Ratio Doesn't Assure Less Crime," *Rocky Mountain News* (November 8):7,18.

Fogel, D. (1975) *We Are the Living Proof: The Justice Model for Corrections*. Cincinnati, Ohio: Anderson.

Foote, C. (1956) "Vagrancy-type Law and Its Administration," *University of Pennsylvania Law Review* **104**:603–650.

Forbes (1975) "Crime in the Suites," *Forbes* (August 15):17–20.

Forbes, M. S., Jr. (1983) "Good Intentions, Bad Results," *Forbes* (February 28):23.

Fort Collins Coloradoan (1974) "Fairer Justice" *Fort Collins Coloradoan* (November 22):6.

Foucault, M. (1979) *Discipline and Punish*. New York: Vintage Books.

Frankel, M. E. (1973) *Criminal Sentences: Law without Trial.* New York: Hill & Wang.

Freeman, H. (1977) "On Consuming the Surplus," *The Progressive* **41**(February):20–21.

Friedrich, O. (1981) "We, the Jury, Find the . . . ," *Time* (September 28):44–56.

Friedrich, O. (1983) "Cheating by the Millions," *Time* (March 28):26–33.

Galliher, J. F., and J. A. Cain (1974) "Citation Support for the Mafia Myth in Criminology Textbooks," *American Sociologist* **9**(May):68–74.

Galliher, J. F., and J. L. McCartney (1977) *Criminology: Power, Crime, and Criminal Law.* Homewood, Ill.: The Dorsey Press.

Gallup, G. (1981) "No One Reason Found for Alarming Hike in Crime." Field Enterprises, Inc. In *The Denver Post* (April 9):31.

Galvin, J. (1983) " 'Dramatic Changes' Seen in Sentencing, Parole," *Justice Assistance News* **4**(September):5–8.

Gans, H. J. (1971) "The Uses of Power: The Poor Pay All," *Social Policy* **2**(July/August):20–24.

Garfinkel, H. (1947) "Research Note on Inter- and Intra-Racial Homicides," *Social Forces* **27**(May):369–381.

Garlock, J. (1982) "The Knights of Labor Courts: A Case Study of Popular Justice." In R. L. Abel (ed.), *The Politics of Informal Justice,* Vol. 1. New York: Academic Press, pp. 17–33.

Geis, G. (1972) *Not the Law's Business?* National Institute of Mental Health Center for Studies of Crime and Delinquency. Washington, D.C.: U.S. Government Printing Office.

Geis, G. (1973) "Deterring Corporate Crime." In R. Nader and M. J. Green (eds.), *Corporate Power in America.* New York: Grossman.

Geis, G. (1974) "Upperworld Crime." In A. S. Blumberg (ed.), *Current Perspectives on Criminal Behavior.* New York: Alfred A. Knopf, pp. 114–137.

Geis, G. (1974) "Deterring Corporate Crime." In C. E. Reasons (ed.), *The Criminologist: Crime and the Criminal.* Pacific Palisades, Calif.: Goodyear, pp. 246–259.

Geis, G. (1978) "The Criminal Justice System without Victimless Crimes." In P. Wickman and P. Whitten (eds.), *Readings in Criminology.* Lexington, Mass.: Heath, pp. 272–276.

Geis, G., and R. F. Meier (1977) *White-Collar Crime: Offenses in Business, Politics, and the Professions,* revised ed. New York: The Free Press.

Geis, G., and E. Stotland (1980) "Introduction." In G. Geis and E. Stotland (eds.), *White Collar Crime: Theory and Research.* Beverly Hills, Calif.: Sage.

Gersten, A. (1981) "Underground Economy's Tunnels Spread," *Rocky Mountain News* (February 8):82,85.

Gest, T. (1981) "Bail or Jail—A Tough Question for Judges," *U.S. News & World Report* (November 16):62.

Gest, T. (1982) "Who Is Watching You?" *U.S. News & World Report* (July 12):34–37.

Gest, T. (1983) "When Employees Turn Into Thieves," *U.S. News & World Report* (September 26):79–80.

Giallombardo, R. (1966) *Society of Women: A Study of a Women's Prison.* New York: Wiley.

Gibbons, D. C. (1982) *Society, Crime, and Criminal Behavior,* 4th ed. Englewood Cliffs, N.J.: Prentice-Hall.

Gibbs, J. P. (1975) *Crime, Punishment, and Deterrence.* New York: Elsevier.

Gibbs, J. (1978) "The Death Penalty, Retribution and Penal Policy," *The Journal of Criminal Law and Criminology* **69**(Fall):294–299.

Glaser, D. (1969) *The Effectiveness of a Prison and Parole System.* Indianapolis, Ind.: Bobbs-Merrill.

Glaser, D., and M. S. Zeigler (1974) "Use of the Death Penalty vs. Outrage at Murder," *Crime and Delinquency* **20**(October).

Glick, H. R. (1979) "Mandatory Sentencing: The Politics of the New Criminal Justice," *Federal Probation* **43**(March):3–9.

Goetz, R. (1980) "Petty Crimes, Severe Sentence," *The Christian Century* (April 16):428–429.

Goffman, E. (1961) *Asylums: Essays on the Social Situation of Mental Patients and Other Inmates.* Garden City, N.Y.: Doubleday Anchor Books.

Goffman, E. (1963) *Stigma: Notes on the Management of Spoiled Identity.* Englewood Cliffs, N.J.: Prentice-Hall.

Goldberger, P. (1971) "Tony Imperiale Stands Vigilant for Law and Order." In G. T. Marx (ed.), *Racial Conflict: Tension and Change in American Society.* Boston: Little, Brown, pp. 397–405.

Goldfarb, R. L. (1974) "American Prisons: Self-Defeating Concrete," *Psychology Today* **7**(January):20,22,85,88–89.

Goldfarb, R. L. (1975) *Jails: The Ultimate Ghetto of the Criminal Justice System.* Garden City, N.Y.: Anchor Books.

Goldman, J. J. (1981) "Guardian Angels; a Godsend for New Yorkers," *The Collegian,* Fort Collins, Colo. (February 18).

Goldstein, H. (1977) *Policing in a Free Society.* Cambridge, Mass.: Ballinger.

Goodell, C. (1973) *Political Prisoners in America.* New York: Random House.

Gouldner, A. (1970) *The Coming Crisis of Western Sociology.* New York: Avon.

Graham, D. (1981) "Legislators Hear Views on Iowa's Obscenity Laws," *The Des Moines Register* (November 17):3a.

Graham, J. M. (1972) "Amphetamine Politics on Capitol Hill," *Trans-action* **9**(January).

Great Britain Committee on Homosexual Offenses and Prostitution (1957) *The Wolfenden Report,* Report/Command No. 247.

Green, C. (1982) "Dill Admits Off-Duty Loopholes," *The Denver Post* (July 25):1,10.

Green, M. J., B. C. Moore, Jr., and B. Wasserstein (1972) *The Closed Enterprise System.* New York: Bantam Books.

Greenberg, D. F. (1977) "The Dynamics of Oscillatory Punishment Processes," *The Journal of Criminal Law and Criminology* **68**(4):643–651.

Greenberg, D. F. (1977) "The Correctional Effects of Corrections: A Survey of Evaluations." In D. F. Greenberg (ed.), *Corrections and Punishment.* Beverly Hills, Calif.: Sage, pp. 111–148.

Greenberg, D. F. (1981) *Crime and Capitalism: Readings in Marxist Criminology.* Palo Alto, Calif.: Mayfield.

Greenberg, D. F., and D. Humphries (1981) "The Cooptation of Fixed Sentencing Reform." In D. F. Greenberg (ed.), *Crime and Capitalism.* Palo Alto, Calif.: Mayfield, pp. 367–386.

Greenwald, J. (1982) "Playing Tax Games," *Time* (April 12):55–59.

Greenwood, P. W. (1981) "Private-Enterprise Prisons?" *Los Angeles Times* (May 11):5.

Greenwood, P. W., J. M. Chaiken, J. Petersilia, and L. Prusoff (1975) *The Criminal Investigation Process: Observations and Analysis,* Vol. III. Study done by the Rand Corporation. Washington, D.C.: U.S. Department of Justice.

Griffin, S. (1976) "Rape: The All-American Crime." In W. J. Chambliss and M. Markoff (eds.), *Whose Law? What Order? A Conflict Approach to Criminology.* New York: Wiley, pp. 225–239.

Griswold, D. B., and M. D. Wiatrowski (1983) "The Emergency of Determinate Sentencing," *Federal Probation* **47**(June):28–35.

Gross, B. (1981) "Is the Left Guilty of Criminal Neglect?" *In These Times* **6**(4):11,13.

Gross, B. (1982) "Stealing the Right's Thunder: Some Anticrime Proposals for Progressives," *The Nation* **234**(5):137–140.

Gross, H. (1979) *A Theory of Punishment.* New York: Oxford University Press.

Gussow, J. (1980) "What Corporations Have Done to Our Food," *Business & Society Review* **35**(Fall):19–25.

Gutmann, P. (1980) "Latest Notes from the Subterranean Economy," *Business & Society Review* **34**:25–30.

Haas, E. J., and T. E. Drabek (1973) *Complex Organizations.* New York: Macmillan.

Hagan, J. (1975) "The Social and Legal Construction of Criminal Justice: A Study of the Pre-Sentencing Process," *Social Problems* **22**(June):620–637.

Hagan, J., J. D. Hewitt, and D. F. Alwin (1979) "Ceremonial Justice: Crime and Punishment in a Loosely Coupled System," *Social Forces* **58**(2):506–527.

Hagan, J., E. T. Silva, and J. H. Simpson (1977) "Conflict and Consensus in the Designation of Deviance," *Social Forces* **56**(December):320–340.

Hall, J. (1952) *Theft, Law, and Society,* 2nd ed. Indianapolis, Ind.: Bobbs-Merrill.

Hall, R. H. (1977) *Organizations: Structure and Process,* revised ed. Englewood Cliffs, N.J.: Prentice-Hall.

Halperin, M. H., J. J. Berman, R. L. Borosage, and C. M. Marwick (1976) *The Lawless State: The Crimes of the U.S. Intelligence Agencies.* New York: Penguin.

Harring, S. (1981) "The Taylorization of Police Work: Policing the 80s," *The Insurgent Sociologist* **10**(4)–**11**(1):25–32.

Harrington, M. (1979) "Social Retreat and Economic Stagnation," *Dissent* **26**(Spring):131–134.

Harris, M. (1983) "America's Capital of Fraud," *Money* **12**(November):225–237.

Harris, M. (1981) *America Now: The Anthropology of a Changing Culture.* New York: Simon & Schuster.

Harris, R. (1977) "Crime in the FBI," *The New Yorker* (August 8):30–42.

Hartjen, C. A. (1978) *Crime and Criminalization,* 2nd ed. New York: Holt, Rinehart & Winston/Praeger.

Haskell, M. R., and L. Yablonsky (1974) *Crime and Delinquency,* 2nd ed. Chicago: Rand McNally.

Hay, G. A., and D. Kelley (1974) "An Empirical Survey of Price Fixing Conspiracies," *The Journal of Law and Economics* **17**(April):13–38.

Hefferman, E. (1972) *Making It in Prison: The Square, The Cool, and The Life.* New York: Wiley.

Helmer, J. (1975) *Drugs and Minority Oppression.* New York: Seabury Press.

Henssenstamm, F. K. (1971) "Bumper Stickers and the Cops," *Trans-action* **8**(February):32–33.

Herbert, H. J. (1983) "Files Show GM Knew X-Car Brakes Locked," *Denver Post* (October 21):1A–2A.

Herman, E. S. (1970) *Atrocities in Vietnam: Myths and Realities.* Philadelphia: Pilgrim Press.

Huemann, M. (1978) *Plea Bargaining: The Experience of Prosecutors, Judges, and Defense Attorneys.* Chicago: University of Chicago Press.

Hightower, J. (1975) *Eat Your Heart Out: Food Profiteering in America.* New York: Vintage.

Hills, S. L. (1971) *Crime, Power and Morality.* Toronto: Chandler.

Himmelstein, J. L. (1978) "Drug Politics Theory: Analysis and Critique," *Journal of Drug Issues* **8**(Winter):37–52.

Hindelang, M. J., M. R. Gottfredson, and J. Garofalo (1978) *Victims of Personal Crime: An Empirical Foundation for a Theory of Personal Victimization.* Cambridge, Mass.: Ballinger.

Hindelang, M. J., T. Hirschi, and J. Weis (1979) "Correlates of Deliquency: The Illusion of Discrepancy Between Self-Report and Official Measures," *American Sociological Review* **44**:995–1014.

Hindelang, M. J., T. Hirschi, and J. Weis (1981) *Measuring Delinquency.* Beverly Hills, Calif.: Sage.

Hirschi, T. (1969) *Causes of Delinquency.* Berkeley: University of California Press.

Hobsbawm, E. J. (1959) *Primitive Rebels: Studies in Archaic Forms of Social Movements in the 19th and 20th Centuries.* New York: Norton.

Holahan, J. F., and P. A. Henningsen (1972) "The Economics of Heroin." In P. M. Wald and P. B. Hull (eds.), *Dealing with Drug Abuse: A Report to the Ford Foundation.* New York: Praeger.

Hopkins, A. (1979) "Pressure Groups and the Law," *Contemporary Crises* **3**(January):69–82.

Hopkins, A. (1981) "Class Bias in the Criminal Law," *Contemporary Crises* **5**(October):385–394.

Hornung, D. N. M. (1970) "Blue-Collar Theft." In E. O. Smigel and H. L. Ross (eds.), *Crime Against Bureaucracy.* New York: Van Nostrand, pp. 46–61.

Horowitz, I. L., and M. Liebowitz (1968) "Social Deviance and Political Marginality: Toward a Redefinition of the Relation between Sociology and Politics," *Social Problems* **15**:3(Winter):280–296.

Huff, C. R. (1980) "Historical Explanations of Crime: From Demons to Politics."

In D. Kelly (ed.), *Criminal Behavior: Readings in Criminology*. New York: St. Martin's Press, pp. 155–174.

Hughes, G. (1982) "Who Should Go to Prison?" *New York Review of Books* (April 1):39–41.

Human Behavior (1979) "Mandatory Sentences," *Human Behavior* (May):60.

Humphries, D. (1979) "Crime and the State." In A. J. Szymanski and T. G. Goertzel (eds.), *Sociology: Class, Consciousness and Contradictions*. New York: Van Nostrand.

Humphries, D., and D. Wallace (1980) "Capitalist Accumulation and Urban Crime, 1950–1971," *Social Problems* **28**(December):179–193.

Hunt, M. (1972) *The Mugging*. New York: Atheneum.

Hurtt, W. A. (1981) "Judges Burned out by Rising Case Loads," *Rocky Mountain News* (May 10):63–64.

Hutchins, R. M. (1976) "Is Democracy Possible?" *The Center Magazine* **9**(January/February):2–6.

Hylton, J. (1982) "Rhetoric and Reality: A Critical Appraisal of Community Correctional Programs," *Crime and Delinquency* **28**(3):341–373.

Ianni, F. A. J., and F. Ianni (eds.) (1976) *The Crime Society: Organized Crime and Corruption in America*. New York: New American Library.

Imlay, C. H., and C. R. Glasheen (1971) "See What Conditions Your Conditions Are In," *Federal Probation* **35**:3–11.

Ingraham, B. (1969) "Political Crime in the United States and Japan," *Issues in Criminology* **4**(Fall):145–169.

Institute for the Study of Labor and Economic Crisis (1982) *The Iron Fist and the Velvet Glove,* 3rd ed. San Francisco: Crime and Social Justice Associates.

Isaacson, W. (1981) "The Duel over Gun Control," *Time* (March 23):13.

ISR Newsletter (1981) "Women in Prison: Harsh Sentences and Little Rehabilitation," *Institute for Social Research* (Autumn):4–5.

Jackson, G. (1970) *Soledad Brother: The Prison Letters of George Jackson*. New York: Bantam.

Jackson, R. L. (1982) "Tax-Cheating Loss $80 Billion a Year, GAO Report Says," *Denver Post* (March 18):1,7A.

James, D. R., and M. Soref (1981) "Profit Constraints on Managerial Autonomy: Managerial Theory and the Unmaking of the Corporation President," *American Sociological Review* **46**(February):1–18.

Jankovic, I. (1977) "Labor Market and Imprisonment," *Crime and Social Justice* **8**(Fall/Winter):17–31.

Johnson, B. C. (1976) "Taking Care of Labor: The Police in American Politics," *Theory and Society* **3**:89–117.

Johnson, J. M., and J. D. Douglas (eds.) (1978) *Crime at the Top: Deviance in Business and the Professions*. Philadelphia: Lippincott.

Jones, J. H. (1981) *Bad Blood*. New York: Free Press.

Jurik, N. (1980) "Women Ex-offenders in the TARP Experiment." In P. Rossi, R. A. Berk, and K. Lenihan (eds.), *Money, Work and Crime*. New York: Academic Press, pp. 319–334.

Justice Assistance News (1981) "Reagan Outlines Crime Control Strategy," *Justice Assistance News* **2**(November):1.

Justice Assistance News (1983) "Blacks, Hispanics Imprisoned Longer Than Whites, Study Says," *Justice Assistance News* **4**(September):4.

Kadish, S. H. (1967) "The Crisis of Overcriminalization," *Annals of the American Academy of Political and Social Science* **374**(November):157–170.

Kadish, S. H. (1971) "Overcriminalization." In L. Radzinowicz and M. E. Wolfang (eds.), *Crime and Justice,* Vol. 1, *The Criminal in Society*. New York: Basic Books, pp. 56–71.

Kairys, D., J. Kadane, and J. Lehorsky (1977) "Jury Representativeness: A Mandate for Multiple Source Lists," *California Law Review* **65**(July):776–827.

Kakalik, J. S., and S. Wildhorn (1971) *The Private Police Industry: Its Nature and Extent*. Vol. 2. Rand Corporation Study for the National Institute of Law Enforcement and Criminal Justice. Washington, D.C.: Government Printing Office.

Kakalik, J. S., and S. Wildhorn (1977) *The Private Police: Security and Danger*. New York: Russak.

Kalette, D. (1983) "GM Pact: A Travesty or a Beginning?" *USA Today* (October 20):B1–2.

Kalven, H., Jr., and H. Zeisel (1966) *The American Jury*. Boston: Little, Brown.

Kaplan, B. D. (1981) "In Poland: Solidarity, Sobriety," Hearst News Service. *Los Angeles Herald Examiner* (March 1):A4.

Kelly, O. (1983) "Why Pentagon Pays $44 for a Light Bulb," *U.S. News & World Report* (August 1):29.

Kelly, O. (1983) "Offshore Tax Havens Lure Main Street Money," *U.S. News & World Report* (August 1):31–33.

Kelly, O., and T. Gest (1982) "Reagan Revolution Takes Firm Hold at Justice," *U.S. News & World Report* (April 26):24–26.

Kennedy, E. M. (1976) "For Mandatory Minimum Sentences," *Rocky Mountain News* (January 4).

Kerby, P. (1981) "Predators in Our Society Aren't Born, They Are Made," *Los Angeles Times* (July 23):Part II, p.1.

Kessler, J. (1981) "Gambling on Sports Comes Out of the Closet." Editorial Research Reports. *The Des Moines Register* (November 14):5A.

Key, V. O., Jr. (1949) *Southern Politics*. New York: Vintage.

King, Larry L. (1975) "White Collar Crime," *New Times* (June 13):8.

Kilpatrick, J. (1983) "Boeing's Greed Shakes Faith in System," *Fort Collins Coloradoan* (September 2):A6.

Kinloch, G. C. (1977) *Sociological Theory: Its Development and Major Paradigms*. New York: McGraw-Hill.

Kinsey, A., W. Pomeroy, and C. E. Martin (1949) *Sexual Behavior in the Human Male*. Philadelphia: Saunders.

Kitsuse, J. I., and A. V. Cicourel (1963) "A Note on the Uses of Official Statistics," *Social Problems* **11**(Summer):131–139.

Kittrie, N. N. (1971) *The Right to Be Different: Deviance and Enforced Therapy*. Baltimore: The Johns Hopkins University Press.

Klare, M. T. (1975) "Rent-a-Cop: The Boom in Private Police," *The Nation* **221**(November 15):486–491.

Kleck, G. (1981) "Racial Discrimination in Criminal Sentencing: A Critical Evaluation of the Evidence with Additional Evidence on the Death Penalty," *American Sociological Review* **46**(December):783–805.

Klein, L. R., B. Forst, and V. Filatov (1978) "The Deterrent Effect of Capital Punishment." In A. Blumstein et al. (eds.), *Deterrence and Incapacitation.* Washington, D.C.: National Academy of Sciences, pp. 336–360.

Klein, M., K. S. Teilmann. J. A. Styles, S. B. Lincoln, and S. Labin-Rosenweig (1976) "The Explosion in Police Diversion Programs: Evaluating the Structural Dimensions of a Social Fad." In M. Klein (ed.), *The Juvenile Justice System.* Beverly Hills, Calif.: Sage, pp. 101–119.

Knapp Commission (1972) *Knapp Commission Report on Police Corruption.* New York: George Braziller.

Knoll, E., and J. N. McFadden (eds.) (1970) *War Crimes and the American Conscience.* New York: Holt, Rinehart & Winston.

Kohn, H. (1976) "The Nixon-Hughes-Lansky Connection," *Rolling Stone* (May 20):41–50,77–78.

Kolko, G. (1963) *The Triumph of Conservatism.* New York: Free Press of Glencoe.

Kolko, G. (1965) *Railroads and Regulations.* Princeton, N.J.: Princeton University Press.

Kotulak, R. (1982) "New Twist to Age-Old Problem: More and More Elderly Turn to Crime," *Chicago Tribune* (June 6):1.

Kramer, R. C. (1982) "Corporate Crime: An Organizational Perspective." In P. Wickman and T. Dailey (eds.), *White Collar and Economic Crime.* Lexington, Mass.: Lexington Books, pp. 75–94.

Kwitny, J. (1981) "The Great Transportation Conspiracy," *Harper's Magazine* **262**(February):14–21.

LEAA Newsletter (1977) **6**(August 7).

Leary, M. E. (1982) "California's Prop. 8: Crackdown on Crime or Political Ploy?" *Des Moines Register* (July 22):9a.

Lee, A. M. (1982) "Letter to the Editor," *The Nation* **235**(18):546.

Lee, M. A. (1982) "CIA: Carcinogen," *The Nation* (June 5):675.

LeGrand, C. (1973) "Rape and Rape Laws: Sexism in Society and Law," *California Law Review* **61**:919–942.

Leiser, B. M. (1979) *Liberty, Justice, and Morals: Contemporary Value Conflicts.* New York: Macmillan.

Lekachman, R. (1979) "The Spector of Full Employment," In J. H. Skolnick and E. Currie (eds.), *Crisis in American Institutions,* 4th ed. Boston: Little, Brown, pp. 50–58.

Lemert, E. (1951) *Social Pathology.* New York: McGraw-Hill.

Lemert, E. (1967) *Human Deviance, Social Problems, and Social Control.* Englewood Cliffs, N.J.: Prentice-Hall.

Lemert, E. M., and F. Dill (1978) *Offenders in the Community.* Lexington, Mass.: Lexington Books.

Lemert, E. M., and J. Rosberg (1948) *The Administration of Justice to Minority Groups in Los Angeles County.* Berkeley: University of California Press.

Lens, S. (1979) "Dead on the Job," *The Progressive* **43**(November):50–52.

Leo, J. (1981) "What Crime Does to the Victims: Grief, Anger, Paranoia and a New Quest for Community," *Time* (March 23):29–30.

Lerman, P. (1975) *Community Treatment and Social Control: A Critical Analysis of Juvenile Correctional Policy*. Chicago: University of Chicago Press.

Levine, J. P. (1976) "The Potential for Crime Overreporting in Criminal Victimization Surveys," *Criminology* **14**(November):307–330.

Lewin, J. (1982) "Future Cop," *Parade* (March 21):4–5.

Lewis, O. (1971) *Five Families: Mexican Case Studies in the Culture of Poverty*. New York: New American Library.

Liazos, A. (1972) "The Poverty of the Sociology of Deviance: Nuts, Sluts, and Preverts," *Social Problems* **20**(Summer):103–120.

Liazos, A. (1978) "School, Alienation, and Delinquency," *Crime and Delinquency* **24**(July):355–370.

Liazos, A. (1982) *People First: An Introduction to Social Problems*. Boston: Allyn & Bacon.

Lienert, P. (1983) "Discrimination Settlement Will Cost GM $42.5 Million," *Denver Post* (October 19):3A.

Linden, G. M., and W. W. Beck (1981) "White-Collar Crime in the Dallas Public Schools," *Phi Delta Kappan* **62**(April):574–577.

Lipman, M. (1973) *Stealing*. New York: Harper's Magazine Press.

Lipson, M. (1975) *On Guard: The Business of Private Security*. New York: Quadrangle/The New York Times Book Co.

Lipton, D., R. M. Martinson, and J. Wilkes (1975) *The Effectiveness of Correctional Treatment: A Survey of Treatment Evaluation Studies*. New York: Praeger.

Lombroso, C. (1876) *L'Uomo Delinquente*. Milan, Italy: Hoepli.

Lundman, R. J. (1980) *Police and Policing: An Introduction*. New York: Holt, Rinehart & Winston.

MacNamara, D. E. J. (1977) "The Medical Model in Corrections," *Criminology* **14**(February):439–447.

MacNamara, D. E. J. (1983) "Medical Model in Corrections: Requiescent in Pace." In J. L. Sullivan, J. L. Victor, and D. E. J. MacNamara (eds.), *Criminal Justice 83/84*. Gilford, Conn.: Dushkin, pp. 237–239.

Magnuson, E. (1981) "The Curse of Violent Crime," *Time* (March 23):16–21.

Magnuson, E. (1981) "The Prison Nightmare," *Time* (June 8):16–18.

Malloy, M. T. (1974) "A Roulette Wheel Spins at the Bar of Justice," *National Observer* (September 14):5.

Maltz, M. D. (1977) "Crime Statistics: A Historical Perspective," *Crime and Delinquency* **23**(January):32–40.

Mankoff, M. (1976) "Perspectives on the Problem of Crime: Introduction." In W. J. Chambliss and M. Mankoff (eds.), *Whose Law? What Order? A Conflict Approach to Criminology*. New York: Wiley, pp. 187–192.

Mankoff, M. (1976) "The Political Economy of Law Enforcement: Introduction." In W. J. Chambliss and M. Mankoff (eds.), *Whose Law? What Order? A Conflict Approach to Criminology*. New York: Wiley, pp. 125–128.

Mann, J. (1981) "Trouble with a 'V' for Video Games," *The Los Angeles Times*. Reprinted in *The Des Moines Register* (November 14):1a,6a.

Manning, P. K. (1974) "Dramatic Aspects of Policing: Selected Propositions," *Sociology and Social Research* **59**:21–29.

Manning, P. K. (1977) *Police Work: The Social Organization of Policing*. Cambridge, Mass.: MIT Press.

Mapes, G. (1970) "Unequal Justice: A Growing Disparity in Criminal Sentences Troubles Legal Expects," *Wall Street Journal* (September 9):1.

Marks, J. (1979) "Sex, Drugs, and the CIA," *Saturday Review* (February 3):12–16.

Martin, D. (1976) *Battered Wives*. San Francisco: Glide.

Martin, J. (1982) "Prisons Mean Business," *In These Times* (February 24):5.

Martinson, R. (1974) "What Works?—Questions and Answers about Prison Reform," *The Public Interest* **35**(Spring):22–54.

Martinson, R. (1979) "Symposium on Sentencing," *Hofstra Law Review* **7**(Winter):243–258.

Marx, K. (1904) *Contribution to a Critique of Political Economy*. Trans. by N. I. Stone. Chicago: Charles H. Kerr.

Marx, K. (1967) *Capital: A Critique of Political Economy*. New York: International Publishers. (Originally published in 1866.)

Marx, K, and F. Engels (1955) *The Communist Manifesto*. New York: Appleton-Century-Crofts. (Originally published in 1848.)

Mattick, H. (1974) "The Contemporary Jails of the United States: An Unknown and Neglected Area of Justice." In D. Glaser (ed.), *Handbook of Criminology*. Skokie, Ill.: Rand McNally, pp. 777–848.

Matza, D. (1964) *Delinquency and Drift*. New York: Wiley.

Maxfield, M. G., D. A. Lewis, and R. Szoc (1980) "Producing Official Crimes: Verified Crime Reports as Measures of Police Output," *Social Science Quarterly* **61**(September):221–236.

Mayer, C. E. (1982) "House Vetoes Disclosure Bill for Used Cars," *Denver Post* (May 27):27a.

McCaghy, C. H. (1976) *Deviant Behavior: Crime, Conflict, and Interest Groups*. New York: Macmillan.

McCaghy, C. H. (1980) *Crime in American Society*. New York: Macmillan.

McCarthy, C. (1981) "Conscientious Hard-Line Judge (Hard on Prevailing Myths)," *Des Moines Register* (November 5):10a.

McCarthy, C. (1981) "It's Christmastime for Poor and Homeless, Too," *Des Moines Register* (December 21):7a.

McCarthy, C. (1982) "The Message Coal Miners Hear: Washington Doesn't Care," *Des Moines Register* (February 24):11a.

McCloskey, P. N., Jr. (1972) *Truth and Untruth: Political Deceit in America*. New York: Simon & Schuster.

McCloskey, P. N., Jr. (1981) "A Challenge to American Justice," *The Los Angeles Times* (October 20):Part II,5.

McConnell, W, H. (1978) "Political Trials East and West." In C. E. Reasons and R. M. Rich (eds.), *The Sociology of Law: A Conflict Perspective*. Toronto: Butterworth.

McCorkle, L. W. (1970) "Social Structures in a Prison." In N. Johnston, L. Savitz, and M. E. Wolfgang (eds.), *The Sociology of Punishment and Correction,* 2nd ed. New York: Wiley.

McCoy, A. W. (1972) *The Politics of Heroin in Southeast Asia*. New York: Harper & Row.

McCullough, W. W. (1981) "White-Collar Crooks *Are* Crooks," *Los Angeles Times* (November 4):Part 1,7.

McDonald, W. F. (ed.) (1977) *Criminal Justice and the Victim.* Beverly Hills, Calif.: Sage.

McDowall, D., and C. Lifton (1983) "Collective Security and the Demand for Legal Handguns," *American Journal of Sociology* **88**(May):1146–1161.

McGarrah, R., and D. Kusnet (1981) "Where Have They All Gone?" *In These Times* (December 6):11.

McGhee, D. (1977) "Workplace Hazards: No Women Need Apply," *The Progressive* **41**(October):25.

McIntosh, M. (1973) "The Growth of Racketeering," *Economy and Society* (February):35–69.

Mehan, H., and H. Wood (1975) *The Reality of Ethnomethodology.* New York: Wiley—Interscience.

Melanson, P. H. (1983) "The Human Guinea Pigs at Bikini," *The Nation* **33**(July 9–16):48–50.

Mendelson, M. A. (1974) *Tender Loving Greed.* New York: Knopf.

Menninger, K. (1971) "Love against Hate." In S. E. Grupp (ed.), *Theories of Punishment.* Bloomington: Indiana University Press, pp. 243–254.

Menninger, W. (1979) "The Pernicious Pattern of Racism in Prisons," *Rocky Mountain News* (April 27):44.

Merton, R. K. (1968) *Social Theory and Social Structure,* 2nd ed. New York: Free Press.

Merton, R. K., and R. Nisbet (1976) *Contemporary Social Problems.* New York: Harcourt, Brace, Jovanovich.

Messinger, S. L. (1973) "The Year 2000 and the Problem of Criminal Justice," Paper presented at the Conference on Criminal Justice meetings, Chicago.

Mianowany, J. (1982) "Nation's State Prisons on Verge of Disaster," *Rocky Mountain News* (January 10):46.

Miller, D. (1980) *Alternatives to Incarceration: From Total Institutions to Total Systems.* Unpublished dissertation. University of California at Berkeley.

Miller, D., A. Rosenthal, D. Miller, and S. Ruzek (1971) "Public Knowledge of Criminal Penalties." In S. E. Grupp (ed.), *Theories of Punishment.* Bloomington: University of Indiana Press, pp. 205–226.

Miller, J. (1976) "Testing the Seeds of Destruction," *The Progressive* **40**(December):37–40.

Miller, M. B. (1974) "At Hard Labor: Rediscovering the 19th Century Prison," *Issues in Criminology* **9**(Spring):91–114.

Miller, T. (1977) "Behind Bars," *The Progressive* **41**(January):13–24.

Miller, W. (1958) "Lower-Class Culture as a Generating Milieu of Gang Delinquency," *Journal of Social Issues* **14**:5–19.

Mills, C. W. (1940) "Situated Actions and Vocabularies of Motive," *American Sociological Review* **5**(6):904–913.

Mills, C. W. (1959) *The Sociological Imagination.* New York: Oxford University Press.

Minnesota Department of Corrections/Research Department (1981) *Minnesota Community Corrections Act Evaluation: General Report.*

Minor, W. W. (1975) "Political Crime, Political Justice, and Political Prisoners," *Criminology* **12**(February):385–398.

Mintz, M., and J. S. Cohen (1971) *America, Inc.: Who Owns and Operates the United States.* New York: Dial Press.

Mitford, J. (1971) "Kind and Unusual Punishment in California," *Atlantic* **227**(March):45–52.

Mitford, J. (1973) "Experiments behind Bars," *Atlantic* **229**(January):64–73.

Mitford, J. (1973) *Kind and Usual Punishment: The Prison Business.* New York: Knopf.

Mitford, J. (1974) "Experiments Behind Doors: Doctors, Drug Companies, and Prisoners," *Atlantic* **231**(January):64–73.

Mitford, J. (1982) "An Update on the 'Prison Business,' " *The Nation* **235** (14):424–426.

Model, F. P. (1981) "The Epiphany of Charlie Silberman," *The Civil Rights Quarterly/Perspectives* **12**(Fall 1980–Winter 1981):29–33.

Moore, R. H. (1981) "The Criminal Justice Non-System." In R. G. Culbertson and M. R. Tezak (eds.), *Order under Law: Readings in Criminal Justice.* Prospect Heights, Ill.: Waveland Press, pp. 40–47.

Morison, S. E., and H. S. Commager (1950) *The Growth of the American Republic,* Vol. 2. New York: Oxford University Press.

Morris, M. (ed.) (1975) *Instead of Prisons: A Handbook for Abolitionists.* Syracuse, N.Y.: Prison Research Education Action Project.

Morris, N. (1974) *The Future of Imprisonment.* Chicago: University of Chicago Press.

Morris, N., and G. Hawkins (1970) *The Honest Politician's Guide to Crime Control.* Chicago: University of Chicago Press.

Mouat, L. (1979) "Are U.S. Cops Brutal? Investigating Investigators," *Rocky Mountain News* (September 9):69.

Moyers, B. (1979) "Keep Out of the Reach of Children," *Bill Moyer's Journal,* Public Broadcasting (April 30).

Myers, S. L., Jr. (1980) "Why Are Crimes Underreported? What Is the Crime Rate? Does It Really Matter?" *Social Science Quarterly* **61**(June):23–43.

Nader, R., and M. Green (1972) "Crime in the Suites," *New Republic* (April 29):20–21.

Nagel, S. (1966) "The Tipped Scales of Justice," *Trans-action* (May–June):3–9.

Nagy, D. (1981) "Safe at Home—Behind a Set of Iron Bars," *U.S. News & World Report* (July 13):55–56.

Nathan, R. S. (1980) "Coddled Criminals," *Harper's* **260**(January):30–39.

National Council on Crime and Delinquency (1980) *A New Correctional Policy for California: Developing Alternatives to Prison.* San Francisco: Research Center West.

National Criminal Justice Information and Statistics Service (1977) *Expenditure and Employment Data for the Criminal Justice System.* Washington, D.C.: U.S. Government Printing Office.

Nelson, J. (1980) "New York's Heroin Connection: The Kids of 115th Street," *Pacific News Service* (September 5).

Nettler, G. (1979) "Criminal Justice," *Annual Review of Sociology* **5**:27–52.

Newman, D. J. (1977) "White-Collar Crime: An Overview and Analysis." In G. Geis and R. F. Meier (eds.), *White Collar Crime*. New York: Free Press.

Newsweek (1972) "How Equal Is Justice?" *Newsweek* (October 30):97.

Newsweek (1979) "Silkwood Vindicated," *Newsweek* (May 28):40.

Newton, C. H., R. G. Shelden, and S. W. Jenkins (1975) "The Homogenization Process within the Juvenile Justice System," *International Journal of Criminology and Penology* **3**:213–227.

O'Connor, J. (1973) *The Fiscal Crisis of the State*. New York: St. Martin's Press.

Ognibene, P. (1979) "The Politics of the Draft," *Saturday Review* (June 23):12.

Olsen, M. (1965) *The Logic of Collective Action*. Cambridge, Mass.: Harvard University Press.

Osborne, L. (1974) "Beyond Stigma Theory," *Issues in Criminology* **9** (Spring):71–90.

Ostrow, R. J. (1982) "Drug Use Is Cause of Crime, Study Finds," *Los Angeles Times* (March 21):1.

Ostrow, R. J. (1981) "Public Puts Crime Control Ahead of Defense, Poll Finds," *Los Angeles Times* (March 28): Part 1,3.

Ostrow, R. J. (1981) "Violent Crime up 13% in 1980," *Los Angeles Times* (April 1):1.

O'Toole, G. (1978) *The Private Sector: Rent-a-Cops, Private Spies and the Police Industrial Complex*. New York: Norton.

Overby, A. (1970) "Discrimination in the Administration of Justice." In Johnston, Savitz, and Wolfgang (eds.), *The Sociology of Punishment and Correction,* 2nd ed. New York: Wiley, pp. 265–270.

Packer, H. L. (1968) *The Limits of the Criminal Sanction*. Stanford, Calif.: Stanford University Press.

Pallas, J., and B. Barber (1980) "From Riot to Revolution," In T. Platt and P. Takagi (eds.), *Punishment and Penal Discipline*. Berkeley, Calif.: Crime and Social Justice Associates, pp. 146–154.

Palmer, T. (1983) "The 'Effectiveness' Issue Today: An Overview," *Federal Probation* **47**(January):3–10.

Parenti, M. (1978) *Power and the Powerless*. New York: St. Martin's.

Parenti, M. (1980) *Democracy for the Few,* 3rd ed. New York: St. Martin's.

Park, R. E., and E. W. Burgess (1924) *Introduction to the Science of Sociology*. Chicago: University of Chicago Press.

Parker, D. B. (1976) *Crime by Computer*. New York: Charles Scribner's Sons.

Parks, E. (1976) "From Constabulary to Police Society: Implications for Social Control." In W. J. Chambliss and M. Mankoff (eds.), *Whose Law? What Order? A Conflict Approach to Criminology*. New York: Wiley, pp. 129–147.

Parsons, T. (1951) *The Social System*. New York: Free Press.

Parsons, T. (1962) "The Law and Social Control." In W. M. Evans (ed.), *Law and Sociology: Exploratory Essays*. New York: Free Press.

Parsons, T. (1977) *Evolution of Societies*. Englewood Cliffs, N.J.: Prentice-Hall.

Passell, P. (1975) "The Deterrent Effect in the Death Penalty," *Stanford Law Review* **28**(1):61–80.

Peirce, N. R. (1982) "Settling Conflicts with a Neighborhood Justice System," *Des Moines Register* (June 18):7a.

Percy, C. H. (1974) *Growing Old in the Country of the Young.* New York: McGraw-Hill.

Perrow, C. (1979) *Complex Organizations: A Critical Essay,* 2nd ed. Glenview, Ill.: Scott, Foresman, and Co.

Pertschuk, M. (1982) "Reaganism Is Harmful to Your Health," *The Nation* (July 24–31): 65,83–84.

Petersen, D. M. (1971) "Informal Norms and Police Practices: The Traffic Tickets Quota System," *Sociology and Social Research* **55**:354–362.

Petroski, W. (1982) "Ferreting Out Welfare Fraud," *Des Moines Register* (March 28):1A,7A.

Petroski, W. (1982) "Each Inmate's Cost Averages $49 per Day," *Des Moines Register* (August 23):3a.

Petti, L. (1982) "Civil Liberties Under Attack from the Right," *Crime and Social Justice* **17**(Summer):83–85.

Pfohl, S. J. (1980) "Deciding on Dangerousness: Predictions of Violence as Social Control." In T. Platt and P. Takagi (eds.), *Punishment and Penal Discipline.* Berkeley, Calif.: Crime and Social Justice Associates, pp. 129–141.

Phalon, R. (1979) "The Game Where Nobody Loses but Everybody Loses," *Forbes* (April 16):55–63.

Phillips, K. (1982) "Private-Enterprise Law Enforcement?" *Des Moines Register* (April 24):4a.

Phillips, L., H. L. Votey, Jr., and D. Maxwell (1972) "Crime, Youth and the Labor Market," *Journal of Political Economy* **80**(May–June):491–504.

Phillips, W. G. (1974) "The Government's Classification System." In N. Dorsen and J. H. F. Shattuck (eds.), *None of Your Business.* New York: Viking.

Pileggi, N. (1981) "The Godfather and the Guards," *New York* (April 27):34–37.

Pious, R. M. (1971) "Pretrial and Nontrial in the Lower Criminal Courts," *Current History* **61**(July):20–26.

Pitts, G. L. (1983) "Merchants' Credit Fraud Epidemic," *Denver Post* (October 27):D1–2.

Piven, F. F., and R. A. Cloward (1971) *Regulating the Poor.* New York: Pantheon.

Piven, F. F., and R. A. Cloward (1982) *The New Class War: Reagan's Attack on the Welfare State and Its Consequences.* New York: Pantheon.

Platt, A. (1972) "The Triumph of Benevolence: The Origins of the Juvenile Justice Systems in the United States." Berkeley: University of California (mimeograph).

Platt, A. (1978) " 'Street' Crime—A View from the Left," *Crime and Social Justice* **9**(Spring/Summer):26–34.

Pope, L. (1978) "Surveys Claim American Businesses Don't Protect Selves in Computer Crime," *Rocky Mountain News "Trend"* (July 16):7.

Porter, S. (1982) "Hiring Safeguards Required to Combat Theft by Employees," *The Denver Post* (March 20):7A.

Posner, R. A. (1980) "Optimal Sentences for White-Collar Criminals," *American Criminal Law Review* **17**(Spring):409–418.

Pound, R. (1942) *Social Control through Law*. New Haven, Conn.: Yale University Press.

Pound, R. (1943) "A Survey of Interests," *Harvard Law Review* **57**(October).

Powers, T. (1979) "Inside the Department of Dirty Tricks," *Atlantic* **244**(August):33–64.

Presidential Commission on Civil Disorders (1968) *Report of the National Advisory Commission on Civil Disorders*. New York: Bantam.

President's Commission on Law Enforcement and Administration of Justice (1967) *The Challenge of Crime in a Free Society*. Washington, D.C.: U.S. Government Printing Office.

President's Commission on Law Enforcement and Administration of Justice (1967) *Task Force Report: The Courts*. Washington, D.C.: U.S. Government Printing Office.

President's Commission on Law Enforcement and Administration of Justice (1967) *Task Force Report: Corrections*. Washington, D.C.: U.S. Government Printing Office.

Press, A. (1980) "The Scandalous U.S. Jails," *Newsweek* (August 18):74–77.

Press, A. (1981) "The Plague of Violent Crime," *Newsweek* (March 23):46–54.

Preston, I. L. (1975) *The Great American Blow-Up: Puffery in Advertising and Selling*. Madison: University of Wisconsin Press.

Price, J. L. (1968) *Organizational Effectiveness: An Inventory of Propositions*. Homewood, Ill.: Irwin.

Public Opinion (1979) "Alternatives for American Growth," *Public Opinion* **2**(August/September).

Quinney, R. (1970) *The Social Reality of Crime*. Boston: Little, Brown.

Quinney, R. (1970) *The Problem of Crime*. New York: Dodd, Mead, & Company.

Quinney, R. (1974) *Criminal Justice in America: A Critical Understanding*. Boston: Little, Brown.

Quinney, R. (1974) *Critique of Legal Order: Crime Control in Capitalist Society*. Boston: Little, Brown.

Quinney, R. (1975) *Criminology: Analysis and Critique of Crime in America*. Boston: Little, Brown.

Quinney, R. (1977) *Class, State, and Crime: On the Theory and Practice of Criminal Justice*. New York: McKay.

Quinney, R. (1977) *The Problem of Crime: A Critical Introduction to Criminology*, 2nd ed. New York: Harper & Row.

Quinney, R. (1979) *Criminology*, 2nd ed. Boston: Little, Brown.

Quinney, R., and J. Wildeman (1977) *The Problem of Crime*. New York: Harper & Row.

Rainwater, L. (1967) "The Revolt of the Dirty Workers," *Trans-action* **5**:2,64.

Ramirez, A. (1981) "Simmering Streets: Miami's Liberty City, Site of Riot in 1980, Is Tense, Troubled," *The Wall Street Journal* (March 30):1,16.

Rankin, A. (1964) "The Effect of Pre-Trial Detention," *New York University Law Review* **39**(June):631–641.

Rankin, D. (1980) "Cheating Found on the Rise," *The New York Times* (April 22):D2.

Reasons, C. E. (1974) *The Criminologist: Crime and the Criminal.* Pacific Palisades, Calif.: Goodyear,

Reasons, C. E. (1974) "The Politics of Drugs: An Inquiry in the Sociology of Social Problems," *Sociological Quarterly* **15**(Summer):381–404.

Reasons, C. E. (1974) "Racism, Prisons, and Prisoners' Rights," *Issues in Criminology* **9**(Fall):3–20.

Reasons, C. E., and R. L. Kaplan (1974) "Tear Down the Walls?: Some Functions of Prisons." Paper presented at the meetings of the American Sociological Association, Montreal (August).

Reasons, C. E., and W. D. Perdue (1981) *The Ideology of Social Problems.* Sherman Oaks, Calif.: Alfred.

Reasons, C. E., and R. M. Rich (1978) *The Sociology of Law: A Conflict Perspective.* Toronto: Butterworths.

Reasons, C. E., L. Ross, and C. Patterson (1982) "Your Money and Your Life—Workers' Health in Canada," *Crime and Social Justice* **17**(Summer): 55–60.

Reckless, W. (1967) *The Crime Problem.* New York: Appleton-Century-Crofts.

Reckless, W. (1973) *The Crime Problem.* Englewood Cliffs, N.J.: Prentice-Hall.

Redlich, F., and S. R. Kellert (1978) "Trends in American Mental Health," *American Journal of Psychiatry* **135**:22–28.

Rehnquist, W. H. (1981) "A Mockery of the Criminal Justice System," *Los Angeles Times* (April 29):Part 2,7.

Reid, E. (1969) *The Grim Reapers.* New York: Bantam Books.

Reid, S. T. (1982) *Crime and Criminology,* 3rd ed. New York: Holt, Rinehart & Winston.

Reiman, J. H. (1979a) *The Rich Get Richer and the Poor Get Prison: Ideology, Class and Criminal Justice.* New York: Wiley.

Reiman, J. H. (1979b) "Prostitution, Addiction and the Ideology of Liberalism," *Contemporary Crises* **3**:53–68.

Reiss, A. J., Jr. (1976) "Police Brutality-Answers to Key Questions." In A. Niederhoffer and A. S. Blumberg (eds.), *The Ambivalent Force.* Hinsdale, Ill.: Dryden Press, pp. 333–342.

Rhodes, R. P. (1977) *The Insoluble Problems of Crime.* New York: Wiley.

Ricchiardi, S., and R. Moore (1980) "Iowa's Jailing Rate of Blacks among Highest," *Des Moines Register* (August 22):1,3.

Rich, V. (1975) *Law and the Administration of Justice.* New York: Wiley.

Richardson, J. F. (1970) *The New York Police: Colonial Times to 1901.* New York: Oxford University Press.

Riis, R., and J. Patric (1942) *The Repairman Will Get You If You Don't Watch Out.* New York: Doubleday.

Ritzer, G., K. C. W. Kammeyer, and N. R. Yetman (1982) *Sociology: Experiencing a Changing Society,* 2nd ed. Boston: Allyn & Bacon.

Roberts, R. E. (1978) *Social Problems: Human Possibilities.* St. Louis, Mo.: Mosby.

Robinson, C. D. (1978) "The Deradicalization of the Policeman: A Historical Analysis," *Crime and Delinquency* **24**(2):129–151.

Rocky Mountain News (1981) "The Tragic Victims of Crime," *Rocky Mountain News,* (February 25):48.

Rocky Mountain News (1982) "Detention," *Rocky Mountain News* (January 4):38.

Rocky Mountain News (1983) "Those Who Bilk U.S. Get Slapped on Wrists," *Rocky Mountain News* (August 3):54.

Roebuck, J., and S. C. Weeber (1978) *Political Crime in the United States: Analyzing Crime by and Against Government.* New York: Praeger.

Rojek, D. G. (1979) "Private Justice Systems and Crime Reporting," *Criminology* **17**(1):100–111.

Rosenberg, H. L. (1976) "The Guinea Pigs at Camp Desert Rock," *The Progressive* **40**(June):37–43.

Ross, H. L. (1982) "Law, Science and Accidents: The British Road Safety Act of 1967," cited in von Hirsch, "Why Punish?" In N. Johnston and L. D. Savitz (eds.), *Legal Process and Corrections.* New York: Wiley, p. 310.

Ross, I. (1980) "How Lawless Are Big Companies?" *Fortune* **102**(December 1):56–64.

Ross, R. A., and G. C. S. Benson (1979) "Criminal Justice from East to West," *Crime and Delinquency* **25**(January):76–86.

Rossi, P. H., E. Waite, C. E. Bose, and R. E. Berk (1974) "The Seriousness of Crimes: Normative Structure and Individual Difference," *American Sociological Review* **39**(April):224–237.

Rossi, P. H., R. A. Berk, and K. J. Lenihan (eds.) (1980) *Money, Work, and Crime: Experimental Evidence.* New York: Academic Press.

Rothman, D. J. (1971) *The Discovery of the Asylum.* Boston: Little, Brown.

Rubinstein, J. (1973) *City Police.* New York: Ballantine.

Ruhl, J. (1981) "Employees Con Millions," *Rocky Mountain News* (March 31):1B–15B.

Rusche, G. (1933) "Labor Market and Penal Sanction." In T. Platt and P. Takagi (eds.), *Punishment and Penal Discipline.* Berkeley, Calif.: Crime and Social Justice Associates, 1980, pp. 10–16.

Rusche, G., and O. Kirchheimer (1939) *Punishment and Social Structure.* New York: Columbia University Press.

Ryan, W. (1976) *Blaming the Victim,* revised ed. New York: Vantage Books.

Sakes, M. J. (1976) "The Limits of Scientific Jury Selection: Ethical and Empirical," *Jurimetrics Journal* **17**(Fall):5–20.

Samuelson, R. J. (1981) "A Nation Confused about Attitudes toward the Poor," *Los Angeles Times* (October 20):Part II,15.

Sandburg, C. (1926) *Abraham Lincoln, The Prairie Years.* New York: Harcourt, Brace.

Savoy, P. (1981) "Legalizing Corporate Murder," *The Nation* (June 20):745,761–764.

Schafer, S. (1974) *The Political Criminal: The Problem of Morality and Crime.* New York: The Free Press.

Schervish, P. (1973) "The Labeling Perspective: Its Bias and Potential in the Study of Political Deviance," *American Sociologist* **8**(May):47–57.

Schinto, J. (1977) "The Breathless Cotton Workers," *The Progressive* **41**(August).

Schneider, J. W. (1978) "Deviant Drinking as Disease: Alcoholism as a Social Accomplishment," *Social Problems* **25**:361–372.

Schrag, C. (1977) "Review of 'Thinking about Crime,' 'Punishing Criminals,' and 'We Are the Living Proof,' " *Criminology* **14**(February):569–573.

Schrager, L. S., and J. F. Short, Jr. (1978) "Toward a Sociology of Organizational Crime," *Social Problems* **25**(April):407–419.

Schuessler, K. F. (1971) "The Deterrent Influence of the Death Penalty." In S. E. Grupp (ed.), *Theories of Punishment*. Bloomington: University of Indiana Press, pp. 181–195.

Schulman, J., (1973) "Recipe for a Jury," *Psychology Today* **6**(May):37–44,77–84.

Schultz, T. (1980) "How Millions Cheat (and Beat) the IRS," *Dallas Times Herald* (March 30):M1–M6.

Schur, E. M. (1965) *Crimes without Victims*. Englewood Cliffs, N.J.: Prentice-Hall.

Schur, E. M. (1969) *Our Criminal Society: The Social and Legal Sources of Crime in America*. Englewood Cliffs, N.J.: Prentice-Hall.

Schur, E. M. (1973) *Radical Non-intervention: Rethinking the Delinquency Problem*. Englewood Cliffs, N.J.: Prentice-Hall (Spectrum Books).

Schur, E. M. (1979) *Interpreting Deviance: A Sociological Introduction*. New York: Harper & Row.

Schur, E. M., and H. A. Bedau (1974) *Victimless Crimes: Two Sides of a Controversy*. Englewood Cliffs, N.J.: Prentice-Hall.

Schwartz, R. D., and J. C. Miller (1964) "Legal Evolution and Societal Complexity," *American Journal of Sociology* **70**(2):159–169.

Schwendinger, H., and J. Schwendinger (1970) "Defenders of Order or Guardians of Human Rights," *Issues in Criminology* **7**:72–81.

Schwendinger, J. R., and H. Schwendinger (1983) *Rape and Inequality*. Beverly Hills, Calif.: Sage.

Scull, A. T. (1977) *Decarceration: Community Treatment and the Deviant*. Englewood Cliffs, NJ: Prentice Hall.

Scull, A. T. (1982) "Community Corrections: Panacea, Progress, or Pretense?" In R. L. Abel (ed.), *The Politics of Informal Justice,* Vol. 1. New York: Academic Press, pp. 99–118.

Seidman, D., and M. Couzens (1974) "Getting the Crime Rate Down: Political Pressure and Crime Reporting," *Law and Society Review* **8**(Spring):457–493.

Siegel, C. M. (1981) "Safety Citations at Dutch Creek Called Average," *Rocky Mountain News* (April 22):24.

Sellin, T. (1938) *Culture Conflict and Crime*. New York: Social Science Research Council.

Sellin, T. (1944) *Pioneering in Penology*. Philadelphia: University of Pennsylvania Press.

Sellin T. (1959) *The Death Penalty*. Philadelphia: American Law Institute.

Senna, J. J., and L. J. Siegel (1978) *Introduction to Criminal Justice*. St. Paul, Minn.: West.

Seymour, W. N., Jr. (1973) *Why Justice Fails*. New York: Morrow.

Shaw, C. R., and H. D. McKay (1972) *Juvenile Delinquency and Urban Areas*. revised ed. Chicago: University of Chicago Press.

Shearing, C. D. (1979) "Subterranean Processes in the Maintenance of Power: An Examination of the Mechanisms Coordinating Police Action." Unpublished paper, Center for Criminology: University of Toronto.

Shearing, C. D., and P. C. Stenning (1983) "Private Security: Implications for Social Control," *Social Problems* **30**(June):493–506.

Shelden, R. G. (1981) "Convict Leasing: An Application of the Rusche-Kirchheimer Thesis to Penal Changes in Tennessee, 1830–1915." In D. F. Greenburg (ed.), *Crime and Capitalism*. Palo Alto, Calif.: Mayfield, pp. 358–366.

Shelden, R. G. (1982) *Criminal Justice in America: A Sociological Approach*. Boston: Little, Brown.

Sheldon, W. H. (1940) *The Varieties of Human Physique: An Introduction to Constitutional Psychology*. New York: Harper & Row.

Sheler, J. L. (1982) "As Unemployment Rises, So Does Benefit Frauds," *U.S. News & World Report* (May 31):72–73.

Shelley, L. (1981) *Crime and Modernization*. Carbondale/Edwardsville, Ill.: Southern Illinois University Press.

Sherman, L. W. (1982) "Deviant Organizations." In M. D. Ermann and R. J. Lundman (eds.), *Corporate and Governmental Deviance,* 2nd ed. New York: Oxford University Press, pp. 63–73.

Sherman, M., and G. Hawkins (1982) *Imprisonment in America*. Chicago: University of Chicago Press.

Shipp, E. R. (1981) "Quality-of-Life Offenses: City Makes a Big Issue of Little Crimes," *The New York Times* (August 30):6E.

Short, J. F., Jr., and F. I. Nye (1958) "Extent of Unrecorded Juvenile Delinquency," *Journal of Criminal Law, Criminology and Police Science* **49** (November/December):296–302.

Silver, A. (1967) "The Demand for Order in Civil Society: A Review of Some Themes in the History of Urban Crime, Police and Riot." In D. J. Bordua (ed.), *The Police: Six Sociological Essays*. New York: Wiley, pp. 1–24.

Simon, D. R. (1981) "The Political Economy of Crime." In S. G. NcNall (ed.), *Political Economy: A Critique of American Society*. Glenview, Ill.: Scott, Foresman, pp. 347–366.

Simon, D. R., and D. S. Eitzen (1982) *Elite Deviance*. Boston: Allyn & Bacon.

Simon, R. J. (1980) *The Jury: Its Role in American Society*. Lexington, Mass.: Lexington.

Sinclair, U. (1960) *The Jungle*. New York: New American Library. (Originally published in 1905.)

Skogan, W. G. (1974) "The Validity of Official Crime Statistics: An Empirical Investigation," *Social Science Quarterly* **55**(June):25–38.

Skogan, W. G. (ed.) (1976) *Sample Surveys of the Victims of Crime*. Cambridge, Mass.: Ballinger.

Skogan, W. G. (ed.) (1976) "Citizen Reporting of Crime," *Criminology* **13**(February):535–549.

Skogan, W. G. (1976) "Crime and Crime Rates." In W. G. Skogan (ed.), *Sample Surveys of the Victims of Crime*. Cambridge, Mass.: Ballinger, pp. 105–119.

Skogan, W. G. (1977) "Dimensions of the Dark Figure of Unreported Crime," *Crime and Delinquency* **23**(January):41–50.

Skogan, W. G., and W. R. Klecka (1977) *The Fear of Crime*. Washington, D.C.: American Political Science Association.

Skolnick, J. (1969) *The Politics of Protest*. Washington, D.C.: U.S. Government Printing Office.

Skolnick, J. (1969) "Dialogue with Jerome Skolnick," *Issues in Criminology* **4**:109–122.

Skolnick, J. (1981) "The Attorney General's Crime Report Has a Familiar Sound," *Los Angeles Times* (August 23):PartIV,3.

Skolnick, J. (1982) "Why a Liberal Supports Curbs on Exclusionary Rule," *Des Moines Register* (September 27):8A.

Skolnick, J., and J. Dombrink (1978) "The Legalization of Deviance," *Criminology* **16**(2):193–208.

Sloman, L. (1978) *Reefer Madness: The History of Marijuana in America*. Indianapolis, Ind.: Bobbs-Merrill.

Smith, D. C. (1975) *The Mafia Mistique*. New York: Basic Books.

Smith, D. C. (1980) "Paragons, Pariahs, and Pirates: A Spectrum-Based Theory of Enterprise," *Crime and Delinquency* **26**(July):358–386.

Smith, R. A. (1961) "The Incredible Electrical Conspiracy," *Fortune* **63**(April):132–137,170–180;(May):161–164,210–224.

Snider, L. (1982) "Traditional and Corporate Theft: A Comparison of Sanctions." In P. Wickman and T. Dailey (eds.), *White Collar and Economic Crime*. Lexington, Mass.: Lexington Books, pp. 235–258.

Snow, R. P. (1978) "The Golden Fleece's Arizona Land Fraud." In J. M. Johnson and J. D. Douglas (eds.), *Crime at the Top*. Philadelphia: Lippincott, pp. 133–150.

Society (1980) "Social Science and the Citizen: Crime and Unemployment," *Society* **17**(July-August):2–3.

Society (1981) "Social Science and the Citizen: Hispanic Victims," *Society* **18**(January–February):4.

Sohn, I. (1976) "Illicit Capital: The Political Economy of Organized Crime." Unpublished paper.

Solomon, F., W. L. Walker, G. J. O'Connor, and J. R. Fishman (1980) "Civil Rights Activity and Reduction in Crime among Negroes," reprinted in *Crime and Social Justice* **14**(Winter):27–35.

Speiglman, R. (1980) "Prison Psychiatrists and Drugs: A Case Study." In T. Platt and P. Takagi (eds.), *Punishment and Penal Discipline*. Berkeley, Calif.: Crime and Social Justice Associates, pp. 113–128.

Spitzer, S. (1975a) "Toward a Marxian Theory of Deviance," *Social Problems* **22:**638–651.

Spitzer, S. (1975b) "Punishment and Social Organization: A Study of Durkheim's Theory of Penal Evolution," *Law and Society Review* **9:**613–635.

Spitzer, S. (1979) "The Rationalization of Crime Control in Capitalist Society," *Contemporary Crises* **3:**187–206.

Spitzer, S., and A. T. Scull (1977) "Privatization and Capitalist Development: The Case of the Private Police," *Social Problems* **25**(1):18–29.

Spitzer, S., and A. T. Scull (1977) "Social Control in Historical Perspective: From Private to Public Responses to Crime." In D. F. Greenburg (ed.), *Corrections and Punishment: Structure, Function, and Process*. Beverly Hills, Calif.: Sage, pp. 281–302.

Spohn, C., J. Grul, and S. Welch (1981) "The Effect of Race on Sentencing," *Law and Society Review* **16:**71–88.

Spradley, J. P. (1970) *You Owe Yourself a Drunk*. Boston: Little, Brown.

Star, J. (1974) "Chesterfield Smith: The Lawyers," *Intellectual Digest* (March): 21.

Steffensmeier, D. J. (1980) "Differences in Patterns of Adult Crime: A Review and Assessment," *Social Forces* **58**(June):1080–1108.

Steffensmeier, D. J., and M. J. Cobb (1981) "Sex Differences in Urban Arrest Patterns, 1934–1979," *Social Problems* **29**(October):37–50.

Steffensmeier, D. J., A. S. Rosenthal, and C. Shehan (1980) "World War II and Its Effect on the Sex Differential in Arrests: An Empirical Test of the Sex-Role Equality and Crime Proposition," *Sociological Quarterly* **21**(Summer):403–416.

Steif, W. (1978) "Drug Price Relief," *The Progressive* **42**(November):13.

Stein, E. (1940) "The Employers' Approach to the Labor Problem." In E. Stein and J. Davis (eds.), *Labor Problems in America*. New York: Farrar & Rinehart, pp. 423–545.

Stein, J. (1981) "Crime Wave," *The Progressive* **45**(October):14.

Sternberg, D. (1974) "The New Radical-Criminal Trials: A Step toward a Class-for-Itself in the American Proletariat?" In R. Quinney (ed.), *Criminal Justice in America*. Boston: Little, Brown, pp. 274–294.

Stone, C. (1975) *Where the Law Ends: The Social Control of Corporate Behavior*. New York: Harper & Row.

Stuckey, G. A. (1976) *Procedures in the Justice System*. Columbus, Ohio: Merrill.

Sudnow, D. (1965) "Normal Crimes," *Social Problems* **12:**255–276.

Sumner, W. G. (1906) *Folkways*. New York: Dover.

Sutherland, E. H. (1940) "White-Collar Criminality," *American Sociological Review* **5**(February):1–12.

Sutherland, E. H. (1949) *White Collar Crime*. New York: Dryden.

Sutherland, E. H. (1961) *White Collar Crime*. New York: Holt, Rinehart, & Winston.

Sutherland, E. H., and D. R. Cressey (1970) *Criminology*, 8th ed. Philadelphia: Lippincott.

Sutherland, E. H., and D. R. Cressey (1974) *Criminology,* 9th ed. Philadelphia: Lippincott.

Sutherland, E. H., and D. R. Cressey (1978) *Criminology,* 10th ed. Philadelphia: Lippincott.

Swartz, J. (1975) "Silent Killers at Work," *Crime and Social Justice* (Spring/Summer):15–20.

Sykes, G. M. (1958) *The Society of Captives.* Princeton, N.J.: Princeton University Press.

Sykes, G. M. (1974) "The Rise of Critical Criminology," *Journal of Criminal Law and Criminology* **65**(2):206–213.

Sykes, G. M. (1978) *Criminology.* New York: Harcourt, Brace and Jovanovich.

Sykes, G. M. (1980) *The Future of Crime.* Washington, D.C.: U.S. Government Printing Office.

Sykes, G. M., and D. Matza (1957) "Techniques of Neutralization: A Theory of Delinquency," *American Sociological Review* **22**:664–670.

Sykes, G. M., and S. L. Messinger (1960) "The Inmate Social System." In R. A. Cloward, D. R. Cressey, G. H. Grosser, R. McCleery, L. E. Ohlin, G. M. Sykes, and S. L. Messinger (eds.), *Theoretical Studies in the Social Organization of the Prison.* New York: Social Research Council.

Sylvester, S. F., J. H. Reed, and D. O. Nelson (1977) *Prison Homicide.* New York: Halsted.

Tabor, M. (1971) "The Plague: Capitalism + Dope = Genocide." In R. Perrucci and M. Pilisuk (eds.), *The Triple Revolution Emerging: Social Problems in Depth.* Boston: Little, Brown, pp. 241–249.

Taft, P., and P. Ross (1969) "American Labor Violence: Its Causes, Character and Outcome." In H. D. Graham and T. R. Gurr (eds.), *The History of Violence in America.* New York: Barton, pp. 281–395.

Takagi, P. (1980) "The Walnut Street Jail: A Penal Reform to Centralize the Powers of the State." In T. Platt and P. Takagi (eds.), *Punishment and Penal Discipline.* Berkeley, Calif.: Crime and Social Justice Associates, pp. 48–56.

Tannenbaum, F. (1938) *Crime and the Community.* New York: Ginn.

Taubman, P. (1979) "U.S. Attack on Corporate Crime Yields Handfull of Cases in Ten Years," *The New York Times* (July 15):1,29.

Taylor, I., P. Walton, and J. Young (1973) *The New Criminology: For a Social Theory of Deviance.* London: Routledge & Kegan Paul.

Taylor, I., P. Walton, and J. Young (1974) *The New Criminology.* New York: Harper Torchbooks.

Taylor, L., and I. Taylor (1968) "We Are All Deviants Now," *International Socialism* **24**:28–32.

Taylor, S., Jr. (1982) "Too Much Justice," *Harper's* **265**(September):56–66.

Taylor, T. (1971) *Nuremberg and Vietnam: An American Tragedy.* New York: Bantam.

Thomas, C. W., and J. R. Hepburn (1983) *Crime, Criminal Law, and Criminology.* Dubuque, Iowa: Brown.

Thomas, J. (1981) "Class, State, and Political Surveillance: Liberal Democracy and Structural Contradictions," *Insurgent Sociologist* **10**(Summer/Fall):47–58.

Time (1974) "Judging Jurors," *Time* (January 28):60.

Time (1978) "The Ultimate Heist," *Time* (November 20):48.

Time (1981) "The Battle of the Bottle," *Time* (June 1):26.

Timmer, D. A. (1978) "Whence the Professional Police." Unpublished paper.

Timmer, D. A. (1980) "The Politics of Correctional Evaluation." Unpublished paper.

Timmer, D. A. (1981) "Organizational and Phenomenological Determinants of Local Crime Control: The Historical Selectivity of Municipal Policing." Ph.D. Dissertation, Colorado State University.

Timmer, D. A. (1982) "The Productivity of Crime in the United States: Drugs and Capital Accumulation," *Journal of Drug Issues* **12**(4):383–396.

Tittle, C. R. (1974) "Prisons and Rehabilitation: The Inevitability of Disfavor," *Social Problems* **21**(Winter):385–395.

Tittle, C. R. (1983) "Social Class and Criminal Behavior: A Critique of the Theoretical Foundation," *Social Forces* **62**(2):334–358.

Tittle, C. R., W. J. Villemez, and D. A. Smith (1978) "The Myth of Social Class and Criminality: An Empirical Assessment of the Empirical Evidence," *American Sociological Review* **43**(October):643–656.

Toby, J. (1979) "Societal Evolution and Criminality: A Parsonian View," *Social Problems* **26**(April):386–391.

Tuky, C. (1981) "What the Underground Economy Costs You," *Money* **10** (April):74–77.

Tullock, G. (1974) "Does Punishment Deter Crime?" *The Public Interest* **36**(Summer):103–111.

United Press International (1979) "False Tax Returns Bilk Government of Millions" (April 23).

United Press International (1981) "More Police May Be Indicted in Corruption Probe in Miami" (July 16).

United Press International (1981) "10 Chicago Police Indicted for Drug Ring Ties" (November 13).

United Press International (1981) "Few Intervene to Prevent Staged Car Burglaries" (November 17).

United Press International (1981) "Illinois: 25 Percent of Pupils Victims of Theft" (August 11).

United Press International (1981) "Crime Plan Focus: Drugs, Violence" (October 24).

United Press International (1982) "Burger Fears Crash of U.S. Law System" (November 19).

United Press International (1982) "Physicians Owe U.S." (May 21)

Unnever, J., C. Frazier, and J. Henretta (1980) "Racial Differences in Criminal Sentencing," *Sociological Quarterly* **21**(Spring):197–206.

USA Today (1983) "Credit Card Frauds Top Holdings," *USA Today* (May 19):1A.

USA Today (1983) "Crime in the U.S.A.," *USA Today* (April 21):8A.

U.S. Bureau of the Census (1979) *Statistical Abstract of the United States*. Washington, D.C.: U.S. Government Printing Office.

U.S. Bureau of Prisons (1975) "Correlation of Unemployment and Federal Prisons Population," Washington, D. C.: U.S. Government Printing Office.

U.S. Chamber of Commerce (1977) "White Collar Crime: The Problem and Its Import." In L. Radzinowicz and M. E. Wolfgang (eds.), *Crime and Justice,* Vol. 1. New York: Basic Books, pp. 314–355.

U.S. Department of Justice (1976) *Survey of Inmates of State Correctional Facilities, 1974.* Washington, D.C.: U.S. Government Printing Office.

U.S. Department of Justice (1977) *Crime in the United States, 1977.* Washington, D.C.: U.S. Government Printing Office.

U.S. Department of Justice (1980) *Capital Punishment, 1979.* Washington, D.C.: U.S. Government Printing Office.

U.S. Department of Justice (1980) *FBI Uniform Crime Reports: Crime in the United States, 1979.* Washington, D.C.: U.S. Government Printing Office.

U.S. Department of Justice (1982) *FBI Uniform Crime Reports: Crime in the United States, 1981.* Washington, D.C.: U.S. Government Printing Office.

U.S. Department of Justice/Bureau of Justice Statistics (1980) *Criminal Victimization in the United States, 1978.* Washington, D.C.: U.S. Government Printing Office.

U.S. Department of Justice/Bureau of Justice Statistics (1982) *Criminal Victimization in the United States, 1980.* Washington, D.C.: U.S. Government Printing Office.

U.S. News & World Report (1975) "CIA Murder Plots—Weighing the Damage to U.S.," *U.S. News & World Report* (December 1):13–15.

U.S. News & World Report (1976) "It's Official: Government Snooping Has Been Going on for 50 Years," *U.S. News & World Report* (May 24):65–66.

U.S. News & World Report (1978) "How Billions Are Wasted in Auto Repairs," *U.S. News & World Report* (September 8):72.

U.S. News & World Report (1979) "Is Your Job Dangerous to Your Health?" *U.S. News & World Report* (February 5):59.

U.S. News & World Report (1979) "As Police Cope with Charges of Brutality . . . ," *U.S. News & World Report* (August 27).

U.S. News & World Report (1979) "Abuse of Authority Is a Very Explosive Situation" (Interview with Paul Takagi), *U.S. News & World Report* (August 27):29.

U.S. News & World Report (1979) "The Underground Economy," *U.S. News & World Report* (October 22):49–56.

U.S. News & World Report (1980) "The Push-Button Criminals of the '80s," *U.S. News & World Report* (September 22):39–40.

U.S. News & World Report (1981) "Violence in Big Cities: Behind the Surge," *U.S. News & World Report* (February 23):63–65.

U.S. News & World Report (1981) "The People's War against Crime," *U.S. News & World Report* (July 13):53–54.

U.S. News & World Report (1981) "Trend toward Bigness in Business Speeds Up," *U.S. News & World Report* (August 24):69–70.

U.S. News & World Report (1982) "Unclogging the Courts," *U.S. News & World Report* (February 22):36–40.

U.S. News & World Report (1982) "Underground Economy: $100 Billion in Lost Taxes," *U.S. News & World Report* (April 19):48–49.

U.S. News & World Report (1982) "An Overloaded Court Cries for Relief," *U.S. News & World Report* (August 23):52–53.

U.S. News & World Report (1982) "American Justice," *U.S. News & World Report* (November 1):35–58.

U.S. Senate Committee on Banking, Housing and Urban Affairs, 96th Congress (1980) *Hearings on Banks and Narcotics Money Flow in South Florida*. Washington, D.C.: U.S. Government Printing Office.

van den Haag, E. (1975) *Punishing Criminals: Concerning a Very Old and Painful Question*. New York: Basic Books.

Vetter, H. J., and J. Silverman (1978) *The Nature of Crime*. Philadelphia: Saunders.

Viviano, F. (1981) "What's Happening in 'Murder City?'" *The Progressive* **45**(September):38–42.

Vold, G. (1958) *Theoretical Criminology*. New York: Oxford University Press.

von Hirsch, A. (1976) *Doing Justice: The Choice of Punishments*. New York: Hill & Wang.

von Hoffman, N. (1980) "Legitimate Business Infiltrates the Rackets," King Features Syndicate. *Rocky Mountain News,* pp. 33,36.

Walker, S. (1980) *Popular Justice: A History of American Criminal Justice*. New York: Oxford University Press.

Wallace, D. (1981) "The Political Economy of Incarceration Trends in Late U.S. Capitalism: 1971–1977," *Insurgent Sociologist* **10–11**(Summer–Fall):59–65.

Wallerstein, J. S., and C. J. Wyle (1947) "Our Law-Abiding Law-Breakers," *Federal Probation* **25**(April):107–112.

Ward, D. A., and G. G. Kassebaum (1972) "On Biting the Hand That Feeds: Some Implications of Sociological Evaluations of Correctional Effectiveness." In C. Weiss (ed.), *Evaluating Action Programs: Readings in Social Action and Education*. Boston: Allyn & Bacon, pp. 300–310.

Washington Post (1977) "AFDC Audit Shows $550 Million Misspent," *Washington Post* (August 5):A12.

Watson, J. (1982) "Death Penalty: Is It an Idle Threat?" *Rocky Mountain News* (November 14):6W.

Webster, W. H. (1979) "Countering White Collar Crime," *Journal of Current Social Issues* **16**(Summer):14–16.

Weinstock, M. (1979) Quoted in *Broadcasting* **96**(January 22):25.

Weiss, R. (1981) "The Private Detective Agency in the Development of Policing Forms in the Rural and Frontier United States," *The Insurgent Sociologist* **10**(4)–**11**(1):75–84.

Weitzer, R. (1981) "Political Crime and Repression in Europe and America," *Contemporary Crises* **5**(April):217–225.

Wellford, C. (1975) "Labeling Theory and Criminology: An Assessment," *Social Problems* **23**(Winter):332–345.

Wellford, H. (1972) *Sowing the Wind: A Report From Ralph Nader's Center for*

Study of Responsive Law on Food Safety and the Chemical Harvest. New York: Grossman.

Wenger, M. G., and T. A. Bonomo (1978) "Crime, Crisis, and Social Revolution: An Examination of the Progressive Thesis in Marxist Criminology," *Transforming Sociology Series.* Red Feather, Colo.: The Red Feather Institute.

Westley, W. A. (1970) *Violence and the Police.* Cambridge, Mass.: MIT Press.

Wheeler, S. (1978). "Trends and Problems in the Sociological Study of Crime." In P. Wickman and P. Whitten (eds.), *Readings in Criminology.* Lexington, Mass.: Heath.

Whiteside, T. (1977) "Annals of Crime: Dead Souls in the Computer," *The New Yorker* (August 22):35–65; (August 29):34–64.

Wicker, T. (1975) *A Time to Die.* New York: Quadrangle/The New York Times Book Co.

Wicker, T. (1981) In "Crime Solutions Guaranteed to 'Revulse,' " New York Times News Service. *Des Moines Register* (August 22):OP/ED page.

Wickman, P., and T. Dailey (eds.) (1982) *White-Collar and Economic Crime: Multidisciplinary and Cross-National Perspectives.* Lexington, Mass.: Lexington Books.

Williams, R. M. (1979) "Arsenic and Old Factories," *Saturday Review* (January 20):26.

Willis, C. L. (1981) "Why Our Justice Is Not Equal," *The Humanist Sociologist* **6**(June):11–13.

Willis, J. (1982) "Time Thieves," *The Denver Post* (February 11):H1.

Willson, S. B. (1979) "More and More Prisons," *The Progressive* **43**(December):14–21.

Wilson, J. Q. (1968) *Varieties of Police Behavior.* Cambridge, Mass.: Harvard University Press.

Wilson, J. Q. (1975) *Thinking About Crime.* New York: Vintage.

Winter, B. (1978) "A Cure for What Ails Us," *The Progressive* **42**(December):11.

Wise, D. (1973) *The Politics of Lying.* New York: Vintage.

Wolfgang, M., and F. Ferracuti (1967) *The Subculture of Violence.* London: Tavistock.

Wright, C. (1980) "Death in Miami," *New Statesman* **99**:808.

Wright, E. O. (1973) *The Politics of Punishment: A Critical Analysis of Prisons in America.* New York: Harper & Row.

Wright, J. D., P. H. Rossi, and K. Daly (1983) *Under the Gun: Weapons, Crime and Violence in America.* Hawthorne. N.Y.: Aldine.

Wylie, J. (1981) "Social Science for Social Control," *The Progressive* **45**(June):27.

Yeager, M. G. (1979) "Unemployment and Imprisonment," *Journal of Criminal Law and Criminology* (Winter):586–588.

Young, J. (1971) "The Role of the Police as Amplifiers of Deviance, Negotiators of Reality, and Translators of Fantasy." In S. Cohen (ed.), *Images of Deviance.* Hammondsworth: Penguin Press, pp. 27–61.

Young, T. R. (1978) "Crime and Capitalism." Paper presented to the annual meeting of the Western Social Science Association, Denver (April).

Young, T. R. (1981) "Corporate Crime: A Critique of the Clinard Report," *Contemporary Crises* **5**(June):323–336.

Young, T. R. (1982) "Crime and Capitalism," *Transforming Sociology Series*. Red Feather, Colo.: The Red Feather Institute.

Yunker, J. A. (1982) "Testing the Deterrent Effect of Capital Punishment," *Criminology* **19**(February):626–649.

Yurick, S. (1970) "The Political Economy of Junk," *Monthly Review* **22**(7):22–37.

Zeisel, H. (1981) "Race Bias in the Administration of the Death Penalty: The Florida Experience," *Harvard Law Review* **95**(December):456–468.

Zeitlin, M., K. G. Lutterman, and J. W. Russell (1977) "Death in Vietnam: Class, Poverty, and the Risks of War." In M. Zeitlin (ed.), *American Society, Inc.,* 2nd ed. Chicago: Rand McNally, pp. 143–155.

Zolbe, P. A. (1980) "The Uniform Crime Reporting Program: 50 Years of Progress," *FBI Law Enforcement Bulletin* **49**(September):2–7.

Zwerdling, D. (1978) "Food Pollution." In R. C. Edwards, M. Reich, and T. E. Weisskopf (eds.), *The Capitalist System*. Englewood Cliffs, N.J.: Prentice-Hall, pp. 19–24.

Glossary

ADVERSARY SYSTEM The American courts are organized on the principle that the prosecution (the state) and the defense (the counsel for the defense) shall engage in legal "combat" on equal terms before a neutral judge.

ANOMIE Robert Merton's theory that crime is the result of the almost universal cultural desire for material security, success, and comfort on the one hand, and the limited opportunities available in society to achieve these things on the other. Anomie refers to the "confused" and "normless" state of the individual faced with this dilemma and increases the likelihood that crime will be used to reach desired goals.

AUBURN PLAN (Congregate hard labor plan) The organizing principle for prisoners begun in Auburn, New York, in 1821 and still prevails. It emphasized common activities, external discipline, hard labor, and forced rehabilitation.

BAIL Money used to secure the release of a defendant accused of a crime and to guarantee his or her appearance at the trial.

BIOSOCIAL CRIMINOLOGY A contemporary resurgence of pre- and nonsociological explanations of the sources of crime that contends the ultimate causes of criminal behavior are found in the physical and biological makeup of the individual offender.

BLAMING THE VICTIM Holding criminal offenders who have been victimized by exploitive social and economic conditions solely responsible for their acts.

CAPITAL PUNISHMENT The ultimate punishment for those guilty of heinous crimes—death.

CAVEAT EMPTOR The Latin phrase "let the buyer beware" that is often used to justify fraudulent behavior.

CIVIL CASE An action decided by the courts involving one party seeking a judgment against another.

COMMON LAW (English) Law that all subjects in England, regardless of geography or social class, were required to obey.

COMMUNITY SERVICE A sentence or court order requiring that an offender do some specified amount of public work for the community or some community agency.

COMPLAIN- ANTLESS CRIME Crimes that typically have a "willing victim" such as gambling, drug use and addiction, prostitution, etc.; where no one complains to the police about the crime.

CONSENSUAL TRANSAC- TION A mutually agreed upon—by two or more consenting adults—exchange of goods and services that often characterizes victimless or complainantless crimes such as gambling and prostitution.

CORPORATE CRIME Deliberate acts by large business enterprises that do physical or economic harm to the environment, their employees, or to their customers (whether in violation of the law or not).

CORPORATE DUMPING The form of corporate crime whereby unsafe products banned in the United States are sold in other countries.

CRIME INDEX (FBI) The most serious crimes, according to the FBI: homicide, rape, assault, robbery, burglary, larceny, and auto theft.

CRIME TARIFF The charge added to organized crime's goods and services for taking the legal risks involved in providing them.

CRIMES OF ACCOMMO- DATION Individual street crimes that, unlike crimes of resistance, do not represent "polit- ical" acts in response to social and economic exploitation and inequality but rather victimize, primarily, other working-class and poor persons.

CRIMES OF RESISTANCE Violent and property street crimes involved in situations such as riots and revolts that have an explicitly political character, in response to social and economic exploitation and inequalities.

CRIMINAL CASE An action in which the law has purportedly been broken and the courts determine guilt or innocence.

CRIMINAL TYPE The idea that there is a distinct and identifiable kind of person with distinct and identifiable personal characteristics that distinguish them from noncriminal persons.

CRIMINAL- IZATION The process of prohibiting some activity by criminal statute; or making some already criminal activity more criminal by law.

CRIMINO- GENESIS All those factors that give birth to, give rise to, cause, or generate crime.

DECARCERA- TION The process of deinstitutionalizing criminal offenders; assigning them to commu- nity programs rather than continuing to confine them in prison.

DECRIMINAL- IZATION The process of making some criminalized activity less criminal by law, for ex- ample, reducing a felony to a misdemeanor, or a simple misdemeanor to a ticket or citation.

DEFOUNDING The process of statistically lowering unsolved felonies to misdemeanors.

DETERMINATE SENTENCE A fixed prison term set by the legislature by type of crime.

DEVIANT GHETTOIZATION	The process of containing the criminal, deviant, and surplus population in deteriorating areas of large cities without benefit of criminal justice system supervision or rehabilitative services.
DIFFERENTIAL ASSOCIATION	Sociologist and criminologist E. H. Sutherland's theory that criminal behavior is the result of an individual's being socialized to criminal values, techniques, and rationalizations in a deviant or criminal subculture. Sutherland contends that whenever criminal socialization and association with criminal subcultures leads to more favorable—as compared with unfavorable—definitions of law-breaking, crime occurs.
DISORGANIZED CRIMES	Crimes of individuals—street, victimless, and white-collar crime.
DIVERSION PROGRAMS	Mental health, welfare, alcohol, drug abuse programs that criminal courts use to remove offenders or alleged offenders from the criminal justice system, usually at an early stage in criminal proceedings.
DUE PROCESS	Court procedures to ensure that the rights of the accused are guaranteed.
ECOCIDE	A war crime in which there is willful and permanent destruction of the environment.
EXCLUSIONARY RULE	The rule that prohibits the use of illegally obtained evidence in court.
EX POST FACTO LAWS	Laws passed after the act is committed, making it illegal.
FEE SPLITTING	A kickback arrangement whereby one party pays another who refers clients to him or her.
FORMAL SOCIAL SYSTEM	The explicit rules and role expectations in a social organization.
FRAUD	The intentional deception to cause another to give up something of value.
GENERAL DETERRENCE	The effect that punishment of an offender has on preventing the general public from committing crimes.
GENOCIDE	A war crime in which there is a willful destruction of an entire people and their culture.
GRAND JURY	A group of citizens selected to hear only the prosecution to decide if there is probable cause to charge a defendant with a crime.
HABEAS CORPUS	The legal procedure whereby a person convicted in a state court can appeal to the federal courts if his or her constitutional rights have been violated.
HALFWAY HOUSES	A component of community corrections programs that provides supervision and services in an actual residence in the community. Assignment to a halfway house may be a condition of probation, parole, or work-release.
INCARCERATION	To be imprisoned.

INDETERMI-NATE SENTENCE The length of sentence is not specified in order for the authorities to release the prisoner when rehabilitated.

INDICTMENT The formal accusation of a crime by a grand jury.

INFORMAL SOCIAL SYSTEM The unwritten rules for appropriate and inappropriate behaviors by the actors in a social organization.

INFORMA-TION A document filed with a court by the prosecution charging someone with a crime.

INTERAC-TIONIST THEORY A key sociological perspective in criminology that focuses on the way in which crime is generated by social control agencies (i.e., the criminal justice system) as they attach stigmatizing labels to individual offenders, who often "live-up" to the criminal identity that flows from labels, and who devote themselves to criminal careers.

JAILS Local lockups for persons awaiting trial and unable to make bail or serving relatively short sentences for minor crimes.

KICKBACK A person in a position of power or trust using that position to grant favors illegally in return for items of value.

LATENT CONSE-QUENCES The unintended and generally unrecognized consequences of social arrangements.

LEGALIZA-TION The process of making legal some activity previously prohibited by law.

LESS ELIGIBILITY The principle of Georg Rusche that prison conditions must always be worse than those of the working poor.

MAFIA A group of ethnic-based "families" (at different times primarily Irish, Jewish, then Italian) that controlled the sale and distribution of illegal goods and services in the vice districts of large cities before Prohibition. During and after Prohibition, organized crime expanded and became more organized, that is, more corporate in its structure and operation, and the Mafia gradually began to disappear.

MALA IN SE CRIMES Acts are crimes because they are assumed to be inherently wrong.

MALA PROHIBITA CRIMES Acts are made crimes only because the law prohibits them.

MANDATORY SENTENCE Terms set by the legislation by type of crime. The legislation may impose minimum and maximum terms or fixed prison sentences.

MEDICAL MODEL The assumption that a problem person is mentally or physically "sick."

MEDICALIZA-TION OF CRIME AND DEVIANCE Decriminalizing certain acts and attempting to control them and their perpetrators socially with medical institutions, rather than with the criminal justice system.

MENS REA   The Latin term referring to criminal intent.

M'NAGHTEN RULE   A person is insane and therefore not guilty of a crime if the individual at the time was unable to distinguish between right and wrong.

MONOPOLY   When a corporation has no competition in a particular market.

MONOPOLY CAPITALISM   The historical stage of capitalization predicted by Karl Marx in which fewer and fewer firms become larger and larger, dominating the economy and eliminating competition.

NOLLE PROSEQUI   ("I refuse to prosecute") When the prosecutor determines that the evidence is insufficient or the case is relatively unimportant, the case is dropped.

ORDER MAINTE-NANCE   The "nonlaw enforcement" activities of the police that serve to create and maintain social order and control. Activities like intervening in domestic and neighborhood disturbances and conflicts.

OVERCRIMI-NALIZATION   The overuse of the criminal law; making too many behaviors illegal; attempting to prevent or control particular behaviors with an overreliance on the criminal law.

PAROLE   The release of a prisoner under the supervision of the state.

PERSONAL CRIME   Individual crimes of violence like assault, robbery, rape, and murder.

PHILADEL-PHIA PLAN   The organizing principle for prisons developed by the Quakers in the early 19th century. It was based on the assumption that the criminal was a sinner and in need of repentence. Hence, prisoners were put in solitary confinement with the Bible to reflect on their crimes.

PLEA BARGAINING   A procedure whereby the accused pleads guilty in return for a deal by the prosecution (reducing the seriousness of the original charge and/or lessening the punishment).

POLICE DISCRETION   The power of police officers to make judgments and decisions about whether or not to use their legal authority to police particular activities, whether or not to make arrests, and so on.

POLICE POWER OF THE STATE   The right of the state to regulate in order to protect the public health, welfare, and morals of its citizens.

POLICE PROFESSION-ALIZATION   The process of formally educating and training the police and introducing management techniques into the police bureaucracy, designed to make it more rational and efficient.

POLICE SUBCULTURE   The typically close-knit association of police officers both on and off the job. This subculture includes police officer knowledge and beliefs about crime and criminals as well as the development of on-the-job methods of getting police work done.

POLITICAL CRIME   Crimes by individuals or groups against the government or crimes by the government against the people.

POLITICS OF CRIME RATES   The assumption of radicals that the official agencies of government focus on the crimes of the powerless to protect the interests of the wealthy and powerful.

POLITIZATION OF PRISONERS
To the degree that inmates feel they are unfairly confined, they will believe they are political victims and reject the social order they believe to be unjust.

POPULAR JUSTICE
Attempts by local neighborhoods and communities to devise informal and non-bureaucratic alternatives to the official justice system (e.g., unofficial neighborhood or community courts and police patrols).

PRE- AND NONSOCIO-LOGICAL THEORIES
A plethora of old and new attempts to explain crime as the result of something "inside" the individual criminal offender, be it their physical, biological, chemical, or psychological makeup that predisposes them to criminal acts.

PREDATORY CRIME
Individual property crimes like theft, burglary, and larceny that are committed primarily for the sake of the perpetrator's survival.

PRESENTENCE INVESTIGA-TION
A component of community corrections programs that prepares a rather detailed background report on an offender and makes a recommendation for sentencing (based on the report) to the criminal court.

PRETRIAL HEARING
The judge examines the facts of the case as presented by the prosecution to determine if the accused can be released or confined before the trial and if released what, if any, bail should be required.

PRETRIAL RELEASE
A component of community corrections programs that assesses the appropriateness of releasing changed individuals before their next court appearance; this release is sometimes granted unconditionally, sometimes with certain conditions attached (such as, for example, regular "check-ins" with the pretrial release staff or regular participation in some community treatment program).

PRICE-FIXING
A collusive agreement among "competitors" to overcharge customers or clients.

PRICE GOUGING
When business takes extraordinary advantage of consumers because of the bias of the law, monopoly of the market, or because of contrived or real shortages.

PRIMARY DEVIANCE
The original violation of a rule or law.

PRISONIZA-TION
The process by which inmates learn and internalize the culture of the inmate social system.

PRISONS
Lockups for offenders of serious crime run by the state and the federal governments.

PRIVATE JUSTICE
The sale of policing and correctional services, of "justice, safety, and protection," by private, run-for-profit security firms and treatment and rehabilitative agencies.

PROACTIVE POLICING
Police activities that seek out suspicious or criminal activity.

PROBATION
A sentence that permits the guilty to remain in the community instead of going to prison but under the supervision of the state.

PROBATION/ PAROLE REVOCATION
A criminal court procedure that determines that an offender has violated the terms and conditions of his or her probation or parole and sends (probation) or returns (parole) him or her to prison.

RADICAL CRIMINOL-OGY
A sociological perspective in criminology that locates the source of crime in the historical development and social structure of capitalist and class societies. More specifically, this perspective emphasizes the ways in which the mode of economic production and the state's intervention into the economy influences the forms and extent of crime in society.

REACTIVE POLICING
A type of police patrol whereby the police only respond to citizen complaints or requests for their intervention.

RECIDIVISM
Reinvolvement in criminal behavior after punishment, usually expressed as the proportion of exprisoners who are arrested for crimes.

REGULATORY VIOLENCE
Efforts by authorities in a prison to control inmates by the use of harmful methods such as beatings, drugs, and solitary confinement.

REHABILITA-TION
The process of changing a criminal into a conforming member of society through punishment, therapy, or other method.

RESIDENTIAL TREATMENT
A component of community corrections programs that confines convicted offenders to a usually smaller and "minimum-security" (as compared with prison) facility that is supposed to provide rehabilitative services for its residents as well.

RESOCIAL-IZATION
The process of learning and incorporating the rules and roles expected in a new setting because the old ones are no longer relevant.

RESTITUTION
A sentence or court order that requires an offender to compensate his or her victim for some or all of the harm or damage brought upon that victim.

RETRIBUTION
Punishment that is proportionate to the crime (an "eye for an eye").

SECONDARY DEVIANCE
From an interactionist perspective, the crime or deviance that results when official agencies of social control (like the criminal justice system) label and treat primary deviance or crime (see PRIMARY DEVIANCE) as deviant or criminal.

SELF-FULFILLING PROPHECY
An event that occurs because it was predicted. The prophecy is confirmed because people alter their behavior to conform to the prediction.

SELF-REPORT STUDIES
Respondents are asked to reveal their past criminality to determine the actual frequency of criminality in all segments of the population.

SHARED MONOPOLY
When four or fewer companies supply at least 50 percent of a particular market.

SOCIAL CONSTRUC-TION OF CRIME
The assumption of interactionists that what is a "crime" and who is a "criminal" are products of a selection process by authorities in society.

SPECIFIC (special) DETERRENCE
The effect that punishment has on preventing subsequent crime by the person punished.

STARE DECISIS
The principle used in the courts of basing decisions on precedent.

STREET CRIME
The conventional or traditional crimes of individuals such as assault, robbery, rape, murder, larceny, burglary, theft, shoplifting, and arson.

SURPLUS POPULATION	The poor, unemployed, deviant, criminal, institutionalized, and imprisoned who are marginal to and unneeded by the system of economic production and distribution.
TAYLORIZA-TION OF POLICE WORK	The application of Frederick Taylor's ''scientific management'' practices to the organization of police work. The impact of this process has recently been felt in many big city police departments: layoffs, cutbacks, increasing specialization of tasks, more reactive and dangerous patrol work, and the use of technology to concentrate authority and control in the hands of police administrators.
TOTAL INSTITUTION	Erving Goffman's concept referring to places such as a mental hospital or prison where inmates are confined in an all-encompassing social environment. The inmates are under the absolute control of officials and stripped of their former identities and resocialized.
TRADITIONAL SOCIOLOG-ICAL THEORIES	A host of sociological perspectives in criminology that locate the origins of criminal acts in the perpetrator's ''immediate social environment'' but generally recommend that crime control is best accomplished by adjusting (reforming, rehabilitating) the individual offender to the established social order.
UNDER-GROUND ECONOMY	Unreported, untaxed, unregulated, and often illegal economic transactions that take place outside of the official and legal economy.
UNFOUNDING	The process of statistically declaring that certain unsolved crimes were never crimes in the first place.
UNIFORM CRIME REPORTS (UCR)	The annual report published by the FBI summarizing the crimes reported by the 15,000 or so local police departments. The crimes reported are limited to street crimes.
UNJUST LAW	A contradiction in terms for traditional sociologists but not so for radicals. According to Martin Luther King, Jr., a law is unjust if it (a) compels a minority to obey but is not binding on the majority, (b) is unfair to a minority that was denied the right to vote on it, and (c) is fair but unjust in its application.
VICTIMIZA-TION SURVEYS	Surveys conducted by the Census Bureau of individuals and business personnel to establish an estimate of the national frequency of crimes.
VICTIMLESS CRIME	Crimes that normally do not have a complaining victim such as gambling, drug use, and prostitution.
VOIR DIRE	(''to tell the truth'') The selection process whereby prospective jurors are questioned by both sides and the judge.
WAR CRIMES	An act during war that violates a standard of morality applied to winners and losers alike.
WHITE-COLLAR CRIME	Illegal acts, committed by relatively high status persons, using nonphysical means, concealment, or guile to obtain money or property, or to obtain business or personal advantage.
WORK-RELEASE	The temporary release of an offender from prison, a community corrections residential facility, or a parole halfway house, for the purpose of working in the community.

PHOTO CREDITS

Chapter 13

Opener: Martin A. Levick/Black Star. Page 469: Erick A. Roth/The Picture Cube. Page 472: Mimi Forsyth/Monkmeyer.

Chapter 14

Opener: Michael O'Brien/Archive. Page: 495: Danny Lyon/Magnum. Page 502: Norman Bergsma/Sygma.

Chapter 15

Opener: Charles Gatewood/The Image Works. Page 544: Bettye Lane/Photo Researchers. Page 546: Owen Franken/Sygma.

Chapter 16

Opener: Bill Bachman/Photo Researchers. Page 569: Alex Webb/Magnum. Page 575: Martin Adler Levick/Black Star.

Index

Where the reference is in a footnote the page number is followed by n.